NAU
FF

We hope you enjoy this book. Please return or renew it by the due date. You can renew it at **www.norfolk.gov.uk/libraries** or by using our free library app. Otherwise you can phone **0344 800 8020** - please have your library card and PIN ready. You can sign up for email reminders too.

5/10/19

24/10/23

D1334183

'Another wonderful sports book on the shelves this summer is a brilliantly presented history of English cricket written by Simon Wilde. Not only does it cover all the major matches, issues and controversies of our national summer game, it is also speckled liberally with fascinating lists and statistics ... The book is simply a treat.'
Jim Holden, *Sunday Express*

'Fellow [cricket] tragics will love this book, issued in the summer of England's 1,000th Test match. Even the title – *England: The Biography* – deserves a round of applause for presuming that the nation is synonymous with cricket ... The book's greatest joys are its footnotes.'
Francis Wheen, *Mail on Sunday*

'This book, indispensable to any serious cricket lover, is an important work of scholarly synthesis which establishes Wilde as one of our foremost cricket historians.'
Peter Oborne, *The Spectator*

'An impressive and comprehensive gem ... superbly researched and brilliantly delivered. It is going to ... be indispensable. It needs to be read, and it deserves to sell well.'
Huw Turbervill, *The Cricketer*

'A collection of 35 thematic chapters rather than a chronological narrative and is packed full of stats and fascinating details.'
*Mail on Sunday,* Sports Books of the Year

# England
# The Biography

## THE STORY OF ENGLISH CRICKET 1877–2019

## Simon Wilde

**SIMON &
SCHUSTER**

London · New York · Sydney · Toronto · New Delhi

A CBS COMPANY

First published in Great Britain by Simon & Schuster UK Ltd, 2018
This paperback edition published by Simon & Schuster UK Ltd, 2019

A CBS COMPANY

1 3 5 7 9 10 8 6 4 2

Simon & Schuster UK Ltd
1st Floor
222 Gray's Inn Road
London WC1X 8HB

www.simonandschuster.co.uk
www.simonandschuster.com.au
www.simonandschuster.co.in

Simon & Schuster Australia, Sydney
Simon & Schuster India, New Delhi

A CIP catalogue record for this book
is available from the British Library

Paperback ISBN: 978-1-4711-5485-0
eBook ISBN: 978-1-4711-5486-7

Typeset in Bembo by M Rules
Printed and bound by CPI Group (UK) Ltd, Croydon, CR0 4YY

# CONTENTS

# FOREWORD – BY ED SMITH, NATIONAL SELECTOR, ENGLAND CRICKET

English cricket has a special place in the history of sport. As the first fully organised team game, cricket is the father figure of all modern sport. Cricket is also uniquely bound up with English identity, in all its complexity and subtlety. The story of English cricket, to some extent, is also the story of England itself.

This is one of our game's great strengths – the breadth of opinion and wisdom, the contrasting landscapes, the different approaches to achievement and success, even the range of its accents. There has never been one route to the top in English cricket and there never will be.

The chalk downs of the south where the game was born; the village pitches where cricketing artisans earned a living and elevated the early professional game; the draw of London life with its sporting theatre and new sources of income; the industrial city and the emergence of deep local pride in county sides; the school and university tradition; the competitive cricket of the northern leagues; the local club, from village green to city park.

All these forces have shaped and contributed to English cricket. They are all bound up with our game's voice and identity, as Simon Wilde's book explores.

The beauty of English cricket is that it can never be contained or owned by one place or faction. English cricket at its best celebrates the breadth and colour of the country it reflects, represents and, at times, inspires.

Anyone who really serves English cricket, whatever their personal journey through the sport and the country, comes to understand that our game is strongest when it draws on all types of talent and ability.

The story of England cricket is often explored through divisions and conflicts – amateur versus professionals, North versus South, modernisers versus traditionalists. Sometimes, I concede, it is hard to avoid those themes.

If, however, we are considering the story of English cricket in the form of a single life ('a biography') then what a great life it has been – full of achievement and adaptability, drama and value, brilliance and resilience. Yes, there have often been tensions inside English cricket. But rich and interesting lives usually have some tension; it is bound up with their creative energy.

As I write these lines, the England one-day side has just scored a scintillating 481 against Australia, breaking its own world record.

Best of all, in the biography of England cricket, the greatest chapters may be yet to come.

*2018*

# CHAPTER 1

# Band of Brothers

In February 2017, a special dinner was held at Lord's to which every living England cricketer, whether they had played Tests, one-day internationals or Twenty20s, was invited. Some were unable to attend, others who had long ago lost contact with colleagues and were no longer involved in the game could not be tracked down, but of the 321 surviving male players, 230 attended – the largest gathering of England cricketers ever assembled in one room. Everyone was given a commemorative tassled cap with their name and personal number on it marking their chronological place in the team's history. Tables had sitting at them a player who was still actively involved: he presented caps to past players and they in turn gave a piece of card with a few words of advice on it to the latest custodian of the national shirt. Old friendships were renewed and memories revived, and there was general praise for the man whose brainchild the occasion was, the managing director of England cricket Andrew Strauss.

Strauss's purpose was twofold. He himself had played 100 Test matches, 50 of them as captain, and was conscious of how fleeting many international careers were and how little connection many players actually had with the England team they represented. Even a player as senior as Andrew Flintoff, the star all-rounder of his day and alongside Strauss an Ashes winner in 2005 and 2009, had in the past spoken about how raw he felt at ending his involvement with international cricket. England cricketers were members of a special club, yet how special did they feel? Of the 690 Test cricketers to represent England, almost half appeared five times or fewer, 94 only once.

Strauss also wanted the present generation to tap into what he described as a 'vast bank of information, knowledge and experience' of past cricketers, and make them aware they had a responsibility to the cap, the shirt and the nation: they represented their country, but they also represented a team with a distinguished if turbulent and sometimes troubled history stretching back 140 years; some of their predecessors had gone through extraordinary experiences before ever making it onto the field in days long before developmental pathways from age-group cricket to the Test arena had been dreamt up: some had been orphans, some overcame life-threatening illness, some fought in world wars. Some who previously represented England were killed in war. While not suggesting that modern-day players had had life easy – some certainly had not – Strauss in 2017 felt it could only improve them, as people and cricketers, if they gained a better understanding of the past, and what it was they were a part of. What they are part of is the story traced by this book.

The England cricket team cannot boast the glorious traditions of some sporting outfits. They are not the equivalent of the All Blacks in rugby, or of Brazil or Germany in football. They have never gone 15 years without losing a series, as the vaunted West Indies side of the 1980s and 1990s did, or remained unbeaten in Ashes series for 18 years, as the great Australians managed between 1987 and 2005. In more than 40 years of trying they have never won the World Cup and when they did win a World Twenty20 they struck gold with an XI pulled together on the eve of the tournament. There have been exceptional periods when they could justifiably claim to be the best Test team in the world – examples include the late 1920s, the mid-1950s and 2010–11 – but sustained success has been hard to secure, especially away from home. Australia, the opponents against whom England test themselves every two years, have generally proved a tough nut to crack.

The doleful truth is that they have been defined as much by their shortcomings as their triumphs. Just as the English public like to grumble about the weather, so they moan about the England cricket team and how frequently the grey days outnumber those when the sun shines. What tests the patience is not just the on-field mishaps (although the capacity to lose to the likes of the Netherlands, Ireland and Bangladesh in global one-day tournaments is vexing, and don't get me started on the batting collapses ...) but also the knack of conjuring out of nowhere an administrative cock-up or soap-opera-style scandal. You cannot chronicle England cricket without dealing with bureaucracy, barmaids and street-brawls, or headbutts. Rarely has it been free of crisis.

Modern audiences brought up on the dynamism of Joe Root, or the scoops and flicks of Jos Buttler and Eoin Morgan, may think England cricket's relationship with flair has always been a close one; in truth, the team was built on generations of temperate-clime battlers, northern opening batsmen with granite-like defences, and bowlers steeped in the craft of seam and swing. This is a tale in which striving and heroism against the odds prominently feature: England may not have produced many vintage cricket teams but being familiar with backs-to-the-wall crises they have provided some vintage escapologists: Willie Watson and Trevor Bailey at Lord's, and Michael Atherton in Johannesburg, batting for hour after hour to save the game; Bob Willis at Headingley, and Ian Botham at Edgbaston, steaming in to win Tests that had looked lost. Captaining such a team, usually with little security of tenure, was no easy matter and the role took a heavy toll on most of those who did it for any length of time, however talented or resilient. The public scrutiny alone made it one of the toughest public offices in the land. Michael Vaughan wore the crown more lightly than many, and in terms of Test wins enjoyed more success than any, yet even he departed shedding tears, worn out by the constant need to wear a 'mask of positivity'.

An early problem was that for many years the team operated on an irregular basis, less a distinct entity than a banner under which ad hoc troupes of players occasionally marched. Not until after the Second World War did they regularly play more than six matches a year. Equally, the teams they played against all came from British

Dominions, many of which saw themselves as outlying branches of the United Kingdom. England's Test matches were not therefore the full-blown tests of national virility they might have been; this perhaps only started to happen once these territories achieved political independence. English cricket quickly learned to take the Australians seriously because they were seriously good at cricket but initially it adopted a paternalistic attitude towards other, lesser opposition and rarely bothered to put out their best available XI. Gradually, England had no choice but to take them seriously as well.

The team was not particularly well run either. English cricket was deeply rooted in the county game and this monopolised the attentions of administrators and players. Until the 1960s, England's home Test matches, and even more so overseas tours, came under the management of Marylebone Cricket Club, the senior amateur club in the land, and MCC duly managed affairs in a manner of its own choosing. The England team contained a healthy smattering of amateurs and was almost invariably led by a member of the amateur class, preferably one with close ties to the club itself. Class often came before country, and the logic behind the selection of some England captains could be hard to fathom. It was a wonder England won as often as they did.

Regardless of such factors, it took a particular type of person to want to play for the team. Some such as Herbert Sutcliffe, Godfrey Evans and Ian Botham positively thrived on the big stage, playing better the tougher the occasion. They were unusual though. Many did not savour the additional pressure or expectation. When Harold Gimblett heard his name announced in an England squad for the first time to face India in 1936 he did not feel elated. 'Far from throwing my hat in the air, I was terrified,' he said. 'Suddenly I realised the fearful responsibilities resting on my shoulders ... I just wanted to go away and get lost. I didn't want to play for England.' Gimblett scored 67 not out but was dropped after two games, much to his relief, though he was recalled for one further game three years later. Eric Hollies, who famously bowled Don Bradman for nought in his last Test, much preferred playing for Warwickshire and had to be cajoled into appearing in that match at The Oval in 1948. Doug

Insole, who won nine Test caps, gave this assessment of playing for England shortly before he retired in 1963: 'I believe that very few players do enjoy it, apart from the general atmosphere and the satisfaction of being selected for one's country ... the steady increase in partisan and even nationalistic feeling doesn't help. The advent of television, the increase in radio and film coverage, and the ever-growing army of press correspondents in recent years have all helped to make Test cricket a far more tense and nerve-wracking business than ever before. Every move, every ball, every action and almost every word may be the subject of minute scrutiny.'

Keith Fletcher, whose England career began in 1968 at around the time when the responsibility for running the team was being transferred from MCC to the Test and County Cricket Board (later the England and Wales Cricket Board), said that the early teams he played in had none of the unity or comradeship he found at Essex. 'It wasn't a collective effort. We were a group of individuals, never a team. We turned up on a Wednesday for a sort of a net, had a dinner in the evening and then played a Test match the next day. It was done on a wing and a prayer and if you had two bad Test matches there was a fair chance you'd be left out.' He said established players never gave him advice on batting or what certain bowlers might be doing with the ball. 'They weren't over-keen on somebody taking their place.' David Lloyd, who debuted as a Test player at Lord's in 1974, was struck by the eerie quietness of the dressing-room. 'I had been used to the buzz and banter of the Lancashire side, full of fun and characters and opinions; by comparison, this was like walking into a public library.'

In such a stultifying environment, it was little surprise that it took outsiders to shake things up. Pelham Warner, though he ultimately became a bastion of the cricketing establishment, was one of the first England captains and selectors to realise the need to prioritise the national team if it was to be successful; with England, Douglas Jardine was the first to deploy a strategy – Bodyline – with absolute intellectual rigour; and Tony Greig was the first to orchestrate and see through a rebellion over pay and conditions by signing up for Kerry Packer's World Series and taking with him several other England players in the process. All three were born and to varying degrees nurtured outside the English system (Jardine and Greig were also of Scottish stock). Similarly, one of the administrators who did most to modernise international cricket in England, Raman Subba Row, was born into an Indian family, while two head coaches who radically overhauled the running of the England set-up, Duncan Fletcher and Andy Flower, were both southern Africans. Eoin Morgan, an Irishman, spearheaded a renaissance in the team's white-ball cricket. Most of these characters would not have won a popularity contest. Jardine and Greig were accused of wanting to win too much, Greig of also caring too much about money, and Subba Row, Fletcher and Flower of demanding too much control. Morgan kept his lips sealed when the national anthem was sung. But without them, and others like them, England cricket might have stagnated long ago.

By historical standards, the England team today is very well run and resourced. In fact, there is not now just one England team but several: one to play Test cricket (red-ball or, in the case of day–night Tests, pink-ball matches) and others for one-day internationals and Twenty20s (white ball). They are not an add-on to the county game but full-time operations in their own right, fulfilling more than 40 fixtures across the three formats every year. 'The increase in the amount of cricket England played was the biggest change in my time,' Vaughan said. 'It turned you into an England cricketer rather than a county player who just represented England. It also made England look more into creating a spirit of "team".' The players are supported by a host of technical coaches, fitness trainers, physiotherapists, masseurs, psychologists and data analysts, while the top performers are contracted to the national side, rarely play for anyone else, and are handsomely paid. England A or Lions and Under-19 teams serve as nurseries for the next generation. The choice of red- and white-ball captains rarely excites anything like the old debates: they are the best-credentialed options from within the ranks. It is no coincidence that results have improved.

That is the good news. The less-good news is that there is a sense that the teams have chiefly become vehicles for making money for the ECB and 11 home international venues desperate for matches to stage, and pouring something – anything – down the gullet of television. Indeed, it seems there is barely a day when an England side is not on duty somewhere in the world, whether it is Cardiff, Cape Town, Kolkata, Colombo or Christchurch. Even devotees find it hard to keep up with what is going on, or remember which series were won and lost. England's best cricketers were once national icons but that stopped shortly after the team touched the rarefied heights of celebrity during the 2005 Ashes: at that point the ECB, acting on a decision taken several years earlier, took television coverage away from terrestrial broadcasters altogether and moved it to subscription channels. The board's defence was that the game needed the money and that the England team needed the money if it was to be successfully sustained, but since that time even 'stars' such as Root, Alastair Cook and James Anderson are less recognised by the average man, woman and child in the street. The price of better funding and better results has been that the England team's place in the national consciousness has shrunk.

It is ironic, too, that so soon after England finally secured the full-time services of the top cricketers for themselves, a fresh rival emerged for their attention in the shape of cash-rich domestic Twenty20 leagues. Whereas playing for England used to be the pinnacle of the game, and the best means of making money, now there was an alternative arena in which significant sums could be earned for a lot less effort. When Kevin Pietersen, another outsider who was born and raised in South Africa, asked in 2012 for time off from England's schedule in order to play in the Indian Premier League, he was rebuffed, but when Strauss became managing director of England cricket three years later he accepted the new reality by accommodating those on central contracts who wished to play in the big Twenty20 leagues. Two years later, two English players – Ben Stokes, born in New Zealand but living in England since the age of 12, and Tymal Mills – joined the IPL on million-dollar deals. Strauss's decision was partly pragmatic. He did not want to lose key players altogether and see his England teams fragment. But he also felt it was time to fully embrace the white-ball formats and endorsed this belief by also appointing as head coach Trevor Bayliss, an Australian who had made his reputation winning one-day trophies, with the express aim of lifting the World Cup on home soil in 2019. It was a revolutionary moment.

The threat of the Twenty20 leagues may have been another reason for Strauss holding his Lord's dinner. He might have calculated that with rival attractions on offer there was no better way to persuade the players to stay loyal to the England cause than appeal to their sense of national pride. Such an appeal seemed more necessary than ever when, less than six months after receiving his IPL windfall, Stokes was suspended by England following his arrest over an alleged assault outside a Bristol nightclub hours after playing in a one-day international, forcing him to miss an Ashes series in Australia (he was subsequently acquitted of affray but fined £30,000 by the Cricket Discipline Commission for various offences). Thankfully, most appreciated that England could offer something Twenty20 could not: the richest of sporting histories.

# CHAPTER 2

# Gentlemen v Players
## The rise of meritocracy

The England Test team spent much of the first 50 years of its existence in a state of glorious complacency. Despite several series defeats – mainly in faraway Australia when England's true strength was not fully represented, but also sometimes at home – a deep-seated belief held firm that English cricket was, still, the best. Talent was habitually alienated and squandered because there was a feeling that such waste could be afforded. The scales only truly fell from people's eyes once a 3-0 home series defeat by Australia in 1921 followed hard on the heels of an unprecedented 5-0 whitewash Down Under the previous winter. There could be no more delusion.

England had lost heavily away from home before but it was difficult assembling anything like full-strength sides to undertake tours that commonly lasted around six months – it was normal for English teams touring Australia to leave in September and return in April – and so if excuses were needed they were not hard to find. Winning in Australia was as challenging then as it is now and to add to the difficulty Test matches there before the Second World War were as a matter of course played to a finish: there was no hope of getting away with a losing draw. At home was different. Before 1921 England had lost only eight matches on their own soil and in terms of series scorelines had never been beaten by a margin of more than one match (although the feted England XI of 1902 came within a whisker of losing 3-0 before pulling off a hair's-breadth one-wicket win in the final Test at The Oval, thanks to the canny Yorkshire pair of George Hirst and Wilfred Rhodes edging them over the line). Admittedly, come the early 1920s, Britain had just gone through an epic war and English cricket, like every other aspect of national life, was recovering its strength, but Australia had fought a war too. The carnage on the Western Front could not fully explain the gulf between the sides.

One measure of how serious things were was that two Tests into the 1921 series Johnny Douglas, a broadly liked captain with pre-war series victories in Australia and South Africa to his name but who lacked imagination (hardly a hindrance to some previous holders of the office), was dismissed from his post. It was the first time England had as a matter of strategy chosen to switch leader in the midst of a home series.* Lionel Tennyson, the man who replaced him, had only come into the side in the previous match at Lord's, the recipient of a late summons from a panicked selection panel. After an initial defeat, which secured for Australia the series, Tennyson oversaw improved performances in the last two Tests, both drawn, but it was of little consequence. Sydney Pardon, the presiding voice of *Wisden* since 1891, wrote: 'During all the years I have edited *Wisden* there has never been a season so disheartening as that of 1921. England was not merely beaten but overwhelmed.'

A sense of entitlement had been one drag on results. Test cricket was established during the height of the British Empire and confidence was not in short supply; England had given cricket to the world and assumptions of superiority were ingrained. But there was one glaring fault-line above all: an invidious social apartheid.

The gentlemanly class that had played the game at the great public schools and universities (principally Eton and Harrow, Oxford and Cambridge) dominated control of the game's levers of power. Armed with time, money and devotion, they populated the committees

---

* Having got a taste for it, the selection panel adopted the same manoeuvre in each of the next two home Ashes series in 1926 and 1930.

that ran both MCC, a private men's club which through its links to the Conservative Party had been for generations close to the seat of governmental power and since 1903–04 had organised all England tours, and the first-class counties that by 1921 had risen to a bloated old-boy network numbering 17. Most significantly of all, on 24 October 1898, a Board of Control governing home Tests first met to determine the number of matches to be played, allocate venues, divide profits, and appoint a panel of selectors, an indication that international cricket was now important enough to require some sort of centralised management. There was also pressure coming from Australia: in 1895 the Australian authorities initially declined the tour of England in 1896 because there was no official host body with which to deal.

With MCC holding an effective majority – with the club president, in possession of a casting vote, joined by five other club representatives on a panel of 12 – the original Board of Control contained an earl, two lords and one soon-to-be lord, a knight and eight others from the amateur class, even if one of them, WG Grace – included because of his status as the greatest exponent of the game there had been to that point – was the grandson of servants and had been educated at a village school. There was not a horny-handed professional in sight.

England had only ever been captained in home Tests by one of the amateur class, and the board's original guidelines, while not saying so in as many words, made it clear that there was no intention of that changing. The first three-man selection panel was made up of prominent amateurs: Lord Hawke, the chairman and captain of Yorkshire, HW Bainbridge, Warwickshire captain, and Grace, who led both Gloucestershire and England. They were to pick the team in two phases. First, the panel would select six players, out of which would be co-opted two amateurs to help pick the rest of the squad. 'In the event of no amateur being selected in the first six,' it was stated, 'the said committee of three shall select all players ... if only one amateur shall be so selected the committee of four shall select all the players.' In other words, no professional cricketer, however senior, was to be consulted. The notion that no amateur might be selected proved academic. Before 1924, England only twice fielded a side in a home Test match with as few as two amateurs: at Old Trafford in 1888, in the days before the creation of the management board when teams were generally selected by the committee of the club staging the match, and at Lord's in 1909 when for particular reasons selection was not straightforward.

The first amateurs to be co-opted were Stanley Jackson and Charles Fry, two men who would have colourful careers that went far beyond cricket. Jackson had appeared with success in two previous home Ashes series, but Fry had yet to play against Australia and, although a Test regular over the next 13 years, he proved a highly unreliable contributor to England's cause. Jackson and Fry duly played in all five Tests of the 1899 series while the selection panel to which they contributed put into the field 24 players in all. This process was complicated by Grace voluntarily stepping down after the first Test and being replaced as captain, and consequently as selector, by Archie MacLaren. MacLaren had already acted as stand-in captain in Tests in Australia but his preferment ahead of Jackson created tension within the panel, Jackson at one point having to be persuaded to play, an early indication of the potential pitfalls of active players being involved in the selection process.

One of the upshots of the new method of selection was that it endorsed the preferential view of amateurs. In the 1899 series, six amateurs were included in the XI that played in the second Test at Lord's and seven in the one chosen for the final Test at The Oval: unsurprisingly, as amateurs tended to specialise in the more gentlemanly pursuit of batting, England racked up 576 but were unable to bowl out Australia twice in a match they needed to win to avoid losing the series. In all, almost half the England caps awarded in 1899 went to nine amateurs; of these nine, seven came out of the public-school and university class that comprised only a fraction of the population. Things were similar in the home Ashes series of 1902 and 1905. The amateur class saw nothing wrong in this; indeed Fry, among others, unashamedly espoused the view that a healthy amateur representation was good for a team and that entirely professional XIs were generally unsuccessful (an opinion without persuasive evidence to support it). As historian Peter Wynne-Thomas observed, 'The upper middle class had hijacked cricket at the highest level.'* It might be argued that the story of the England team since traces the efforts of the lower orders to wrest control back again.

The creation of a management board provided an opportunity to eradicate class divisions that were obstructing the development of the England team; instead in many respects it merely entrenched much of the mistrust and suspicion between the classes that had existed since the earliest days.

Revealingly, on those rare occasions when professionals had been in a position to select England sides, they too tended to favour their own (though perhaps their hand was forced to the extent that few self-respecting amateurs wanted to join a professionally run enterprise). Professionals – in the shape of Sussex's James Lillywhite, who led England in what is now regarded as the first-ever Test match, and the Nottinghamshire pair of Alfred Shaw and Arthur Shrewsbury – had with admirable entrepreneurial zeal conceived and managed several tours of Australia between 1876-77 and 1887-88, all but the last of them with financial satisfaction. The nearest they came to picking an amateur on all but the last of these tours was when Reginald Wood, a former Lancashire amateur who had emigrated to Australia, was recruited by the 1886-87 side for several matches including one Test in Sydney as a replacement for Billy Barnes, the Notts all-rounder, who had damaged his hand throwing a punch at Percy McDonnell, the Australia captain.† But at the time of his call-up Wood was engaged in Melbourne as a professional.

The amateurs, in turn, had sent a team to Australia under the leadership of Lord Harris in 1878-79; the original aim was not to involve any professionals but, lacking depth in bowling, his lordship commandeered two Yorkshiremen, Tom Emmett and George Ulyett.

---

* Wynne-Thomas also noted that the football field, by contrast, was more open to the working class.

† Barnes was an obstreperous character, his mood swayed by drink; on an earlier tour of Australia he had refused the request of his captain Shrewsbury to bowl in a Test at Sydney which England lost by seven runs; in the previous match he had returned figures of nine for 81.

As it happened, a riot during a match against New South Wales in Sydney triggered by the run-out of local hero Billy Murdoch, which led to the cancellation of the second of two Tests, left Harris particularly grateful for their presence as Emmett and Ulyett sought to defend him from the mob with stumps in hand.* Thanks in part to Harris's conciliatory attitude after that incident, the first Test match staged in England took place under his captaincy in 1880, but the side contained eight amateurs and only three professionals (Ulyett and Emmett were not among them). Two years later, when Australia won a Test on English soil for the first time, the England XI contained seven amateurs, while the following winter, when Ivo Bligh, a 6ft 4in 'dashing' bat from Eton and Cambridge, successfully led a mission to reclaim the 'Ashes' of English cricket, his team included seven amateurs in three of the Tests and eight in the other. The English amateur class paid scant regard to the tours of Australia run by professionals and it took an Australian journalist Clarence Moody in 1894 to include them in what became the first accepted list of early Test matches. English publications such as *Wisden*, decidedly sympathetic towards the amateur viewpoint, did not list as standard England Test caps won in Australia until the 1920s.† In 1921, Pelham Warner was referring in the columns of *The Cricketer* to the 1880 Test at The Oval as 'the first Test match'.

Class antipathy alone would be too crude an explanation for the make-up of some of the early teams, especially those sent on tour, when matters of cost also compelled the inclusion of a corps of amateurs. The South African authorities in particular were anxious that not too many professionals were brought with an English visiting team as they lacked the funds to pay them. Not that all amateurs came cheap of course.

---

* This is one of only two England Tests cancelled following the commencement of a tour, the other being the Guyana Test in 1980-81, cancelled when the Guyanese government objected to Robin Jackman's playing links to apartheid South Africa.

† In fact, this also delayed recognition to more than 20 amateurs who made their only England Test appearances in Australia before 1914. These included Sandford Schultz, a member of Harris's team, who changed his German-sounding name during the First World War when anti-German feelings ran high in Britain. He became Sandford Storey, but *Wisden* always listed him under his original name.

Just how far apart the two social groups were became apparent when in 1887-88 both organised and dispatched rival teams to Australia – to the detriment of each, as well as to their rival backers in Melbourne and Sydney. The amateur trip lost £4,000 while the professionals, under the management of Lillywhite, Shaw and Shrewsbury, ended £2,400 out of pocket (all of which fell to Shaw and Shrewsbury as Lillywhite defaulted).* The professionals did, however, include four amateurs in their 12-man party, one of whom, Aubrey Smith of Sussex, was made captain, in Alan Gibson's words 'possibly in an attempt to give Sydney some social status comparable with that of Melbourne'.† However, the two teams played only one Test match: in an effort to salvage something from a ruinous situation, they came together in Sydney to play what is now regarded as a Test, with Walter Read, one of three amateurs selected in the XI, given the captaincy – as with Smith, presumably in deference to social norms. With the players from Melbourne refusing to turn out for Australia, the attendance for the match, which lasted three days, was just 1,971, the lowest recorded figure for any England Test. 'It is certain that such a piece of folly will never be perpetrated again,' *Wisden* reported. 'Wherever the blame lay, the effect was to throw a complete damper on the visits of English cricketers to the Colonies.' There was not another tour of Australia for four years.

One of the main causes of friction was money. Lillywhite's all-professional tour of 1876-77 partly arose out of his experiences touring Australia three years earlier in a group of seven professionals and five amateurs led by Grace, when he and his fellow professionals took umbrage at being paid £150 each, and generally treated as second-class citizens in comparison with the 'gentlemen', while Grace received £1,500 plus expenses, exposing his amateur status as the sham most knew it was. The professionals boycotted an end-of-tour banquet in protest. Jack Conway, a talented Victoria player with an eye for business, invited Lillywhite to return with his own

---

* For all his pioneering tours, Lillywhite was falling on hard times. He later turned to first-class umpiring and spent the last 28 years of his long life working in a stone quarry.
† The amateur-arranged tour actually consisted of seven amateurs and six professionals.

team, which he duly did. This time the players received £200 each, co-existed harmoniously and drank such copious quantities of champagne that it probably contributed to their defeat in what is now regarded as the inaugural Test match at the Paddock in Melbourne, the precursor to the MCG. Having lost three times to teams from Victoria or New South Wales consisting of 15 men, it was agreed that the Englishmen would meet an Australia team on equal terms – 11 men per side – in what was termed a 'Grand Combination Match'. Lillywhite and Conway forged a fruitful alliance that did as much as anything to get Test cricket up and running: Conway managed Australia's first tour of England in 1878 with Lillywhite acting as local agent, roles they later reversed on two tours of Australia.

The social segregation rankled, especially for matches in England, where the amateur-run clubs in varying degrees required that professionals be kept to separate changing areas, separate lunch tables and in some cases different entry gates to the field of play; the 'dressing-room' was originally purely an amateur privilege and professionals were expected to get ready in windowless pavilion basements or huts set aside for the purpose, sometimes in distant parts of the ground. George Lohmann, a socialist-minded professional at Surrey, complained in an interview in *Cricket* in July 1896 that in many places, though no longer at The Oval, professional changing-rooms were 'so arranged that if a Player wants to watch a match he has to go out among the crowd', and that English grounds would have in the end to follow the example of the less class-bound Australia where facilities for all players were much superior.

Despite the more democratic arrangements overseas, touring was where relationships were truly tested. Tour parties often had to be assembled over several weeks as amateurs were sounded out about their availability; their agreement probably depended on what like-minded company there might be for the long voyages, train journeys and hotel stays. It says something that Jackson and Fry never joined a major Test tour overseas. Only three amateurs joined the first MCC-led tour of Australia in 1903-04 and all were Oxford University men: Pelham Warner, the captain, RE Foster, who also acted as assistant manager, and Bernard Bosanquet. Bosanquet had been a contemporary of Foster's at Oxford and was a Middlesex team-mate of Warner, whom he had already accompanied on all-amateur tours of the United States and Australia. When Warner wrote to Jack Mason of Kent to sound him out about the 1905-06 tour of South Africa, his main point of persuasion was telling him that fellow amateur batsmen Ted Wynyard and Frederick Fane had already agreed to go.* In his letter he made no mention of which professionals might be joining the tour. Amateurs were generally keener to tour South Africa than Australia; the travel and cricket were less arduous and their hosts eager to lavish them with hospitality.

It was noticeable that some of England's most successful tours were those conducted under captains willing to relax the social distinctions: Bligh's players in 1882-83 (eight amateurs, four professionals) all travelled first-class on the outward voyage to Australia and dined together on the boat, while under Warner in 1903-04 the three amateurs and 11 professionals stayed in the same hotels for the first time (an experiment not much repeated until many years later). In 1911-12 when England recorded their greatest win in Australia during this period, Douglas leading the side in the Tests because Warner was ill, Douglas though tactically limited was popular with the professionals because, in the words of wicketkeeper Tiger Smith, 'he was one of us'. Smith explained: 'Warner always wanted the pros to look up to him and to let them realise he was the boss [but] there was none of this "Mr Douglas" nonsense with him ... He was one of us, more of a professional amateur than an amateur of the old school.'

Unfortunately, even-handed leaders were not easy to find. Smith said Fry, who led England at home in 1912, was not a good captain because 'he didn't understand our feelings', terming him a 'martinet'. Joe Darling, who regularly played for Australia against England between 1894 and 1905, wrote in his memoirs, 'I have heard some English captains speak to their professionals like dogs.' Ben Wardill,

---

* Mason was a full-time solicitor and turned down the offer. In fact, unbeknown to Warner, Mason had earlier been approached by MCC about leading the tour party himself.

Australia's tour manager, thought the reason for their victory in England in 1899 was – in the paraphrasing of Derek Birley – down to their 'more democratic views on captaincy and rejection of the debilitating philosophy of gentlemen and players'.

This assessment was echoed by umpire Jim Phillips, who stood in 15 out of 16 Ashes Tests between 1893 and 1898 as well as in many domestic matches in both Australia and England. 'In general-ship the Australians are easily first. They play more in unison, they exchange views in the dressing-room, and their captain is thereby assisted materially in many of his plans . . . Off the field an Australian captain receives the benefit of the opinions of his comrades as if he were chairman of a board of directors. The average English captain is more of an autocrat. He rarely seeks advice from his men. If a consultation be held it is invariably confined to the amateurs and the batsmen, not the professionals and the bowlers. I can recall instances when I have been standing umpire when able and intelligent professional players on an England side have seen the fallacy of some plan of their captain, but nothing has been said by them, no suggestion made, to remedy the mistake . . . Surely, if a man is good enough to play on the same side he is good enough to dress in the same dressing-room. It is there most useful hints and ideas are exchanged when a game is in progress, which cannot be done so well on the field.'

Victor Cohen, manager of the 1893 Australians, said 'some of the men were drunk time after time' and Victor Trumper's diary of the 1902 tour described the Australians getting drunk after their two wins in that series: it is hard to imagine the English amateurs and professionals sitting down together to do the same in such circumstances. Tensions between the two groups on the issue of pay came to a public head during the 1896 Tests when a cabal of professionals threatened to go on strike unless match fees were raised from £10 to £20. Fees for home matches had not gone up in a long time – in fact, the three professionals chosen for the first-ever Test in England in 1880 (Barnes, Shaw and Fred Morley, all of Nottinghamshire) were paid £20 each by the Surrey authorities – and the professionals were aware that some amateurs received as much if not more than that in expenses. They contemplated action in the first two Tests of the series before five high-profile players made their demand ahead of the decider at The Oval.

Lohmann, Bobby Abel, Tom Hayward and Tom Richardson were all Surrey cricketers and may have reckoned that the club was going to do well enough out of staging the game to accommodate them; Lohmann had successfully negotiated a doubling of his bonus money from Surrey in 1889 from £25 to £50, and he, Hayward and Richardson all benefited from multi-year deals at the club at a time when these were a rarity. Lohmann would also have known about an 1893 court case involving Walter Read, the Surrey and England amateur, and Edwin Ash, a sometime Surrey committeeman, resulting from a tour of South Africa in 1891-92 when the chief financial backer James Logan, a Scottish adventurer based in Matjiesfontein, had successfully sued over the recovery of £750 which he said was a loan rather than an advance on expenses and had been dishonourably spent on the 'so-called amateurs'. Ash argued that the sum was only to be returned if profits from the tour allowed (which they had not). The Supreme Court in Cape Town heard that Read had originally demanded £850 to lead the tour and that Murdoch, the former Australia star now playing for Sussex as an amateur, had been paid £350; Lohmann had himself been a candidate to captain the English side and was in the Cape at the time of the court case recovering his health with the support of Logan.*

The fifth player William Gunn played for Nottinghamshire, home to the most politically belligerent professional cricketers in the country and scene of an incendiary pay dispute in the early 1880s led by Shaw and Shrewsbury. Gunn, along with Shrewsbury, had refused to join a tour of Australia led by Grace, also in the winter of 1891-92, in protest at what they knew would be Grace's outrageously advantageous terms; in fact, he received a staggering sum of £3,000, ten times what was paid to the professionals. Lohmann went on that tour,

---

* While in South Africa, Lohmann joined Logan as a member of the Worcester Cape Colony lodge of the Grand Union of England freemasons in 1893, making him probably the first England Test cricketer to become a freemason. (Basil Grieve, who became a freemason in 1885, played in two matches in 1888-89 subsequently regarded as Test matches, but only in the early 1900s.)

so he had personal knowledge on two fronts of the extent to which England's leading amateur cricketers might be enriched.

The threatened strike was not well planned and Surrey quickly and shrewdly lined up three professionals (rather than amateurs) as replacements should they be required. Three of the five rebels backed down in time to play and the two who did not were under less financial pressure to comply. Lohmann, though an avowed socialist, was the son of a stockbroker and had as a matter of choice opted to play as a professional, while Gunn ran a thriving sports equipment firm and was already affluent enough not to need the money. (Ironically, he would eventually be appointed to the Nottinghamshire committee, a rarity for a former professional at any club.) Though the strike action failed, a spotlight had been cast on the injustices of the system and Andrew Stoddart, the Middlesex amateur who had successfully led an England team in Australia two winters previously, was sufficiently embarrassed by the attention he received from the popular press to withdraw from the match (though he would play for, and lead, England again). At the end of the season, Surrey renegotiated the terms by which Read acted as their assistant secretary.

One of the priorities of the new Board of Control was therefore to bring some order to pay and expenses. The last thing it wanted was further embarrassing disruption during Australia's tour in 1899. Professional Test fees were duly raised to £20 but further, less placatory, changes followed ahead of Australia's next visit in 1902. In a letter to clubs staging Test matches dated 17 February 1902, the board specified that 'No collection shall be allowed on any ground during a Test Match'. This was significant: collections were an accepted means of spectators rewarding exceptional performances by professionals, and in 1899 Hayward had scored 137 in the final Test on his home ground at The Oval and benefited from a collection among the crowd worth £131. The ruling also put paid to any professional being given a Test as a benefit match as Surrey's Maurice Read (a professional, unrelated to Walter) had in 1893 when the Oval Test earned him a handsome £1,200. Lohmann had been promised a similar privilege but it never materialised. The cricketing establishment viewed these as unacceptable riches. The same letter stipulated that amateur expenses should amount to reimbursement of rail fares plus 30 shillings a day, up to a total of five days per Test, which conveniently approximated to around the £10 per match Surrey admitted to paying Grace during the furore surrounding the 1896 strike when he came to play Tests at The Oval. Now, every amateur was to be treated as generously.

The board's letter also stated that the hotels used to put up amateurs should be of good quality (a point reiterated ahead of the 1909 Ashes series). Nothing was said about host clubs arranging accommodation for professionals, and things had clearly not improved by the time of the seminal 1921 Ashes when a leading cricketer was spotted wandering about town late on the eve of a Test in the north of England in search of a bed. Several writers took that incident as the cue to suggest it was time for all team members to be put up in the same hotels as a matter of course. But even then nothing was done.

C Stewart Caine, who succeeded Sydney Pardon as *Wisden* editor, restated the case for this to happen ahead of Australia's next tour in 1926 as part of wider reforms: 'Players chosen for England should be allowed to travel at a reasonable hour on the day preceding the match and on arrival should find themselves comfortably housed. Indeed, the appointment of a special manager for such occasions might be taken into consideration.' His proposals received a fresh airing in the newspapers during England's home series defeat to South Africa in 1935, when at least some county matches started earlier so that players chosen for Test matches could 'avoid all-night journeys'. However, nothing permanent was put in place and amid consternation the counties refused a similar arrangement ahead of the final Test at The Oval in 1938, meaning special plans had to be made to transport Walter Hammond, the captain, and five Yorkshire players from Scarborough where a championship match was scheduled to finish on the eve of the Test. In the event the match at Scarborough finished a day early, greatly to the benefit of Len Hutton, who batted for the first 13 hours of the match at The Oval for a Test-record score of 364.

All in all, the Board of Control's changes did little to improve the lot of professionals in relation to amateurs and, with the management of the England team now formally in the hands of an all-amateur body, progress appeared harder to achieve than ever.

No wonder some professionals spoke out. In 1906, Albert Knight, the Leicestershire professional who had helped Warner's team win in Australia, wrote an outspoken book in which he criticised MCC for supporting a system which saw 'many an "amateur", so termed ... more heavily remunerated than an accredited professional' and condemned 'these miserable and hateful labels and distinctions which sicken most honest people by their unfairness'. Knight never represented England, the Players, or MCC again.*

In fact, although the creation of the Board of Control cemented many of the practices engaged in at home, some amateurs did lose out from MCC taking control of major tours overseas and from Lord Hawke in particular taking such a central role in England affairs. On the many tours he led he was a stickler for amateurs being paid only travel and accommodation (drawing the line at food and laundry) and this may explain the absence of big-name amateurs from most such expeditions: Hawke could afford his amateur scruples but they could not. Not every tour was led by Hawke though, and many other captains who took sides overseas effectively acted as manager as well as on-field leader and so were in a position to negotiate personal terms with the tour organisers in return for ensuring a strong team; on the captain's reputation and influence a tour might stand or fall. This was how WG Grace secured such big guarantees when he went to Australia.

When the expenses row was at its height, Stoddart denied having been directly paid as captain in Australia but conceded he was given discretion in ordering champagne, which he did liberally ('with the weather we experienced there this was almost a necessity'). Revealingly, MacLaren, who frequently needed financial assistance from his county Lancashire in order to play regularly, declared he was unavailable when Hawke first attempted to put together a Test tour on MCC's behalf, but when that plan collapsed he stepped forward to deal with the Australians himself and lead a side on what were probably highly advantageous personal terms. This was the sort of thing Hawke and MCC were determined to stop.

---

* Knight did, however, coach at Highgate School in the 1920s a future England captain, chairman of selectors and influential MCC administrator Walter Robins.

Of course, professionals and amateurs were not always at logger-heads. Most professionals kept their grumbles to themselves, called the amateurs Mister, ran runs hard when they were batting with them, and bowled into the wind when asked. Equally, most amateurs appreciated how reliant the team was on the contributions of the professionals. Nor was every amateur the same: some thought cricket's class divide an anachronism, and not all were good enough to command special treatment, or impecunious enough to demand it. In the heat of Test-match battle, the two groups, forming an extraordinary assortment of high life and low – some first trained as machine-operators or foundry-workers while others were born into great landowning fam-ilies or political dynasties – generally came together and co-operated in common cause, as Ulyett, Emmett and Lord Harris did in Sydney.

On Bligh's tour four years later during a series in which both sides accused the other of using their studs to cut up the turf to their advantage, Walter Read came to the aid of Dick Barlow, the Lancashire professional, during a pavilion fracas with Fred Spofforth. Jack Crawford, the Surrey amateur, had his MCC invitation with-drawn to join a Test tour of South Africa under Henry Leveson Gower, his county captain, after refusing to lead the county against the 1909 Australians when several professionals were left out appar-ently for disciplinary reasons following some high jinx during a visit to Chesterfield which attracted the attention of an officious policeman. Crawford protested to the club president Lord Alvestone at the absence of what he termed 'three essential players' and no one appraising him of what they had done wrong: 'Had I been told ... I would have upheld the official captain.' Crawford, as wayward a personality as he was gifted a cricketer, left the club soon after, emi-grated to Australia and never played for England again.*

---

* Crawford was the first teenager to play for England when he toured South Africa in 1905-06, scoring 281 runs and taking nine wickets in five Tests. He was also one of the few to have played for England in glasses; among others to do so were Dick Young, a contemporary of Crawford's at Repton, who kept wicket in two Tests in Australia in 1907-08, and Paul Gibb, a wicketkeeper in three of his eight Tests. Percy Fender, Bill Bowes, Tommy Mitchell, MJK Smith, Geoff Boycott, David Steele, Chris Old, Paul Allott, Devon Malcolm, Richard Dawson and Jack Leach all played in glasses.Boycott switched to contact lenses in 1969 after 35 of his 108 Tests.

In any case, rigorously though the amateurs ruled, Test cricket would in time do as much as anything else to prove their undoing. By its very aspiration – the game played at its highest pitch of excellence – it challenged the fundamental order of English cricket's class-based system. Ultimately how good you were came to matter more than your social background. And the more importance that attached to contests with Australia, the stronger became the case for making the England team the best it could be. Given the structures in place, it took an agonisingly long time to bring about a genuine meritocracy, but the process was as inevitable as it was irreversible. The higher standards became, the harder it was for amateur cricketers to attain and maintain the necessary levels of performance in the few years typically available to them between school or university and moving into business, though a few managed to play regularly for much longer through cricket-related work as assistant secretaries or journalists (roles which, by convenient convention, were deemed not to breach amateur status).

Many preferred not to try, content instead to play occasional county cricket and appear in the Gentlemen v Players matches in which there were always 11 places available. But results in the most prestigious Gentlemen v Players contests played annually at Lord's traced an unarguable decline in amateur power: after 1906, the Gentlemen won only five times (in 1911, 1914, 1934, 1938 and 1953). When England won a Test series in Australia 4–1 in 1911-12, their best result to date, the side contained just two amateurs (Johnny Douglas and Frank Foster) in each of the five matches. No wonder there was such delight among the old-school-tie brigade when MacLaren rolled back the years by raising an XI of ten amateurs and the South African all-rounder Aubrey Faulkner to beat the Australians in a festival fixture at Eastbourne towards the end of their all-conquering tour in 1921.

Inevitably, confidence in the professional ranks grew as this shift in power unfolded, a mirroring of wider changes in British society in the years leading up to a world war which usefully served to divert attention from the rise of the suffragette movement, mounting troubles in Ulster and trade union strikes over poor living conditions. As Eric Midwinter observed, 'some saw socialist revolution on the way'. When it was put to the professionals that their tour of South Africa 1909-10 be extended by three weeks without more pay so that the amateurs could visit Victoria Falls and go game-hunting, they firmly declined – a course condemned by the *Winning Post,* a sports paper, as effectively strike action. This time, unlike in 1896, there were no repercussions.

When MCC tried to assemble a touring party to go to Australia in 1920-21, it seemed oblivious to quite how much the world had changed. Charles Fry and Reggie Spooner, both ageing amateurs, were considered as potential captains. Fortunately, perhaps, neither was willing to accept. Sydney Barnes, England's greatest bowler of the pre-First World War era and still a great bowler at 47, was invited to tour but declined when MCC refused his request to bring his wife; Douglas, the captain, was accompanied by his entire family including his parents but MCC was not prepared to extend such privileges to professional members of the team. Douglas was one of only three amateurs who appeared in the Tests on that disastrous tour, but nine amateurs were tested and largely found wanting during the five Tests that followed in England.

Things had changed, however, by the time it came to picking the side for the next tour of Australia in 1924-25. For a brief but agonising period, it appeared that Jack Hobbs, England's finest batsman, would be unable to join the tour because of health issues and because, like Barnes, he was not allowed to take his wife with him. Hobbs chose instead to accept a place on a private, non-Test tour of South Africa on which his wife could join him at no expense to himself. He was actually left out of the England side for the fourth of the five home Tests against South Africa while this crisis played out. Only once Lord Harris, now MCC's president, got to hear of it was Hobbs asked if he would tour Australia if his wife was after all allowed to travel. Hobbs agreed, although he was still required to pay for his wife himself, while MCC dressed up their climbdown in claims that new medical advice meant Hobbs could now safely travel. The fact was though that Hobbs 'had quietly named his terms and achieved them'.*

---

* The accommodation of Hobbs's demands did not stop life being difficult for lesser players. When Frank Watson, the Lancashire professional, turned down an invitation to tour New Zealand in 1929-30 he was asked to write to MCC expressing his contrition. He never played for England.

The terms offered to all the professionals on the 1924-25 tour were much the best they had been: they received £400 plus £2 per week incidental expenses after travel, taxis, hotel and laundry costs had been met by MCC. Before this, tour fees had hovered around £300 since the days of the professionally managed tours of the 1880s, with only spasmodic improvements in travel arrangements and incidental costs. Even when Tom Hayward, George Hirst, Dick Lilley and Johnny Tyldesley – all key players – rejected terms for the 1907-08 tour, MCC made no attempt to accommodate them. But after the disasters of 1920-21 and 1921, and faced with the risk of losing such a pivotal player as Hobbs, MCC and the Board of Control softened their stance. England again lost heavily but the margin between the sides was closer than a 4-1 scoreline suggested, and in the series that followed in England in 1926 the Ashes were regained with a team overwhelmingly dominated by professional talent and with Hobbs to the fore in the finale. The wheel had turned.

## How England's Amateur Numbers Declined

In the era before the distinction between amateurs and professionals was scrapped in November 1962, amateur cricketers won 30 per cent of all caps awarded to England players in the 183 Tests played against Australia. Generally, they were better represented in home Tests as it was harder for them than professionals to commit to spending several months in the winter on tour. Overall, amateurs enjoyed their strongest period between the mid-1890s and the First World War, when their share rose to 34.9 per cent. The English tours of Australia in 1881-82 (four Tests) and 1884-85 (five Tests) were entirely professional affairs; subsequently, professionals won 46 caps out of 55 in 1920-21, and 45 out of 55 in 1911-12, 1924-25 and 1946-47. At home, they won 43 out of 55 in 1948. Amateurs won 29 caps during Ivo Bligh's largely amateur expedition to Australia in 1882-83, after which their best tallies came at home in 1899 (26 caps) and 1905 (23 caps).

Although for the first time since 1905 the number of amateur caps rose above 20 in 1956 and 1958-59, the status of some amateurs had become highly questionable which was what led, in part, to the abolition of the distinction.

## Test Matches v Australia

| Period | Home Tests | Amateur caps | % | Away Tests | Amateur caps | % |
|--------|------------|--------------|------|------------|--------------|------|
| 1877-1893 | 16 | 70 | 39.8 | 22 | 51 | 21.1 |
| 1894-1912 | 26 | 114 | 39.9 | 30 | 101 | 30.6 |
| 1920-1938 | 24 | 65 | 24.6 | 25 | 63 | 22.9 |
| 1946-1961 | 20 | 67 | 30.5 | 20 | 71 | 32.3 |
| Total | 86 | 316 | 33.4 | 97 | 286 | 26.8 |

# CHAPTER 3

# 'WG' Lights the Spark
## How he motivated Australia and England

WG Grace may have annoyed England team-mates by earning vastly more money than they could while parading as an amateur, but this was not entirely his fault. As Derek Birley wrote in his dissection of the class structure of the English game, *The Willow Wand*, 'the distinction between gentlemen and players was never a matter of money, but rather of caste.' What the professionals needed to remember, and be grateful for, was that Grace not only popularised cricket but did an enormous amount to put wind into the sails of the Test game. When Grace captained England on the one Test match tour he made of Australia in 1891-92, the average attendance for the three Tests topped 48,500, the best for any England–Australia series to that point. Without him, there might not have been Anglo–Australian tours for them to sign up for, and a tour of Australia was an attractive way to spend a winter in the days before the bigger counties such as Yorkshire, Lancashire and Surrey introduced winter pay. A tour fee of £300 compared favourably to a miner, builder or ironworker earning about £70 a year, as typically they did in the 1890s. If anything, Grace's example galvanised professionals in their own business ventures.

If he lit a spark though, it was more by accident than design. Grace had little interest in fostering an England Test team – such an idea had scant meaning when he played his first Test match in 1880 at the advanced age of 32 – and if he thought about the importance of international fixtures it would have been primarily as a money-making opportunity. He had no time or talent for the off-field requirements of leading representative teams: speech-making, diplomacy and man-management. When James Southerton, who toured under Grace in 1873–74, described him as a 'damn bad captain', these were probably the areas he was thinking of rather than on-field leadership. Grace did not turn the England team into a national institution as much as he did himself.

None of this mattered. Grace's mere involvement gave Test cricket its imprimatur: if it was to gain traction as the ultimate test of ability, and as a great public spectacle, it needed the very best players taking part, and no one doubted Grace was the very best there had been to this point. The Australians also realised that, if they were to show they could compete with England, it had to be in matches involving England's greatest cricketer. This was why Grace received repeated offers from Richard Wardill and his younger brother Ben on behalf of the Melbourne Cricket Club to play in Australia. Grace's involvement transformed the commercial viability of any tour, hence the huge fees he commanded.

His first tour of Australia in 1873–74, when he was at around his peak, was the product of several years of negotiations and proved a huge inspiration to the locals; Grace's side only met teams numbering 15, 18 or 22 but when there next arrived a party of Englishmen (under James Lillywhite, and without Grace, who had medical training and family commitments to attend to) an Australian XI was ready to face them on equal terms and duly beat them in what is now regarded as the first Test match in March 1877. Even Nottinghamshire professionals Alfred Shaw and Arthur Shrewsbury, no great admirers of Grace, unsuccessfully tried to persuade him to join their 1886–87 tour, something that needs to be borne in mind when Shrewsbury's carping letter to Shaw about Grace's conduct on the tour of 1891–92 is recalled ('If he hadn't taken Grace out, Lord Sheffield would have been £3,000 better off at the end of the tour, and also had a better team. I told you what wine would be drunk by the amateurs. Grace himself would drink enough to swim a ship'). A year later, in 1887–88, Grace was again approached, this time from both the English and Australian ends, about accompanying the amateur organised tour of that winter, but he again declined.

When he was finally persuaded to make a second tour of Australia, though it may have proved costly to Lord Sheffield, it did much to raise Australian cricket from the doldrums. No English team had visited for four years, England had won every series between the sides since 1882 and had Grace not agreed to go the tour simply would not have happened. The size of Grace's deal may have meant less money for others – and to the serious detriment of the team's strength Shrewsbury and William Gunn both declined to go – but England's 2-1 defeat was less important than the mere fact that the tour took place. Australia's enthusiasm was rekindled. Had Grace visited in the 1880s, Australian cricket might not have briefly atrophied as it did.

Grace thus made only one Test-match tour of Australia but a more accurate measure of his importance was that he was virtually ever-present in the Test matches played in England: by the time he finally retired after the first match of the 1899 series at the age of 50 (one of only three cricketers to play Tests in his fifties), he had appeared in 19 of England's first 20 home Tests; only a hand injury prevented him from appearing in the other one. The next most regular performer for England during this period was Surrey's Walter Read with 12 appearances and unlike many leading amateurs Grace never made himself unavailable for a home Test. Grace was easily the side's best batsman for most of this time, his 934 runs being double that of any other player at home bar Shrewsbury; his scores included 152 in 250 minutes in his first Test in 1880 and 170 in 270 minutes in the final Test of the 1886 series, which stood as England's best Test score at home until 1921. Australian suspicions that he benefited from pref-erential treatment from umpires cowed by his towering personality may not be without substance – though a rarer form of dismissal in those days, he was never out lbw in Tests – but even so this record suggests he was not as unfit for service as some historians, pointing to his expanding waistline once he had entered his thirties, would have us believe. He scarcely bowled for England, having been a prodigious all-rounder in county cricket in his early days, but the fact he took 39 catches in 22 Tests suggests he was either lucky to be in the right place, or remained sharp close to the wicket.

It does appear, though, that Grace used his influence to negotiate hours of play that suited him and perhaps his advanced years. In his only Tests in Australia, in 1891-92, play was confined to four and a half hours per day whereas immediately before and after that tour play in Australia typically spanned five hours. Similarly, the first Test match played in England after his retirement in 1899 saw the hours extended from five and a half hours to six, although this was a series in which it became clear that attempting to achieve a positive result in three days of play was likely to be difficult. It is worth remembering though that this was an era in which many of what would now be termed playing regulations lay in the hands of the captains more than they did the umpires. If Grace wanted short hours, to get his way he probably only had to persuade his opposite number.

Grace, above all, showed his contemporaries how to bat: bat and pad together as a defensive bedrock on what were rough pitches by later standards, but also armed with the strokes to score fluently. Before the mid-1890s few could blend both methods but others, mainly northern professionals, followed his example as best they could: Bobby Abel from Surrey; Shrewsbury, a master of back-foot watchfulness, and the three Williams, Barnes, Scotton and Gunn, all from Nottinghamshire; and George Ulyett from Yorkshire. All played innings for England lasting four hours, but the only one who could score as freely as Grace was 'Happy Jack' Ulyett, whose sunny disposition was reflected in his fondness for striking hard. His 149 at Melbourne in 1882 was England's first Test hundred on Australian soil and remained their highest score on the opening day of a Test in Australia until Bob Barber's 185 in 1966. A common argument was that the dour professionals damaged the game and that without the dash and spirit of amateur batting cricket would be the poorer, but in Test matches application was always an essential ingredient. The Australians, conditioned to playing to a finish at home and mindful of the gate money, demonstrated that.

Grace was also captain in the last 13 of his 22 Tests, the first man to provide any real continuity in the role. Australia teams may have been of variable standard but eight of these games were won and only three lost, WG's vast playing experience guaranteeing he was tactically sound if not as imaginative as some Australian counterparts who emerged in the 1890s. For the first Test match in England in 1880, social convention dictated that Lord Harris should lead the team but, in the absence of a formal selection committee, Grace – who had himself tried to arrange the fixture at Lord's earlier in the season – was closely involved in helping his good friend Harris pick the side. (Grace's involvement may have been a factor in his brothers Edward and Fred also playing in this match, the only instance of three brothers playing for England in the same Test. Tragically within days of the game Fred, aged 29, passed away through a sudden illness, the first England Test cricketer to die.)

Grace's centrality to the affairs of the England team was further confirmed by his inclusion on the inaugural Board of Control for Test Matches in England set up in 1898. The precise sequence of events leading to Grace's departure from Test cricket the following year is unclear, but it was plain that he was in terminal decline as a player and going through an irreparable split with Gloucestershire. The conclusion must have been obvious to both himself and Lord Hawke's fledgling selection committee: his race was run as a Test cricketer.

Grace's contribution went further. Australia's emergence as a cricketing force spurred him on at a time when he was running out of fields to conquer, and even someone with his enormous zest for the game was in need of refreshing; his competitive juices duly stirred, he in turn pushed Australia to strive harder. The starting point was an Australian victory over the amateur might of MCC, led by Grace, in a single day's play at Lord's early on in their first tour of England in 1878; some reports even termed the vanquished team as 'England'. Although it was not officially billed as a Test, this was a far more significant event than the first Test match in Australia the previous year as English cricket, as well as its best player, was challenged in its notions of superiority. Battle was now joined. When, later in the tour, Grace discovered that Billy Midwinter – who was born in Gloucestershire and divided his time between playing for Victoria in Australia in the winter and for Grace's county side in the summer – was about to start a match for the Australians at Lord's when Grace was expecting him at The Oval, Grace (according to one account) headed off in a hansom cab to 'kidnap' him. However it happened, Midwinter ended up playing for Gloucestershire and not the touring team, and it required an apology from Grace to ensure the Australians fulfilled a subsequent fixture against Gloucestershire, which they proceeded to win in vengeful fashion.*

Grace subsequently played an important part in the creation of the Ashes, which arose out of the historic Test at The Oval in 1882. With Australia leading by 75 in their second innings with four wickets in hand and their captain Billy Murdoch at the crease, Grace ran out Murdoch's partner Sam Jones in contentious fashion, Jones having left his crease to pat down a divot. Grace's appeal was upheld by umpire Bob Thoms as Jones had just completed a single and the ball was still in play, but it incensed the Australians, especially their star bowler Fred Spofforth who, according to legend, went into the England dressing-room at the end of the innings to berate Grace as a 'cheat'. Fuelled by righteous indignation, Spofforth then bowled unchanged for 28 (four-ball) overs, mostly in tandem with Harry Boyle, to win the match for his side by seven runs despite Grace, having walked out to the middle to a volley of invective from the close fielders, scoring 32.

England only needed 32 more when Grace was fourth out, and they added another 13 before the next wicket triggered a whole-sale collapse as the pressure became too much for them and most onlookers. 'Men who were noted for their coolness at critical moments were shaking like a leaf – some were shivering with cold – some even fainted,' Charles Alcock, the Surrey secretary, wrote. 'The reaction after the severe tension of the last half-hour left the

---

* Midwinter, who had already played two Tests for Australia, subsequently played four for England in Australia in 1881-82, before reverting to representing Australia; he remains the only man to appear for both teams in England–Australia matches. He managed to finish with a losing record for both. He died in a Melbourne asylum at the age of 39 following the death of his wife and two children.

spectators almost paralysed [and] it is said that the reporters, whose duty it was to telegraph to the evening papers, were so overcome as to forget to transmit the result.' Such a sensational first Australia Test victory on English soil, with Grace in the opposition, sparked the Anglo–Australian rivalry into life, prompting Reginald Shirley Brooks's mock obituary of English cricket in the *Sporting Times* and calls for a team to go to Australia and redeem English honour. This duly happened, Ivo Bligh's side – initially charged with playing three matches against the Australians who had just proved victorious in England – returning home with 'the Ashes' eight months later, the notion given physical substance by some Melbourne ladies (one of whom Bligh married almost a year later) presenting him with a small urn in a velvet bag.*

Grace never shed his reputation in Australian eyes for sharp practice; Joe Darling, who first toured England in 1896, recounted how he was warned to watch out for Grace as he was a 'great bluffer'. Tales of Australian grievance should be heard with caution though. Australians were not averse to gamesmanship either: the 1891-92 series in which Grace was suspected of all manner of skulduggery began with Jack Blackham seemingly duping Grace over the toss of the coin ahead of the first Test in order to ensure his side batted first when their key bowler Charlie Turner was ailing and in need of recovery time. Grace, a qualified doctor, also fixed Turner's finger during the Manchester Test of 1893, without which Turner would have been unable to play a match-saving innings.

---

* An additional fixture against a 'Combined Eleven', including players who had not toured England, was won by the Australians, leading to later claims that the 'series' was drawn 2-2. However, Scyld Berry and Rupert Peploe in their definitive account of the tour, wrote: 'In the aftermath of the third Test in Sydney, the general opinion in both hemispheres was that Bligh's men had succeeded in their quest.' The 4in-high urn remained in the possession of Bligh, who became Lord Darnley in 1900, until his death in 1927 when it was bequeathed to MCC and subsequently put on display at Lord's. There have been occasional demands, steadfastly resisted by MCC, for the urn to be treated as a trophy and handed over to whichever side won the Ashes; legally, the urn is a privately held keepsake in trust with MCC. It has twice been sent to Australia for display: for the country's bicentenary in 1988 and when England toured in 2006-07. In modern times, replica urns have been held aloft by winning captains and a Waterford Crystal representation of the urn has also been presented to the Ashes winners since 1998-99.

Without Grace, not only would Anglo–Australian cricket have been less viable, it would have been less vibrant.

## England's Families

The Graces were the first of 33 families to have provided England with multiple Test cricketers; in all, 70 of England's 690 Test cricketers – or 10 per cent of the total – have been closely related to one another. These included 13 fathers and sons, two grandfathers and grandsons, 12 sets of brothers, four uncles and nephews, and four sets of cousins.

| Family | Test caps | England Test cricketers (eldest first, with date of debut) |
|---|---|---|
| Grace | 24 | Edward 1880, WG 1880, Frederick 1880 (brothers); *all three played together in one Test* |
| Studd | 9 | George 1882, Charles 1882 (brothers); *played together in four Tests* |
| Hearne | 16* | George 1892, Frank 1889, Alec 1892 (brothers), Jack 1892 (their cousin); *in one Test, George and Alec played for England and Frank for South Africa* |
| Gunn | 32 | William 1887 (uncle), John 1901, George 1907 (brothers; nephews) |
| Wilson | 3 | Clem 1899, Rockley 1921 (brothers) |
| Tyldesley | 45 | Johnny 1899, Ernest 1921 (brothers) |
| Harris/Haig | 9 | Lord Harris 1879 (uncle), Nigel Haig 1921 (nephew) |
| Tate | 40 | Fred 1902 (father), Maurice 1924 (son) |
| Russell/ Freeman | 22 | Jack Russell 1920, Tich Freeman 1924 (cousins) |
| Ranji/Duleep | 27 | Ranjitsinhji 1896 (uncle), Duleepsinhji 1929 (nephew) |
| Gilligan | 15 | Arthur 1922, Harold 1930 (brothers); *both captained England* |
| Townsend | 5 | Charles 1899 (father), David 1935 (son) |

* Frank Hearne also played four Tests for South Africa.

| Family | Test caps | England Test cricketers (eldest first, with date of debut) |
| --- | --- | --- |
| Hardstaff | 28 | Joe snr 1907 (father), Joe jnr 1935 (son) |
| Mann | 12 | Francis 1922 (father), George 1948 (son); *both captained England* |
| Parks | 47 | Jim snr 1937 (father), Jim jnr 1954 (son) |
| Richardson | 35 | Peter 1956, Dick 1957 (brothers); *played together in one Test* |
| Edrich | 116 | Bill 1938, John 1963 (cousins) |
| Hutton | 84 | Leonard 1937 (father), Richard 1971 (son) |
| Greig | 60 | Tony 1972, Ian 1982 (brothers) |
| Cowdrey | 120 | Colin 1954 (father), Chris 1984 (son); *both captained England* |
| Smith | 70 | Chris 1983, Robin 1988 (brothers) |
| Stewart | 141 | Micky 1963 (father), Alec 1990 (son) |
| Butcher | 72 | Alan 1979 (father), Mark 1997 (son) |
| Hollioake | 6 | Adam 1997, Ben 1997 (brothers); *played together in one Test* |
| Sidebottom | 23 | Arnie 1985 (father), Ryan 2001 (son) |
| Jones | 33 | Jeff 1964 (father), Simon 2002 (son) |
| Tremlett | 15 | Maurice 1948 (grandfather), Chris 2007 (grandson) |
| Broad | 151 | Chris 1984 (father), Stuart 2007 (son) |
| Bairstow | 67 | David 1979 (father), Jonny 2012 (son) |
| Compton | 94 | Denis 1937 (grandfather), Nick 2012 (grandson) |
| Ali | 59 | Kabir 2003, Moeen 2014 (cousins) |
| French/Ball | 20 | Bruce French 1986 (uncle), Jake Ball 2016 (nephew) |
| Curran | 11 | Tom 2017, Sam 2018 (brothers) |

Several England Test cricketers were related to players who appeared in Test cricket for other countries. They include: Albert Trott 1899 (brother Harry played for Australia); Duleepsinhji 1929 (nephews Hanumant Singh and Indrajitsinhji played for India); the Nawab of Pataudi snr 1932 (son Mansur Ali Khan Pataudi played for India); Roger Tolchard

1977 (cousin Roger Twose played for New Zealand); Roland Butcher 1981 (cousin Basil Butcher played for West Indies); Dean Headley 1997 (father Ron and grandfather George played for West Indies); Darren Pattinson 2008 (brother James played for Australia); Gary Ballance 2014 (uncle David Houghton played for Zimbabwe). A further four families have provided England with a Test player and a one-day player (Test player named first): brothers Alan Wells 1995 and Colin Wells 1985; father MJK Smith 1958 and son Neil Smith 1996; father David Lloyd 1974 and son Graham Lloyd 1996; father Peter Willey 1976 and son David Willey 2015.

# CHAPTER 4

# Demon Spofforth and the Australians
## England meet their match

There would have been no need for a regular England team had there not been someone worth playing. For a long time, there wasn't and such teams as were titled England did not take the field as nationally representative XIs. During Hambledon's greatness of the late 1700s, they played teams called England that were really the 'Rest of England' or 'Anyone but Hambledon'. England sides later faced the likes of Surrey, Kent, Sussex and MCC on a similar basis; WG Grace's first first-class century was for England v Surrey in 1865. None of the famous All England or other wandering XIs that toured the United Kingdom between the 1840s and 1870s saw themselves as representing the nation. Why would they? They were spreading the gospel of the game for commercial gain, passing on skills with one hand, selling equipment and gathering gate receipts with the other.

It was when this entrepreneurial spirit took players abroad – to North America in 1859-60 and then, with North America off limits due to the American Civil War, to significant acclaim to Australia in 1861-62 and again in 1863-64 – that the seeds of international competition were sown. Two Surrey cricketers, Charles Lawrence and William Caffyn, stayed behind after early tours of Australia to coach in Melbourne and Sydney, Lawrence subsequently acting as captain and coach to a little-regarded Aborigine team that toured England in 1868, and Caffyn tutoring Charles Bannerman, scorer of the first Test-match century.

Other Englishmen settled in Australia with cricket in their blood: Bransby Cooper, a member of Australia's first Test XI, was born in India, educated at Rugby school and played for Middlesex and Kent before emigrating in 1869; five others in the team were born in England. Australian cricketers were soon sufficiently enterprising to strike out on tours of their own. The tour they undertook in 1878 was astonishing in its scope and ambition: encompassing matches in Australia, New Zealand, England, Scotland, the United States and Canada, it lasted more than a year. By initially visiting Britain every other year, the Australians crowded out the North Americans, making seven tours by 1890 to Philadelphia's two, and providing England with their only serious competition until South Africa's faltering emergence.

Australia's cricket developed at such a rate as to surprise not only their opponents but themselves. The rise was actually too precipitous to sustain, their first Test victory in England in 1882 being followed by only one more there in the next 14 years (and that, at Lord's in 1888, termed by *Wisden* a 'fluky defeat . . . on a mud-heap') before a more sustained flowering in the 1890s. Australia may have possessed a national cricket team before it possessed a nation – a federation of the states only arrived in 1901 – but so long as the rivalry between Melbourne and Sydney did not get out of hand, the players (although many of them continued to regard themselves as 'Englishmen') shared a collective purpose in a way the English amateurs and professionals could not.

One purpose was to simply prove themselves worthy of the contest. Australians arguably did more towards creating the Ashes 'legend' which cemented these matches than Englishmen: Florence Rose Morphy, who later married Ivo Bligh and was among the group of ladies who presented the urn to him, belonged to an Australian family and was acting on Australian press reports that made great play of Bligh's 'quest'; the lines of verse praising Bligh's team which were pasted to the front of the urn came from *Melbourne Punch* (praise for England cricketers was something the Australian media quickly grew out of). In the wake of the interest aroused by the 1882 win at The Oval, almost 170,000 Australians watched the four Tests against Bligh's team. It was also Australian cricketing publications and newspapers that did most to propagate the term 'Test match', which began to gain wide currency from 1884 when it was used by the *Melbourne Argus*.

Brash the Australians may have been, but all in all England could not have been luckier to find such opponents – good, competitive players who were likeminded in outlook and complementary in approach. They were brothers as much as they were enemies, and arguments were almost always repaired. Frederick 'The Demon' Spofforth, Australia's first great bowler, and Billy Murdoch, their first Test captain in England, both emigrated to England; Spofforth was another of solid English stock.*

Harold Larwood and Frank Tyson, two of England's greatest destroyers in Australia in future generations, settled there in retirement. It was a rivalry that had a happy knack of renewing itself, England's victory in Australia in 1894-95 and Australia's in England in 1902 cementing themselves in the psyche of both countries at important times. When England lost to Australia by three runs in Manchester in 1902, the atmosphere was fiercely partisan, reflecting a nationalism that was asserting itself thanks to Joseph Chamberlain and the Anglo–Boer War, especially the siege of Mafeking, and the increasing militarisation of Europe following Germany's victory over the French in 1871. This would only grow in the years leading up to the First World War. When English teams sailed for Australia in 1903-04 and 1911-12 they did so to large public send-offs. 'Every man was animated by one thought – the honour of English cricket,'

---

* Murdoch and Spofforth were among a number of prominent Australian cricketers who played county cricket in the pre-First World War era. Others included Jack Ferris, Albert Trott and Frank Tarrant. Australia decided against involving Murdoch or Ferris in their 1893 tour of England because they were now settled there (and in fact had joined an English tour of South Africa in 1891-92 and played in a match there which is now regarded as a Test). Trott also joined an English tour of South Africa in 1898-99. Tarrant came close to being chosen to play for England (*see* page 88).

Pelham Warner wrote of the 1911–12 side. But more still bound England and Australia than separated them. When Britain became involved in a European war in 1914, Australia still pledged to support the Mother Country, the prime minister Andrew Fisher promising to 'help and defend her to our last man and our last shilling'. If there was a point of division, the bitter legacy of that conflict – 60,000 Australians dead – provided it.

Australians were teaching cricketing lessons to the English almost as soon as matches on level terms began, forcing them to raise their game. Spofforth, every bit as feisty and competitive as WG, generally bowled medium pace but his variations in pace, spin and flight were so sophisticated as to make him almost unplayable. 'The Australians have mastered the art of bowling more thoroughly than we have,' Lord Harris wrote after England's 1878–79 tour during which Spofforth took 13 wickets in the only Test. 'They try to perfect themselves in it more than in the other departments of the game … In a few years, I believe as good a team will be turned out of the Colonies combined, as can be out of the Old Country.' Spofforth put down Australia's famous victory at The Oval in 1882 to superior tactics, describing how a single was given to Alfred Lyttelton in order that he and Harry Boyle could bowl at the men they were more likely to get out.

George Lohmann, whose Test career briefly overlapped with Spofforth's, gratefully mimicked his methods and in turn passed on what he knew to Bill Lockwood. Murdoch, the scorer of the first Test-match double-century, showed he could bat as long, if not longer, than Grace. The Australian fielding set new standards, from Jack Blackham's wicketkeeping to the agile Syd Gregory at point; Spofforth claimed Australian fielders were generally much faster over the ground than their English counterparts. Their captains set more inventive fields and ran more disciplined teams, as *Wisden*'s praise for Joe Darling's leadership of the Australians in 1902 indicated: 'In this all important matter of physical well-being they undoubtedly owed much to the precept and example of their captain. In his own sphere of action, Darling is a born leader. When he comes to England, he comes simply and solely to play cricket, and he has the rare power of being able to keep a whole team up to something approaching his own standard. He has immense concentration of purpose and under his guidance the players were just as keen at the end of three months' cricket as they had been at the beginning.' Monty Noble, who followed Darling, was just as shrewd and able.

Unencumbered of the caste system that so divided the English game and England teams, many of the early Australian teams approached tours with the same mindset, as speculative ventures on which a healthy share of gate receipts (established then and long maintained for all visiting teams to England at 50 per cent) was theirs for the taking. The players were their own masters to a degree their English counterparts could only dream of, for instance electing their own captains and managers. The English authorities looked askance, and the English professionals enviously, at the Australian players enriching themselves to the extent they sometimes did: the players who invested a £50 stake in the mammoth tour of 1878 returned home with £1,000 each, around £75,000 in today's money. MCC objected to Australians describing themselves as amateurs while clearly earning so well and it was only after they agreed to come to England as amateurs with the initial funding provided by others (though when it was provided by the Melbourne Cricket Club that caused ructions too) that Lord's was prepared to countenance them stepping through the gates. Gradually, the Australians modified their ways to the sensibilities of the English system, to show what Gideon Haigh termed 'colonial obeisance to English class niceties'.*

Australian rapacity set a disruptive example. When a large crowd turned up to one of their matches at The Oval in 1878 the Australian players raised their ticket prices from sixpence to a shilling, prompting a request from the English professionals (Shaw and Shrewsbury again prominent among them) for £20 rather than £10 when the Australians returned to The Oval later in the tour; this was rejected and replacement players found but the episode may have persuaded

---

* Gideon Haigh has suggested that it may have been as a result of the stringent demands made of the 1882 Australians to adhere to Corinthian principles that the English side sent to Australia in the winter of 1882–83 was, in an 'ensuing spirit of amity', unusually laden with amateurs.

the Surrey committee to pay the England professionals £20 each when the inaugural Test match on English soil was staged two years later.

Tours of England apart, Australian cricketers at home took to the field only sporadically and held regular jobs from which they took time off to play; hence their early view of tours as investments and hence the subsequent practice of them receiving compensation in lieu of lost earnings; occasionally, the size of this compensation became an issue, as it was ahead of the 1897-98 Ashes series. This may have further encouraged England's incoming Board of Control to restore the £20 fee in 1898. As power, and control of the purse-strings, gradually shifted from the Australian players to an amateur-run Australian Cricket Board, mirroring the shift in England from professional players to MCC, further disputes materialised, the most incendiary of which saw a group of leading players refuse to go to England in 1912. Broadly speaking, Australia's pre-1914 international players were at least as well paid as England's and readier to tour. This was another reason why England came under pressure to assemble their very best XIs. It was the only way to keep up.

# CHAPTER 5

# Boom Time
## The development of England's
## Test match grounds

The opening day of the 1896 Ashes ranks as one of the most sensational in Test cricket. So many people flocked to Lord's that Monday that the ground authorities and police could not cope. With 25,414 paying spectators and members combined, the full attendance reached around 30,000, the largest crowd to have witnessed a day of Test action to this point. If Thomas Verity's magnificent pavilion acted as some sort of pen to MCC members, out in the public areas the scene was chaotic. Inevitably, as spectators continued to pour in, they spilled onto the edges of the playing area, one report suggesting they actually encroached 10 to 15 yards onto the field, meaning 'many a ball which would ordinarily have been fielded for two, scored four'. With spectators at the back denied a view, some resorted to throwing handfuls of gravel wrapped in newspapers at those in front. 'Lord's has scarcely before been the scene of so much noisiness and rowdyism,' *The Times* reported.*

---

* Crowds at big Test matches were for many years packed into grounds in a manner that would not be allowed in the modern era, with people seated on the grass just beyond the boundary rope; this practice continued into the 1970s. Nowadays, with fielding so much more athletic, the area beyond the boundary marker is required territory for fielders.

The players were naturally unsettled, particularly the Australian batsmen who were bundled out by Tom Richardson and George Lohmann in an hour and a quarter for a total of 53. *Wisden*'s view was that 'lack of nerve on the part of the Australians must have been largely answerable for such an astounding collapse', one that inevitably cost them the game.

The turnout took the organisers by surprise, but it should not have done. The previous Ashes series in Australia in 1894–95 was the most exciting yet played and was won by England after they chased down 298 in the fifth and deciding contest thanks to an attacking hundred from Yorkshire batsman Jack Brown (who would die in 1904 aged 35). That match in Melbourne was watched over five days by the first total gate to exceed 100,000, the series drew more than 275,000, and the tour as a whole made a profit of £7,000 for the Melbourne and Sydney authorities, a boon after the expensive failure of Lord Sheffield's mission in 1891–92.* The media coverage in Britain was extensive, with the *Pall Mall Gazette* investing in regular updates. When the Australians humbled the might of MCC in 1878, reports reached Australia by means of the innovative submarine telegraph the next day, but information now travelled faster still. 'News was telegraphed every few minutes, [and] was awaited with extraordinary interest,' recounted Grace, who was among the many gripped from afar. There had never been such interest in England about an overseas series.†

That alone would have been enough to guarantee huge interest in the three 1896 Tests, but as social historian Asa Briggs calculated, this year marked a watershed in the growth of a national communications network, with the founding of the *Daily Mail*, Marconi introducing his wireless invention to the Post Office and the first cinema shows in the West End. With London increasingly at its

---

* Despite losing £2,000 on his first venture, Lord Sheffield was interested in financing another tour of Australia in 1894–95, but whereas he wanted only three Tests Melbourne and Sydney wanted five, something Stoddart agreed to.
† By the time of the 1903–04 series, the All-British Cable company was able to transmit news of the close of Australia's first innings of the first Test from Sydney to London in three and a half minutes. (*Wisden* 1922, p232)

centre, England was unified in a way it had not been before, and growing enthusiasm for a national cricket team was one manifestation of this. *Cricket*, an affordable national weekly magazine founded in 1882 by Charles Alcock, Surrey secretary and a visionary figure in the development of several sports, promoted the leading players as national heroes.

The first morning at Lord's served as a warning. Within three weeks the MCC committee sanctioned additional temporary seating for Australia's next visit to the ground the following month ('urge the means for providing as much accommodation as possible in this way at once') and instructed Frank Verity – son of Thomas, who had died in 1891, the year after his pavilion was opened – to submit designs for the construction in the winter of what became the Mound Stand. The subsequent Tests at Old Trafford in Manchester and The Oval duly passed off without incident, even though 44,000 watched Australia win by three wickets in Manchester despite a great counter-attacking innings of 154 from the Indian-born cricketer Ranjitsinhji in his first match for England, and 55,000 seeing England come off best again in the decider in Kennington. As a whole, the series saw an almost doubling of the aggregate attendance for the three Tests compared with Australia's visit in 1893.

In an era when revenues were almost wholly generated by gate receipts, this was a development that could not be ignored – and wasn't. The five professionals who threatened to strike ahead of the Oval Test knew what they were doing: with interest at such unprecedented levels, their action was certainly not going to go unnoticed by the wider world. The administrators, for their part, began a wholesale review of the way Test cricket was organised which included following the Australian model and arranging five Tests rather than three for the next series in England in 1899, establishing a formula that has largely been adhered to ever since.

It was said that WG Grace inspired the building of half the great cricket grounds in England, but the advent of Test cricket was the really significant factor. The big county clubs based in the major conurbations grew wealthier on growing memberships, but Test cricket was good business from the outset and, then as often now, a prize worth pursuing for the hosts. The three grounds that had so far staged Tests (The Oval, Old Trafford and Lord's) plus others that aspired to join them (Trent Bridge, Headingley and Edgbaston) had all either purchased the land on which they stood or secured long-term lease arrangements, and were in the process of significantly upgrading their facilities. With the move to five home Tests in the offing, that process continued apace, although there was anxiety for Nottinghamshire when, at the inaugural meeting of the Board of Control in 1898, 'substantial claims' were also made on behalf of Gloucestershire's ground at Bristol. Bristol's facilities were clearly inferior and the bid could only have been the work of WG Grace, though Nottinghamshire's history of rebellion could have counted against them too, especially as during the meeting itself they proposed – unsuccessfully – that MCC should receive less than the proposed 20 per cent of receipts from the Tests they staged. In the event, Nottinghamshire won the ballot among the 12 members.

Strikingly, the pavilions built during this period at Trent Bridge (1886), Headingley (1889), Lord's (1890), Old Trafford (1895) and The Oval (1898) were so well designed and constructed that they still stand today, albeit that those at Headingley, Old Trafford and The Oval no longer house the dressing-rooms. They are a tribute to their architects: Thomas Verity, an established theatre designer and creator of the Albert Hall who built the Lord's pavilion; Thomas Muirhead, who built those at Old Trafford and The Oval; and HM Townsend, a Peterborough firm, whose design for the Trent Bridge pavilion inspired the one at Headingley built by Smith and Tweedale. Both Trent Bridge and Headingley staged their first Tests in 1899 and Edgbaston put on its first Test three years later. So successful did they prove as venues that England needed to commission no new Test ground between 1902 and the arrival of the Riverside stadium in Durham in 2003.

In terms of organisation, Surrey and Lancashire set the standard. Charles Alcock was the first in England to exploit the potential for a match on equal terms between England and Australia and, after Lord's refused to host the Australians during their 1880 tour partly because of their questionable amateur credentials and partly because of the trouble in Sydney in 1878-79, he with Lord Harris's help set up at short notice the first Test staged on English soil that September, paying Sussex £100 to cancel their fixture with the Australians in order to create space in the fixture list.

Largely at Alcock's instigation, The Oval had already staged many of the early football and rugby internationals, as well as most of the FA Cup finals, although in front of relatively small crowds. The Australians attracted big attendances for their matches at The Oval in 1878 following their famous defeat of MCC at Lord's, and the logistical challenges those fixtures presented, with swathes of people overrunning the turnstiles at the first of them, prepared Alcock for the 1880 Test which was watched by more than 20,000 paying spectators on each of the first two days.

Two years later, and with the Surrey committee now more receptive to hosting the Australians, similar numbers attended the two days of cricket that culminated in Australia's sensational first Test victory on English soil; four appearances on the ground by the touring team gave a significant boost to Surrey's coffers; match receipts for the season totalled £12,329 whereas in 1881 they had been £2,260. The briskly efficient Alcock acted as local organiser, or agent, for a number of the early Australian touring teams as well as those from other countries until the creation of the Board of Control for Test Matches in England, by which time he had secured for The Oval a place that it still holds today as the traditional venue for the final Test of the summer and, in Australia years, of Ashes-winning celebrations. As such, no other English ground can lay claim to quite so many cherished memories.*

Old Trafford, under the stewardship of WE Howard, also acted quickly to capitalise on the popularity of the 1878 Australians by erecting temporary stands for Lancashire's fixture against them, garnering handsome receipts of £730. By the mid-1880s, Old Trafford

---

* The Oval staged the second Test and Old Trafford the third and final Test when Australia toured in 1888, 1890 and 1893, but The Oval was restored as venue for the final Test in 1896, a position it has held ever since whenever Australia tour.

boasted a ladies' tea room and special facilities for newspaper reporters and scorers.

Lord's, which in 1884 staged its first Test 11 days after Old Trafford
made its debut, was ill-run by comparison until Francis Lacey, later the
first man knighted for services to cricket, took over as MCC secretary
in 1898 in time to pick up the pieces of the 1896 fiasco. A barrister
by profession, Lacey brought a more businesslike approach to affairs,
although even under him Lord's was slower than other grounds to
respond to the needs of the press. 'I cannot see why MCC should be
so reluctant to build a proper press box as a continuation of the new
Mound Stand,' *Wisden* editor Sydney Pardon complained in 1901.
'MCC have spent thousands of pounds during the last few years to
increase the accommodation for their members and the public and they
might surely do for the newspapers what has been done at Manchester,
Leeds and Nottingham ... It is hardly the thing for the first cricket
club in the world to thus lag behind the counties in such a manner.'

For the Tests of 1902 and 1905 the newspapers reported from the
Mound Stand before the press box was destroyed in a storm, after
which they were moved to the pavilion. When, in the late 1950s,
press-men were housed in the new Warner Stand, along with radio
and television broadcasters, *Wisden* went on the attack again: 'the
long-leg or third-man view should not have been inflicted on those
people whose day-to-day duties are to give a faithful description of
the cricket.' Nothing, though, could disturb the ground's status as
headquarters of MCC and, for many generations, as nerve-centre
of the world game, a position that attracted both veneration for its
hallowed turf and resentment of its dictatorial bearing.

Elsewhere, territorial battles were fought for supremacy. In
Yorkshire, Bramall Lane, Sheffield was the base of the county club
from the 1860s until Headingley, Leeds, in a move engineered by
Lord Hawke, began hosting the majority of the county's home
matches in the 1890s. Even though Headingley staged its maiden
Test in 1899, Sheffield was preferred in 1902 but the fixture was not
a success, and not just because England lost; the facilities were unre-
markable and the ground was surrounded by factories and foundries
which scattered black dust over the field. The following year, the

Yorkshire committee decided to permanently relocate to Leeds, and although Bramall Lane continued to stage county matches until the 1970s, it never hosted another Test.

Having seen off Bristol in the 1898 ballot, Trent Bridge soon had to contend with competition from Birmingham, 50 miles to the southwest. Trent Bridge's preparations for its first Test included the construction of a ladies' pavilion, extensive areas of covered seating for non-members, as well as indoor nets, believed to be the first in the country, and total expenditure was put at £4,000. However, come the match it hardly helped itself by continuing to display such an abrasively independent streak, the crowd heckling irreverently at WG Grace for his lack of mobility in the field. This spirit of rebelliousness in Nottinghamshire cricket had manifested itself in its involvement in the early pay disputes, and would again through its role in the Bodyline and Packer controversies, creating an uneasy relationship with Lord's. The club's influence on England cricket has been occasionally profound but perhaps not as weighty as it ought to have been. Startlingly, it has not provided England with a Test captain since Arthur Carr, one of the architects of Bodyline; indeed, Carr is the only Nottinghamshire player ever to captain England in a home Test.

In 1902, Trent Bridge lost out to Birmingham but, fortunately for Nottinghamshire, Warwickshire had difficulty enticing the public through Edgbaston's gates in good numbers. Largely as a result, Birmingham was granted only four Tests before 1957, when, having undergone some significant post-war redevelopment which included a distinctive new scoreboard built in 1950, it staged a Test in the same summer as Nottingham for the first time and finally joined the regular Test-match roster*. This proved the start of a remarkable renaissance which would lead to Edgbaston becoming the happiest of all England's hunting grounds, but the ground might easily have suffered a similar fate to Sheffield.

Roland Ryder had arrived as Warwickshire secretary in 1896

---

* Trent Bridge also unveiled a new scoreboard in 1950. This showed all the players' names, a feature not replicated in England until the advent of electronic boards in the 1990s.

and organised the building of a new permanent stand and two temporary ones – commandeered from Aston Villa Football Club and
drawn across the city by horse – plus accommodation for reporters.
Unfortunately, after George Hirst and Wilfred Rhodes sensationally
dismissed Australia for 36 on the second day of the 1902 Test, still
their lowest score against England, heavy rain flooded the ground on
the final morning. In anticipation of a blank day, the committee paid
off half the gatemen and released half the police, but the players and
umpires waited, a sizeable crowd gathered outside, and at 2pm a hot
sun came out. The crowd stormed the gates. 'To save our skins we
started play at 5.20[pm] on a swamp,' Ryder recalled. Warwickshire
finished heavily out of pocket and were obliged to launch an end-
of-season fundraising appeal for £3,000.

Generally speaking, though, the ground investments paid off
handsomely. The 1899 Ashes Tests were a huge success, with almost
250,000 people attending the 15 days of the series even though the
final day of the Leeds Test was rained off. *Wisden* thought Trent
Bridge went to unnecessary lengths in erecting new stands round
a great portion of the ground but the Test there drew more than
40,000 people. The greatest hit was Old Trafford where each of the
first two days was watched by about 30,000 with 10,000 more turned
away. Crucially not just the host grounds shared in the financial consequences: one precept of the incoming Board of Control was that
there should be an equitable apportioning of revenues (half of gate
receipts plus money taken at the stands and enclosures less expenses)
and it was deemed that while the host venues would receive 30 per
cent, 60 per cent would be distributed among the other first-class
counties and MCC, and 10 per cent to the Minor Counties.* The
broad principle that money generated by the England team should
benefit all counties to some degree even if they had not staged an
international match or provided players survives to this day, and it
has helped keep the counties afloat.

Although the amateur class which took such pride in its batting
might not have liked it, and the public-school educated historians

---

* The other half of gate receipts went to England's opponents.

may not have recorded it, many spectators preferred to cheer the professional artisans nurtured from the same earthy soil as themselves – Tom Hayward and Bobby Abel, Tom Richardson and George Lohmann, Hirst and Rhodes, and the perennially youthful Johnny Briggs, who tragically fell ill during the Leeds Test of 1899. 'These were the cricketers who became the heroes of the working-class fans in the sixpenny stands,' wrote Ric Sissons in his seminal *The Players: A Social History of the Professional Cricketer.* 'Ordinary people readily identified with players who shared their class background and who, in theory, offered their own sons the chance of a temporary exit from the routine drudgery of work ... In the context of the major contribution the professionals made to popularising cricket as a national institution they were undervalued and underpaid.'

Bigger attendances subtly raised the stakes. Such large crowds were more partisan, if not downright hostile to the visitors: when England toured Australia in 1897-98, they found themselves persistently barracked by crowds bigger than even three years earlier; in turn, Australia found some less-than-welcome receptions in 1902. A line had been crossed and it meant that for the biggest fixtures selection needed to take account of a player's temperament, or at least ought to have done. Arthur Shrewsbury, the first England batsman to score 1,000 Test runs but someone who had long been of fragile disposition, declined to make himself available for the third Test of 1899, believing that at 43 the strain would be too great for him; he did not play for England again. Charles Fry, who found public and press criticism hard to take, and tended to suffer from nerves on big occasions, several times changed his mind about playing for England. When he was finally appointed England captain in 1912 at the age of 40, he missed the simplest of catches against South Africa at Lord's and promptly retreated into the deep field, where he squandered another chance.* Colin Blythe, though on occasions a match-winner,

---

* Fry's appointment as England captain was greeted in some quarters with scepticism, but he received the support of the 'Pavilion Gossip' column in *Cricket*, on 12 May 1912: 'Some people don't fancy Charles Fry as a Test match leader. One says he is nervous ... and another that he has never done much in Test matches anyway ... Highly strung? Yes – so are many of the best leaders in all of life's activities. Nervous? No.'

became so stressed by the prospect of Test cricket that he was medically advised not to play at Lord's in 1909.

The ground redevelopments presented opportunities to review the treatment of amateurs and professionals. In London, at Lord's and The Oval, the feudal division was maintained, with separate changing facilities and separate gates onto the field of play, though the new 1898 pavilion at The Oval made improvements for both. 'The best places for following the game have been given, and quite rightly, to the gentlemen engaged in the cricket; their dressing and sitting rooms command an exact end-on view of the cricket pitch, while the professionals have an almost equally good position,' *The Times* reported. 'The Surrey committee are to be commended for striking out a fresh line in their thought for the players' comfort. The old professional box tacked on to the pavilion at Lord's is always an eyesore to many of the Marylebone Club members.'

There may have been a reversion of these arrangements though; as late as the 1930s, Hobbs complained about the cramped basement quarters given to professionals. At Lord's the segregation policy extended even to its dining arrangements, Hobbs describing the lunch provided to professionals as 'always one of the worst in England' – at least until 1922, when they were finally taken to eat with the amateurs. Alec Bedser said that even in the 1930s, 'To see play from the pros' room at Lord's it was necessary to stand on a chair or on tiptoe.' Even when the rules were relaxed, it seemed old habits died hard. Patsy Hendren, writing in *Wisden* in 1938, stated that professionals 'had the option' at Lord's of going through the centre-gate on to the field, 'but they probably think it too much trouble to walk along there from the dressing-room'.

Things were more relaxed in the provinces. At Trent Bridge in 1898 the amateur changing-room was moved from the east side of the pavilion to the west where the professional facilities were already located (admittedly in the basement; they were now moved upstairs). This meant that from the very start of the ground's time as a Test venue, all the players used the same staircase and the same gate onto the field. Similarly, at Old Trafford, although the new pavilion had three bathrooms for amateurs and only one for professionals, this was an improvement on the previous arrangements that saw professionals change in a cramped room on the other side of the ground. For the 1902 Test, when Lancashire's own Archie MacLaren was England captain, amateurs and professionals entered the playing area side by side, one newspaper reporting: 'As the players went to the wicket there was an outbreak of cheering – the citadel of conservatism had at last been stormed!' A contemporary photograph shows MacLaren leading the players down the pavilion steps followed by amateurs Lionel Palairet and Ranjitsinhji and the professional Len Braund. This would hardly have endeared Lancashire to Lord's, who probably mistrusted Old Trafford's strong-willed committee and strong-minded captains almost as much as it did Trent Bridge's.

Though small, these changes must have lent greater cohesion to the England team and enhanced esprit de corps, even if the physical segregation of the dressing-rooms continued to hinder the development of strategy – assuming, of course, a captain was prepared to heed the input of senior professionals.

The problem of over-congestion at Test matches in England, especially Ashes matches where there was a great temptation to pack in the crowds, was not however solved by the building programmes of the late-Victorian era. There was another case of administrative bungling at the gates on the opening day of the Lord's Test in 1921, the first played there after the First World War, when according to *Wisden* 'many ticket holders being greatly delayed and inconvenienced in getting through . . . MCC came in for some sharp criticism, and were compelled to put forward an explanation.' Eyewitness accounts testified to women fainting amid the crush, as well as lavatory arrangements being spectacularly inadequate at the back of the Mound Stand. Similarly, with interest again high after the Second World War, when more than 500,000 watched the five Tests played by Bradman's Invincibles, boundaries were again pushed in. 'Some of the hits that passed for boundaries in the 1948 series deserved no more than two runs,' Jack Fingleton wrote.

## England's Record in Home Test Matches

| Ground | First Test | Tests | Won | Lost | Drawn |
| --- | --- | --- | --- | --- | --- |
| The Oval, London | 6 Sep 1880 | 101 | 42 | 22 | 37 |
| Old Trafford, Manchester | 10 Jul 1884 | 77 | 28 | 14 | 35 |
| Lord's, London | 21 Jul 1884 | 135 | 54 | 32 | 49 |
| Trent Bridge, Nottingham | 1 Jun 1899 | 62 | 22 | 18 | 22 |
| Headingley, Leeds | 29 Jun 1899 | 76 | 33 | 25 | 18 |
| Edgbaston, Birmingham | 29 May 1902 | 51 | 28 | 8 | 15 |
| Bramall Lane, Sheffield | 3 Jul 1902 | 1 | 0 | 1 | 0 |
| Riverside, Chester-le-Street | 5 Jun 2003 | 6 | 6 | 0 | 0 |
| Sophia Gardens, Cardiff | 8 Jul 2009 | 3 | 2 | 0 | 1 |
| Rose Bowl, Southampton | 16 Jun 2011 | 3 | 2 | 0 | 1 |
| Total | | 515 | 217 | 120 | 178 |

*Up to 23 July 2019*

In addition, two scheduled Test matches against Australia at Old Trafford (in 1890 and 1938) were abandoned without a ball bowled.

# CHAPTER 6

# Hawke, Warner and the Amateur Coup

## Yorkshire become England's greatest asset

No man did more to give shape and direction to the England team than Martin Hawke, or Lord Hawke as he became following the death of his father, the sixth baron, in 1887, an event which forced Martin's early departure from a tour of Australia. Yorkshire's regular championship captain from 1886 until 1908, Hawke was the prime mover behind the administrative changes of 1898, one result of which was that he chaired the newly created Test selection panel for its first ten years. By taking such initiative at this early stage in the evolution of the national team, Hawke did much to cement MCC's position as executors of England affairs while also establishing Yorkshire as the most powerful contributing county to the national cause, a position it has frequently occupied since. Like Lord Harris, Hawke did much as a young man to help England's Test team which his reactionary behaviour in later years should not overshadow.

By showing an interest in each player under his charge whatever his background, and caring for retired players who had hit hard times, Hawke set a standard in captaincy. He also oversaw improvements in pay at county and international level that, although limited, allowed professionals to achieve greater affluence and influence.

However, his contribution was ambivalent: he helped ensure that the captaincy and management of the national team remained in amateur hands for the next 50 years: the declining representation of amateurs in the England team was not mirrored in the corridors of power. By the 1920s Hawke was well out of touch with changes in public mood, as shown by the immediate hostility to his infamous comment at Yorkshire's annual dinner in 1925, 'Pray God, no professional shall ever captain England.' Yet, so firm was the amateur executive's grip on power that this prayer stayed answered until 1952, although shortly before he died Hawke saw a former professional, Walter Hammond, lead England competently enough against Australia in 1938 to elicit his praise.

This should not overshadow the good that he did. Hawke took it upon himself to turn Yorkshire into the best and most disciplined county side and was so successful that it virtually guaranteed a steady supply of top-quality players to the national team. When Wilfred Rhodes made his championship debut for the club against Somerset in May 1898 he was one of nine players in the team, including Hawke, who either had or would play in matches now designated Tests. Yorkshire had won the championship in 1893 and 1896, and would do so again that season and five times more before Hawke stepped down. It was first proof of a saying that has never died: 'When Yorkshire are strong, England are strong.' Yorkshire have provided more Test players to England, and won more England Test caps, than any other county, and the quality was consistently high too. 'I do not remember a single instance of a plain, unmistakable failure in Test cricket by a chosen Yorkshireman,' Neville Cardus wrote in 1938. In a large county which by 2017 was calculated to provide 12 per cent of the entire cricket-playing population of the country, the strength has generally resided more in the west around Leeds, Bradford and Sheffield than Hull to the east or Middlesbrough to the north.

Turning Yorkshire into an indestructible cricketing institution was not easy. Born into a family with a tradition of service in the army and navy, Hawke persuaded himself (and his father) of another course after progressing through Eton and Cambridge; the sheer size of the task was the challenge. Yorkshire had rarely been short of talent – they provided five players to the first England Test XI – but under the professional leadership of Tom Emmett an unhealthy drinking culture developed (Emmett himself sported a famously red nose). It was said that Hawke had charge of 'nine drunks and a chapel parson', a reference to opening batsman Louis Hall being a lay preacher and teetotal (as was John Tunnicliffe, who succeeded Hall at the top of the order). The claim was exaggerated – Billy Bates, who took the first hat-trick for England in a Test in Melbourne in 1883, was known for his clean living and sartorial elegance – but contained an essential truth. Hawke sacked both Ted Peate and Bobby Peel for insobriety when they were still seen as England cricketers as well as Yorkshire ones (Archie MacLaren described Peel as 'the cleverest bowler in my time').

On what proved to be his final Test tour, Peel bowled England to a sensational ten-run victory in Sydney only after being thrust under the shower to sober up following a night on the town; Peel thought that Australia, needing 64 to win with eight wickets in hand, were sure to win, only for overnight rain to transform the pitch in favour of England's bowlers. If Hawke's actions were severe, the aim was achieved: Rhodes, who inherited Peel's place, became exactly the sort of respectable professional Hawke envisaged doing service for club and country.

Hawke started out as often the only amateur in the Yorkshire team and this gave him insight into the lives of professionals; unlike some captains, he had no qualms dealing with them. He did much to improve their welfare, introducing a system copied by other counties of awarding bonus payments according to performance and, although some grumbled about not being better rewarded, things would have been worse without him. Hawke, for instance, saw the legitimacy of the threatened strike by Test players in 1896. When Billy Bates found his career ended by a freak eye injury in Australia and, despairing of his future, tried to commit suicide on the voyage home, Hawke helped organise a benefit fund. Also, when Dick Barlow, a former Lancashire and England all-rounder-turned-umpire, was summoned to Lord's to explain a dispute with Sussex captain Ranjitsinhji during a county match, Hawke ensured Lancashire stuck to their agreement to reimburse Barlow's expenses. He helped George Hirst find a coaching position at Eton. 'He gave to professional cricket a status of dignity and pride, and by his insistence upon an attractive standard of payment and living conditions he could ask for a correspondingly high standard of conduct, so drawing to professional cricket men of admirable character,' Jim Kilburn wrote.

With guaranteed income from company directorships, Hawke devoted time to the game in summer and winter, organising and leading largely amateur teams to Australia (1887), India (1890 and 1892), the United States and Canada (1891 and 1894), South Africa (1895 and 1898), West Indies (1896) and Argentina (1912). Pelham Warner called him the 'Odysseus of cricket . . . the first to preach the gospel of cricket throughout the Empire'. Hawke stimulated a process that led to the provision of more Test-match opposition for England while also gaining greater insight into the nature of touring, something his contact with the Yorkshire professionals who travelled on Test tours also provided. Full England tours were in as much need of reform as Yorkshire cricket: some of the early expeditions, especially those under professional control, were rough affairs on which betting was alleged – in at least one instance in a match against Victoria on the 1881–82 tour of Australia match-fixing by two players, George Ulyett and John Selby, was suspected – while excessive drinking was commonplace.*

Ted Pooley, wicketkeeper on the tour of 1876–77, missed the two Tests because he was languishing in jail in New Zealand having assaulted a local man, Ralph Donkin, over a dispute relating to a bet on a match against 18 men of Canterbury.† As a consequence,

---

* It was alleged Ulyett and Selby were offered money to lose to Victoria in a game which the English XI won by 18 runs, and that William Scotton was unsuccessfully approached to join them. James Lillywhite wrote to *Cricket* on 1 June 1882 refuting the claim: he was team manager and also umpired that game and the four Tests and insisted he saw no evidence of anyone not trying; Selby and Shaw, the captain, also tendered a written denial to MCC on 12 June. Selby never played for England again but Ulyett remained a Test regular until 1890.

† In a subsequent trial, Pooley was acquitted of breaking into and trashing Donkin's hotel room. Pooley eventually arrived back in England a month after the rest of the team. He never played Test cricket.

for the tour of 1881-82, Lillywhite, Shaw and Shrewsbury drew up a memorandum of agreement with the players – 'Professional cricketers of England' – which included a clause that £20 would be withheld in case of 'impropriety or misconduct' and redistributed among the rest, a practice that MCC adopted once it took control of tours. Withholding a portion of tour fees in lieu of good behaviour was a practice that survived until well after the Second World War.

Alfred Shaw, an experienced tour manager, said that with care a professional could return home with between £100 and £150 but because of 'expensive habits ... feasting and merrymaking' often returned home with almost nothing. 'Everyone who is at all behind the scenes in cricket knows perfectly well that in the case, both of English XIs in Australia and Australian XIs in England, the brightest hopes have sometimes been wrecked through want of self-control,' wrote Sydney Pardon in 1903. The first English team to tour South Africa in 1888-89, consisting of six professionals and seven amateurs, saw players partying hard during several early defeats, though it is unclear which members of the group were most culpable. *Wisden* reported: 'It is no libel to say that, for a time, generous hospitality had a bad effect on the cricket.'

The amateur class needed no second invitation to believe that it alone could manage things properly but many including Hawke were converted to the cause after the fiasco of two English teams, one predominantly professional, the other mainly amateur (of which Hawke was briefly a member), heading to Australia in 1887-88. The Cricket Council was created to avoid such confusion in future but the body withered when its chairman Lord Harris became Governor of Bombay in 1890. It was during a speech at Bedale to welcome George Hirst and Ted Wainwright back from the 1897-98 tour of Australia that Hawke aired his belief that MCC, on whose committee he sat, was the proper body to run England's affairs and he pointed to the Cricket Association of Australia overseeing the Australia team as an example to be followed. (In fact the Australian body soon collapsed but was replaced by an Australian Cricket Board in 1905.) Much of what Hawke advocated in his speech became policy once the counties endorsed the introduction of an MCC-instituted Board of Control.

Hawke's motives were not entirely selfless. He felt Yorkshire had sacrificed too much on England's behalf considering how many players they provided and that the club had never hosted a Test despite having a ground at Headingley 'second to none'. He wanted the host clubs' share of Test-match takings cut and the counties providing England players to be fairly rewarded. He issued in his speech a none-too-subtle threat. 'If the matches in future were arranged on the principles he suggested, he was sure they would give satisfaction to the cricket world in general, and there would be an end to the cavilling,' *Cricket* reported. 'He was also sure that if a change were not made Yorkshire would take a strong stand, and not allow their players to take part in a Test match unless it was arranged by MCC to whom they owed allegiance as the head of cricket. As the other counties were being asked for their opinions on these matters, it was as well that those of Yorkshire should be known.'

This was no idle threat: selection for home Tests, resting in the hands of the club committees hosting the matches (to this point, Surrey and Lancashire as well as MCC), was fairly parochial, with a tendency to back local favourites, and Yorkshire along with other counties had sometimes refused to release their professionals, while some amateurs preferred to play for their counties. In one notorious instance in 1893, Stanley Jackson and Bobby Peel had turned out for Yorkshire against Sussex rather than in a deciding Ashes Test at Old Trafford, even though Yorkshire had already secured the championship title.

Hawke's proposals were broadly adopted: the 12-man Board of Control – consisting of MCC's president, five members of its sub-committee and representatives of six first-class counties as selected by the club – was constructed in such a way as to give MCC an effective majority; Yorkshire joined the roster of Test-match hosts in 1899; and profits were dispersed to all first-class counties. However, Hawke's suggestion that counties providing England players be fairly rewarded was not taken up.

This was an important moment. The right had been asserted of the major clubs, armed with the best players and grounds best able to stage Test matches, to a stake in the national team. A Board of

Control might oversee the England team, but there was not one owner but several stakeholders and keeping them happy would be a constant challenge. Nor could the voice of the first-class counties who did not stage Tests (ten of them by 1899) be ignored: they provided players and wanted a slice of revenues too. Some of these issues survive to this day.

Not everything went smoothly for Lord Hawke thereafter. As chairman of selection he presided over three defeats in four home Ashes series, and a great deal of turbulence; like others after him, he found the job harder than captaincy. His committee got into almost immediate difficulty when it had to find a new leader to replace WG Grace after the first Test of 1899. By appointing Archie MacLaren (who apart from anything else had not played a first-class match for nine months), he alienated Stanley Jackson, Hawke's vice-captain at Yorkshire and son of WL Jackson, MP for Leeds North and a former Cabinet minister, who sat with Hawke on the board of the Leeds Cricket, Football and Athletic Company that owned Headingley. Stanley Jackson too had recently taken Hawke's place on the MCC committee when Hawke was obliged to temporarily stand down after serving a maximum of four consecutive years. Jackson was sufficiently aggrieved to miss the Roses match in which MacLaren played for Lancashire and he had to be cajoled into playing the remainder of the Test series.

The breakdown in their relationship was short lived. Jackson would be invited three times by Hawke to lead Ashes series and, although he declined twice for personal reasons, accepted in 1905 with glorious consequences. Yet before long Hawke, for whom diplomacy was never a strong point, had fallen out even more drastically with MacLaren after Hawke's attempts, encouraged by Ben Wardill of the Melbourne Cricket Club, to raise an MCC-managed Test tour of Australia for the first time failed when several amateurs declared their unavailability. Hawke, aged 41, had intended to manage and possibly even lead the side himself, although he conceded in a letter to Charles Townsend, a prospective member of the tour, in January 1900 that MacLaren 'was the probable captain'. MacLaren's subsequent decision to accept an invitation from

Melbourne Cricket Club to take a team himself in 1901-02, only months before Australia were to tour England, incensed Hawke chiefly because it defied his view, supported by Melbourne and the counties, that major tours were best run by MCC, not private individuals. His predictable response was to carry out the threat issued during his Bedale speech and refuse to release Hirst and Rhodes for the tour.* The subsequent bitterness between them was to have a detrimental impact on the 1902 Ashes.

Hawke and MCC did not make the same mistake for the next scheduled Test tour of Australia, in 1903-04, assembling the best team they could – Australia had after all won the last four series – and going ahead even though they had only three amateurs on board, none of whom had played Ashes matches before. This proved the start of more than 70 years of major England tours conducted under the aegis of MCC, which provided administrative stability and financial liability, although in the case of losses incurred on some early Ashes tours these were made good by the Australian board. In going with Pelham Warner as captain after Stanley Jackson had declined, Hawke created a controversy more heated than MacLaren v Jackson in 1899: the popular papers, noting Warner's lack of experience, felt MacLaren was the sounder choice, but Warner received strong backing from the cricketing establishment, Charles Alcock in *Cricket* defending him as 'the most abused man of the day'. It pitched North against South in a way that would become familiar in the years to come.

In Hawke's eyes, Warner (unlike MacLaren) could not have been more on-message. Warner was a long-standing friend with whom he had toured West Indies and South Africa and who had taken over the captaincy and management of a non-Test match tour of Australia and New Zealand the previous winter when Hawke himself withdrew because his mother was ill – key grounding for Warner for

---

* This action has often been cited as evidence of Hawke's willingness to put Yorkshire before England; in fact, it equally reflected his determination to place the administration of England cricket in the hands of MCC. Surrey shared his view and only released one player, Tom Hayward, for MacLaren's tour. Hawke was not alone among prominent figures in English cricket in regarding the expansion of Test cricket as detrimental to the county championship.

the assignment that now lay ahead. When Ben Wardill approached Warner during that tour about returning with a Test team, Warner did what MacLaren probably would not have done and directed him to MCC 'as the proper body'. Warner was as near to a protégé as Hawke had: along with Alfred Lyttelton, who was MCC president when Hawke's plans for a Board of Control were passed and in whose London legal chambers Warner had worked, Hawke had been instrumental in persuading Warner to pursue a cricket career after leaving Oxford. Warner had also played at Oxford under Henry Leveson Gower, another influential member of the MCC committee who succeeded Hawke as chairman of selectors.

Warner's devotion to the game was as impeccable as his connections. He lacked Hawke's wealth and supplemented his income through journalism, and was not quite a batsman of the first rank, but he was committed to England's cause. As a player, captain and administrator spanning more than half a century, Warner contributed as much to the affairs of the national team as any man ever has. He was passed over in favour of Jackson for the home Ashes of 1905 – Hawke co-opted him onto the selection panel instead – but with Jackson virtually giving up playing thereafter to follow his father into business and politics, Warner was asked the following winter to lead a goodwill series in South Africa for the first Test tour there since the Anglo–Boer War. He was also appointed to lead again in Australia in 1911-12, although once there illness confined him to a managerial role which played a not insignificant part in England's victory. Warner was not as strict a captain as Hawke but learned from him man-management and took a similar interest in the pastoral care of the professionals. He was instrumental in Jack Hearne and Patsy Hendren joining the Middlesex committee and was godfather to 'Young' Jack Hearne, whose selection he urged for the 1911-12 tour in the interests of long-term planning (then a novel concept). The decision was justified by Hearne scoring a match-winning century in the second Test aged 20; no one younger hit a hundred for England until Denis Compton in 1938.

Warner's appointment as captain fitted a blueprint that was to be increasingly fashionable; a captain whose loyalty and diplomacy could be depended upon even ahead of his playing ability. With cricket spreading to every corner of the Empire, leadership of an England team overseas was seen as an extension of national foreign policy. Similar requirements were made of tour managers; Frederick Toone, a man well known to Hawke as Yorkshire secretary from 1903 until his death in 1930, was appointed to manage the 1920-21, 1924-25 and 1928-29 tours of Australia, after which he was knighted for promoting good relations between 'the Commonwealth and the Mother Country'. Those chosen as captain were even expected to give their support in the committee rooms once they quit playing. Warner, again, was the exemplar: he was the first to defend Hawke when he prayed no professional would ever captain England. Hawke repaid the favour by backing Warner's appointment as a joint-manager of the 1932-33 tour of Australia (had Toone lived he would surely have managed that tour as well and the Bodyline crisis might then have been diminished).

Not everyone though met requirements quite so well as Warner, or was as available as he was, and compromises had to be countenanced. MacLaren was sounded out about leading another side to Australia in 1907-08, but predictably he was reluctant; for someone as impecunious as him, spending the winter in India in the employment of Ranjitsinhji (recently appointed head of a princely state) was more attractive.* When Jackson, the first choice, declined to come out of retirement to lead in the home Ashes series of 1909, despite the guarantee of leading for the whole series, MacLaren did indeed step in on the same terms, even if at the age of 37 he did so with a certain reluctance; his form with the bat had long been mediocre and he tended to score more heavily in Tests on truer Australian pitches. He was widely blamed for the ensuing fiasco and at one point offered his resignation, but was persuaded to carry on.

---

* Arthur Jones, who had just led Nottinghamshire to the championship, was instead appointed captain ahead of Warner, who may not have been considered because he had a young family. Jones fell ill with the pneumonia that would contribute to his early death at the age of 42, and Frederick Fane led in three of the five Tests in his place. Jones was credited with inventing the gully position. He was also a respected rugby referee, who officiated in five internationals between 1906 and 1912.

'MacLaren was a pessimist by nature and did not inspire his men to believe in their own prowess . . . to make your men believe in themselves is a very important factor in cricket leadership,' wrote Warner, who played one Test under MacLaren in 1909. The temperamentally erratic Charles Fry was less trusted still. He was a keen student of technique, as was demonstrated in the books he wrote in conjunction with the pioneering action photographer George Beldam, but this did not translate into good leadership. He left Sussex for Hampshire after being only intermittently available as captain and having a poor relationship with the professionals; he also embarrassed himself by protesting at Warner's appointment as captain of the Gentlemen in 1908. He was not invited to join the 1907–08 tour and, although he played and acted as selector during the 1909 series, he hardly shone on either front. He captained England for the first and only time in 1912 when in his 40th year but never led a tour. He only took the job that year on the proviso that he too was appointed for the entire summer. He got his way and led England to five wins in six Tests.

MacLaren may have captained England more often than anybody intended but he never made a Test tour under MCC's aegis, a reflection of the club's mistrust of privately run England tours and those who had had anything to do with the running of them. Bill Ferguson, the Australian scorer who travelled with many different touring sides, described MacLaren on a non-Test tour of New Zealand in 1922–23 as 'a spendthrift who got everything he could out of his tour, with never a thought about profits exceeding losses'. MacLaren's MCC membership was a constant bone of contention as he habitually let his subscription lapse; in June 1912 it was agreed that MacLaren should be reinstated as a member but that the secretary should write to him, pointing out that as he had been reinstated on three previous occasions the club was making an exception in his favour.

Andrew Stoddart found himself similarly unwelcome, a man the authorities preferred to forget. Details of the first of the two tours of Australia he led, victoriously in 1894–95, had surely filtered back to Lord's. With five of that 13-man touring party being amateurs, the organising Melbourne Cricket Club might have reckoned on keeping the costs down. 'In this hope,' Alan Gibson wrote, 'they may have been slightly disappointed, so far as the expenses went.' In the eyes of some, Stoddart had merely confirmed his 'shamateur' status by withdrawing from the England team amid the furore of the professionals' threatened strike action ahead of the Oval Test of 1896; he had, too, announced his retirement from regular cricket in the spring of 1899 with the arrival of the next Australian touring team imminent. Once retired, he wrote to the press in defence of his amateur status, which suggested the issue still rankled.

Shortly before Stoddart's suicide in 1915, a request for reinstatement of his MCC membership had been denied and his hopes of being found work at the club had come to nothing. His death went unrecorded in the club's minutes. The MCC president at the time was Lord Hawke.

# CHAPTER 7

# The Myth of Captaincy

## . . . and tackling 'sticky dogs'

The England captaincy usefully reinforced the caste system but for a long time that was about all it did: the job on the field was very limited compared with later times. Perhaps this was why men of such modest talent were able to fill the post, provided they were the 'right type', and why the authorities had few qualms about switching incumbents. Discounting the 13 Tests in which professionals led the team on early tours of Australia, England got through 20 captains in 81 Tests against Australia in the pre-First World War period, and even by the mid-1920s only four men had ever led England in ten Tests: WG Grace, Archie MacLaren, Pelham Warner and Johnny Douglas; of these only Grace would have felt secure in the post. Even victory over Australia provided no guarantees: after Warner won there in 1903–04 and Douglas in 1911–12, neither led England in the next home Tests. MacLaren captained in five series but rarely started as the preferred choice.

MacLaren had his qualities. He learned from the Australians the art of tailoring his fields to different players: Charles Fry likened facing a Lancashire side under his command to playing against a brain, and Monty Noble, a regular adversary in Ashes Tests, described him as 'a master of field placing'. Johnny Moyes, a former Australia state player-turned-critic, praised his 'vision, vitality, and intensity'. But Fry concurred with Warner in thinking him unduly negative in outlook, calling him 'an iron and joyless captain ... under him you entered every game bowed down with the Herculean labour of a cricket match against Australia; you went as in a trance to your doom'. Moyes referred to MacLaren having an obstinacy that was detrimental to the interests of his own team, perhaps an allusion to his spats with Lord Hawke.

The loyalty captains were expected to show towards the cricketing establishment was rarely reciprocated; professionals were not alone in feeling undervalued. An amateur captain might be chosen on social rank but that rarely protected him if it became apparent he was not good enough to command a place or could not handle the pressure; as we have seen, before the 1950s it was not the habit of selectors to assure a leader that he was in post for the entirety of a home season. This was the case even after greater care was taken over the running of the team. Henry Leveson Gower even dropped himself part way through a series in South Africa in 1909-10 (the only Tests he ever played), while Johnny Douglas had to stand his ground after Frederick Toone, his tour manager, floated the idea that he be replaced by Percy Fender two Tests into the series in Australia in 1920-21.* Fender said Douglas, who won an Olympic gold medal as a middleweight boxer at the London Games of 1908 and was exceptionally fit, never spared himself for the team; 'any problems arose because he seldom appreciated that others weren't necessarily as physically or mentally hard as he was.'† One of the few who seemed unaffected by the burden of leadership was Stanley Jackson, who in 1905 topped the batting and bowling averages, won all five tosses and led England to a 2-0 win, a triumph so celebrated that it had a book

---

* Douglas's leadership also briefly came into question in Australia in 1911-12 when he deputised for the unwell Pelham Warner for the whole series and took the new ball himself ahead of Sydney Barnes in the first Test. A disgruntled Barnes did not bowl well and England lost the Test, leading to a crisis meeting – instigated by Warner – to discuss Douglas's leadership. Jack Hobbs and Herbert Strudwick, two of the leading professionals, were supportive and Douglas survived.

† Douglas drowned in December 1930 aged 48 trying unsuccessfully to save his father, a timber merchant, when the boat in which they were returning from a business trip to Finland collided with another vessel in fog off the coast of Denmark.

devoted to it by Alan Gibson called *Jackson's Year*. But it was Jackson's only series in charge and he never played another Test.

Although there were exceptions, captains were usually influential in selection, particularly in assembling a tour party, when they might actually be the chief recruiter, especially in the days before MCC took control of tours in 1903–04. Some captains, MacLaren and Warner among them, were considered good judges of a player, MacLaren in particular deserving credit for backing Sydney Barnes and Gilbert Jessop when others doubted both, in the case of Barnes sometimes despite extreme provocation from Barnes himself. MacLaren even summoned Barnes to play in Sheffield in 1902 when the official selection panel left him out; Barnes received his summons at home in Manchester at 9am on the morning of the game and arrived at the ground after the start; he then took two wickets in his first over. MacLaren also vouched for Jessop's ability to bowl sufficiently long spells in lobbying for his return to the side for the final Test of the 1902 series. Although Jessop subsequently informed Lord Hawke, the chairman of selectors, that he might be unable to meet this demand as his fast-bowling days were all but over, Jessop was nevertheless selected to play and, in the event, although he bowled only six overs, struck one of the most brilliant centuries ever made for England. Going in at 48 for five with England needing 263 to win, he scored in an hour and a quarter 104 off 80 balls, reaching his hundred in 76 deliveries, still the fastest for England in Tests. Amid scenes of almost unbearable tension, England went on to win by one wicket.

Warner was reckoned a sympathetic handler of men but during this early period there were many fewer ways than later in which a captain could affect a game. For many years the Laws were simply too rigidly framed to allow scope for captains to show much imagination or talent for strategy – or perhaps the captains simply lacked sufficient imagination or talent for strategy to demonstrate that the Laws needed relaxing and revising. It might not have helped that the great public schools appeared set on cultivating men to lead rather than think: such adventurous captains as there were tended to have been educated elsewhere.

Captains obviously had a choice at the toss, but convention

dictated they bat first. England captains inserted only four times against Australia before 1926 and only once did this result in a victory. For long after this, any captain who opted to field first risked opprobrium if the move backfired (when Bob Wyatt did so at The Oval in 1935, *Wisden* termed the move 'probably the most daring ever adopted in Test cricket'). A second new ball was only an option in Australia from 1897-98 and in England from 1907, and then only if the opposition scored 200 runs, an unhelpful stipulation that stayed in place until 1946 when overs on the ball became the determining factor. The follow-on remained compulsory when the lead was of a certain size until 1900, when captains were finally given discretion after two incidents exposed the folly of the Law the way it was.

In 1894-95, England won a Test at Sydney after following on 261 behind by taking advantage of tired bowling to score 427 second time before Australia were caught on a rain-affected pitch on the last day and lost by ten runs. Their destroyer was Bobby Peel, who the night before had imbibed too well in the belief that the game was a lost cause and arrived at the ground with Bill Lockwood 20 minutes late. Australia's generosity in delaying the start until they arrived cost them dearly, as the pitch only became stickier under a hot sun during the hiatus.* Then, at Old Trafford in 1899, England's bowlers were the ones to suffer as Australia batted 181 five-ball overs in the follow-on. 'Their bowling was fairly worn out,' *Wisden* reported. 'It is quite hopeless to expect a side to stay in the field for two days without making mistakes.'

The most constraining Law in time-limit games in England was one prohibiting declarations until 1889 – and even after that only in quite specific circumstances in the second half of games. What this meant was that teams with plenty of runs on the board would deliberately throw away wickets to finish their innings, as happened when Australia scored 551 at The Oval in 1884 and Alfred Lyttelton, taking off his wicketkeeping pads, took four for 19 bowling lobs. Stanley Jackson was the first England captain to win after making a declaration, his decision at Trent Bridge in 1905 creating time for

---

* This was the only Test won by a side following on until England did so again at Headingley in 1981.

Bernard Bosanquet to take eight wickets and bowl out Australia. Less happily, there was acute embarrassment at Old Trafford in 1921 when the Australians corrected the England captain Lionel Tennyson, in charge of only his second Test, after he attempted to declare less than 100 minutes before stumps in what had become a two-day match following a first-day washout. Tennyson had to withdraw the declaration and apply it next day.*

Perhaps because there were so few aspects of on-field play that they could control, captains tended to exercise power over something they could influence: the batting order. Some even changed it substantially from innings to innings, let alone match to match. When England needed just 57 to win their first home Test in 1880, Lord Harris sent in Nos 8 and 9 to open; five wickets were lost before the runs were knocked off. Four years later, the tempestuous Walter Read was so incensed at Harris sending him in at No.10 – apparently the upshot of an argument between the two – that he smashed 117 runs in two hours; no other England batsman has struck a hundred so low down the order. In 1882, when England suffered their famous seven-run defeat at The Oval, 'Monkey' Hornby, MacLaren's mentor and a man with a volcanic temper, made every member of his team bar Ted Peate, the No.11, occupy a different position in the second innings than they had in the first, a curious tactic which failed to pay off.†
Charles Studd, who scored two centuries against the Australians that year and subsequently opened the batting for England in Australia with some success, was dropped four places to No.10 and did not face a ball.‡

However, in one specific and important respect captains required genuine strategic nous and that was with regard to rain-affected

---

* A similar breach of the Laws was made by George Mann on the first day of a three-day Test at Lord's in 1949 but Walter Hadlee, New Zealand's captain, lodged no protest and the declaration stood.
† Five months before this Hornby had captained the England rugby team against Scotland in Manchester. He led England twice at cricket and once at rugby, and is one of only two men to lead England in both sports, the other being Andrew Stoddart, four times at rugby (1890-93) and eight times at cricket (1893-98).
‡ Two years later, in 1884, Studd was inspired by an illness to his brother George, who also played four Tests for England, to abandon his former life and take up Christian missionary work in China, India and Africa.

games. It is hard for modern audiences to appreciate the full impact of Test cricket being played in England until autumn 1978 under Laws that dictated that, once a match had commenced, the pitch – and during the period up to 1913 the run-ups – stayed largely unprotected from the elements. If it rained, the nature of the contest underwent a dramatic change, especially if the sun came out to turn drying turf into a 'sticky dog' which provided extravagant grip for those spinning or cutting the ball. Batsmen who could cope with such conditions were as valuable as bowlers who could exploit them: Arthur Shrewsbury was among the best early batting exponents on wet wickets, one reason for WG Grace's famous response when asked which player he would first pick in his team, 'Give me Arthur!' Jack Hobbs, Wally Hammond and Len Hutton were all great wet-wicket batsmen. It was not just a test of skill either but courage: batsmen could expect to be hit by the faster bowlers, as Bill Edrich found when he was estimated to have been struck ten times while scoring 16 in an hour and 45 minutes against Ray Lindwall, Keith Miller and Ernie Toshack on a 'sticky dog' at Brisbane in 1946.

Captains who won the toss when heavy rain had fallen on the first morning of a game were also to be prized. This happened twice to dramatic effect in 1888 when batting became harder the longer the match went on. Australia won at Lord's by 4.25pm on the second afternoon in a match that produced only 291 runs, the lowest-scoring Test that England have been involved in, and England won at Old Trafford when the finish arrived before lunch on day two, their shortest completed home Test. Grace, entering his 40th year, made the highest individual scores on both occasions: 24 and 38.

If the weather was fine at the start it was natural for a captain to opt to bat first and make use of the pitch while it was in good order; if rain came later, the runs on the board became all the more valuable.* The challenge for selectors was picking a balanced squad that catered for both wet weather and dry; the challenge for a

---

* Such was the perceived advantage to batting first that MCC debated at its AGM in 1905 the role of the toss, though no change was made. Ironically that summer Stanley Jackson won all five tosses against Australia and England, batting first each time, won the series 2-0.

captain was picking from that squad the right XI given the expected weather. Understandably, mistakes were made. The selectors left Wilfred Rhodes, Yorkshire's slow left-armer, out of the squad for the Headingley Test in 1899; when it rained heavily the night before the match it became clear his presence would have been an advantage.

Three years later, Lord Hawke refused to include Schofield Haigh, a fine wet-wicket bowler, in the squad for the Old Trafford Test on the grounds that Yorkshire were already providing Rhodes, Hirst and Jackson and he wasn't prepared to release a fourth player from the club when Haigh was not certain to play. In the event, a lot of rain fell ahead of the start but MacLaren, piqued at the squad he had been sent ('My god, look what they've sent me!') and still at odds with Hawke over the previous winter's tour of Australia, left out Hirst and included the uncapped Fred Tate of Sussex who had been sent as Haigh's locum.* Like Haigh, Hirst was skilled at keeping his foothold on muddy turf and bowling well on it; without either, Tate bowled poorly and MacLaren was unable to call on his fastest bowler Bill Lockwood, who needed firm footholds, until Australia were 129 for no wicket. Lockwood went on to take 11 wickets in the game but England lost the Test by three runs and with it the Ashes. The petty behaviour of Hawke and MacLaren did neither credit.

MacLaren's tactical skills were thoroughly tested during the wet summer of 1902. When rain prevented play until 3pm on the second day of the first Test at Edgbaston, England having scored 351 for nine on the first, MacLaren, acting on the advice of his wicketkeeper Dick Lilley, whose home ground it was, instructed his last-wicket pair to bat on for a while until the pitch reached optimum tackiness. The declaration when it came was perfect: Australia were dismissed for 36, their lowest-ever score against England, Hirst taking three wickets and Rhodes seven.

Situations such as these demanded nerves of steel. When it rained in Melbourne ahead of the fourth Test of the 1911–12 series, Johnny Douglas endured some anxious moments after putting in Australia

---

* This famous comment appears to have been first attributed to MacLaren by Jimmy Catton in *Wickets and Goals* (1926).

because under a hotter sun the drying process would be faster than in England: the score reached 53 before the first wicket fell but, with batting becoming increasingly difficult, Australia were all out for 191 and England, enjoying the best batting conditions after the pitch had completely dried, went on to win by an innings and 225 runs. It was the first time an England captain had won after choosing to field first. At Leeds in 1926, Arthur Carr put Australia in to bat and got it wrong: although there had been rain in advance of the game there was not then enough hot sun to make the turf sticky, and Australia totalled 494. Carr hardly helped matters by dropping Charlie Macartney off the fourth ball he faced in what turned out to be a dazzling innings of 151, or by leaving out left-arm spinner Charlie Parker, and although England escaped with a draw he was sacked after the following Test.

Rain affected the pitch during the final match of the series to such an extent that Herbert Sutcliffe feared England would not make 70 in their second innings; in fact, he and Jack Hobbs batted brilliantly to put on 172 for the first wicket and England totalled 436, going on to win easily. Umpire Chester described Hobbs's performance as 'the greatest innings I ever saw and on the worst wicket'. Hobbs was reputed to have pretended to be in difficulties against the off-breaks of Arthur Richardson in order to kid Herbie Collins into keeping Richardson bowling rather than turn to the pace of Jack Gregory when the pitch was at its most treacherous.

It was not until the Barbados Test of 1935 that Bob Wyatt dared to be the first England captain to declare with his team behind, his intention being to make West Indies bat again while a rain-affected pitch was at its most treacherous. West Indies responded by declaring their second innings at 51 for six and setting England 73 to win, but England won by four wickets, and Wyatt's decision was vindicated, thanks to a masterly display by Wally Hammond. It was versatile performances such as this that encouraged a number of English players to rate Hammond as a better batsman than Don Bradman.

Knowing when to send in which batsmen according to the state of a 'sticky wicket' involved delicate calls of judgement. In the second innings in Barbados, Wyatt sent his bowlers in first and held back

Hammond to No.6 in the belief conditions would by then have marginally eased, and he was proved right. (Perhaps emboldened by this success, Wyatt reversed his batting order again when England were left 325 to win the next Test in Trinidad, even though the circumstances were conventional; his aim, he said, was to shield his best batsmen from the new ball on a matting pitch. But the ploy failed and England lost the match off the penultimate scheduled delivery. *Wisden* called it an 'amazing and inexplicable course'.)

Similarly, Australia's captain Joe Darling reversed his batting order for the second innings against England at Melbourne in 1901-02: the last five wickets added 305 and Australia went on to win the game by 229 runs, although there were allegations that the groundstaff had illegally dried the pitch overnight when Australia were 48 for five. There were also suspicions of skulduggery at Melbourne during the second Test of 1894-95, when the allegation was that the ground authorities rolled the pitch more than they should have done following rain on the rest day; both teams had been dismissed cheaply in their first innings and there were fears that a short game would hurt gate receipts. 'Such a proceeding would never for one moment have been allowed in England in so important a match, no matter what difference it would have made to the gate,' Arthur Shrewsbury wrote. With batting conditions easier, the match continued into a fifth day.

One of the reasons Pelham Warner's side won in Australia in 1903-04 was that they performed better in two games affected by rain: the second Test in Melbourne and the fourth in Sydney. In Melbourne, Lancashire's Johnny Tyldesley, a brilliant batsman on difficult pitches, scored 97 and 62 (out of a team total of 103); he was 46 not out at the end of the first day when rain arrived. Rhodes, capitalising on the favourable conditions, bowled unchanged throughout the match and took 15 wickets.

Warner said England won the series because in their bowling they had 'a man for every type of wicket', and that they had won 'fairly and squarely'. In fact, some Australians suspected his team prevailed because of their captain's underhand tactics during the match against New South Wales shortly before the fourth Test in which he altered his XI after the start following the loss of early wickets (including Warner himself for a duck), swapping a bowler Arthur Fielder for Albert Knight. As *Cricket* noted, 'This move, which occasioned such comment, proved very fortunate for the Englishmen.' Knight's second-innings century not only enabled MCC to beat NSW but prepared him well for the subsequent Test match in which he played a vital innings to help England secure the series and the Ashes. 'The locals felt so aggrieved that the scoreboard operatives deliberately put the name of the previously selected player into the frame to ensure that the crowd were aware of the subterfuge.' Warner's actions led to the Australians introducing in their own country the practice of captains exchanging team-sheets before the toss, and on their insistence this happened at the Triangular Tournament in 1912.

Discounting matches on matting pitches in South Africa, statistically the three greatest bowling performances for England before Jim Laker's historic feat in 1956 were all achieved by left-arm spinners on rain-affected pitches. Rhodes's 15 wickets was matched by Colin Blythe against South Africa at Headingley in 1907, also operating unchanged throughout, then by Hedley Verity bowling at Australia at Lord's in 1934 when in fact the main damp patch, the result of a leak in the covers, was in the words of Frank Chester 'as big as a tray', but Verity – whose impeccable length was one of his greatest assets – was good enough to keep hitting it. Such turkey-shoots were generally not shown much respect by commentators: too much was owed to chance, and the notion of fair play was left as bedraggled as everything else by rain. 'A less satisfactory Test game has seldom been played,' *Wisden* said of the Headingley 1907 match. 'The Englishmen had no great reason to congratulate themselves on their victory.' Of Melbourne 1904, it said: 'The significance of the win was altogether discounted by the fact that ... rain had ruined the pitch.'

After the First World War, Australia began completely covering their pitches in domestic state matches, unsuccessfully appealing to MCC to follow suit in England, a divergence that left Australia's batsmen – Don Bradman included – ill-equipped in the arts of wet-wicket survival. Their vulnerabilities were exposed by Verity, who took 14 of his 15 wickets in the 1934 match on the third day, a

Monday, after a weekend of rain had turned the pitch into something that, 'although not much more than a slow turner, was foreign to the Australians'. Bill Voce, England's left-arm paceman, similarly helped Verity destroy Australia's batting on a rain-damaged surface at Sydney in 1936. 'The Australians had a holy dread of English bowlers in such conditions,' EW Swanton, the broadcaster and journalist, wrote.

During that 1936–37 Ashes series, won by Australia from 2–0 down in an unusually wet Australian summer, rain played a part in four of the five matches, to England's advantage in the first two Tests and to Australia's in the third and fifth. Gubby Allen, the England captain, faced two particularly tricky decisions. The first came in the second Test in Sydney over whether to enforce the follow-on after Australia had been caught on a 'sticky dog' first time round; batting conditions eased, but keen to deny Tiger O'Reilly the chance to bowl on a pitch which would help him, he bowled again and Australia, though they reached 162 for one, collapsed to an innings defeat. Then in the next Test in Melbourne, where rain turned the pitch into a glue-pot by the second afternoon, Allen had to consider whether to cut short England's innings and get Australia batting again. In fact, he delayed his declaration and in the event Australia got through to the close only one wicket down. Bradman in any case reversed his batting order while awaiting an improvement in conditions and, thanks an immense innings of 270 at No.7 from Bradman himself, Australia went on to win by a huge margin. Allen admitted how difficult his dilemma was: 'The decision rested on the weather. The clouds were very low, threatening rain at any moment or a successful appeal against the light. If play is not going to be suspended you declare: if it is, you "stay put", hoping to reduce the arrears … I got the decision wrong because I assessed the weather incorrectly.'

The events of that series strengthened the view that rain-damaged pitches left the batting side with virtually no chance in Australia, where a hotter sun tended to have a more dramatic effect on the sodden turf. The series led to calls from former players of both sides for pitches there to be covered in the event of rain during the scheduled hours of play rather than left open to the elements, as was then standard practice in Test matches in Australia and England (although there had been in both countries scope since around 1910 to protect the *ends* of the pitches where a bowler required firm ground for his delivery strides). Nothing was done immediately but, minds perhaps concentrated by England being twice caught on 'sticky dogs' in Brisbane on their next two visits, MCC acquiesced when England returned in 1954-55, and also when they went to South Africa in 1956-57.

By 1960, Test pitches in England were also being covered at all times outside the scheduled playing hours, or once play was called off for the day; this practice was briefly withdrawn between 1963 and 1965 for fear of the detrimental effect it was having on spin bowling, before being restored. From there it was a small step to Test pitches being covered the moment rain interrupted play rather than only once play had been abandoned for the day.

One of the last great wet-wicket performances by an England bowler was Derek Underwood twice destroying Pakistan in 1974 with his slow-medium left-arm spin, the pitch's condition made worse in the second innings by heavy rain seeping down the Lord's slope and under the covers. The Pakistan management lodged an official protest at what it considered MCC's 'appalling show of negligence and incompetence in not covering the wicket adequately', and some suspected that the unhappiness of the Pakistanis played its part in the calling-off of play on the final day which began with England needing just 60 to win with all wickets intact. According to one England player, Keith Fletcher, 'the powers-that-be in the TCCB panicked and play was called off . . . This was the beginning of the end for uncovered pitches.' Another hefty shove came when England were themselves caught out at Edgbaston in 1975, Mike Denness choosing to bowl first even though some forecasts predicted rain later in the game; the rain duly came, England lost by an innings and Denness paid with his job.*

---

* One of the concerns about covering pitches, especially with tarpaulins laid straight onto the turf, was that it would lead to fungal growths. A Fusarium fungus was blamed for the state of the Leeds pitch in 1972 which took spin from the first day and on which Underwood took ten Australia wickets in a match that lasted only three days.

English reluctance to follow practices elsewhere was based partly on the purist belief that a contest on unprotected turf provided more of a challenge – and perhaps played to their advantage. Certainly, pitches completely protected from the elements made for a less varied and interesting game, if perhaps a fairer one. Life for batsmen became easier but for finger spinners, once so deadly, more precarious. Once a regulation was introduced in 1973 allowing for up to 60 minutes of lost time to be made up on the first four days, the scope for sides to be caught out on rain-affected turf broadened. Lord's too was hit by another controversy during the Centenary Test of 1980 when, after numerous interruptions for rain, umpire David Constant was involved in a brief scuffle with frustrated MCC members as the umpires and captains returned to the pavilion on the Saturday afternoon, resulting in the two officials being given a police escort when play subsequently resumed. The area of concern was two old uncovered pitches. A few months later it was decreed that not only the pitch and 20 yards of run-ups were to be covered, but also the entire square.

# CHAPTER 8

# Lord Harris's South African Deal
## The creation of the ICC: the first 'Big Three'

If the entrepreneurism of professional players did much to bring about the early contests between England and Australia, this was nothing compared to the economic and imperial motivations behind the gentlemanly class granting equal status to South Africa, a process formalised by the creation of the Imperial Cricket Conference in July 1909. As with the Australian colonies playing together as a team prior to federation in 1901, so South Africa was not even a nation at this point, the Union of South Africa coming into being only in May 1910. It was a decision owing as much to political and commercial expediency as to the cricketing ability of the South Africans. They had performed well on their first Test tour of England in 1907 but failed to inflict on England the kind of seismic defeat managed by the 1882 Australians.

While some of England's so-called amateur cricketers benefited financially from playing the game, others used the internationalisation of the sport to cultivate business opportunities. Lord Hawke made a playing tour of Argentina where he had railway interests and, for all his dislike of the locals, Douglas Jardine had financial concerns in Australia, chairing the New South Wales Land and Agency Company Limited. Few places were riper for exploitation than South Africa after the gold- and diamond-mining boom of the late 1800s. Aubrey Smith, a 6ft 4in fast-medium bowler and captain of what is now regarded as the first England Test team to play there in 1888-89, stayed on after the tour to set up a stockbroking firm with Monty Bowden, who deputised for him in the second Test when Smith was ill and who – aged 23 years 144 days – is now remembered as England's youngest ever Test captain.

Their new venture proved an abject failure. Smith fell ill with pneumonia and was erroneously reported as dead, while Bowden joined Cecil Rhodes's pioneer column used to annex Mashonaland, now part of Zimbabwe, and died in wretched circumstances in 1892. Smith returned home, focused on acting and by 1895 was appearing in the West End; the following year he played his last match for Sussex at the age of 33. He subsequently progressed to Hollywood stardom, generally playing archetypal Englishmen.* Henry Leveson Gower, another aspiring stockbroker, similarly remained in South Africa after the 1905-06 tour, albeit briefly, before returning as captain four years later having exercised his knowledge of South African affairs by representing them at the inaugural ICC meeting and again in 1912; Leveson Gower was a director of South African Coal Estates Limited. Above them all stood the peppery Lord Harris who, like Leveson Gower and Hawke, was an MCC officer or committee man during the years leading up to and including South Africa's promotion to cricket's top table.

Harris was the game's foremost administrator, and architect with Alfred Lyttelton of the 1884 code of the Laws of Cricket that stood for 60 years; almost every major strategic cricketing decision carried his imprimatur, but when he spoke about cricket's power to bind the imperial family, as he often did, he might also have mentioned its capacity to secure and safeguard business. From 1895, Harris developed a career in the City of London, specialising in South African undertakings. Chief among these was chairing Consolidated Gold Fields of South Africa, a company founded by Rhodes and which declared a profit in 1895 of £2.1 million, 'a larger return than had ever been shown in one year by a limited liability company registered

---

* Smith never lost his passion for cricket. He set up the Hollywood Cricket Club in 1932, commandeering British actors to play in his XI, and hosted Gubby Allen's England team when they passed through Los Angeles en route home from Australia in 1937. He was knighted for services to Anglo–American amity in 1944.

in London'; it was a post Harris held for more than 30 years. In the build-up to the second Anglo–Boer war in 1899, the company gained notoriety for putting its interests ahead of the sort of wider imperial concerns that Harris liked to link to cricket, Harris telling Joseph Chamberlain, the Colonial Secretary, at a meeting in London that Consolidated was inclined to accept the terms of a proposed deal with the Boers rather than join the consensus for war. 'Chamberlain was chilly and blunt: the company could make their choice and follow their own business, but the British public would accuse them of selling their cause and compatriots cheap.'*

The enthusiasm was every bit as strong at the South African end. Shipping magnate Sir Donald Currie, who would carry many English teams on his Union Castle Line, helped support the original tour of 1888-89, which was also guaranteed against losses by Rhodes himself, though the tour was the brainchild of an English army major, Gardner Warton, who had long been based in Cape Town.† Despite political tensions in South Africa thwarting some plans, four subsequent tours between 1891-92 and 1905-06, and South Africa's first three non-Test tours of England, took part with the help of funding from James Logan, the Scotsman who fell out with Walter Read over the 1891-92 tour, Abe Bailey, an English-educated mining magnate and protégé of Rhodes, and the South African authorities, whose £3,000 support for the first tour of England in 1894 included £500 from Rhodes himself.

The Second Anglo–Boer War only led to a redoubling of efforts: after Lord Hawke's 1895-96 team was disconcertingly caught up in the fall-out of the Jameson Raid that effectively triggered the war, Logan's backing ensured Hawke brought out another side only three years later; then, after hostilities were officially declared at an end, a South

---

* When war was declared Harris was appointed acting adjutant-general to the Imperial Yeomanry; he took advantage of his short time in Africa in 1901 to visit several gold-mining concerns.

† Warton, who umpired several of the tour matches including the two subsequently regarded as Tests, raised the team during a return to England in the summer of 1888 and the relative weakness of the side probably owed something to his disconnection from county cricket. Three of the chosen amateur players – Charles Coventry, Basil Grieve and Emile McMaster – had not appeared in first-class cricket before and Grieve and McMaster did not do so again. McMaster played only in the second of the two Tests which finished in two days; his England Test career remains the shortest on record.

African team was sent to England in 1901 in the midst of the conflict (the South African players were criticised by Arthur Conan Doyle, who himself went out to assist in hospital work, for not staying home to fight the Boers).* After the war ended in 1902, further tours were seen as a way of cementing peace. Lyttelton, a King's Counsel, was dispatched by Chamberlain to oversee reconstruction, before then succeeding Chamberlain as Colonial Secretary and later dying as a result of an abscess caused by a blow from a cricket ball. The first England team to play a five-match series of Tests in South Africa, under Pelham Warner's captaincy in 1905–06, was organised by MCC but guaranteed against financial loss by the South Africans; Warner's side was well short of England's full strength and lost 4–1 but a measure of how unimportant these matches were in the wider context of rapprochement is that four of the five Tests were jammed into the final month of a four-month tour.†

Then, during 1908, Harris chaired a series of meetings of the Advisory County Cricket Committee, formed in 1904 'to bring the counties into closer touch with MCC', to consider a proposal from Abe Bailey that teams representing England, Australia and South Africa should take part in an 'Imperial Cricket Contest' in England. Leveson Gower seconded a motion that the counties agree to the proposal in principle and on 3 July it was voted 9–6 to tell Australia, slated to tour in 1909, 'that the counties are so strongly in favour of the Triangular Contest that MCC would not be in a position to invite any Colonial XI in 1909, except for that purpose'. But the Australians, though they provided troops to the Boer War, had commercially and politically less to gain and stood firm. The Triangular Tournament was put back until 1912, when England emerged victorious from a format consisting of each team playing three Tests against the others. In cricketing terms it was not a success – it was a wet summer and

---

* Several England Test cricketers fought in the war: Jack Ferris, Christopher Heseltine, Stanley Jackson, Frank Milligan, Frank Mitchell and Teddy Wynyard. Milligan, who stayed on after the end of the 1898-99 tour, was killed in action during the siege of Mafeking in March 1900, and Ferris also died in South Africa later that year after leaving the army.

† The England team that toured South Africa in 1913-14 showed its support for the Union authorities by enrolling as special constables in Johannesburg to help deal with a transport strike in support of white miners' demands.

South Africa, who mostly played on matting pitches at home, were inexperienced on rain-affected turf, though total receipts amounted to £12,463 – but these were not primary considerations. Bailey said the tournament would not be in vain if the outcome was 'the strengthening of the bonds of union within the Empire'. The presence of King George V when South Africa played Australia at Lord's suggested his wish would be fulfilled. The Triangular Tournament was never repeated but its architects would have reckoned it did not need to be.

The tournament was part of a wider ICC agreement to exchange more tours, an agreement which reflected the sort of collaborative decisions the ICC was created to make rather than act as a global governing body, which was what it later came to be cast as. England had previously played South Africa in only two official Test series in South Africa in 1905–06 and England in 1907, though chroniclers had begun by 1912 to retrospectively confer Test status on eight matches in South Africa between 1888–89 and 1898–99. Yet, between September 1909 and September 1929, England played South Africa 33 times – precisely as many Tests as they engaged in with Australia during the same period. Fiercely protective of their special relationship with England, Australia condescended to meet South Africa just 11 times during this period and six of these were played in South Africa during stopovers on Australia's return home from tours of England. In all this time South Africa tasted victory just once in 21 Test matches overseas; though they won six times at home – all against England and all on matting pitches – England sent teams of only moderate strength, a practice which only ended after South Africa's successive series wins at home in 1930–31 and in England in 1935.

The South African authorities recruited English professionals on winter coaching contracts but its cricket still lacked depth or infrastructure. Many of the players it drew on were actually well-connected English settlers. William Milton, who played in what are now regarded as the country's first three Tests, captaining in two, had emigrated at the age of 24, was an associate of Rhodes and became administrator of Southern Rhodesia. Frank Hearne stayed on after the 1888–89 tour, setting up as a sports outfitter in Cape Town and representing South Africa against the English sides of 1891–92 and

1895-96 (the first of which contained two of his brothers); a son, born in England shortly before Frank left, also played for South Africa. Barberton Halliwell, who kept wicket to Hearne's bowling in an 1891-92 Test, was himself born in England and emigrated; he was a senior figure on three tours of England. Yorkshire batsman Frank Mitchell toured with Lord Hawke's second team, returned to fight in the war, then relocated to Johannesburg to act – as Milton had done – as Abe Bailey's secretary, before developing a career in tin-mining.

Mitchell's appointment to lead South Africa on the 1904 tour and then at the Triangular Tournament, having played no meaningful cricket for eight years, only made sense as an appointment palatable to his English hosts; he averaged 4.66 in three matches at the Triangular before dropping himself. Reggie Schwarz, one of the key figures on the field in South Africa's rise, spent the first 27 years of his life in England, during which he, like Mitchell, was educated at Cambridge and played rugby for England; he too then left to work for Bailey, although not before acquiring from Bernard Bosanquet at Middlesex the art of googly bowling. He was South Africa's leading wicket-taker on the 1907 tour; Dave Nourse, the leading run-maker, had been born in Croydon and went to South Africa as an army drummer-boy at the age of 17. James 'Bonnor' Middleton, born in Chester-le-Street, was bought out of the British army by the Cape Town club and subsequently took 24 wickets in what are now regarded as six Tests. George Lohmann, who spent time in the Cape for his health, having been one of England's finest cricketers, managed South Africa's 1901 tour of England shortly before his tragically early death. In all, more than one in five of South Africa's Test cricketers up to 1914 were born in England, Ireland or Scotland, and when the influx dried up it told; HL Crockett, an administrator in Natal, described South African cricket in the 1920s as 'very near the border line'.*

---

* Nor did it help that some talented players gave up on South African cricket, including Schwarz, who stayed on in England after the Triangular Tournament; he served in the First World War, was awarded the Military Cross and died in France of Spanish flu in 1918, seven days after the armistice, aged 43 (bequeathing £1,000 to Bosanquet). Six other South Africa Test cricketers of pre-First World War vintage who were born in Britain had returned there by the time of their deaths, among them Frank Mitchell.

The influx dried up because England, Australia and South Africa agreed, in drawing up some basic rules for Test matches at the original meeting of the ICC in 1909, that to be eligible to play for a territory required a cricketer to have been born there or resided there for four years (the residential rule in county cricket at the time was a more lenient one year). For the first time, therefore, players were asked to formally establish an allegiance. This had by far the biggest impact on South Africa, squeezing the supply of talent from English cricket. England themselves had yet to seriously recruit from abroad. Discounting four former Australia Test players who had taken up county cricket and joined early English tours of South Africa, only six England Test cricketers in the pre-1914 era were born outside Britain and most of them belonged to colonial or army families (including Lord Harris and Pelham Warner, both born in Trinidad). A rare exception was the Indian-born Ranjitsinhji, chosen by England in 1896 only after an internal debate and the consent of the Australian team, but he had been living in the country for eight years after initially arriving to attend Cambridge University.

Some cases had highlighted the need for guidelines. In South Africa in 1895-96, Lord Hawke's team tried to recruit Robert Poore after one of their batsmen went down injured. Poore, who was born in Ireland and had developed his batting in the British army, had only been in South Africa nine months but after scoring runs for Natal against Hawke's side it was clearly intended that he should play for the South Africa representative team. The South Africa Cricket Association protested and under pressure Poore declined Hawke's invitation, though this did not stop the local press questioning whether he was actually entitled to play for South Africa.

Then, in 1902, by which time Hawke was chairman of the England selection panel, he picked the all-rounder Charles Llewellyn in the squad for the first Test match against Australia in Birmingham. Llewellyn was born in Pietermaritzburg but, even more pertinently, had played for South Africa in the 1895-96 matches against Hawke. It was not until some years later that these games became regarded as official Tests but, given the trouble there had been over Poore, Hawke might have wondered whether Llewellyn's summons might raise questions. Llewellyn, like Poore, had only recently moved to his 'adopted' country, having played one season of county cricket for Hampshire. In the event, Llewellyn did not play against Australia, but under the 1909 rules he would have been ineligible to do so; he subsequently played further Tests for South Africa. In 1909 itself, Lord Hawke was said to be considering Sydney Smith, a left-handed all-rounder born and raised in Trinidad who settled in England and qualified for Northamptonshire after touring with West Indies in 1906; in the event nothing came of it. Even more contentiously England toyed with selecting the Melbourne-born Frank Tarrant, who briefly played for Victoria before moving to England at the age of 22 and becoming one of the leading county all-rounders with Middlesex; he played for Victoria again in 1907–08 (including against the visiting MCC touring team). He was picked for an England Test Trial match in 1911 but was not taken to Australia in 1911–12 amid suggestions that his presence would have triggered objections. He was nevertheless invited to join a Test tour of South Africa in 1913–14 but declined, citing prior coaching commitments in India. It was not until the Cape Coloured Basil D'Oliveira in 1966 that England first chose for Test cricket someone who had been born, and played a significant amount of early cricket, overseas.

Though it may have been seeded in commercial self-interest, there were some far-reaching consequences to the Imperial Cricket Conference's creation. It was agreed, for instance, that membership would be confined to those who accepted the British monarch as head of state. In a sense, this only reflected the reality that most cricket-playing territories were part of Britain's Empire rather than independent nation states, but it was a decision that cemented English cricket, and MCC, at the centre of the game: for many years the ICC met only very occasionally, but when it did its meetings were chaired by the MCC president, while the MCC secretary filled the same role for ICC.

For decades, few decisions were taken at ICC that did not meet MCC's approval, and when this practice changed, as it had to, the decoupling proved painful. The demand for fealty to the crown also alienated some whose involvement in the game might have blossomed. Philadelphia had undertaken several cricket tours of England, and also received English sides in return, as well as attracting players such as Thomas Armitage, a member of England's first Test XI, to emigrate to play and coach.* Its voice had previously counted for something in the game, but it was now left marginalised by America's status as a republic, and destined for decline.

The South Africa Cricket Association, too, favoured the interests of the minority English-speaking white population precisely because it consolidated links with Britain. Afrikaners, who were originally enthusiastic cricketers, could not give their allegiance to the British monarchy and such a requirement so soon after the Anglo–Boer War stopped Afrikaner cricket in its tracks. 'The Boers did not feel either welcome or inclined to participate in the game, which remained very much an expression of Anglo-Saxon separateness and superiority in the eyes of Afrikaner farming people,' Richard Holt wrote. 'Test cricket between South Africa and England was an Anglophile "family" affair.' (Noticeably, after South Africa became a republic and left the Commonwealth in the early 1960s, Afrikaner enthusiasm for the game revived.) The English side of 1891-92 played against a team of Malays, but this was the last time a team of black South Africans faced a touring side for more than 80 years. Broadly, the causes of all non-white cricketing communities were set back by the creation of a body dominated by the white elite.

English cricket's eagerness to tie the knot with South Africa stored up all sorts of problems for the future. Whereas England's relationship with Australia was sufficiently competitive to ensure they maintained a respectful distance, the one with South Africa was simply too close for comfort, meaning that the English cricketing establishment found it nigh on impossible to disavow South Africa's apartheid regime, or resist the allure of a number of high-profile players who followed D'Oliveira in switching camps with far less persuasive reasons for doing so. In fact, commerce again was the chief driver. There are also tangible physical remains of this special relationship. Sir Herbert

---

* Armitage, having first worked as a professional in Philadelphia in 1886, later settled in Chicago, where he lived up to his death in 1922.

Baker – a British architect who, during almost 20 years working in South Africa, remodelled at Cecil Rhodes's request the prime ministerial home in Cape Town as well as designing the Union buildings in Pretoria – was subsequently commissioned to build at Lord's the Grace Gates (1923), the original Grand Stand (1926) and a memorial garden to Lord Harris himself (1934). In addition, Baker presented as a gift to MCC the Father Time weathervane which now stands on top of the clock tower.

## England Cricketers Who Played Tests For Two Countries

| | |
|---|---|
| William Midwinter | Australia (8 Tests v England, 1876-77 to 1886-87) |
| | England (4 Tests v Australia, 1881-82) |
| John Ferris | Australia (8 Tests v England, 1886-87 to 1890) |
| | *England (1 Test v South Africa, 1891-92) |
| William Murdoch | Australia (18 Tests v England, 1876-77 to 1890) |
| | *England (1 Test v South Africa, 1891-92) |
| Frank Hearne | *England (2 Tests v South Africa, 1888-89) |
| | †*South Africa (4 Tests v England, 1891-92 to 1895-96) |
| Sammy Woods | Australia (3 Tests v England, 1888) |
| | *England (3 Tests v South Africa, 1895-96) |
| Albert Trott | Australia (3 Tests v England, 1894-95) |
| | *England (2 Tests v South Africa, 1898-99) |
| Frank Mitchell | *England (2 Tests v South Africa, 1898-99) |
| | *South Africa (1 Test v Australia, 2 Tests v England, 1912) |
| Nawab of Pataudi snr | England (3 Tests v Australia, 1932-33 to 1934) |
| | India (3 Tests v England, 1946) |
| Boyd Rankin | England (1 Test v Australia, 2013-14) |
| | Ireland (1 Test v Pakistan, 2018) |

---

* Matches between England and South Africa from 1888-89 and 1898-99 were only retrospectively regarded as of Test status.
† Frank Hearne played one Test against his brothers George and Alec Hearne, who toured South Africa with an England team in 1891-92.

Five other cricketers have represented England and another country in Tests, one-day internationals or Twenty20s: Gavin Hamilton (England 1999, Scotland 1999-2010), Dougie Brown (England 1997-98, Scotland 2006-07), Eoin Morgan (Ireland 2006-09, England 2009-19), Ed Joyce (England 2006-07, Ireland 2011-18) and Geraint Jones (England 2004-06, Papua New Guinea 2014).

# CHAPTER 9

# Speed, Swing and Spin
## Tom Richardson, SF Barnes and 'Bosie'

Gradually the quality of pitches improved and batsmen learned how to build bigger innings. The Test at Old Trafford in 1896 was the first in England in which more than 1,000 runs were scored and almost one-fifth of the runs came from the bat of one man, Ranjitsinhji, who patented the leg-glance and demonstrated that it was possible to exploit every area of the field. The aggregate of 1,182 runs at The Oval in 1899 stood as a record for Tests in England until they were extended from a minimum of three to four days in 1930. RE Foster's 287 at Sydney in 1903 represented a Bob Beamon-style leap for the highest individual score in Tests, a record that also stood until 1930 and a feat all the more impressive for Foster playing only seven first-class matches in the previous 12 months, scoring one half-century. Bowlers were being forced to work and think harder about what they were doing. Conclusions ranged from bowling the ball faster, to swinging it more, to spinning it in new ways.

Genuinely fast bowling played a relatively small part in Test cricket during this period. Historian HS Altham, writing with a heavy bias towards the Edwardian amateur 'golden age', gave a lengthy list of pacemen, many of them athletic, enthusiastic amateurs, who featured around the counties at the turn of the century, but some were only fleetingly at a peak and most appeared briefly if at all for England.

Charles Kortright, rated by many as the fastest of all, never toured and missed the 1899 season when Australia visited, while Gilbert Jessop sustained a back injury during his debut Test in 1899 and was finished as a bowler of real speed by the age of 26. Neville Knox, described by Jack Hobbs as 'the best fast bowler I ever saw', appeared in only two Tests before injuries possibly brought on by an overly long run-up finished him by his mid-twenties.*

With the championship programme growing significantly for the leading counties between 1894 and 1905, the volume of cricket placed special demands on anyone bowling at top pace week in, week out, and the absence of a second new ball in England until 1909 hardly encouraged anyone to keep bending their backs. There were also justified concerns about the legality of some fast bowlers' actions: Lord Harris declined to captain England at Old Trafford in 1884 because the Lancashire committee included the suspected 'chucker' John Crossland in the Test squad; AN Hornby, Crossland's captain at Lancashire, filled the breach but in the event Crossland did not play in that Test or any other. Arthur Mold, another Lancashire bowler, who played three Tests in 1893, was widely suspected of throwing and was eventually drummed out of the game in 1901 amid a general purge. Such was the climate that few escaped suspicion, including Tom Richardson, England's first great Test fast bowler.

The biggest handicap was the instruction that pitches and (before 1910) run-ups should be left exposed to the elements once a game began. Fast bowlers needed firm turf on which to operate and if rain fell heavily they were denied that. If a pitch was considered particularly soft before the start of a game, a fast bowler might not even play; if he did, he probably would not bowl until conditions dried out. The idea of opening the bowling with *two* out-and-out fast bowlers was almost never entertained in Tests, especially in England's more temperate climate, until the covering of run-ups was permitted

---

* Knox, like Aubrey Smith, turned to stage acting in the West End where he understudied Basil Foster, brother of RE Foster, under whose captaincy he played his two Tests against South Africa in 1907.

and England's attack was spearheaded to deadly effect by swing and seam on harder surfaces in Australia in 1911-12. Typically, the new ball was shared between a fast or fast-medium bowler and a spinner. In 22 home Tests between 1899 and 1909, England's first-innings attack was opened by a spinner more than half the time, although the bowler most frequently used was the fast-medium George Hirst, who had a reputation for keeping his footing whatever the conditions. This practice died out as pitch covering became more common; since 1928, a spinner has opened the bowling for England in the first innings of a Test only three times, most recently when Gareth Batty did so in Chittagong in 2016.

The most trusted fast bowlers were Bill Lockwood and Tom Richardson, who appeared in 12 and 14 Tests respectively and both played for Surrey, benefiting from the hard Oval pitches that suited their work.* Even for their county, though, they did not routinely open the bowling together and when they toured Australia in 1894-95 Richardson opened the bowling with left-arm spinner Bobby Peel in all five Tests while Lockwood, who had a poor tour, came on at third, fourth or even fifth change.† In fact Lockwood, whose skills included subtle variations of pace learned from George Lohmann, only once opened the bowling in the first innings of any Test. Richardson and Lockwood were associated, but not as a new-ball pair for England.

Lockwood was a mercurial character but for six years Richardson maintained an unprecedented blend of speed and accuracy before the workload told. Had there been a better understanding of managing fast bowlers, Richardson's career might have been prolonged; as it was, when he took an overdue rest in the winter of 1898-99 he put on weight and was never as good again. His performances in Australia

---

* Ironically, the only Test Richardson played at The Oval was affected by rain and he bowled just six overs. He, like Lockwood, had difficulty with his footholds on wet wickets. Richardson died aged 41 in Aix-les-Bains, France in July 1912 and on the day of his funeral flags flew at half-mast during the Gentlemen v Players match at The Oval, probably the first time this gesture was extended to a former England Test cricketer.

† Lockwood's problems included getting into trouble after he ignored shark warnings and attempted to swim ashore during a boat trip around Sydney Harbour after the first Test; he had to be rescued by passing yachtsmen.

in 1894-95, when in five Tests he got through 291.1 six-ball overs and took 32 wickets, marked a watershed by disproving a common notion that fast bowlers could not succeed on Australia's billiard-table pitches. As George Giffen, the Australia all-rounder, put it: 'Tom Richardson swept down on us ... and cast all these theories to the four winds of heaven.'

Australia's response was to put faith in their fastest and most powerful bowler Ernest Jones, who lacked Richardson's control but was at least as fast, and he shocked England in 1896 by breaking Stanley Jackson's rib and almost putting a ball through WG Grace's beard in a tour match at Sheffield Park.* Coping with extreme pace became a necessity and in 1899 the threat of Jones was a contributory factor in Grace's Test retirement and Bobby Abel's omission from all five Tests (Abel was among the most prolific batsmen in the country but showed a tendency in Gentlemen v Players matches to back away against the pace of Kortright and others, some reports suggesting he was 'obviously scared'); Jones's ten-wicket haul was instrumental in Australia winning the Lord's Test. Australia soon produced another very fast bowler in Tibby Cotter, whose bouncers, one of which hit Johnny Tyldesley, drew the ire of the crowd at Trent Bridge in 1905.

The precarious nature of their involvement made life fraught for fast bowlers, and for those selectors charged with judging whether they should play. Public feelings could run high on the issue too, never more so than during the 1909 Ashes when England went into both the Lord's and Oval Tests without a paceman. *Wisden* editor Sydney Pardon squarely blamed Archie MacLaren, the captain, for not picking the Essex fast bowler Claude Buckenham for the final Test, and in a famous phrase went considerably further: 'The idea of letting England go into the field in fine weather, on a typical Oval wicket, with no fast bowler except [batting all-rounder Jack] Sharp

---

* Jones's action was another to come under suspicion and he was no-balled for throwing by Jim Phillips, the touring team's Australian-born umpire, when AE Stoddart's XI faced South Australia in 1897-98; it was believed his action had improved by the time of Australia's 1899 tour of England.

touched the confines of lunacy.'* CB Fry, one of the selectors, laid
the fault at the door of Lord Hawke, the chairman, describing him
in later years as 'much too observant of what he thought was public
opinion'. *Bailey's Magazine* accused the selectors of having 'betrayed
England to Australia'.

For the Lord's Test, decision-making was complicated by Hawke
being absent through ill-health and Fry being required in a law suit;
it also rained around the time the squad was selected so the ability
of the bowlers to perform on what might have been a wet surface
had to be closely taken into account. Walter Brearley, spearhead
of MacLaren's county Lancashire and the best fast bowler in the
country, was left out in favour of the uncapped Thomas Jayes of
Leicestershire, only for Jayes not to be summoned to Lord's on the
morning of the game; George Beldham wrote a few days later that,
'He [MacLaren] wanted Jayes, but [Schofield] Haigh was given him!'
As it happened Brearley was at Lord's but, indignant at his treatment, he declined MacLaren's eleventh-hour pleas to play; his kit,
he said, was already in Tonbridge for Lancashire's next match and he
refused to send for it. According to Leveson Gower, the third designated selector, Brearley stood outside the boxes and gave a loud and
prolonged account of why he should have been playing. Brearley's
reputation as a 'difficult' man probably owed much to this incident. Predictably, the match was lost. A week later, Brearley broke
Leveson Gower's hand while bowling at him in the championship
at The Oval, probably the only case of an England player breaking
the bones of a selector who had just left him out of the side. Point
made, Brearley played the next Test.

Pace was an asset but by its nature a game played in a temperate
English climate on generally soft turf was going to see seam and
swing movement playing a more significant role: this type of bowling

---

* Amid stiff competition, England's selection for this series ranks high among the most
shambolic of any summer. MacLaren needed persuading to play the latent genius Jack
Hobbs in the first Test and for the second Test the in-form Gilbert Jessop was left out
while the patently unfit Tom Hayward played. *The Times* called for the setting aside
of 'small jealousies and petty pique' so that England's strongest side could be picked.

has won England more Test matches than any other. Manipulating the ball off the pitch was a skill learned earlier than swing; bowlers had for generations understood the need to keep the seam 'proud'.* Swing was a more mysterious art. Tiger Smith, who kept wicket in 11 Tests between 1911 and 1913, claimed that fast bowlers liked to keep the ball clean and would be annoyed if they saw spinners rubbing it in the dirt, which they did to improve their grip, but they never talked about gripping the ball in a particular way to achieve inswing or outswing; nor were they in the habit of polishing it (the only one he could recall doing so was Johnny Douglas).† Kortright concurred: he had never worried about the seam's position in his hand and thought most contemporaries were of the same view. 'Yet [they] could make the ball swerve and seam off the pitch,' Smith said. 'A natural body action helped them get their movement and pace off the pitch.' Smith was perhaps being economical with the truth; during the 1911–12 Ashes series there were suspicions that bowlers of both sides used resin to keep the ball polished, with the Australians believing Douglas frequently shook hands with the gauntleted Smith because his gloves had resin on them.

The first England cricketers to achieve some mastery of swing were George Hirst and Sydney Barnes. Hirst, a left-armer at Yorkshire, was called the father of swing bowling by English commentators but Barnes, who began his career at Warwickshire before moving to Lancashire, developed the art around the same time and refined it after touring Australia in 1901–02 and observing Monty Noble, to whom the label more deservedly applied. Noble's experience as a baseball pitcher taught him about flight and he was baffling England's batsmen as early as 1897–98 by making the ball swerve late. Hirst went on that tour but it was not until spring 1901 that he chanced to make the ball swing himself in practice. 'Sometimes when the wind

---

* The MCC minutes for November 1911 address ball-tampering in a match involving Surrey and Worcestershire although the committee suspected the seam was lifted or damaged 'to give the bowler a better finger-hold or to enable the fielding side to demand a new ball', rather than to better make the ball deviate off the pitch. MCC ruled it illegal and sent a warning to county captains, 'so that it may not become a practice'.
† Rubbing the ball in the dirt was outlawed in 1980.

was in the right direction the ball swerved,' Hirst said. 'I studied it. I found I could do it best with a new ball and when I was bowling into the wind rather than against it. When I got extraordinary swerve I called it one of my "funny" days.'

Hirst would hold the seam upright between his first two fingers with thumb underneath, and found that by putting his right foot down in the direction of second slip the arc of his body over the leg and what Jim Kilburn termed a 'not notably high' arm served to exaggerate the inswing (standard technique today but not then). Just 12 months after his epiphany, Hirst helped dismiss Australia for 36 at Edgbaston and, although he took three wickets to Wilfred Rhodes's seven, critics thought he sowed the seed and Rhodes reaped the harvest. In the corresponding fixture of the 1909 Ashes, Hirst took nine for 86 in the match, *Wisden* commenting that he was 'making the ball swerve in his most puzzling fashion'.

Hirst's skill, though, was limited to making the ball swing in to the right-hander, hence his deployment of leg slips and hence his unexceptional overall Test record; had he been able to consistently swing the ball away too he would have been doubly dangerous at the highest level. Even so, so potent was Hirst's magic that England searched for bowlers who could replicate it, though with little success. The number of bowlers summoned and sent away unused during the 1909 Ashes was ascribed by the writer Home Gordon to 'the exaggerated cult of Hirst as a bowler'.

According to his biographer, Barnes – tall, lean and supple – could already swing the ball both ways before approaching Noble in Australia to ask him how he swung the ball one way before making it break off the pitch in the opposite direction – a combination of swing and seam movement or spin that constituted an additional layer of complexity again. Noble generously passed on details of a drill that involved swinging the ball between two poles, one 10 or 11 yards from the bowling crease, the other five or six yards from the batsman, before making it break back off the pitch; Barnes, being the obsessive student he was, practised religiously until he had mastered it. He bowled Victor Trumper with just such a ball at Sydney in 1907, Charles Macartney, the non-striker, describing it as 'the sort of ball a man might see if he was dreaming or drunk', and removed Australia's top four in his opening spell at Melbourne in 1911, one of the great bowling performances of the period. Clem Hill, one of his victims, said Barnes had the ability to swing the new ball both in and out very late. Barnes also commanded a leg-break and off-break – crucially without any discernible change of action – but bowled the ball faster than a conventional spin bowler; his normal run-up involved 13 paces.

Despite this, Barnes was not an automatic choice for England's Test side until near the end of the decade. He and Hirst were seen as alternatives rather than allies: Barnes owed his original selection for England to Hirst's unavailability for the 1901-02 tour, Barnes having played just six championship matches at the time, and in the next three Ashes series Hirst played 12 times to Barnes's once. Hirst had two advantages: he was a useful lower-order batsman who in partnership with Rhodes famously saw England home amid unbearable tension at The Oval in 1902; and he was a sunny, popular character assured of Lord Hawke's support. Barnes, by contrast, was moody and argumentative, and his determination after 1903 to take the better pay in the leagues rather than play county cricket did not make him any easier to know or (from the establishment's point of view) trust.* After the First World War, the authorities, acting on a resolution moved by Yorkshire, sought to prevent players deserting to the leagues by ruling that to be selected for representative matches and overseas tours cricketers had to be available for county cricket.

Hirst played his last two Tests alongside Barnes in 1909, when at Edgbaston Arthur Jones, fielding at forward short leg for Hirst's inswing, took a famous catch to dismiss Monty Noble, moving low to his left to take the ball off the full face of the bat. Barnes was finally deemed indispensable but another left-arm bowling all-rounder emerged in Frank Foster to form with him England's first genuine new-ball spearhead in Australia in 1911-12. Foster, like Hirst,

---

* The establishment perhaps never quite forgave him. Following Barnes's death in 1967, at the age of 94, MCC Committee minutes record that a request for his ashes to be scattered at Lord's was turned down. They were placed at the Edgbaston ground instead.

specialised in sharp inswing but he could mirror the Noble–Barnes trick of making his inswingers move away off the pitch. Operating from round the wicket to a line on middle and leg to right-handers, with a four-man leg-trap, Foster was an early pioneer of leg-theory which would ultimately morph into the Bodyline tactics of 1932-33 and on which he was consulted by Douglas Jardine.

A more immediate concern was finding a wicketkeeper capable enough down the leg side to deal with his methods and one was found in his Warwickshire team-mate Tiger Smith after Herbert Strudwick struggled with Foster's bowling in the first Test in Sydney. That was the game in which Johnny Douglas, the captain, who himself swung the ball both ways, opened the attack with Foster, much to Barnes's fury. Not only was Barnes slighted by the demotion; it was now understood – by some – that bowlers could do things with a new ball that they could not with an old one, even if they did not fully realise how to prolong its efficacy; in a nutshell, Barnes was eager to get his hands on it. Fortunately, Douglas quickly acknowledged his mistake and, having lost the first match, England won the next four.

The Barnes–Foster alliance lasted no longer than the nine months spanning the Australia tour and the Triangular Tournament. Foster, an amateur, was unavailable for England's next series in South Africa in 1913-14 and never played Test cricket again. In his absence, and in what transpired to be his own final series, Barnes opened the bowling with four different bowlers in four matches after the first of them, Major Booth, who could also swerve the ball, was injured in a car crash and did not reappear until the fifth Test (a match Barnes missed because of a dispute with the local authorities over expenses). Not that Barnes was inconvenienced: he took a record 49 wickets in the series including 17 for 159 in the second Test in Johannesburg which stood as England's best match figures until Jim Laker's 19 for 90 in 1956.*

*

---

* Foster and Booth would have been young enough to resume playing for England after the First World War but Foster injured a leg in a motorbike accident on army duty in 1915 and Booth was killed on the Somme on 1 July 1916.

If the skills and strategies of fast and fast-medium bowling were honed by professionals, it was amateurs who were at the forefront of the riskier types of spin bowling. An amateur, Bernard Bosanquet, introduced to Test cricket the googly, one of the greatest innovations the game has seen, using it to help England win two Ashes series.

Bosanquet started out as a medium-pace bowler before experimenting at Oxford with a delivery that looked like a leg-break but spun the other way. The problem for all spin bowlers who turned the ball only one way – which was almost all of them – was predictability, so the element of doubt the googly created in the minds of batsmen was a revolutionary step and guaranteed it longevity. After eventually applying it with success for Middlesex, Bosanquet was chosen for the tour of Australia in 1903-04 under the captaincy of his county colleague Pelham Warner who believed in its potential. Bosanquet bowled England to an Ashes-clinching victory in the fourth Test in Sydney and Australia's batsmen found him similarly unfathomable on the final day of the opening Test in England in 1905 when he took eight for 107.

Unfortunately, Bosanquet lacked the control to make his mix of leg-breaks and googlies as potent as they might have been; Warner said he bowled more bad balls than anyone he knew. Also, wrist spinners encountered the same problem as genuine fast bowlers in that English pitches rarely suited them; they too were far more dangerous on surfaces offering generous bounce. In the very next match after bowling England to victory in 1905, Bosanquet was not called on to bowl at all during a damp Test at Lord's, and after one more appearance he was dropped. He did not tour South Africa under Warner the following winter and soon he was playing for his county (but not his country) essentially as a batsman. His international career was over after 18 months.

This typified England's relationship with wrist spin: the selectors would back it, but not for long, and tended to view it as something to be deployed overseas where conditions were often more favourable. This may have been pragmatic but it hardly encouraged anyone to make a career out of it. Bosanquet's invention, meanwhile, was quickly taken up and refined in South Africa and more lastingly in

Australia, where a golden tradition developed of bowling the leg-break and googly (commonly known in Australia as the 'Bosie').

Many of those who purveyed the riskier forms of spin in England were men like Bosanquet whose livelihoods did not depend on their speculative methods bearing fruit. Generally, too, they wanted the option of spinning the ball back into the right-hander, a line of attack not much pursued by the leading professional spinners, who tended to specialise in orthodox slow left-arm up to the Second World War: Johnny Briggs, Bobby Peel, Wilfred Rhodes, Colin Blythe and Hedley Verity were all focused on threatening the outside edge of the right-hander, as was Frank Woolley, a considerable all-rounder, who took ten for 49 in just 17.2 overs on a rain-affected pitch against Australia at The Oval in 1912. These were days when left-handers were much less common than they are in the modern era, partly because left-handers were actively discouraged to bat that way (Lord Hawke, for example, was naturally left-handed but told as a young-ster to switch to holding a bat right-handed). Alternative means of attack were occasionally needed, though not always forthcoming. Between Billy Bates in the 1880s and the mercurial Cecil Parkin in the 1920s no specialist off-spinner made a serious impact for England.

This breach was filled, after a fashion, by adventurous-minded ama-teurs. AG Steel – who played 13 Tests as a genuine all-rounder in the 1880s, four of them as captain – was probably the first England bowler who spun the ball both ways with off-breaks and leg-breaks. He was described by HS Altham, in the 1920s, as 'the best leg-break bowler in history'. The last of the few underarm lob bowlers who performed for England was an amateur, George Simpson-Hayward, who took 23 wickets in the 1909-10 series in South Africa on matting pitches which helped his sharply spun off-breaks.* 'Mr Simpson-Hayward has been a great success,' *The Times* reported during the series. 'With the exception of Mr White, Mr Snooke, Mr Faulkner and Mr Nourse,

---

* Lob bowling was not the exclusive preserve of amateurs. Thomas Armitage, a Yorkshire professional who played in England's first two Tests, occasionally bowled underarm, and Walter Humphreys, a professional at Sussex, toured Australia in 1894-95 aged 45 but did not play in any of the Tests. In all first-class cricket between 1871 and 1900 Humphreys took 718 wickets.

none of the opposing batsmen in the Test matches played the lobs with confidence. Mr Sinclair, Mr Schwarz and Mr Zulch have been mastered by him on almost every occasion they have met him, and the value of this kind of attack has been thoroughly demonstrated.' But Simpson-Hayward's methods, like Bosanquet's, found a more fertile response overseas, with Australia's Clarrie Grimmett adopting his grips and using them in his deployment of over-arm leg-spin.

Most of England's early leg-break and googly bowlers were amateurs too, among them Douglas Carr, a 37-year-old Kent school-teacher picked for the final Test of the 1909 Ashes series after just six first-class matches. He was followed by Percy Fender, Greville Stevens, Ian Peebles, Walter Robins, Freddie Brown and 'Father' Marriott in the inter-war period. At Warner's instigation, Robins was booked into Aubrey Faulkner's indoor school in London in 1926, and Peebles – before he had even played county cricket – was sent on a Test tour to South Africa in 1927-28 as secretary to the captain, Ronnie Stanyforth, and bowled well enough to play in four Tests. However, Peebles's leg-break was not as good as his googly, which Don Bradman in 1930 admitted he could not pick, and (as well as through bowling too much too young) Peebles was finished as an England player by the age of 23. Brown was also tutored at Faulkner's school. Of the eight unorthodox spinners who took 20 wickets for England up to 1938, six were amateurs while the two professionals were not gamblers by nature: Len Braund never developed a googly and Tich Freeman bowled flat and straight, his stock ball the top-spinner.

There was a period shortly after the Second World War when England, bereft of pacemen, drew on the services of three profes-sionals who bowled leg-spin – Doug Wright, Eric Hollies and Roly Jenkins – and on seven occasions even fielded two of them in the same Test. However, Wright, the only unorthodox spinner to have taken 100 Test wickets for England, and Jenkins were expensive and inconsistent, and Hollies, though he looked to contain more, was fundamentally unhappy about playing Test cricket and even after confounding Don Bradman with a googly in the final Test match of 1948 still declined to tour South Africa the following winter. However, as the ranks of amateurs thinned so too did the number of home-grown unorthodox spinners. They were an indulgence, a luxury English cricket could rarely afford, and also one that it did not need to afford following the rise of world-class off-spinners such as Jim Laker and Fred Titmus.* Their declining numbers did nothing to help English batsmen hone their skills against a type of bowling they could count on being confronted with in Australia and elsewhere.

Since the advent of the all-professional era in 1962, only a handful of specialist leg-spinners have played Tests for England: Robin Hobbs, Ian Salisbury, Chris Schofield, Scott Borthwick, Adil Rashid and Mason Crane, none of whom lasted more than four matches at the outset. Hobbs took 1,099 first-class wickets yet was chosen for only seven Tests, Salisbury took 884 first-class wickets and played 15. Hobbs said he was treated like something that had dropped from the moon. Salisbury noted that in practice ahead of his debut Jack Russell, the England wicketkeeper, could not pick his leg-breaks from his googlies.

Rashid's five-wicket haul against Pakistan in Abu Dhabi in October 2015 was the first by a member of this subset since 1959. The following winter he took 30 wickets in seven Tests in Bangladesh and India but was peremptorily dropped for England's home Tests the following summer. England appeared to regard him, as they had Salisbury, as too expensive to be a Test regular and left him to pursue a career as a white-ball specialist. By the time he turned 30, he had withdrawn from first-class cricket, partly blaming ECB scheduling that took away championship matches from the centre of summer. He was not alone: most international leg-spinners struggled to excel across red- and white-ball formats at the same time. England turned their attention instead to nurturing Crane, a young leg-spinner from Hampshire, who at the age of 20 made his debut at Sydney in January 2018, the youngest wrist spinner to play for England since Brown 87 years earlier. Predictably, he struggled. Then, with the arrival of Ed Smith as national selector, Rashid was startlingly recalled to the Test side in August 2018 despite not playing championship cricket

---

* The rise of the off-spinner was attributed in some quarters to the change in the lbw law in 1935, which allowed for batsmen to be out to balls pitching outside off stump; it was reckoned that while this helped the off-spinner it did nothing for leg-spinners and slow left-armers who spun the ball the other way.

that summer. He was used sparingly but nonetheless played his part in series wins over India and Sri Lanka. Then, with the arrival of Ed Smith as national selector, Rashid was startlingly recalled to the Test side in August 2018 despite not playing championship cricket that summer. He was used sparingly but nonetheless played his part in series wins over India and Sri Lanka.

England wrist spinners have suffered acutely from the expectation that they will run through sides when conditions are in their favour, but it has not helped that they have routinely been viewed with suspicion and mistrust, unable to provide the control demanded of all England spinners. Their inability to hold down regular Test places, though, is in part an indictment of those who manage them.

## England's High-risk Spinners

Players chosen as specialist bowlers of leg-breaks, googlies or lobs; minimum 20 wickets; professional unless stated.

| Bowler/Type | Span | Tests | Wickets | Average |
| --- | --- | --- | --- | --- |
| Len Braund (LB) | 1901-08 | 23 | 47 | 38.5 |
| Bernard Bosanquet (LBG; amateur) | 1903-05 | 7 | 25 | 24.2 |
| George Simpson-Hayward (lobs, amateur) | 1909-10 | 5 | 23 | 18.3 |
| Percy Fender (LB, amateur) | 1921-29 | 13 | 29 | 40.9 |
| Greville Stevens (LB, amateur) | 1922-30 | 10 | 20 | 32.4 |
| Tich Freeman (LBG) | 1924-29 | 12 | 66 | 25.9 |
| Ian Peebles (LBG, amateur) | 1927-31 | 13 | 45 | 30.9 |
| Walter Robins (LBG, amateur) | 1929-37 | 19 | 64 | 27.5 |
| *Freddie Brown (LBG/RM, amateur) | 1931-53 | 22 | 45 | 31.1 |
| Eric Hollies (LBG) | 1935-50 | 13 | 44 | 30.3 |

---

* Freddie Brown mainly bowled spin in Test matches, although he took 18 wickets in five Tests bowling predominantly medium pace in Australia in 1950-51.

| Bowler/Type | Span | Tests | Wickets | Average |
|---|---|---|---|---|
| Doug Wright (LBG) | 1938-51 | 34 | 108 | 39.1 |
| Roly Jenkins (LBG) | 1948-52 | 9 | 32 | 34.3 |
| Ian Salisbury (LBG) | 1992-2000 | 15 | 20 | 77.0 |
| Adil Rashid (LBG) | 2015-19 | 19 | 60 | 39.8 |

Bob Barber (1960-68, 42 wickets at 43.0 in 28 Tests) and Ken Barrington (1955-68, 29 wickets at 44.8 in 82 Tests) both bowled leg-breaks and googlies but were primarily chosen as frontline batsmen.

Johnny Wardle (1948-57, 28 Tests, 102 wickets, average 20.4) bowled orthodox left-arm spin and left-arm wrist spin. He tended to bowl wrist spin overseas, where his record was: 13 Tests, 45 wickets, average 20.0.

# CHAPTER 10

# The Culture of the Cap
## Three lions, one crown

RE 'Tip' Foster's England career typified the fleeting glory of the amateur cricketer in the supposed 'golden age'. After a gilded sporting career at Malvern and Oxford, he was chosen as player and assistant manager of the first tour of Australia organised by MCC, where he set a then Test-record score with an innings of 287 in his first Test match at Sydney, despite having played only a few matches the previous summer because of business commitments. His work as a stockbroker restricted him to only three more Tests, as captain, at home to South Africa in 1907 which were meant as preparation for taking the English team to Australia the following winter, but in the event, he could not make the tour. In respect of international cricket, Foster's legacy was mixed: his ability to play to a high standard without regular match practice briefly encouraged the suspect idea that it was possible to go into Test matches without much preparation, but he also contributed to the creation of the badge which England cricketers wear to this day.

As England's captain in 1907, and a member of the MCC committee, Foster was consulted when the club took the decision at a cricket subcommittee meeting in October of that year to create a specially designed cap for those chosen to play Test cricket at home. By March 1908, MCC committee minutes noted that a cap had been selected, 'the design being three lions under a crown, in silver, on a blue cap, subject to the consent of HM the King'; a subsequent minute recorded that Edward VII's consent had been obtained. It was Foster's suggestion for silver lions on 'a cap for all England' and the design appears to have been directly borrowed from the badge long worn on shirts by the England football team, itself derived from the symbols used for England on the United Kingdom's Royal Coat of Arms. Significantly, Foster had represented England five times at football, including once as captain, between 1900 and 1902; his suggestion therefore was that cricket should simply follow football's example. Foster remains the only person to have captained both the England cricket and football teams.

Not only were caps to be awarded contemporaneously but also to those past players 'approved by MCC to be entitled to wear' them. It was the first sign that representing England at the highest level constituted membership of a select club, rather like election to MCC itself. The crucial difference was that it was open to amateurs and professionals alike, and was therefore a fundamentally democratic and cohesive step. Although it may not have been the intention, the cap helped further erode class distinctions, if only gradually. It was decided to award the cap only to those who represented England in home Test matches because teams travelling overseas by then already had the uniform of MCC colours: on the tour of Australia in 1903–04 that Foster went on, players were given sweaters and ties, caps bearing a St George badge, and blue blazers with red and gold piping, a uniform that acted – at least in the eyes of those who conceived it – as a guarantee of decency and fair play. Teams also travelled with an MCC flag.* The need for a dress code for home matches was less pressing but it may have been significant that the England cap was introduced at the time that talk of a Triangular Tournament was gaining strength. The Australians had been using touring caps bearing a 'national' coat of arms since 1890 (long before an official one came into being in 1908) and wearing designated caps in home

---

* When England beat Australia at The Oval in 1926 to regain the Ashes, an MCC flag taken to Australia in 1903–04 and 1911–12 was flown from the pavilion flagstaff. The MCC flag was routinely taken on tour until 1997, when England stopped touring in MCC colours.

Tests since 1902; by April 1908 the Australian board announced the team was officially adopting colours of gum-tree green and gold that had been commonly used with pride for some years. The South Africans that faced Foster's England team in three Tests in 1907 wore blazers with a springbok emblem. There may have been a feeling that England needed to show a similar esprit de corps.

The early caps, with smaller peaks than those of later vintage, were made by H Ludlam of Albemarle Street, London, of which some have survived: those retrospectively presented to Edward Grace, who played in the inaugural Test in England in 1880, and Harry Wood, whose one home Test appearance came against Australia in 1888, both recently appeared at auction, as did one awarded to JW Hearne, probably in 1912, made by EC Devereux of Eton. A cap belonging to Tom Richardson has also survived. Lord Harris himself, who was captain in three of England's first four home Tests, was photographed wearing his cap even though he turned 57 years of age in 1908, suggesting it was a matter of great pride for him to wear one. This, and the general awarding of caps to past and present amateurs and professionals, confounds the theory that Harris had little enthusiasm for the England team. He was never formally involved in selecting England teams for home Tests but sat on several MCC committees convened to pick major overseas tours.

Up to this point, teams representing England had been seen in a patchwork of headwear. Professionals generally wore their county caps, which betokened their calling and were an essential part of their self-esteem, while amateurs tended to prefer caps that identified their old schools or universities. On those Test tours undertaken before MCC became involved, some sort of uniform was usually created, though they varied from one expedition to another; when Andrew Stoddart was assembling his side for Australia in 1897-98, a letter to Teddy Wynyard whom he was hoping to persuade to join the tour included details about the 'colours' to be worn – ties and hat ribbons, tour caps and coats.* Stoddart's team took the field

---

* In fact, Wynyard, an army officer, was ultimately denied leave to join the tour by the War Office.

wearing hooped caps.* By the time of MacLaren's team of 1901–02, a link had been established with more 'patriotic' symbols; the players sported navy-blue caps bearing in red the Royal Coat of Arms of the United Kingdom.

Receipt of an England cap was also clearly a matter of great pride to many professionals. Jack Hobbs was photographed wearing one as he walked out to open the batting with CB Fry at Edgbaston in 1909 in the first home Test after their introduction. Hobbs also wrote an article in *Wisden* in 1935 to mark his retirement from first-class cricket in which he regretted England awarding so many home fixtures to South Africa, West Indies, New Zealand and India: 'The honour of wearing the England cap with the three silver lions on it has, I am afraid, become rather cheap since its inception. These caps should have been awarded only to cricketers who have appeared in England against Australia.' Harry Lee of Middlesex in 1931 requested a cap and blazer after playing the previous winter as an emergency opening batsman in Johannesburg in place of Andrew Sandham, who had been injured in a car crash. However, Pelham Warner, the chairman of selectors and a former Middlesex captain of Lee's, refused because of claims (which Lee denied) that he had failed to obtain leave from coaching duty.† Lee's predicament highlighted a loophole in the system; he was not entitled to the sort of cap awarded to players appearing in home Tests but nor was he an official member of an MCC tour party so he would not have received the MCC kit issued at the outset of the tour. Lee was 40 years old and this was his only Test. Even some professionals, though, wore the caps only

---

* Charles Townsend, who played two Tests, both at home in 1899, wrote in a letter to *The Cricketer* in 1949 that thanks to AC MacLaren and Ranjitsinhji, among others, a cap was produced for him which was 'dark blue with the crest of a single lion rampant surrounded by a circle of lighter blue, with the word "England" worked into the circle'. This may have been one used by Stoddart's 1897-98 team, of which MacLaren and Ranjitsinhji were members. Townsend also recalled later being given an England cap, the description of which matches the 1908 model, although he misattributes the presentation to 1899.

† Fighting on the Western Front in May 1915, Lee was shot in the leg and, given up for dead, lay for three days between the lines; by the time news reached England of his survival, a memorial service had already been held. His injuries left him with one leg permanently shortened but he recovered to play county cricket for another 15 seasons.

sporadically. Hobbs was using a non-England cap when he took the field at Old Trafford in 1926 as acting captain after Arthur Carr had been taken ill – a historic moment as no professional had previously led the side in a Test in England.

Amateurs seemed less enthusiastic about the England cap and for some time after 1908 continued to be photographed wearing 'old school' headwear, as though their approval of the new national colours and emblems, and of the notion of being indistinguishable from their professional colleagues, was qualified. Charles Fry and Gilbert Jessop wore England caps during the 1909 home series but Douglas Jardine, like Pelham Warner before him, liked to be seen in a Harlequins cap which denoted his former associations with Oxford University. Jardine's insistence on this particular style of cap, along with his enthusiasm for wearing cravats, cemented his unpopularity with Australians when he toured in 1928-29 and 1932-33, identifying him as a man apart. Australians who could remember Warner wearing the same cap when he visited as a player may have mistrusted him all the more as the joint-manager of the 1932-33 tour.*

Other rituals eventually attached to membership of the 'England club'. These included for those who played Tests in England a sweater, also bearing the crown and three lions, and a tie; these were respectively introduced in 1948 and 1949; there was also a blazer.† Further permission had to be sought for use of the crown, the Home Office stressing to MCC that its use must be appropriate.

Ian Peebles, writing in 1958, said that 'owing to restrictions on the use of the royal insignia for sporting purposes it [the tie] must only be worn on important cricket occasions'. England stopped being described as an MCC team on tour after the winter of 1976-77, playing thereafter in non-representative matches as an England

---

* Although they had their difference over Bodyline, Warner and Jardine were both freemasons: Warner joined Douglas Lodge in Maidstone, Kent, in January 1910; Jardine was initiated into the Apollo University Lodge in Oxford, while an undergraduate there aged 19, in October 1920. Other members of the Bodyline tour who were freemasons included Herbert Sutcliffe, Hedley Verity, Bill Bowes and Maurice Tate, as were Yorkshire and England cricketers of later vintage Len Hutton and David Bairstow.
† With the exception of the captain, who wears one at the toss, modern England players do not wear blazers; they dress in suits for official functions.

XI, but continued to wear MCC colours on tour until the winter of 1996-97, when Lord MacLaurin, incoming chairman of the newly created England and Wales Cricket Board, instructed that they be replaced with an 'England' kit.*

During this period, players who only played Tests overseas were awarded MCC blazers and caps rather than England ones. Only since the creation of the ECB in 1997 has England kit been standardised regardless of whether the team was playing at home or abroad: MacLaurin restored the crown and three lions where previously the motif on the shirt was a lion in front of a set of stumps. However, the crown was replaced by a coronet because of restrictions on reproducing the crown on replica gear. MacLaurin's thinking about unifying the kit was influenced by commercial considerations: sponsors would expect the kit to be worn by England teams on a consistent basis, home and away. For many years from the 1972 Ashes onwards, England's sweaters and caps were supplied by Kent & Curwen. England teams were slow to abandon white clothing in the one-day arena: they began wearing coloured clothes overseas only in 1982-83 and at home in 1999, long after other sides accepted them as the norm.

At the suggestion of Duncan Fletcher after he became head coach in 1999, a distinction was drawn between the blazers worn by players as opposed to backroom staff such as himself who had not played for England: those who had played for England had the crown and three lions on their badge while those who had not had the coronet and three lions, which was the ECB's logo.

In 1992, at the suggestion of a member of MCC's ground working party, an honours board was put up in the dressing-room which now lists all batsmen scoring centuries, and bowlers taking five wickets in an innings and ten in a match, in Test matches and ODIs at Lord's. This practice was soon followed at England's other venues, and at other major grounds around the world. Making it onto the honours board, especially at Lord's, became a major ambition of many players,

---

* Lord MacLaurin's decision to scrap MCC colours did not go down well and even 20 years later he said: 'MCC will never forgive me for that' (*The Times,* 3 January 2017).

and some have been known on reaching their landmark to gesture to the dressing-room to stick up a piece of paper with their name on it straightaway.

It became customary for the captain or chairman of selectors to present a player making his debut with his cap on the outfield, a tradition that began when Lord MacLaurin learned from Nick Knight that when he had recently made his first Test appearance there was simply a box of caps on a table; 'I just took one that fitted me.'* This ceremony was not always strictly observed: Steve Harmison remembered his first Test in 2002 being marked by Nasser Hussain tossing his cap at him from across the Trent Bridge dressing-room. More recently former England players have been invited to take part in this ceremony, thereby bonding the present generation with those of the past and adding greater significance and merit to induction into the club of England cricket. These were practices copied from the Australians who by the 1990s had turned reverence of the 'Baggy Green cap' – an item in earlier times left forgotten in garages and lofts or handed out to acquaintances without a thought – into a cult. The Australians also patented the idea of giving each player his own unique number derived from his place in a chronological list of Test and one-day caps; the numbers were initially worn on caps but when England copied the practice they started putting them on their shirts in 2001 as well.

Originally, caps were presented once and once only. A player was expected to keep it for the duration of his England career. Geoff Boycott, who played 108 Tests between 1964 and 1982 in an era before batting helmets were de rigueur, said that his became so battered and stained with sweat that he demanded a new one but Donald Carr of the TCCB only granted him one after much persuasion. In more recent times, special caps have been awarded for England players winning 25 caps, 50 caps, 75 caps and so on, with the appropriate number on them.† The idea of presenting past

---

* At Edgbaston in 1992, Ian Salisbury was given his cap in the dressing-room but before team-sheets were exchanged rain delayed the start and England changed their XI: Salisbury was left out and had to return the cap. He debuted at Lord's two weeks later.
† This practice was in place by May 2001 when Darren Gough was given a special cap for his 50th Test; the cap was stolen from his car a few days later.

and present players with commemorative caps at Andrew Strauss's instigation in 2017 was not thought to be an original concept: similar caps have been awarded to England football and rugby players, and England cricketers from Lord MacLaurin's era remember him handing out commemorative headgear.* Commemorative silver caps or bats were subsequently presented to the 14 players who had won 100 Test caps (the late Colin Cowdrey's cap being collected by his grandson Fabian).

In 2004 the ECB added another ritual when it began playing the Jerusalem 'anthem' before the start of play at home Test matches: for the opening Test of that summer, MCC refused to allow it to be played at Lord's so it was first heard at Leeds two weeks later; MCC later relented. Around the time of the 2005 Ashes, a team song was introduced to celebrate victories; a later variant, led by Graeme Swann, was used at the World Twenty20 in 2010 and during the Ashes tour a few months later.

Broadly speaking, the rituals surrounding kit worked because these items were much prized. Dennis Amiss used to sleep with his England sweater under his pillow and Basil O'Oliveira did the same with his England cap. Poor Wilf Slack, who collapsed and died while playing in a minor match in the Gambia in 1989 at the age of 34, was buried in his England blazer and with his bat by his side. Recent players treasure their international caps and jumpers perhaps all the more for so often being obliged to wear sponsors' caps. When England in 2008 abandoned the old-style cream knitted jumpers in favour of a bright-white synthetic material it caused an outcry. 'I wouldn't fancy a career in one of those,' said one player. To acclaim, the knitted jumper, with the three lions restored to its centre, was brought back for the 2017 home season by England's new kit suppliers New Balance, an American firm, who replaced Adidas. Common kit was one of the ways in which a sense of togetherness among an essentially transitory band of brothers was forged.

---

* Modern players such as Darren Gough, Andrew Flintoff and Kevin Pietersen among others have sought to display more permanent allegiance to the team by having the 'Three Lions' tattooed on their arms – or, in Bill Athey's case in the 1980s, the Union Flag.

# CHAPTER 11

# Hobbs and Rhodes
## England's first batting partnership

No two professionals did more to democratise the England team than Jack Hobbs and Wilfred Rhodes. They were near-automatic selections throughout their Test careers and too good, and too experienced, for their opinions not to count with captains, managers and selectors regardless of their social background. Hobbs was never dropped for a match against Australia; he played in every Ashes Test from his debut in 1907-08 until his retirement in 1930 except six for which he was unavailable because of injury or illness. He opened all but twice in 71 innings and his runs (3,483) and centuries (11 out of 12 in all) in this role remain records for England against Australia; he was also a superb fielder who ran out 15 batsmen on the 1911-12 tour of Australia. Rhodes between 1899 and the first Test of 1921 missed only four matches against Australia apart from the 1901-02 tour from which he was withheld by Yorkshire; even from some of those four games his omission caused intense debate. He started as a bowler, reinvented himself as a batsman, and is one of only two England players to do the 1,000 runs-100 wickets in Ashes Tests (Ian Botham being the other).

When Johnny Douglas's leadership came into question during the 1920-21 tour, his form being poor and his focus distracted by the presence of his family, it was Hobbs and Rhodes, as well as another senior professional Frank Woolley, whom manager Frederick Toone consulted about replacing him with Percy Fender (in the end Douglas survived). When England thought they had a realistic chance of regaining the Ashes in 1926, provided they take every care, they co-opted Hobbs and Rhodes as selectors, got Hobbs to act as stand-in captain when Arthur Carr was incapacitated after the first day at Old Trafford (briefly breaking the long-standing taboo about professionals captaining England), and persuaded Rhodes to come out of international retirement aged 48 to play in the deciding match at The Oval. Capitalising on Hobbs's brilliant second-innings hundred on a 'sticky dog' by Hobbs, Rhodes bowled England to victory.

They were not by instinct revolutionaries. Hobbs's reluctance to press himself forward for the England captaincy annoyed some of his professional colleagues and towards the end of his career he expressed regret at the decline of amateur numbers because they helped 'knit a team together'. But nor did they cede ground for the sake of it. Their personalities in respects may have been different – Hobbs being cheerful, affable and kind, Rhodes cautious, taciturn and detached – but both hailed from similarly disadvantaged backgrounds. Hobbs was the eldest of 12 children to a Cambridge roof-slater, and before starting in county cricket he worked as an errand boy, college servant and gas-fitter; 'I had the inferiority complex to a marked degree,' he said. Rhodes grew up on a farm and first worked as a railway apprentice; rarely satisfied with how administrators treated cricketers, he considered himself 'a VIP who was in a sense a hired servant on a low wage'. With Yorkshire's senior professionals exerting greater influence over a succession of weak amateur leaders than they could have dreamt of doing with Lord Hawke, Rhodes was reckoned by the 1920s to be effectively their on-field captain. Proud of their calling as professional cricketers, Hobbs and Rhodes were always immaculately attired (Rhodes's shirt was always buttoned up) and, as Lord Hawke and Lord Harris would have wished, they set a standard others were eager to follow. Hobbs and Rhodes were prominent among the professionals who refused to stay on in South Africa in 1909-10 without extra pay for the convenience of the amateurs in the side. As we have seen, Hobbs in 1924-25 secured the right for his wife to join him on a tour of Australia, the first professional to do so.

The 1909-10 tour of South Africa saw Hobbs and Rhodes break the power of the amateurs in another way. Just as a captain led out his team when they were fielding, so it was seen as the duty of at least one amateur batsman to walk out and start the innings. Even if it was no more than a symbolic act, in the eyes of the gentlemanly class who ran the game it was still a ritual to be observed. Where there was at Lord's one gate onto the playing area for amateurs and another for professionals, it would not have looked good if the amateur gate remained shut at the outset of an England innings. In today's game, a stable opening pair is viewed as essential, but for many years there was little understanding of the value of sticking with the tried and trusted; seeing off a pair of fast bowlers of extreme pace was not yet part of the job description. In the period up to 1909 England's most regular pairing, Archie MacLaren and Tom Hayward, went in first together in only two series, and in only 13 innings. When Hobbs opened with Hayward at Lord's in 1909, Charles Fry having pulled out of the game at the eleventh hour, it was the first time two professionals had ever gone in first for England in the first innings of a home Test, a comment on contemporary mores if ever there was one. Too often the selectors preferred the brilliance of an amateur to the steadiness of a professional.

With MacLaren and Hayward having played their last Tests, Rhodes, who had moved up the order with success in the final match of the 1909 series, was sent in first with Hobbs in South Africa. They immediately established a rapport, sharing stands of 159 and 36 in the first Test, 94 and 48 in the second, and 221 in the fifth, after which they became accepted as England's natural openers, home or away, until 1921. Their overall record (2,146 runs, average 61.31, with eight century stands) was superior to anything that had gone before, although Hobbs's subsequent first-wicket association with Herbert Sutcliffe would outstrip theirs by a distance. Despite the series in South Africa being lost 3-2 Rhodes and Hobbs made an enormous contribution towards England winning 4-1 in Australia in 1911-12. More by picking their length than the action, Hobbs countered the threat of the new googly bowlers better than anyone (unlike Hayward, who was baffled by them).

Hobbs and Rhodes were as different in style as they were in personality. Hobbs, armed with a lot of strokes and a knack for playing the ball at the last instant, was capable of scoring runs on all types of surfaces against all types of bowling; in the years before the First World War he was a flamboyant strokemaker only to tailor his methods afterwards as scoring levels rose and the need to play bigger innings grew. 'I was only half the player after the war,' he said, but as far as England were concerned he remained their most dependable batsman. Rhodes was predominantly a defensive player who looked to score via deflections behind the wicket: he worked the ball rather than drove or hooked it.

What they had in common was an aggressive attitude to running. Hobbs said that, of all his batting partners, Rhodes was the best between the wickets; he backed up well and was always ready to run. Hobbs himself was a fast runner, just as he was fast over the ground as a cover fieldsman, and when on strike liked to set off almost before he had completed his stroke. Whichever of them was non-striker would call or just run; there were often few words spoken, rather an almost-imperceptible sign to go. However it worked, there was rarely a mix-up; there was only one run-out between them in all the Tests they played together (Rhodes in Adelaide in 1920-21) and the nearest thing to friction was Hobbs's penchant for pinching the bowling with a single off the last ball of an over. In their biggest Test stand of 323 at Melbourne in 1911-12 – still a first-wicket record for England against Australia – running between wickets was a key element in its success.

It was a relationship built on trust in what the other was doing and the kind of rapport that no amateur–professional combination perhaps ever achieved.

# CHAPTER 12

# The Shock of Gregory and McDonald

## Countering the power of pace

The nature of the defeats suffered at the hands of Australia in 1920–21 and 1921 not only convinced the English authorities that things could not carry on as they were, but shaped the course of international cricket up to and beyond the Second World War. Jack Gregory and Ted McDonald, ruthlessly orchestrated by Warwick Armstrong and helped by new practices regarding the protection of run-ups which meant they could always put everything into their actions, were the first pair of express fast bowlers to spearhead a Test attack, and the trauma they induced was profound. No amount of humbug in the committee rooms at Lord's could any longer convince anyone of Albion's innate superiority. But without the nightmares visited on them by Gregory, McDonald and Armstrong, England would not have subsequently acquired such a ruthless mindset themselves; nor probably would they have devised, let alone carried through with, the merciless Bodyline strategy. From this point on, Test teams aspired to a pair of fast bowlers – and opening batsmen who could counter them.

Armstrong used Gregory and McDonald as shock troops. To the consternation of the English camp, he would open up with both, but later in the innings use them separately so that one was always fresh and ready to be summoned when required. Both were a threat with the short-pitched ball, which neither was reluctant to use, but McDonald's real talent was in moving the ball around dangerously from a good length. Gregory, as ungainly as McDonald was graceful, was the more intimidating: coming in off a long run, he leapt high in delivery, often positioning himself wide on the return crease so the ball angled at the batsman's body, and was disturbingly erratic, an effect Armstrong maximised by always giving him the wind at his back.

'Never in my life did I have bowlers like Armstrong had, but the way he shuffled them about, the "thrust" at a new batsman, the "holding" operation if required, the field-placings for different batsmen, these were the sort of things Armstrong showed me were possible and which no other captains seemed to think about in the same way,' said Percy Fender, who played in five Tests against Armstrong's Australians and applied what he learned as an imaginative captain of Surrey for 11 seasons. As a tactician, Armstrong was regarded by English commentators as a man of uncanny ingenuity and resourcefulness, while also utterly uncompromising. These were qualities his hosts registered, if grudgingly, as they reflected on how they might themselves improve. He was streets ahead of the unfortunate Johnny Douglas and Lionel Tennyson.

The opening match of the series in Nottingham, which saw England beaten in two days for the first time since 1888, crystallised the destroying image. Some of England's batsmen had faced Gregory in 1919 when he played for an Australian Imperial Forces side, and Gregory and McDonald together in Australia, where they teamed up for three Tests, but their impact was never greater than during this opening match as they shared 16 wickets. Crucially, the skies over Trent Bridge on the first morning were grey and the pitch damp; a mid-morning shower enlivened it further. The ball flew off the wet turf and Gregory and McDonald were all the more lethal precisely because they were operating on firm ground in their delivery strides: the practice of covering ends introduced shortly before the First World War, and which extended to rainbreaks during play while the pitch itself was left exposed to the elements, was hugely beneficial to two bowlers of such athleticism and speed.

How closely match venues stuck to the MCC guidelines on covering is unclear but the pressure to see cricket played became greater as the popularity of big matches grew, and rules were surely bent. Later in the series at Old Trafford hundreds of impatient spectators flocked onto the playing area when drizzle prevented play on the opening day and it required what *Wisden* described as 'a strong force of police' to restore order (there was similar unrest at the same ground during a South Africa Test three years later). By the time of Australia's next tour in 1926, each ground was allowed to follow its own practices in terms of covering the pitch in advance of a match getting underway.

Unlike fast bowlers of earlier generations for whom the prospect of rain jeopardised their chances of even taking part, Gregory and McDonald were able to run in confident of their footing at all times, greatly enhancing their capacity to bowl fast. Previously, a rain-affected pitch meant a spinner could make hay; now, so could fast bowlers. England had got a first taste of the deadliest bowling yet seen in Test cricket four months earlier when rain, followed by a hot sun, turned the pitch at Melbourne into a virtual minefield. Herbert Strudwick was hit three times over the heart by Gregory, an episode that had made it especially tough for the Englishmen to share the boat back home with their opponents.

'In older days the area in and around the stumps was not protected during rain, and a fast bowler often found the greatest difficulty in standing up. It has been very noticeable in recent years how often a fast bowler has been successful on a slow or sticky wicket, and this has been especially the case at Lord's and the Oval,' Pelham Warner wrote in *Cricket Between the Wars*. One of the things that convinced Jardine that Bradman might be susceptible to bowling on the line of the body was the difficulty he had in dealing with Harold Larwood's bowling as the ball kicked off wet turf following rain at the Oval Test in 1930; one ball struck Bradman over the chest, he stepped back from other deliveries and the scoring-rate plummeted.

On the first day at Trent Bridge, Gregory and McDonald bowled unchanged save for three maiden overs from Armstrong and had England all out for 112 by half past three. Gregory had begun the carnage by claiming the first three wickets in a flurry during his third and fourth overs, culminating in Patsy Hendren's off stump cartwheeling out of the ground. When England batted a second time, and mustered 147, the Nottingham spectators were incensed to see Ernest Tyldesley knocked out cold by a bouncer, showing their disapproval of the relentless diet of short-pitched bowling by barracking Gregory. Memories of this game burned bright with Nottingham folk when Australians later protested at the Bodyline tactics of local heroes Harold Larwood and Bill Voce.

The sight of flying stumps and bruised flesh was to be common. Of the 46 wickets Gregory and McDonald took between them in the series (which proved to be McDonald's last as he soon settled in England to play county cricket) precisely half were bowled. If an indictment was needed of English technique or temperament in the face of hostile bowling, this doleful fact provides it. Although it was unfortunate that because of injury and illness Jack Hobbs did not bat once in the series and JW Hearne only twice, this could not be used as an excuse; Australia's bowling – backed by far more athletic catching than their slovenly opponents could manage – was simply too fast and too good. A few batsmen showed resolve but so chaotic was England's selection process that even some of them were incomprehensibly dropped; the nerves of others were plainly broken. Though he scored 95 and 93 in the second Test, Frank Woolley was battered black and blue, and said in retirement he never had to work so hard for his runs as he did in that match. The mayhem was typified by Andy Ducat's dismissal at Headingley, where a delivery from McDonald shattered his bat: the ball deflected into the hands of a slip fielder, while a shard of willow cannoned into the stumps. He was thus out twice in one ball (the catch took precedence). Research in Australia after the Bodyline series, by RH Campbell in *Cricket Casualties*, found that Gregory struck 20 'blows' on opposing batsmen in Anglo–Australia Tests compared to 34 by Larwood.

England's selectors – Harry Foster, John Daniell and Reggie Spooner – were as much out of their depth as many of the 30 players they summoned in the five matches (a record for one series). None of them had experience of captaining England and only Spooner had played Test cricket; he had in fact been invited ahead of Douglas to lead the tour of Australia the previous winter even though he hardly played during the 1920 season and was affected by wounds sustained in the war; he eventually declined.* Their reflexive response to the unfolding crisis was to turn to those who had had a good war, perhaps reflecting the pervasive influence the war still had over society as a whole (England's captain Johnny Douglas was frequently styled 'Colonel Douglas'). Following the rout at Nottingham, the selectors summoned for the Lord's Test Johnny Evans and Nigel Haig; neither was Test class but both were decorated for war service, Evans escaping several times from prison camp while Haig was wounded on the Somme (he was also a nephew of Lord Harris and cousin of General Haig). An invitation was also sent to Commander CB Fry, now in his 50th year, but he demurred.

At the eleventh hour, Lionel Tennyson, a nephew of the poet Alfred, Lord Tennyson, was asked to play and accepted; Tennyson had also survived the Somme and been wounded several times before being invalided out of the war in November 1917. His two brothers were both killed. The experience changed his life, the adventurous approach he brought to his cricket being mirrored by a love of fast horses, faster women and gaming tables. 'My whole later career was based upon what happened in France,' he said. He was routinely referred to as Major Tennyson until he succeeded to the baronetcy in 1928. Unlike Evans or Haig, Tennyson proved a success: taking on Gregory and McDonald fearlessly if luckily, he made three half-centuries in four matches, one at Headingley virtually one-handed after sustaining an injury while fielding. Struck

---

* Spooner's preferment at No.3 ahead of George Gunn of Nottinghamshire for the Triangular Tournament in 1912 had been a puzzle, Gunn having just done well in that position in Australia. Now, the surprise was that Spooner and his fellow selectors did not pick the in-form Gunn for any of the 1921 Tests.

over the heart by a ball from McDonald at The Oval, he carried on unfazed. Appointed captain in place of Douglas after just one game, by his belligerence he first rekindled England's hope that the Australian juggernaut could be halted. Not everyone was capable of matching his example. Walking out to join Evans in the middle at Lord's he found someone 'so nervous that he could hardly hold his bat, while his knees were literally knocking together. I endeavoured to put some heart into him by a few timely words ... but it was useless; his nerve was gone, and the first straight ball was enough for him.'

The panic extended to selectors who genuinely did not seem to know what they were doing, on one occasion accosting Haig as he left the dressing-room at Lord's and telling him to force the pace, an instruction which contradicted what Haig had been told by his captain. Haig popped his head back around the dressing-room door and asked: 'Johnny [Douglas], the selectors are telling me to have a go. What shall I do?'

Tennyson's example encouraged the idea that, although amateur cricket was in such decline that amateur numbers in county cricket would halve during the 1920s, fearlessness was an important attribute that an amateur captain could bring to his leadership, and England subsequently bestowed the job on several others who had good wars. Frank Mann, three times wounded and three times mentioned in dispatches, and Ronnie Stanyforth, who was awarded the Military Cross and admitted to the Royal Victorian Order, led the sides that toured South Africa in 1922-23 and 1927-28, even though in Stanyforth's case he had yet to play county cricket. The teams sent to New Zealand and West Indies in the winter of 1929-30 were captained respectively by two former pilots Harold Gilligan and Freddie Calthorpe, to whom Stanyforth, now an army major, acted as deputy; Gilligan survived 72 hours in the North Sea after ditching and was awarded the Military Cross. Jack Holmes, another war-time airman, was appointed captain of a tour of India in 1939-40 that was ultimately cancelled because of the Second World War, having the previous winter managed a Test tour of South Africa; subsequently, and by now a Group Captain, he chaired the Test selection panel from 1947 to 1949. Tennyson himself led several non-Test tours to South Africa, West Indies and India.*

The war also had a marked influence on those just too young to be involved. Percy Chapman, educated at Uppingham and Cambridge, played with the same carefree, upbeat spirit as Tennyson but was a better batsman and a superb fieldsman, good enough to merit a place in a strong side that he led to nine successive victories after surprisingly being chosen to replace Arthur Carr for the decisive Test of 1926. Standing over 6ft, with curly blond hair, Chapman, in the words of Ian Peebles, 'radiated a debonair gaiety which immediately captured the imagination of a public yearning for the inspiration of a colourful hero'. Peebles estimated that after Chapman retained the Ashes in Australia in 1928-29, his prestige as England captain 'stood higher than that of any predecessor'.

Whereas Tennyson's greatest weakness was a gambling habit that cost him his home in 1939, Chapman's problem was an addiction to drink fuelled by his work for a distillery, and this probably contributed to him being controversially sacked ahead of the final Test against Australia in 1930 after his grip on tactics, never profound, failed him under the onslaught of Don Bradman's bat. Even before the series began, Pelham Warner reckoned that Chapman needed to lose two stone in weight. Having already been appointed for the forthcoming tour of South Africa, Chapman took back the reins from Bob Wyatt in the winter, but that series merely confirmed that his behaviour was at odds with the more serious mood of international cricket.†

Douglas Jardine – born seven weeks after Chapman and educated at a public school in Winchester which sent a disproportionately large number of young men to their deaths on the Western Front – took

---

* There were seven England Test cricketers who survived the First World War and were decorated: John Hartley (Distinguished Service Order); Johnny Evans, Frederick Fane, Harold Gilligan, Ronald Stanyforth and George Wood (all Military Cross); and Nigel Haig (Air Force Cross) (*The Cricket Statistician*, Summer 2015, p44).

† Tennyson and Chapman both died at the relatively young age of 61: Tennyson sitting up in bed, smoking a cigar and reading the racing page, Chapman a victim of depression and alcoholism.

a more ascetic approach to life. Having played against the 1921 Australians for Oxford University (scoring an unbeaten 96 that might have been a hundred had the Australian captain been more generous about allowing play to continue at the end of the game) and being a protégé of Percy Fender at Surrey, Jardine knew all about how ruthlessly cricket was played under Warwick Armstrong. He absorbed the lessons well. For him, cricket would be his chance to conduct war by other means.

Tennyson's freewheeling approach boosted morale, but searching for war heroes who could play cricket was no way to select a team. England needed to improve their methods of unearthing cricketers of genuine class. The solution was to revive the Test Trial, briefly used in the lead-up to the 1911-12 tour of Australia and the Triangular Tournament, and when weather permitted these worked well through to the early 1950s, by which time England had embarked on one of the most productive periods of results in their history.* County cricket, it was clear, could not be trusted as a measure of who might perform well against the strongest opposition, and many Gentlemen v Players matches were lopsided affairs. The days of the gilded amateur turning up for a Test with little game-time behind him, or declining an invitation at the eleventh hour, were also consigned to the past. The Test Trial helped bring greater professionalism to the selection process.

The trials were also designed to allow the likely XI to knit together. 'Our teams suffered a good deal from the casual and unsystematic ways in which things were managed,' Sydney Pardon wrote of the 1921 series. 'Men ought not to be in doubt 24 hours

---

* The formal Test Trial was dropped after 1953, before a fleeting revival in 1973 and 1974; both times, the criticism was that front-rank players did not need such matches. At Bradford in 1950, Jim Laker returned the astonishing analysis of eight for 2 as The Rest were dismissed for 27; at Worcester in 1974, Geoff Boycott scored 160 not out and 116 for England. In its absence other fixtures were sometimes treated as quasi-trials: Gentlemen v Players at Lord's, which regained some credibility in the 1950s before being scrapped in 1962; early-season matches between MCC and counties such as Surrey and Yorkshire, or a touring team; later the annual MCC v champion county fixture, first at Lord's and later in Abu Dhabi.

beforehand as to whether they are going to play in a Test match. I think the side should always be chosen well in advance of the day, [save for] an extra bowler being held in reserve in view of a sudden change in the weather.' In the build-up to subsequent Ashes series or tours, two or three trial matches were sometimes staged, but typically the main one, pitting England against The Rest, was held a week to ten days before the first home Test of the summer. This too was a beneficial move.

The Test Trials helped identify Maurice Tate and Harold Larwood as bowlers of star potential and Percy Chapman as a batsman of rare enterprise; after a good performance in a trial match in 1924 he was given a Test debut before he had played for Kent in the championship. Above all, the trials revealed Herbert Sutcliffe as the man to open the innings with Jack Hobbs, who had largely fought Gregory and McDonald alone at the top of the order in Australia in 1920-21. What set Hobbs apart was his impeccable judgement in playing only at those deliveries he had to. 'Both these bowlers made the ball fly high and disconcertingly,' wicketkeeper Bert Oldfield recalled. '[Hobbs] at the very last fraction of a second would draw his bat away from the line of the ball just sufficiently to avoid the possibility of being caught behind or in the slips.' With Wilfred Rhodes struggling to rediscover his form of pre-war days, and Hobbs sidelined during the 1921 series, England in their first nine post-war Tests got through eight different opening pairs who managed just two fifty stands between them. But in Sutcliffe, Hobbs found a likeminded technician and when they were first paired together for England, against South Africa in 1924, Sutcliffe had already proved himself in two Test Trials the previous summer, in one of which at Lord's he had batted in every bit as masterly a fashion as Hobbs on a difficult pitch.

Sutcliffe's determined, unflappable personality was built on the bleakest of upbringings. His father, a sawmill worker and publican, died from a rugby injury when Herbert was four years old; his mother died of tuberculosis when he was eight. Brought up by three aunts in Pudsey, his early jobs included working in a boot factory and as a book-keeper in a textile mill, and, although he did not see active service, he spent most of the war in uniform and was commissioned as a second lieutenant; his entry into first-class cricket was thus delayed until he was 24 years old. 'If I am beaten all ends up and get away with it, I have forgotten about it as soon as the bowler starts his run for the next delivery,' he once said.

Hobbs's quiet encouragement enabled Sutcliffe to quickly settle into his new role with England, and Sutcliffe's gentle reminder to Hobbs to 'leave the new ball alone' when they were negotiating a tricky period to stumps in the first Test in Australia in 1924-25 convinced Hobbs of his credentials: 'I knew we'd found the right opener for England.' In the next match of that series in Melbourne, in putting on 283, the two of them batted throughout the third day, the first time any pair had done this in a Test and still the only time it has been done for England. Twice during the series in England in 1926 they held firm in fiercely difficult conditions, saving the game at Headingley then setting up a win in the decider at The Oval on a pitch which, in the words of umpire Frank Chester, 'kept the ball popping and turning like a mad thing'; given the significance of the game, this ranks as one of the greatest of all partnerships for England. As Hobbs had done with Rhodes, they judged quick singles to perfection.

Hobbs and Sutcliffe blunted the new ball as effectively as any other combination has ever done – not just for England, but for any Test side. They were central not only to England regaining the Ashes in 1926 but retaining them in 1928-29 when a partnership of 105 on a sticky wicket set their side on the way to scoring 332 to clinch the series in Melbourne; this remains England's highest-ever successful run-chase. Sutcliffe continued to be an influential figure after Hobbs retired from Tests in 1930; he was the joint leading run-scorer in the 1932-33 Ashes series when he shared century stands for the first wicket with Bob Wyatt in the first Test and Douglas Jardine in the fourth. The solidity of the starts provided by Hobbs and Sutcliffe gave England a huge advantage over Australia, whose openers often struggled to keep the likes of Tate and Larwood at bay; when Bill Woodfull and Bill Ponsford posted two big stands during the 1930 series, it paved the way for double-centuries from Don Bradman.

Hobbs and Sutcliffe's value became even more evident once they were gone. No amount of Test Trials managed to provide anything better than short-term fixes to the problem of their replacements until Len Hutton, a protégé of Sutcliffe's from Pudsey, emerged as an England player in 1937 with an approach every bit as phlegmatic and a technique every bit as polished. After Hobbs's retirement, Sutcliffe opened with seven different partners in 18 Tests; these included Percy Holmes, a long-standing ally at Yorkshire who had been unfairly jettisoned after the opening Test of 1921 in which he had shown great fight against Gregory and McDonald. By now 45 years old, Holmes failed to do himself justice: his time had gone. It was not until after the Second World War when Hutton, having rebuilt his technique after a war-time accident resulted in his left arm being shortened by two inches, teamed up with Cyril Washbrook, another batsman tutored against the moving ball in the north of the country, that England found another opening pair on whom they could truly rely.

All this reflected the difficulty of the opener's role but also how adroitly Hobbs and Sutcliffe had gone about their work. Hobbs was rightly feted as a master of his craft but he was also a hard-nosed professional who shamelessly used his pads as a second line of defence, a ploy that exploited the law as it then stood permitting lbw decisions only to balls pitching directly in line with the stumps. Thus a ball that came back into the batsman but landed outside off stump – a classic inswing bowler's delivery, or off-cutter – could be safely padded away, all the more in Hobbs's case because, as John Arlott noted, 'his standing was such that he was unlikely to be given a bad decision'. Hobbs was far from alone in using this technique after the First World War – Wilfred Rhodes and Douglas Jardine were others – but he deployed it to full advantage. In fact, so open-chested did his stance become so that he could cover his stumps with both legs that he was left frequently looking to work the ball through the on-side; Arthur Gilligan, who captained the 1924-25 tour of Australia, said that this contributed to the strength of Hobbs's partnership with Sutcliffe because Sutcliffe preferred scoring through the off side: 'Their partnership almost amounts to that of a right-hander and a left-hander together.'

The 'two-eyed stance' was denounced by many of the older generation (who had the luxury of not actually being engaged in trying to
win Test matches) as an infringement of the spirit of cricket. Although
there were other factors at work such as the fall-out from Bodyline, it
may have been significant that in the season after Hobbs retired from
first-class cricket, MCC introduced an experimental law permitting
batsmen to be lbw to balls pitching outside off stump. Batting averages
and the number of drawn matches fell, and the experimental law was
swiftly approved as permanent. 'A batsman dare not "cover-up" to the
ball that was coming wide of the off stump,' Sydney Pardon wrote in
reviewing the changeover season of 1935.

'There came a decided check to those interminable first-wicket
partnerships which were so detrimental to the game. It was not
surprising that, facing the swerve with the ball brand new, the early
batsmen found their task harder.' For left-handed batsmen, the new
law created the added complication of bringing into play the rough of
the bowlers' follow-through, as well as heightening the threat of the
leg-spinner. Sutcliffe found the changed law particularly challenging
and admitted, 'I have perhaps succumbed to the new lbw rule more
than anyone else.' He was lbw in each of his first three innings against
South Africa in the 1935 Tests, and did not play for England again.
Another outspoken critic was Bob Wyatt, who captained England
that summer and saw his first-class average almost halve between
1934 and 1936, before recovering. He said the new law discouraged
off-side play, an opinion shared by an increasing number of influential figures including Gubby Allen and Cyril Washbrook.

Pad-play was also blamed for encouraging Bodyline, insofar as an
open-chested batsman left the bowler little else to bowl at other than
the body, and left him good reason to pack the leg-side field. When
Hobbs criticised England's Bodyline tactics, the mild-mannered
Larwood publicly rebuked him: 'Does Jack really think that an
action which robs the bowler of a wicket to be fair cricket? I know
it is not against the Laws of Cricket but neither is my fast leg-theory
bowling ... Actually it was pad-play that was partly responsible for
the leg-side attack. So if the latter's not cricket, those who use their
pads too much must shoulder at least some of the blame for it.'

## England's Best Opening Pairs

(Qualification: 1,500 runs, average 40)

| Partners | Period | Innings | Runs | Average | Century Stands |
|---|---|---|---|---|---|
| Jack Hobbs/Herbert Sutcliffe | 1924-30 | 38 | 3249 | 87.81 | 15 |
| Jack Hobbs/Wilfred Rhodes | 1910-21 | 36 | 2146 | 61.31 | 8 |
| Len Hutton/Cyril Washbrook | 1946-51 | 51 | 2880 | 60.00 | 8 |
| Michael Atherton/Graham Gooch | 1990-95 | 44 | 2501 | 56.84 | 7 |
| Andrew Strauss/Marcus Trescothick | 2004-06 | 52 | 2670 | 52.35 | 8 |
| Geoff Boycott/John Edrich | 1964-72 | 35 | 1672 | 52.25 | 6 |
| Marcus Trescothick/Michael Vaughan | 2002-05 | 54 | 2487 | 48.76 | 6 |
| Alastair Cook/Andrew Strauss | 2006-12 | 117 | 4711 | 40.96 | 12 |

England's wait to unearth fast bowlers of the calibre of Gregory and McDonald was so prolonged that they were always likely to maximise their impact when they finally came along.

Johnny Douglas's team headed to Australia for the first post-war series imbued with memories of the triumph of 1911-12 and in the hope of recreating Frank Foster's success took with them Abe Waddington, a left-arm seam and swing bowler with a fine action. The move failed – Waddington, suffering ill health, took one wicket in two Tests – but none of England's fast/fast-medium bowlers proved a success and Australia actually lost more wickets to run-outs than they did to any one bowler of this type.

The death of Second Lieutenant Major Booth, killed in action during the war, was keenly felt. Booth was a right-arm seam and swing bowler who could have been especially effective in England and would have been 34 at the time of the 1920-21 tour; the average age of the side that played in the final Test was 36. When Booth died on the first day of the Somme offensive, Waddington, a fellow member of the West Yorkshire Regiment, was with him and cradled him in his arms as his life ebbed away.* Waddington was himself hit by shrapnel in the chest and legs and, although he recovered from his wounds and survived the war, he remained haunted by Booth's death and gained a reputation as an awkward character on and off the field.† England's frustration at their lack of firepower was only exacerbated by Harry Howell in Melbourne and Bill Hitch at The Oval bowling spells of genuine pace only to be unable to sustain such form; then Arthur Gilligan, not yet 30 and capable of genuine pace, was hit over the heart during a Gentlemen v Players match in 1924 and never achieved full pace again; three weeks earlier he had taken six for 7 as he and Maurice Tate routed South Africa for 30 at Edgbaston, then the joint-lowest total in a Test.

Tate was not a bowler of the highest speed but by breathing fire and brimstone at Australia's batsmen in 1924–25 he gave warning of England's intent. Tate, who was England's first second-generation Test cricketer as his father Fred played one Test in 1902 when he was widely though unjustly blamed for a three-run defeat, earned comparisons to Sydney Barnes for his sheer intensity of effort, but his methods were different. Whereas Barnes spun the ball, Tate cut it; he also hit the pitch hard with an upright seam so that the ball spat this way and that with snake-like venom and a relentlessness that no England 'seamer' had managed before. Tate's efforts in Australia actually eclipsed those of Barnes in 1911–12 in terms of wickets; his 38 victims remain the most by an England bowler in a series Down Under. More remarkable still was the amount of work he got through as he largely carried the attack on his own shoulders. By bowling 316 eight-ball overs he sent down more deliveries (2,528) than any other England bowler in any series. Tate was never as deadly again,

---

* Colin Blythe, one of England's finest slow left-arm spinners who took 100 wickets in 19 Tests, was also killed during the First World War, but would not have resumed playing after the war had he lived; shortly before he was killed in action in 1917 his retirement from county cricket had been announced. Roy Kilner, at whose wedding Major Booth had been best man in 1912, sustained a damaged wrist on the first day of the Battle of the Somme, but after the war he took up left-arm spin and played nine Tests for England as an all-rounder before his early death in 1928.

† At the invitation of Len Hutton, the captain, Waddington accompanied the England team to Australia in 1954–55.

but he remained a consistent performer for several years and shared the new ball with Larwood when England won at The Oval in 1926 and at Trent Bridge in 1930, as well as in every Test in Australia in 1928-29, when he again got through a staggering amount of work.

Larwood played his first full season of county cricket in 1925 at the age of 20, and two years later he was joined in the Nottinghamshire side by Bill Voce, a left-armer still a few weeks short of his 18th birthday. Both were of mining stock from Kirkby-in-Ashfield and the hardier for it. Though the shorter by five inches at only 5ft 8in, Larwood with the help of their coach Jimmy Iremonger developed a superbly efficient run-up and delivery that maximised his pace: his Test debut at the start of the 1926 series was secured by a period of three weeks in which he bowled Jack Hobbs twice in a county match, the England captain Arthur Carr (also his county captain) in a Test Trial and the 'unbowlable' Australia opener Bill Woodfull for the North of England. It was a talent he never lost: almost half his Test wickets, and more than half his first-class wickets, were bowled.

Two years after Voce arrived, Bill Bowes made his debut for Yorkshire aged 20. Bowes was 6ft 4in and took direct inspiration from playing in Roses matches against Ted McDonald, who had joined Lancashire in 1924 and whose recommended approach to batsmen was: 'Have no mercy ... Give 'em hell.'* Gubby Allen, a Middlesex amateur who played when his work on the Stock Exchange allowed, was also capable of fitful bursts of speed and took all ten wickets (including eight men bowled) against Lancashire, champions of the past three seasons, in 1929. Of this quartet only Larwood went to Australia in 1928-29, where he won the Test at Brisbane, but all four were dispatched in 1932-33. It was a ground-breaking number.

The appetite for vengeance consumed the very top of the English game because Armstrong's Australians had in particular exposed the

---

* It was unusual for high-profile overseas Test stars to sign up for county or league cricket at this time, as it effectively meant the end of their Test careers, but some such as McDonald were persuaded. He was 33 years old in 1924 but still good enough in the next seven years to take more than 1,000 wickets for Lancashire. Bill Ponsford was on the verge of playing league cricket for Blackpool in 1927 when a local fundraising campaign kept him in Australia; he played four more Ashes series. A move to take Don Bradman to Accrington in the early 1930s was also thwarted.

pitiful inadequacies of what remained of the nation's amateur ranks following the carnage on the fields of Flanders. In ten Tests against Armstrong's side, the highest score by an England amateur was just 75; professionals went better than that on 12 occasions, including seven hundreds. Nor was this pattern to be arrested any time soon. Freddie Calthorpe, the Warwickshire captain, was never the same batsman again after being hit in the chest by a ball from McDonald during a county match in 1925, while as an article of faith most amateurs were reluctant to follow professionals in using their pads as a second line of defence. Admirable perhaps, but hardly a formula for success: little wonder, then, that not one of the 49 Test hundreds scored for England between December 1913 and June 1929 was made by an amateur. Little wonder too that Lord Hawke prayed the day would not come when a professional led the team.

Hawke was not alone in identifying the Test matches of 1921 as the origin of the Bodyline crisis. Wilfred Rhodes asserted in the *Yorkshire Evening Post* that Larwood and Voce were not as formidable as the Gregory that 'hit a few men' in that series. Voce himself, who was only 11 when Armstrong's bowlers cut down England's batting at Trent Bridge, justified Bodyline by claiming he and Larwood were only imitating the concentrated aggression of Gregory and McDonald.

Tennyson gave his backing to Jardine's tactics specifically on the grounds that past Australian bombardments ought to be repaid with interest and, even before Jardine's team departed, revenge appeared to feature prominently in the thoughts of the *Manchester Guardian*'s Neville Cardus when he wrote: 'If the Australians are to be tackled, give me a captain who smiles only when the enemy are being rubbed into the dust.'

## Where England's Test Cricketers Were Drawn From

England have drawn on 690 players and 80 captains during their 1010 Test matches to 23 July 2019. They were playing for the following clubs at the time of their selection:

| County | Players | Caps | Most caps | Captains | Tests | Most Tests captained |
|---|---|---|---|---|---|---|
| **SOUTH-EAST** | | | | | | |
| Essex | 32 | 756 | AN Cook 161 | 6 | 168 | AN Cook 59 |
| Hampshire | 26 | 255 | KP Pietersen 66 | 3 | 12 | CB Fry 6 |
| Kent | 58 | 903 | MC Cowdrey 114 | 6 | 72 | MC Cowdrey 27 |
| Middlesex | 66 | 1182 | AJ Strauss 100 | 12 | 152 | AJ Strauss 50 |
| Surrey | 75 | 1309 | AJ Stewart 133 | 8 | 79 | PBH May 41 |
| Sussex | 43 | 525 | MJ Prior 79 | 7 | 62 | ER Dexter 30 |
| **NORTH** | | | | | | |
| Derbyshire | 24 | 274 | RW Taylor 57 | 1 | 1 | DB Carr 1 |
| Durham | 10 | 224 | PD Collingwood 68 | 0 | 0 | – |
| Lancashire | 68 | 1060 | JM Anderson 148 | 7 | 98 | MA Atherton 54 |
| Notts | 45 | 698 | SCJ Broad 126 | 4 | 19 | A Shrewsbury 7 |
| Yorkshire | 83 | 1421 | G Boycott 108 | 8 | 135 | MP Vaughan 51 |
| **MIDLANDS** | | | | | | |
| Leics | 26 | 260 | DI Gower 106 | 2 | 63 | DI Gower 32 |
| Northants | 25 | 298 | AJ Lamb 79 | 2 | 18 | FR Brown 15 |
| Warwicks | 32 | 693 | IR Bell 118 | 4 | 63 | MJK Smith 25 |
| Worcs | 31 | 392 | GA Hick 65 | 3 | 5 | RE Foster 3 |
| **WEST** | | | | | | |
| Glamorgan | 16 | 118 | RDB Croft 21 | 1 | 8 | AR Lewis 8 |
| Gloucs | 28 | 369 | WR Hammond 85 | 2 | 33 | WR Hammond 20 |
| Somerset | 28 | 329 | IT Botham 85 | 3 | 18 | IT Botham 12 |

A further 11 cricketers won a total of 21 caps: seven made all of their Test appearances for England before playing for one of the 18 counties, while four never played for a first-class or minor county; most were amateurs and had links to MCC, and all but two played before the

First World War. The two exceptions were Ronald Stanyforth, an army cricketer who led a tour of South Africa in 1927-28, captaining in four Tests, shortly before first playing for Yorkshire, and David Townsend, who averaged 12.83 as an opening bat in three Tests in West Indies in 1934-35 between leaving Oxford University and first representing Durham, then a minor county, in 1935.

Sydney Barnes, having played four Tests in 1901-02 while with Lancashire, also won 23 Test caps between 1907 and 1914 as a Staffordshire player.

Twenty-nine cricketers won England caps with two of the 18 counties, and four (Ian Botham, Phillip DeFreitas, Chris Lewis and Monty Panesar) with three.

Sixteen cricketers represented England before making their final first-class appearances for Oxford or Cambridge University. Of these, six did so after 1935, all while at Cambridge: John Dewes (one Test, 1948), Hubert Doggart (two Tests, 1950), David Sheppard (four Tests, 1950-51), John Warr (two Tests, 1950-51), Peter May (four Tests, 1951-52) and Derek Pringle (one Test, 1982).

# CHAPTER 13

# West Indies, New Zealand and India Join the Club

## The rise of bilateral tours and England's workload

The greater attention given to the management of the national team was timely because England's relationship with other regions of the cricketing world began to acquire greater importance, leading to a significant increase in their Test-playing commitments. West Indies, who subsequent to their third full tour of Britain in 1923 began a painstaking process of creating a regional governing body, aspired to Test-match status, as did New Zealand, whose ruling council had been formed in 1894.

As a result, two meetings of the Imperial Cricket Conference in London in the summer of 1926, the second chaired by Lord Harris, received delegates from both. These meetings effectively threw open the doors to West Indies and New Zealand joining the Test-match fraternity and it was clear that once India, who had first sent a broadly representative side to England in 1911, also set up an organising body, which it formally did in December 1928, it too could request meetings, send delegates and thereby arrange Test tours. By early 1934, England had played Tests home and away against all three newcomers while maintaining their traditional exchanges with Australia and South Africa, and as a result their life as a team – insofar as it could be regarded as a single organism – was never the same again. Whereas Test tours were once something of a novelty, they now became established features of the calendar. Since 1928, every English summer outside the war-time period of 1940–45 has staged at least one Test series.*

This development perhaps deliberately reflected British government attempts to incorporate and manage certain colonies in response to the emergence of nationalist political forces, particularly in India where the independence movement was gaining momentum, and in the colonies there were Imperialist natives supportive of these efforts. In the autumn of 1926 the Balfour Declaration that arose from an Imperial Conference of Empire leaders declared the United Kingdom and the Dominions to be 'autonomous communities within the British Empire, equal in status, in no way subordinate one to another in any aspect of their domestic or external affairs, though united by a common allegiance to the Crown, and freely associated as members of the British Commonwealth of Nations' – an acceptance, in other words, of the growing political and diplomatic independence of the Dominions, if not also recognition of the 200,000 Dominion lives sacrificed on behalf of the Empire in the First World War.† Among these were 53,000 Indians and more than 1,200 from the Caribbean.

Cricket tours therefore had a diplomatic dimension to them, as they would until post-colonial times. 'I have from the very outset regarded these tours primarily as imperial enterprises, tending to

---

* Although no official Tests are now deemed to have taken place in England in the 1970 season, a scheduled tour by apartheid South Africa was cancelled and replaced by five matches between England and a Rest of the World side which were designated by the TCCB as Tests at the time. However, in 1972, mainly on the initiative of South Africa and Australia, the ICC annual meeting stated that they were not official Test matches and in 1980 Norman Preston, *Wisden* editor, reluctantly dropped them from the Almanack's records.

† A legal basis for the independence of the Dominions was established by the Statute of Westminster in 1931, largely at the insistence of South African and Irish interests. Others were less keen: the statute was not adopted in Australia until 1942 and New Zealand until 1947.

cement friendship between the Mother Country and her Dominions,'
wrote Frederick Toone, a long-serving secretary of the Yorkshire
club who managed all three tours of Australia in the 1920s with
thoroughness and sagacity. 'Players, therefore, selected to take part
in them – and this has always been borne in mind by MCC – should
not be chosen for their cricket qualities alone. They must be men of
good character, high principle, easy of address, and in every personal
sense worthy of representing their country, in all circumstances.'

This was all well and good but teams increasingly wanted to
win. The war, which saw the introduction of passports, had led to a
sharper sense of national identity as well as a sharpening of nationalist
sentiment, especially in Europe where many new nation states were
formed, and this was reflected in a more partisan aspect to international sporting competition. It was something which even infected
the British, who had previously liked to take their superiority for
granted. Derek Birley cites the work of Sir Theodore Cook who in
1927 published *Character and Sportsmanship*, a paean to 'the sporting
instinct that brought us safe through the Great War'. Don Bradman
said his own ruthlessness was partly shaped by the way England
played when he made his debut appearance in Test cricket at Brisbane
in 1928 and Australia, with two men absent, were crushed by 675
runs. Then came Bodyline. For England's opponents, cricket was
one of the most effective bonds of nationhood, and beating England
in a Test match represented a defining event on the path to political
and social maturity. It may not be a coincidence that the first football
World Cup was staged at around this time, in 1930 (though England
declined to send a team).

What should pass for nationality consequently became a more
important issue. When Duleepsinhji, nephew of Ranjitsinhji and
sent by him to be educated at Malvern and Cambridge, chose to play
for England it caused more disquiet than had been the case with his
uncle. This was because Duleep now had a choice: he could have
thrown in his lot with India, the land of his birth, as he was implored
to do by Indian cricketing officials. England themselves were ambivalent and, after picking him for the first Test against South Africa in
1929, left him out of the rest of the series, despite his golden form

with the bat, ostensibly for fear of offending South Africa, who only selected from their white population.*

Duleep was subsequently picked only for matches against New Zealand and Australia. Even so, in 1932, after he and the Nawab of Pataudi (who had similarly opted to play for England rather than India after being educated at Oxford) had been chosen to tour Australia, Duleep received a death-threat from an anonymous, racist correspondent: 'How can you play for England? Play with your black brothers from India, that is your place ... You two may go to Australia but you will never come back. At least not alive.'† England's selection in 1930 of Gubby Allen, who was born in Sydney but only lived there until he was six, also caused debate in a way it would not have done in earlier times; he, like Duleep, had learned his cricket in England and satisfied ICC's qualification rules which required four years of residence in his adopted country.

The ICC in fact tightened up the qualification rules at a meeting at The Oval in July 1931 which effectively made the poaching of players harder. Each country, it was stated, was responsible for 'submitting in reasonable time for the approval of the Imperial Cricket Conference the names of any cricketers likely to be selected to play in any approaching series of Test matches, furnishing their qualifications and stating if any player has during the four immediately preceding years played for the country of his birth. In the case of cricketers qualified by residence, they shall further state the periods of residence upon which such residential qualifications are founded.' It was also spelled out for the first time that once a cricketer had played in a Test match for one country he would not be eligible to play in a Test match against that country without the consent of the Board of Control. After this, there were no more contentious selections for

---

* Duleep said that an England selector told him the South Africans objected to an Indian appearing for England, an explanation the touring team refuted. The chairman of selectors was Henry Leveson Gower who, as we have seen, led an England side to South Africa and had business interests there; he also once represented South Africa at ICC. Also on the selection panel were Jack White (Somerset captain, who played the first three Tests in 1929) and Nigel Haig (Middlesex captain).

† Duleep in fact withdrew from the 1932-33 tour through illness but Pataudi did go to Australia.

more than a generation; while Britain and its cricket-playing colonies were engaged in the sensitive process of political decoupling, England stuck stolidly, save for a few harmless exceptions, to drawing on cricketers born inside the United Kingdom.*

England's additional commitments created for the first time workload issues. The 1926 conference defined Test matches 'as matches played between sides duly selected by recognised governing bodies of cricket representing countries within the Empire' but England's fellow members interpreted this as chiefly a mechanism for playing England rather than each other. This quickly led to difficulty, with MCC agreeing to send England sides concurrently to New Zealand and West Indies in the winter of 1929-30: there were actually points at which England sides were taking part in Test matches simultaneously in Christchurch and Barbados, then Auckland and Guyana (British Guiana as it then was), although this was not fully appreciated at the time as the West Indies Tests were barely viewed as such: the 1931 *Wisden* termed them as 'Representative Matches' and only those in New Zealand as 'Test Matches', although three years later it categorised them as Tests (the status of the West Indies Tests was still being argued in the pages of *The Cricketer* in 1938).

Parallel tours were similarly arranged to South Africa and India the following winter but the India tour was cancelled as the result of the unrest caused by Mahatma Gandhi's civil disobedience campaign, India being invited to tour England instead, resulting in the first official Test between the sides at Lord's in 1932. C Stewart Caine, the editor of *Wisden*, warned in 1927 of the dangers of burnout and suggested paying players to stay at home might be the best way to preserve the leading professional fast bowlers: 'Naturally men earning their living by the game cannot be expected to refuse opportunities of making money, but in the best interests of English cricket it would be well if matters could be so arranged that great bowlers

---

* Attempts were made by Douglas Jardine among others to persuade Alan Melville, who was born and raised in South Africa, to switch allegiance to England during a period between 1930 and 1936 in which he played for and captained Oxford University and Sussex. Melville declined, returned to Johannesburg to work as a stockbroker and played the first of 11 Tests for South Africa against England in 1938-39.

without loss of income, were enabled to conserve their energies for the summer.' It was an idea about 70 years ahead of its time.

The response of the English authorities was to send sub-strength teams to tour their newer opponents, often in the winters preceding home Ashes series when there was an obvious advantage to resting star performers. Only five of the 25 players who appeared for England during the inaugural Test tours of New Zealand and West Indies featured in the 1930 Tests against Australia; the team sent to the Caribbean actually contained six players in their 40th year or beyond and had an average age of almost 38, making it England's oldest tour party.* Similarly, English sides toured India in 1933-34 and 1937-38 ahead of the 1934 and 1938 incoming visits by Australia. Both were essentially second-string sides, although the first was led by Douglas Jardine, who at the time of departure remained the incumbent England captain but confirmed during the tour that he had no wish to face Australia again following the Bodyline furore. The 1937-38 tour was not even accorded full status; it required the sponsorship of Lionel Tennyson, now Lord Tennyson, who captained the side and turned 48 during the trip, and involved only an unofficial Test series which was won 3-2 by the Englishmen, just three of whom subsequently played in the 1938 Ashes.

Even these measures proved insufficient and England raised the matter of the burden the international programme was placing on their players at the ICC meeting of 1938, even though the counties feared the financial impact of fewer Test tours. At a correspond-ing meeting ten years later, the MCC selection and planning subcommittee, chaired by Pelham Warner and also containing three other England captains in Gubby Allen, Walter Robins and Ronnie Stanyforth, gave a bleaker assessment still in presenting a detailed report on the future of international tours in which it said that an increase in standards in receiving countries meant that only the best English teams should play abroad in order to 'satisfy the

---

* Wilfred Rhodes remains the oldest man ever to play a Test, aged 52 years 165 days when the final Test in Jamaica ended; nor has anyone older scored 250-plus in a Test match than Andrew Sandham, aged 39, who in the same game made a then Test record 325 using his captain's bat and Patsy Hendren's shoes.

hosts and for the prestige of international cricket'; if this was not done, tours should not rank as official or involve full Test matches. It implored other member countries to arrange more visits among themselves.

This verdict came from bitter perspective: as the subcommittee was reporting, England were in the midst of a heavy defeat at the hands of Bradman's Invincibles, while only a few months earlier a below-strength team led by the 45-year-old Allen had returned from the Caribbean soundly beaten despite summoning Len Hutton from home, where he had been resting ahead of the 1948 Ashes, to reinforce a side depleted by injuries and illness mid-series. This experience left Allen well placed to judge how tours should best be conducted (Allen deserved some blame for taking upon himself the captaincy of such a challenging assignment at so advanced an age).* There were various consequences: to India's consternation, MCC postponed a planned Test tour of India in 1949-50 (it eventually took place two winters later); Australia's next scheduled visit to England was put back 12 months to 1953; and it was announced that England would tour for not more than two winters in a row, and never in the months leading up to a home Ashes series, a practice that survived until the early 1960s. In reality, although England in future sent strong sides to South Africa and West Indies, it continued to dispatch second-string teams to India and Pakistan until the 1970s.†

The dynamics in any case were changing. Britain's colonies, perceiving imperial weakness, aspired in the aftermath of the Second World War to full political independence; this India attained in August 1947, bringing with it the creation of Pakistan. This more outward-looking approach was soon reflected in a more diverse international

---

* At MCC's AGM in May 1948, the committee let members know 'that at no time was the standard of West Indies cricket underrated, and that, in the circumstances stated, the best team was selected from the players available', a view partly contradicted by the findings of the selection and planning subcommittee which suggested that the spate of injuries on the tour might have been due to the age of the players and 'some deficiency in diet'.

† MCC also asked South Africa, India, West Indies and New Zealand to cover 'the entire expenses of [incoming] tours, including overhead costs of every kind'.

fixture list. It was not before time: of the 289 Test matches played up to October 1947, all but 32 of them involved England.*

As had been the case with South Africa, Englishmen were heavily involved in assimilating these new teams into the Test-match arena, although more in terms of administration than English-born players relocating to a second country. Pelham Warner was from early days a champion of West Indies cricket. He had been born in Trinidad into a former slave-trading family and educated in Barbados, and his elder brother Aucher, later attorney-general of Trinidad, captained the first West Indies side to tour England in 1900, so he understood both the region's cricketing potential and the issues of race and class that might compromise it. He lobbied for black representation in the early West Indies touring sides and, by making the black Learie Constantine captain of a Dominions XI against England at Lord's in 1945, he contributed to the campaign to break the white elite's hold on the West Indies Test captaincy. In keeping with MCC providing secretarial support to ICC, Warner twice represented West Indies at ICC meetings (as well as South Africa). Harry Mallett, a former Durham captain, chairman of the Minor Counties Cricket Association and a member of the MCC committee, provided the diplomatic skills needed to bring the territories together and create a West Indies board in 1927; he also scheduled and managed several of their early tours.

Harold Gilligan occupied a similar role to Mallett for New Zealand, arranging their first four Test tours of England and representing them for 30 years at ICC, having captained England's first Test matches in New Zealand on the 1929-30 tour. Another of New Zealand's early ICC delegates was Arthur Sims, who played cricket in New Zealand but later settled in England and set up business as a meat importer. Tom Lowry, captain of New Zealand's first full tour of England in 1927 on which they showed themselves capable of playing Tests when they next visited, enjoyed the closest ties with

* Australia had played South Africa 24 times, West Indies five times and New Zealand once (in 1945 in a match accorded Test status only in March 1948); South Africa had played New Zealand twice.

England, having been educated at Cambridge, played several seasons at Somerset and even toured his own country with an MCC side. His sister married Percy Chapman in 1925 (the marriage did not survive Chapman's drinking).

India's bid for Test cricket was initially driven by the British expatriate community: two Calcutta businessmen A Murray Robertson and William Currie happened to be in London in 1926 at the time the ICC gathered in the hope of persuading MCC to send a team to challenge India's European cricketers, Indian cricket being largely organised in pre-independence days on communal lines.* In fact, the team MCC agreed to send the following winter, led by Arthur Gilligan, Sussex captain and a member of the MCC committee (and Harold's elder brother), played teams representing all communities. Once he saw his side outplayed by a representative side of native cricketers in Bombay, Gilligan encouraged India to set up a governing body in accordance with ICC's instructions and even attended the inaugural meeting.† The Indian board was formed under the presidency of RE Grant Govan, a British industrialist. John Glennie Greig, an English army officer, chaired a panel that selected the 1911 India tour party otherwise made up of Parsis, Hindus and Muslims. India's first Test tour of England in 1932 was managed by an Englishman Major EWC Ricketts, and Alec Hosie, another member of Calcutta's European community, even chaired India's selection panel for the first home series against England in 1933–34, to the ire of nationalists.‡

Although they lost five of their first six Tests in England by an innings, West Indies quickly proved the strongest of the three new sides and brought with them also a refreshing vibrancy, especially

---

* The leading tournament in India at the time was the Bombay Quadrangular in which sides representing Europeans, Hindus, Muslims and Parsis competed.

† The Gilligans remain the only brothers to captain England in Tests.

‡ It was even mooted, though rejected, that India should be captained in their first Tests by an Englishman on the basis an Englishmen would best unify the side; according to Mihir Bose, Douglas Jardine's name was mentioned, although this would not have been possible under the ICC's new qualification rules, and Hosie was among other possible candidates. In fact, no Europeans ever represented India in Tests. In the event, Jardine captained England in their first Tests in India.

to their fast bowling and fielding epitomised by Learie Constantine from Trinidad. They were a match for the early sub-strength England sides sent to the Caribbean, drawing the first series and winning the next two before storming the game's citadel with a 3-1 series win in England in 1950. They possessed a truly great batsman in George Headley and an array of powerful, athletic fast bowlers, a feature that would endure. Even at the risk of retaliation, they took pride in ruffling the feathers of master batsmen such as Wally Hammond and Herbert Sutcliffe, who said he had never faced finer fast bowling, and used Bodyline tactics against England to good effect in 1933. Bob Wyatt had his jaw broken in several places by Manny Martindale in Jamaica in 1935.

They might have been even more effective had not inter-island rivalry and the insistence on white captains militated against the selection of their strongest XI. CLR James, an anti-colonial writer from Trinidad who saw cricket as a means of nation-building for Caribbean countries, feared that a white captain such as the Cambridge-educated Jackie Grant would be reluctant to challenge his white 'cousins' as aggressively as black players after the mood among English administrators began to turn against Bodyline; if this happened, he said, 'the West Indians should flay him [Grant] alive'.

England awarded West Indies the most matches and most regular tours of the three. New Zealand – subsequent to originally hosting England in 1929-30 for what was planned as a three-match series only for a fourth Test to be added after rain affected the game in Auckland – received visits through to the 1960s for one or two Tests only as an add-on to England playing in Australia. This was actually the consequence of them having exceeded expectations in England in 1931 when originally only one Test at Lord's was scheduled: New Zealand played so well, putting England under pressure after being 230 behind on first innings, that they were awarded two extra Tests that summer, then Jardine's 1932-33 side to Australia stopped off for Tests in Christchurch and Auckland (Walter Hammond scoring 227 and 336 not out, the latter a then Test record). That set an unfortunate precedent which New Zealand were not strong enough to break, especially after a clutch of players – Charles Dacre, Stewie

Dempster, Ken James, Bill Merritt and Tom Pritchard – opted to play county cricket rather than Tests. New Zealand did not manage to win a Test home or abroad until the 1950s; nor did India, who found their opportunities up to the Second World War even more restricted, England not coming to play Tests again after the visit of Jardine's side until 1951-52.

MCC's aristocrats may have talked of spreading cricket's gospel, and virtual second XIs may have been put in the field, but England nevertheless showed little mercy: their home record against the three newcomers between 1928 and 1949 was played 26, won 12, drawn 14, lost 0.* These teams were even treated differently: England played them over shorter matches than Australia or South Africa, and the pitches on which these sides played their first Tests on English soil were not even covered before play began, unlike for visits by Australia and South Africa.† Nor did Nobby Clark, a fiery red-headed left-armer from Northamptonshire, spare India's batsmen the short-pitched stuff on the 1933-34, with opener Naoomal Jeoomal being stretchered off during the third Test. India had fast bowlers of their own to respond with but they, like West Indies, might have fared better had their selection not been compromised by tensions arising from race and class. Princes of feeble cricketing ability took the captaincy ahead of genuinely talented players who risked exclusion from the side if they dared to protest – not that, in this respect, things were vastly different from how they were in England.

---

* It was a long time too before England's Tests against West Indies, New Zealand and India were treated properly by the game's record keepers: *Wisden* did not list England Test caps won against these teams until its 1948 edition. Caps won against South Africa were included from the 1936 edition, the year after South Africa first won a Test match in England.

† At an ICC meeting in September 1930, MCC objected to the practice, introduced to Tests in England in 1926, of pitches being covered before the game on the basis that it advantaged the side batting first, although it withdrew its disapproval from 1934 onwards. West Indies had incurred MCC's wrath after completely covering pitches during the 1929-30 matches against England in infringement of the Laws (*Wisden* 1970, p138).

# CHAPTER 14

# Professionals Flex their Muscles
## Hammond and Ames

The late 1920s and early 1930s was a golden period for the England team. There continued to be a high turnover of players but for the bigger matches especially the side was blessed with a core of true greats. This was particularly the case in the batting but there were also some fast bowlers and wicketkeepers of exceptional talent and, from 1931, a left-arm spinner of genius in Hedley Verity. With the exception of the captaincy, which remained precariously in the hands of the 'elite' class, selection was now focused on finding the best players for each position and there were few weak links. There were, too, extenuating circumstances to the only two series defeats between 1925 and 1934, when the fall-out from Bodyline began to takes its toll on results: an unprecedented avalanche of runs from Don Bradman's bat was the determining factor in the Ashes of 1930, while the only match lost in South Africa in 1930-31 came on matting rather than turf. England were unbeaten in 21 consecutive home matches between 1921 and 1930, and no England side since has matched the achievement of the 1928-29 and 1932-33 sides of winning four matches in Australia against a full-strength Australian team.

This was specifically a professional golden age. Jack Hobbs, Frank Woolley and Bert Strudwick had all successfully played Test cricket before the 1914-18 war but made more appearances for England after it than before. Joining the team came Patsy Hendren (in 1920-21), Ernest Tyldesley, Johnny's younger brother by 16 years (1921), George Duckworth, Herbert Sutcliffe and Maurice Tate (1924), Harold Larwood, the fastest bowler England had had to this point (1926), Wally Hammond (1927-28), Maurice Leyland (1928), Les Ames (1929), Bill Voce (1929-30) and Verity (1931). Of these 11, all but the first two toured Australia together in 1932-33. Sydney Pardon, writing in *The Times* in 1922, reckoned that had there been a Test series that summer the only amateur who would have got into the England side on merit was Percy Fender.

When there next was a Test series in England, against South Africa in 1924, the fifth and final match did indeed see only one amateur make the team, the captain Arthur Gilligan. As also happened in the third Test of that summer, the top seven places in the order were all occupied by professionals. When England regained the Ashes in 1926, the XI never contained more than two amateurs, a fact that may have contributed to the decision taken ahead of the second game at Lord's to have amateurs and professionals sharing the same dressing-room for the first time for a home Test match. For the final Test of the 1928 series against West Indies, the captain was again the only amateur: Percy Chapman. Of the 126 Test hundreds scored for England between the wars, 112 were made by professionals.*

The northern counties were largely responsible for this domination. In 18 seasons between 1922 and 1939, the championship remained solely in their hands: Yorkshire won 11 titles, Lancashire five, and Nottinghamshire and Derbyshire one each. Well balanced and well drilled, Yorkshire set an example of how smoothly a team could run, and their England players took this quiet determination into Test matches. When chairman of selectors Pelham Warner praised Sutcliffe for his part in saving a Test at Headingley in 1926, Sutcliffe whispered back: 'Mr Warner, I love a dog-fight!' Recalling this comment, Warner wrote: 'And by heaven! These Yorkshiremen

---

* These figures count Walter Hammond purely as a professional, which he was throughout his England career until 1938 when he turned amateur in order to take on the captaincy. He scored five Test hundreds as an amateur in 1938-39.

do. I like them on my side. I do not care to go into action without them.' The most courageous England bowler of an era that required considerable bravery in the face of batsmen who knew the game was loaded in their favour was Verity, who sometimes could be criticised for pushing the ball through too quickly but held his nerve better than most at the prospect of bowling so much at Bradman, whom he dismissed a record eight times.

This shift was central to the evolution of the England team. The professionals were specialists in ways amateurs could not be: they had the time, inclination and motivation to strive for the highest standards. They could feed off each other too. Larwood and Voce were closely tutored in the science of fast bowling by Jimmy Iremonger, the Nottinghamshire coach, who never played Tests but toured Australia in 1911-12. Verity was mentored in slow bowling by Wilfred Rhodes. Sutcliffe helped make Len Hutton, whom he knew from Hutton's earliest days in and around Pudsey, into an opening batsman in his image. This kind of holistic guidance was superior to the advice given by retired professionals coaching future generations of amateurs at public schools. A gap with the old Corinthian approach opened up and, with Australia possessing likeminded players of their own, led by the indefatigable Bradman, and competition growing from the newer Test teams, it needed to. Maurice Leyland was another Yorkshire player of influence: as a left-hander, he was seen as a strategic counter to Australia's leg-spinners Clarrie Grimmett and Bill O'Reilly and was a near-automatic pick in Ashes Tests for this reason. He was also a fine fielder, especially in the deep. On the few occasions Leyland did not play, Eddie Paynter, a left-hander from Lancashire, stepped in and was every bit as effective. Between them they averaged 62 and scored eight hundreds against Australia.

The incentive to forge a successful career had never been greater. Economically, times were hard in post-war Britain, made severely worse in the northern industrial regions by the Great Depression starting in 1929 which saw unemployment rocket. The life of a professional cricketer was precarious, with some county clubs forced to cut wages and cap talent money, but provided he stayed in work it was good compared with the rest of the working class, especially as the cost of living, which had risen over the years of the First World War, fell by more than one-third between 1920 and 1938. Some came to cricket from mining communities and the colliery clubs; England players who followed this route included Larwood, Voce, Sam Staples and Walter Keeton, all of Notts, and Bill Copson and Tommy Mitchell of Derbyshire; Copson and Mitchell both got into cricket during the break in work forced by the General Strike of 1926.* A significant number supplemented their county income by winter coaching in South Africa, Australia and India, or playing professional football, which had the added advantage of maintaining fitness. Hendren played professional football until 1927; he was one of the England's fleetest outfielders and played 44 Tests after turning 35.† Hendren was 46 when he played his last Test, Hobbs and Woolley both 47. With livelihoods to make, few retired early.

Importantly, for those who played regularly for England it was now possible to be financially successful and enjoy incomes that, in the words of Fred Root, a stalwart at Worcestershire who appeared in three Tests, 'are far beyond the dreams of the average county cricketer'. England's long-awaited Ashes victory in 1926 generated huge interest at the turnstiles: it was estimated that 10,000 were unable to gain admittance on the first day of the Lord's Test and the deciding match at The Oval, extended to four days, drew the first aggregate attendance of more than 100,000 for a Test in England. The Lord's Test of 1930 set a new record of just under 115,000 and the second day of the Lord's Test in 1938 drew a ground record for one day of

---

* The mining communities continued to produce England fast bowlers after the Second World War, when Les Jackson (Test debut 1949) and Fred Trueman (1952) first appeared. 'He was puissant in back and long in arm, just like all the mining fast bowlers [that] Yorkshire, Derbyshire and Nottinghamshire have whistled up to the surface,' Frank Tyson wrote of Trueman. The influence of colliery clubs diminished with the decline of the mining industry. The last England cricketers who were products of colliery clubs were Bruce French (16 Tests, 1986–88) and his nephew Jake Ball (4 Tests, 2016–17) both of whom played for Wellbeck Colliery CC (now Wellbeck CC) near Mansfield.

† Thirty-three England Test cricketers have played English league football; of these, ten made their Test debuts in the 1877–1914 period, 12 in the inter-war period and only 11 since 1946. The last to join this list was Arnie Sidebottom, who played his only Test match in 1985 having played league football between 1972 and 1979.

33,800, with the ropes being brought in to allow many spectators to sit on the grass.

The bigger grounds in Australia drew a total attendance of 692,242 for the 1924–25 series (the first time any series had drawn more than half a million) before new records were set in 1928–29 (857,600) and then again in 1936–37 (948,498). Test match fees rose accordingly: by the early 1930s, professionals were paid £40 for a home Test against Australia, £27 for South Africa and £20 for West Indies, New Zealand or India. These differentials reflected Ashes Tests from this point being scheduled for a minimum of four days rather than three, as well as the contrasting status of the opposition. There was also a win bonus of up to £50 for those taking part in the 1926 series, depending on appearances. Tours of Australia were the big earners: for 1928–29 and 1932–33, MCC paid the professionals a basic fee of £400 with the possibility of bonuses of up to £350 depending on discipline and merit. In 1932–33, Hammond, Sutcliffe and Larwood all received £350 each in additional payments and the other professionals who played regularly in the Tests £300. A good tour could also result in a subscription fund, as happened for Sutcliffe and Tate after the 1924–25 tour, and Larwood and Voce after 1932–33 (which netted the pair £776). By the time cricket resumed after the 1939–45 war, fees for the first tour of Australia had risen to £550 (plus a possible win bonus, unclaimed, of £275) while each appearance in the home Ashes of 1948 was worth £75.*

Fuelled by fast-expanding media coverage and the desire of the masses for escape from the hardship of everyday life, the top England players (but especially the professionals) became popular champions to an extent not seen before. When Roy Kilner, primarily a Yorkshire hero but also an England all-rounder of note, died of enteric fever at the age of 37 his funeral drew more than 100,000 to the streets of Wombwell. Many were readily identifiable to the ordinary man in their quiet dedications to their craft and early hardships: Hobbs, Sutcliffe and Hendren, whose parents like Sutcliffe's died when he

---

* Some of these figures are taken from Ric Sissons's seminal *The Players: A Social History of the Professional Cricketer* (1988).

was young, all had difficult upbringings, as did Hammond, whose father, an army officer, was killed in the war.

But they also aspired to, and achieved, respectable middle-class status. Hobbs promoted products such as tailored suits, fountain pens and armchairs. Hammond drove a sponsored car, a Saloon Graham Paige, the first England player to do so. Hobbs's biographer Leo McKinstry estimated he earned £1,500 a year from all his income streams which included a sports shop set up with money invested from his first benefit; John Arlott argued that Hobbs earning more from his business than cricket marked a significant moment, 'a major step in the elevation of the professional cricketer – indeed the professional games player in Britain – above dependence'. Hendren's biographer Ian Peebles calculated he earned a similar figure from all sources, among them a cricket school in Acton.

Sutcliffe, like Hobbs, set up a sports outfitters and was as thorough and orderly about his business affairs as he was in compiling Test centuries; Bill Bowes described how, after getting out, Sutcliffe would return to the dressing-room, open his briefcase and attend to his papers. Like Hammond, he had a penchant for Savile Row suits. He lived in a former mill-owner's house in seven acres near Pudsey, drove a Rolls-Royce and addressed amateurs by their Christian names rather than as 'Sir' or 'Mr' as was the norm among professionals. Nor did his advocacy of professionals captaining England endear him to the amateur class; Gubby Allen, having lost the England captaincy to Wally Hammond in 1938, peppered Sutcliffe with short balls at that year's Scarborough festival, earning a rebuke from umpire George Hirst.

Speaking of their tours of Australia, Ames said: 'Where there is a pretty lady, you will find Herbert.' Ames himself saved enough from his first tour of Australia to buy a house; he too used benefit money to fund his own sports outfitting business. Ames and Hammond, who had by then adopted amateur status as a cricketer, along with Bill Edrich, all ended their service as Squadron Leaders in the Royal Air Force, the newest and socially most relaxed of the services; here was evidence that the divide between the social classes was gradually narrowing, but also of the upward mobility of these individuals.

Having resumed his playing career after the war, Edrich followed Hammond in turning amateur.

Ames was the first great wicketkeeper-batsman from any country. Previously keepers were not expected to score runs: the only England keeper to have made a century in a Test was Harry Wood in Cape Town in 1892 (in a match not recognised as a Test at the time), while the two longest-serving England keepers, Dick Lilley and Strudwick, averaged with the bat in Tests respectively 20.52 and 8.14. Duckworth, whom Ames replaced in Ashes Tests after an error-strewn performance behind the stumps at The Oval in 1930, averaged 20.50. According to Warner, it was said that by the time Ames made his championship debut for Kent at the age of 20 he was already in quality an England cricketer. He not only scored eight hundreds for England but made six of them batting in frontline positions, at No.5 and No.6, though more importantly he provided crucial ballast as a run-scoring No.7, a role which was not emulated until Jim Parks and Alan Knott in the 1960s.

Ames's all-round excellence set new standards and largely killed off the tinkering that had gone on with the wicketkeeping position since England's earliest days. Before the creation of a national selection panel, host clubs picking the team for Tests at their grounds tended to favour their own keepers (perhaps because in an era of more variable pitch conditions, local knowledge really counted for something): Wood's only home Test was on his local patch at The Oval, and Dick Pilling of Lancashire played his only three Tests in England at Old Trafford. Selecting an amateur keeper was also a means of ensuring another 'gentleman' on tour. After Ames's introduction, standards with regard to the wicketkeeping position became more stringent and selection more stable, and only in six further Tests did amateurs keep wicket.*

---

* Ames was the 30th keeper England had used in 171 Tests; they have since capped only 37 more, of whom four were as amateurs: Hopper Levett (one Test, 1933–34), Paul Gibb (three Tests, 1946 and 1946–47), Billy Griffith (two Tests, 1948–49) and Don Brennan (two Tests, 1951). The next wicketkeeper capped after Ames was 'Tich' Cornford, who in the winter of 1929–30 wore the gloves in New Zealand while Ames toured West Indies; at 5ft 2in, Cornford remains the shortest man to play for England.

The downside was that there were no comparable deputies and his absence after the second Test in 1938 with a broken finger arguably caused England defeat in a grippingly low-scoring match at Headingley which Bradman described as 'the greatest of modern times', and thereby the Ashes.

In fact, by this time Ames was finding it increasingly difficult to combine keeping wicket with batting duties and after returning home from the tour of South Africa in 1938-39 he followed medical advice and gave up the gloves in order to ease the strain on his back, even though it brought an end to his England career.

Ames was at the start of a tradition of Kent providing England with its best wicketkeepers, one with which he remained closely involved for 30 years after the Second World War when he continued to play for Kent as a batsman before joining the management of the club; he also managed several England tours in the late 1960s. Godfrey Evans, between 1946 and 1959, and Alan Knott, from 1967 to 1981, both of Kent, respectively kept wicket in 91 and 95 Tests, the most for England, and touched new heights with the meticulousness of their glove work, while Knott himself was an extremely resourceful if unorthodox batsman. Evans, whose movement was honed through a secondary career as a boxer in his youth, let through just one bye in his first three Test innings while India scored 331 and Australia 659 for eight declared and 365, and Knott did not concede any byes on his debut when Pakistan were dismissed for 140 and 114. Evans was reckoned to have not missed one catch during a series in Australia in 1950-51 but to have created several through his agility. With Paul Downton in the 1980s and Geraint Jones in the 2000s also playing 30 or more times, Kent keepers have been behind the stumps in more than 300 England Tests.

The top professionals could not only expect a better quality of life, they could also expect a longer life. Of the nine professionals in the XI that faced Australia at The Oval in 1926, Tate alone failed to make his eighth decade and they lived to an average age of 83. By contrast, of the seven professionals involved in the corresponding match 40 years earlier, only one, Dick Barlow, lived beyond 47. Two committed suicide and another, Billy Bates, attempted suicide when he feared that his playing career, and therefore his means of earning a living, was over. The average age of that team was just 45.*

The growing confidence of the professionals manifested itself in the willingness of some of their number – even if they were in a minority – to publicly question the credentials of those amateurs captaining England. The cricketing ability of England's Test leaders during this period was hardly inferior to that of earlier incumbents – indeed, in some instances it was much better – but where previously there had been deference, if occasionally grudgingly given, now came more open dissent. This reflected a changing society: Britain had its first Labour-led government under Ramsay Macdonald in 1924 and all women over the age of 21 were eligible to vote by 1928. There was, too, a common fear of Bolshevism making its way from Russia and anyone who spoke out in favour of change – or simply spoke his mind – was liable to be branded a political agitator. 'The whole crusade against the so-called dividing line between amateur and professional is Communistic, if not Bolshevistic in tendency,' EHD Sewell wrote in 1926, not entirely inaccurately.† The counter-argument was that by keeping the captaincy in amateur hands an ageing establishment class, led by Lord Hawke and Lord Harris who had once helped develop the national team, was now wilfully putting class before country, a case sections of the press were increasingly willing to articulate. Arthur Gilligan, who captained the tour of Australia in 1924-25, was a member of an anti-communist group, the British Fascists, as was the manager Frederick Toone.‡

---

* It is thought that eight cricketers who played Tests for England committed suicide: William Scotton (died 1893), Arthur Shrewsbury (1903), Albert Trott (1914), Andrew Stoddart (1915), Leonard Moon (1916, on war service), Albert Relf (1937), Harold Gimblett (1978) and David Bairstow (1998). Jack Ferris (1900) may also have done so. Bairstow was discovered at home by his family including his eight-year-old son Jonny, who would go on to play for England with distinction.

† Sewell's loyalties lay with the amateur class but he played briefly for Essex as a professional.

‡ The British Fascists was a minor precursor of the British Union of Fascists formed in 1932. Author Andrew Moore has speculated that Gilligan and Toone, who came to the notice of the Australian secret service, distributed literature that helped create British Fascist chapters in Sydney and Melbourne. The group was virtually defunct by 1926.

The England team had itself become a powerful force for change. When the desire to beat Australia was as strong as it was in 1926, the decision to put amateurs and professionals together in the same dressing-room was unsurprising. Even Jack Hobbs – who as someone inured to long-standing practice resisted the attempts of Percy Fender, one of the more enlightened county leaders, to do something similar at Surrey – gave his approval, saying, 'it gave us a better chance to discuss tactics.'* For the most important games, there was no longer room for unnecessary compromises, as Pelham Warner wrote: 'All concerned seemed determined that nothing should be left to chance, and that nothing should be left undone which might contribute to success.'

The previous winter, during an MCC tour of West Indies (on which no Test matches were played), Tiger Smith, the senior professional, recalled that 'once I'd sorted out with the amateurs that the pros should be treated equally we got on fine'. Of necessity, England teams abroad routinely travelled and changed together, and mostly shared the same accommodation. Les Ames said that England tours did much to break down social barriers, a view echoed by Patsy Hendren who wrote: 'When on tour, amateurs and professionals "mix" splendidly. They are all part of one team; all live together, all change together.' Hobbs was too self-deprecating to push himself forward at anyone's expense, but was aware that the public resented the distinction between amateur and professional 'still more than we do'. Hobbs even privately called Lord Harris an old bore.

A flashpoint came during the home series against South Africa in 1924 when Cec Parkin, the Lancashire bowler, used a column in the *Weekly Dispatch*, and in contravention of a ban on players commenting on England matches in which they were playing, to denounce Gilligan for giving him only 16 overs out of more than 150 bowled by the team in the first Test match at Edgbaston. 'I never felt so humiliated in the whole course of my cricket career ... I feel that I should not be fair to myself if I accepted an invitation to play in any

---

* Separate dressing-rooms continued to be used in county cricket for some time after this, in some cases well into the 1950s and close to the abolition of amateur status in 1962.

further Test match,' he wrote, under a headline: 'Cecil Parkin refuses to play for England again'.

Parkin was an unpredictable character and reaction to his outburst was mixed; Tiger Smith said that Parkin was in fact carrying an injury and out of order in saying what he had. Parkin subsequently apologised to the Board of Control, only to renew his attack on Gilligan in another column after the second Ashes Test in Australia the following winter, saying that Gilligan should never have been chosen for the tour (Gilligan had himself sustained an injury during the summer that seriously impaired his bowling) and that if there was not a suitable amateur Jack Hobbs should have led the side. Parkin was on safer ground here, as there were widely held reservations about Gilligan's on-field leadership in Australia: he was reckoned naive and, in Warner's estimation, too ready to concede on cricketing points to his opposite number Herby Collins. But Parkin's support for Hobbs was misplaced inasmuch as Hobbs, though he often led Players against Gentlemen, had little ambition to captain England.

It was Parkin's comments which prompted Lord Hawke to declare, 'Pray God, no professional shall ever captain England.' It was an ill-judged remark which, however, needed to be seen in the wider context of a man in his mid-sixties bemoaning the decline of amateur cricket. Hawke went on: 'I love and admire them all [professionals] but we have always had an amateur skipper and when the day comes when we shall have no more amateurs captaining England it will be a thousand pities.' There could be no excuses though: Hawke was insulting the very players the public so much admired and who were at that time doing battle in Australia – the likes of Hobbs, Sutcliffe, Woolley, Hendren and Tate among 12 professionals who appeared in the Tests compared to three amateurs. As a group, they wired to London that Hawke's remarks were 'disparaging to professionals'.

Condemnation from the younger generation was unanimous. Percy Fender in an interview in the *Daily Herald* described Hawke's words as a 'gratuitous insult to the main body of professional crick-eters' and said he would be happy to play under a professional if it were in the best interests of the side. This intervention spoiled what-ever hope remained of Fender captaining England; he had already crossed the establishment with some unhelpfully frank pieces of journalism, including one in which he suggested Lord Harris and MCC had wilfully breached its own regulations on pitch-covering at the Scarborough festival, and also by leading his amateurs and professionals through the same gate at Lord's (as Lionel Tennyson, the Hampshire captain, had done). Fender conceded he could be too outspoken for his own good and had probably cost himself a chance of the England captaincy; he was right.

As chance had it, in England's next series against Australia in 1926, Arthur Carr was taken ill during the fourth Test at Old Trafford, leaving Greville Stevens, playing only his second match for his country and at 25 the youngest man on the team by six years, as the only amateur. Feeling Stevens was too much of a risk, Pelham Warner, the chairman of selectors, took the unprecedented step for a home Test of inviting first Strudwick, as the senior professional in terms of age, and then Hobbs to lead the side. Strudwick declined but Hobbs accepted, though only after Warner rejected his attempt to defer to Stevens.

When it was announced at Old Trafford that Hobbs would lead the side onto the field it created a sensation among the crowd. However, though Hobbs was reckoned by Warner and others to have done a sound job, he was not kept on when Warner's selection panel (which included Arthur Gilligan as well as Hobbs and Wilfred Rhodes as co-opted members) decided to sack the erratic Carr for the decider at The Oval, Warner asking him to stand down 'for the sake of England'. (Carr had already volunteered to stand down as captain before the third Test at Leeds in the belief that he was not worth his place, and then erred first by inviting Australia to bat, and then by dropping a crucial catch.)

Instead they turned to another amateur, Percy Chapman, who had never captained in a first-class match before and was four months younger than Stevens, though he had played in the first three Tests of the series. This was a gamble and one all the greater for Hobbs providing a credible alternative if the selectors could set aside their anxiety at the precedent it would set; Chapman's appointment created plenty of debate, the *Daily Express* questioning why the side could not be led by Hobbs or Rhodes, who was recalled to the side after a five-year absence at the age of 48. Fortunately for Warner and Chapman, England won. Rhodes would later suggest that Chapman in the field 'did what me and Jack told him'. At least Chapman was shrewd enough to let them. Carr was subsequently bitter about his treatment and critical of Hobbs, whom he appeared to wrongly suspect of assisting in his removal for his own advantage.

Hobbs possessed the stature but not the personality to break the amateur hold on the leadership; his view, later expressed, was that professionals were naturally reluctant 'to boss their own fellows'. When Australia next toured in 1930, and the selectors again found themselves contemplating a change of leader going into the deciding match – this time with Chapman as the man under pressure – Hobbs once more emerged as a possible stand-in. His appointment would have been easier for opponents to countenance as it was known that the Oval Test would be Hobbs's last and his captaincy of England would therefore be a one-off event. It was strongly rumoured that he was offered but declined the position during a meeting of the selectors, chaired by Henry Leveson Gower, and also involving Frank Mann and Jack White as well as Hobbs himself and Rhodes as the co-opted professionals.

When he learned of what had happened, Sutcliffe was said to be deeply disappointed, saying, 'For the sake of the professional cricketer, he [Hobbs] should have accepted.' Sutcliffe's feelings were the sharper for his own experience at Yorkshire where the committee – chaired by Lord Hawke and striving for improvement after seeing Lancashire win back-to-back titles under an amateur captain who averaged 29.96 while Yorkshire's averaged 8.84 – had voted to invite him to captain the side for the 1928 season and allow him to remain a professional while doing so. However, the committee then asked him to withdraw when their intentions threatened to divide the club, it having become public that Hawke himself had voted against and Wilfred Rhodes as senior professional was unhappy that he had not been asked first. Sutcliffe acquiesced, though according to his biographer he regretted doing so.

Yorkshire continued to appoint amateur captains and did not win another championship until 1931, an experience that contributed to Maurice Leyland's famous remark: 'I never counted the captain in the Yorkshire side – but we won a few championships with the handicap of one.'

Selecting and captaining England sides was not for the faint-hearted. When Warner spoke at a West Country dinner in 1929 and praised Wally Hammond and Jack White but not left-arm spinner Charlie Parker, he found himself accosted in a hotel lift by Parker who was still incensed at being left out of the Headingley Test three years earlier, a widely criticised decision commonly laid at Warner's door. According to reports, Parker grabbed Warner by the neck, ripped his bow-tie and uttered some unparliamentary language, and needed restraining by Reg Sinfield, a Gloucestershire team-mate. Parker never added to his one Test cap.

Tommy Mitchell, the Derbyshire leg-spinner, similarly never played for England again after telling Bob Wyatt during England's defeat to South Africa at Lord's in 1935 that, 'You couldn't captain a box of bloody lead soldiers,' after Wyatt had stood at mid-on and told Mitchell how to bowl. Wyatt had fought hard with the selectors for Mitchell to play ahead of Walter Robins and may have been prompted to offer advice as he saw his decision unravel before his eyes. Wyatt had first led England after Hobbs's refusal at The Oval in 1930 and, with Hobbs's appointment having been anticipated in some sections of the press, his elevation was not popular. Wyatt thought deeply about the game but was too dogged to be a successful captain; he lost the England captaincy to Gubby Allen in 1936 and was effectively sacked as Warwickshire captain the following year amid questionable claims that he hindered the development of young players.

What was striking was not so much that the leadership of Carr, Chapman and Wyatt may have been wanting in some respect, but that Parkin, Parker and Mitchell were prepared to act as they did.

The amateur class was in little position to argue. While the best professionals had never had it better, few of the leading amateurs good enough to play regularly for England any longer had the means to support such a career. Some were obliged to juggle cricket with work in the City, as happened with Gubby Allen and Douglas Jardine, or virtually give up altogether, as was the case with Greville Stevens. Many simply had more important things to do in a world which had changed out of all recognition since pre-war days. A growing proportion of those who still wanted to play sought employment as their county club's secretary or assistant secretary, roles deemed (by curious convention) as not infringing an amateur's status: among those who took this route to England's advantage were Cyril Walters at Worcestershire, Maurice Turnbull at Glamorgan and Wyatt at Warwickshire, an arrangement that enabled Wyatt to be easily England's most capped amateur between the wars.* With amateurs less readily available, and the quality of many of those who were free to play unexceptional, counties increasingly used their most experienced professionals as occasional captains, and in 1935 Leicestershire became the first county to officially appoint a professional as captain when they gave the position to Ewart Astill, aged 47, who played Tests for England on tours of South Africa and West Indies.

Of more direct significance to England, Gloucestershire in 1932 appointed Wally Hammond vice-captain to Bev Lyon, whose business interests meant he was frequently away, and he led the county to five of their six wins. 'It was considered that a professional of such wide experience would prove a more capable leader than any of the young amateurs who might join the team from time to time ... Hammond often showed shrewdness and judgment [and] got more out of his colleagues that any untried amateur,' *Wisden* reported. Hammond's grammar-school background lent him a veneer of respectability in the eyes of the establishment, as was the case with Ames and Duckworth, and later Cyril Washbrook. Hammond, who actually began his county career as an amateur, returned to amateur status in 1938 in order to take on the England captaincy, while Ames

---

* Wyatt played 40 Tests, in which he scored two hundreds and averaged 31.70; the first of those hundreds against South Africa in 1929 was the first by an amateur for England since 1913. The next most appearances among amateurs between the wars was Chapman with 26 Tests.

and Washbrook were the first professionals to become full national selectors.

This was a successful era for England but the blurring of lines between amateurs and professionals was causing tension even before Douglas Jardine took the team to Australia in 1932-33.

# CHAPTER 15

# Jardine Creates the First System

## Bodyline, the rise of the media and England's climbdown

Douglas Jardine's Bodyline strategy was radical for reasons that went beyond deploying leg-theory at such pace to packed leg-side fields that the physical well-being of the batsmen became a concern. It broke new ground by being a 'system' that demanded an unprecedented unity of purpose from the England team: for the plan to be effective, the fast bowlers had to be highly accurate and stick closely to their captain's instructions, while those fielding close on the leg side – and there were usually up to five short legs with three others set deeper – needed courage and discipline. Most of Jardine's players bought into it, but not all. It was the professionals who stuck to the task most readily; for some amateurs used to being free to show off their individual skills – that was the point of them, in a way – the idea of toeing a win-at-all-costs line from a man so strong in his opinions as Jardine was irksome. To Jardine, everything had to be yoked to his scheme and what Arthur Mailey, the Australia spinner-turned-pundit, called his 'relentless Napoleonic attitude'.

Few if any of England's previous captains had shown such resoluteness of purpose but if Australia, and specifically Bradman, were to be stopped, it required someone as calculating and methodical as Jardine. Explaining Jardine's selection as England captain in 1931, an appointment made with the express aim of regaining the Ashes in Australia in 1932-33, Pelham Warner wrote: 'He was a keen student of the game and a close and intelligent observer ... he had a genius for taking pains.' Even on the Bodyline tour itself, after his relationship with the captain became strained, Warner conceded 'he [Jardine] is very efficient'.

Jardine only arrived at his strategy after deep research and thought. Importantly, he had played most of his cricket at Surrey under the tactically astute and imaginative Percy Fender, whose enthusiasm for analysis and planning he inherited before taking over from him as Surrey leader in 1932, and Fender was to help develop his plans. Having attended the Oval Test of 1930 in a journalistic capacity, Fender relayed to Jardine, who did not play in the Ashes that summer, an account of Bradman's discomfort against Larwood. Two years later he passed on correspondence recounting how Australia's right-handers, including Bradman, had responded to South Africa's pace bowling in a series in Australia by moving over to off stump to play the ball through the less populated leg side. It was also through Fender's auspices that in the late summer of 1932 Jardine met Harold Larwood and Bill Voce, along with their county captain Arthur Carr, in the grill-room of the Piccadilly hotel in London, and asked Larwood whether he could bowl on leg stump and make the ball come up into the body to force Bradman to play to leg, where fieldsmen would be positioned accordingly.

Like Fender, Jardine recognised that the English game was dominated by good, hard-headed professionals. He enjoyed Surrey's matches against the strong northern counties laden with professionals such as Yorkshire, Lancashire and Nottinghamshire and recognised that the professionals must form the core of a successful England side. In his seven Tests before being made England captain, Jardine played alongside only three amateurs – Percy Chapman, Jack White and Vallance Jupp – and he had little time for Chapman's freewheeling leadership of the 1928-29 tour, telling

Bob Wyatt that if there had been a revolver available he would willingly have shot Chapman.*

Jardine was party to the selection of five amateurs in his first four Tests as captain, all at home, but of these only Gubby Allen and Freddie Brown were taken on the Bodyline tour and Brown was not called on in the Tests. If Australia were to be beaten, the co-operation of the leading professionals, used to being patronised or ignored by amateur captains who often knew less about the game than them, was vital. Few England captains before Jardine had sat down to dinner with his professionals to discuss tactics, as he did with Larwood and Voce, or outlined his thinking to them in private meetings on the voyage to Australia, as he did with his fast bowlers and probably also senior batsmen Herbert Sutcliffe and Wally Hammond. How many previous England captains would have gone to the Australian dressing-room, as Jardine did in Adelaide, to protest at Larwood, his star fast bowler, having apparently been called a 'bastard', or after the series was over given him an ashtray engraved with the words, 'To Harold for the Ashes – 1932-33 – From a grateful Skipper'? (To 'Harold', note, not 'Larwood'.) How many captains before him were considerate enough to send his professionals' wives and girlfriends gifts, as he did?

The professionals' loyalty was forthcoming all the more readily because Jardine willingly put himself in the front line; he sold his wicket as dearly as any of them, was nerveless in the face of hostile fast bowling, and a fearless fielder. The Yorkshire players particularly admired his grit. Sutcliffe called him 'a stern master but every inch a man' and said that on the Bodyline tour 'he planned for us, he cared for us, he fought for us'. Hedley Verity named his second son after him. Bill Bowes described him as 'my friend and greatest of captains', even though he fell out with Jardine during the 1932-33 tour about the fields he should bowl to, before being won over by his captain's firmness and logic. Maurice Tate's relationship with Jardine was

---

* Vallance Jupp, who played eight Tests between 1921 and 1928, was convicted of manslaughter and jailed for nine months after being at the wheel of a car that struck and killed a young factory worker on a motorbike in 1934.

fragile (though in truth Tate was surplus to requirements in Australia and lucky to make the tour), and Hammond and Duckworth were both to later express reservations about Bodyline, but no professional ever disparaged his leadership in the way Cec Parkin did with Arthur Gilligan, or Tommy Mitchell with Wyatt.

Eddie Paynter, a pocket-sized and late-developing left-hander who had once worked in a brickyard, was central to the first-innings recoveries in Adelaide and Brisbane, where in one of the most celebrated acts of heroism by an England batsman, he discharged himself from hospital after going down with tonsillitis to bat for four hours for 83 over the course of two days, returning to his sickbed between times. Suffering from aching muscles and muzzy vision, and wearing a scarf around his neck and panama hat to keep the sun off his head, he broke off at times to take more medication and had to be highly selective in his shot-making. Jardine visited Paynter in hospital on the rest day of the game 'and put the thought into his batsman's head that even if he had to "bat on crutches" he would do so'.* Jardine appeared to feel that it was encumbent on Paynter to try, stating in his autobiography that Paynter must have known about his condition before the match and 'should certainly have reported to me that he was not fit'.

Jardine's relations with his amateurs were a different matter. The Nawab of Pataudi initially refused to field in the leg trap and, although he appeared to follow orders in the second Test, he was dropped from the side thereafter, despite having scored a century in his first innings of the series. Gubby Allen consented to field on the leg side but was seemingly reluctant throughout the series to bowl leg-theory, although Bowes said he was not accurate enough to do so and Wyatt suggested that he was not seriously asked to bowl it, as Jardine saw benefit in Allen bowling in orthodox fashion outside off stump to batsmen grateful for respite from Larwood and eager for the chance to take liberties; Allen finished with 21 wickets in the five Tests.

There was a revealing exchange when Jardine went to Allen

---

* Paynter came to England's rescue in another fashion during the Lord's Test of 1938 when, despite scant experience of the role, he kept wicket throughout Australia's second innings after Les Ames broke a finger. He conceded only five byes and held a catch.

before the second Test and said that Larwood and Voce thought it absurd that Allen was not bowling bouncers and they believed he was refusing to do so purely in order to preserve his popularity (Allen was born in Sydney, had extensive family and friends there, and spent as much time in the city as he could manage during the tour: more than 40 days in all). Nothing highlighted how much things had changed: professionals criticising an amateur to their captain, essentially accusing him of putting himself before the team's interests, and a captain implicitly endorsing that criticism by passing it on. It was more than Allen could take and his response, recounted in his own words in a letter home, said it all: 'Well! I burst and said a good deal about swollen-headed, gutless, uneducated miners.' It has been claimed that Wyatt, Jardine's vice-captain and the only other amateur to play in the Tests, was also against the tactics, but if so it had no material impact.*

When reports surfaced after the third Test in Adelaide of divisions within the England camp – reports that Larwood blamed on a disgruntled Pataudi, who was by now out of the team – Jardine asked his players to confirm whether they were happy to continue; after a meeting chaired by Sutcliffe, they issued a statement denying 'definitively and absolutely' that there was dissension or disloyalty in the team, and assured everyone that they were 'utterly loyal to their captain'.

Jardine was therefore navigating some tricky social waters. That he bore a solitary air does not mean he looked down his nose on the professionals as mere servants, as some did, even if that was a common assumption. On the contrary: the evidence points to him

---

* Allen would subsequently be cast – and would cast himself – as a principled voice of dissent within Jardine's ranks, but research by Brian Rendell, who gained access to Allen's uncensored letters home to his parents in England, shows Allen to be an unreliable and inconsistent witness. Allen's private expressions of hostility towards Jardine were influenced by Jardine's cricketing demands which interfered with Allen's social arrangements in Sydney; Allen was also – as Larwood and Voce alleged – concerned that if he too adopted the controversial leg-theory it would be awkward for his family in Australia. By the later stages of the tour, Allen appeared to conclude that leg-theory endangered the spirit of the game but in a letter written on 2 March 1933, after the team had left Australia, he nonetheless echoed the sentiments of Jardine and Larwood when he described Bradman as 'a terrible little coward of fast bowling', a view that was only published after Bradman's death.

being anything but a traditionalist intent on propping up the old order, and this may have offended the game's ruling class as much as his questionable tactics; he was never greatly appreciated in the corridors of power and was one of the few captains to lead an MCC-organised Test tour overseas to never sit on the club's committee.

Leg-theory in itself was nothing new. It had been used for years by Englishmen and Australians as a means of containing batsmen from scoring freely when other options were exhausted, and it was to an extent an inevitable consequence of an lbw law that demanded that balls pitch in line with the stumps if they were to win leg-before verdicts. Bowlers who naturally made the ball break back, or swing in, to right-handers felt they had little alternative but to bowl on the stumps with protection on the leg side; if they bowled outside off stump batsmen were under no compunction to play at their deliveries and could not be lbw if the ball came back into them. Larwood and the left-armer Voce both knew this from personal experience and had used leg-theory in Test matches before.

With the new ball's effectiveness in Australia short-lived, Jardine was looking for means of keeping run-scoring in check after that phase had ended. His solution was to deploy 'leg-theory at pace' rigorously for specified periods when Australia's right-handers – including Bill Woodfull and Bill Ponsford but particularly Bradman – were facing; he knew he possessed bowlers of sufficient pace that if they could bowl accurately on leg stump to packed leg-side fields on hard, dry pitches, Australia would find it very difficult to score, especially if they continued to move over towards off stump. It was an ambitious plan and, after their initial meeting with Jardine at the Piccadilly hotel, it was only after weeks of experimentation that Larwood and Voce felt comfortable with it. Larwood's explanation of why England won the incendiary Test in Adelaide was simplistic but nonetheless revealing: 'It was won because Australia's batsmen cannot play fast bowling that pitches on the wicket and off it on the leg side, instead of, futilely, wide on the off side.'

Though Stan McCabe played a brilliant counter-attacking innings in the first Test, and Bradman by moving over towards leg to put the ball away through the unprotected off side managed to average

56.57, Australia's methods were mainly inadequate. Bradman himself – through what many, including some team-mates, regarded as unnecessarily theatrical dancing around the crease – largely escaped the body blows he had sustained at The Oval in 1930, but Jack Fingleton, McCabe, Woodfull and Ponsford, whose method was to turn his back and let the ball strike him, were often hit.

Such was the dominance of England's pace attack that they would probably have won without the use of Bodyline, but it was a tactic whose time had come: a logical consequence of leg-theory in an era in which sports teams in general were striving to operate as efficiently as machines. Warwick Armstrong had built his Australian side around Gregory and McDonald and by the mid-1920s Herbert Chapman was transforming the role of football manager by getting his Huddersfield Town squad to stand around a magnetic board studying tactics. The league titles he won with them were then replicated in 1931 and 1933 at Arsenal, where he got all 11 players functioning like a finely calibrated engine. In cricket as in football, players who in earlier times had aspired to play with style and individuality were now expected to work together in the most efficient manner possible.

Jardine was certainly not alone in his unsentimental approach. The series in which he made his Test debut in 1928 saw the England and West Indies attacks make uncompromising use of fast short-pitched bowling, as they did again in the Caribbean in 1929-30, when Learie Constantine was only eventually persuaded by the English camp to desist from bowling short at the body of the 39-year-old Andrew Sandham. In England in 1933, the West Indies attack – with the controversy still fresh in everyone's minds – adopted Bodyline to spicily good effect, well enough to bruise the chin of Wally Hammond, with whom Constantine had long duelled, but not well enough to prevent Jardine from battling his way to a century at Old Trafford.

Jardine may have conceived Bodyline as a means of dealing with Bradman, but he led ruthlessly whoever the opposition. In 1932, he got Voce and Bowes, against their inclinations, to bowl a full toss an over against India, playing their inaugural Test, because it was proving difficult to sight the ball at Lord's, and in India in 1933-34 he used Stan Nichols and the left-arm Nobby Clark to bowl with such hostility, sometimes to Bodyline fields, that three batsmen – Dilawar Hussain, Naoomal Jeoomal and Vijay Merchant – left the field with ugly head injuries. Mohamed Nissar retaliated with some Bodyline bowling of his own. CLR James, a close friend of Constantine, argued that Bodyline was but a manifestation of wider society. 'Bodyline was not an incident, it was not an accident, it was not a temporary aberration. It was the violence and ferocity of our age expressing itself in cricket . . . The totalitarian dictatorships cultivated brutality of set purpose.'

The English cricketing establishment, taken aback by the strength of Australian protests and torn about whether to condone or condemn a strategy most had not seen with their own eyes, eventually chose the course of appeasement and disowned the tactic. It was already planning to bypass Jardine when he let it be known while in India that he did not wish to play in the next Ashes series. He was in any case 33 years old, a late age for an amateur batsman to do well in Test cricket.* More questionably, neither Larwood nor Voce, aged respectively 29 and 24 at the start of the 1934 season, was chosen for any of the Ashes Tests that year, and in the first Test match of the series, which Australia won handsomely, England took the field with just one fast bowler, Ken Farnes, whose ten wickets on debut showed that he could have done with more support. Farnes, who stood 6ft 5in, was capable of rare pace from a short run-up when the mood took him but after a quiet match in the following Test at Lord's, the selectors dropped him for the rest of the series.

Larwood, in fact, would have been chosen that summer had he agreed to put his name to a letter – delivered by Sir Julien Cahn, Nottinghamshire's patron, in advance of the series – apologising for his bowling in Australia and agreeing to bowl legitimately in future, but Larwood's honesty and stubbornness made it impossible for him to acquiesce. 'I've nothing to apologise for, sir,' he replied. Larwood also knew, deep down, that his bowling had lost 'bite'.

---

* Only three England amateur batsmen had to that point scored Test hundreds when older than Jardine would have been at the start of the 1934 Ashes: WG Grace, Charles Fry and Archie MacLaren.

With Australia's visit out of the way, the following summer Larwood and Voce were approached privately by what MCC termed in a later statement as responsible officials, 'as to their attitude towards taking part in representative cricket', but both said they wished only to play for Nottinghamshire, hardly surprising given the conditions attached. Larwood steadfastly stuck to this position and never played for England again but Voce gave ground and was restored to the England side in 1936 after non-negotiable solicitations from Gubby Allen, the captain, ahead of the next Australia tour. Voce was aware that he would be expected to bowl differently from the way he had before. Having defended Larwood and Voce and the tactics he helped evolve, and which he continued to deploy on occasions during the 1934 season, Arthur Carr was forced out of the Nottinghamshire captaincy by the end of the year. It was a betrayal articulated best by Fender: 'For the first time in my cricket career England had appointed a determined and resolute captain; a man cast in the toughest Australian mould, à la Armstrong if you like, with the character and vision to plan for victory and the will-power and players to see it through. And what happened? It all went wrong and was followed by the climbdown when the counties thought the 1934 Australian visit was in jeopardy. It was as big a tragedy in sport as I ever knew.'

Though Bodyline was outlawed, the new ruthlessness of international cricket was not, and when Bradman found himself in the late 1940s equipped in Ray Lindwall and Keith Miller with a pair of fast bowlers to match the hostility of Larwood and Voce, he spared his opponents nothing. England themselves took a long time to recover from the fall-out as the restoration of good relations with Australia took priority. It was not until the appointment in 1952 of Len Hutton as the first professional captain of modern times that they again displayed the sort of ruthlessly co-ordinated will to win shown under Jardine.*

---

* At the time of Jardine's death in June 1958, England were led by another ruthless captain of Surrey and England in Peter May, and Jardine's methods no longer seemed so repugnant. The MCC and New Zealand flags flew at half-mast during the Lord's Test.

## England's Captains 1877-1947

There was little stability to the England captaincy until after the Second World War. In 252 Test matches up to 1 May 1947, 40 captains were used, giving them an average tenure of just 6.3 matches. Since then, 40 captains have led England in 758 Tests, an average of 19.0 matches each. Only eight men led England in ten or more Tests before May 1947.

| Captain | Period | P | W | L | D | Win % |
|---|---|---|---|---|---|---|
| WG Grace | 1888-99 | 13 | 8 | 3 | 2 | 61.5 |
| DR Jardine | 1931-34 | 15 | 9 | 1 | 5 | 60.0 |
| APF Chapman | 1926-31 | 17 | 9 | 2 | 6 | 52.9 |
| JWHT Douglas | 1911-24 | 18 | 8 | 8 | 2 | 44.4 |
| PF Warner | 1903-06 | 10 | 4 | 6 | 0 | 40.0 |
| WR Hammond | 1938-47 | 20 | 4 | 3 | 13 | 20.0 |
| RES Wyatt | 1930-35 | 16 | 3 | 5 | 8 | 18.8 |
| AC MacLaren | 1897-1909 | 22 | 4 | 11 | 7 | 18.2 |

What was also distinct about the Bodyline series was the prominent role played by newsreel, radio and newspapers. It was not that the media – Australian or English – was malicious in the way events were covered; rather, it was better able than before to inform and thereby crystallise public opinion in Australia against the English team and their tactics, while the authorities were still coming to terms with the ways in which the media could interact with key participants. Newspapers were instrumental in revealing the opposition to Bodyline of Bill Woodfull, the Australia captain, and Pelham Warner, the MCC assistant manager. The former came via a leak from the Australian camp, the latter through an article written by Warner several months before the tour which came back to bite him and his team, all the more when he shrank from openly confirming whether this was still his position. Both greatly increased the pressure on Jardine and his players and, through his evasions, Warner unwittingly did as much as anyone to raise doubts over the morality of their methods.

The Tests were attended by large numbers of people who saw for themselves what happened, but those Australians who were not present had increasingly sophisticated means of drawing their own conclusions. For the first time, an England series was covered ball-by-ball on radio and the commentary captivated the Australian nation; radio licence-holders were estimated at 370,000. In addition, three newsreel companies filmed what proved to be the most contentious match in Adelaide. The footage of Woodfull and Bert Oldfield being hurt by Larwood's bowling on the Saturday of that game (Bodyline fields were not set at the time, though to the ire of spectators Jardine adopted one directly after Woodfull was hit) created an unprecedented shock when it was shown in cinemas around the country. Film, though subsequently lost, had been shot of England Test matches as early as 1902 but the quality was now much superior, as was the extent of distribution. The image – captured with a telephoto lens by Herbert Fishwick, an English émigré working for the *Sydney Mail* – of Oldfield being struck had a similar impact on newspaper readers. Only since the First World War, when the telephoto lens was developed as a means of reconnaissance, had intimate action shots of Test matches in progress been possible.

For all that, it was the leak from the Australian camp that turned the public, and ultimately the Australian board, decisively against Jardine's strategy. Although the Australian board was not keen on participating players engaging in media work, it allowed them to speak to radio broadcasters at the end of a day's play (though none took the opportunity to complain about Bodyline) and to write about cricket, with permission, if journalism was their full-time profession, as it was for Jack Fingleton who played in the first three Tests. Don Bradman had a contract with the *Sydney Sun* and wanted this rule relaxed; he had already incurred a fine when *Don Bradman's Book* was serialised in England in 1930 in breach of his tour contract.

On the Monday morning following the incendiary Saturday play in Adelaide, reports appeared in several Australian newspapers of an exchange between Woodfull and Warner, who had visited the

Australian dressing-room after stumps to enquire after Woodfull's well-being. Woodfull's remark, 'I don't want to see you, Mr Warner. There are two teams out there. One is trying to play cricket and the other is not,' revealing that the Australia captain, though he had declined to publicly say anything critical, privately disapproved of Bodyline, was potentially explosive, as anyone among those who heard it would have recognised. The source of the leak was never conclusively established: Fingleton was originally widely suspected, and probably paid a price as a result, being dropped for the two remaining Tests and omitted from the tour of England in 1934, but it was later claimed, including by Fingleton himself, that Bradman was responsible; Bradman's links with the *Sydney Sun* pointed directly to the journalist thought to have shared the information, Claude Corbett. Either way, once Woodfull's true feelings were known, they had a decisive impact on Australian public opinion.

The mood was already febrile. Australians had for years routinely barracked visiting English teams in a manner they were not subjected to elsewhere; Jardine's own dislike of Australians dated from his experiences in 1928-29. Their hostility was now heightened by broader feelings of hurt and isolation arising from the economic depression; belt-tightening measures designed to prevent Australia being any more beholden than it was already to Britain and others for financial loans were having a severe effect while migration to the country had virtually stopped. Woodfull himself observed in a letter to the Australian board his concern that in Australia and England, 'large sections of both countries are embittered'. But this did not mean the tour was not valued; indeed, the Australian Cricket Board had cabled MCC as early as June 1931 stating that the tour was essential. The events of the Saturday in Adelaide would not have felt quite so combustive had there not been in attendance a crowd of 50,962, well beyond what was considered to be the usual capacity and a figure not bettered at the ground until January 2015.

Little wonder then that, four days after this and two days after the publication of Woodfull's comments to Warner, and with the Adelaide Test heading for an England victory, the Australian board voted, though only by a margin of 8-5, to send a cable of protest to

MCC at England's tactics. As only four of the 13 delegates attended the third Test it is fair to assume the views of many were shaped to some extent by the media coverage. That Bill Jeanes, the board secretary, read out the contents of the cable to the press the same day further suggested that placating the Australian public was a prime consideration.

As the board only sent its cable at the normal rate, rather than express, journalists addressed by Jeanes were able to alert colleagues in London before the cable arrived, which resulted in Viscount Lewisham, the MCC president, being raised from his bed at 2.30am for a response to something he had not yet read (he may have been the first English cricket administrator to whom this had happened, but he would not be the last). If that was hardly likely to endear the Australian board to him, nor were the contents of the cable, which was not well-judged. Its central demand – that Bodyline bowling be 'stopped at once' – was impractical as MCC's committee men had not seen Bodyline in action, while the description of the England team's methods as 'unsportsmanlike' was bound to raise hackles. Even though there was a three-week gap before the next Test, realistically nothing could be done during the series short of cancelling the last two matches. ICC protocol, flimsy creation though it was, suggested Australia should request a meeting to air its grievances.

It took a series of cables, as well other channels of diplomacy, including at government level, to resolve the situation in time for the fourth Test to take place as planned. MCC, relying on an inner circle that included Lewisham, his two immediate predecessors as president and two former England captains in Lord Hawke and Stanley Jackson, and drawing on messages from Jardine and Warner to the club secretary William Findlay, responded with predictable robustness to the 'unsportsmanlike' charge, but otherwise returned the ball firmly to Australia's court by saying that if the Australian board 'wish to propose a new law or rule it shall receive our careful consideration in due course', and if it considered it desirable to cancel the remaining Tests 'we would consent with great reluctance'. Inevitably the Australian board rowed back, iterating that the remainder of the series was not in doubt, that the sportsmanship of the English team was not in question, and that it hoped such bowling could be eradicated from future series. All of this might have been said in a more judicious first cable.

This episode threw a spotlight on the quality of information flowing back to the English administrators and public. David Frith's forensic study of the series, *Bodyline Autopsy*, published in 2002, highlighted that they were not as badly informed as was long believed: BBC radio provided short daily round-ups, employing after the first Test the eyewitness testimony of Alan Kippax, who was dropped from the Australia team after that game – a direct response to a two-hour synthetic radio commentary based on cables provided by Le Poste Parisien from 6am each morning which used the service of Alan Fairfax, who had played for Australia in the 1930 series.

Newsreel reports first shown in Australia reached British cinemas within three weeks. However, one of the reasons they were not better informed was that none of the England players was allowed to do as Fingleton did and write for a newspaper, or several of the Australians did and speak to radio broadcasters after play, as had happened also after the conclusion of the final Test in England in 1930. During the 1932-33 Tests, Australian players 'would be hustled into cars at close of play and hastened to the studio to record their impressions of the day's play'. Jardine, focused on the task in hand, instructed his players not to communicate with the media, while MCC had since 1921 barred active players from putting their names to newspaper columns. This contributed to only a meagre corps of reporters being sent from England to accompany the team.*

The MCC ban was the result of past problems, especially in Australia. Journalism had been a means by which former players, and some active ones, mainly amateurs, could supplement their income. It was frowned upon in some quarters as undignified work

---

* They consisted of Gilbert Mant for Reuters, Bruce Harris for the *Evening Standard* and Jack Hobbs, who had retired from Test cricket in 1930, ghosted by Jack Ingham for the *Star*. In the aftermath of the Ashes being won in Brisbane, Harris persuaded Jardine to give a telephone interview to the *Evening Standard* in London. Hobbs, who was still playing for Surrey under Jardine's captaincy at the time, expressed only uncontroversial views on this most controversial of tours.

for gentlemen but proved of vital financial assistance to the likes of Fry, Ranjitsinhji, Jessop, MacLaren and Warner during tours and Test series. In 1902, Fry wrote for the *Daily Express* lengthy reports of matches in which he was playing, which may have contributed to his failure in three Tests before he was dropped. Players writing under their own names had to measure their words carefully and inevitably there were occasions when offence was caused, which was why the Australians had introduced a ban on their players writing on tour around the turn of the century on pain of a £100 fine.

For England players, the tipping point came on the 1920-21 tour when vice-captain Rockley Wilson and Percy Fender, filing reports home for respectively the *Daily Express* and the *Daily News*, were reckoned to have crossed a line. Wilson was critical of the umpiring during the first Test and Wilson and Fender both criticised the crowd for barracking Jack Hobbs during the fifth Test when he was carrying an injury; this merely led to Wilson and Fender being barracked themselves later in the game, prompting Wilson to take issue with the crowd. Two days after the team's boat reached home, the Board of Control for Test Matches announced that it had advised the selection committee, 'that when inviting anyone to play for England, it shall be on the condition that the player does not contribute a report or a statement of any kind to the press, until the end of the season, as regards any Test Match for which he is selected and in which he plays'.

It was this rule that Parkin flouted when he criticised Arthur Gilligan during the first Test of 1924 and this rule that Jardine used as a vehicle for making himself unavailable for the 1934 Ashes series; he informed MCC that he had been engaged to write on the Test matches in the press. It also became relevant once the 1934 Tests were underway when Larwood gave vent to his feelings of frustration in the *Sunday Dispatch* following the secret overtures he received from MCC to apologise for his part in Bodyline. The headlines on the article stated: 'I refuse to play in any more Tests – Politicians trying to hound me out of Test Cricket – They feared I would burst the Empire'. By doing so he merely gave the establishment another stick with which to beat him: had he not written what he did, it was said, he might have been chosen, even though by then he had already been ignored for the first Test.

'No greater disservice was ever done to English cricket than when Larwood was induced to dash into print and become responsible for statements which put him beyond the pale of being selected for England,' Sydney Southerton wrote in the 1935 edition of *Wisden*. 'I think I am right in saying that he would have been chosen for the Test match at Lord's – to mention only one – but for the article under his name which appeared shortly before that game. No selection committee worthy of the name could possibly have considered him after that.' But Southerton was either ignorant of, or chose to overlook, MCC's insistence that Larwood apologise first. Bill Voce, who did not commit his feelings on Bodyline so fulsomely to print, was able to return to Test cricket.

In 1938, even before the series began, the selectors apparently lost interest in picking Bob Wyatt after learning that he was contracted to cover the Tests for the *Daily Mail*, Wyatt having concluded that his days as an England player were numbered when he was over- looked for the home Tests the previous summer. Once asked about his availability for the first Test, Wyatt suggested that he might be able to extricate himself from his newspaper deal, but to no avail. 'It was then decided that as I was under contract to the *Daily Mail* I should not be invited to play in the first Test,' he wrote. In his place, Eddie Paynter scored 216 not out, and Wyatt never played for England again.

The rule did not silence players altogether as they were free to comment on a series in which they were not involved. Parkin was thus able to be critical of Gilligan again in print several months later because he was not a member of the team touring Australia in 1924– 25; similarly, Percy Fender wrote in support of Parkin because he was another non-tourist.

MCC tour contracts routinely contained clauses relating to the public pronouncement of players. The ones drawn up for the sched- uled tour of South Africa in 1968-69 (the last Test tour before the TCCB took control of England affairs, though it was eventually cancelled and replaced by a trip to Ceylon and Pakistan) stated that players should not make public pronouncements – including contributions to any book, magazine, periodical or newspaper, or radio or television broadcast – without prior consent of the manager or MCC secretary. The contract remained valid until March 1971, two years after the tour was scheduled to finish.

The Board of Control badly erred in not extending the ban more thoroughly to those involved in administering the England team. In 1928 it had ruled that no member of the selection panel could report on any Test or Trial match, a consequence of Warner, who had turned to full-time journalism after retiring as a player in 1920, attempting to justify his decisions as chairman of selectors during the 1926 Ashes. He did this in the *Morning Post*, of which he was cricket correspondent, and *The Cricketer* magazine, which he edited, as well as in a BBC radio broadcast during the Lord's Test in which he praised the efforts of the team.

With the connivance of the *Morning Post* Warner eventually got round the ban by writing on everything but Tests and Trial matches and this was tacitly endorsed when he was appointed chairman of selection in 1931 for two years, *Wisden* reporting: 'It was intimated that Mr Warner could make arrangements to conform with the rule of the Board of Control which debars anyone on the Test match selection committee from contributing a report or statement to the press.'* Then in early 1932 he accepted an invitation from Lord Hawke to manage the forthcoming tour of Australia which he would help select. The potential for trouble was fully realised when Warner covered a match between Surrey and Yorkshire at The Oval in August 1932 and was required to pass judgement on Bill Bowes adopting a Bodyline field to Jack Hobbs.† His criticism of Yorkshire's tactics ('they will find themselves a very unpopular side if there is a repetition of Saturday's play . . .') were gleefully thrown back at him after the first Test in Australia, WM Rutledge in *The Referee* calling Warner a 'double personality' in finding what was 'abhorrent to him

---

\* This rule, or convention, retained sufficient force that when Ted Dexter took charge of England selection in 1989 he gave up his job with the *Sunday Mirror*.
† Warner watched the episode among angry Surrey members in the pavilion rather than from the press box, which some believed coloured his judgement.

in English county cricket, the very essence of true sportsmanship in Australia'. Suitably chastened, Warner left the *Morning Post* before even returning to England.

Jardine, who captained Surrey in that match, had little time for Warner on the tour, Wyatt describing their relationship as 'profoundly unhappy' after they had a disagreement during the outward voyage. Jardine dismissed Warner as unimportant in terms of the conduct of the series and had no time for his moral hand-wringing.

What was remarkable was that, from the time the Bodyline row erupted until the end of the tour, the England players withstood so well the immense pressure they came under. Even though he appeared to privately concede during the Adelaide Test that a stop would be put to Bodyline after the series, Jardine publicly gave every impression of being unfazed by the criticism, and his steadfastness only raised him further in the estimation of most of his players.* He stuck by the players and they stuck by him, reacting as most teams under siege would by drawing closer together. Jardine's subsequent book on the tour laid much of the blame on the reaction of the crowds and the press, as did his players. Larwood said: 'If certain critics had not made such an effeminate outcry [after Adelaide] the whole bother would be too childishly ludicrous to merit further consideration by grown-up men.' Jack Fingleton eventually concurred. Speaking in 1977, he said: 'Looking back, the Australians perhaps made too much fuss about it.'

England won the Bodyline war but, as Jardine anticipated, lost the peace. The consequences of what happened in Australia had a wide-ranging and long-lasting impact on the England team.

In 1935 the Laws were changed, provisionally at first but later formally, with a view to eradicating 'direct attack' bowling, as MCC called it. Umpires were charged with halting as unfair what they deemed to be 'persistent and systematic' short-pitched fast

---

* On the rest day following the explosive Saturday in Adelaide, Jardine told his host at a party: 'I've got an instrument in my hand whereby I can win a series against the little man [Bradman] ... But don't worry. It'll be stopped.' (Quoted in *Bodyline Autopsy*, p.193).

bowling. The lbw law was also broadened to include balls which pitched outside off stump, a move which greatly assisted exponents of inswingers and off-cutters; had this change been made, as it should have been, when scoring-levels rose afresh in the 1920s and leg-theory first became prevalent, Bodyline probably would have never happened. Intimidatory bowling was not killed off forever – hence the amendments to the Laws, in 1960 and 1991 respectively, empowering umpires to order a bowler out of the attack if he persisted with short-pitched fast bowling and limiting the number of above-shoulder bouncers per batsman per over to one, the latter amendment following on from the failure of an informal pact in the 1970s to spare 'non-recognised batsmen' the worst bouncer barrages – but in the short term the 1935 amendments had a profound effect on England in particular.*

The Australian board's protests helped force action upon MCC, who initially favoured self-regulation, only for Nottinghamshire to break ranks. The board followed up its original demand that Bodyline should be stopped at once by seeking assurances before sending a team to England in 1934 that this type of bowling would not be practised during the Tests that summer, then complaining through official channels when it appeared English bowlers were 'departing from the agreement'. Their concerns included short-pitched bowling by Bill Bowes and Nobby Clark during the Tests and Bill Voce giving vent to his indignation at being overlooked by England by bowling aggressively for Nottinghamshire against the Australians, which scotched any chance of Voce being recalled for a must-win fifth Test. During the second Test at Lord's, Bob Wyatt went across to Bowes to inform him that he had just received a message from the pavilion asking for Bowes to not bowl short.

'And what do you say as captain?' Bowes asked.

'Well, if they want it friendly, perhaps they'd better have it that way.'

---

* The limit on the number of fieldsmen behind square on the leg side to two is often thought to be a direct consequence of Bodyline but it was actually introduced by ICC almost 40 years later in the hope that it would, in the words of *Wisden*, 'materially discourage negative leg-side bowling and the excessive use of bouncers, and would make for brighter and more attractive cricket'.

All this marked a watershed. 'Australia, by practically claiming the right to make laws, automatically ranked herself as equal first [with England] in cricketing nations,' according to the *Barbados Advocate*.

It was no coincidence that Australia strove to flex its muscles at a time when the international cricket community had expanded to the detriment of Australia's special cricketing relationship with England. Between the Ashes series of 1926 and 1932-33, England played 40 Test matches and only ten of these were against Australia, hence perhaps the gloomy view of the Australian board chairman Dr Allen Robertson in October 1932 that 'cricket is doomed in Australia'.

Under instruction, England's bowlers continued to pull their punches beyond Australia's visit in 1934, which may explain why defeat in that series was followed by others in West Indies in 1934-35, at home to South Africa in 1935 and in Australia in 1936-37, before a 1-1 draw was secured against Australia in 1938, though only thanks to a consolatory win at The Oval when the Ashes were already lost. This also had an impact on English batsmen who were denied exposure to short-pitched bowling in county cricket. 'For many years after Larwood went out of the game it could be said that no young fast bowler was permitted to bounce the ball at all, without earning a reprimand,' Walter Hammond wrote. 'The result was that most English batsmen ceased to be able to play the fast bouncer at all.'

England took every precaution that their return to Australia went smoothly, sending an MCC side there under Errol Holmes in 1935-36 for some goodwill matches before selecting as captain of the Ashes series itself the following winter Gubby Allen, a favoured son of the establishment and the one fast bowler on Jardine's tour to refuse to bowl Bodyline (although, as has already been outlined, his motives were essentially self-serving).* Even with Voce back in the fold, Allen's attack pitched the ball up and away from the body – and lost the series despite going 2-0 up, the only time this has happened to any side in a five-match series.

---

* Allen's favoured status possibly extended to being the illegitimate offspring of Pelham Warner. David Frith has argued some persuasive circumstantial evidence which included Bob Wyatt, when the possibility was put to him, saying: 'We all knew that.' Frith regrets not clarifying whether Wyatt was referring to the rumour or to the fact.

When there appeared a possibility of the truce breaking down as a result of Australia selecting for the deciding Test Laurie Nash, a fast bowler who made the ball rise awkwardly, Dr Robertson, chairman of the Australian board, took the unusual step of calling together the umpires and captains and expressing the hope that nothing untoward would happen, reminding the umpires they had the powers to ban intimidatory bowling. The match passed off peacefully – and Australia won.

Though many questioned in the aftermath of Bodyline whether Test matches were worth the trouble, and the MCC vote to invite Australia in 1934 was only passed 8–5, English cricket's desire for reconciliation was cloying. It was driven by the awareness that without Test matches the game in England would financially collapse. In 1937 the Findlay Commission, charged with inquiring into the state of county cricket, revealed that the counties were annually in debt by a combined £27,000 despite receiving on average over a four-year cycle £16,500 a year from the visits of overseas teams, of which £11,600 came from tours by Australia. 'The effect on the counties generally of any serious decline in the popularity of Test match cricket is so apparent as to need no further comment,' it reported. The 1934 Tests against Australia produced gates worth more than £88,000, and the 1936–37 tour made a record profit.

The Bodyline series also fuelled the media's enthusiasm for Test matches at a time when technological advances enabled radio and television to become more widely available. Although active players remained barred from passing written comment, the services of former England players were in greater demand than ever, particularly from mass-market newspapers among whom competition was fiercer than ever. Jardine, recruited by the *Evening Standard*, was among those sitting in the press box for the 1934 Ashes. That series also saw the first live radio commentary of Tests in England. This had been a feature of Tests in Australia since the 1924–25 series when a Sydney station 2BL provided 'commentary and scores' of the two Sydney Tests. Whereas Australian listeners could enjoy all-day coverage of their home Tests, in England broadcasters confined themselves to short passages of commentary, and close-of-play summaries largely for fear that cricket's tempo was too slow to make entertaining listening.*

Thanks, however, to the excellence of Howard Marshall – the man who broke fresh ground by commentating on the Lord's Test of 1934 (Verity's match) from a space in the Tavern rented from MCC for 20 guineas – and John Arlott after the war, the BBC's coverage became highly popular; when Australia chased 404 to win at Headingley in 1948, seven million people tuned in at various times of the day. In that series, commentary was restricted to two hours 50 minutes per day and this had only expanded to three hours 15 minutes by 1956. Full ball-by-ball coverage only arrived with the advent of *Test Match Special* in 1957. Peter Baxter, the longest-serving producer of *TMS*, believed that Jim Laker's 19 wickets at Old Trafford the previous year was the catalyst for the move, although there had been general complaints from Robert Hudson, a senior executive, about key periods of play being missed.

The restrictions did not apply to listeners of BBC radio services overseas though: those in Australia received full ball-by-ball coverage from the BBC of the Ashes series in England in 1948, 1953 and 1956, and other Test series were similarly available in the territories England were hosting. Arlott, with his poetical turn of phrase and Hampshire accent, first made his name reporting on the 1946 India tour of England which was put out on the BBC's Eastern Service to Southeast Asia and he acquired many devotees there, as he did in the West Indies, even though he never worked in those regions. All India Radio spread the gospel across India when England played Tests there in 1951-52. This coverage helped foster interest around the world and inspire players from Brisbane to Barbados, and Calcutta to Cape Town, to strive to come to places such as Lord's and attempt to beat the Mother Country and the seat of Empire at their own game. 'A Test match today is an imperial event,' Pelham

---

* What was described as the world's first broadcast by the England cricket team was made from the studios of the New South Wales Broadcasting Company in Sydney on Sunday, 11 November 1928, three weeks before the first Test of the series. It involved an early start for the players as the hour-long broadcast began at 5.15am Sydney time, which was 7.15pm the previous day in London, though they were then served breakfast.

Warner wrote in the 1940s. 'Almost every ball is broadcast to the uttermost ends of the earth.' In Bray, south of Dublin, Jimmy Joyce, father to two sons and two daughters who would play international cricket for Ireland including Ed Joyce, who also represented England, was first hooked on the game by listening to BBC radio commentary of the 1950 Tests with West Indies.

Although in England in the early days there was less eagerness than in Australia to interview the players themselves, an exception was made when Len Hutton broke the Test-record score in 1938. EW Swanton, who was at the time making his way with the BBC and attended the game, recalled, 'the ashen-faced young Yorkshireman, his trousers grey with the Kennington dust, wearily climbing the ladder to the broadcasting perch at the top of the Ladies' Stand after he was out, to be interviewed by Howard Marshall'.

Radio companies soon realised the value of former international players giving their considered opinions. One of the first former England players to make a name for himself as a summariser was Arthur Gilligan, who worked on 'Hutton's match' of 1938 and after the war, apart from assisting the BBC, was also part of cricket coverage produced by the Australian Broadcasting Commission (later the Australian Broadcasting Corporation). Other former England captains to work after the war as summarisers were CB Fry, Norman Yardley and Freddie Brown, while two other former England players Trevor Bailey and Fred Trueman became lasting fixtures on *TMS*. The first radio broadcasts from England's overseas Tests were delivered by Swanton for the BBC in South Africa in 1938-39; he provided 15- or 30-minute spells of commentary and summary at the end of a day's play and on his second day captured a hat-trick by Tom Goddard.* After the war, Rex Alston was the first BBC correspondent to regularly cover England's overseas Test tours – although, in further evidence of the low regard in which these series were held, India and Pakistan 'were never seriously considered'.

---

* Goddard's hat-trick is one of only four taken by England spinners in Tests and was the last before Moeen Ali claimed one against South Africa at The Oval in 2017. The others were taken by Billy Bates in 1883 and Johnny Briggs in 1892, both against Australia. Ten have been taken by fast or fast-medium bowlers, two by Stuart Broad.

The first Test broadcast by television was the Lord's match of 1938 when pictures were provided by three cameras, and Teddy Wakelam, already an experienced radio reporter, acted as commentator. Although viewers were confined to the London area and only 5,000 people owned TV sets, the public response was again positive and the Oval Test in that series was also shown. Yardley, England's captain, recalled the Australia players during the Lord's Tests of 1948 watching the match (or the tennis at Wimbledon) on a TV set in their dressing-room, 'one eye on the set and the other watching play out of the window', and Lindsay Hassett claiming he was cross-eyed as a result when Yardley dismissed him for nought.

Once technical developments allowed, Test matches outside London were also televised, from Nottingham in 1950, and Leeds and Manchester in 1952, when for the first time every match in a series in England was shown. As with radio, the hours of coverage were restricted: up to a maximum of two and a half hours on some weekdays, and four and a half hours on others, and to two hours on Saturdays. Anything more was deemed a risk not worth taking: the BBC paid only small sums for the privilege and the Board of Control was fearful of the impact on attendances at the Tests themselves and county matches; in 1953 for example, the BBC paid only 75 guineas to cover five Ashes Tests whereas gate receipts brought in £200,000. Only following an increase in the BBC's fee in 1959 were the hours expanded. In 1960, near-immediate action replays were being used for the first time. By the mid-1960s, virtually the entire day was being shown, and indeed Test-match attendances against all but the strongest opposition did tail off during this time. Percy Fender, who had done some radio work in the 1930s, was used by BBC television in 1946 and by the mid- to late-1950s former Test cricketers were being used as summarisers on a regular basis. Denis Compton, Ted Dexter and Jim Laker all enjoyed lengthy careers in this field.

An early pattern was established that radio and TV were more reverential in tone than newspapers, whose sales had long depended on the vigorous airing of opinions. Wyatt complained in a letter how he was treated during the 1934 Tests: 'given a rough ride by the cheap press without a real knowledge of the game and always looking for a sensation'. But radio did not escape criticism. Pelham Warner, in a letter to England captain Len Hutton after the first Test of the 1953 Ashes, signed off with the words, 'Don't, I beseech you, listen to [EW] Swanton on the wireless ...' According to the Australian Jack Fingleton, who covered the same series as a writer, there were accusations of 'one-sidedness' in the BBC's coverage. A meeting was held mid-series to discuss the issue. When Australia next toured England in 1956, Fingleton himself was employed as part of BBC television's team covering the Tests.

# CHAPTER 16

# The Welsh and Irish Connections

## From Maurice Turnbull to Simon Jones, Timothy O'Brien to Eoin Morgan

Among those who took the field for England at Lord's in their first Test match after returning home from the Bodyline tour were Maurice Turnbull and Cyril Walters. Turnbull had played Tests in New Zealand and South Africa but never before at home; Walters was appearing for the first time and was widely praised for the stylish manner of his half-century against the West Indies pace attack.* Both were born and bred in Wales: Walters had joined Worcestershire in 1929 but Turnbull, though educated at Downside and Cambridge, remained close to his roots as captain and secretary at Glamorgan and was the first player to appear for England while at the club. A few months before this, Turnbull twice represented Wales at scrum-half in the Home Nations rugby championship, debuting in a famous 7–3 victory over England at Twickenham.†

Turnbull marked the start of an anomalous but productive

---

* In conjunction with Maurice Allom, the Surrey fast bowler, Turnbull wrote two of the more entertaining tour books recounting the visits to New Zealand and South Africa, *The Book of Two Maurices* and *The Two Maurices Again*.
† Turnbull remains the only sportsman to have played Test cricket for England and rugby for Wales.

relationship between Welsh cricket and the England team. Glamorgan have provided England with only 16 Test players (fewer than any other first-class county bar late-arrivals Durham), and those 16 players have won only 118 caps (less than half the tally of Hampshire, the lowest on the list of English counties, except Durham), but the club's impact extends beyond the scoring of runs and taking of wickets.* Of the five men who captained Glamorgan between 1930 and 1972, Turnbull, Johnny Clay, Wilf Wooller and Ossie Wheatley (who was actually born in Durham and played first for Warwickshire) all acted as Test selectors. Wheatley was also an influential chairman of the TCCB's cricket committee who vetoed Mike Gatting's reappointment as England captain in 1989, while Tony Lewis was the first Glamorgan player to captain England, on a tour of India and Pakistan in 1972-73.

Swansea staged one of England's earliest one-day internationals against New Zealand in 1973, though the ground would never reappear on the schedule apart from during the 1983 World Cup, and Cardiff hosted its first England one-day international in 2006, its first Test match in 2009 and first international Twenty20 in 2010.†

England also benefited from an array of off-field figures drawn from Glamorgan's championship winning season of 1997. Opening batsman Hugh Morris was subsequently appointed technical director at the ECB, was instrumental in the creation of a national academy, and later became the first managing director of the England team. Chairman David Morgan became deputy chairman of the ECB and subsequently chaired the board for six years, while Morgan's own deputy Gerard Elias QC oversaw all aspects of ECB discipline until 2016. Duncan Fletcher, the southern African coach, was in 1999 appointed England's head coach, partly at the instigation of

---

* A 17th player, Alan Jones, took the field for England in what he understood was a Test match at the time against the Rest of the World at Lord's in 1970; the series was subsequently denied Test status by ICC and Jones never played another match for England. When Andrew Strauss held a dinner in 2017 for former England players, Jones was included. 'It was the right thing to do to make sure he feels part of that England cricket family,' Strauss said.

† Cardiff had previously staged five one-day internationals involving sides other than England between 1999 and 2005.

Morris and Morgan, while Matthew Maynard, the captain, who was born in Lancashire but grew up on Anglesey, worked as Fletcher's assistant with England. Four of the 1997 side appeared in Tests for England but the most innovative of all Glamorgan's England players first appeared in the championship the following year. Simon Jones, whose father Jeff played 15 Tests as a fast bowler in the 1960s, fought a long-running battle with injuries but in 2004 and 2005, when he won most of his 18 caps, demonstrated a mastery of reverse-swing bowling into and away from the batsman that no other England bowler has matched.* However, after Jones there followed a lengthy drought in terms of Glamorgan producing England players.

As with the Scots and Irish, the Welsh viewed themselves as junior partners in their cricketing relationship with England; with several of their counties (Carmarthenshire, Glamorgan and Monmouthshire in the industrial south and Denbighshire in the north) having competed in the Minor Counties championship before the 1914-18 war, they aspired to be ranked equally with English county sides rather than the England team itself, and geographically a Welsh side was better placed to fulfil a county championship programme than one from Scotland or Ireland (although eventually Scotland and Ireland for a time took part in English domestic one-day competitions). Pre-First World War captains Tom Whittington and Norman Riches, as well as Harry Mallett, chairman of the Minor Counties Cricket Association, used their connections at MCC to secure a deal whereby Glamorgan could join an already crowded championship provided nine counties agreed to play fixtures against them; this they did in 1921.

With finances parlous and their playing strength over-reliant on second-rate amateurs, Glamorgan might have been forced to retreat but for the dynamic leadership of Turnbull and Clay, who – having played for the county since first-class status was achieved – also acted as treasurer from 1933 to 1938. To raise funds and improve playing

---

* Jeff Jones averaged only 4.75 with the bat in Tests but by surviving the final over of the final Test from Lance Gibbs in Georgetown in 1968 he secured England a famous series win against West Indies.

standards Turnbull, one of eight brothers from a Penarth ship-owning family, broadened the team's appeal beyond Glamorgan's borders, deliberately fostering a Welsh identity as well as bringing to the team the passion and organisation of the rugby field (as did Wooller, who was capped 18 times by Wales). For many, Glamorgan came to represent Wales, never more so than when taking on touring teams in what became quasi-internationals; they beat the West Indians in 1923 and 1939, the Indians in 1936 and 1959, the New Zealanders twice in 1937, the South Africans in 1951, the Pakistanis in 1962, and the Australians in 1964 and 1968. Crowds in excess of 25,000 and even 30,000 were drawn to Swansea for the visits of the Australians. 'We were not only playing for Glamorgan, but playing for a nation as well,' said Lewis.* When Robert Croft, Glamorgan's most capped England Test cricketer, became head coach of the county in 2016, he described Glamorgan as 'the national team of Wales'.

Nor were some afraid to turn down England. Turnbull declined the opportunity to tour India with Jardine's side in 1933-34 in order to concentrate on putting Glamorgan's affairs in order, while for business reasons Wooller passed over the vice-captaincy of a Test tour of South Africa in 1948-49 and the captaincy to India in 1951-52.† Clay effectively declared himself too old to play for England and when he was recalled anyway for the first Test of 1938 he withdrew citing an injury. When Allan Watkins made his Test debut at The Oval in 1948, the season in which Glamorgan won their first championship, he recalled: 'Nobody spoke to me. There was no joy in the side at all.' Not that everyone got the opportunity. Don Shepherd took more than 2,000 first-class wickets but never played

---

* It was only during Fletcher's reign as England coach and Morgan's as ECB chairman that an England v Wales fixture was finally instituted: a one-day warm-up ahead of England's summer one-day internationals was held annually in Cardiff in 2002-04; however, the Wales team was virtually indistinguishable from the Glamorgan side and in 2004 'Wales' fielded a player, Alex Wharf, born in Bradford, who appeared for England later in the summer.

† However, Turnbull might well have captained England after the 1939-45 war had he not been killed in action during the Normandy landings in August 1944, aged 38. Clay said he was the best of his generation who never captained England.

a Test for England; 'They [the selectors] might appear in Wales once in a couple of seasons and if you didn't play well then you had had your chance,' he reflected. Peter Hain, MP for Neath, introduced an Early Day Motion in 1993, 'noting the obstinate refusal of the selectors to choose any Welsh players'.

Ireland and Scotland were until modern times less intimately involved in England's story even though their best players knew there was a route available to them into the England team. Cricket was broadly popular with the Irish in the late 19th century, as the Irish origins of some of Australia's early Test cricketers indicates, but only the well-connected found their way into the upper echelons of the English game. The few Irish-born cricketers who played Tests for England in the pre-1914 era had links to the British garrisons, civil service, or gentry, including two who captained England as stand-ins on overseas tours: the fiery Sir Timothy O'Brien, whose grandfather earned a baronetcy for organising Queen Victoria's visit to Dublin in 1849, and Frederick Fane, born in the Curragh camp.* Like some later Irishmen, O'Brien was an unorthodox batsman whose repertoire of shots included the reverse sweep.

Gradually the sport fell victim to poor administration and an emerging nationalist movement that viewed cricket as tainted by its British associations. The influential Gaelic Athletic Association barred from 1902 to 1970 anyone who played or even watched 'foreign' sports from taking part in traditional Irish games, admittedly to limited effect, and the war of independence and establishment of the Irish Free State in 1922 further loosened ties. The Irish Cricket Union, belatedly formed in 1923, kept cricketers on both sides of the new border united, but only in parts of the north and middle-class pockets in the south such as Cork and Dublin did the sport stay robust.

It was not until Ed Joyce in 2006 that a cricketer who learned the game in Ireland again represented England, in his case in one-day

---

* O'Brien is the only man to captain England and Ireland in first-class cricket, leading an Irish tour of England in 1902.

internationals rather than Tests.* Joyce in fact blazed an important trail. Raised in Bray, south of Dublin, among a large cricketing family, he first represented Ireland at the age of 18 but within two years, following a recommendation from Mike Hendrick, a former England fast bowler who was Ireland's coach, he was playing for Middlesex. By 2005 Joyce had qualified for England by residence and rather than continue to play for Ireland, whom he helped to reach the 2007 World Cup, he opted to pursue a career with England and ended up playing five matches for them at that tournament (including one against Ireland).

Among those who followed Joyce to Middlesex were Eoin Morgan, who grew up on a north County Dublin housing estate, and Boyd Rankin, who came from farming stock in the north and was also helped by Hendrick. When they too chose to play for England the response in Ireland was unfriendly, especially in the case of Morgan, who defected during a World Cup qualifying campaign in South Africa in 2009. The England careers of Joyce and Rankin quickly stalled and they resumed playing for Ireland, but Morgan thrived as a white-ball player for his adopted country and was eventually appointed captain of England's ODI and Twenty20 teams. As Irish cricket blossomed thanks to increasing numbers learning their craft with English counties, Morgan blanked all questions relating to his former home, even though he could be seen reading the *Irish Independent* in the dressing-room, while also declining to sing the national anthem when it was played before England matches. 'Nationality is a difficult subject for him,' wrote Irish sportswriter Peter O'Reilly.

Scotland was enthusiastic enough to have its own county championship (founded in 1902) but the best cricketers headed for England if they could. AG Steel was born in Liverpool to a Scots family and grew up in Lockerbie before attending Marlborough and Cambridge, but he maintained links beyond the border. The week after taking part in England's first home Test match, at The Oval in 1880, he travelled to Raeburn Place, Edinburgh to face the Australians again,

---

* Martin McCague, who played three Tests for England in 1993 and 1994-95, was born in Co Antrim but was raised in Australia before relocating to Kent.

this time for a Scotland team. Gregor MacGregor, the first Scottish-born cricketer to play for England and still the youngest to keep wicket for them in a Test, learned his cricket south of the border, at Uppingham, Cambridge and Middlesex, but nevertheless played rugby for Scotland. Ian Peebles was educated at Glasgow Academy before refining his bowling at Aubrey Faulkner's cricket school in London, and with Middlesex and Oxford.

The first England cricketer to have been born in Scotland and played seriously there was Mike Denness, whose father had played with Peebles; it was while appearing for Ayr and Scotland that Denness was spotted by county sides and recruited by Kent in 1962. He played 28 Tests, 19 as captain, and for what he probably knew at the time was his last press conference in charge chose to wear tartan trousers. His successor as England captain, Tony Greig, was born in South Africa to a Scottish father. Douglas Jardine, who had Scottish ancestry and spent his early school holidays with relatives there, always viewed himself as a Scot, a facet of his personality that perhaps helped explain his well-chronicled detachment. When he died in 1958, his ashes were scattered in Perthshire.

Calum MacLeod, who was born in Glasgow and educated at the city's Gaelic School, played for Warwickshire as well as Scotland, which led to him fielding as a substitute for England in a Test against Australia at Edgbaston in 2009.

The inextricable link between Welsh and English cricket was driven home when one-day cricket broadened the scope for more countries to play official internationals. While Ireland and Scotland were able to play as distinct entities in ODI cricket on a regular basis from 1999 and 2006 respectively, with Ireland also granted Test-match status with ECB support in 2017, Wales enjoyed no such independence, to the frustrations of nationalists who called on them to go it alone under the Welsh flag.* Logistically and financially this

---

* The ECB may have supported Ireland's application for Test status, but it drew resentment from Ireland and Scotland for backing a reduction in the size of the World Cup from 14 teams to ten for the 2019 tournament, which England were scheduled to stage. Neither Ireland nor Scotland made it through qualifying. Scotland exacted swift revenge, beating England for the first time in an ODI at Edinburgh in June 2018.

was all but impossible. Constitutionally, Welsh cricket was a constituent part of English domestic cricket, hence a Wales Minor Counties team playing in the county one-day knockout competition between 1993 and 2005. Indeed, the relationship with England was cemented by the Test and County Cricket Board being renamed the England and Wales Cricket Board in 1997.

# CHAPTER 17

# On the Mat

## The challenge of touring outside Australia

One of the biggest challenges facing England teams when they toured places other than Australia was dealing with matting wickets. These were standard features of Test matches in South Africa until the 1930s and England continued to play Tests on the mat rather than turf on visits to the Queen's Park Oval at Port of Spain, Trinidad (though not grounds in other West Indian territories) until 1954. In certain parts of India and the newly formed Pakistan – chiefly those in arid hinterland away from the affluence and infrastructure of the big conurbations – the mat remained a feature at international level until 1959 and in domestic cricket well beyond that. However, while England played up-country matches on matting, they never actually took part in a Test on the subcontinent on matting.

The main advantage of matting wickets was that they were cheap to maintain and lessened the demand for water, a scarce commodity in many regions. Experience too demonstrated that local cricketers were better versed in how to play on the mat and even when turf pitches became more practical there was a reluctance to give up something that worked well for the host side. At a time when they were vastly superior on turf, England lost as many Tests as they won on matting – 11 apiece – in South Africa between 1906 and 1931, and lost three and drew one of their six series there in that time.

But well before the end of this period South Africa reluctantly accepted that their cricketers would have little success on turf pitches in England, and elsewhere, until they learned to develop the necessary skills in their own environment, and from 1926 they began staging domestic matches on turf. By the time England toured in 1930–31, Durban and Cape Town had made the switch to turf, Johannesburg following a few years later (South Africa won the 1930–31 series thanks to a solitary win on matting). It was no coincidence that South Africa won their first Test and series in England soon after, in 1935.* The same argument eventually persuaded other countries to abandon the mat and gradually they too came to terms with turf pitches. A West Indies win on the mat in Trinidad, inspired by the all-round brilliance of Learie Constantine, who was brought up on matting wickets, contributed to a 2–1 series win over England in 1934–35.

The ICC meeting in London in August 1929 urged other countries to follow South Africa's efforts to establish turf pitches, 'where the climatic and other conditions permit', reflecting England's desire not to have the problems they encountered in South Africa replicated elsewhere. During the time matting pitches were in use in Test cricket, England only made two Test tours of India – in 1933–34 and 1951–52, on both of which they were allocated the bigger centres – and never played Tests in Pakistan, although the 'unofficial Test' they lost to Pakistan in 1951–52 which expedited Pakistan's elevation to Test status took place on a coir-matting pitch in Karachi. Other teams were not so lucky: Australia and New Zealand both played Tests on matting in Pakistan, and West Indies in both Pakistan and India.

England probably reckoned they had had their fill of the mat. In all, they played 39 Tests on matting wickets – almost one in four of all the Tests they played overseas between 1877 and 1954.

A succession of England touring sides therefore had to come to

---

* Although England's defeat at Lord's in July 1935 was their first on turf to South Africa, they had by then lost two Tests on turf to West Indies, who beat them in Georgetown, British Guiana (now Guyana) in 1930 and in Kingston, Jamaica in March 1935. These were England's only Test defeats on turf to sides other than Australia before the Second World War.

terms with alien conditions in South Africa. The players who visited
under Walter Read in 1891-92 found their canvas boots ill-suited to
matting and only solved the problem by laying their hands on what
opening batsman William Chatterton described as, 'a good heavy
pair of lawn-tennis boots with India-rubber soles'. Wally Hammond
encountered similar difficulties in 1927-28 when he found his studs
getting caught in the fibres of the mat. Ernie Hayes, who toured
in 1905-06, described how even some of the outfields were bare
of grass – 'a monotonous study of brick red' – and after a few overs
the ball took on the colour of the outfield: 'Players unused to these
conditions find it difficult, especially if a dusty wind is blowing, to
follow its flight.'

Ian Peebles was a member of the last two England touring teams
to play on matting pitches in South Africa when the Old Wanderers
ground in Johannesburg was 'red gravel and looked like a huge hard
tennis court'. In an attempt to get in some advanced preparation,
Henry Leveson Gower's 1909-10 side took with them a mat which
was nailed to the deck of the *RMS Saxon* for the 17-day voyage to
Cape Town; they still lost the Test series 3-2. It may have been significant that when the next side won 4-0 in 1913-14 it contained six
players with previous experience of playing Tests in South Africa.
Johnny Douglas, the captain, afterwards described the matting
pitches as 'very good, all of them. I wonder we don't use matting
wickets here.'

Matting tended to favour bowlers who could spin or cut the ball
rather than those of pace, who would see many of their deliveries
bounce clear of the stumps. Leveson Gower's side even resorted to
opening the bowling with Jack Hobbs's little-used medium-paced
swing in three of the five Tests. Peebles noted that, 'the ball roughs
up very much more quickly so that the seam bowler, in modern times
a very potent performer, has only a fleeting period before becoming
a stop gap until the arrival of the next new ball . . . the main force of
the attack is confined to the spinner or cutter of brisk pace.'

The grip on the ball provided by the mat was a key element in
South Africa's development of leg-break and googly bowling which
won them victories in 1905-06 and 1909-10. Pelham Warner, who

captained England in the first of those series, wrote: '[Reggie] Schwarz, [Aubrey] Faulkner and [Bert] Vogler were suited exactly by the matting wickets on which it is so difficult to jump out to drive, and on which the ball not only turns twice as much and twice as quickly as on grass, but occasionally gets up a little.' Sydney Barnes proved even more difficult to negotiate with his medium-paced cutters and, by claiming 49 wickets in four Tests for England in 1913-14, set a record for any country in any series. 'He was practically unplayable on matting,' Hobbs said. 'His command of length and flight was superb and he made the ball turn so much that three or four times in one over he would beat the bat and miss the stumps . . .' George Geary's leg-cutters won England the first Test at Johannesburg in 1927-28 and had he not broken down injured in the next match they might have taken the series rather than drawn it.

Some bowlers tutored on matting pitches found it hard to adapt their skills to turf. Jimmy Blackenberg and Buster Nupen, two of South Africa's most successful bowlers up to the Second World War, took 110 Test wickets between them, only seven of which came on grass. The 1930-31 series, which involved the first and fourth Test being played on the mat in Johannesburg and the second, third and fifth on turf in Cape Town and Durban, proved particularly testing. After Nupen failed to bowl as well in the second Test as he had in the first with his mix of fast off-breaks and leg-cutters, South Africa dropped him from the two remaining matches on grass. Peebles similarly enjoyed more success with his leg-breaks in the two Tests on the mat and was left out of the third Test in Durban. Another factor in the case of matches played in Johannesburg was the altitude of 1,750 metres which made the work of fast bowlers especially hard.

For the batsmen, the challenge of matting wickets could be a stern one but could ultimately prove beneficial to their all-round game. Lord Hawke said that CB Fry's experience of playing on the mat in South Africa in 1895-96 helped turn him into the prolific batsman he became shortly after.

The way a mat behaved also depended on what it was laid on. Turf, soil and sand were other options but Peebles said gravel provided the truest surfaces and said that 'for sustained interest I have never seen better than the play at Johannesburg in the last days of matting wickets'. The early mats were made of coir, from coconut hair, but jute began to be used in West Indies and then India as the bounce was thought to be closer to that produced by turf. In fact, jute matting provided such easy-paced surfaces for batting that many games ended in draws – not something contests on coir were known for – and expedited a full transition to turf. The last Test England played on matting, in Trinidad in 1954, resulted in a tedious draw after West Indies scored 681 for eight declared and England replied with 537. 'Those who knew the nature of the Trinidad jute-matting pitch prophesied a certain draw and at no time in the match did any other result look possible ... The complete subjugation of bowlers took away much competitive interest and the cricket was enjoyed only by those who delight in utter dominance by batsmen,' *Wisden* reported. A few months later, the first turf pitch was laid on the red soil of the Queen's Park Oval.

Matting also lacked the breadth of variation in bounce and turn offered by a turf pitch deteriorating over several days, although the tension of a mat would affect the way it played: the tauter it was, the more bounce it generated; the slacker it was, the better the ball gripped and spun. Nummy Deane, the South Africa captain, put England into bat three times during the 1927-28 series at a time when such a ploy was unusual, which suggested he believed the mat would behave differently as the game went on and there was something to be gained from bowling first; South Africa claimed a first-innings lead on all three occasions and won twice. Richie Benaud, who led Australia in Pakistan in 1959-60 in the last series to involve Tests on matting, suspected that the groundstaff deliberately pegged the mat tautly when the home side was due to bat and loosened it off when the visitors were to do so; to counter this, he sent his twelfth man to the ground a couple of hours early to stand sentry. Generally, a matting pitch was good for batting as the bounce stayed truer than on turf, enabling batsmen to play confidently and aggressively, but long innings were rare: in Tests, Jack Hobbs converted only one of nine scores of fifty into a hundred and Wally Hammond none in five.

Ayub Khan, Pakistan's president, who was also president of the

Pakistan Cricket Board, heeded Benaud's urgings that Pakistan should extend turf pitches beyond Lahore to improve their cricket. In fact, this merely ended a pattern of Pakistan winning more often than they lost on matting and losing more often than they won on turf, and replaced it with a series of stalemates on new turf pitches lacking all life. England won the first Test they played in Pakistan, at Lahore in October 1961, but it was not until 1984 that they experienced another positive result, 12 meetings later. It took Pakistan until 1987 to win a series in England and that result owed more to their leading players benefiting from spells in county cricket than the advent of turf pitches at home.

Probably the last fixture played on matting by a properly representative England team took place in Suva, Fiji during a stopover en route to New Zealand in January 1984. What was virtually an England second XI played two matches on matting against the Netherlands in Amstelveen in 1989.

## England's Test Record on Matting Pitches

| Venue | Period | P | W | L | D |
|---|---|---|---|---|---|
| St George's Park, Port Elizabeth | 1889-1914 | 3 | 3 | 0 | 0 |
| Newlands, Cape Town | 1889-1927 | 10 | 8 | 2 | 0 |
| Old Wanderers, Johannesburg | 1896-1931 | 15 | 6 | 7 | 2 |
| Lord's, Durban | 1910-14 | 3 | 1 | 1 | 1 |
| Kingsmead, Durban | 1923-28 | 4 | 1 | 1 | 2 |
| Queen's Park, Port of Spain, Trinidad | 1930-54 | 4 | 1 | 1 | 2 |
| Total | | 39 | 20 | 12 | 7 |

## Highest Scores for England on Matting

| | |
|---|---|
| 205 not out | Patsy Hendren v West Indies, Trinidad, 1930 |
| 187 | Jack Hobbs v South Africa, Cape Town, 1910 |
| 181 | Phil Mead v South Africa, Durban, 1923 |
| 152 | Wilfred Rhodes v South Africa, Johannesburg, 1913 |

## Best Bowling for England on Matting

| | |
|---|---|
| 17-159 | Sydney Barnes v South Africa, Johannesburg, 1913 |
| *15-28 | Johnny Briggs v South Africa, Cape Town, 1889 |
| *15-45 | George Lohmann v South Africa, Port Elizabeth, 1896 |
| 14-144 | Sydney Barnes v South Africa, Durban 1913 |
| *13-91 | Jack Ferris v South Africa, Cape Town, 1892 |
| *12-71 | George Lohmann v South Africa, Johannesburg, 1896 |
| 12-130 | George Geary v South Africa, Johannesburg, 1927 |
| 11-118 | Colin Blythe v South Africa, Cape Town, 1906 |
| 11-149 | Bill Voce v West Indies, Trinidad, 1930 |

---

* England's first eight Tests in South Africa between 1888–89 and 1898–99, all on matting and all won, were only retrospectively viewed as Test matches.

# CHAPTER 18

# England's Talent for Attrition
## Timeless Tests and five-day matches

The tone of England's Test cricket changed profoundly during a period either side of the Second World War. Only in 1930 were Tests in England extended from three days to four, yet by 1948 – discounting the war years, only 12 seasons later – a swift transition began to five-day matches. Whereas an attacking mindset was needed if a win was to be forced on a good pitch inside three days, a contest lasting more than half as long again, and with time for the pitch to naturally deteriorate to the benefit of the spinners, could be much more attritional, with a draw representing a genuine achievement for a side on the wrong end of things for the first two or three days.

England teams had prior to this regularly played matches to a finish in Australia and occasionally at home in series deciders, and these more elongated games tended to suit the temperament of English sides. The broader move to longer matches marked a permanent change in favour of those who expressed themselves best through defiance and durability rather than the flair that would be so essential (and in England's case was often found wanting) when the one-day international and Twenty20 formats took hold. Some of the defining moments in England's history involved marathon feats of batting when crease occupation was the priority in situations that simply would not have arisen in shorter contests. The likes of Ken Barrington, Geoff Boycott, Michael Atherton and Alastair Cook typified this approach right up to the modern day.

Probably the most celebrated and still the highest innings for England was Len Hutton's 364 against Australia at The Oval in 1938 in a match played to a finish. Mindful of Don Bradman's presence in the opposition, and Bradman's scores of 232 and 244 in the timeless Tests that concluded the 1930 and 1934 series in Australia's favour, Wally Hammond instructed Hutton – aged 22 and playing only his sixth Test – to bat as long as possible. The Yorkshireman carried out this demand to perfection by staying in for 13 hours 17 minutes. Bradman eventually snapped an ankle bone while bowling, shortly after which Hammond declared on 903 for seven (still England's highest Test score); spirits broken, Australia were beaten by an innings and 579 runs the next day.

Hutton's score represented a record for Tests that stood until 1958 and brought him international celebrity, not least because he had put in the shade Bradman's mightiest efforts. He was moreover playing against type because as a youngster he was a free-flowing batsman at Yorkshire, though after the war, during which he suffered an injury which resulted in his left arm being two inches shorter, he adopted a more cautious approach, reflecting his status as England's best batsman as well as the more protracted nature of Test cricket. This outlook extended to his leadership following his appointment as England's first professional captain since the 1880s: when England narrowly regained the Ashes under him in 1953, their run-rate of 2.08 was their lowest for any home Ashes series. A key event was Willie Watson, another Yorkshireman, and Trevor Bailey, an all-rounder at Essex with an extraordinary capacity for self-denial in England's cause, staying together for most of the fifth and final day to secure a draw at Lord's. Freddie Brown, whose own England side barely scored any faster in Australia in 1950-51, firmly blamed time-limitless Tests and the move to Test matches lasting 30 hours: 'English batsmen seem to be infected with a defensive virus.' The need for 'brighter cricket' was a constant refrain during the 1950s and into the 1960s.

The impetus for a move to five-day Tests began with the earlier matches in the 1938 Ashes series, which from an English perspective produced the frustrating situation of them having the better of high-scoring games at Trent Bridge and Lord's without being able to force a win, then losing a lower-scoring contest at Headingley. Former England captain Arthur Gilligan, writing in *The Cricketer* ahead of the Oval match, argued that it was time for five- or even six-day Tests: 'I am strongly advocating that six days should be allotted for future Tests in this country ... it does not follow that these Test matches will last the full six days, but it is a tremendous advantage to know that a definite result is practically assured.' He accepted though that a move to five days was more likely, and that was indeed what happened.

The transition was not smooth, the number of days over which England were willing to play their various opponents at home betraying the differing regard in which they held their various opponents: during the 1940s they allocated five days for Australia and four for South Africa but only three for West Indies, New Zealand and India. Three-day Tests had long been a target of condemnation: Archie MacLaren, the England captain, vented his frustration at being unable to force a series-levelling win against Australia in 1899 by denouncing them as 'the so-called Test which is no Test'. But *Wisden* editor Sydney Pardon argued in 1903 that three-day Tests in England were more interesting than the timeless matches in Australia where batsmen avoided risk 'with laborious care', adding: 'Time being of no consequence, the game would, I fear, lose its brilliant qualities and become little more than a matter of endurance.'

But when at Australia's persistent urging it was decided to lengthen Ashes Tests in England to four days following the sterility of the first four games of the 1926 series, the move was not mirrored in home matches with other sides until South Africa toured in 1947, even though from the outset four-day Tests produced good cricket and enhanced attendance figures.* The privilege the South Africans

---

* England would have hosted South Africa for four-day Tests in 1940 but South Africa's tour was cancelled because of war.

enjoyed was not immediately extended to the newer Test sides even though by then England and Australia had agreed to go further by playing matches over five days in England in 1948. This decision gave rise to what some considered the gloomiest day in England's Test history to date when Norman Yardley, needing a win to keep the series alive, set Australia 404 on the fifth day at Headingley. Thanks to a litany of errors and great batting by Bradman and Arthur Morris England were beaten by seven wickets, the first time a Test was lost against a declaration.

'The great crowd ... were so stunned and disappointed that there was only some perfunctory clapping as Bradman and [Neil] Harvey returned to the pavilion ... one and all felt that the match had been thrown away by indifferent leadership and bad fielding,' reported *The Cricketer*, which added that England needed a captain with tactical acumen and the capacity to inspire others. The *Manchester Guardian* termed England's fielding an 'ill-assorted shambles'. Yardley offered to resign before the final Test but with suitable amateur alternatives thin on the ground he was persuaded to see out the series.

No thought was given to going back to four days. Bradman's Australians may have been much the superior side but the public appetite for sporting spectacle after the war was vast and commercially the 1948 Tests were an enormous success. What were then the three highest attendance figures for Tests in England were recorded at Lord's (132,000), Old Trafford (133,740) and Headingley (158,000, still a record for any Test in England), and for the series as a whole paying spectators and members totalled more than 520,000. When Australia next visited in 1953, this unprecedented tally was improved upon again, with 549,650 watching England finally wrest back the Ashes.

As far as England's other opponents were concerned, a turning point came with New Zealand's tour of 1949. Reckoning they could not take 20 wickets themselves in three days, and determined to scotch the idea that they were not worth Tests of longer duration, Walter Hadlee's team set out to draw every Test. By packing their side with batting they managed to do so with ease, being dismissed for under 300 only once. England after two Tests suggested extending the remaining games to four days but New Zealand insisted on sticking to the original itinerary, and other moves that might have broken the deadlock also failed; these included England switching captains from George Mann to Freddie Brown, picking five bowlers for the third Test and six for the fourth. Denis Compton, England's most adventurous cricketer, described it as the most boring series he played in.

As a consequence, the Board of Control took the drastic step of recommending that the following summer's Tests against West Indies be lengthened from three days to five, not purely in recognition of West Indies' improvement (though they had emphatically beaten a mid-strength England side in the Caribbean in the winter of 1947–48) but that they might prove even harder than New Zealand to break down. *Wisden* editor Hubert Preston understood the thinking, writing that, 'an unbroken run of draws makes a series almost farcical and demonstrates clearly the want of clever hostile bowlers', but detected the dangers inherent in longer matches: 'The longer the period of play, the greater the temptation to make sure that you will not lose'; only once a team could see a way to victory would they 'put forth the special effort needed to achieve that end'.

In fact, speculation that the West Indies selectors would think defensively proved well wide of the mark as England's bowlers were cut to ribbons by the 'three Ws', Frank Worrell, Everton Weekes and Clyde Walcott, and their batsmen bamboozled by the spin of Sonny Ramadhin and Alf Valentine. The only upshot of five-day matches in 1950 was that they created scope for England's humiliation to be all the greater: England were dogged by injuries, but the margins of defeat – by 326 runs at Lord's, ten wickets at Trent Bridge and an innings and 56 at The Oval (despite a brilliantly defiant double-century from Len Hutton) – were among the heaviest they had suffered at home. In what was a record during a home series, they made eight changes to their XI between the third and fourth matches, including bringing in Freddie Brown as captain for the second summer in succession, this time at the expense of Norman Yardley.

From this point on, all Tests in England were scheduled for five days, though few in the early days were as vibrant as these.* Indeed, it gradually became clear that the longer the time allowed, the less inclined were many players to get on with things. Norman Preston, the editor of *Wisden*, blamed the dull play in the county championship in 1959 on the example set by Test players. 'Such tactics could in time kill first-class cricket,' he wrote. But when South Africa proposed that their Tests in England in 1960 revert to four days, the suggestion was rejected by counties eager not to see their share of gate receipts cut, especially as India managed to take only one of their five Tests in England in 1959 into a fifth day. When first planned, Sri Lanka's inaugural Test in England in 1984 was set to be played over four days in order to shorten the absences of the England players from their counties, but the idea was eventually dropped.

England's overseas Tests followed different patterns, though the differentiation between opponents remained. Their Tests in Australia involved five hours of play a day rather than the six in England, but matches there were played to a finish – what *Wisden* in 1927 described as 'the severe ordeal of games played to a finish however long they may last'.† Scoring was heavier than in England, though the tempo more sedate, and some very long games ensued. The 1924-25 Ashes series featured three seven-day Tests and spanned 31 days; the matches in 1928-29 got longer as the series went on, culminating in Australia pulling off a whitewash–avoiding win in Melbourne on the eighth day of the match and the 33rd day of the series, the longest ever. The most successful English batsmen in these

---

* When Tests in England were lengthened from three to four days, and then four to five, concerns were expressed that it would more often deprive the counties of their best players and lead, in the words of *Wisden* in 1927, to 'the great annual [county] competition being consequently robbed of all real importance'. The Almanack suggested longer but fewer Tests, but accepted that was unlikely to happen: 'The money question threatens to dominate the situation.' To counter the advent of five-day Tests, the counties increased their championship fixtures from 26 to 28 in 1950, thereby merely raising everyone's workload.

† Ralph Barker and Irving Rosenwater stated that time-keeping in early Tests was lax. Of the Lord's Test of 1905, they wrote: 'A prompt start at the advertised time was so rare in this period that it was liable to be praised as "commendable punctuality" ... a day's play in England generally meant 6–6.5 hours on paper, and in Australia 4.5–5 hours.'

attritional conditions were Herbert Sutcliffe, who faced 2,022 balls for 734 runs in 1924-25, and Wally Hammond, whose 2,521 deliveries faced and 905 runs scored in 1928-29 are records for any England batsman in any series. Hammond played 'in a quietly determined, self-denying way quite different from his normal method at home' and stuck to that method on subsequent visits though without quite the same success as Australia heeded Monty Noble's observation that in 1928-29 their bowlers had 'neglected to persevere with the attack on Hammond's obvious weakness – the leg stump'; he nevertheless averaged 55.00 in 1932-33 and 58.50 in 1936-37.

Bowlers too were subjected to huge amounts of work. For a spinner such as Jack White to send down 2,440 deliveries, as he did in 1928-29, was one thing, but for a fast-medium pacer, Maurice Tate, to bowl 2,528 balls for 38 wickets in 1924-25 was astonishing; it remains an unsurpassed workload for an England bowler in a single series.

It was only when Ashes Tests resumed after the Second World War that England and Australia agreed to standardise the playing hours for matches between themselves to 30 hours (an idea that was being pushed by the Australians in 1938), initially with the possible exception of the final Test being played to a finish in certain circumstances; there would be six days of five hours in Australia and five days of six hours in England. England continued to play six-day Tests in Australia until 1958-59 and with similar consideration to the testing combination of strong opposition and oppressive heat they also played matches over six days in the Caribbean until 1959-60. Yet, however many days were involved, the 30-hour Test match gradually became the norm, though other countries took their time falling into line, with India and Pakistan not doing so until the 1980s.* It was not before time: someone such as Hammond, whose Test career spanned the years from 1927 to 1947, took part in Tests lasting three, four, five, six, seven, eight and ten days. It was with the

---

* India and Pakistan, like West Indies, long favoured playing five or five-and-a-half hours each day because of a combination of factors, including heat, morning dew and early sunsets. Pakistan were the last to make the move, doing so in time for England's tour in 1987-88.

aim of fulfilling 30 hours of play that the Jamaica Test of 1968 was extended into a sixth morning to make up 75 minutes lost on the fourth afternoon to a riot triggered by the dismissal of Basil Butcher and quelled only with the use of tear-gas; England, who might have won by an innings at this point, lost momentum and ultimately had to scramble to secure a draw.

England were not quite done with four-day Tests after 1950. The last side they agreed to play over five days was New Zealand but on the second occasion, in Auckland in 1954-55, New Zealand were dismissed for just 26, the lowest total in all Test cricket, so that the game did not even reach a fourth day.* Further disparity followed in England in 1958 when only rain prevented Peter May's side winning all five matches in three or four days (in the event, they took the series 4-0). As a result, England reverted to four-day Tests for their visits to New Zealand and this only changed after Bev Congdon's New Zealand side pushed England to the limit in three five-day matches in England in 1973.

The third time the sides met after that, in 1977-78, New Zealand beat England for the first time – at the Basin Reserve, Wellington on the fifth day – their side containing two sons of Walter Hadlee who had led the team with such stubborn effectiveness in England in 1949. With the teams level at 1-1, it was agreed to play the deciding match in Auckland over six days and, no doubt to their intense satisfaction, New Zealand could still not be beaten even over that distance. India's feeble resistance in England in 1959 prompted *The Times* to express the hope that their matches would be limited to four or even three days when they next visited, but India baulked at any reduction and proved their fighting spirit by scoring 510 in the follow-on, and taking the match well into a fifth day, in the first Test match of their 1967 tour. This did not stop Norman Preston again suggesting that

---

* On the same ground in March 2018, New Zealand nearly exacted total revenge when Trent Boult and Tim Southee reduced England to 23 for eight in the first session of the first day-night Test between the sides; thanks to Craig Overton striking 33 not out at No. 9 they rallied to 58 all out. New Zealand were 175 for three at stumps, making it the worst first day England had experienced after batting first, surpassing The Oval 1948 (England 52 all out, Australia 153 for two).

it might be better if England played their home games against India, New Zealand and Pakistan ('the three weaker cricketing countries') over four days rather than five.

England also played two four-day Tests in Pakistan in 1968-69 on the last-minute orders of President Ayub Khan, who wanted to curb the momentum of a student movement in Lahore and secessionist agitation in Dacca (now Dhaka). Both matches were drawn and when the final Test in Karachi was scheduled for five days in the hope of producing a definite result it was halted on the third day by a riot.

In addition to their timeless Tests in Australia, England developed a tradition of playing the final home match of the summer against Australia to a finish, provided something rested on the outcome, which was the case five times in six Australian visits between 1912 and 1938; occasionally the practice was also adopted on tours of South Africa and West Indies where matches were usually limited to four or five days.* This was eventually replaced by some series 'deciders' being extended by an extra, sixth day if necessary; the first time this happened was in West Indies in 1947-48 and then in England in 1953 (though both matches finished without the need of a sixth day).

Such contests – timeless Tests or extended ones – were originally popular with the public and therefore also with administrators with an eye on gate receipts, but they were often sterile affairs lacking variety. In the desire to produce surfaces that would last, groundsmen from the time that Tests were extended from three days to four tended to over-prepare them, with the upshot that they gave little assistance to bowlers of pace and seam. This was strikingly the case in the first summer of four-day Tests in 1930 when Bradman amassed a record haul of 974 runs and the fast bowlers of both sides struggled.

In the case of timeless Tests, this process was only exaggerated:

---

* Provision was made for the final Tests of two earlier Ashes series in England, in 1905 and 1909, to be extended but in the event this was unnecessary. 'Although the "play to a finish" clause was present in the playing conditions ... the real intention for the 1905 match (as later declared by the Board of Control) was for a four-day limit; in 1909 the match was "to be played to a finish but the match not to extend beyond the sixth day".' (Barker and Rosenwater, p304)

'Bosser' Martin boasted that his pitch at The Oval in 1938 would 'last till Christmas', and it might well have done. Teams holding big first-innings leads would therefore not necessarily enforce the follow-on, as they wanted to rest their bowlers and make the opposition bat last. This ploy, while possibly sensible in theory, proved costly in practice for both England at Jamaica in 1930 and South Africa at Durban in 1939, when their opponents batted so stubbornly in the fourth innings – West Indies for the best part of two days on the former occasion when they were set a record 836, and England for three days on the latter in pursuit of 696 – that the games had to be abandoned as draws because the England players needed to voyage home. At Durban, where Wally Hammond, Paul Gibb and Bill Edrich all batted for almost six hours or more, England got within 42 of their enormous target with five wickets in hand and would surely have won had rain not prevented play after tea on the tenth (and as it transpired final) day.*

The first play-to-a-finish Test in England came at the Triangular Tournament of 1912 in which a clear-cut winner was naturally needed. Contemporary reports present a confusing picture as to how it was intended to achieve this, with *The Times* even reporting three days before the final match, between England and Australia, that an extra Test might be arranged. In the event, it was agreed that whichever side won at The Oval would be tournament winners, 'the match being played to a finish even if it lasted a week' – what Charles Fry, the England captain, called 'a straight knockout fight'.

It seems that there was actually a six-day limit on the contest but this was in essence the same thing and in the event England won comfortably in four days; with 44,717 paying at the gate despite unseasonable weather, the game was deemed a success. The opportunity for a repeat did not occur until 1926, Australia having wrapped

---

* There were discussions between Hammond and tour manager AJ Holmes and the South African authorities about how they might modify the touring team's travel plans in order to complete the game but it was decided the match would end on the tenth day come what may, the local authorities announcing on the ninth evening that the next day would be the last.

up the 1921 series at an early stage. By then, another successful time-less Test had been staged in Durban on the 1922-23 tour of South Africa led by Frank Mann, father of George, who sat on the MCC committee which cabled its approval for the last Test to be played to a finish with the series level at 1-1. England won by 109 runs – though it took them six days to finish the job because of rain – thanks to centuries in both innings from Jack Russell, the second of them at No.6 as he battled illness. Russell was rewarded with a collection among the crowd worth £90 (collections had been banned at Tests in England since the 1890s but not overseas).

England's celebrated victory in the 1926 timeless finale – approval for which was granted at an ICC meeting the day after the fourth Test produced yet another draw – cemented the popularity of the format. The four days of the game were watched by a total of 103,000 people, the first attendance in England of more than 100,000. This was eclipsed by the 110,000 who watched Australia triumph in 1930 after dwarfing England's first-innings score of 405 with a total of 695, enabling them to win by an innings in five days of actual playing time.

However, public opinion began to shift against timeless Tests, so predictable was much of the play. Gubby Allen related in his tour report of 1936-37 to the Board of Control that he had detected growing support in Australia for time-limit Test matches since his last visit four years earlier and Don Bradman wrote in *Wisden* in 1939 that 'people left The Oval tired of watching the unequal fight' in the final Tests of both the 1934 and 1938 Ashes deciders. The timeless Test at Durban was only three days old when the South African board declared itself unanimously opposed to further games of this sort, a view it reiterated at an ICC meeting the same year. However, a strong body of opinion in Australia remained behind timeless Tests and, with justification, blamed the nature of the pitches on the tedious cricket seen at The Oval and Durban.*

---

* The refusal of MCC to agree to South Africa's request for covered pitches for the 1938-39 series was a contributory factor to the farce in Durban. Three times overnight rainfall followed by a fresh rolling of the pitch effectively prevented any deterioration in the surface.

However, when cricket resumed after the Second World War, England and Australia again agreed that if an Ashes series was alive going into the final match it would be played to a finish; in the event this was unnecessary. Only in 1953 did they adopt a plan previously in place for the final home Tests against sides such as India and New Zealand of scheduling an extra day's play. This was indeed what happened at The Oval that year, although England needed only four days rather than six to complete a victory that regained them the Ashes for the first time since 1934 in front of an aggregate attendance of 115,000. England also played six-day final Tests in Australia in 1970-71, in the West Indies in 1973-74, at home to Australia in 1972 and 1975, and in New Zealand in 1977-78. At The Oval in 1975, England secured a draw after following on 341 behind by batting almost 15 hours in their second innings, Bob Woolmer occupying the crease for more than eight hours for 149. In terms of playing time, it stands as the longest of England's home matches. At Auckland in 1978, Clive Radley took eight hours seven minutes to reach his hundred.*

The principle that a standard Test match should last up to 30 hours stood unchallenged until the 1980s when a gradual transition was made towards a minimum of 90 overs per day, and therefore 450 overs per match, to counter declining over-rates. England's home Tests against India and Pakistan in 1982 and New Zealand in 1983 involved 96 overs per day but this was too much for some sides; 90 overs per day began in England in 1988 and was formalised by the ICC three years later. Overs rather than time became the chief determining factor in the span of a Test match. Various methods were used in an effort to ensure teams adhered to the 90-overs-a-day requirement, including an additional 30 minutes being available each day, plus potential fines and suspensions for the captains of tardy bowling sides.

---

* Although the match in Auckland was England's last six-day Test, two England players, Andrew Flintoff and Steven Harmison, were subsequently involved in a six-day Test when they represented a World XI v Australia at Sydney in 2005. Provision was made for England's final home Test against South Africa in 1970 to last up to eight days to accommodate 30 hours of play as insurance against bad weather and anti-apartheid demonstrations; in the event the tour was cancelled.

With public interest in Test cricket dwindling in some quarters – though in England less than elsewhere – some prominent voices championed a move to four-day Tests of seven hours (or 105 overs per day), a model successfully pioneered by Kerry Packer in his World Series 'Supertests'. Ian Chappell, who played in those games, said such contests were less taxing when they were played as day–night fixtures in cooler temperatures. Supporters included Geoffrey Boycott, who argued in his Cowdrey Lecture in 2005 for such a change, as well as Tom Harrison and Colin Graves, respectively chief executive and chairman of the ECB. Eventually, in October 2017, the ICC approved a trial period during which teams could bilaterally agree to play Tests over four days. England were set to make first use of this with an inaugural meeting against Ireland at Lord's in July 2019.

## England in Timeless Tests

| Host country | Period | Played | Won | Lost | Drawn |
|---|---|---|---|---|---|
| *Australia | 1877-37 | 77 | 34 | 41 | 2 |
| England (all v Australia) | 1912-38 | 5 | 3 | 2 | 0 |
| South Africa | 1923; 1939 | 2 | 1 | 0 | 1 |
| West Indies | 1930 | 1 | 0 | 0 | 1 |
| Total | | 85 | 38 | 43 | 4 |

---

* All early Tests in Australia were intended to be played to a finish but two matches in Melbourne during the 1881–82 series were abandoned as draws on the fourth day because players had voyages to catch; both are counted in the above table. The Tests in Kingston, Jamaica in 1930 and at Durban in 1939 were similarly abandoned as draws because England teams needed to catch return voyages home.

## England's Longest Tests

| Days | Result |
| --- | --- |
| 10 | South Africa drew with England, Durban, 3-14 March 1939 (no play day 8) |
| 9 | West Indies drew with England, Jamaica, 3-12 April 1930 (no play days 8 and 9) |
| 8 | Australia beat England by 5 wickets, Melbourne, 8-16 March 1929 |
| 7 | England beat Australia by 70 runs, Melbourne, 23 February-1 March 1912 (no play days 3 and 6) |
| 7 | Australia beat England by 193 runs, Sydney, 19-27 December 1924 |
| 7 | Australia beat England by 81 runs, Melbourne, 1-8 January 1925 |
| 7 | Australia beat England by 11 runs, Adelaide, 16-23 January 1925 |
| 7 | England beat Australia by 3 wickets, Melbourne, 29 December-5 January 1928-29 |
| 7 | England beat Australia by 12 runs, Adelaide, 1-8 February 1929 |

All the above were matches intended to be played to a finish, although in the event those in Durban and Jamaica were abandoned as draws. EW Swanton, who reported on the match, estimated that the Durban Test lasted roughly 45 hours of play. In terms of balls bowled, England's longest matches were those at Durban in 1939 (5,447 balls) and Melbourne in March 1929 (4,244 balls).

## Longest Scheduled Tests in England

Five Tests in England have been played to a finish and three others were scheduled to last six days: all were the final Tests of the series and viewed as 'deciders'.

| Planned length | Days played | Result |
| --- | --- | --- |
| Timeless | 4 | England beat Australia by 244 runs, The Oval, 19-22 August 1912 |
| Timeless | 4 | England beat Australia by 289 runs, The Oval, 14-18 August 1926 |
| Timeless | 6 | Australia beat England by innings & 39, The Oval, 16-22 August 1930 (no play day 5) |
| Timeless | 4 | Australia beat England by 562 runs, The Oval, 18-22 August 1934 |
| Timeless | 4 | England beat Australia by innings & 579, The Oval, 20-24 August 1938 |
| Six days | 4 | England beat Australia by eight wickets, The Oval, 15-19 August 1953 |
| Six days | 6 | Australia beat England by five wickets, The Oval, 10-16 August 1972 |
| Six days | 6 | England drew with Australia, The Oval, 28 August-3 September 1975 |

England's longest home Test in terms of balls bowled was against West Indies at Lord's in 1950, which spanned five days and 3,645 deliveries.

# CHAPTER 19

# Hammond's Sacrifice
## A 'professional' takes charge

By the late 1930s, after a string of setbacks on the field, England's selectors were under severe pressure to get the team back to winning ways. Not only were Australia, led by Don Bradman, almost impossibly hard to beat but it seemed that South Africa and West Indies could not be held at bay without careful planning. When in 1937 Herbert Sutcliffe said that he believed England possessed a team capable of beating Australia the following year if only the selectors could be induced to pick it, his views chimed with those who felt the time had come for a professional to lead the side and to abandon the practice of picking solely amateur captains, some of whom were not worth their place in the side. Another former England player, Bob Wyatt, and an amateur captain at that, also questioned the wisdom of selecting captains not worth their place at around the same time.

The problem was that the establishment was not yet ready to accommodate such revolutionary thinking, as Wilfrid Brookes, the editor of *Wisden*, made clear: 'It is common knowledge that the number of amateurs who can devote the necessary time to the game is not increasing. If this fact is disquieting to sticklers for tradition, the end of the convention which for so many years has directed that England's captain must be an amateur is by no means in sight.'

The solution arrived at was controversial. Walter Hammond, the country's best and most famous cricketer, was encouraged to turn amateur, with steps taken to make sure a job outside cricket was found for him. The baronial chiefs chose their man well: Hammond was only too amenable to the idea. He, like Sutcliffe, hankered after social betterment and was in his own word 'desperate' to captain England against Australia. 'I would almost have given my ears for it,' he wrote in one of his books. Tactically, he was certainly competent enough to do the job. He brought to the position the experience of 65 Test matches and five previous Ashes series; no incoming England captain before him could draw on such a wealth of knowledge.

Where he was less able, it was said, was in empathising with or encouraging less gifted performers; his rootless upbringing as the son of an army officer killed in the First World War left him a shy and remote figure to many, and his fame only isolated him further. 'I suffered from hero-worship,' he once said. 'I know it was offered in all kindness but it embarrassed.' Denis Compton recounted in critical terms how Hammond, in his first Test as captain at Trent Bridge in 1938, chastised Compton, then just 20 years old, for getting out straight after reaching his century. But in this instance Hammond may have been right to do so: he had been around long enough to know that a score of 102 was not in itself enough against Bradman's Australia. Hammond's hardness towards lesser mortals may have been less forgivable at Gloucestershire, but in any case charges of aloofness ought to be taken with a pinch of salt, too: of how many England captains before Hammond might it have been said that they failed to connect with their men? Some of Hammond's critics had highly selective memories.

Those wedded to the ancien régime were only too happy to see Hammond's captaincy fail – and sure enough at the last hurdle it did when, against his better judgement and the advice of the Gloucestershire chairman FO Wills, he agreed at the age of 43 to a request from Lord's to take England to Australia in 1946-47. So ill-equipped were England as a bowling and fielding side that whoever led the side would have returned beaten, but Hammond's reputation, which ought to have been unimpeachable so great a player had he been, suffered irreparable damage. Nevertheless, he showed enough strategic capability in his 20 Tests in charge to smooth the path towards Len Hutton becoming England's first professional captain in 1952. Hutton acknowledged the debt and described Hammond as the greatest batsman he had played with or against (i.e. better than Bradman) while also quietly denouncing those senior players who on that ill-fated Australia tour had been more interested in partying than supporting their captain.

The selection panel was running out of options when it turned to Hammond. When Pelham Warner was brought back in 1935 for a third spell as chairman of selectors with a view to overseeing plans for the Ashes in Australia in 1936–37 and England in 1938, the man who had already made England captains out of Percy Chapman and Douglas Jardine quickly sought to replace Bob Wyatt with Gubby Allen ahead of England's first Test matches in Australia since Bodyline.* The logic was clear if contentious: Allen would be a palatable choice to Australia as he had not bowled leg-theory in 1932–33, and was also intimately connected to the country through birth and family, while Wyatt had been Jardine's deputy and remained close to him.

Wyatt suspected, probably rightly, that Warner had a bias for southerners with an Oxbridge background but Allen was a dynamic leader and proved a popular choice with most of his players; Hammond recalled this Australia tour, his last without the cares of captaincy, as his happiest. The problem was that Allen needed to keep up his work in the City and played only infrequently for Middlesex; he was also a fast bowler at inherent risk of breaking down.† *The Times* was among those critical of his appointment. Sure enough, Allen found the dual burden of captaincy and bowling

---

* Warner had lobbied unsuccessfully for Allen to lead England in the 1934 Ashes when Wyatt got the job, but Warner was not then on the selection panel.

† Only seven players have taken more than 20 Test wickets bowling fast or fast-medium while captaining England: Johnny Douglas (1911-24; 37 wickets in 18 Tests as captain), Arthur Gilligan (1924-25; 27 in 9), Gubby Allen (1936-48; 42 in 11), Ted Dexter (1961-64; 33 in 30), Ian Botham (1980-81; 35 in 12), Bob Willis (1982-84; 77 in 18) and Andrew Flintoff (2006-07; 34 in 11).

fast in Australia arduous and, faced with diminishing returns and mental exhaustion, he had to be dissuaded from sitting out the final Test. Warner accepted Walter Robins, the Middlesex captain and Allen's deputy in Australia, as captain against New Zealand in 1937 in the hope that Allen would be re-energised in time for the Ashes in 1938 (Robins himself conceded he served as mere caretaker). However, with Allen in his mid-thirties and increasingly troubled by back problems, the time was ripe for the readying of Hammond as an alternative.

Warner had known Hammond a long time. He had spotted him as a special talent as early as 1923 and visited him three years later when Hammond was close to death in a hospital in Bristol suffering from what is now suspected to have been syphilis. This support earned Warner Hammond's lasting gratitude. Warner would have been aware that Hammond had been considering turning amateur for some time. Hammond earned good money as a professional cricketer but there was scope to make more if he could find the right job outside the game, while this would also facilitate his ambition of captaining England, although on that front time was running short: it was becoming ever more likely that another war in Europe was on the way. He had been offered in 1936 the post of assistant secretary and with it the joint captaincy of Gloucestershire if he turned amateur, but he declined because it would have brought him less than the £450 he received as senior professional.

Then in November 1937, following approaches from influential members of MCC, Warner probably among them, the Bristol branch of Marsham Tyres invited him to join its board of directors with a salary of £2,000, with the understanding that he would be free to play as much cricket as required. It was a mutually beneficial arrangement: the greater Hammond's celebrity, the greater his value to the firm in terms of bringing in sales. Warner later wrote that from that point there was never any doubt that Hammond would be captain, but Warner still encouraged Allen to be involved in the Ashes and arranged for him to lead The Rest in a Test Trial against an England side captained by Hammond. In the event Allen withdrew, citing fitness problems, and did not play for England again until after the

Second World War.* In the event, Wyatt, Allen and Robins never played in an England side led by Hammond.

The Test series Hammond led against West Indies in 1939 was overshadowed by the imminent war in Europe. During two of the three Tests at Lord's and Old Trafford, Hammond was recruited during the games to make speeches asking for volunteers for national service. The final Test at The Oval took place with barrage balloons overhead, and shortly after it ended the remaining tour matches were cancelled.

In the three series Hammond led before the war, there was broad praise for his grasp of on-field matters, if some regret that he could not force more results in South Africa, where England won the five-match series 1-0 thanks to seven wickets from Ken Farnes in an innings victory in the third Test at Durban.

On that tour, Hammond fostered a good spirit among the players, something Eddie Paynter attributed to Hammond's experience of professional and amateur status. *Wisden,* having originally suggested he lacked experience for the job (though he had captained in 31 first-class matches to that point), swiftly revised its opinion: 'Hammond showed unmistakably that he was well fitted for the post; indeed, having regard to his limited experience of leading an XI ... he surprised his closest friends by his intelligent tactics. Undoubtedly Hammond proved himself a sagacious and inspiring captain.'

South Africans were equally impressed. Alan Melville, South Africa captain, rated his opposite number highly and Louis Duffus, a noted local chronicler, wrote: 'He [Hammond] maintained rigid discipline, set his field shrewdly, and was forever besetting the batsmen with new strategies. Indeed, he introduced

---

* Gubby Allen's biographer, EW Swanton, became a staunch critic of Hammond's captaincy but his account was not always accurate and his opinion changed. He wrote that during the winter of 1937-38 the England captaincy was between Allen and Robins, only for Hammond to announce in spring 1938 that he was turning amateur (when in fact he did so in November 1937). His pre-war reports were actually sympathetic, in one of which he called Hammond a 'sagacious tactician'; only later did he assert that Hammond was 'ill-equipped temperamentally as a leader of men, except in so far as he could inspire by example'. He suggested Allen was in line to captain the 1938-39 tour of South Africa after Lord Cobham, MCC treasurer, asked as to his availability, but Allen was still unfit.

new methods to South Africa cricket by his policy of continually changing his attack and using his bowlers in short spells. He was an exemplary captain.' For all that he was reputed to lack concern for others he showed great faith in Bill Edrich, who had scored 88 runs in 11 Test innings before Hammond counter-intuitively moved him up to No.3 and Edrich repaid him with a double-century in Durban.*

When serious cricket began finding its feet after the war, Hammond immediately showed that, although he had lost his athleticism, he remained the natural choice to lead England. He had no obvious rivals: in the Test Trial of 1946, The Rest were led by an Oxbridge amateur Bryan Valentine, who had played a few Tests before the war with success and now led Kent, but he had been badly wounded in action and was not a credible choice. Hammond, by contrast, went into the trial having scored six centuries in his previous seven first-class innings (scoring an unbeaten 59 in the other), although thereafter his gifts would quickly desert him. In 1945 he had led an England side in a series of five three-day matches against Australian servicemen-cricketers, dubbed Victory Tests but not official internationals. The series was hugely popular, with 367,000 people attending, and widely praised for its enterprising play and good spirit. Both countries were counting their losses – former England Test cricketers Ken Farnes, George Macaulay, Maurice Turnbull and Hedley Verity were among those who died while on service – and reconciliation was in the air. The rival teams shared dressing-rooms, hotels and transportation, and the hope was expressed that, when Test cricket resumed, the attritional mood of pre-war contests would be abandoned.

This did not happen. The manager of the Australian Services side, Keith Johnson, successfully lobbied Lord's for England to tour Australia as early as 1946–47, though England's preference was to hold off another 12 months to give them time to gather a stronger

---

* Bizarrely, this innings failed to secure Edrich a place for the home Tests against West Indies a few months later. Wyatt called him 'a great slayer of moderate bowling without being a really great player against bowling of the highest class'.

side.* Johnson's view prevailed at an ICC meeting in January 1946, with the trade-off that Don Bradman, the great draw-card, would lead Australia in England in 1948. Bradman had been invalided out of the war on health grounds and had not been party to the Victory Tests or their Corinthian spirit; he was physically frailer, but once he was persuaded to resume playing he did so intent to play as hard a game as he had before the war, to the dismay of some in his own team. Then, in Brisbane in 1946 in the first Test of what was dubbed the Goodwill Tour, Bradman survived what the England players were convinced was a fair catch to Jack Ikin in the gully on 28, and Hammond was reportedly heard to comment: 'That's a bloody fine way to start.' Publicly his view was more measured – 'I thought it was a catch but I may have been wrong' – but from that moment Hammond's disenchantment grew as his will to win diminished. Bradman went on to score 187 and, after England suffered a massive defeat, Hammond shared a car journey with Len Hutton and Cyril Washbrook to Sydney during which he barely uttered a word.

Hammond had left home intending that it should be a happy tour. He gave his players free rein – most had endured enough regimentation during the war and Australia was a land of plenty compared to austere Britain – but some abused the privilege. When Bill Edrich returned after 'an all-night binge' he was protected by his Middlesex 'twin' Denis Compton. Compton himself let down Hammond in other ways. In what were now time-limit Tests in Australia, Hammond wanted his batsmen to sell their wickets dearly, mirroring the caution that had served him well on earlier visits, but Compton found such an approach alien to his instincts. Hutton confided many years later that he thought Edrich and Compton were sufficiently unprofessional to warrant being sent home. To add to his problems, Hammond was afflicted with fibrositis, causing him to miss the final Test, while details of the collapse of his first marriage hurtfully appeared in the Australian newspapers. Unsurprisingly, well before

---

* It was not just a matter of England finding good enough cricketers to play at Test level; even those who were good enough were not necessarily ready by 1946–47. Alec Bedser, for example, struggled to bowl after tea on the first day of that series because of stomach trouble, which was a consequence of his war service in Italy.

the end of the tour Hammond gave notice of his intention to retire, citing 'pressure from business'.

Joe Hardstaff, who was on the tour, said that the captaincy was more than Hammond could take but, however unsatisfactorily from the England players' point of view, the mission got Ashes cricket up and running again, and Hammond's contribution towards that was appreciated by many. Norman Yardley, Hammond's deputy, said that their 'enormous extraneous duties' – by which he meant media commitments and social functions – left Hammond and Major Rupert Howard, the manager, little time to devote to their players or to cultivating team spirit. Spared some of these duties, the captain would have been free to mix with his men, spend time at practice and strategic planning: 'He would be a player like the rest, not a sort of touring god.' Clif Cary, an Australian broadcaster, said of Hammond: 'He displayed tact and diplomacy in the interests of the game.'

Gerald Howat, one of Hammond's biographers, observed: 'If he had stayed in Test cricket too long, he had done it for the best of motives, to help the post-war game recover. There was nothing in it for him and he knew it.' On his return home, Hammond agreed to a request from MCC to make a broadcast on BBC Radio to dispel the notion that the tour had been a failure in goodwill terms. 'Our visit has done something to cement the relationship between this country and Australia and New Zealand,' he said. 'As a goodwill tour it was a complete success ... no nicer or happier side ever travelled.' This was a gracious interpretation of events. Even before the furore over the Ikin catch, he had found himself criticised in the *Yorkshire Evening Post* by Brian Sellers for his handling of players and tactics, a bizarre and inflammatory intervention from an active England selector but perhaps an indication of the qualified regard in which Hammond was held by the establishment (Sellers apparently disapproved of Hammond's ongoing divorce from a Bradford woman).*

Hammond – who soon emigrated with his second wife to South

---

* Sellers thus breached the principle that selectors did not contribute a report or statement to the press while a home series or tour was in progress. He was removed as a selector for 1947 but returned for 1949–50 and 1955.

Africa, where he became a curiosity for English visiting sides who came across his barely recognisable figure around Durban – subsequently showed little affection for cricket's amateur class that he had so publicly signed up to, or for its insistence that professionals should not captain England. 'Apparently it is only the nominal status, not the man or his characteristics, to which objection is taken,' he wrote in *Cricket's Secret History* in 1952. 'I can say this because I captained England, after most of a cricket life-time as a professional. I was the same man as before, or perhaps I even had a slightly declining skill by that time. But because I changed my label all was well ... I submit this is illogical.' He would also argue that it was time for amateurs to take 'honourable pay and compete on equal terms with those who make a living from cricket' and for those amateurs who intended to give up a first-class career after a year or two, as so many had, 'to say so and stand down from Test teams'. He added: 'It may be flattering to vanity to say they have played a couple of times for England ... Young professionals feel this keenly and it is time someone brought it into the open.'

These were strong words but reflected a wider sense that English cricket needed to change with the times: Britain had been transformed not only by war but by the election of a Labour government. But expectations that the old amateur–professional divide might quickly be swept away proved wide of the mark. Cricket's amateur class might have been a shell of what it once was, and the professionals – a significant number of whom had like Squadron Leader Hammond achieved notable rank in the services – might have been shaking off the last vestiges of their former serfdom, but power was not easily wrested from its old citadels. When Hammond quit the England captaincy the job passed to Norman Yardley, another amateur of the old school, a decent enough cricketer and captain, but not of the first rank. He might have been a more sympathetic leader of men, happy to call professionals by their first names, but the notion that this in itself would improve England's prospects was absurd: Yardley was not remotely tough enough to cope when faced with the ruthlessness of Bradman's 1948 side, and he presided over an even heavier defeat than Hammond.

# The Rise of England's Professionals

1877-87:   James Lillywhite jnr, Alfred Shaw and Arthur Shrewsbury organise and
           manage four tours of Australia, captaining 11 Tests between them.

1909:      Jack Hobbs and Tom Hayward provide the first instance of two
           professionals opening the batting in the first innings of a home Test.

1926:      Jack Hobbs and Wilfred Rhodes are co-opted as Test selectors, beginning
           a pattern of senior England professionals assisting in selection meetings at
           home and abroad. Jack Hobbs deputises as captain during a Test match at
           Old Trafford.

1938:      Walter Hammond becomes the first former professional to officially captain
           England at home, having turned amateur the previous year. He leads
           England in 20 Tests.

1950:      Les Ames, a former professional, becomes a full member of the selection
           panel.

1950-51:   Denis Compton is the first professional to be appointed vice-captain of a
           major tour.

1952:      Len Hutton is appointed England's first professional captain since 1887;
           he regains the Ashes the following year. He leads his first major tour, to the
           West Indies, in 1953-54.

1953:      Hobbs is knighted for services to cricket.

1955       Hutton becomes the first active professional appointed an honorary
           member of MCC. He is knighted the following year.

1962:      Amateur status is abolished. Ames, Hutton and Alec Bedser join the MCC
           cricket subcommittee.

1966-73:   Brian Close and Ray Illingworth, who played as professionals in the pre-
           abolition era, lead England in seven and 31 Tests respectively.

1969:      Bedser is appointed chairman of selectors, a post he holds until 1981.

2004:      Tom Graveney is the first former professional England Test cricketer to be
           appointed MCC president.

# England Test Cricketers Who Died on War Service

| | |
|---|---|
| Lieutenant<br>FRANK MILLIGAN | – died during the siege of Mafeking, Ramathlabama, South Africa, 31 March 1900, aged 30 |
| Second Lieutenant<br>MAJOR BOOTH | – killed in action on the first day of the battle of the Somme, near La Cigny, France, 1 July 1916, aged 29 |
| Lieutenant<br>KENNETH HUTCHINGS | – killed in action during the battle of the Somme, Ginchy, France, 3 September 1916, aged 43 |
| Second Lieutenant<br>LEONARD MOON | – died of self-inflicted gun wounds, near Salonika, Greece, 23 November 1916, aged 38 |
| Sergeant<br>COLIN BLYTHE | – killed by a shell on a railway line, near Passchendaele, Belgium, 8 November 1917, aged 38 |
| Lieutenant-Commander<br>GEOFFREY LEGGE | – killed in a flying accident while serving in the Fleet Air Arm, Brampford Speke, Devon, 21 November 1940, aged 37 |
| Pilot Officer<br>GEORGE MACAULAY | – died while serving in the Royal Air Force, Sullom Voe, Shetland Islands, 13 December 1940, aged 43 |
| Pilot Officer<br>KENNETH FARNES | – killed on a flying exercise while serving in the Royal Air Force, near Chipping Warden, Northamptonshire, 20 October 1941, aged 30 |
| Captain<br>HEDLEY VERITY | – died of wounds sustained during the invasion of Sicily, at Caserta, Italy, 31 July 1943, aged 38 |
| Major<br>MAURICE TURNBULL | – shot dead by a sniper during the Normandy landings, Montchamp, France, 5 August 1944, aged 38 |

George Macaulay's death was commonly ascribed to pneumonia but recent research by Anthony Bradbury found that Macaulay's death certificate stated cardiac failure linked to alcoholism. Macaulay's widow was subsequently denied a war pension, a *Yorkshire Post* report in 1947 referring to evidence given at a war pensions review tribunal that Macaulay 'had been drinking heavily during the past 10 days [before his death]'.[*]

Jack Ferris, who served in the second Boer War, died as the result of a fall from a tram in Durban, South Africa, in November 1900, aged 33, a month after being discharged from the army for misconduct. His biographer Max Bonnell has suggested it may have been an act of suicide.

---

[*] See *The Cricket Statistician*, the journal of the Association of Cricket Statisticians and Historians, autumn 2017, p.4.

# CHAPTER 20

# The Politicisation of Test Cricket
## England's treatment of Pakistan and the South Africa problem

The defeat England suffered at the hands of West Indies at Lord's in 1950 came at an important moment in their relationship with the newer cricketing powers. It was their first home defeat to a Test team containing non-white players and the result gave impetus not only to cricket in the Caribbean but also in the Indian subcontinent at a time when, with Britain divesting itself of its Empire, sport was a ready vehicle for nationalist sentiment. At Lord's, West Indian immigrants, two years after the arrival of SS *Windrush*, provided for the first time a significant and vibrant presence within an English crowd cheering on the visiting side. 'The Lord's Test was the scene of the first "cricket carnival" in England,' Hilary Beckles wrote. 'The ground exploded in dance, song and bacchanal, West Indian style, and signalled the beginning of a process that was to refashion the culture of cricket crowds in England. Lord Kitchener and Lord Beginner [calypso artists] . . . led jubilant West Indians across the field in a procession of improvised singing.'

Two years later, India recorded their first Test victory over England in Madras (now Chennai) in their first five-match series against England, one that captivated many classes across the

subcontinent through the medium of All India Radio's live broadcasts, and was played out in the shadow of King George VI's death,
which was announced on the first day. A further two years after that,
against widespread expectation, a fledgling Pakistan team won a
Test on their first tour of England.* Their winning XI at The Oval
contained many players affected by the trauma of Partition and was
led by a man who had previously played against England for India,
Abdul Hafeez Kardar, who sculpted a team that was 'the near-
exact expression of the vision of Pakistan's founder, Mohammad
Ali Jinnah'.† By 1963, expatriate West Indians were turning out in
force in several English cities to watch their team. 'West Indians
from all walks of life arrived at the ground to see their heroes,'
the *Birmingham Post* reported of that year's Edgbaston Test. 'There
were bus-crews and postman's uniforms, gaily-coloured shirts and
wide-brimmed hats.' When the gates at The Oval were closed on
a crowd of 25,350 to see West Indies take the series victory, it was
estimated that two-thirds of the spectators were West Indians resi-
dent in London. After Basil Butcher had struck the winning runs,
the field was invaded by jubilant fans. 'Those who were present will
never forget the fantastic final scene,' *Wisden* stated.

In 1950 the sensational spin bowling of Sonny Ramadhin and Alf
Valentine, and batting feats of Frank Worrell, Everton Weekes and
Clyde Walcott, inspired people from all these regions to believe that
they could be the equal of Britain. At the same time, the galvanising
event politically was India's independence in 1947, which brought
with it the creation of Pakistan and gave momentum to the independence movements in regions of the Caribbean, chiefly Jamaica
and Trinidad (who each achieved autonomy in 1962) and Guyana
and Barbados (both 1966).

International cricket was thus very different for England after the
Second World War. Their matches with India, Pakistan and West

---

* Pakistan remain the only visiting team to win a Test match on their first tour
of England.
† AH Kardar is one of only two players to represent two countries in Tests against
England. The other is Kepler Wessels, who played for Australia and South Africa
between 1982 and 1994.

Indies were weightier affairs, the outcomes of national importance to their opponents, and defeat therefore a calamity to be avoided. Such was the cautious, negative mood that pervaded many of these contests that often even five or six days was not enough to arrive at a positive outcome: when England toured India and Pakistan for eight Tests in the winter of 1961–62, five ended in draws, and when they returned to India for five more Tests two winters later, neither side could force even one win. (During the Test in Delhi, an unruly crowd took to flashing mirrors in the eyes of batsmen.)

England triumphed in the West Indies in 1959–60 and 1967–68 both times by 1-0 margins with four draws, and when a misjudged declaration by Garry Sobers enabled England to win in Trinidad during the second of these series he was widely condemned. The attritional mindset was not confined to these encounters; in what was now a fast-expanding international fixture list, most series were infected.* 'I sometimes wonder if the fact that we are spreading the gospel of cricket from the traditional home of the game prevents us from playing international cricket as hard as our opponents,' Frank Tyson wrote in 1961. In fact, England at home were not above some of the more questionable practices such as tailoring of pitches, time-wasting and home–town umpiring; indeed, they often led the way. On the Saturday of the Trent Bridge Test in 1955, the crowd resorted to 'a mild form of slow hand-clapping' as South Africa spent almost six hours scoring 144 runs.

The dourness left cricket vulnerable to rival interests imported from America, including in Australia where the Ashes rivalry had sustained people for so long. 'As a sporting attraction, cricket in the 1950s would yield to the great American–Australian tennis rivalry in the Davis Cup, and the global spectacle of the [1956] Olympic Games in Melbourne,' Malcolm Knox wrote. 'Not until the advent of non-Anglo–Australian cricketing gods would the game discover a new identity and break out of what became, in the 1950s, perceived as a pre-war Anglo-centric fustiness.' Winning at cricket still mattered

---

* England's involvement in all the Test matches played around the world dropped from 89 per cent before October 1947 to 55 per cent between then and October 1964.

to Australians though. Peter May said that when in 1958-59 he led England to Australia, he found a country 'in a high state of nationalistic fervour about its cricket', having not beaten England since 1950-51.

Nor did England always get their way in the corridors of power. Whereas previously Dominion representatives had generally shown deference in their dealings with MCC and England, they now brought to the table issues to debate and demands to be met, and the discussions were often discordant. Imperial Cricket Conference meetings that had been occasional became biennial, then annual, and by 1958 all members were armed with one vote where previously England, Australia and South Africa had wielded two (though no major change could now be passed without the agreement of two of the three founding members). The ICC finally meant something more than an exclusive whites-only club, and as a consequence the issue of South Africa's apartheid policy, applied with force following the election of the Afrikaner National Party in 1948, received a regular airing, to the acute discomfort of MCC.

A forceful indication of the shifting landscape came when England toured the Caribbean in 1953-54, a tour which would be described by *The Times* as 'the second most controversial tour in cricket history'. 'A distressing point in my view is that white people are no longer connected with the administrative side of cricket in the West Indies,' Len Hutton wrote in his captain's report. 'It was disappointing too to see so few white men in the teams we played. I would say that a liberal estimate of the number of "whites" who played against us was five and this includes [Jeffrey] Stollmeyer and [Gerry] Gomez . . . On New Year's Eve we were invited to the Kingston CC dance and the hospitality was the worst I have ever experienced on an MCC tour. Many of the players left the dance early . . . and it was apparent to most of them that their presence was not desired . . . Our friends in the West Indies actively connected with cricket, I felt, could be numbered on one hand.' Trevor Bailey, Hutton's vice-captain, said that white West Indians and expatriate Englishmen had told the players that an England win was imperative if the balance of racial power in the region was not to be disturbed – 'or, as a Victorian would have put it, "[it would] make the natives uppity".'

When during the final Test in Kingston, Hutton came off the field at tea having batted more than five sessions and failed to fully acknowledge Alexander Bustamente, the nationalist leader and Jamaica's first chief minister, it triggered a minor diplomatic crisis which it took the tour manager Charles Palmer – first aware of the problem when he was manhandled by a burly member of Bustamente's staff – hours of conciliatory talks to resolve.

A series defeat was avoided, England coming back from two down to draw 2-2, but their uncompromising approach, and very public dissatisfaction at some poor umpiring, went down badly. Worrell, appointed in 1960 the first black captain of West Indies, said, 'The MCC team of 1954 pushed British prestige in the West Indies to an all-time low. The men who could have been such great ambassadors turned out to be providers of ammunition for the "enemy".' Walcott said, 'Some of the language directed against our players was appalling.'

MCC, as articulator of English policy and secretariat of ICC, hardly helped matters. Their officers continued to be largely drawn from aristocracy or retired military brass tied to the old imperial ideal. Nor was the ICC constitution suited to the changed political world and it had to be hastily revised in order that membership was linked to the new British Commonwealth rather than the old Empire. Until this process was complete India, as a republic, was permitted to stay within ICC only on a provisional basis. They were confirmed as full members again in 1950. Pakistan too, rather than be granted automatic membership of ICC, were cast out and told to prove themselves worthy of re-entry, even though the territories of West Pakistan had previously provided several cricketers who toured England with India sides.

On Partition, Pakistan lost their Hindu players and many administrators, while the Indian cricket board retained all of the assets. Anthony de Mello, the India board secretary, was actually in favour of India and Pakistan playing as one team and this view was endorsed by the Earl of Gowrie and Pelham Warner, respectively MCC presidents (and therefore chairmen of ICC) in 1948 and 1950, even though by then Pakistan had formally founded a board of control.

'There are few signs of willingness to help Pakistan to secure election,' *The Times* reported from Pakistan before the ICC meeting in 1950. Highlighting the technical and procedural reasons for delay put forward by MCC, it added: 'These have often been couched in terms which could certainly have been more happily phrased when dealing with a new and loyal Dominion of the Commonwealth.' Only after a Pakistan team beat MCC in Karachi in December 1951 was there a change of heart. MCC the following year seconded India's proposal that Pakistan be granted Test status and an invitation was extended to them to make their first Test tour of England in 1954.* Pakistan did not forget these slights.

Pakistan from the outset possessed some great players such as Fazal Mahmood, an English-style medium-pacer who delivered the historic first Test win in England, and a batsman made for five-day matches in Hanif Mohammad, but they were handicapped by an undeveloped domestic system, which was played mainly on matting pitches in major centres such as Karachi and Lahore by the middle classes. (Six of the XI that won at The Oval in 1954 attended Islamia College, Lahore.) A first-class national championship was only launched in the months before the first England tour.

No Test team began so friendless, although they did have one important ally in Alf Gover, a former England fast bowler, whose coaching school in Wandsworth, south London, provided a nursery for several Pakistan players from 1949 onwards. Gover was in attendance when England were toppled at The Oval, and greeted the result with the words: 'We have won! We have won!' But even after this success Pakistan, to their frustration, were merely granted a visit by an MCC A team in 1955-56 and did not play another Test against England until the winter of 1961-62. England did not make a standalone Test tour of Pakistan (as opposed to combining matches there with a visit to India) until 1977-78. England's attitude was plain: they preferred touring Australia and South Africa, and viewed tours of the

---

* Ceylon, or Sri Lanka as it became, also gained independence on Partition but was made to wait until 1965 to be admitted to ICC.

subcontinent as opportunities to rest their star players and to blood newcomers. When stories emerged of players returning home three stone lighter after suffering from dysentery, as Geoff Pullar did after the four-and-a-half-month tour of India and Pakistan in 1961–62, this approach appeared to have some justification.

'This business of leading players declining certain tours needs consideration by the authorities,' wrote Leslie Smith in his report for *Wisden* of the 1961–62 tour, which was led by a third-choice captain in Ted Dexter after Peter May, contemplating retirement, and Colin Cowdrey, a seasoned player with more than 50 caps to his name, declined. 'India rightly point out that they have never seen a full-strength MCC side and resent the fact that the star players make a habit of turning down the trip. Admittedly English players find the tour harder and less comfortable than any other, but this scarcely justifies players, once they are established, picking and choosing which tour they want to make. It is no secret that in general the men who go to India, Pakistan and Ceylon regard themselves as a "second eleven", often play like it and are caustic about the stars who stay at home ... The English players never did accustom themselves to the different type of food, the all-too-many functions and the unusual living conditions.'

Traditional practices that had served England so well came under threat. Pakistan – who, like India, made a point of sending their own delegates to ICC meetings rather than accepting proxies as Australia, South Africa and New Zealand did – proposed in 1955 that ICC meetings be sometimes held away from the usual venues of Lord's or The Oval, and offered themselves as hosts. India in 1958 also supported the idea of meetings being hosted by rotation, only for it to be scuppered by the Maharajah of Vizianagram out of reverence for the status of Lord's as the game's headquarters. The ICC did not hold a meeting outside London until 1991.

A regular complaint was the preferential treatment accorded Australia and South Africa in England's touring schedule, which was drawn up an extraordinary distance in advance: in 1950, the programme was outlined until 1965; in 1960 it was pencilled in up to 1978. The defence was that Australia and South Africa were 'traditionally England's oldest opponents'. However, events conspired to shift the debate. The South Africa team that toured England in 1960 was unusually weak, while the following winter a West Indies side – now playing under their first black captain in Frank Worrell following a successful campaign led by Worrell himself and CLR James to topple the white leadership in Caribbean cricket – captured the imagination of the world with their exciting play during a spine-tinglingly taut series in Australia which included the first-ever tied Test.

With public opinion behind them, West Indies demanded a review of a schedule that did not have them touring England between 1963 and 1971, and then not again until 1978, while South Africa were granted three visits during this period. 'They now clearly rank as one of the three Great Powers of Cricket,' Alan Ross wrote in the *Guardian* of West Indies during their 1963 tour of England and ahead of the ICC's annual meeting, making it clear he felt a 'colour line' was in operation. After Worrell himself turned up to the meeting, MCC was forced into a rethink and the following year issued a revised schedule which included West Indies returning for five Tests in 1966.* Meanwhile, the overall programme was eased by the introduction in 1965 of split tours, which meant two teams visiting England in the same summer to play three Tests each (of which one in each series would be at Lord's). Although some parties needed persuading, notably India and Pakistan, this offered a welcome solution to the problems experienced when, in a rare show of even-handedness, England hosted five-match series against New Zealand (in 1958), India (1959) and Pakistan (1962) which turned out to be horribly one-sided. Only Australia were guaranteed not to be involved in these new arrangements: they would continue to tour for the whole summer at least once every four years.†

---

* Another indication of the new allure of West Indies was the inception in 1963 – the centenary of the *Wisden* Almanack – of a Wisden Trophy for competition between England and West Indies.

† According to EW Swanton, the idea of split tours was first put forward by Jack Dashwood, a well-known sportsman, in a letter to the *Daily Telegraph* on 26 June 1963, three weeks before the ICC meeting (*Gubby Allen: Man of Cricket*, pp.281-2).

Entwined in these developments was the increasingly toxic issue of South African politics and the fact that the body whose representatives were sent to ICC, the South African Cricket Association, operated exclusively for the benefit of whites even though a new unified non-white organisation, the South African Cricket Board of Control, had been in existence since 1947. Following the Sharpeville massacre of March 1960, the Pakistan board proposed to ICC that Test status be withdrawn from South Africa until the country revised its apartheid policy in sport, and showed a willingness to play all Test opponents regardless of colour, but the proposal came too late for inclusion in the agenda for that year's meeting.

The following year, Jeffrey Stollmeyer, representing West Indies, suggested the ICC should state its opposition to apartheid in cricket but MCC's loyalty to its white South African friends ran too deep. Gubby Allen, on MCC's behalf, stated that retaining cricketing ties with South Africa was a form of bridge-building, not only with South Africa but the African continent in general (even though little or no effort was made at the time to develop cricket in other African countries). The stalemate was formalised at the annual meeting in 1962 when, in the face of continued lobbying for action from Pakistan, India and West Indies, it was decided, chiefly at the instigation of Australia and New Zealand, that each country should decide for itself if they were to play South Africa. This was especially controversial as South Africa had the previous year in response to mounting criticism withdrawn from the Commonwealth altogether, thus breaching its ICC membership. 'The status quo was retained with never a suggestion that the constitution of the conference might be altered to allow South Africa in,' The Times reported. Pakistan's ICC representative Muzaffar Husain was strongly critical of this 'solution', calling it 'dangerous' to bend the ICC's constitution and warning of a threat to the very existence of the ICC itself.

Thus, England, Australia and New Zealand continued to play South Africa – in matches they decreed as official Tests despite South Africa's equivocal status – and the three non-white members did not play them.* MCC support for South Africa was unyielding. Frank Worrell's suggestion at the 1963 meeting that South Africa's potentially embarrassing tour of England in 1965 be deferred was rebuffed. Then, when Gubby Allen outlined a draft itinerary for 1969-72 containing a full rather than a split tour of England by South Africa in 1970, it raised protests from West Indies and India at a decision that 'might be construed as an insult to full member countries'.

In 1965, in an attempt to spread cricket around the world it was finally agreed that it was no longer necessary to be a member of the Commonwealth to be a member of the ICC, which duly changed its name from Imperial Cricket Conference to the International Cricket Conference (and from 1989 the International Cricket Council), but India, Pakistan and West Indies ensured South Africa were not readmitted.†

Politics not only drove a wedge between MCC/England and the non-white bloc of cricketing nations, it also created a divide between administrators and those England players – not many in number but nevertheless an influential minority – who were either opposed to supporting the South African regime or had grave doubts about whether cricketing relations should be maintained with it. Some such as David Sheppard, who played 22 Tests between 1950 and 1963, two as captain, and Mike Brearley, a multiple Ashes-winning captain in the late 1970s and early 1980s, were prominent in their public opposition.

Some England players had their eyes opened to the political reality only after touring South Africa. Alan Oakman was driving a car, with Jim Laker as passenger, on the 1956-57 tour when he was involved in an accident with a black man on a bicycle. Laker described how no one took any notice of the man as he lay on the ground while a policeman encouraged the idea among witnesses, too fearful to dispute the point, that the man was drunk and therefore

---

* Not only did England, Australia and New Zealand regard the matches they played against South Africa as Tests, so too did *Wisden*, which continued to include them in its records.
† Another important consequence of this rule change was that ICC could admit associate members unconnected to Commonwealth or Empire, such as the United States.

at fault for the incident. 'This, thought Alan, too bemused to do anything, is what white men call justice,' Laker wrote.

Sheppard, who had decided to pursue a life in the church, originally declared his unavailability for the 1956-57 tour, and later turned down a request from the captain Peter May to join the tour part way through as a replacement; Sheppard pleaded other commitments but there was a common assumption that in both instances he was reluctant to go to South Africa on political grounds. He hesitated to confirm this supposition but certainly refused on a point of principle to play against the South Africans when they toured England in 1960, making his views public despite Harry Altham, MCC president, seeking to dissuade him from doing so.

Sheppard's anti-apartheid views were ultimately to scupper his candidature to lead the England side in Australia in 1962-63 after being lured out of early retirement by those, the new chairman of selectors Walter Robins included, who felt he might be capable of encouraging in his players an attractive style of play (though in fact many of these players doubted whether Sheppard ought to be granted such a prized role, having committed so little to the side in the past).* EM Wellings, who covered the 1962-63 tour and was himself a Sheppard supporter, identified Gubby Allen as the man who acted to protect cricketing relations with South Africa.

'The situation suddenly changed when Gubby Allen reappeared as a voting selector,' Wellings wrote. 'He had retired as chairman of selectors a year earlier. He agreed to join the Robins selectors solely in an advisory capacity, when they reached the point of choosing the touring players. When it came to that he surprisingly became a voting selector, and his presence influenced the decision against Sheppard in favour of [Ted] Dexter. Many of us felt at the time that Allen should have stayed gracefully in retirement ... on the eve of selection it [Sheppard's opposition to apartheid] was brought

---

* Frank Tyson was strongly opposed to Sheppard's selection for the final Test in 1956 because clerical duties had confined him to only a few championship appearances: 'His inclusion was a guess on the part of the selectors.'

to life again in the guise of a red herring. What, it was suddenly asked, would be his reaction if questioned on tour about the White Australian policy? Would his answer be embarrassing to MCC? Did it never occur to the selectors to settle the matter by asking him what he would reply? Thus Sheppard was cast out . . ."* However, Alec Bedser, a member of the 1962 selection panel, felt that Robins in any case regarded Dexter as first choice during this debate.

Brearley and Tom Cartwright, two members of the England side that toured South Africa in 1964-65, held grave political reservations. Brearley, who visited factories and townships, stayed on for three weeks at the end of the tour to find out more for himself. Cartwright's withdrawal from the planned tour of South Africa in 1968-69 because of an injury that had severely hampered his county season attracted speculation that he was deliberately excusing himself out of dislike for the South African regime and a wish to precipitate the crisis that followed when Basil D'Oliveira, a Cape Coloured, was called up in his place. Cartwright said that in fact D'Oliveira's name was not mentioned as a likely replacement when he discussed his fitness issues with Doug Insole, the chairman of selectors, and MCC officials, but he did have reservations about whether joining another tour of South Africa was the right thing to do. He recalled reading a report in the *Daily Express* about how – when the England team was originally announced without D'Oliveira in it – the South African parliament, in session in Cape Town, stood and cheered. 'When I read that, I went cold,' he said. 'And I started to wonder whether I wanted to be part of it . . . There were such an awful lot of things in the mix.'

Sheppard and Brearley were also to the fore among a group of dissident members of MCC who successfully lobbied for a special general meeting of the club, held at Church House, Westminster in December 1968; one resolution regretted the club's handling of the

---

* Sheppard, who was ordained in 1955, played ten Test matches on his return to the England side in 1962-63 and is the only ordained minister to play Tests for England. Vernon Royle, who played one Test in 1878-79, Clem Wilson, two Tests in 1898-99, and Tom Killick, two Tests in 1929, all moved into the church in later life. Killick died while batting in a diocesan clergy match in 1953.

crisis, and another stated there should be no more tours of South Africa without evidence of greater racial integration. The criticism was that MCC failed to acquire proper assurances from South Africa that whatever their selection it would be accepted. Sheppard and Brearley were the main speakers in favour of the resolutions, while Colin Cowdrey, the England captain, spoke on behalf of the club by in effect denying that the selectors had been pressured to leave out D'Oliveira. The motions were carried in the hall but defeated overall. Sheppard was unrepentant: 'What is more important than votes . . . is that ideas have been ventilated. Nothing will be quite the same in English cricket after the debate.' Brearley concedes that he felt freer than most to speak out because in the late 1960s he wasn't playing regular cricket.*

John Arlott, an English journalist and broadcaster, was also con- verted by his experiences on England's 1948-49 tour, when he saw at first hand the mistreatment of non-whites and the squalor in which they were condemned to live. Arlott became a vociferous opponent of South Africa in a way many players felt they could not be without jeopardising their careers, and he played an important role in helping D'Oliveira first come to England to play league cricket. He refused to cover subsequent series involving South Africa, though he wrote an account of their tour of England in 1960 called *Cricket on Trial*. In anticipation of trouble following the recent Sharpeville massacre, MCC gave the South Africa board the option of calling off the tour, which it declined to do, but in fact the protests that accompanied the tour were mild. Some Warwickshire members refused to attend the Edgbaston Test but after that, according to Arlott, the boycott was barely noticeable: 'The English public concluded that it was not fair to blame Sharpeville on South Africa's cricketers.' Demonstrators confined themselves to distributing pamphlets and parading with banners, one of which asked, 'What about Subba Row?' in reference

---

* It has been claimed that Peter Lever, the Lancashire fast bowler who played 17 Tests in the 1970s, refused to play against the 1965 South Africans, but in fact he played against them at Blackpool in the final weeks of the tour. He also played in the England v Rest of the World series involving several South African players, which replaced the South Africa tour.

to the England batsman of Indian origin, who would play four Tests that summer.

Some players may have suspected that the English cricketing establishment readily kow-towed to John Vorster's apartheid government, but others were themselves content to deal closely with South Africa, seeing it as a convenient winter destination to play and coach, even after international fixtures were suspended. When copies of Father Trevor Huddleston's book exposing the iniquities of apartheid, *Naught for Your Comfort*, were handed to the England players as they sailed out of Southampton at the start of their 1956–57 tour, many were reportedly tossed overboard unread. Similarly, when following the D'Oliveira Affair the English cricket authorities sought to proceed with South Africa's scheduled tour in 1970 despite a more concerted 'Stop the Tour' campaign and South Africa's recent expulsion from the Olympic movement, several prominent past and present England players supported the raising of funds to meet the costs of protecting the proposed venues from political protestors. They included Cowdrey, Brian Close and Alec Bedser. A referendum of the Cricketers' Association in January 1970 found that 81 per cent supported the 1970 tour. (Meanwhile David Sheppard, now the Bishop of Woolwich, was appointed chair of a group that planned a protest march on the Saturday of the Lord's Test.) How many if any players might have refused to make themselves available to play in the 1970 Tests can only be guessed at, although the minds of some might have been concentrated by the receipt of letters from TCCB informing them that their lives were to be insured for £15,000 each. In the event, the tour was cancelled on the instruction of the British government ten days before it was due to start.*

---

* The loss of the tour, even though it was replaced by a series against the Rest of the World, had a financial impact on the counties and led to the TCCB demanding compensation from the government. Attendances for the five Rest of the World matches totalled 177,500, well down on the total for just three South Africa Tests in 1965. On 31 March 1971 the government awarded the TCCB £75,054. The Cricket Council had hoped for £200,000 and Billy Griffith, MCC secretary, said the sum fell far short of expectations. It was the possibility of such claims that led government reluctance to instruct sporting bodies to cancel events on political grounds, a subsequent bone of contention in respect of England visits to Zimbabwe.

Peter May, who in 1959 married a daughter of Harold Gilligan, who had extensive business interests in South Africa, was another who was sympathetic to South African cricket, if not the political regime, and this caused a lasting rift between himself and Sheppard, whom he had known since their days at Cambridge. 'Peter was very upset with David over the affair,' May's wife Virginia said. 'They were in two camps. My father and Peter sincerely hoped that all cricketers would support cricket. They saw this as a genuine option and the way forward.' May maintained his stance even after becoming chairman of selectors in 1982, shortly after 15 English players were banned by the TCCB for three years for undertaking a rebel tour of South Africa.

May implied these bans were nothing to do with him and he would pick the players again when they were available (which he did). When the following year there were moves led by John Carlisle MP for MCC to send a minor team to tour South Africa, May wrote privately: 'I firmly believe that South African cricket needs some encouragement for the tremendous efforts which have been made to integrate their cricket. In many ways therefore I would find it difficult to support a committee decision to ban the tour.' Nonetheless the committee came out against, with their case put at a special general meeting by Hubert Doggart, a former club president, and Cowdrey, who abandoned his earlier position, with support from Sheppard. The proposal was rejected but Carlisle's group, which commandeered the support of Denis Compton and Bill Edrich, mustered almost 40 per cent of the overall vote. Raman Subba Row, in his role as administrator in the 1980s and despite his own racial background being anathema to South Africa's regime, admitted to maintaining low-key contact with Ali Bacher in anticipation of the day when normal relations could be resumed. This finally happened in the early 1990s with the dismantling of the apartheid system.

## England's Post-War Programme

In 20 years after the Second World War, England played more Tests against their traditional opponents Australia and South Africa than the other Test teams combined.

| Opposition | Tests | Won | Lost | Drawn |
|---|---|---|---|---|
| Australia | 55 | 10 | 22 | 23 |
| South Africa | 38 | 17 | 6 | 15 |
| Total | 93 | 27 | 28 | 38 |
| India | 27 | 10 | 3 | 14 |
| New Zealand | 25 | 14 | 0 | 11 |
| Pakistan | 12 | 6 | 1 | 5 |
| West Indies | 28 | 8 | 10 | 10 |
| Total | 92 | 38 | 14 | 40 |

*1 May 1946 to 1 May 1966*

# CHAPTER 21

# How Hutton and May Made England Hard to Beat

## A golden era for English bowling

The captaincy reigns of Len Hutton and Peter May provided England with one of the most stable and successful periods in their history. From Hutton's ascension in May 1952 to May's final Test match in August 1961, the team went undefeated in 62 of their 77 Tests, and in 15 of their 17 series, and Australia were beaten in three successive five-match series for the first time. For star quality, the XI that secured the Ashes at home in 1953 bore comparison to Douglas Jardine's 1932-33 side. But the glorious results were not altogether matched by the methods the two men adopted. With Hutton coming late to captaincy at the age of 35 and May early – being at 25 the youngest official England captain since Percy Chapman – and neither of them having previously had much experience of leadership, both were cautious and uncompromising in approach. England were not the only team to play this way amid a general move to put containment first in five-day matches – with Don Bradman blamed in some quarters for setting the trend in 1948 – but through their very success they gave a powerful lead to others, to the detriment of the game as a spectacle.

With scrutiny and expectation greater than ever, especially on

Hutton as England's first modern-day professional captain, the strain and solitariness of the job took a heavy toll on the health of both Hutton and May, neither of whom relished the glare of publicity that their status demanded. Hutton found leading the team on tour, when he was so much in the spotlight, particularly arduous; he said the West Indies tour took two years off his career, and only after a delegation of management and senior players to his bedside on the morning of the game did he agree to risk what was cited as an attack of fibrositis and play in the pivotal third Test at Melbourne in 1954-55. George Duckworth, the former Lancashire professional and England wicketkeeper-turned-tour baggage-master and scorer, was a crucial support.*

Hutton returned home exhausted and quit playing altogether within months. May missed 11 Tests towards the end of his reign through an illness eventually diagnosed as hemorrhoids and exacerbated by him returning to action before he was fully recovered from surgery. In other circumstances, they might have played longer, but Hutton's race was run by the time he was 38 and May's before he turned 32. May was among the last genuine amateurs to play Test cricket. Having recently married and started a young family, he needed to develop a business career, but that was only one motive for stopping; after six years as England captain he no longer enjoyed the game, and was weary of the criticism attached to it. May's decision to take his fiancée on the Australia tour, and the press attention this attracted, only accelerated this process. May's disillusionment was a state of mind that, increasingly, England captains reached at some point or other.

Had Hutton been appointed earlier, things could have been different in many respects. Instead, after Wally Hammond retired, the practice of amateurs being put in charge continued for the next five years. Like so many before them, these players were either not worth their place or could not commit to Test cricket all the year round, as was now more necessary than ever with such a busy international

---

* Cyril Washbrook, also of Lancashire and England, said of Duckworth: 'He became one of the shrewdest observers of the game and his advice was always available and eagerly sought by cricketers of every class and creed.'

schedule. The victory England achieved at Port Elizabeth in the final Test of 1948–49 – when, at the urging of their captain George Mann, they chased down a target of 172 in 95 minutes with a minute to spare – provided a classic example of what spirited old-style amateur leadership and play might offer, but whatever its advocates hoped, it was an approach whose days were numbered.* The nadir came with Nigel Howard, described by Tom Graveney as 'a very ordinary cricketer and that's putting it kindly', leading the side to India in 1951-52.

Even during these five years, though, there were indications of a softening of the establishment position. In July 1949, during the Duke of Edinburgh's presidency of the club, MCC for the first time began granting honorary cricket membership to professionals, and started by admitting 26 former England Test 'greats'. The following year Les Ames became the first professional to become a full-time selector and Tom Dollery, Warwickshire's professional captain, was a contender to lead the tour to Australia; when the job went to Freddie Brown, a professional was appointed his vice-captain. Unfortunately, the choice fell not on Hutton but Denis Compton, and might have gone to Cyril Washbrook, Hutton's staunch opening partner from across the Pennines, had his involvement in the tour not been initially in doubt. Hutton and Compton had played most of their Test cricket together but were never brothers-in-arms in the way Hutton and Washbrook were.

Hutton's record-breaking score of 364 before the war put pressure on him not to fail that never applied to Compton, who was temperamentally best suited to playing Cavalier rather than Roundhead. Compton touched rare heights of brilliance in the years immediately after the war, scoring 753 runs in the series against South Africa in 1947 and 562 in the one against Australia in 1948 – at the time the two best aggregates achieved by an England batsman at home. He

---

* England were responding to a declaration from South Africa who were seeking a series-levelling victory. In the previous match, Mann had set South Africa 375 to win in the equivalent of 86.4 six-ball overs at Ellis Park, Johannesburg but they declined to go for the runs. Mann's father Frank also captained England on a winning tour of South Africa (in 1922-23) and like him played for Cambridge and Middlesex. Both men played all their Tests as captain, an indication as to where their credentials lay. George Mann was later chairman of the TCCB from 1978-83.

wooed the crowds in a way few players have ever done, but by 1950–51 the damage he had done to his knees playing football for Arsenal was taking its toll and his Test returns overseas, when there were distractions, were rarely what they should have been for a player of his class. 'The relationship between Hutton and Compton was never of the easiest,' Alan Gibson wrote. 'They could never have become kindred spirits.' As it happened, Brown preferred in Australia to consult Hutton and wicketkeeper Godfrey Evans rather than Compton, and Hutton's contributions with the bat totally outshone those of Compton, but the long wait for acknowledgement that he could be trusted with a position of authority only made the adjustment for Hutton as England captain all the greater.

Compton's peak coincided with a time when cricket attendances also scaled rare heights, in part because of the presence of demobilised servicemen on leave: it was estimated that in 1947 three million people went through the gates into first-class cricket and several daily attendances at the Test matches reached 30,000. 'I have not been so deeply touched on a cricket ground as I was in this heavenly summer when I went to Lord's to see a pale-faced crowd, existing on rations, the rocket bomb still in the ears of most folk – to see this worn, dowdy crowd watching Compton,' Neville Cardus wrote. Attendances for England's Tests in Australia in 1946–47 were even healthier, averaging more than 30,000 per day.

In the end, the urge to arrest years of underachievement by the national team compelled Hutton's promotion at home to India in 1952, with the next Ashes series a year away. Alternatives were in short supply, although a case could have been made for Reg Simpson, who scored 156 not out in the final Test in 1950–51 to give England their first win over Australia since the war; that he captained the historically rebellious county of Nottinghamshire probably counted against him less than what Hutton among others came to perceive as a lack of ruthlessness. The selection panel that plumped for Hutton, while hardly of radical bent, was made up of four men – Norman Yardley, Bob Wyatt, Brown and Ames – with personal experience of how difficult it was to beat Australia and how vital it was to pick the best man, a view Wyatt had expressed before the war. Wyatt and Brown, too, were members of the MCC committee that would have been required to give Hutton's appointment its blessing, so they could have relayed these views in person. Ames, though a former professional, had the previous year been offered the captaincy of Kent (on the proviso he turned amateur, which he declined to do). Even so, when it came to it, Wyatt was sent as emissary to Hutton and suggested he might follow Hammond's example and turn amateur, but Hutton indicated that such a move would be a betrayal of his upbringing. This was a brave step on Hutton's part but the right thing to do. His appointment stood.

This was a significant event but the social divide within the England camp was already narrowing. John Dewes said that amateurs, of whom he was one, were discouraged from mixing freely with the professionals on the 1950-51 tour of Australia; however, Alex Bannister of the *Daily Mail* recalled that when invitations to temporary membership of a club in Adelaide were extended only to the four amateurs and to those of the press who were members of MCC it was politely declined. John Woodcock, who covered Hutton's tour of Australia in 1954-55 for *The Times*, said that there was often little telling the players apart. The main difference, it seemed, was the way they were financially rewarded (and in some cases even that was a thin distinction). Colin Cowdrey remembered batting with Hutton in a Test match on this tour and finding batting particularly hard going. 'Ay, and what's more you're not getting paid for it, are you?' said Hutton.

In Hutton, English cricket turned to a man steeped in the bitter past. He was in particular resentful of some of the accommodations made towards England's opponents, such as the post-war decision to permit a second new ball after just 55 overs, to the obvious advantage of his great tormentors, Ray Lindwall and Keith Miller. Like Douglas Jardine, Hutton felt that only by applying body and soul to the task could he hope to accomplish his mission. 'He became convinced that successful cricket was a business requiring as much study and concentration and devising as any other successful business,' Jim Kilburn wrote. 'Without becoming arrogant he lost tolerance towards cricketers not prepared to follow his own single-minded devotion.'

Relations between England and Australia had been largely cool since Hammond and Bradman crossed swords in Brisbane in 1946; when the youthful David Sheppard joined the 1950-51 tour, he was asked by a senior colleague, 'Do you think you can learn to hate these Australians for the next six months?' Hutton did nothing as captain to change this mood; indeed, he actively encouraged his players not to fraternise with the enemy after close of play, instructions that to his annoyance were ignored by Bedser in Australia and Trueman in West Indies. On the tour of the Caribbean, Evans said his captain's attitude was: 'We've got to do 'em. You mustn't speak to 'em on or off the field.'

Hutton handled his players adroitly, especially fast bowlers whom he saw as the means to extract revenge on Australia for their victories under Lindwall and Miller, but there was little room for sentiment. Bedser was Hutton's champion bowler in 1953, when he took what was then a record 39 wickets by an England bowler in a series, but he was unceremoniously dropped in Australia in 1954-55, Hutton being too preoccupied with the impending battle to break the news to him with the solicitous words Bedser deserved. Bedser outlined why he preferred to play under Freddie Brown, describing him as, 'straight, honest, flexible (an admirable trait in a captain), a man's man and a first-rate captain and leader,' before adding: 'Look at Freddie Brown on the field and you could almost read his thought processes ... Look at Len Hutton to try and read his thoughts, and you were seldom the wiser.'

But Hutton was right: he was convinced of Tyson's capabilities in Australia after Neil Harvey took off his pad to rub his leg after being hit by Tyson during an early match against New South Wales, and stuck with his raw pace even after he had a poor opening Test. Tyson, having reduced his run-up without sacrificing pace but gaining accuracy, proved the chief destroyer of an Australian batting line-up that displayed genuine signs of fear. He also won for England the first Test of May's reign as captain against South Africa at Trent Bridge. During this time Tyson, wearing sturdy bowling boots modelled on those used by Harold Larwood, bowled as fast as any England bowler has ever done, but fitness issues contributed to him appearing only

sporadically thereafter.* Neville Cardus described Hutton's preference of Tyson over Bedser as exhibiting 'a firm-mindedness and
shrewdness never excelled by any other captain'.

Hutton sought control through cautious batting and a funereal
over-rate that helped preserve his fast bowlers in the heat. During
England's victory in Sydney which began the turnaround in the series,
Hutton's pace attack bowled in a five-hour day 54 eight-ball overs,
which equates to 72 six-ball overs – barely tardy by today's standards
but shockingly low for the period. 'The business of waiting for what
seemed like hours for every delivery, slowed the game down in an
astonishing and, at times, boring manner,' wrote Richie Benaud,
one of the Australian players. The crowd booed its disapproval but
Benaud himself admired Hutton's methods, describing him as 'one
of the most efficient captains I have seen'. Colin Cowdrey – making
his first tour with England and a professed admirer of a man who
took him under his wing after Cowdrey discovered early in the
tour that his father had died – also defended his captain in an autobiography written in 1976: 'He was accused of keeping a brake on
the game with a slow over-rate but no captain, before or since, could
have handled his bowling better or set his fields more effectively ...
he was manipulating everything as though playing a very tight and
ruthless game of chess.'

Defensive batting was fundamental to England's victory over
Australia in 1953, when they scored at a collective strike-rate of 33
runs per 100 balls, which plunged to 24 during the match in Leeds.
The draw they secured there to keep alive hopes of regaining the
Ashes also required blatant time-wasting in the closing stages when
they got through only 12 overs in the final 45 minutes (again,
slow for the day, but typical today), narrowly managing to thwart
Australia's run-chase. Six of these overs were bowled by Trevor

---

* There were claims in the Australian press, which were officially denied, that the
Melbourne pitch during the third Test during the 1954-55 series was illegally watered
on the rest day, helping to bind a cracked surface. Tyson concurred: 'Black patches, not
previously apparent, were visible on the wicket and its surrounds. The wicket was soft! It
had been watered.' But by the time Australia batted last the surface nevertheless behaved
treacherously. Australia were all out for 111, Tyson taking seven for 27.

Bailey, operating off his long run to use up more time and deliberately aiming on or outside leg stump. Hutton was nevertheless cheered to the rafters when England won the final Test at The Oval to beat Australia in a series for the first time in 19 years. The public and press was less tolerant when such tactics failed, and Hutton's team came in for heavy criticism when they lost the first two Tests in the West Indies, in the second of which in Barbados they advanced their first-innings score on one day by only 128 in 114 overs.

Bailey resorted to bowling negatively again in the West Indies and earned a sharp rebuke from headquarters. Norman Preston, editor of *Wisden*, lambasted Hutton for returning to 'the ultra-cautious policy that he showed and was condemned for when he first captained England in 1952 against India . . . I feel certain that Hutton's anxiety about his fellow batsmen would disappear if he would encourage them to play their natural game, particularly by his own example. In any case it would be far better to lose playing attractive cricket than go down the way England did at Kingston and Bridgetown.' In fact, some of Hutton's players actively urged their captain to let them try a more attacking approach in the second innings in Bridgetown, among them Compton, who termed the earlier approach 'cricket in handcuffs'. Tom Graveney was by nature a free-flowing player and, chastised by his captain for playing in too relaxed a fashion against Australia at Lord's in 1953, became one of the chief culprits in the Barbados go-slow; he had a distaste for grafting against tighter bowling and fielding and never quite came to terms with the demands of playing under Hutton or May. He was rarely sure of his place in the team or the batting order.

The criticism Hutton received for his tactics in the West Indies left him with little warmth for the reporters who accompanied the tour, and in his report to Lord's he said of them: 'Their presence at times is very embarrassing, particularly the odd type who is working on sensational lines . . . it would be better if the press and players could travel and live separately.' He also said: 'I am sure the press has an effect on players, particularly the young ones who play for counties with a small press following.' However, several months later he handled the media to skilful advantage in his first press conference in Australia, given on board ship in Fremantle and attended by 60 or 70.

'He played it so superbly that his character dominated the whole room,' wrote Cowdrey, who slipped in at the back of the gathering. 'The Australian press, I suspect, were expecting a lot of bravado, even bombast. They received the opposite. When they phrased a question to bring a head-on collision Hutton sat there, smiling slightly, turning the words over and over in his mind. Sometimes the pauses lasted fully 30 seconds ... When the answer came it would be shrewd, pointed and dryly witty ... It was a brilliant achievement. He took the wind out of their sails with almost every reply. He had the whole room poised, waiting for his next answer, and when the answer came it told them nothing at all.' Few if any previous England captains had attempted to exploit the media; amateur leaders may have felt little need to justify themselves, or perhaps that justifying themselves might be too hard. Hutton, however, was in a different position and was happy to lower expectations. 'His idea, I suspect, was to play the part of the humble, unsophisticated cricket professional,' Cowdrey added. 'It probably required a good deal of nervous energy that he could not spare when the Test series got underway.'

Hutton was a hard man to fathom but he commanded the respect of his players by dint of his own performances and his certainty of touch as a strategist. As Cowdrey said, 'His streak of isolationism ... may have made him the great captain he was.' In return, Hutton backed his players, sometimes to a fault. Reg Hayter, writing in *Wisden* of the West Indies tour that was laced with controversial incidents, felt he was too lenient: 'He showed reluctance to take what at times appeared to be necessary corrective action with the more headstrong.' Compton, Evans and Graveney might all have been censured for various acts of indiscipline on or off the field, and Hutton delivered some harsh words about Johnny Wardle in his report ('Wardle showed jealousy, bitterness and envy at times, which was most embarrassing for me and for several other members of the team'), but only Fred Trueman, making his first Test tour, was actually punished. Hutton recommended Trueman's £50 tour bonus be withheld, informing Lord's that, 'Trueman gave me much concern and until a big improvement is made in his general conduct and cricket manners I do not think he is suitable for MCC tours', although he went on to add, 'ultimately I think something can be done with him under capable leadership.' Trueman was made to wait until 1958–59 to tour with England again while Wardle went to Australia the next winter.

In effectively ruling Trueman out of Australia, Hutton was hurting his own plans to retain the Ashes through pace bowling, because Trueman – armed, in Hutton's own phrase, with shoulders like a battleship – had shown from the moment he entered Test cricket in 1952 in Hutton's first series as captain that he possessed rare talent. In the second innings of his debut match, India lost their first four wickets in 14 balls without a run on the board, three of them to Trueman, and in his third match he took eight for 31 at Old Trafford. This was like rain on parched earth for an England team that had been without a bowler of genuine pace since the war, so much so that Bill Edrich, charging in off 11 paces for a few overs, had occasionally been used as a new-ball proxy.

However, Hutton may have felt that Trueman's immature and volatile conduct in the Caribbean gave him little alternative. Trueman had broken the arm of the legendary George Headley in a warm-up match in Jamaica and then the jaw of Wilf Ferguson, a Trinidad tailender, after deliberately stepping through the crease; in both instances he showed no immediate remorse or concern for the welfare of the stricken batsmen. The most damaging incident to Trueman's cause was when he allegedly racially abused umpire Cecil Kippins during a match against British Guiana (now Guyana) during a spell of bowling in which he was denied a number of lbw verdicts. Trueman's protestations of innocence fell on deaf ears but in an extraordinary retraction many years later Kippins stated that he wrongly identified Trueman and the bowler at fault was actually Wardle. Kippins did not correct his error at the time because he had fallen out with Hutton, who was more interested in taking issue about rejected lbws than anything his bowlers had said. (After the game, Hutton blocked Kippins from standing in the Georgetown Test.)

Hutton's methods aroused concern in the corridors of

power – concerns relentlessly articulated by EW Swanton in the *Daily Telegraph* – and when he was reappointed captain for the summer of 1955, he was told by chairman of selectors Gubby Allen to improve England's over-rate, which at 14.7 per hour had fallen well short of Australia's 19.6 the previous winter. The message was also sent out that players risked being dropped if they scored slowly. In the event, Hutton was afflicted in the early weeks of the season with lumbago and withdrew from the first Test against South Africa before announcing his retirement a few weeks later, resulting in Peter May's rapid elevation to the captaincy. Invited by Allen to take over the side on the Saturday, May was leading out England at Trent Bridge on the Thursday, although precise details of the handover are disputed. 'Gubby says that he also made it a condition that I stepped up the over-rate, but I do not remember that,' May stated. Allen's claim may have been designed to cover his own back as England, under May, were to play every bit as cautiously as they had under Hutton, and insomuch as he kept reappointing him – Allen remained chairman of selectors throughout May's reign – he allowed him to continue doing so. Colin Cowdrey, writing in 1976, thought that May 'became fully captain of England as perhaps only Don Bradman had been captain of a Test team since the war.'

May grew up in a tough school, at Surrey under Stuart Surridge, who led the county to the first five of their seven consecutive championships between 1952 and 1956 before May took over, as well as under Hutton with England. Surridge was a more demonstrative character than Hutton but was driven by a similarly competitive urge and in both environments the most exacting standards were demanded. May chastised Don Smith for walking, rather than waiting for the umpire's decision, during his debut Test at Lord's in 1957. May was, with the odd notable exception, popular with his players because, as Trueman once said, 'There was no, "us and them". In the team he was unmistakably one of us'; but if he felt they had let him down May could be unforgiving.

These sentiments were echoed by Doug Insole: 'He never forgives anybody who lets him down, but returns with interest the loyalty of those who do their darnedest for him.' One of May's rare errors in diplomacy was accusing to his face Jim Laker, Surrey and England's best spinner, of not trying during a county match in 1958, which led Laker to contemplate not touring Australia the following winter under a captain who appeared not to trust him. ('There was no doubt in my mind that he meant precisely what he said,' Laker said.) Eventually, without formally apologising, May indicated that his words were not meant to be malicious, and Laker agreed to tour, but the bitterness lingered, contaminating the tour, partly because Laker on the eve of departure announced his intention to retire once the tour was over. Laker subsequently published a book, *Over to Me*, in which he aired various grievances, leading to his MCC honorary membership being withdrawn.

Frank Tyson accused May of lacking the common touch in his dealings with his men off the field. 'Peter, at his best, combined the drive of Surridge with the tactical tightness of Hutton,' said Trevor Bailey, a senior England player under Hutton and May. 'Considerable personal charm tended to camouflage his toughness.' As a batsman, May shared Hutton's capacity for self-discipline and concentration; both men stood head and shoulders above regular team-mates in respect of runs and average during their time as captain. May was widely acknowledged as the most accomplished batsman in the world during the mid- to late 1950s.

May had no reason to feel, as Hutton had, that he was not socially qualified to lead England. Indeed, he had seemed destined for this position from his earliest days at Charterhouse, though by the time he reached Cambridge his prospects were temporarily eclipsed by David Sheppard, who was preferred by his peers as captain. Soon enough though, Sheppard's future prospects were muddied by his interest in the church. May's problem, come 1955 and Hutton's early retirement, was that his cricketing experience was still lacking; he was young and had to that point captained his county in only four championship matches. To compensate, he aimed to replicate his predecessor. 'He was a fervent admirer of Hutton and he tried to captain England in a similar style to Leonard ... rather cautious,' Laker recalled. Alan Gibson concurred: he thought May, 'crammed himself into the mould of Hutton', and that 'there was little observable difference in their approaches'; he estimated that, 'another couple of years without the responsibility might have given him [May] the confidence to be more adventurous.'

In May's first series in charge, England scored even more slowly than they had under Hutton during the 1953 Ashes, and their tempo fell still further on the tours May led to South Africa and Australia. Nor did their over-rate improve: there were spells in the West Indies in 1959-60 when it dipped below 14 an hour, slower even than with Hutton's side in Australia. At the start of the 1959 season – with a fresh start being sought following the disastrous defeat in Australia, and a line drawn under the career of the arch-blocker Trevor Bailey, soon to be followed by that of veteran keeper Godfrey Evans – Allen's selection committee implored May and his team to smarten up their game. 'The chairman informed him of the committee's determination to instil into the team, through the captain, a more aggressive approach to the game,' minutes of the meeting read. 'Particular reference was made to the number of overs bowled per hour, fielding, and the tempo generally. In the light of Mr May's undertaking to do his best to achieve improvement in these departments of the game, he was invited to captain England for the whole series.' However, things only got worse, with delight at England recording the first series win in the Caribbean in their history tempered by the means of its accomplishment – under May in the first three Tests and Cowdrey in the last two after May's illness forced him to withdraw.

'The cricket was by no means of the highest standard and several controversial issues arose, but they served only to make the English players more resolute and determined,' Leslie Smith wrote in *Wisden*. 'The main points were time-wasting, short-pitched bowling and throwing ... they developed to such an extent that no longer could the Imperial Cricket Conference afford to ignore them. Time-wasting had been seen occasionally before, but never to such a concentrated or planned extent as in this series. England must take the biggest share of responsibility, for after winning the second Test they realised that only under exceptional circumstances would they repeat the victory ... Field-placings reached a fine art ... and by bowling to a large extent outside the off-stump to a cleverly placed field the England bowlers, particularly the spinners, managed to contain all the West Indies batsmen ... Such bowling and fielding tactics were legitimate even if they did not provide much interest for the spectators.' May caused further ill-feeling when, against convention, he denied Rohan Kanhai a runner during the third Test.*

May's most celebrated innings was also contentious in its methods. His unbeaten 285 spanned ten hours against West Indies in 1957, for most of which time he was accompanied by Colin Cowdrey in what remains at 411 the highest partnership for England in Tests, and was fashioned in response to the threat posed by Sonny Ramadhin, the spinner who with a fast arm and no discernible change of action could spin the ball either way. Ramadhin had enjoyed great success in England in 1950 and began the 1957 series ominously by capturing seven wickets in the first innings in Birmingham. When May and Cowdrey came together on the fourth morning of the game, England, 288 behind, were facing imminent defeat at 113 for three, with Ramadhin having claimed two further scalps.

Fortunately, the rest day had allowed time for reflection and May, in consultation with Cowdrey and Wilf Wooller, one of the selectors, who had noticed Ramadhin was bowling his leg-break slightly higher and slower, devised a plan to get well forward when Ramadhin came over the wicket, as he preferred to, and play him as an off-spinner. Crucially, with the lbw law as it was then constituted, a batsman could only be lbw to balls that struck the pad in line with the stumps, even if the batsman was not attempting a shot, so provided May and Cowdrey got their front leg far enough forward and met the ball outside the line of off stump they were at little risk of being given out. Even if they were struck in line, the ball still had

---

* After the controversies of the 1953-54 tour, Peter May and Walter Robins, the tour manager, sought to maintain good relations with the press in 1959-60 and in his tour report May judged that the team and the press had built up a happy relationship 'with the notable exception of Mr EW Swanton'. May went on: 'I regret to say that he is liable to interfere with the running of MCC tours. This I think is most undesirable and at times most embarrassing to the captain and vice-captain. I feel it would be an excellent thing for MCC to make this abundantly clear to Mr Swanton.' According to Doug Insole, his vice-captain, May was also 'courtesy and co-operation personified' in his dealings with the press in South Africa in 1956-57, although again Swanton was an ignoble exception, being ostracised by the team for his persistent and virulent criticism.

so far to travel that an umpire was unlikely to give the batsman out and to Ramadhin's frustration umpires Charlie Elliott and Emrys Davies turned down his appeals him time after time. 'Colin kicked him [Ramadhin] to death,' said Tom Graveney, England's 12th man. 'He never tried to play him with the bat.'

Although the partnership saved the game (and in fact nearly set up a win as West Indies lost seven wickets before the end) and was widely feted in English circles, it represented a further negation of the game and led to widespread imitation. Ramadhin found his bowling being kicked away for the rest of the tour and was so disenchanted that he refused to tour when West Indies returned in 1963. Eventually, after a short period of experimentation, the ICC agreed in 1971 to the parameters of the lbw law being broadened to permit batsmen to be given out lbw if they were not attempting a shot to balls pitching outside off stump, or even hitting their bodies outside the line of off stump. This change was to have a big impact on eradicating negative play.

EM Wellings, writing in 1963, surveyed the manner of England's defeats to Australia in 1958–59 and 1961 under Peter May. 'English cricket had settled into a depressing groove. Cricket thinking had become negative. It was obsessed by defensive considerations. Four years ago England had played miserably negative cricket throughout Australia, emerged with a dismal playing record and left England's cricketing reputation in shreds. Nothing was done at home two years later to put things right.'

The loss to Australia at Manchester in the fourth Test of the 1961 series encapsulated English shortcomings, as the task of scoring 256 runs at a rate of 3.3 per over, as they had to do if they were to regain the Ashes, proved beyond a team conditioned to putting defence first. A magnificent innings of 76 in 84 minutes from Ted Dexter kept them in the hunt but they were eventually denied by Richie Benaud going round the wicket and aiming at the bowler's footmarks (reckoned to be chiefly those of Trueman, who was dropped for the next match in punishment). Benaud's tactics were not then as common as they later became and were rightly regarded as a defensive ploy designed to frustrate England's progress. In fact, he quickly dismissed

Dexter, bowled May behind his legs rashly attempting to sweep his second ball, and took two further wickets in 20 minutes before tea. Unable to regroup, England lost with 20 minutes remaining.

That England won 11 out of 23 Tests under Hutton and 20 out of 41 under May was in large part due to an array of exceptionally good bowlers – more than could be accommodated at one time, including the best all-rounder the team had had since Wilfred Rhodes (setting aside Walter Hammond as a batsman who bowled on occasions) in Trevor Bailey – operating on sporting pitches at home that Bill Bowes, the former England fast bowler, writing in 1959 condemned as making 'all international games in England a near farce'. High-scoring games on doped pitches became a distant memory. May himself, in reflecting on the quality of the bowling at his disposal and the supposed 'golden age' English cricket enjoyed in the 1950s, regretted 'there was no such abundance of Test-class batsmen and especially opening batsmen'.

Between Hutton and Washbrook last opening in tandem in 1951 and Geoff Boycott and John Edrich opening together regularly in the late 1960s, no pair of England openers posted more than two century stands, and a bewildering array of different combinations was tried – 19 alone during May's 41 Tests in charge. Peter Richardson, who opened most often for England between Hutton and Boycott, had 12 opening partners. Cowdrey himself might have provided a solution as he was technically good against pace bowling and in an era before helmets he repeatedly showed his courage against the likes of Wes Hall and Charlie Griffith (and would do so again against Dennis Lillee and Jeff Thomson when he was recalled to the Test side in his forties wearing an improvised chest guard to protect him from the numerous blows he took in his determination to stay in line), but he was a reluctant convert and generally batted in the middle order. Lancashire left-hander Geoff Pullar was pressed-ganged into service on Washbrook's recommendation, never having opened before in serious cricket, and proved a success for four years before injury and illness forced him out of the side, for what proved to be for good, at the age of 27.

This was a sharp difference from the immediate post-war period when numerous openers scored heavily in county cricket because, according to Doug Insole, 'there was not a fast bowler in England'. Insole added: 'England's lack of success against the Australian speed attack was hardly surprising when one considers that our batsmen were never obliged to face bowling of anything like the same speed in county cricket.' Six of the batsmen taken to Australia in 1950-51 were regular county openers but only two were when the side went there in 1954-55, by which time the balance of power had shifted.

England's shortage of Test-class bowlers in the immediate post-war period was in part a consequence of a new generation needing time to learn their skills. Alec Bedser, who had briefly appeared in first-class cricket before the war and was 27 when England resumed playing Tests, nobly carried the attack well into the 1950s but he wanted for support: he opened the bowling with 15 different partners in 51 appearances. Operating off a short run-up, Bedser concentrated on swinging the ball into the right-hander late, or cutting it away off the pitch, a method that worked better at home than abroad. His style echoed that of Maurice Tate and, like Tate, he was axed during a tour of Australia when faster options were finally available. Frank Tyson and Brian Statham did not move the ball in the air like Bedser but they had the speed and, in Statham's case, the relentless accuracy to pose problems. Tyson struggled for fitness and rhythm and his Test career was only short-lived but Statham, lean and lithe, proved unusually durable, playing in 70 Test matches, more than any England fast bowler until Bob Willis beat that tally in 1982.

In 1957, Statham settled into a regular new-ball partnership with the rehabilitated Trueman that lasted for most of the next six years. By studying the methods of Lindwall, Trueman developed into a sophisticated bowler who could pitch the ball up and swing it away late at a time when inswing was the vogue; he could also bowl off-cutters, which at the suggestion of May he used to win a Test match against Australia at Leeds in 1961. Trueman thus did more with the ball than Statham, and was perhaps marginally the more dangerous, but Statham was the more accurate and controlled, and nipped the ball back in at waspish pace. According to Tyson, Statham could calibrate the extent to which he seamed the ball off the pitch. They were an ideal combination. In Jim Kilburn's words, 'Statham obliterates opposing batting like the inexorable flood tide; Trueman shatters by tempest.' Bedser had been the first England bowler to 200 wickets but Trueman was the first to both 250 and 300; by 1965, Trueman, Statham and Bedser were with Richie Benaud among the four greatest wicket-takers in Test history. Among long-serving England new-ball pairs, Trueman and Statham are rivalled only by Willis and Ian Botham, and James Anderson and Stuart Broad.

Even though he had been struck by the difficulties into which the Australian batsmen got when they were caught on turning pitches during the 1953 series, by Laker and Wardle at Old Trafford and Laker and Lock at The Oval, Hutton saw only a limited role for spin in Australia in 1954-55 and both Laker and Lock were left at home. However, he did have with him Bob Appleyard, a Yorkshire team-mate who had only recently recovered from tuberculosis and the removal of a lung, and who could bowl both seam and swing or off-spin. Appleyard deployed flight and variations in pace to take 11 wickets in the series, all of them top-six batsmen, at 20.36 apiece. 'Sometimes he was like Alec Bedser, sometimes like Jim Laker,' Wardle said. Ray Illingworth rated him higher than Laker: 'He had a bigger heart.' Sadly, injuries contributed to him playing only two further Tests on his return home.*

All these bowlers were made even better by having behind the stumps Godfrey Evans, a wicketkeeper of rare energy, who obviously enjoyed Test cricket and was unfazed by his occasional errors. 'Godfrey Evans behind the stumps was worth two ordinary mortals,' Tyson wrote. 'He expected everyone to give to the game what he himself gave – a supercharged everything. He was more than the stumper of the side: he was the chief whip of the party ... In a Test match, his whole heart was on the field and in his keeping.' Evans expanded the scope of what was possible for a wicketkeeper, covering ground over a wide arc and pulling off some brilliant catches down the leg side, including one off the left-handed Neil Harvey at Melbourne in 1954 which Tyson, the bowler, felt decided the series.

---

* Before playing for England, Appleyard overcame extraordinary adversity beyond his illness. On the outbreak of war in 1939, he returned home from a stay with his grandmother to find his father had gassed himself, Appleyard's stepmother and his two half-sisters.

By standing up to the stumps, Evans made Bedser bowl the fuller length that was required if he was to be at his most dangerous; the price was countless bruises to arms and chest. Evans was not infallible, and his mistakes cost England victory at Headingley in 1948 which contributed to him losing his place in South Africa the following winter, and his fondness for partying with Compton and Edrich was sometimes frowned upon, but he was England's preferred choice of keeper for 13 years during which he missed only 19 out of 110 Tests.*

It was only once Hutton gave way to May that spin started to feature more consistently in England's plans. Laker, who took a long time to shake off being hit out of the attack in the Headingley Test of 1948 and to Hutton's eye retained an inferiority complex, became a master of flight and accuracy. By turning the ball into the right-hander with an array of short legs lying in wait, he gave Australia no respite in 1956 when he took 46 wickets in five Tests, including his world-record haul at Old Trafford. According to Insole, Laker never bowled badly in his last four or five years playing for England and 'tamed the best attacking batsmen in the world on perfect wickets ... [though] he was too frightened of being hit'. Like Laker, the aggressive, attacking left-armer Lock was more dangerous on tailored home pitches than overseas, but in Wardle, difficult character though he may have been, England possessed someone who could bowl both orthodox left-arm spin as well as wrist spin and take advantage of the bouncier pitches of Australia and South Africa. Wardle actually averaged slightly less in Tests overseas than he did in England. Lock was also one of the best close fielders England have ever had, taking 59 catches in 49 matches.

For home Tests, the selectors were especially spoilt for choice when it came to pace bowlers. 'We certainly had the bowlers, especially for damp English summers and unpredictable pitches,' May wrote. 'Some of our longest selection committee meetings owed their length to painful decisions which had to be made to leave out bowlers of proven class just because others might be more effective on the type

---

* One of Evans's most remarkable efforts was batting with a fractured finger in plaster, and scoring a hard-hitting 36, in a bid to save the Old Trafford Test of 1955; South Africa won with three minutes to spare.

of pitch expected, or were thought to be fitter or in better form.' Cowdrey wondered whether England might not have sometimes been better backing the new breed of seam bowlers that developed on green English pitches. 'By unshakeable tradition fast bowlers picked for Test matches are genuinely fast,' he wrote. 'Trueman and Statham were automatically selected for Test matches at Lord's when they were not automatically the bowlers best suited to the conditions. Lord's during those years was a seamer's paradise and had England picked [Les] Jackson of Derbyshire . . . plus [Derek] Shackleton of Hampshire and [Tom] Cartwright of Warwickshire, we would have been more successful . . . The trouble was that we never had the courage to come to terms with the power of seam bowling.'

## Longest Unbeaten Home Runs

| Team | Period | Played | Won | Lost | Drawn |
|------|--------|--------|-----|------|-------|
| Pakistan | 1980-86 | 26 | 14 | 0 | 12 |
| Australia | 2003-08 | 25 | 22 | 0 | 3 |
| West Indies | 1978-88 | 25 | 15 | 0 | 10 |
| England | 1956-61 | 24 | 17 | 0 | 7 |
| Australia | 1999-2002 | 22 | 19 | 0 | 3 |
| England | 1921-30 | 21 | 10 | 0 | 11 |

## England's Captains 1947-75

England's scoring-rate in the 1950s was, at 2.23 runs per over, their lowest in any decade of Test cricket. Their opponents were little more dynamic, scoring at 2.31 per over, the lowest recorded against England's bowlers in any decade since the 1880s. Len Hutton and Peter May's teams were among the slowest scorers in England's history and all the slowest teams come from the period between 1947 and 1975.

| Captain | Period | P | W | L | D | Runs per over |
|---------|--------|----|----|----|----|------|
| L Hutton | 1952-55 | 23 | 11 | 4 | 8 | 2.17 |
| PBH May | 1955-61 | 41 | 20 | 10 | 11 | 2.26 |
| NWD Yardley | 1947-50 | 14 | 4 | 7 | 3 | 2.28 |
| FR Brown | 1949-51 | 15 | 5 | 6 | 4 | 2.42 |
| R Illingworth | 1969-73 | 31 | 12 | 5 | 14 | 2.47 |
| MJK Smith | 1964-66 | 25 | 5 | 3 | 17 | 2.48 |
| MH Denness | 1974-75 | 19 | 6 | 5 | 8 | 2.49 |
| MC Cowdrey | 1959-69 | 27 | 8 | 4 | 15 | 2.52 |

*Minimum: 12 Tests*

## Bowlers With Best Home Records

Three of the seven lowest averages recorded by Test match bowlers on home soil were achieved by England players in England during the period between 1948 and 1965.

| Bowler | Country | Period | Tests | Wickets | Ave | Ave elsewhere |
|--------|---------|--------|-------|---------|-----|------|
| JC Laker | England | 1948-58 | 31 | 135 | 18.7 | 27.1 |
| K Rabada | South Africa | 2011-19 | 21 | 119 | 18.4 | 28.7 |
| VD Philander | South Africa | 2011-19 | 31 | 135 | 18.7 | 27.1 |
| Imran Khan | Pakistan | 1976-92 | 38 | 163 | 19.2 | 25.8 |
| GAR Lock | England | 1952-63 | 28 | 104 | 19.5 | 34.6 |
| M Muralitharan | Sri Lanka | 1992-2010 | 73 | 493 | 19.6 | 27.8 |
| Ravindra Jadeja | India | 2012-18 | 28 | 144 | 19.7 | 35.6. |
| FS Trueman | England | 1952-65 | 47 | 229 | 20.0 | 26.1 |

*Minimum: 100 wickets; to 13 February 2019*

# CHAPTER 22

# Selectors: Too Close or Not Close Enough?

### Basil D'Oliveira and the need for men of good character

Freddie Brown did much to help England's post-war recovery. He was not a player of the first rank but without his energetic and perpetually optimistic leadership Australia's superiority and the emergence of West Indies as a serious force might easily have swamped English spirits. A brusque, plain-speaking manner that served well in war-time service did not work to the benefit of every player who served under him – he should have done more as captain to look after the young Brian Close in Australia in 1950-51, and spent less time as manager in Australia eight years later insisting on the players calling Peter May, 'Mr May' or 'Skipper' – but he laid some of the ground for the success under Hutton and May.* However, Brown's judgement let him down when as chairman of

* Close was only 19 years old when he was chosen with Brown's support to tour Australia, but after being dropped following a poor performance in the second Test in Melbourne he was left an isolated figure. He wrote home to a close friend: 'My brain seems to be muzzy and keeps wandering into all kinds of thoughts and my nerves are on edge. Oh, to hell with it all, I just feel like doing away with myself.'

selectors in 1953, and in what he had already declared would be his final season in first-class cricket at the age of 42, he picked himself for the second Test of the series at Lord's, the only time a chairman has ever done this.

The reasons were twofold and neither was satisfactory. One was that the leg-breaks Brown occasionally dispensed for Northamptonshire – he sometimes bowled medium-pace out-swingers – would serve England better than those of a younger candidate. As Brown even in his pomp some 20 years earlier had never commanded a regular Test place, and was not a first-choice player when he was appointed captain in 1950, this seemed implausible. The second, not publicly articulated, was that as an amateur and former England captain Brown was a figure behind whom those who still doubted that a professional could do a good job of leading the country might rally. In an attempt to counter criticism, both Brown and Hutton issued statements saying they were happy with the situation, but few were satisfied. 'It seems rather sad that, as chairman of selectors, he [Brown] must accept a large share of the responsibility for his own selection – which is not the surest guarantee of confidence,' John Arlott wrote. 'Moreover, the presence of the chairman of selectors in the dressing-room must, inevitably, have some effect upon the relationship between the players and a captain who is being chosen from Test to Test . . . it seems a grudging attitude, emphasised, in many minds, by the fact that Hutton is a professional.' Jack Fingleton concurred: 'It is possible Hutton might not have been altogether confident of his future as England's captain when this Lord's Test began.'

Whatever he might have said publicly, Hutton was clearly perturbed. His back played up and he dropped several catches in Australia's first innings that he would normally have taken, damaging his hand in the process. (While he was off the field, Brown took command, waving his arms about with the bearing of a man accustomed to wielding power.) He recovered poise sufficiently to score a masterful century when England batted and to show who was actually in charge in the field by pointedly not consulting Brown (which would not have been so striking had they not worked well together in Australia when Brown was in charge). Hutton even dispatched him to field on the boundary. England held on for a draw thanks to the famous rearguard of Trevor Bailey and Willie Watson, but Australia's captain Lindsay Hassett might still have forced a win had he at the end targeted Brown with the pace of Ray Lindwall and Keith Miller which had troubled him in the first innings.* Brown dropped himself for the next Test in Manchester, and Douglas Jardine, in his capacity as newspaper pundit, speculated that Brown feared subjecting himself to the straight-speaking spectators of the north.

When the Ashes were next held in England in 1956, another selection panel – this time chaired by Gubby Allen – concluded after a defeat at Lord's that they too should take the unusual step of picking one of their own, recalling Cyril Washbrook of Lancashire after a five-year absence at the age of 41. His case was first pressed by fellow-selector Wilf Wooller, who was himself an active player with Glamorgan, and supported by two other members of the panel, Allen and Les Ames. However, Peter May, the captain, was unconvinced. As a young leader, May was eager to build a new team and he greeted the idea in lukewarm fashion. 'Surely the position is not as bad as all that,' he said. In the end, May was talked round by Allen and the decision was vindicated, Washbrook scoring 98 and sharing in a partnership of 187 with May which created the platform for an innings victory, but when Washbrook's selection was first announced it met with widespread criticism. Some termed it another 'FR Brown ploy'. Bruce Harris of the *Evening Standard* called for a ban on selectors choosing themselves.†

These incidents highlighted how delicate was the relationship

---

* Brown's apprehension when confronted by Lindwall and Miller did not prevent him from criticising England's batsmen for their reluctance during the series to get onto the front foot in an article in the next year's edition of *Wisden*.

† In fact, although no ban was introduced, no serving selector has played for England since Washbrook except for those captains who, as a consequence of their appointment, joined the selection panel. The only non-captains to be chosen to play for England while also working as formal (as opposed to co-opted) members of the selection panel were: CB Fry (three Tests, 1909), Jack White (one Test, 1930), Freddie Brown (one Test, 1953) and Cyril Washbrook (three Tests, 1956); only Brown was chairman. Wilfred Rhodes was a co-opted member of the panel when he was famously recalled for the final Test in 1926.

between captain and chairman of selectors, who at least until the arrival in the late 1980s of a full-time manager/head coach was the most powerful figure in the day-to-day running of the England team at home. They also emphasised how complicated things were when some selectors were themselves active players, which was common-place until the mid-1970s. Not that selection was ever easy – and when England lost, the selectors were inevitably targets of public opprobrium. 'Selectors in the natural order of things are the anvil for the hammer of every critic,' said Alec Bedser, England's longest-serving chairman of selectors.

One generally accepted principle of selection was that the cap-tain should where possible go onto the field with the players he wanted. A captain might not always know best, but his opinions deserved respect and must be factored into equations. After all, once a match starts it is down to him to deliver, and no one else. Wally Hammond, who as captain was co-opted onto the selection panel in the 1930s and 1940s, asserted that the captain 'has the last word about any doubtful name'. He cited as an example the case of Bob Wyatt holding out during a protracted selection meeting for the inclusion of Tommy Mitchell ahead of Walter Robins at Lord's in 1935, though it backfired on him as Wyatt and Mitchell failed to hit it off and England were beaten for the first time at home by South Africa. After the game, Pelham Warner, the chairman, received an unsigned telegram which read simply, 'Robins Robins Robins Robins Robins Robins'. But Warner should not have been blamed for allowing a captain his preferences.

Doug Insole, chairman from 1965 until 1968, wrote: 'It is clearly wrong to select any player who is completely unacceptable to him [the captain].' Alec Bedser, who succeeded him, echoed his words: 'The last thing selectors want to do is to send into the field a team which the captain does not feel reasonably happy with.' Bedser, though, was unsure that a captain should actually be a formal member of selection: 'Over the years I invariably found captains to be the most cautious members of the panel, particularly when it came to the introduction of young or new players.' Mike Brearley, who as captain only worked with Bedser, wrote: 'It was rare I didn't get what I wanted.' Keith Fletcher as manager did not agree with the non-selection of David Gower for the tour of Asia in 1992-93 or against Australia in 1993, when Gower's left-handedness would have been an asset against Shane Warne, whose dismissal of Mike Gatting with his first ball in Ashes Tests shocked the England dressing-room, but Fletcher's 'ingrained notion of selection' was that the captain – in this case Graham Gooch – should have the team he wanted. In hindsight, Fletcher conceded that he should have insisted on Gower's selection for India. On the same basis, Fletcher publicly supported Michael Atherton's decision to declare when Graeme Hick was two short of a maiden Ashes hundred at Sydney in 1994-95 even though he personally disagreed with it; Fletcher later described it as 'the worst decision Atherton made as captain in my time [as manager]'.

However, there have been times when a captain did not get the team he wanted. As we have seen, Archie MacLaren and Lord Hawke were heavily at odds in 1902 following their falling-out over arrangements for the 1901-02 tour, and they let their feud get in the way of picking the best team. Atherton and Ray Illingworth were similarly out of kilter in the early years of Atherton's reign as captain: Illingworth appeared to favour reverting to the old-school method of picking the best-performing players in county cricket, while Atherton wanted to keep faith with the younger, more promising players he already had alongside him in the Test team before Illingworth became chairman of selectors. Illingworth had secured the power of veto over the selection of individual players (though not the captain) and applied it more than once. Trevor Bayliss, head coach from 2015, when asked at the time of Joe Root's appointment as captain whether in his experience as a selector England captains tended to get their way, said: 'Most of the time if not 100 per cent of the time ... To my way of thinking, the captain is the one in charge. He's the guy out in the middle, the one that's got to direct the troops, and he's got to be comfortable with who he's got in the team and how he's going to use them.'

The chairman's role was tricky because he needed to be adviser but also master. In the first instance, the chairman and his panel generally selected the captain; as late as 1999, Nasser Hussain's appointment as captain was initiated by David Graveney, as chairman of selectors, in consultation with ECB chairman Lord MacLaurin. The chairman and his panel, too, were empowered to appoint and retain captains on a match-by-match or series-by-series basis. (This only formally ended with the introduction of central contracts in Hussain's time, although when Alec Stewart was appointed captain in 1998 he was given an initial term of 12 months.)

However, the chairman's own role was circumscribed inasmuch as the appointment of the captain required rubber-stamping from a higher authority to ensure the chosen man was 'the right type'. For a long time, this power of veto rested with MCC or its appointees on the Board of Control for Test Matches in England; subsequently, following the disbandment of the Board of Control in the late 1960s, it passed to a representative of whichever body wielded overall control of the professional game – now the England and Wales Cricket Board. When Ossie Wheatley blocked Mike Gatting's appointment as England captain in 1989 he did so in his capacity as chairman of the TCCB's cricket committee, although largely as a result of this incident the counties forced the veto to pass five years later to the higher authority of the TCCB (now ECB) chairman, who today approves the appointment of all England captains. In fact, since the advent in 2007 of a managing director of England cricket, his voice has counted for most: Hugh Morris was heavily involved in the departures of Kevin Pietersen and Peter Moores as captain and coach in 2009 and when Colin Graves, the ECB chairman since 2015, had concerns about Eoin Morgan captaining the white-ball teams he opted to leave the decision to Andrew Strauss.

The chairman of selectors was himself originally appointed by the Board of Control, as was his panel, which has varied in size from three to five full-time members.*

Once a captain was in place, the chairman's task became that of

---

* Between 1899 and 1937, the panel consisted of three full-time selectors (plus occasional co-opted members). Since 1938, it has consisted of three or four members except in 1994, 1996, 1998 and 1999 when there were five. In 2018, it was cut to three for the first time since 2007.

co-strategist, helping the captain assess pitch conditions and finalise his starting XI, and even being consulted about tactics during matches. This involvement occasionally strayed into controversial territory. After Australia won the Lord's Test of 1956 on a greentop, the pitches for the remaining games in the series at Headingley, Old Trafford and The Oval all to a striking extent favoured England's spinners Jim Laker and Tony Lock, and although Gubby Allen rejected Australian accusations that he was the chief culprit, the testimony of the Old Trafford groundsman Bert Flack implicated him as far as 'Laker's match' was concerned. On the eve of the game, Allen inspected the pitch and told Tommy Burrows, the Lancashire chairman, whose responsibility it was to oversee preparations, that he was not satisfied. Burrows relayed the message to Flack: 'The chairman wants more [grass] off. Take a little more off, Bert, and that'll please him.' When Allen had left, Flack said: 'That's stupid. The match won't last three days. The surface is not all that well-knit.' Things were little better the following year when West Indies toured, Clyde Walcott describing three of the five Test pitches as 'suspect', and in Allen's last year as chairman Australia were again unhappy at the state of a 'piebald' Leeds pitch on which Trueman twice bowled them out.*

Australians also scapegoated another chairman of selectors, David Graveney, when in 1997 there was a switch of pitches two weeks before the Headingley Test; the ECB's response to their formal complaint was that Graveney was merely kept informed of developments. What sometimes complicated matters was that the chairman might be a former England captain whose CV dwarfed that of the captain he was dealing with, and he had to resist the temptation to do what Lord Hawke, Freddie Brown and Ray Illingworth did and promote their own views at the expense of the men they were supposed to

---

* There was further controversy over the state of an English Test pitch when, during the Lord's Test of 1961, there were complaints of deliveries rising sharply from an infamous 'ridge' at the Nursery End of the pitch. 'Immediately the match ended MCC called in a team of experts to survey the pitch. They discovered several depressions and MCC stated that they would make an attempt to put things right before the start of 1962' (*Wisden*). In fact, the Lord's 'ridge' long remained a topic of debate even after the offending area was eventually dug up.

be helping. However, a chairman did have to be more mindful than the captain of wider considerations such as long-term planning. He also had to guard against overreacting in a crisis.*

Acknowledging a captain's views as important was one thing, but finding the best means of accommodating them was another. Captains have sometimes been made voting members of the selection panel for home Tests, as most recently happened between 1989 and 2002. At other times they have been informally consulted without wielding a vote, on the basis that this best protected their relationships with the players on whom they were passing judgement; this system has operated since the start of the 2003 season. An example of the pitfalls of a captain being directly involved in selection occurred when MCC members called a vote of no confidence in the selectors following the omission of David Gower, Jack Russell and Ian Salisbury from the 1992-93 tour of India and Sri Lanka; Graham Gooch, the captain, rather than Ted Dexter, the chairman, became the focal point of criticism.† (The motion was ultimately defeated.)

On the other hand, the problem with a captain not being a voting selector was that he was less likely to get his way, which was what happened when Darren Pattinson, a late call-up as cover, played in the Leeds Test of 2008 when Michael Vaughan, the captain, would have favoured Steve Harmison had he been able to get him in the original squad. (Vaughan denied reports that he favoured a recall for Simon Jones.) Vaughan's publicly expressed dissatisfaction led to a crisis meeting between himself and the chairman of selectors Geoff Miller. Though they did not formally wield a vote, recent England Test captains such as Andrew Strauss, Alastair Cook and Joe Root were in the habit of sitting in on some selection meetings, which hardly spared Cook widespread abuse on social media and elsewhere

---

* The focus was often on the relationship between captain and chairman of selectors. Less was heard about how well a captain got on with other selectors. Although Alec Bedser described Tony Greig as the best England captain he worked with during his chairmanship, Len Hutton, a member of Bedser's panel, found Greig too strident, and left the panel after the 1975 season in which Greig took over as captain.

† However, when Dexter's resignation as chairman was announced over the public address during the Edgbaston Test in August 1993, the crowd cheered.

when he was widely believed to have been party to the axeing of Kevin Pietersen from all England's sides in 2014, paying an even heavier price than Gooch had over the Gower issue.

In the days when captains did vote, the importance given their views was for a long time reflected in them being granted a casting vote (hence Gubby Allen's strenuous efforts to win round Peter May in 1956). This practice was in place by at least the 1920s and only ended in 1976 when Tony Greig as captain insisted on the selection of the 45-year-old Brian Close – the oldest man to be picked by England since Freddie Brown – as part of his general plan to pack the side with gritty, experienced batsmen against a West Indies side with a powerful pace attack. (John Edrich, David Steele, Chris Balderstone and Mike Brearley, all chosen that summer, were also highly seasoned players.) Alec Bedser, as chairman, felt a captain's short-term wishes conflicted with his own long-term considerations and successfully – if questionably – argued for the veto to pass to him.*

Another key consideration was how closely involved with the game a selector should be. Should he be a well-placed player or a full-time observer? The advantage of an active player was that he was equipped with first-hand knowledge of candidates, even at the risk of entrenched friendships or animosities colouring his views. A retired player could watch more widely and perhaps assess more impartially and dispassionately, but he risked being in less direct contact with events; if retired, how long retired should he be? Could he have a coaching or administrative role at a county club and still remain independent? These issues have aroused heated debate, but the historical trend has seen a shift from selectors-as-players towards selectors-as-observers so that – apart from England captains who joined selection panels by dint of their office, a practice which itself

---

* Steele, brought into the side at the age of 33 for the second Test against Australia in 1975 following Mike Denness's departure as captain, had gloriously vindicated his selection with 365 runs in three Tests batting at No. 3 against Dennis Lillee and Jeff Thomson. Grey-haired and bespectacled, and dubbed 'the bank clerk who went to war', Steele was named BBC Sports Personality of the Year. However, despite further displays of courage against West Indies, he was overlooked for the tour of India in 1976-77 because of a perceived weakness against spin and was not recalled even after Greig and others defected to Kerry Packer. He never played for England again.

formally stopped in 2003 – no active professional cricketer has served as full-time selector since Mike Gatting in 1998.

It took time for selectors to be even regarded as observers or scouts. The first official panel in 1899 established a pattern of selectors being almost exclusively drawn from the ranks of county captains. Though their clubs were sometimes geographically diverse, there was no guarantee that any of them would have seen certain candidates, and none of them, it seemed, was dispatched to watch a particular player. Information was gathered slowly via pavilion gossip and correspondence, and undoubtedly deserving players escaped notice. Little wonder that selection was so haphazard and erratic.

Charles Fry claimed that when he was asked to captain in 1912 he insisted on being appointed for the whole summer and working with two selectors – John Shuter and Henry Foster – who were not active players, perhaps because he wanted to protect his patch from rivals; he himself had been both selector and player in 1909 when Archie MacLaren was captain. The formula worked well inasmuch as England won the Triangular Tournament and Fry got his wish that the batting remained stable.* The previous year he had written in *Fry's Magazine* about the harmful effects on batsmen of inconsistent selection: 'A team which plays regularly together favours that easy and confident state of mind which is all so much to the good in batsmen ... [and] is more likely to bat up to the true individual form of its members than a virtually scratch team. England teams in England are at a disadvantage in this respect. But the worst disability under which they labour is that the batsmen feel that they are "playing for their places".' When England next played a home Test series in 1921, Foster, as chairman, was one of two members of the panel who were effectively retired players but the group's floundering merely led to calls for change in how England teams were chosen.

With Pelham Warner's appointment as chairman in 1926 the

---

* Shuter, the chairman, had played his last full season for Surrey in 1893, and Foster played only two late-season matches for Worcestershire in 1912. Fry claimed in his autobiography that they held just one initial meeting but this is unlikely; England called on 17 players in six Tests.

position passed to someone prepared to provide the thoroughness required. Having worked as a journalist since his retirement in 1920, Warner was used to watching cricket closely and assessing the merits of cricketers, and he applied the same principles to selection. In another significant departure, Peter Perrin, one of Warner's co-selectors, expressly took time off from captaining Essex to fulfil selection duties, something he was better able to do as selectors now received expenses. However, not until 1979 were selectors actually remunerated for their services, Alec Bedser as chairman being paid £2,500 and the others on the panel £20 per day. Until that point, therefore, for many years selection remained the preserve of those of financially independent means or who remained active as players. Selection was not a job, less still a career.* It was not until the mid-1990s that the panel was largely made up of full-time selectors.

Just as some professional cricketers became less deferential during the inter-war years, so criticism of selection became more pointed. Following England's home defeat to Australia the previous year, Sussex put forward a motion at a Board of Control meeting in March 1931 that the county captains, rather than MCC, should elect the subcommittee which appointed the selectors. The criticism of Henry Leveson Gower, Frank Mann and Jack White was of them 'not watching much'. They also provided another instance of a selection panel picking one of their own: White played in the Lord's Test.† In addition, Sussex may have been motivated by the mistreatment of their star batsman Duleepsinhji, whose omission from the England side after the first Test of the 1929 series against South Africa was suspected to have a racial dimension; he was subsequently overlooked for the tour of South Africa in 1930-31. Sussex's proposal was rejected but the whole panel was replaced: Warner and Perrin were recalled

---

* Among the first paid selectors was Charlie Elliott, still the only selector appointed largely by dint of his experience as an umpire. Elliott served as selector from 1975-81 having retired from 19 seasons of umpiring in 1974. He stood in 42 Tests.

† A favourite refrain then, as so often, was that the selectors were biased in favour of players based in the home counties; as late as 1988 Ray Illingworth accused the selection panel of not watching enough cricket north of Watford. There is some substance to the claims: of England's 80 Test captains, 42 played for the six south-east counties of Essex, Hampshire, Kent, Middlesex, Surrey and Sussex (see table on p.135).

and joined by Thomas Higson for a two-year term leading up to the 1932–33 Ashes tour. Duleepsinhji would have been a member of that tour but for illness.

Every panel from then until 1937 comprised only observer-selectors but, with England under pressure to regain the Ashes in 1938, Warner and Perrin were joined by two county captains, Brian Sellers of Yorkshire and Maurice Turnbull of Glamorgan, and after the Second World War active players, the majority of them county captains, featured strongly until 1953. (In 1951, all four selectors were fully engaged in playing first-class cricket, the only time this has happened.) This was partly out of necessity – post-war auster-ity left few former players with time to act as unpaid selectors, and Perrin and Turnbull had died – but the quality of decision-making was poor, notably in 1948 when Jack Holmes, the chairman, Johnny Clay and Walter Robins, in conjunction with Gubby Allen who attended all meetings in a non-voting advisory role, plus co-opted captain Norman Yardley, dropped Len Hutton for one Test in the belief that Hutton had developed a problem against Lindwall and Miller – displaying, according to Yardley, 'a fatal tendency to flash at rising balls outside the off stump'.

Their subsequent decision to leave out Doug Wright probably cost England the Leeds Test ('the lesson of that day remains for future selections; a leg-spinner is essential,' Yardley wrote). Some of the Australians said that Holmes's panel never picked more than seven players who they would have had in their best England XI; they were particularly contemptuous of Robins's judgement and worked him over with the short ball when he played for the Gentlemen against them late on the tour. Bob Wyatt, who served as a selector between 1950 and 1954, said he would have liked more intelligent people on the committee, though he exonerated Les Ames; 'there were certain people who didn't know enough about the game.' According to Alex Bannister of the *Daily Mail*, contact between MCC and the working press was minimal in the early post-war years: 'Selectors offered no public reasons for their decisions.' However, by 1952, when there were suspicions that information was being leaked to the media, an informal meeting between members of MCC and the press was held.

The decision regarding Hutton was an eyebrow-raiser in the Freddie Brown class. Hammond felt it highlighted the need on the panel for a professional in close contact with the game: 'What the selectors did not know, but every professional cricketer (and a good many other people) in the country knew quite well, was that Hutton had received a sharp knock on the hip-bone from [Bill] Johnston, which slowed his footwork and also made him loath to risk a second blow in the same place. Many batsmen would have retired [hurt] after getting that injury ... his courage cost him his place in the next Test.' Two years later Les Ames, who was nearing the end of his playing career at Kent, became the first professional appointed to a home selection panel; he served for eight of the next nine years and Gubby Allen rated him the best of the selectors he worked with during his seven years as chairman.

A more lasting pattern of rebuilding shaped around the cycle of Ashes matches began after the shock 4-0 defeat in Australia in 1958-59, England's heaviest since the defeat to Bradman's Invincibles. A clear-out of senior players began and Gubby Allen, chairman of selectors, announced a long-term plan to beat Australia when the sides next met in 1961. Allen's panel cast the net wide for the following winter's tour of the West Indies, initially picking a squad of 29 'possibles'. The reigns of subsequent chairmen, Walter Robins (1962-64) and Doug Insole (1965-68) – both of whom were incidentally from relatively modest backgrounds and educated at minor grammar schools in a further sign of the erosion of the game's old social order – were also designed to end with a home series against Australia, though neither was successful in regaining the Ashes.*

It was during this period that the distinction between amateur and professional players was finally scrapped in November 1962. It was not before time. The questionable status of many 'amateurs' – often employed by their county clubs who required them to do little or no work as 'assistant secretaries' or funded by local

---

* The practice of a chairman's term ending with a home Ashes series was sporadically adhered to subsequent to 1968: Alec Bedser stepped down after 1981, Ted Dexter resigned with one match remaining in 1993, and Geoff Miller retired after 2013.

businesses who only expected them to turn up when cricketing commitments allowed – was the cause of widespread disgruntlement among professionals. Now the issue acquired special urgency because England's batting was dominated by amateurs such as Colin Cowdrey, Ted Dexter, Peter May, Peter Richardson and Raman Subba Row, as well as all-rounder Trevor Bailey, all of whom toured Australia in 1958-59. MJK Smith, who had made his England debut at home during the 1958 season, was another who fell into the category.

A special committee on amateur status, dubbed the 'Star Chamber' and chaired by the Duke of Norfolk, considered several cases of dubious status which effectively led to Subba Row being forced out of the game (he played his final Test series in 1961, scoring a hundred on his last appearance against Australia) and Richardson turning professional. However, far from clearing up the issue, the committee's investigations merely highlighted the fragility of amateur status; even David Sheppard, who played for Sussex and England as an amateur, argued in favour of abolition. The truth was that precious few players could afford to be genuine amateurs. The issue was causing particular tensions within the Test team. 'It does little to improve the morale of a touring team when it is known that the amateurs may even receive more money in expenses than the professional earns in money, when tax has been deducted ... scarcely an amateur in the country can truthfully call himself financially independent of the game,' Frank Tyson, who also toured in 1958-59, wrote in 1961.

Tyson also felt that the England selectors gave preferential treatment to amateurs even when there was a former professional sitting on the selection panel. 'This amateur–professional apartheid does nothing but harm to any team and particularly to a touring side,' he said. 'It only makes team spirit all the more difficult to maintain.' The Advisory County Cricket Committee's ruling, subsequently endorsed by the MCC committee, met with popular approval. The *Daily Telegraph* condemned what had been a 'form of legalised deceit', and the *Daily Mail* welcomed the death of 'humbug and the need for petty deception'.

In another step towards modernisation, player-selectors also began to be phased out: those who did still play (Wilf Wooller, Willie Watson and Insole) were approaching retirement and took the field only occasionally, allowing them time to gather and process data. Ray Illingworth's name was put forward for selectorial duties after his sacking as captain in 1973 but was rejected, possibly because he was deemed to be too close to many of the England players. Insole, who served ten years from 1959 and 1968, said the aim was to watch all leading candidates before the first Test of the summer; thereafter a selector would be detailed to act as manager for each home Test, overseeing transport, hotel and practice arrangements, thereby lightening the load on the captain. Insole as chairman also strove to treat rejected players more humanely and inform them of their omission rather than let them discover their fate via the media, though this protocol was followed erratically until the 1990s.*

Insole was probably influenced by his own experiences as a player: for his Test debut at Trent Bridge in 1950, he was requested to turn up at 10.30am on the morning of the game, which he understandably thought 'quite extraordinary'; he reached Nottingham's railway station at 10pm the night before where he discovered Norman Yardley phoning for a batsman as there were injury worries about Len Hutton and Harold Gimblett; in the event John Dewes was summoned. When he next played a home Test, in 1955, Insole found things had improved sufficiently for him to be asked to turn up at 3pm the day before the game; at dinner that evening with the selectors, 'there was an immediate impression of being part of a team'.

Traditionally, for home Tests, players were informed of their selection through a letter of invitation from the chairman, and this continued into the 1980s, though in fact they often first heard the news on the radio. As late as the mid-1990s, players were learning of their call-ups from journalists before they had been notified by

---

* When Insole stepped down, in 1968, he was presented with a salver signed by all the players picked for England while he was chairman, organised by Colin Cowdrey. Insole described it as 'my most prized cricketing possession'.

official channels. On tour, the responsibility fell on the captain, manager or head coach, in which regard Mike Denness was reckoned to have fallen short when in the West Indies in 1973-74 Mike Hendrick learned of his omission for the Barbados Test from a reporter.

Since 1974, only three active county players – ex officio England captains aside – have served as selectors. Norman Gifford was 42 years old and in his last season at Worcestershire when he joined the panel in 1982, but withdrew the following year after moving to Warwickshire, where he revived his fortunes as a slow left-armer with 104 wickets in the season; he subsequently captained England in two one-day internationals in Sharjah in 1984-85.* Graham Gooch and Mike Gatting, while respectively playing for Essex and Middlesex, were appointed shortly after retiring from international cricket – Gooch in 1996 and Gatting in 1997; both stopped playing county cricket a year after joining the panel and continued their selection work.

Ray Illingworth, chairman of selectors, didn't like Gooch working as a selector in 1996 because Gooch could not go and watch players as Illingworth wanted; when a request was put in to Essex, asking for Gooch's release from playing duties to watch a match at Worcester, the county refused. Similarly, Illingworth felt David Graveney, a candidate for the panel in 1994, could not select while continuing to play for Durham: 'I honestly felt he could not see enough cricket to justify a place on the committee [as a current player].' Graveney joined the panel the following year after hanging up his boots as a player. Gooch and Gatting had been appointed through a ballot of constituent members of the TCCB – namely the 18 counties, MCC and Minor Counties – but were relieved of selection duties midway through the 1999 season by the England Management Advisory Committee after a panel of five selectors had wrestled unsuccessfully to produce a coherent strategy. The previous year head coach David Lloyd had stepped off the panel because he felt it was simply too large.

---

* Gifford also controversially chose himself at the age of 45, while serving as assistant manager, for an unofficial Test for England B against Sri Lanka in Kandy in 1985-86 despite instructions to play only if there was a shortage of players.

Insole was an early advocate of a full-time team manager running England affairs in conjunction with a panel of selectors, but it was 18 years after his chairmanship ended before this happened. The managerial post was originally offered to Ray Illingworth but his demand for full control over selection killed the deal; only then was Micky Stewart recruited for the winter of 1986-87. It was an initiative expedited by the fundamental weakness in the reign as chairman of Peter May, who was unwilling to devote as much time to the job as his predecessor Alec Bedser and who proved incapable of communicating clearly with press and players. At least three England captains during his time were removed without proper explanation, one of whom, Chris Cowdrey, was fined after complaining in print about his treatment. Cowdrey was even May's godson. The gulf between chairman and team was reinforced by Ian Botham's description of May and his panel as 'gin-swilling dodderers'. Finally, in November 1988, shortly after the cancellation of the India tour and to general relief, May resigned. No England cricketer was so feted as a player and so condemned as an administrator.

May's immediate successors as chairman were similarly big-name former captains in Ted Dexter and Illingworth (who again demanded special powers of control and was this time granted them) but they, like May, were accused of having been out of the game too long. Many players simply could not comprehend Dexter and his eccentricities. Gradually, the chairman's role was downgraded, and the method by which selection was conducted was overhauled, as first the head coach (as the manager was retitled) and then the director of England cricket – a post created in 2007 to oversee broad strategy – assumed many of the powers previously invested in him.* These included the power to appoint the captain: although officially the selectors initiated the process by making their recommendation,

---

* When David Lloyd, as the new head coach, joined the selection panel in 1996 he was surprised to find the meeting taking place 'over a nice dinner, with some bottles of decent wine'. Writing in 2000, he added: 'I'm told it has always been this way ... but at the time I still felt it was an inappropriate way to conduct the business of picking a team.' Subsequently, selection became a more businesslike affair. James Whitaker, who served more than ten years on the panel from 2007, said selection meetings were no-frills affairs without wine or dinner.

the director of cricket Andrew Strauss was the central figure in the appointment of Joe Root as England's Test captain in February 2017 (before being endorsed by the ECB chairman). The director of cricket also recruits the chairman of selectors. Perhaps as sop to his territory being trimmed by the arrival of a managing director, the chairman of selectors was in 2008 given a new title of national selector as well as a hefty pay rise. However, with Ed Smith's appointment as national selector in 2018, Strauss restored some of the old power to the role.

The introduction of central contracts in 2000 had limited the scope of the selection panel, whose work became more about talent identification, with specialists such as David Graveney (after he had been replaced as chairman of the full England selection panel) appointed to oversee the progress of England Under-19s and prospective England Lions players, and Mo Bobat acting as player identification lead at Loughborough. This process was taken to another level when a new panel was appointed in 2018 with Strauss demanding greater use of data analysis. One consequence of this was that it seemed less necessary that the selectors themselves had played at the highest level, although historically many successful selectors had not in any case played Test cricket.* Of the five men who served on England selection panels between 2014 and 2017, only two had played Test cricket and one of those, James Whitaker, played only once. Ed Smith, appointed in Whitaker's place, played three times for England.

Until modern times, the way England touring teams were chosen was more intricate than at home. Before MCC took control of organisation, the players were assembled by tour managements which varied from one tour to the next, and the captain in particular tended to handpick his men. Once MCC became involved, the club initially appointed its own selectors: the first Test team sent by

---

* A rare instance of the lack of Test experience among selectors becoming an issue occurred in 1974-75 when three of the four members of Alec Bedser's panel had not played for England (Ossie Wheatley, Brian Taylor and Jack Bond). England's heavy defeat in Australia that winter contributed to the recruitment of Len Hutton, Ken Barrington and Charlie Elliott, a former Test umpire.

MCC to Australia in 1903-04 was put together by a panel chaired by AG Steel, and several subsequent Test tours were arranged under the chairmanship of Lord Harris; neither ever chaired a formal panel of selectors for home Tests. Later, as Test cricket became a regular event home and away, MCC was content when it came to selecting touring parties to supplement the panel in operation at home (plus the elected tour captain) with some senior figures of its own in a consultative capacity. 'They did not as a rule give technical opinions,' EW Swanton wrote of MCC's appointees. 'They were present primarily to oversee the acceptability as tourists of those chosen.'

The MCC view was that, as the team was travelling under its flag, the club had an obligation to ensure that the players chosen upheld its reputation on and off the field – or, as Frederick Toone put it, tours were 'imperial enterprises' for which those selected needed to be 'men of good character'. For this reason, tour managers such as Toone also routinely sat in on the original pre-tour selection meeting, without formally wielding a vote. Once a tour was underway, discipline was imposed through a good-conduct bonus awarded only once the teams had returned home and captain and manager had filed their tour reports and recommendations. As we have seen, Fred Trueman was denied his bonus after a tour of West Indies in 1953-54. When on an A team tour of Pakistan in 1955-56, the MCC players 'ragged' a local umpire, the entire squad wrote a letter to Lord Alexander of Tunis, the club president, expressing regret that they had placed him 'in the unfortunate position of having to apologise in public for the conduct of an MCC team overseas'.

The sense that touring players needed vetting for what amounted to ambassadorial duty overseas survived MCC's replacement by the TCCB as the body responsible for the England team. AC Smith, the TCCB chief executive, sat in on the selection meeting for the West Indies tour of 1993-94 and, being famously anxious about information leaks, actually began the meeting by getting on all fours to search for bugging devices he feared might have been planted by the media. The following year Tim Lamb, Smith's successor, joined the five-man panel of selectors that had served at home when they met at the Copthorne hotel in Manchester to pick the team for Australia.

The practical impact of vetting could be profound. Bill Edrich – who had a history of partying while on international duty, receiving a written reprimand for his 'bohemian jollities' during a non-Test tour of India in 1937-38 and raising eyebrows over his conduct in Australia in 1946-47 – was not chosen for a tour of Australia following his nocturnal behaviour during a Test match against West Indies at Old Trafford in 1950: returning late to his room he inadvertently disturbed the chairman of selectors in the room next door. Similarly, MCC withdrew an invitation to Johnny Wardle to tour Australia in 1958-59 after he criticised in print among others his county committee and the club's autocratic captain Brian Sellers, following Yorkshire's announcement that they intended to release him. (Wardle's newspaper pieces, plus Laker's outspoken remarks in *Over to Me* which appeared in 1960, resulted in the Advisory County Cricket Committee and MCC looking into ways to tighten up the contracts of all first-class cricketers to prevent them writing or broadcasting anything detrimental to the game, and a clause to this effect was common in the tour contracts of England players in the years that followed.) Mike Brearley recounted being told of a time when the selectors decided not to include in any touring party two particular players together: 'As a pair, they had apparently behaved atrociously on a previous trip.'

As we have seen with Gubby Allen's intervention over the captaincy for Australia in 1962-63, when David Sheppard's anti-apartheid stance was deemed potentially awkward, what constituted a suitable tourist could be construed in many ways, although as a general rule it helped in terms of captaincy if you had gone to Oxford or Cambridge or, better still, were involved with MCC.* Allen also interceded in controversial fashion when he overrode the wishes of the selectors, including the captain Mike Denness, and

---

* Those chosen to captain major England Test tours while serving on the MCC committee included Henry Leveson Gower (1909-10), Pelham Warner (1911-12), Frank Mann (1922-23), Arthur Gilligan (1924-25), Percy Chapman (1930-31), Gubby Allen (1936-37 and 1947-48) and Peter May (1956-57 and 1958-59). RE Foster sat on the committee when he was invited to captain a tour of Australia in 1907-08 but declined for business reasons. Doug Insole was appointed to the MCC committee in 1956 and chosen as Peter May's vice-captain for the tour of South Africa later the same year.

blocked John Snow's selection for the 1974-75 Australia tour on the grounds of past misconduct, Snow having barged to the ground the India batsman Sunil Gavaskar during a Test match at Lord's in 1971. Snow had paid a price at the time, having been dropped for the next Test and made to apologise in writing to the chairman of the selectors and the secretary of the TCCB, but Allen did not think that sufficient when it came to an overseas tour.* Keith Fletcher described Snow's omission as 'a dreadful selectorial blunder' which allowed Australia to prepare uneven, grassed pitches for Lillee and Thomson in Brisbane and Sydney knowing England had nothing with which to retaliate.

On tour itself, a selection committee would be formed to pick the final XI. For many years this usually consisted of manager, captain and vice-captain (a post England traditionally filled on tour but not at home, at least until very modern times), plus perhaps two senior players, meaning that unlike at home players actually engaged in the Tests commanded a majority. In more recent times, this committee has shrunk to just the head coach and the captain, although there is usually informal input from other backroom staff and senior players. The involvement of the manager could sometimes look odd, depending on how substantial his cricketing credentials were. In the case of Peter Lush, who managed several major tours from 1986-87 to 1990-91, they were positively diaphanous, but Lush insists that although he sat in on selection he never interfered in the wishes of Micky Stewart and the England captain.

That the selection of touring teams could involve such a broad range of personnel and considerations provides important context to the most notorious decision any England selection panel has made. When Basil D'Oliveira was omitted from the original squad to tour South Africa in 1968-69, the insistence that the selectors had left him

---

* It has also been claimed that Snow further blotted his copy-book by bowling under-arm during a Test Trial match at Worcester in 1974 but this has been denied by several participants. Snow did, however, have a sharp exchange with one of the selectors, Ossie Wheatley, when he entered the dressing-room on the last afternoon of the game and encouraged the young batsman Frank Hayes to make a game of it when senior players such as Geoff Boycott and John Edrich had used the match for batting practice.

out purely on cricketing grounds – rather than because they were conscious that the inclusion of a Cape Coloured risked opposition from South Africa's apartheid government – aroused general suspicion. Cricketing grounds had never been the sole criterion in the selection of MCC touring teams and the presence in the selection meeting alongside the four selectors, Colin Cowdrey, the captain, and tour manager Les Ames, of four influential MCC figures – president Arthur Gilligan, treasurer Gubby Allen, secretary Billy Griffith and his assistant Donald Carr – suggested that, as usual, wider issues were at stake.

However, the situation was complex. Political considerations must have played a part in the thinking of at least some of those present, but some at the meeting knew more than others about the likelihood of the tour being cancelled. Gilligan, Allen and Griffith had knowledge of a letter from Lord Cobham, a former MCC president who had met South Africa prime minister JB Vorster several months earlier, advising that D'Oliveira's selection would be unacceptable; other guidance, known to all, was more sanguine.

Also, an aspect that was widely underplayed was that D'Oliveira had jeopardised his selection with his conduct on the West Indies tour the previous winter where his drinking, and his conduct while 'in drink', became a concern to the team management. 'Basil D'Oliveira is a very nice chap but I'm not best pleased with the hours he keeps,' Cowdrey wrote in one of his regular airmailed letters to Griffith. Ames had also taken D'Oliveira aside on one occasion during the tour to remind him of his responsibilities. David Brown, who roomed with D'Oliveira on the tour, and Tom Graveney, another team-mate, confirmed that D'Oliveira was frequently out late, while Keith Fletcher, who also roomed with D'Oliveira on subsequent tours, said he would trash furniture after drinking too much. Pat Pocock has described how briefly violent he could become.

Although a detailed contemporaneous account does not exist of the selection meeting which took place on the last evening of the final Test of 1968 in which D'Oliveira scored 158 having been summoned as replacement for Roger Prideaux, it is understood that Ames raised the issue of D'Oliveira's inappropriate behaviour in the

West Indies and whether it could be guaranteed that he would not prove a diplomatic liability in South Africa.*

Clearly, the political capital the South African government could have made out of a Cape Coloured misbehaving would have been immense and this seems to have weighed with Ames and Cowdrey. 'If the management of that previous tour had been 110 per cent behind him it would have made an enormous difference,' Insole said. On another occasion, Insole termed it 'an absolutely genuine selection process'. Peter Oborne's sympathetic biography of D'Oliveira concedes – somewhat reluctantly – that D'Oliveira's chances of touring South Africa 'were severely damaged' by events in the West Indies. Thus, there were actually two motives for leaving out D'Oliveira – one political, the other disciplinary. In the end, after injuries (and a political storm of protest) encouraged a revision of plans over the original squad, D'Oliveira was selected, and the tour consequently cancelled.

Another candidate for the 1968-69 tour, Barry Knight, was ruled out of consideration by Allen and Gilligan because Knight's personal life was in disarray. Nor was Colin Milburn taken. Milburn was one of the most attacking batsmen in the country, who scored an unbeaten 126 on his second Test appearance against West Indies in 1966 and according to *Wisden* was 'one of the few personalities the public craved to see'; he was dropped two matches later because of concerns that his size meant he was too cumbersome in the field. He too had toured West Indies in 1967-68 without appearing in the Tests but was in the England XI for the final Test of the Australia series.

There was no disguising MCC's ingrained sympathy for South African cricket and, some argued, by extension its political regime, and the club's handling of the D'Oliveira affair thereby did lasting damage to its reputation. In any case, 1968-69 was the last winter of

---

* The absence of detailed notes from the South Africa tour selection meeting has been taken as suspicious but minutes of selection meetings were sporadically kept; what fragments of information survive from the pre-1969 era are notes relayed by the MCC secretary to the club committee. Prideaux's withdrawal from the Oval Test provided another intriguing subplot. He was said to have a cold but he is now understood to have pulled out on the basis that the only way he could lose out on a tour spot was if he played, and failed, in the final match of the series.

Tests over which MCC presided. If cricket was to receive government funding from the newly created Sports Council it needed to be run by a properly constituted governing body rather than a private club, and as a result English cricket was reconstituted into a new body called the Cricket Council, which first met in January 1969. It was made up of three elements, but the TCCB emerged far stronger than MCC or the National Cricket Association, taking responsibility for the financial welfare of the first-class game and the affairs of the England team at home and abroad.*

Although MCC officers initially filled many of the most important positions at the TCCB and looked after much of its administrative work into the 1980s, the club's reluctance to let the new branches of administration develop without interference met with an abrupt response. First, Raman Subba Row resigned from the council's reorganisation subcommittee, then Cedric Rhoades, the feisty Lancashire chairman, proposed that the TCCB should break away altogether and set up a base away from Lord's, suggesting Nottingham as an alternative. As a result, a restructuring in 1974 left MCC's voting power reduced from almost twice that of the TCCB to the same, and by 1982 the TCCB held 50 per cent of the votes and MCC less than 20 per cent – a situation that provoked the resignation of the arch-conservative Gubby Allen. A few years later Jack Bailey resigned as MCC secretary over a number of wrangles with the TCCB relating to the staging of big matches at Lord's.

Those at MCC may not have wanted to accept that the TCCB to all intents and purposes now ran the English game, and relations between the club and the TCCB remained tense for many years, but that was the new reality. The long-standing grip on England team affairs applied by a line of MCC patriarchs dating back through Allen to Walter Robins, Pelham Warner, Lord Hawke and Lord Harris was finally broken. Those who had been arguing for years for the abolition of MCC's dictatorship of English cricket finally had their way.

---

* One consequence of this was the demise of the Board of Control for Test Matches at Home, which had been created in 1898.

## England's Chairmen of Selectors/National Selectors 1899-2019

| Chairman | Period | Age* | Seasons as chairman |
|---|---|---|---|
| Lord Hawke | 1899-1909; 1933 | 38 | 6 |
| *John Shuter* | *1912* | *57* | *1* |
| *Henry Foster* | *1921* | *47* | *1* |
| Henry Leveson Gower | 1924; 1928-30 | 50 | 4 |
| Pelham Warner | 1926; 1931-32; 1935-38 | 52 | 7 |
| Stanley Jackson | 1934; 1946 | 64 | 2 |
| *Peter Perrin* | *1939* | *62* | *1* |
| *Jack Holmes* | *1947-49* | *47* | *3* |
| Bob Wyatt | 1950 | 48 | 1 |
| Norman Yardley | 1951-52 | 36 | 2 |
| Freddie Brown | 1953 | 42 | 1 |
| *Harry Altham* | *1954* | *65* | *1* |
| Gubby Allen | 1955-61 | 52 | 7 |
| Walter Robins | 1962-64 | 55 | 3 |
| Doug Insole | 1965-68 | 39 | 4 |
| Alec Bedser | 1969-81 | 50 | 12 |
| Peter May | 1982-88 | 52 | 7 |
| Ted Dexter | 1989-93 | 53 | 5 |
| Ray Illingworth | 1994-96 | 61 | 3 |
| *David Graveney* | *1997-2008* | *44* | *11* |
| Geoff Miller | 2008-13 | 55 | 6 |
| James Whitaker | 2014-18 | 51 | 4 |
| Ed Smith | 2018-19 | 40 | 1 |

* Age is that on 1 May in first year of appointment; entries in italic were those who never played Test cricket for England.

## Most Home Test Seasons on the Selection Panel

Alec Bedser 23 (1962-85; excluding 1970), Geoff Miller 14 (2000-13), David Graveney 13 (1995-2007), Peter May 11* (1965-88), Peter Perrin 10 (1926-39), Doug Insole 10 (1959-68), James Whitaker 10 (2008-17)

---

\* Excludes his seasons as a co-opted member of the panel when he was England captain.

# CHAPTER 23

## The Rise of the Umpire
### Frank Chester, nationalism and the art of neutrality

Frank Chester was spoken of as a future England cricketer when he was 18 years old. No one had scored a championship hundred at a younger age and he added three more centuries before turning 20. Then the First World War came. While on active service in Greece, he was struck by shrapnel, the wound became gangrenous and he lost his right arm below the elbow. Chester's playing career was over but he turned to umpiring and by the age of 29 was standing in his first Test. He remains the youngest English umpire to officiate in what was recognised at the time as a Test match.* In a career spanning more than 30 years, he stood in 48 Tests and, equipped with his trademark trilby and metal arm, took umpiring to new heights. Don Bradman rated Chester the best umpire he played under, not only for the soundness of his judgements but because he willingly took control of the game. He was not afraid to give out the captains whose written reports to the authorities

---

* John Hickson (umpired one Test in 1888-89) and Audley Miller (two Tests in 1895-96) were born in England and younger than Chester, but stood in matches in South Africa only retrospectively viewed as Tests.

could make or break an umpire's reputation, or to chide bowlers for bad appeals.

After the Second World War, Chester increasingly fell foul of the Australians, to whose persistent appealing he took exception, publicly criticising them in 1948 when he was also seen making disapproving gestures from square leg. 'I thought [they] went too far in their appealing, which often they accompanied by excited leaping and gesticulating,' he wrote. 'Apart from being distasteful to the home players, as well as to the cricket-loving public, this sort of behaviour made umpiring a somewhat nerve-wracking business ... An exaggerated chorus of appeals can spoil the game, as well as bring upon an umpire the hostility of the crowd.'

Apologists put down his irascibility to stomach ulcers, but when in 1953 he began turning down appeals in a sarcastic voice Lindsay Hassett, the Australia captain, complained to MCC. Hassett felt Chester's umpiring of the Leeds Test crucially favoured England batsmen Denis Compton and Reg Simpson and that Chester should have intervened when Trevor Bailey blatantly bowled down the leg side to thwart Australia's last-day run-chase. Chester was stood down from the deciding Test at The Oval, although his removal was publicly put down to ill health and expanded to include all matches for the rest of the season. By the time Australia next visited, he had retired. It was a significant rebuke for English umpiring, which had to this point been regarded, at least in England, as the best in the world. Chester's belief, expressed in an autobiography in 1956, that, 'the English temperament is the safest insurance against losing the spirit of the game', probably did little to smooth relations.

Chester was not the only English umpire to cause consternation among visiting sides at this time. In the deciding Test of 1955, England enjoyed the benefit of a number of decisions from umpires Dai Davies and Tom Bartley. Peter May was only four runs into his match-winning innings of 89 not out when Bartley turned down a confident appeal from Hugh Tayfield. 'I know South Africa to their dying day swear I should have been lbw,' May wrote. 'My own thoughts at the time were that ... I had been lucky.' To compound matters, the next day Russell Endean and Jackie McGlew were adjudged lbw sweeping, though both had their front leg far down the pitch. Doug Insole, who played for England in the 1955 series, wrote in his autobiography that the Australians in 1953 actually objected to two English umpires and both were stood down and the South Africans similarly lodged a protest against one umpire with the same result, but England's wishes in respect of officials for the fifth Test in South Africa in 1956–57 and second Test in Australia in 1958–59 were not met.

By this time, the nature of international umpiring was changing. As a consequence of Britain's altered relationship with its Dominions, the old processes by which Lord's might determine who officiated in England Test matches, whether abroad or at home, were no longer appropriate. When England last toured India before the war, all three Tests involved English and Australian umpires rather than Indian ones; such high-handed bypassing of local officialdom was unthinkable once India secured political independence. Similarly, England's last pre-war tour of the Caribbean in 1934–35 had seen an Australian stand in two of the four games; that too would not happen again until the appointment of neutral umpires. After the Second World War, umpiring was purely a matter for the 'locals'. These changes mirrored an earlier transition in Australia, where the assumption of political independence on 1 January 1901 marked an end to the use of English-sponsored umpires.* But with the establishment of home umpires came suspicions of partisan umpiring, especially in the new post-war world in which everyone was hungrier for national success.

Umpiring competence came under scrutiny immediately as international cricket resumed after the Second World War, when in the first Ashes Test at Brisbane in November 1946 the Australian umpire George Borwick gave Bradman not out despite Bradman seemingly being caught in regulation fashion by Jack Ikin at second slip, chopping at a wide ball from Bill Voce. The English players, and Clif Cary, watching through binoculars while broadcasting,

---

* The last English umpire to stand in an England Test overseas was Charles Elliott at Christchurch in 1971, but he was in New Zealand on a Churchill Fellowship and did so at the invitation of the New Zealand Cricket Council.

felt that the catch was so obvious that Bradman might have simply walked off without waiting for the umpire – and the fact he didn't badly soured relations between the sides – but Borwick's failure to act was in itself striking.

There were other incidents during the tour which drew the ire of the English players, though with admirable restraint Walter Hammond, who had been 'blazingly angry' over the Ikin incident, declined to ascribe errors to partial umpiring. Eighteen months later, the ICC reiterated its protocols regarding the appointment of Test umpires: the home authority would nominate a panel of umpires to officiate in a series, after which any captain had the right to privately submit objections to any umpire who had been put forward, but he could not nominate which umpires he preferred; in effect, all umpires regardless of nationality were to be treated as equals. It was this right of objection which Hassett exercised when vetoing Chester in England in 1953.

The English game provided the greatest scope for umpires to gain experience but the system was hardly conducive to best practice: first-class umpires were 'paid' hands whose career prospects depended on good references from county captains, and most lacked the self-confidence of a Frank Chester to give out those captains for fear of the consequences. Nor had many umpires actually played Test cricket themselves: before 1921, only four umpires standing in Test matches in England had ever played at that level, and all four of them only stood once at home.* Ironically one of these four, Dick Barlow, did not stand again because the Australians privately took exception to his solitary performance at Trent Bridge in 1899, where England escaped with a draw. Ahead of their next visit in 1902, the Australians requested prior approval of Test umpires, but were turned down by MCC.

Joe Darling also expressed his dissatisfaction with the umpiring on his fourth and last tour of England in 1905; his general complaint was that English umpires were afraid to give out prominent amateurs,

---

* Allen Hill (one Test in 1890), and Richard Barlow, Mordecai Sherwin and James Lillywhite junior (all one Test in 1899).

and he cited WG Grace and Stanley Jackson among beneficiaries. Monty Noble, Darling's successor, asked after just one Test of the 1909 tour that MCC choose the two best umpires and let them stand for the remainder of the series, but MCC identified four umpires and allocated matches by ballot. A further request by the Australians ahead of the Triangular Tournament in 1912, this time supported by Pelham Warner, that MCC should adopt the Australian system of the captains identifying suitable candidates was again rejected; instead a panel of six umpires recommended by the county captains was assembled and allotted Tests by ballot, although a cable was sent to the Australian and South African boards stating that 'any umpire objected to on previous occasions had been omitted from the list'. County captains, as the top of English cricket's social hierarchy, thus played a role in the pre-1914 era both in the selection of England's Test umpires and players.

Australians were perhaps emboldened to speak out on this issue in the knowledge that they had produced the first 'great' international umpire. Jim Phillips was born in Victoria and for many years commuted between Australia and England as player and umpire, standing in 29 Test matches and winning the lasting gratitude of the game's establishment for rooting out bowlers who 'threw', among them Arthur Mold of England and Ernie Jones and Tom McKibbin of Australia. 'His presence in a match between England and Australia is a guarantee that, at least at one end of the wicket, there will be an umpire whose decisions will be absolutely impartial and unbiased,' WA Bettesworth wrote of Phillips after the 1905 series. Phillips was not without his critics. Some felt he was too zealous in his campaign against 'chuckers', whom he would identify in advance to press-men and anyone else within earshot, and the Australians blocked him from standing in the 1903–04 series for this reason, but like Chester he was not cowed by anyone on the field. Sadly, no other Australians were able to follow his example and Phillips remained the only non-English umpire to stand in a Test match in England until neutral umpires were introduced in 1994.

As Test matches grew in popularity, so attention grew on umpiring as with all aspects of the game. During the deciding Test of the

Triangular Tournament of 1912, Australia batsman Warren Bardsley was judged run out by umpire John Moss following brilliant work by Jack Hobbs at cover point. 'There was a lot of discussion about the decision, several famous cricketers in the pavilion expressing a positive opinion that Bardsley was not out,' *Wisden* reported. 'However, Moss, the umpire, when interviewed after the match, said that he had no doubt whatever on the point. Here one may leave a question that will probably be talked about for years to come.' Here was an early case of a Test umpire being tried in the court of public opinion, with former players as chief prosecutors. There would be plenty more.

When Joe Hardstaff junior broke into the England team against South Africa in 1935, it was readily acknowledged that his father Joe senior, who had umpired Test matches every summer since 1928 and was described by Chester as 'one of the outstanding Test umpires of all time', would have to be removed from international duty; he stood in the final Test of the series for which his son was not selected, but not thereafter.

English teams travelling overseas had little faith in local officials and habitually grumbled about their competency and honesty; most had stood much less often in first-class cricket than English umpires. Grace in 1891-92 was probably not the first, merely the most famous, England player to try to intimidate inexperienced Australian umpires. In 1897-98, Tom Richardson wrote in his diary of the local umpiring that, 'on several occasions it was simply disgraceful'. Tiger Smith described the umpiring in 1911-12 as 'terrible', while nine years later Percy Fender and Rockley Wilson ventured into print with their criticisms. Not all of the scepticism was unfounded. Bradman described a decision in his favour at Adelaide in 1937 – given by an umpire, John Scott, whose home town Adelaide was – as the second-worst he experienced. (The worst was presumably the reprieve he received from Borwick nine years later, though he did not state as much.)

On several Test tours England sides took with them, or co-opted on arrival, men designated as their own umpires and guarantors of fair play. There was logic to this inasmuch as if there were to be disputes, it was surely better to have adjudicators drawn from both sides; the counter-argument was that some of these appointees proved less independent than advertised, and their very presence fostered a suspicion among the players of partisan umpiring, and in fact cast the two umpires into opposing camps. When Lord Harris's team toured Australia, the riot during the New South Wales match was directly linked to Sydney-siders, probably with money at stake, taking issue with a run-out decision made by an umpire recommended by the Melbourne Cricket Club to stand on behalf of Harris's team. George Coulthard, a professional cricketer and noted Australian Rules player, had not officiated in a first-class match before and was only 22 years old; he is still the youngest person ever to umpire a Test.*

James Lillywhite was involved as captain, organiser and promoter of some of England's earliest tours but he also umpired all four Tests of the 1881-82 series, as well as the second one in 1884-85, before the Australians, doubting his impartiality, refused to let him stand again (although this did not stop him reappearing as umpire in one Test in England in 1899). When on another of Lillywhite's tours in 1886-87, local umpire John Swift was unavailable on the final day in Sydney, it was agreed that one of the England players, William Gunn, would umpire the rest of the game, which was delicately poised. Australia were 101 for five, chasing 222, and England won by 71 runs. It is the only instance of a participating player acting as umpire in a Test match.† Unsatisfactory episodes such as these contributed to Stoddart's two teams taking with them to Australia their own full-time umpire in Jim Phillips.

Subsequent practice in Australia up to the Second World War was for the captains to actively propose the umpires they wanted – no panels, no ballots, as in England – with the English captain having had a chance to scrutinise candidates during the state matches. Pelham Warner ran into difficulties with the NSW cricket association over the choice of umpires for a Test in Sydney in 1903-04 but

---

* Coulthard also stood in another England v Australia Test match during the 1881-82 series, in which he also appeared for Australia as a player. He died of tuberculosis in 1883, aged 27.

† It was also agreed that one of the Australians, Charles Turner, would field for England in Gunn's absence. He took a catch.

eventually got his way, although only after some of his correspondence had been leaked to the press.* Similarly Douglas Jardine and Bill
Woodfull 'approved' the umpires for the 1932-33 series (the same
two, George Hele and George Borwick, stood in all five Tests). On
the following Ashes tour of 1936-37, Gubby Allen's objections to a
certain umpire were only acknowledged with difficulty. 'I expressed
a very strong wish that a certain umpire whom they favoured should
not be appointed and after some rather awkward discussions they
acceded to my request,' Allen wrote in his tour report. His assessment of the Australian umpiring on the tour was that it was 'at times
inaccurate but with one exception (the 1st NSW match) certainly
not prejudiced'.

In South Africa, at least one umpire born in or sanctioned by
England stood in every Test England played there until the 1920s, a
reflection of the rudimentary and Anglocentric nature of early South
African cricket. For the first MCC-organised Test tour there in
1905-06, England again recruited Jim Phillips and he stood in all five
Tests. Before then, as in Australia, some touring teams simply took
the duties upon themselves. Major Gardner Warton not only organised the first English tour of 1888-89 but umpired the two matches
subsequently ranked as Tests, while in 1895-96 Audley Miller acted
as umpire in the second and third Tests having played for England in
the first. Such an approach might have been a necessary intermediary
step until local standards of officiating improved, but it appeared to
work to England's advantage. Pelham Warner survived a stumping
appeal early in his innings of 132 not out at Johannesburg in 1899,
which umpire Soames later admitted was a grave mistake that cost
South Africa what would be regarded now as their first-ever Test
victory. When England crept home by one wicket at Cape Town
in 1922, the match would have ended in a tie had not a strong lbw

---

* The appointed umpires, Bob Crockett and Philip Argall, both respected officials,
were the unwitting cause of one of the worst cases of crowd disorder at an England Test
when on the Saturday, with 35,000 in the ground, they took the players off the field
several times for rain. Bottles were thrown across the cycle-track which ran around the
playing area. 'A small number of people attempted to rush the ground, but soon retired
on the appearance of the police,' *The Times* reported. 'The bottle-throwing, however,
continued.'

appeal been rejected; the umpire was George Thompson, a former England player who had never before umpired a first-class match (and after the following Test would never do so again). Johnny Douglas, England captain in South Africa in 1913-14, did not think the locals were in much need of education: 'Umpiring was not too good, on the whole,' he wrote. 'But there were exceptions. A few umpires we came across were, in my opinion, better than any we have at home.'

When England first played Tests in West Indies in 1929-30, they took with them Joe Hardstaff senior, who stood in all four matches, and although they did not take with them an umpire on their next visit to the Caribbean in 1934-35, they recruited Arthur Richardson – the former Australia Test player, who had stood in island matches the previous year – to officiate in Trinidad and British Guiana (now Guyana). Although the switch to wholly local umpires was made by the time England returned in 1947-48, Gubby Allen objected to Perry Burke standing in the Jamaica Test on the basis that Burke was only 21 years of age. The West Indies board acquiesced and replaced him with his father Sam Burke, who had shared umpiring duties with his son in the preceding Jamaica v MCC match. Perry Burke would later establish a reputation as one of the most reliable umpires in the West Indies.

England's first Tests in India in 1933-34 were officiated by Bill Hitch, a former England fast bowler, and Frank Tarrant, an Australian-born all-rounder who spent a lot of his later life in the employ of Indian princes, but Douglas Jardine had Tarrant removed for the third and final Test of the series after Tarrant warned the England captain during the Calcutta Test that he would order Nobbie Clark out of the attack if he did not curb his short-pitched bowling. Jardine already felt that Tarrant had favoured India with too many lbws, and had cabled MCC for advice. Tarrant was replaced for the third Test by John Higgins, a former Worcestershire amateur.

England touring teams were even more sceptical of foreign umpires once it became established after the Second World War that they would stand in all overseas Tests, and to doubts about their competency and experience were added suspicions of their intention to uphold regional pride. In the case of West Indies tours, the situation was more complex still, with relations between local white and non-white communities tense and the black population prone to view umpires as retainers of affluent white anti-nationalists. Each territory, too, wanted its Test match supervised by its own officials and this – combined with Len Hutton vetoing two local umpires for the Test in British Guiana – meant that the eight umpires used in the four Tests in 1953-54 had only previously stood in seven Tests between them. One of these, Badge Menzies, the Bourda groundsman, had never stood in a first-class match before. Perry Burke's family was assaulted after he gave out local batsman JK Holt leg-before for 94 in Jamaica; Menzies needed protection after adjudging another local player Clifford McWatt run out in Georgetown, a decision that ended a partnership of 99, thereby thwarting bets among the crowd, who responded to McWatt's dismissal by throwing bottles onto the outfield and causing a delay of ten minutes.* A more serious riot occurred among a crowd of 30,000 during the Trinidad Test on England's next tour in 1959-60, which resulted in the third day's play being abandoned shortly after tea. The trigger was the run-out of a local player, but the umpire's decision was not seriously disputed, it was simply the last straw in an abject batting collapse.

Len Hutton in his 1953-54 tour report described the umpiring, rather ambiguously, as 'appalling, though I do not for one moment suggest that these umpires were dishonest but rather biased incompetent', sentiments echoed by tour manager Charles Palmer. However, his players may not have shared this view; denied a slip catch during the fourth Test in Trinidad, Tom Graveney threw the ball to the ground and shouted at Ellis Achong: 'That's the fourth f***ing time you've cheated us!' What is beyond argument is that they made their displeasure plain, Crawford White of the *News Chronicle* writing: 'I have never known any company of cricketers as incensed by gross injustices and flagrant decisions as this England side ... [but] one must sympathise as well as condemn.'

---

* Denis Compton was full of praise for Len Hutton's decision to stay on the field during this delay: 'Len never had a greater moment. He was cool, nerveless, quite unconcerned about the demonstrating crowds which surrounded him in angry thousands.'

When MCC were beaten by Pakistan on their tour of the sub-continent in 1951-52, in a result that contributed to Pakistan being awarded Test status, reports in sections of the British media suggested the outcome was due to bad umpiring, with more than 30 appeals disallowed. Such claims incensed the Pakistan captain AH Kardar who, fearing they might damage Pakistan's hopes of promotion, wrote a letter of protest to *The Times*. Further trouble, with far more significant consequences, followed when an England A team visited in 1955-56 under the captaincy of Donald Carr. Idris Begh was reputed to be Pakistan's best umpire but his decisions invariably seemed to go against Carr's team.

When, after an evening of drinking in Peshawar, a few of the players decided to 'kidnap' Begh from his hotel and douse him in water, a prank previously inflicted on members of their own party, they quickly found themselves in deep opprobrium. Kardar, now Pakistan manager, fired off complaints to London and only frantic diplomacy and an apology from MCC president Lord Alexander of Tunis prevented the tour being abandoned. Questions were asked in parliament and English embarrassment was acute; Carr was severely reprimanded.* An incident the previous winter shed less kindly light on Begh, with Lala Amarnath, the manager of the India team making their first Test tour of Pakistan, accidentally witnessing an exchange on the eve of the final Test in which Begh asked Kardar: 'Any instructions for tomorrow's game, Skipper?' Begh was per-emptorily removed from match duties but nonetheless survived to officiate many more important games, including England A's visit and five more Tests, though none involving England.

The Begh incident in Peshawar was held as a classic example of British arrogance towards its former colonies, and long remained a thorn in the side of England's cricketing relations with Pakistan.

---

* Six players who either had or would play Test cricket for England were directly involved in the prank: Carr, Ken Barrington, Brian Close, Jim Parks, Peter Richardson and Roy Swetman. Carr's censure did not harm his career: after retiring as a player he served as an administrator at MCC from 1963 and the TCCB from 1974-86. However, when he became an ICC match referee and was assigned a match in Pakistan in 1991 there were, according to his obituary in *The Times*, 'howls of protest'.

Kardar's early response was to propose the use of neutral umpires, but it was more than 30 years before the idea was taken up.*

England's complacent faith in the integrity of their own umpires stored up trouble that finally erupted with the throwing controversy of the late 1950s. Had umpires policed more rigorously bowlers with suspect actions, and had they been supported more robustly by the authorities, the crisis that engulfed the international game might have been avoided. Frank Chester was ready to call Cuan McCarthy of South Africa for throwing during the Trent Bridge Test of 1951, but when he sought out two MCC committee men at lunch to see if he would receive official support for doing so, 'they were not prepared to say'. As Chester's livelihood depended on him remaining on the Test panel, he – for once – took no action.

The throwing controversy forced welcome change: at a meeting of the Imperial Cricket Conference in London in July 1960, which was viewed so seriously that members sent their own representatives rather than using English proxies, umpires were given greater powers to deal with throwing – which was defined more clearly as 'a sudden straightening of the bowling arm' prior to delivery – and a number of other aspects of play which international teams were cynically exploiting. Umpires did not overnight become fearsome law-enforcers but they were better equipped to control Test matches, and the better ones made more concerted efforts to do so.

Some observers were in no doubt as to why teams selected bowlers whose actions they knew to be suspect. 'The very thing which is helping to damage cricket [is] the increasing nationalism and the win-at-all-costs attitude which has developed,' wrote Leslie Smith in *Wisden*. 'Indeed, all around us we can see examples of such nationalism and the bad feeling it causes. Almost every international sporting occasion is riddled with it and the public must be getting heartily sick and tired of the perpetual squabbles on and off the field. Dwindling

---

* Peter Oborne, in his history of Pakistan cricket, rejected the notion that Begh was biased against the England team in 1955–56 but seems unaware of the incident witnessed by Amarnath and cited by Mihir Bose in *The Cambridge Companion to Cricket*.

gates in practically every major sport reflects the public reaction. First-class cricket, confined as it is to a handful of countries within the Commonwealth, ought to rise above such pettiness.'

The problem for England started with Tony Lock, a left-arm spinner who was widely suspected of throwing his faster ball. When Lock, aged 23, was no-balled three times for throwing by umpire Fred Price, a former England wicketkeeper, while playing for Surrey against the Indian touring team in 1952, it caused a sensation; Lock had made his Test debut only a week earlier. Price knew what he was about because it was the fourth time he had stood in a match involving Lock that season. England's selectors were undeterred. They retained Lock for the last Test of the summer and picked him twice against Australia in 1953 before sending him to the West Indies in 1953-54. As has already been noted, the standard of umpiring in the Caribbean was not high, but the local officials knew a bent arm when they saw one and Lock was called for throwing by Perry Burke during the first Test in Jamaica, and by both umpires, Harold Walcott and Cortez Jordan, in the following match against Barbados.*

Lock discarded his faster ball and lost some of his effectiveness as a result but, with Hutton unhappy at his peremptory treatment, he stayed in the Test side for the remainder of the tour. He was chosen by England for the next four years, mainly at home where he was only supervised by English officials. Before selecting him in 1955, chairman of selectors Gubby Allen and fellow selector Les Ames went incognito to study Lock's action in a championship match, thought it looked 'a little bit funny', but agreed he could be chosen for England anyway. There were also mutterings about Peter Loader, also of Surrey and England, a skilful fast bowler who could move the ball either way but whose bouncers were noticeably faster than his other deliveries; 'he can certainly generate a great deal of speed for a man who is of slender build,' wrote Frank Tyson, an occasional England colleague. But no umpire ever called him.

---

* Lock remains the only bona fide England bowler to be called for throwing in a Test match. David Gower, who delivered only 36 legitimate balls in a career of 117 Tests, deliberately threw the last ball of a match against New Zealand at Trent Bridge in 1986 for the novelty of being the first England player to be called for throwing in a home Test.

Price, who began umpiring in 1949, was not summoned for Test match duty until 1964, by which time the throwing controversy had subsided. 'Umpires who had called a bowler for throwing were looked on as "stirrers" or publicity seekers,' wrote Peter May, who captained Surrey when Price called Lock. 'The tendency was to sweep such unpleasantness under the carpet. A bowler banned for throwing would, after all, be deprived of his livelihood if he was a professional.'

The treatment of Lock in particular left England compromised when questions over the legitimacy of bowlers from other countries surfaced. When May's team were crushed 4–0 in 1958–59, Australia fielded four bowlers with suspect actions, the most prominent Ian Meckiff, who took 17 wickets in four Tests and whose methods were widely denounced by former England players and the English media, and less stridently by some former Australian players.* None was called for throwing and Freddie Brown, the tour manager, wanted to lodge a complaint with the Australian board but was stopped by May, who feared accusations of double standards (and sour grapes). May believed Australia were in no hurry to take action against their chuckers because their cricketers were being eclipsed by their successful swimmers and tennis players; there was also a lingering grievance at the doctoring of pitches in favour of Jim Laker and Lock during the 1956 series.

'I sometimes see the 1958–59 tour of Australia referred to as the greatest failure of my career as England captain,' May wrote. 'I myself often think that it may have been one of my greatest successes. At the end of it, England and Australia were still speaking.' But his players did not share this satisfaction, Frank Tyson calling it 'diabolical' that the management failed to protest at the time, though May and Brown told Bradman they intended to make 'a very strong report to Lord's' once they had returned home.

It was hardly their fault, either, that the Australian board

---

* England's problems were compounded by Meckiff and Alan Davidson bowling fast left-arm, a style of attack they had little experienced since the war; Davidson had played ten Tests against them but he was an altogether different and more effective bowler.

seemingly reneged on the understanding that visiting teams could veto an umpire with whom they were dissatisfied; after the first Test, May and Brown asked, as was their right, that Mel McInnes not stand again, only for their objection to be overruled. 'I cannot remember an occasion when this has happened in England,' May wrote pointedly in 1985. When England returned to the West Indies the following winter, questions about the action of Charlie Stayers of British Guiana were rebuffed with the response that Lock had got away with it, so why shouldn't he? In the event, despite being included in the squad at the start, Stayers did not feature in any of the Tests. Leslie Smith in *Wisden* estimated that, even so, two bowlers with suspect actions did play regularly in the Tests.

England belatedly realised they would have to act themselves if they expected others to, and they began a purge before the seminal ICC meeting in 1960. Suspect bowlers in domestic cricket were identified and umpires urged to take action. Lock was among those no-balled in county cricket in 1959, although by then he was set on remodelling his action after being shown film by Geoff Rabone, the New Zealand captain, earlier in the year. He returned to Test cricket in 1961, but only after he was told not to attempt certain variations considered suspect. Then, in 1960, South Africa brought to England a young fast bowler in Geoff Griffin who had already been called in domestic cricket. He was no-balled for throwing by six umpires in three warm-up games but South Africa still selected him for the first two Tests. In the second of these he was no-balled frequently by Frank Lee (younger brother of Harry Lee) and again by Syd Buller in an exhibition match staged after the Test finished early; Griffin did not appear again in the series and never played for South Africa again.

However, with Gubby Allen in the vanguard, MCC was desperate to preserve good relations with other nations during this politically sensitive period and, following South Africa protests at Griffin's treatment, it was agreed Buller would not stand in the remaining Tests. This caused a public outcry in England among those who felt Buller had suffered simply for doing his job, while in his homeland Griffin was cast as victim and Allen as persecutor.*

The ill-feeling generated over this episode, and fears of a political backlash, may have contributed to the leeway granted Charlie Griffith when West Indies toured in 1963. Griffith had been called in the Caribbean and England players such as Ken Barrington and Fred Trueman among others were convinced he threw. Early on, one of Trueman's Yorkshire team-mates, John Hampshire, was badly hit on the head by Griffith, a blow that left Hampshire with a lasting vulnerability, though he went on to play eight Tests. Trueman subsequently claimed that while in the bath during the Lord's Test he overheard Walter Robins, who had succeeded Allen as chairman of selectors, telling umpires Buller and Eddie Phillipson not to no-ball Griffith; neither they nor any other umpires that summer did so.

When West Indies toured again in 1966, Arthur Fagg no-balled Griffith for throwing once from square leg during an early game against Lancashire, but the incident escaped general notice until the Lancashire players drew attention to it. Then, on the eve of the third Test, Barrington – whose views about Griffith were public knowledge – withdrew on the eve of the game, though nothing was directly said about this being connected to Griffith. *Wisden* confined itself to saying merely, 'England caused much surprise just before the match began by omitting Barrington on the grounds that he was suffering from physical and nervous strain through playing too much cricket in the past six years.'

Barrington did not play a first-class match for a month.† Although Griffith was cautioned by umpire Charlie Elliott following a vicious bouncer to Tom Graveney during the next Test in Leeds, this carried none of the opprobrium of a no-balling. It was preferred that

---

* Buller did not suffer long. The county captains nominated him for the Test panel in 1961 and he umpired in Tests every year thereafter until his death in 1970.
† Barrington's month-long absence largely coincided with a 35-day break between the third and fourth Tests due to England hosting the football World Cup but although he then returned to the Surrey side he did not take part in the remaining Tests of the series. The five-week break equals the longest gap between matches in a Test series in England; there were 35 days between the second and third Tests against West Indies in 2000 to accommodate a triangular ODI series.

concerns were expressed privately. Chairman of selectors Doug Insole wrote privately to the MCC secretary, asking him to pass on concerns to the West Indies board (which he did) and stating that Griffith's bowling was the main reason why the atmosphere between the teams was not better during this series. Griffith, he stated, was a player 'known throughout the cricketing world to be a thrower, and who is admitted as such in private conversation by most West Indies players and administrators'.

Fagg was to find himself more broadly at odds with the West Indian players who toured in 1973 when, led by the captain Rohan Kanhai, they persistently showed their displeasure at him denying them an appeal for a catch against Geoff Boycott during the Edgbaston Test. Fagg threatened at the end of the second day's play to withdraw from the rest of the match, and indeed his place was taken by a substitute – Alan Oakman, the Warwickshire coach and a former first-class umpire and England Test cricketer – for the first over of the Saturday morning, but after discussions with the West Indies team manager Esmund Kentish and England's chairman of selectors Alec Bedser he was persuaded to continue. He and Dickie Bird called the teams together at lunch and threatened to call off the match unless things improved, after which West Indies played out the game in grudging spirit. Fagg, who did not receive the apology he asked for, said in a statement: 'If they will not accept decisions, there is no point carrying on.' John Woodcock in *The Times* described Kanhai's behaviour as 'reprehensible'.

In a conciliatory vein similar to that used with Griffith, MCC agreed to an Australian request that any bowler suspected of throwing during their tour of England in 1961 would be reported only confidentially and would remain free to play at Australia's discretion. The umpires, it seemed, were not quite as independent as the steps taken in 1960 suggested.

In fact, Australia did not select Meckiff or any of their other suspect bowlers for the 1961 tour, but England and Australia concluded that non-selection of potential culprits was not enough and public shows of strength (against their own bowlers if not those of the opposition) were necessary. Australia recalled Meckiff in 1963 for a

Test against South Africa only for him to be immediately no-balled, and effectively cast out of the game for good, an act welcomed by England captain Ted Dexter. Meanwhile Harold Rhodes – one of the fastest bowlers in England, whose selection for two Tests in 1959 suggested he was not then on the blacklist – was no-balled for throwing by Buller in a county match in 1965 (having earlier been reported by an opponent, Fred Titmus, the Middlesex and England all-rounder). Rhodes was reckoned unfortunate: most chuckers bowled with chest-on, splay-footed actions; his was classically side-on. With film increasingly helping to achieve meaningful dissections of technique, Rhodes was eventually cleared in 1968 when it was accepted that a perceived straightening of the arm was due to hyperextension, but by then England had lost a potentially significant cricketer.

Umpires had also long been lax about enforcing the back-foot no-ball rule in the face of 'dragging', a method by which fast bowlers landed their back foot behind the line then dragged it forward before their front foot landed and they delivered the ball, allowing them to gain an extra yard (or more) down the pitch. Some bowlers had become skilled at elongating this movement. Australia's Ray Lindwall was no-balled by Dai Davies during the Old Trafford Test of 1948 and Griffin was also no-balled for dragging in England in 1960, but many escaped unpunished. In 1958-59, England's problems were compounded by some of Australia's chuckers being, like Griffin, draggers as well. ('Having the ball thrown at you from 18 yards blights the sunniest disposition,' May wrote.)

The 1960 meeting supported an experimental move to a front-foot no-ball law; this was formalised in 1962. Umpires were also empowered to order a bowler out of the attack if he persisted with short-pitched fast bowling, while various measures were introduced to tackle negative play, including a limit of no more than two fielders behind square on the leg side. Umpires had already been notified at the ICC meeting of 1959 of a 'danger area' in front of the stumps which bowlers should avoid during their follow-through. The impact was mixed. Seasoned observers scratched their heads to recall a fast bowler being ordered off for bowling too many bouncers, and time-wasting would get worse rather than better, but these changes shaped

WG Grace gave Test cricket its imprimatur and was the first man to provide continuity to the role of England captain.

Lord Hawke turned Yorkshire into a rich supplier of talent, proposed the first England management structure and was the first chairman of selectors.

Pelham Warner, seen here (standing second from the right) leading England in Australia in 1903-04, contributed as much to the affairs of the national team as any man ever has, as player, selector and administrator.

SF Barnes was an early master of swing bowling but was mistrusted by authority and waited a long time for an extended run in the England side.

No two professionals did more to democratise the England team than Wilfred Rhodes (seated far left) and Jack Hobbs (seated second from the right).

Walter Hammond scored 1,657 runs at an average of 55.23 in 20 Tests as captain but was unfairly blamed for England's defeat in Australia in 1946-47.

Douglas Jardine presents Bill Voce and Harold Larwood, his principal strike bowlers in Australia in 1932-33, with money donated by the people of Nottingham.

Len Hutton, the side's first modern professional captain, leads out England at Old Trafford in 1952.

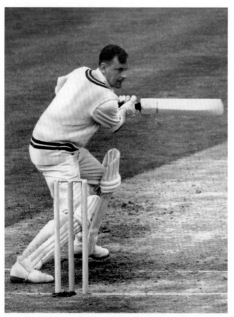

Peter May, like Hutton, was England's best batsman and a tough, uncompromising captain. No one in the 20th century led England to more wins in Test cricket.

Few England fast bowlers proved as devastatingly effective in Australia as Frank Tyson in 1954–55.

John Snow, Ray Illingworth and Geoff Boycott, stars of the Ashes win in 1970–71 when tensions with manager David Clark highlighted the gulf between players and administrators.

Tony Greig was arguably the most influential England cricketer of all time. Born in South Africa, he was among the first of the modern influx of foreign-born players to break into the national side, and was instrumental in a transformation in pay and conditions.

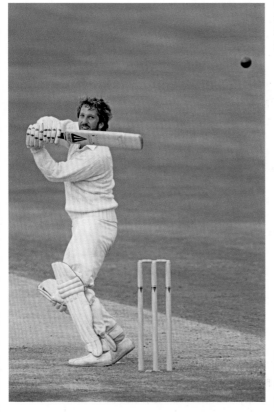

Ian Botham, batting here at Headingley in 1981, was a supreme athlete during the early years of his England career.

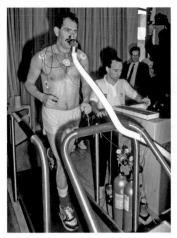

Graham Gooch as captain challenged England's players to follow his example and become fitter.

Duncan Fletcher, the best technical coach England have had, and Nasser Hussain dragged the team out of the doldrums.

Michael Vaughan hid the pressure well whether as batsman or leader.

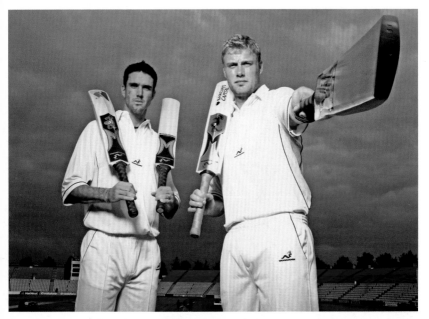

Kevin Pietersen (left) and Andrew Flintoff, whose superstar status threatened the fragile balance of the team.

Andrew Strauss (left), Ashes winning captain of 2009 and 2010-11, with perhaps his most valuable player, off-spinner Graeme Swann.

Alastair Cook, James Anderson and Stuart Broad, three modern champions of Test cricket.

White-ball pioneer: Eoin Morgan led a revolution in England's ODI cricket.

the game as it is played today and made umpires, more than captains, stewards of the game's conduct.

One of the consequences of a turbulent period, however, was that there was a decline in applicants looking to join the list of English first-class umpires, and in 1965 it was agreed to increase their pay, with Test fees rising from £65 to £75 plus expenses.

## 'England-Accredited' Umpires in England Tests Overseas

Before neutral umpires were phased into Test cricket by the ICC, England showed a strong preference for their matches being offici- ated by Englishmen in the belief that they were inherently best at the job. With the exception of Jim Phillips, who was born in Australia but played and officiated in England as well as his homeland, umpires born in England stood in every Test in England up to 1994; also, some English-born umpires were assigned to accompany England on several early tours, or were co-opted to appear in overseas Tests once the team was there.

The following England Tests overseas before 1994 involved umpires born in England or, in a few cases, Australians co-opted to assist the touring team.

### In Australia

1878-79: George Coulthard, born in Australia, accompanied the team for six matches, including the only Test

1881-82: James Lillywhite jnr, tour manager and promoter, stood in all four Tests

1884-85: James Lillywhite jnr, tour promoter, stood in the second of five Tests

1886-87: William Gunn, who was playing in the match, stood on the final day of the second Test as replacement for the absent local umpire John Swift

1887-88: Jim Phillips, born in Australia, stood in nine matches, includ- ing the one Test

1894-95: Phillips accompanied the team throughout and stood in all five Tests

1897-98: Phillips accompanied the team throughout and stood in all five Tests

## In South Africa

England teams played eight matches between 1888-89 and 1898-99 which are now ranked as Tests. Understandably given the recent settlement of southern Africa, most of the umpires were born in England, but some umpiring was done by members of the touring side: Gardner Warton, who managed the tour, stood in both Tests in 1888-89 and Audley Miller stood in the second and third Tests of the 1895-96 series having played for England in the first. AA White travelled with the 1898-99 team as umpire.

1905-06: Jim Phillips accompanied the team throughout and stood in all five Tests; Frank Smith stood in three Tests and Frank Hearne in two

1909-10: Alfred Atfield stood in four Tests and Frank Smith in one

1913-14: Atfield stood in four Tests, Douglas Smith in one

1922-23: George Thompson stood in two Tests and Walker Wainwright in one

## In West Indies

1929-30: Joe Hardstaff snr accompanied the team throughout and stood in all four Tests

1934-35: Arthur Richardson, a former Australia cricketer, stood in two Tests

## In India

1933-34: Bill Hitch stood in all three Tests; John Higgins stood with him in one and Frank Tarrant, who was born in Australia, in the other two

## In New Zealand

1970-71: Charles Elliott stood in one Test

## England Cricketers Who Played and Umpired Tests

In chronological order of first Test appearance

Allen Hill (2 as player, 1 as umpire), James Lillywhite jnr (2, 6), Dick Barlow (17, 1), Mordecai Sherwin (3, 1), *Frank Hearne (2, 6), Harry Butt (3, 6), Audley Miller (1, 2), Sailor Young (2, 3), Len Braund (23, 3), Joe Hardstaff snr (5, 21), George Thompson (6, 2), Bill Hitch (7, 4), Tiger Smith (11, 8), Arthur Dolphin (1, 6), Harry Elliott (4, 7), Arthur Fagg (5, 18), Fred Price (1, 8), Norman Oldfield (1, 2), Jack Crapp (7, 4), Ken Palmer (1, 22), John Hampshire (8, 21), Jack Birkenshaw (5, 2), Peter Willey (26, 25), Mark Benson (1, 27), Richard Illingworth (9, 23), Neil Mallender (2, 3)

Ian Gould, who played 18 one-day internationals for England, had stood in 73 Tests by 17 February 2019; he is the only English-born umpire to stand in Tests in England since 2001, officiating in two Pakistan–Australia matches at Headingley and Lord's in 2010.

William Gunn (at Sydney in 1886-87) and Alan Oakman (at Edgbaston in 1973), both Test cricketers, briefly umpired as emergency replacements, Gunn in a match in which he was playing.

---

* Hearne additionally played in four Tests for South Africa.

# CHAPTER 24

# The Fight for the Soul of the Game
## Illingworth retrieves a lost decade

By the early 1960s, English cricket was facing a crisis of confidence. With relations with the other Test-match powers under strain from politics, the throwing dispute and gamesmanship, its mindset had become less assured, more defensive. An ideological battle had developed over how the national team should play, and those in favour of a more entertaining approach than Hutton and May's teams offered were seemingly willing to see England lose more often if necessary. If only the right captain could be found, the argument went, England could play in the same fashion as Australia and West Indies in their spellbinding series in Australia in 1960-61, and attendances for the English first-class game – which had steadily fallen since the boom just after the Second World War – might rally.

But unsurprisingly the captain and players against whose names Test results went were not easily persuaded, even those with amateur credentials. Neither the old Tonbridgian Colin Cowdrey, who often deputised for May and would lead the side on and off until 1969, nor the Radley-educated Ted Dexter, who led England for most of the three years that followed May's last Test appearance in 1961, sought a more adventurous path. The hierarchy may have wanted enterprising captains but the men they appointed – though their privileged schooling, like May's, may have suggested a free-spiritedness – were undoubtedly

Test class as players but temperamentally unsuited to the task. Cowdrey found responsibility a constant struggle, being too diffident and indecisive. Dexter was less sure than he appeared and, although always fond of a theory, was too detached to connect with his players.

According to Ray Illingworth, Cowdrey 'never seemed able to make a decision about anything, he never had the courage of his convictions, and he had to be talked into things', while Dexter 'hadn't the powers of concentration that captaincy requires'. He wasn't alone in these views. Numerous players also testified to Cowdrey's amazingly relaxed manner on the pitch, even when facing the most ferocious fast bowling, but off it he worried constantly. 'Of all the really top-class batsmen, he is the least sure of himself and the most subject to violent fluctuations of form,' Doug Insole wrote. Of Dexter, Micky Stewart said: 'As a man he could be shy at times, and he had to conquer that as captain. But with a bat or a ball in his hand he was a different man. Full of arrogance.'

The selectors, belatedly realising their shortcomings, even put the two men through a beauty contest during the home series with Pakistan ahead of the Australia tour in 1962-63, placing Dexter in charge for the first and second Tests before asking him to play under Cowdrey in the third. Cowdrey would probably have led in the fourth as well but he fell ill. In the end, Dexter took the side Down Under, but his appointment was greeted with widespread scepticism and the series that followed was turgid. The following year, Dexter first displayed a talent for the new limited-overs county cricket, captaining Sussex to success in the first Gillette Cup (a feat he repeated the following year), but his tactics were essentially based on deploying five seam bowlers operating to defensive fields, and drew criticism. When Sussex won their first final against Worcestershire, the match finished with Dexter posting all his fielders on the boundary.

To an extent the manner in which the England team have played their cricket has been a perennial debate (Tom Harrison, the ECB chief executive, in March 2017 called on Joe Root's Test side to play entertaining cricket regardless of the outcome, an idea Root swiftly sidestepped) but with the amateur class in terminal retreat – a process culminating in the overdue abolition of the distinction between amateur and professional playing status in November 1962 – this became a more pertinent issue than ever. Amateur administrators were determined to uphold the old code. This tussle extended into the captaincies of MJK Smith and the grammar-school educated Brian Close, who was sacked as England captain for time-wasting in a county match, and it was not until the dour, thinking Illingworth emerged by chance after Cowdrey snapped an Achilles tendon that a leader was found with sufficient self-confidence to stick to his instincts, and straight enough in his dealings (if sometimes a little blunt) to command the trust of his players. Under his tactically shrewd leadership in Australia in 1970-71, against considerable odds, the Ashes were regained after a 12-year hiatus. Like Hutton and Herbert Sutcliffe before him (and Matthew Hoggard subsequently), Illingworth's formative years were spent in or around Pudsey, West Yorkshire. He attended a state school and, like Hutton and Close, found himself an uncomfortable bedfellow of the game's establishment.

Unlike his immediate predecessors, Illingworth on that tour was able to resist managerial meddling – in this instance from David Clark, who had managed the tour of India 1963-64 and been appointed again in the expectation that he would be working alongside Cowdrey. In a brief playing career, Clark had been Cowdrey's first Kent captain. Illingworth's key player, fast bowler John Snow, said the tour highlighted a gulf between players and administrators, and that he was 'sick of the biased attitude and incompetence which was apparent in cricket administration'. Snow was 27 years old and in his prime, having had an outstanding tour of the West Indies in 1967-68 where he took 27 wickets in the Tests. He had a reputation as a difficult man who did not always appear to give 100 per cent to net sessions and warm-up matches, to the irritation of team-mates as well as management, but he was used to being managed directly by Illingworth, who one match into his reign in 1969 had been instrumental in Snow being dropped as a wake-up call. Hitting the seam regularly, Snow took 31 wickets in five and a half Tests in Australia.

The gulf Snow referred to had been increasingly apparent since the war. Gubby Allen and Walter Robins, who between them chaired the selection panel between 1955 and 1964, and Freddie Brown, who managed the tours of South Africa in 1956–57 and Australia in 1958–59, all wielded considerable influence long after they stopped playing. None of Allen, Robins and Brown was popular with the rank and file of England players. They had enjoyed little sustained success as England players themselves, and were perhaps seeking compensation as administrators.

Fred Trueman, a former miner, appeared to get on reasonably well with Robins, but he described Brown as a snob and a bigot, and had little affection for the Bentley-driving Allen, who publicly embarrassed him in the nets on his home ground at Headingley in 1956 after putting a handkerchief down on a length and instructing him to bowl at it. Doug Insole defended Allen on the grounds that Trueman was going through a bad patch and needed help, but it was the schoolmasterly manner of the exercise that hurt. Allen was involved in another incident at the same ground the following year when he took aside an unidentified member of the England team to advise him that 'his mistakes were generally made when he was "showing-off"'. According to EW Swanton, Allen and his co-selectors were anxious that standards of behaviour should be maintained 'for the benefit of the millions now viewing on television as well as spectators on the spot'. Trueman clashed in Australia with Brown, who told him after he missed the first Test with lumbago that he'd be going home if he was unfit. Trueman complained to Peter May who, according to Trueman's biographer Chris Waters, 'ordered Brown to give Trueman a wide berth and told him to act in a manner more befitting someone with managerial responsibility'.

Allen was also suspected of being one of the chief reasons why Les Jackson – who, like Larwood, Voce and Trueman, was of mining stock – played only twice for England despite taking 1,733 first-class wickets. Fred Titmus played twice in Allen's first year as chairman but then had to wait until Robins took over for a recall seven years later; he had refused to accept Allen's criticism that he bowled too flat. Titmus in fact was a master of drift. He eventually played 53 Tests and took 153 wickets. Allen's unpopularity may have had its origins in the equivocal role he played in the Bodyline series and its aftermath. Allen, like Robins, formed a firm alliance with Don Bradman. Robins and

Bradman, who shared a mistrust of the game's patrician class, were warmer friends, Robins often putting up Bradman when he was in England, but Allen and Bradman were intimate enough to share rounds of golf and in the 1950s and 1960s work closely as the leading cricket administrators in their respective countries. 'The influence of former amateur captains continued after they had moved into cricket administration,' Raman Subba Row, an England player of the late 1950s and early 1960s and later an administrator himself, said. 'They had grown up as autocrats and persisted with the same attitudes.'

Malcolm Knox has argued persuasively in his book *Bradman's War* that they were both party to the post-war decision to allow a second new ball after just 55 overs – Robins sat on the MCC subcommittee that revised the Laws – knowing that Bradman wanted the law changed. Similarly, Robins was an official member of the selection panel, and Allen involved in an advisory capacity, in the summer of 1948 when Hutton was dropped from the England side. As Knox again pointed out, in the days leading up to the decision, Robins socialised with Bradman a lot. Although most people were baffled by Hutton's demotion, Bradman always maintained it was justified, even though Hutton's subsequent record against Australia suggested it was not.*

Allen's handling of the 1947-48 tour was another contentious matter: his attempts to order about an inexperienced side did not meet with the approval of Joe Hardstaff junior, a senior professional. Allen, bridling at Hardstaff's belligerence, told him on the boat home that he would not play for England again, and Hardstaff proposed a bet of £100 on it. When Hardstaff was chosen for the first Test of the 1948 Ashes, Allen sent him a cheque, which Hardstaff tore up. However, Hardstaff was dropped for the next match at Lord's – perhaps significantly, Allen's 'territory' – and never played again.† Also among Allen's charges was Gerald Smithson, a young left-handed

---

\* If further evidence of the intimacy of the relationship is needed, Robins and Allen acted as Australia's proxies at ICC meetings on ten occasions (Robins eight times, Allen twice).

† Allen and Hardstaff had first clashed in Australia in 1936-37. In the West Indies, Hardstaff rebuffed Allen's demands that he ensure players did not keep late hours and they also fell out over Allen's handling of Nottinghamshire fast bowler Harold Butler, who like Hardstaff soon found himself surplus to England's requirements.

batsman from Yorkshire who had spent the previous three years in National Service working at a mine near Doncaster and required special dispensation to join the tour, which was only granted after questions were raised in the House of Commons over an initial decision by the Ministry of Labour to deny him leave. EW Swanton, Allen's biographer, claimed Smithson was chosen on the strength of one innings, though he actually scored 887 runs in the season despite making only one championship appearance before late June, including 107 not out against Surrey and 98 against Lancashire. Allen himself had played only once in the championship. Smithson played two Tests on the tour but never reappeared for England.

The corrosive effect on the morale and self-confidence of players from such arbitrary treatment was incalculable, but it was the England captain who had most to concern him. Hutton found this from the moment of his promotion. 'Much unofficial – and some quasi-official – opposition to the appointment [of Hutton] was surprising and all but shocking,' John Arlott wrote. 'In some quarters reaction towered far above that form of team-support which is sometimes called patriotism.'* Hutton, it was felt, could not be altogether trusted: hence Freddie Brown as chairman of selectors picking himself for a Test match at Lord's; hence also the bespectacled amateur Charles Palmer, having briefly and unexpectedly taken Leicestershire to the top of the championship, being appointed player-manager of the West Indies tour in 1953–54, which created the absurd situation of Hutton being both junior and senior to him.

When he returned home, Palmer recommended that a player should never again act as manager; even EW Swanton called it 'just about the worst decision ever to come out of Lord's'. Then, when Hutton missed two Tests through exhaustion the following summer and the England side was captained in his absence by David Sheppard, Robins (by now a selector) led a push for Sheppard rather than Hutton to take the side to Australia. Although in the end, and

---

* Richard Holt has suggested that Hutton's appointment, as well as other concessions to the professional ranks, were intended to ensure that 'Britain's national summer game remained in the hands of a small group who, in the best Whig traditions, had formed a policy of reforming to conserve'.

after a lively debate in national press, the selectors voted to stick with Hutton, this was both disloyal and unhelpful.*

Robins caused further consternation when – as manager of the side that went to the Caribbean in 1959-60, England's first tour since the catastrophic defeat in Australia – he performed, in Colin Cowdrey's words, 'extraordinary histrionics' in telling Peter May, even before the boat had passed Land's End, how the team should operate and seeking to impose 'military-style discipline'. Ray Illingworth, on his first England tour, was surprised to find the distinction between amateur and professionals even more pronounced than at home. Things came to a head on the final day of the final Test when Cowdrey, by now captain in the absence of the unwell May, played safe to protect England's 1-0 lead. Afterwards, Robins tore into him in front of his players; his 'public dressing down of his captain in the dressing-room only served to spoil what I thought had been a successful day for English cricket,' Cowdrey wrote.

Robins's proposal met with no support and, according to David Allen, the exchange ended with Trueman throwing him out of the room: 'You ain't no bloody business in 'ere. Get out!' Cowdrey's relationship with Robins never recovered. 'Apart from a few formal greetings over the next few years he had little time for me,' Cowdrey added. When in 1962, with Robins now chairman of selectors, the choice of captain for the tour of Australia came down to himself or Dexter, Cowdrey knew he had little chance, and so it proved.

Robins's problem was perhaps that, while he had been an enterprising player and captain, he failed to fully appreciate how much more tough and attritional international cricket was after the Second World War, with the result that his urgings as a selector and chairman of selectors for England to play in more attacking fashion were doomed to failure. 'As manager and selector, he became cantankerous and inconsiderate,' Mike Brearley wrote.

Cowdrey had various spells leading the side between 1959 and 1968 but was not a success. That he lacked the instinctive ruthlessness of

---

* *Wisden* corrected its original claim that only by a single vote did the selectors opt to retain Hutton, to a unanimous verdict.

a Hutton or May was demonstrated during his first Test in charge, when – with the series against India already won – he chose at Manchester not to enforce the follow-on so that the spectators would have some cricket to watch. In fact, according to *Wisden*, 'the purposeless cricket was derided by the majority of the crowd' and India eventually took the game into the final afternoon. He even needed persuading to go for the runs in Trinidad that delivered him his greatest triumph as captain in 1967-68; according to Geoff Boycott, Cowdrey was ready to accept a draw at tea, when England needed 142 runs in the final session with nine wickets in hand. It may have been such ingrained caution that prompted Garry Sobers to make such a generous declaration in the first place: he simply did not believe Cowdrey would accept the challenge. May felt too that Cowdrey had a good enough batting technique to be more attacking than he was: 'The pity was that as he grew older he seemed to lose the confidence to use that technique in attack.' Keith Fletcher, who was among the younger generation coming through, identified Cowdrey as among those in the 1970s who put the emphasis on grinding down the bowling rather than putting it to the sword. Illingworth wrote that Cowdrey 'was condemned to ultimate failure as a captain through essentially being an amateur trying to make himself into a professional'.*

If Robins hoped for better from Dexter then he was to be disappointed. Events conspired against Dexter when he captained the side to India and Pakistan in the winter of 1961-62 and lost the toss seven times in eight Tests. England were not at full strength and had yet to find an adequate replacement for Trevor Bailey as all-rounder; Dexter, though he performed heroically with bat and ball in the last Test of the tour in Karachi, was not quite a good enough bowler to fill that role himself. In the one Test in which he won the toss, England came closest to recording a win in India, but Dexter's team was plainly lacking in initiative. 'Until they [the England players] learn to treat cricket as a game to be enjoyed and not only as a means

---

* Cowdrey was also deeply hurt by an episode early in his Test career when, two weeks after starting national service in 1955, he was excused because of a problem with his feet. Three weeks later, he was back playing for England against South Africa. 'The press came down on me like a ton of bricks ... The letters poured in.'

to a commercial end, players will remain discontented with their lot,'
Leslie Smith wrote in *The Cricketer*, implying that the impending era
of full-on professionalism was not a cause for celebration.

When Robins formally took over as chairman in spring 1962, he
made it clear Dexter needed to up his game. 'We want a captain –
above everything else a leader – who must answer every bid or
challenge Australia make,' he declared. 'We do not want someone
who might wait for victory to come.' But with David Sheppard's
candidacy blocked by Gubby Allen and Cowdrey's shortcomings
all too apparent, the selectors had little alternative but to stick with
Dexter, with all too predictable results in Australia the following
winter. EM Wellings, who covered the tour, was scathing: 'The
appointment of Dexter as captain was a surprise about which few of
the critics were more than lukewarm. As a leader he was curiously
moody. He had not been a success at the head of MCC in India and
Pakistan ... He seemed essentially a cricketer who should be left to
develop his own brilliant play while someone else with more flair
for leadership captained the team.'

In a bizarre effort to ensure that MCC's intentions of livelier
cricket would be carried out – or, in Robins's words, 'influence
Dexter towards the right sort of play' – MCC plucked from its own
committee Bernard Fitzalan-Howard, the 16th Duke of Norfolk,
whose seat at Arundel and occasional involvement with the Sussex
club had brought him into contact with Dexter before, to act as manager. The Duke's appointment was met with widespread incredulity
as he had little understanding or experience of the duties involved. 'I
had to do all the work as the Duke wasn't familiar with cricket tours
at all,' said Alec Bedser, his assistant manager.* The same message

---

* The original intention was for Billy Griffith, MCC secretary, to manage the tour
but he became tied up with the amalgamation of amateur and professional status. The
Duke attracted enormous attention for his extracurricular activities on the tour, before
returning home early for reasons of state, thus allowing Griffith to join the tour after
all. According to Ian Wooldridge, the Duke announced to the press before the tour:
'Gentlemen, I wish this to be an entirely informal tour. You will merely address me as,
"Sir".' When he met up with the team in Colombo with three of his daughters in tow,
he told the players: 'You may dance with my daughters, you may take them out and wine
them and dine them, but that is all you may do.' His eldest daughter Anne Elizabeth,
later Lady Herries, married Colin Cowdrey in 1985.

went out to Dexter's players. Titmus, having scored a pedestrian 70 in the last-ever Gentlemen v Players match at Lord's, was told by Robins: 'If your captain says to you in Melbourne this winter you've got to get on with it, you had better get on with it.' In the event, though England started brightly and pulled off a surprise win in the second Test, they lost badly in Sydney and were unable to rouse themselves for the last two games.

England could hardly complain when opponents played them at their own game. Defensive bowling on leg stump had become a fashionable tactic and South Africa deployed it well against England in 1955, so much so that England picked five left-handers in what proved to be an unsuccessful attempt to counter Trevor Goddard in the fifth and deciding Test match.

The Lord's Test of 1963 produced one of the most famous of all finishes, the drama heightened for TV viewers by the BBC breaking away from its early-evening news bulletin, but a contributory factor was West Indies bowling their overs slowly to stymie England's pursuit of 234 on the final afternoon. At the climax, Colin Cowdrey – his arm having been broken by one of a string of short balls from Wes Hall – walked out with his arm in plaster to join David Allen, who played out the last two balls of the game with six runs needed for victory. With Hall and Charlie Griffith bowling for most of the afternoon the West Indies over-rate dropped to 14 an hour, much the same as England's tempo under May in the Caribbean. Brian Close, cast as scapegoat at Manchester in 1961 for attempting to hit Benaud off his length, had more success disrupting Hall and Griffith's length by bravely advancing down the pitch, sustaining many bruises in the process, but his tactics were again widely debated. Insole, an England selector, claimed somewhat fancifully that this was 'the first really obvious and overt example of an over-rate being slowed down in Test cricket'.

When Dexter's team were beaten at home in 1964 by an unexceptional Australia side led by Bob Simpson, his captaincy was finished. England lost only once, but such was the manner of the defeat at Leeds that Dexter's reputation was permanently scarred. Not only did he opt to take the second new ball in an effort to wrap up the

Australia second innings when his spinners Titmus and Norman Gifford were doing well, but he and Trueman could not then agree tactics against the one frontline batsman left at the crease, Peter Burge: Trueman wanted a man out on the hook, Dexter refused to give him one. Trueman's insistence on bowling short anyway, at no more than medium pace, while Burge sped to 160, fully warranted his dropping for the next match, but Dexter had lost the plot too. 'He couldn't skipper a rowing boat,' declared Brian Sellers, the former Yorkshire captain and England selector. Needing only a draw to secure the Ashes, Australia painstakingly batted into the third day at Old Trafford for 656. With nothing left to play for but pride, England replied with 611, of which Ken Barrington made 256 and Dexter 174. It was an excruciating spectacle.

Dexter actually initiated his own departure by standing for parliament as a Conservative in a General Election that took place on the day the 1964–65 tour of South Africa began. Had he been elected MP for Cardiff South East he would not have joined the tour at all but he was beaten by nearly 8,000 votes by James Callaghan, the future Labour Prime Minister, and arrived a week after the rest of the team to act as deputy to Mike Smith.* Although he played another nine Tests, Dexter never led the side again, an arrangement with which he seemed content. 'He seemed more relaxed and at ease than at any previous time in his career and made a major contribution to what was always an excellent dressing-room atmosphere,' Basil Easterbrook wrote in *Wisden* of his part on the South Africa tour. Although during a brief comeback he played two more Tests in 1968, Dexter was soon gone from regular Test cricket at the age of 30, explaining many years later: 'I had been everywhere and what beckoned was repetition.'

---

* Like Dexter, Charles Fry stood unsuccessfully for parliament, in his case three times as a Liberal in the 1920s. Alfred Lyttelton and Stanley Jackson, who both played Tests for England, served as Members of Parliament, Lyttelton from 1895 to 1906, Jackson from 1915 to 1926. Six England Test cricketers have sat in the House of Lords: Ivo Bligh (Lord Darnley 1900–27), George Harris (Lord Harris 1872–1932), Martin Hawke (Lord Hawke 1887–1938), Lionel Tennyson (Lord Tennyson 1928–51), David Sheppard (Baron Sheppard of Liverpool 1998–2005) and Colin Cowdrey (Baron Cowdrey of Tonbridge 1997–2000).

It may not have been a coincidence that England proved happier and more successful travellers once a captain was found in Mike Smith with a modicum of talent for man-management. Although some were less effusive, Tony Lewis described him as 'an outstanding reader of opposition techniques ... and a shrewd reader of temperaments'. Smith, who played under Cowdrey at Oxford, had like Trevor Bailey and Reg Simpson sustained a county career as an amateur through working for his county as assistant secretary, though he was under no illusions: 'Effectively I was a professional.'

The first man to lead England on three successive winter Test tours, he drew 0-0 in India in 1963-64 (Dexter was unavailable and Cowdrey, after being appointed captain, withdrew through injury, though he subsequently joined the tour as a replacement), won 1-0 in South Africa in 1964-65 (when Cowdrey curiously stated he was unavailable for family reasons), and drew 1-1 in Australia in 1965-66 (having gone 1-0 up).* Given that England were now without Trueman and Statham and short of new-ball penetration (the young John Snow played only two Tests during this time, both at home), it was understandable that Smith chose to sit on his lead once England had won the first Test in South Africa, and he would probably have sought to do the same in Australia had it not been for a nightmarish performance in Adelaide.

Singling out Smith and Donald Carr, the manager, for praise in South Africa, Basil Easterbrook wrote: 'MCC have sent more powerful teams from Lord's than this one, but never one superior in terms of corporate effort on the playing pitch and harmony in the pavilion. Manager and captain set the tone by behaving naturally and unchangingly to all with whom they had to deal. On any occasion which offered for fun or relaxation they identified themselves as members of the team.' Billy Griffith, manager in Australia, helped

---

* Smith was also invited to captain England on their tour of India and Pakistan in 1972-73 at the age of 39, but declined. Under Smith, England went unbeaten through two major Test tours, in India in 1963-64 and South Africa 1964-65. The only other times this happened when ten or more first-class matches were played was under Hammond in South Africa 1938-39, George Mann in South Africa 1948-49 and Cowdrey in West Indies 1967-68. Smith was also England's last cricket–rugby double international.

coax out of the batsmen a more enterprising approach, but he was fortunate to have in Bob Barber an instinctively attacking opener whose game had been galvanised by the early limited-overs county cricket. In Sydney, Barber struck 185 from only 255 balls. Griffith had less success getting England to bowl their overs at a healthy rate.

England's performance in Bombay (later Mumbai) in Smith's second match in charge typified the esprit de corps he cultivated. With one man injured and three others unwell, he had only 11 players to choose from, and by tea on the first day Micky Stewart, who had himself shaken off illness, had succumbed again, leaving them armed with two specialist batsmen, two wicketkeepers, two spinners and four fast bowlers. India loaned out a twelfth man, Kripal Singh. 'This must be the oddest England side ever to have played in an official Test match,' John Woodcock wrote in his match report the next day. But the ten men of England fought a heroic rearguard and secured a draw with something to spare. *Wisden* described their spirit as magnificent: 'They put the sort of fire into their out-cricket that distinguishes the best Celtic rugger pack, and they fought splendidly with the bat.'* The team had had a narrow escape in the first Test in Madras (later Chennai), when on the third day England were batting and five of the six men waiting to bat were in bed at the team hotel. After the rest day, all had recovered sufficiently to bat and save the follow-on.

Hopes that a corner had been turned were soon dashed. For all his qualities, Smith was not really worth his place in the side as a

---

* Had Stewart not recovered before the start, England would have been in grave difficulty finding an 11th player. They would probably have commandeered David Clark, the manager and only non-playing member of the touring party. Clark, 44, averaged 15.8 with the bat during his short career with Kent, which ended in 1951. He confirmed to press-men on the eve of the Test that his most recent match had been a fathers-and-sons game in Oxford the previous year, although he had had a net in Madras the previous week. Henry Blofeld, 24, who played 16 first-class matches for Cambridge University in 1959 and 1960, and had played once for Norfolk in the minor counties championship in 1961, was covering the tour for the *Guardian* and was apparently another option – with Clark himself alerting Blofeld to the possibility – although one that prompted Micky Stewart to say to Clark, 'You're kidding, aren't you?' John Woodcock, covering the tour for *The Times*, does not remember much being made of the Blofeld option at the time. Blofeld claimed in 2017 that he came 'within half an hour of playing in a Test match'.

batsman – he was not chosen against Australia in 1964 and scored one hundred in 25 Tests as captain. After one Test at home to West Indies in 1966 he was dropped and Cowdrey recalled. Cowdrey lasted three Tests before being replaced by Brian Close, whose established record of winning trophies at Yorkshire initially overrode reservations about his unnerving habit of speaking his mind and genuinely thinking he could do everything. (He batted at No.9 in his first Test and No.2 in his last, could bowl seam or spin, and was one of the great short-leg fieldsmen.) Close's involvement with England as a player had been chequered, and like Smith he was not an automatic selection, but once he had led the team to an innings win in his first match in charge – thanks in large part to England's last three wickets freakishly adding 361 – he was guaranteed the job when India and Pakistan, neither of whom had won a Test series in England, toured in 1967.

With the first Test of the summer, the issue of slow play resurfaced when Geoff Boycott spent almost ten hours taking an unbeaten 246 off a toothless India attack at Headingley. Doug Insole's panel promptly dropped him for one match as punishment, a disciplinary measure they had previously meted out to Ken Barrington in 1965 when he had spent more than seven hours scoring 137 against New Zealand (at one stage his score remained on 85 for 20 overs). Insole was in effect carrying out the threat Robins had issued when he became chairman that England players needed to show 'intent'. Privately, he told Barrington, 'It appeared as though all you wanted was a hundred – which looks very selfish.' Keith Miller, writing in the *Daily Express*, said: 'Barrington set the cricket clock back to the Dark Ages ... A painful crowd-killer and the stuff that is emptying the cricket grounds of England.' But Percy Fender directed blame at the team's management, arguing that Barrington was only acting in the interests of his side. Barrington returned after a one-match absence and scored 163 in speedier fashion. Boycott's dropping created more controversy and when Michael Parkinson, writing in the *Sunday Times*, alleged that the England selectors had been actuated by 'unworthy and discreditable motives', the selectors responded with an action for libel and secured an apology in the Queen's Bench Division before Mr Justice Nield.

Although technically capable of scoring runs at Test level, neither Boycott nor Barrington was the most confident of players, Barrington worrying about his place in the side even when his consistent record of run-scoring for England made him in most people's eyes an automatic pick. He struggled to sleep or eat before Test matches, puffed anxiously on cigarettes, and retired at 37. Like Boycott, who would open the batting in more than 100 Tests, Barrington had a tough role to fill as a rock-like presence at No.3. It was a position that had in the past often been occupied by men armed with more strokes than any other player in the side, such as Wally Hammond and Ted Dexter, but in this more cautious era Barrington's first duty was to occupy the crease, not entertain crowds.

This was the backdrop to Close's sacking as England captain for time-wasting while captaining a championship match at Edgbaston, where Yorkshire bowled only six overs in the last 30 minutes, and two in the last 15, to leave Warwickshire stranded nine runs short of their target.* This incident occurred in the week before the final Test of the summer, though it did not prevent Close captaining that match, which resulted in another England win, giving him five wins out of six against India and Pakistan, four of them in three or four days. Purely in terms of results, therefore, Close held an unarguable case for taking the team to the West Indies, even if Illingworth, his right-hand man at Yorkshire, thought him a better leader when things were going well: 'On a slow flat wicket when nothing was happening he switched off, which you can't do as captain.'

The selectors met to consider the tour party the day after the time-wasting incident, and at that point were in majority support for Close, but a final decision was delayed until the outcome of an executive committee meeting of the Advisory County Cricket Committee chaired by MCC president Arthur Gilligan. This concluded Close was guilty of deliberately slowing down the game in order to avoid defeat. When the selectors reconvened, they were split 3-3. 'Three

---

* This incident led to the introduction of a law stipulating that 20 overs had to be bowled in the last scheduled hour of a match, which survived in Tests until the ICC accepted 15 overs an hour as the standard requirement.

members considered that . . . it would be most undesirable to appoint Close,' the minutes of the meeting read. 'They believed that there would be a most unfavourable public reaction, particularly in the West Indies, to such an appointment.'

This estimation may have been influenced by a letter sent to MCC several weeks earlier from a correspondent describing himself as an 'Old West Indies Cricketer', who began by saying: 'The general rumour in Trinidad is that B Close will be appointed captain of the English side which will come out here later this year. Right here I will tell you that that kind of decision is among the worst mistakes English cricket has been making in late years by appointing 3rd or 4th class types of men to lead their cricket teams both at home and abroad.' He concluded: 'Why not go back to your old policy of appointing university graduates as captains?'

At the bottom of the letter the initials 'DBC' (presumably those of Donald Carr, MCC's assistant secretary) accompanied a scrawled note: 'We must keep this letter as it clearly represents my views.' Some may also have remembered Hutton's warning in his tour report of 1953-54 which stated: 'In future tours to the West Indies I feel that an experienced captain must be sent. The situations at times require very careful handling and I do feel that it would be unfair to expect a young man to cope.' Close's fate was sealed when the MCC committee declined to endorse him as captain – another instance of MCC's imprimatur regarding tour appointments being required. The Oxford-educated Cowdrey was chosen in place of the northern grammar-school boy.

In fact, on the eve of the final Test, Close had been summoned to Lord's to explain himself and Insole had told him he could save himself if he just said sorry, but Close could not bring himself to do so. Perhaps he wondered why he should when so many captains before him had dragged their heels in the field and won national acclaim for doing so. He was unrepentant and the fear that he might commit some similar act of expedience in the West Indies sealed his fate. Close said he had been warned in advance of the Edgbaston incident by Crawford White of the *Daily Express* that moves were afoot to remove him. 'Crawford phoned me,' he said. 'He advised me to watch my step as word was going round that the establishment wanted me out of the way and their own man in my place with any excuse to get rid of me.' Yet not all the establishment felt the same: Insole admitted during a press conference at Lord's not only that the vote against Close had been by the narrowest possible margin, but that he personally favoured Close's retention.*

Administrative initiatives designed to bring about more enterprising play were having little effect. The professional mentality was taking an ever-stronger grip on the game, and whatever the imprecations coming out of Lord's, no player was going to die in a ditch to stop it, certainly not Illingworth. He was not the establishment's preferred candidate but after Cowdrey's injury in the early weeks of the 1969 season, he was a compelling choice, though the credentials of Roger Prideaux – a former Cambridge Blue who had played three Tests – received an airing.

Illingworth had recently left Yorkshire, the club chairman Brian Sellers having rejected out of hand his novel request for a long-term contract, and was now captaining Leicestershire.† He was another who had rarely felt sure of an England place, partly because he was competing for the same role of off-spinning all-rounder as Titmus, as well as David Allen, whose bounce and loop made him a good option on harder surfaces overseas. It was only after Titmus, by now vice-captain, suffered a freak accident in the Caribbean in 1967-68 when he lost four toes on the propeller of a boat that Illingworth's Test prospects improved.‡ His response was immediate: he took 13 wickets in three Tests against Australia in 1968, including six for 87 at Headingley, and in his second match as captain scored a maiden Test hundred.

---

* In fact, Close was to lead England again. With Ray Illingworth injured, Close was asked to captain the side in three one-day internationals against Australia in 1972, the first played on home soil, and took the series 2-1.

† A year later Brian Sellers also forced Close out of Yorkshire after giving him the option to resign or be sacked as captain; Close was felt to be not encouraging the younger players. Close moved to Somerset where he nurtured a number of future England players including Ian Botham, Brian Rose and Vic Marks.

‡ Titmus recovered to resume his first-class career, and even played four more Tests in Australia in 1974-75 at the age of 42. Titmus received only £90 from MCC in compensation for his injury, leading to a reform of insurance policies in respect of England cricketers on duty overseas.

Nevertheless, Cowdrey's supporters remained vocal – EW Swanton trotting out the customary grumbles about dreary batting and slow over-rates – and Illingworth came to the understanding that his appointment for Australia was only secured by a 3-1 vote, with the chairman Bedser backing a return to Cowdrey. Bedser, for his part, had to see off a push for Gubby Allen, now 68 years of age, to rejoin and probably therefore chair the selection panel the following year. Like Illingworth, Bedser was not prepared to be pushed around: he ended up staying as chairman until 1981, the longest run anyone has ever managed.

The old saws about North v South, Professional v Amateur and New School v Old School came into play when Illingworth led England in Australia and found himself saddled as manager with David Clark, who since managing the 1963-64 tour of India had in 1967 authored a significant report into the state of county cricket. Ominously, one of his report's conclusions stated that the future of the game depended on 'the ability of administrators to encourage the proper approach [from the players]'. Illingworth was already acutely conscious that the former Oxbridge men, Cowdrey, Dexter and MJK Smith, had all not selected him at various stages of their captaincies.

Clark's interference in cricketing matters incensed both Illingworth and Snow from the early stages of the tour. First, Snow was rested from a state game after bowling 52.5 eight-ball overs in the first Test, only for Clark to tell him he still had to take full part in a practice session; Snow, whose fuse was never long, stormed off and was not seen until the next day.* Then after the second Test, Clark decried to the press the cautious nature of the play, criticised England for their short-pitched bowling and suggested he would prefer to see Australia win 3-0 than watch four more draws. After they had heard of these remarks, Illingworth and Snow met with Clark in Adelaide

---

* Clark seemed less strict about making Cowdrey, Illingworth's vice-captain, attend nets. 'There were days when Cowdrey didn't even turn up at all at the nets,' Illingworth wrote in his autobiography. 'I expected him to be organising the nets. I asked the manager ... where Colin was and he didn't know.' Their antipathy appeared to date from an incident on the 1962-63 Ashes tour when Illingworth had been ill in hospital and Cowdrey asked him to do 12th man duties as he and his wife wanted to go to the cinema see the premiere of *Mutiny on the Bounty*.

but, according to Snow, 'after an hour, we were no nearer a mutual understanding and just gave up'.

Then, when rain washed out the next Test in Melbourne over the New Year period, Clark and Gubby Allen had agreed with Don Bradman, chairman of the Australian Cricket Board – and without consulting Illingworth or the players or making provision for them to receive extra payment – to the staging of a one-day match to provide entertainment for the crowd (what is now regarded as the first one-day international), as well as an additional Test tagged onto the end of the series, creating in effect an unprecedented seventh Test, including the wash-out.* After the players voted strongly to support Illingworth's proposal that they refuse to play the extra Test without a proportional increase in their tour fee, the TCCB eventually agreed to each man receiving an additional £100 after an opening offer of £25.† Clark had initially refused any increase even though it was known Australians were getting $200 each. Bob Willis, who played the first of his 90 Test matches on this tour, wrote that the relationship between Clark and Illingworth 'was by some distance the worst I have ever known between a captain and manager'.

Illingworth recalled that at one point on the tour, 'I was forced to tell him [Clark] that I honestly believed he was more of an asset to the Australians than to us. I told him he was there as team manager, not as an ambassador of goodwill on behalf of MCC.'

With the players exhausted by the protracted schedule, and England holding a precarious 1–0 lead, the most incendiary episode of a febrile tour arrived on the second evening of the extra Test match in Sydney. Snow bowled a short ball at Terry Jenner, a tailender, which struck him on the back of the neck. As Jenner was helped from the field, Lou Rowan – who had a reputation for interpreting umpiring

---

* One of the recommendations in David Clark's report into the state of county cricket was that there should be more one-day cricket, which had since happened with the introduction of a Sunday league, sponsored by John Player, in 1969. These were 40-over matches. The first one-day international in Melbourne consisted of 40 eight-ball overs per side.

† Only two players did not support Illingworth's motion: Derek Underwood, who said he would be happy to play for England without pay, and Colin Cowdrey, the man passed over for the captaincy, who failed to show for the meeting.

as an extension of his regular job as a policeman and had warned England's strike bowler earlier in the series at Perth about overdoing the bouncer – told Snow to ease up on the short-pitched deliveries.

Snow was furious, as was Illingworth, as neither felt Snow's bowling had been consistently short enough to warrant such a reprimand (Jenner himself later conceded he was at fault). 'You can't caution him,' Illingworth said. 'Hell, I'll report you.' At the end of the over, Illingworth sent Snow to the fine-leg fence, which proved a mistake as Snow was soon grabbed by the shirt by a spectator, other fielders rushed over, and the crowd began throwing empty beer cans onto the field. Illingworth first told his players to sit down then, when the situation deteriorated further, he led them from the field, though without informing the umpires, only to be met by Clark telling him to get back onto the field. When umpires Rowan and Tom Brooks threatened him with forfeiture if he did not resume the match, Illingworth agreed provided police protection was provided, but frank words were exchanged before this happened. 'Snowy joined in and got rather a lot off his chest,' Illingworth wrote.

England went on to win a thrillingly taut game by 62 runs despite Snow being incapacitated by a hand injury – Illingworth leading the way with three for 39, having top-scored with 42 in the first innings – but the captain did not let the matter rest. He duly wrote a letter of complaint to the Australian board about Rowan and the fact England's bowlers were denied any lbws during the series. Then, once home, he threatened that all hell would break loose if any of his players was denied a good conduct bonus. This did not happen – though Snow and Boycott, who threw his bat down in disgust at being run out during the Adelaide Test, were summoned to Lord's for a lecture from Billy Griffith. Yet, in future, greater efforts were made to ensure that tour managers and players were, in Snow's words, 'more of a like mind', or as Jack Bannister put it in the 1990s, the troubles of this tour led to 'a more enlightened method of choosing the manager, with the captain now usually chosen first, and then his views taken into account'. Snow, though, would not experience those improved relations at first hand: he was never chosen for another Test tour.

## Alma Maters

As long as the amateur–professional divide existed, it was common for England captains to be drawn from the leading English private schools and universities. Of England's first 51 captains, 31 went to Oxford or Cambridge (although Timothy O'Brien's attachment to Oxford appears to have been a purely cricketing one); of the subsequent 29, only three did so (Tony Lewis, Mike Brearley and Michael Atherton), and only two (Chris Cowdrey at Tonbridge and Andrew Strauss at Radley) were primarily educated at a leading private school. Lewis and Cyril Walters were both products of Neath Grammar School and Neath Cricket Club. Ilford CC nurtured Graham Gooch and Nasser Hussain and Sheffield Collegiate both Michael Vaughan and Joe Root. Five captains attended Pembroke College, Cambridge, and four captains Trinity, Cambridge and St John's, Cambridge.

Educational establishments have played less of a role in the development of cricketers in the modern era: their priority is academic excellence and the 18 first-class counties have age-group systems which nurture elite players from an early stage. Root, who spent his last two years of education at an independent school, said the move to Worksop College was actually a hindrance to his cricketing development: 'They were strict about schoolwork and about school fixtures taking precedence over Yorkshire academy and second XI cricket, which was frustrating.'

## Leading providers of England captains
*(year given is that of first match as captain)*

Senior schools

ETON 7 (Lord Harris 1879, Ivo Bligh 1882, Lord Hawke 1896, Lionel Tennyson 1921, Ronnie Stanyforth 1927, Gubby Allen 1936, George Mann 1948)

HARROW 3 (AN Hornby 1882, Archie MacLaren 1897, Stanley Jackson 1905)

CHARTERHOUSE 3 (C Aubrey Smith 1889, Frederick Fane 1907, Peter May 1955)

DULWICH 3 (Monty Bowden 1889, Arthur Gilligan 1924, Harold
    Gilligan 1930)
REPTON 3 (Charles Fry 1912, Freddie Calthorpe 1930, Donald Carr 1952)
MALVERN 2 (RE Foster 1907, Frank Mann 1922)
WINCHESTER 2 (Henry Leveson Gower 1910, Douglas Jardine 1931)
SHERBORNE 2 (Arthur Carr 1926, David Sheppard 1954)
TONBRIDGE 2 (Colin Cowdrey 1959, Chris Cowdrey 1988)
RADLEY 2 (Ted Dexter 1961, Andrew Strauss 2006)
NEATH GRAMMAR SCHOOL 2 (Cyril Walters 1934, Tony Lewis 1972)

## Universities

CAMBRIDGE 21 (Ivo Bligh 1882, AG Steel 1886, C Aubrey Smith 1889,
    Lord Hawke 1896, Stanley Jackson 1905, Arthur Jones 1908, Frank
    Mann 1922, Arthur Gilligan 1924, Percy Chapman 1926, Freddie
    Calthorpe 1930, Gubby Allen 1936, Walter Robins 1937, Norman
    Yardley 1947, George Mann 1948, Freddie Brown 1949, David
    Sheppard 1954, Peter May 1955, Ted Dexter 1961, Tony Lewis 1972,
    Mike Brearley 1977, Michael Atherton 1993)
OXFORD 13 (Lord Harris 1879, Tim O'Brien 1896, Pelham Warner 1903,
    RE Foster 1907, Frederick Fane 1907, Henry Leveson Gower 1910,
    Charles Fry 1912, Ronnie Stanyforth 1927, Greville Stevens 1928,
    Douglas Jardine 1931, Donald Carr 1952, Colin Cowdrey 1959, MJK
    Smith 1964)

## England Players Who Also Managed Test Tours

Once MCC became directly involved with England Test tours in 1903-
04, the teams were generally managed by men with experience as
county secretaries (Frederick Toone managed three tours of Australia in
the 1920s) or the services (Rupert Howard, Mike Green and TH Carlton-
Levick, all army men, and Geoffrey Howard, formerly of the RAF, all
supervised two tours). They needed to be resourceful: Geoffrey Howard
had to open a personal bank overdraft to pay for incidental expenses
in the early stages of the Australia tour in 1954-55.

Only from the late 1950s were former England players appointed manager with a view to helping captains more specifically with the cricket; on some tours assistant managers were also appointed to help with coaching. Between 1956-57 and 1986-87 when England travelled for the first time with a head coach (originally called, confusingly, a team manager), only six Test tours were handled by non-Test players (Tom Pearce, the Duke of Norfolk, David Clark and Tony Brown) and they were not notable successes. Pearce, indeed, was chided by one of the players Bob Barber for drinking too freely at social events on the subcontinent in 1961-62: 'I was one of three amateurs and the pros wouldn't say too much as they were on a bonus,' Barber said. 'I had a go at him and told him that perhaps he should hold his tongue.'

In the era of head coaches, the role of tour manager reverted to men who, though some played to a good standard, were not internationals: Peter Lush (1986-87 to 1990-91), Bob Bennett (1991-92, 1992-93, 1997-98), John Barclay (1996-97) and Phil Neale (who worked on every Test tour between South Africa 1999-2000 and Sri Lanka 2018-19).

| Former player | Tours |
| --- | --- |
| James Lillywhite | Three to Australia 1876-77 to 1887-88 (one as player-manager) |
| Alfred Shaw | Two to Australia 1884-85 and 1886-87 |
| AE Stoddart | Australia 1894-95 (captain-manager) |
| George Lohmann | South Africa 1898-99 |
| Archie MacLaren | Australia 1901-02 (captain-manager) |
| Harold Gilligan | New Zealand 1929-30 (captain-manager) |
| Pelham Warner | Australia 1932-33 (joint-manager) |
| Gubby Allen | West Indies 1947-48 (captain-manager) |
| Charles Palmer | West Indies 1953-54 (player-manager) |
| Freddie Brown | Two to South Africa 1956-57 and Australia 1958-59 |
| Walter Robins | West Indies 1959-60 |
| Billy Griffith | Two to Australia 1962-63 (part) and 1965-66 |
| Donald Carr | Three to South Africa 1964-65, India/Pakistan 1972-73 and West Indies 1973-74 |

| Former player | Tours |
|---|---|
| Les Ames | Two to West Indies 1967-68 and Pakistan 1968-69 |
| Alec Bedser | Two to Australia 1974-75 and Australia/India 1979-80 |
| Ken Barrington | Two to India/Australia 1976-77 and Pakistan/New Zealand 1977-78 |
| Doug Insole | Two to Australia 1978-79 and 1982-83 |
| AC Smith | Two to West Indies 1980-81 and New Zealand/Pakistan 1983-84 |
| Raman Subba Row | India/Sri Lanka 1981-82 |
| MJK Smith | Two to West Indies 1993-94 and Australia 1994-95 |
| Ray Illingworth | South Africa 1995-96 |
| Graham Gooch | Australia 1998-99 |

# CHAPTER 25

# Leaving, On a Jet Plane

## Shorter tours, Sunday play, the end of rest days

In 1965-66, England for the first time flew all the way, both ways, for a Test tour of Australia and New Zealand. On the outward leg they stopped over in Colombo, where they played two one-day matches, but in actual flying time the journey from London to Perth took just under 60 hours. On the way back they broke their journey in Hong Kong, playing two more one-day games. Even with these breaks – which would be gone by the late 1970s as jet travel became speedier still – this was a radically faster means of travel than players on earlier tours had enjoyed. When England first went to Australia after the Second World War, the voyage took about 24 days; back in the 1870s, when the first Test tours were made, the P&O steamships typically took around double that time to plough across the oceans.

England's Test team had flown before, but the difference was that the longest journeys had now been negotiated safely and the authorities were persuaded that flying was the way forward. They had taken a long time to get to this point. On the previous tour of Australia in 1962-63, the team only flew as far as Aden before boarding the *Canberra* and sailing from there to Colombo and then on to Fremantle. This proved to be the last time an England Test team travelled by sea, as they returned at the end of the tour by plane. Even when the players flew to and from South Africa in 1964-65 though, the party was split into two groups and placed on different planes. 'I think they [the administrators] still had the Munich air crash in mind,' said one of them, Tom Cartwright.

Not everyone was convinced by the advent of this racier world in which Heathrow airport displaced Tilbury docks as the traditional point of departure. Once England's players had levered themselves out of their cramped economy-class seats and stepped onto the tarmac in Perth in October 1965, several of them went down with stomach disorders and viruses over the following days which affected their early preparations. At around the same time, similar problems afflicted rugby union and rugby league teams flying from Britain to Australia.

'It is a fair assumption that rapid transportation into different conditions is at least in part the cause of such maladies, which were not suffered when teams travelled more slowly by sea,' wrote Lyn Wellings, who covered the 1965–66 tour for the *London Evening News* and was a writer who never knowingly agreed with the authorities. He called on MCC in *Wisden* to review its travel arrangements. Wellings also regretted talk of future England tours of Australia being shortened. 'That, I believe, would be a sad mistake. Tours involving England and Australia are the great events of cricket. If they are worth doing, they must be done thoroughly, without any skimping ... A tour of 16 first-class matches and three minor games would mean a tour of 18 weeks, and it should not be any shorter than that.' In fact, even with the introduction into the schedule of one-day internationals, no England tour of Australia has exceeded 18 weeks since 1986–87.

Air flight transformed the lives of international cricketers and the nature of international cricket. Marriage between cricketers and air-hostesses was only one consequence. The tours themselves lost much of their old pomp and ceremony, as visiting teams began to fulfil their commitments with greater efficiency. Colin Cowdrey, reflecting on his first tour of Australia in 1954–55, recounted how the night before sailing from Tilbury the team gathered at Lord's for a dinner in the Long Room in which they were addressed by the MCC president 'as though we were just off to Agincourt instead of Adelaide'.

Early tours were stuffed with official functions at most of which the captain – and if not him the manager – was expected to make a speech. (WG Grace gave the same speech at each one, simply changing the name of the place he and his players were delighted to be in.) The voyages themselves were for many players among the most attractive parts of the adventure: a time for enforced relaxation, sightseeing in Pompeii and Alexandria, and making friends with Australians who would invite them to visit once the tour proper was underway.

EW Swanton, whose experience of touring Australia spanned England's first eight tours after the Second World War, rued the transition towards a more brutally modernist means of transport: 'No such lovely, leisurely, luxurious start as the old sea voyages through the Med and Suez and with the stretching of sea-legs in the one-day game at Colombo: no dusty train journeys . . . no putting up at faded old country hotels, seemingly not decorated since the gold rush . . .' Not that he was much enamoured with the outward voyage in 1946–47, of which he said: 'Nearly a month at sea on a crowded ship run on austerity lines by the Government – no classes and no drink.'

MCC's reluctance to embrace air travel in part reflected the fact that the early flights – international and internal – were not always the smoothest affairs. They were hit by delays and mechanical problems, and many travellers were unwilling to endure the risks. When Gubby Allen missed a state match during the 1936–37 tour, he needed special dispensation from MCC president Lord Somers in order to fly from Melbourne to Hobart to catch up with the rest of the team.

However, MCC's stance softened during the timeless Test at Durban in 1938–39, when it cabled an offer to transport the team by flying boat if it would allow them to stay and finish the game. After a conference between Wally Hammond, the tour manager and the South African authorities, it was decided to abandon the match anyway to let the England players catch their appointed boat home (although in fact Hammond himself flew from Durban to Cape Town to meet the boat while the rest of the team went by rail). The first time an entire England party took what was described as 'an ocean flight' was for the relatively short hop from Sydney to Auckland in March 1947, but for a long time players appear to have been allowed to choose whether they flew or sailed home. Godfrey Evans was among a group who returned home from the 1946-47 tour by flying boat and described being treated like emperors: 'At Cairo we landed on the Nile, then launched off, black tie, to dine and nightclub before leaving at dawn the next day. Bliss.'

At the end of the 1950-51 tour, though most of the team flew back from New Zealand via San Francisco and New York, three players – Bob Berry, Brian Close and Eric Hollies, who were not required for the New Zealand leg – preferred to sail and still got home only six days after the others. Four years later, Cowdrey described sitting next to a 'yellow-green' Len Hutton on a bumpy internal flight in Australia; when the tour finished, Hutton was among those who opted to return by boat; they arrived back 15 days later than their colleagues.

The 1953-54 tour of the West Indies was the first on which the England team flew out en masse by plane, though they returned by boat; they had to refuel in Ireland and were then diverted to Newfoundland, but two days after leaving Britain they were engaged in a two-day fixture in Bermuda. On the 1961-62 tour of the subcontinent, when the players flew both ways, they were subjected to a particularly arduous schedule with few days off. Due to a hold-up on a flight from Colombo to Karachi, the team arrived for a match without sleep and made a delayed start at 1.30pm. This was a tour which several senior players opted out of (among them Cowdrey, Brian Statham and Fred Trueman), and their absence created some ill-feeling among those who did make the trip, among whom were seven new caps. Only for the 1970-71 tour of Australia were steps first taken to counter jet-lag, the players being given a week to acclimatise before beginning their opening fixture against a South Australia Country XI in Port Pirie.

Those who harked back to the time before planes as some sort of golden age tended to forget the time-consuming and occasionally hazardous nature of travelling by boat and train. Ivo Bligh's team was aboard the *Peshawur* en route to Australia when it was involved in a collision with another boat at Colombo, and Fred Morley suffered a broken rib which is said to have contributed to his early death two years later at the age of 33. Seasickness afflicted the likes of William Gunn, Gilbert Jessop, Jack Hobbs, Tony Lock and Trueman, among many others. Thomas Armitage, who played in the first of all Test matches in Australia in 1877, arrived from New Zealand only the day before the game, suffering badly from the sea-crossing.

The first Test tour of South Africa in 1888–89 took place before the railway had reached Johannesburg and most journeys were undertaken by ox-wagon. 'More time was spent in getting from place to place than in actually playing cricket,' lamented one account. The England team of 1920–21 lost a week of practice when they were quarantined on arrival in Australia following a typhus outbreak on their boat. Gubby Allen was unable to move his neck after undertaking the marathon train journey from Perth to Adelaide in 1932–33; 'I have had Turkish baths and massage in the hope of getting rid of it.'

When in 1947–48 the England party sailed for the Caribbean out of Liverpool, they looked askance at the empty banana boat called the *Tetela* provided for their two-week voyage over Christmas and New Year. 'It was a small ship, only 2,500 tons, and it looked as if it would bob up and down on the great seas of the Atlantic like a rowing boat on the Serpentine,' Godfrey Evans wrote. After enduring rough weather, Gubby Allen again found himself in the wars. In an effort to keep fit he went on deck with a skipping rope and promptly pulled a calf muscle which put him out of the first Test. On the way out to South Africa in 1938–39, Norman Yardley slipped on deck and cracked a rib, while 20 years later Willie Watson damaged his knee getting out of a deckchair and was flown on ahead from Colombo to Perth for treatment. 'The idea that it [travelling by boat] gave you a chance to get to know one another was always a farce,' MJK Smith said. 'If anything, it gave you a chance to fall out with each other.'

Arthur Shrewsbury said of travelling in Australia and New Zealand in the 1880s: 'Twenty to thirty hours at a stretch in a railway carriage slowly creeping along with bad sleeping and refreshment accommodation is an experience not to be desired.' Pelham Warner calculated that on a tour of South Africa in 1905–06 he and his players travelled 6,348 miles by rail and spent 22 nights on trains, in addition to a sea voyage between Durban and East London. Similarly, Frederick Toone, manager of the team touring Australia in 1928-29, estimated that they spent between 20 and 30 nights on trains, including three nights in a row from Perth to Adelaide, and another three from Melbourne to Perth. 'The whole tour means a round journey of between 40,000 and 50,000 miles,' he wrote. Until it became standard for teams to travel together by coach, instances of players being involved in car crashes on tour were also not uncommon; Major Booth and Andrew Sandham, both on tours of South Africa, and Peter Loader and Statham, in Australia, all missed Tests followed such accidents.

When an airline strike ruined England's travel arrangements during the tour of India 1992-93 they discovered how brutal journeys by train could be: the team was stuck for 18 hours on one train and had to play a Test the next day. When photographs appeared of them looking dishevelled as they arrived, they were widely condemned.

The option of flying transformed the abilities of touring teams to summon replacements. With Gubby Allen's side in the West Indies plagued by injuries, an SOS was sent for Denis Compton, Bill Edrich or Len Hutton to be released by their counties; all three had stayed at home in preparation for the 1948 Ashes. Eventually Yorkshire relented, Hutton was rushed to Heathrow and after three days of travel he reached Georgetown 13 days after Allen put out his request.

Statham and Roy Tattersall experienced an even more tortu-ous journey when they were called up for the 1950-51 tour. They travelled from Manchester to London by train, then took flights to Rome, Cairo, Karachi, Singapore, Darwin, Sydney and Melbourne, where they finally met up with the team. Their first two flights were hampered by electrical problems. Neither had ever flown before. At the start of the same tour, Cyril Washbrook, after initially declining a place, changed his mind and caught up with the main party by flying out whereas they had gone by boat. Flying out replacements was an expensive business but once the practice became established the onus shifted to the selectors responding quickly and judiciously to requests for extra men. In 1958-59, Gubby Allen's panel was criticised for not acting faster to ensure that Ted Dexter and John Mortimore arrived in time to be realistic picks for the first Test in Brisbane.*

As with Statham and Tattersall, some mercy dashes involved protracted journeys. Barry Wood in 1974-75 was summoned to Auckland all the way from the West Indies, where he was touring with an English Counties team. Having travelled for 63 hours, his reward was to be out for a first-ball duck. Alastair Cook and James Anderson were also in transit for three days from Antigua to Nagpur when they were called up for England's 2005-06 tour of India; Cook was sufficiently unfazed to bat for nine and a half hours on debut, scoring 60 and 104 not out.†

The value of plane travel was never better appreciated than when it enabled England's players to make a swift exit from a chaotic situation in Karachi in March 1969.‡ It was immediately clear on arrival in Pakistan that the country – both its East and West wings – was in a state of civil unrest caused by secessionist agitation in the former and student calls for democracy in the latter. Peter Oborne said the tour was 'sanctioned and encouraged' by the British Foreign Office because Ayub Khan's faltering military dictatorship had been established with British and American support, and Keith Fletcher probably articulated the feelings of many of the England players when he later wrote, 'we were no longer cricketers, it seemed, but ambassadors being paid a tour fee to keep the peace.'

Les Ames, the MCC manager, acting on the advice of High Commission officials, calculated that England could not call off the tour without making the team themselves a target, while the Pakistan cricket board, being effectively an arm of government, remained adamant that the three Tests would go ahead, one of them

---

* Ted Dexter became sufficiently enthusiastic about flying to pilot himself and his family to Australia when he covered the tour for the *Sunday Mirror* in 1970-71.
† One of the more unlikely emergency flights to a Test match involved Denis Compton, who broke down in his car on the way to Old Trafford to play South Africa in 1955. He was flown to Manchester in a light aircraft piloted by a friend. Compton arrived with no kit except for his boots but scored 158 and 71 using a bat borrowed from Fred Titmus.
‡ This tour, which started with four matches in Ceylon (now Sri Lanka), was arranged in lieu of the cancelled trip to South Africa. It was originally proposed that England should also visit India but prime minister Indira Gandhi refused to release the necessary foreign exchange.

in East Pakistan even though the England players had insisted on not going there. When they got there and some players expressed a wish to leave, John Snow recalled that they were informed 'in no uncertain terms that our coach would not reach the airport'. Snow described the week in Dacca (now Dhaka) as 'probably the most nerve-wracking in my life', adding: 'Day and night we could hear gunfire – some of it only yards from our hotel.' Others, such as John Murray and Fletcher, have less alarmist memories of their five weeks, although Fletcher reckoned the captain Colin Cowdrey did feel in danger and did not want to be there. 'Personally, I never felt as though I was really in danger,' Fletcher said. 'The trouble wasn't targeted at us. They were using us to make headlines. The person who held that tour together was Les Ames.'

With police and army struggling to maintain order during two heavily interrupted days of the final Test in Karachi, it was agreed at a meeting between the Karachi Cricket Association and the two captains, Cowdrey and Saeed Ahmed, that the next act of disruption would result in the match being abandoned. This duly happened the following morning when, in the words of John Woodcock in *The Times*, 'a mob, having made its way out from the city, broke into the stadium, tore up the stumps, savaged the pitch and wrecked the officials' enclosure ... For the first time, I sensed a wild and uncontrollable fury in the hearts of those who leaped over the pickets.' Within 12 hours, the England team – including Colin Milburn, who had flown in from Australia where he had been playing state cricket only two days before the game, and then scored 139 – was on a plane out of Karachi.*

The major long-term consequence of air travel, first by economy but more recently by business class, was that it led to more frequent but shorter tours: since 1976-77, England have played Tests every

---

* This remains the only England Test match abandoned because of public disorder. The end was ill-timed for Alan Knott, who was only four runs short of a maiden Test century and was, according to John Murray, the last player to leave the field. Although the circumstances in which the three Tests were played were wholly unsuitable, the England players were never, fortunately, a direct target. *The Times*, in a leading article on 10 March 1969, and perhaps thinking also of the cancelled tour of South Africa, stated: 'What is clear is that the planning of overseas tours will have to take far more account of the political climate than could have been imagined even a year ago.'

winter in at least one country or region, often two, and in two instances three (in 1987-88 and 2003-04).* A reduction in the length of tours was in fact overdue: to the disgruntlement of the players, England took part in nine first-class matches in the lead-up to the first Test in South Africa in 1956-57, and six more outside the Test series once it had started.

Following complaints that the 1961-62 tour was too long, England returned to India two years later to play five Tests in an itinerary spanning just ten matches in all and lasting less than nine weeks. This proved an unwise gamble when illness and injury struck a squad consisting of only 15 players, meaning additional players had to be summoned. 'It is too much to expect the same nucleus of 12 or 13 players to undertake four Test matches within 30 days in a country where Europeans go down like ninepins until they become accustomed to the change of diet and climate,' John Woodcock wrote at the height of the crisis.

In 1970-71, England completed the last four Tests in Australia and two in New Zealand with just one 'side' match of more than one day, a three-dayer against Northern New South Wales that did not carry first-class status. Increasingly, fixtures outside the international games became seen as no more than glorified practice sessions, and by the time of the 2016-17 tour of Bangladesh and India, which involved seven Tests, England were seemingly content with just practice sessions, the programme consisting of no other matches whatsoever, although Colin Graves, the ECB chairman, denounced the schedule as unsuitable and promised it would not happen again.

Air travel also made it feasible for England to visit New Zealand separately from Australia, and Pakistan separately from India – they visited both these countries back to back in 1977-78 and again in 1983-84 – and to fly in additional one-day specialists once ODIs became established as a distinct part of overseas tours in the late 1990s.

*

---

* England did not play any Tests in the winter of 1988-89 but they were scheduled to tour Sri Lanka and India. The Sri Lanka leg was cancelled due to political unrest on the island and India was cancelled due to India's objections to the South African connections of several England players including the captain Graham Gooch.

A further compression of the schedule came with the arrival of Sunday play, which in turn paved the way for the scrapping of the rest day, a standard feature since the days of timeless Tests, and the move in 1921 to Test matches in England starting on a Saturday.* With the removal of the rest day, Test cricket became even more a battle of endurance and put a premium on greater fitness, especially among fast bowlers. The shortcomings of English players in this respect were a contributory factor in the struggles of the Test team in the 1980s and 1990s as five straight days of play became the norm.

Sunday play was first introduced into English county cricket as a radical means of arresting the decline in attendances. From 1965 an International Cavaliers side began playing televised matches in England on Sundays. The following year some championship games featured play on both days of the weekend. Because of Sunday trading laws, gate money could not be charged, though programmes and scorecards could be sold, and play could not begin until the afternoon, but the success of these ventures led to the launch of a county Sunday league in 1969, by which time gate money was allowed. The league was hugely popular, but the restriction on the start time, as well as fears – unfounded, as it transpired – of opposition from the Lord's Day Observance Society meant the TCCB did not attempt to play Test matches on a Sunday until 1981, when Nottingham, Birmingham and Manchester hosted games in which the hours of play were set back on the Sunday to 12pm-7pm.†

Significantly, Sunday play was by then already an established feature of Test cricket in Australia. The England team first played on a

---

* Once Tests in England expanded to four and then five days, the most common starting day became Thursday. This remains the case, although Wednesday and Friday starts have also featured since the ICC introduced a statutory three-day gap between back-to-back matches. Starting days of England's 515 home Tests have been as follows: Thursday 367, Saturday 64, Friday 37, Monday 33, Wednesday 13, Sunday 1, Tuesday 0. The first match of England's series with the Rest of the World in 1970, recognised at the time as of Test status, began on a Wednesday with the Thursday a rest day because of a General Election.
† In another break with past practice, the normal start time was brought forward during the 1981 series from 11.30am to 11am, a move according to Peter Lush designed to counter problems experienced with bad light during Tests staged in late summer. Tests in England have generally started at 11am ever since; during a brief period when Channel 4 held broadcast rights play usually began at 10.45am.

Sunday there on 29 November 1970 in Brisbane and in three subsequent matches in the same series, one at Perth and two in Sydney.*
Not only that: in striking a peace deal with Kerry Packer and his Channel Nine television company which was to cover international cricket in Australia, the preferred position of the Australian board from 1979 was to play home Tests straight through without a break, as had happened in Packer's Supertests. Other countries fell into line but not England, who resisted this option when they toured Australia for three Tests the following winter and consented to doing away with the rest day in only one of the five Tests when they returned in 1982–83 (the one they won in Melbourne) and 1986–87.

Between 1981 and 1983, England hosted eight Tests with Sunday play, most memorably at Birmingham in 1981 when Ian Botham clinched the match with a sensational spell of bowling on a sun-drenched Sabbath. But while Sunday play was embraced by public and broadcasters, there were influential voices within the game ranged against playing Tests straight through. 'I think it wrong to stage Test matches without a rest day at all,' Mike Brearley, England's captain in 1981, wrote. 'After three days the players and umpires need a break, for relaxation and to give themselves an opportunity to recover from aches and pains.'

Bob Willis, who led England in Australia in 1982–83 and as a fast bowler had a particular interest in the issue, said a rest day should be statutory. 'It is not a cricketing decision but a promotional one [to go without a rest day] ... a Test is already quite demanding enough without taking away the one opportunity to wind down, recharge and rest those niggling injuries which so often occur in the five-day game.' Although fast bowlers have become conditioned to playing without rest days, Willis's generation of quick men might argue that their successors have sacrificed speed for survival.

England had legitimate cause for concern in the 1980s inasmuch as their bowlers were committed to a heavy schedule of county cricket

---

* These were not the first Test matches England had played on a Sunday; up to this point their Tests in India and Pakistan, dating back to 1933–34, routinely involved scheduled Sunday play.

between home Tests. It was only after it was agreed at the TCCB's spring meeting in 1990 that England players should be allowed to leave their counties two days in advance of a Test, rather than meeting up on the day before, that an irrevocable transition towards Test matches without rest days began. England manager Micky Stewart said the tipping point was when he found himself being quizzed by journalists before the Old Trafford Test of 1989 as to why Ian Botham had not taken a full part in Wednesday practice when Botham had just driven up from Hove having bowled 40 overs there on the Monday and 25 more on the Tuesday.

This process took several years to complete – England's last rest day occurred at Nottingham in 1996 – and was not a painless exercise as the selectors for some time after this struggled to identify a group of fast bowlers who could last the course. Typical was England's experience in New Zealand in early 1992, when none of the Tests had rest days and the team was unable to follow up victories in Christchurch and Auckland with another in Wellington; injuries led to a rejigging of the pace attack and Phillip DeFreitas then broke down early in the game with a groin strain. 'England could not summon up the energy to make a clean sweep of the series,' *Wisden* reported. In a sequence of ten Tests played without rest days later that year and in 1993, England took all 20 wickets only once and were beaten nine times.

The extra day of preparation was not only a help to fast bowlers but all the players, who benefited from the extra time to get their minds off county cricket, focus on the task ahead, and gel with their England team-mates before crossing the boundary rope.

## England Tours: How They Got Shorter

England tours of Australia were typically enormous expeditions until jet travel transformed transcontinental journeys: following the introduction of regular five-Test series in 1894-95, all but one before 1958-59 involved the team being away from England for more than 200 days; the exception was the 1911-12 tour which spanned 190 days. From the 1930s onwards, tours of Australia were further elongated by additional

matches afterwards in New Zealand. The longest five-Test tour before
the Second World War tour was 229 days, in 1894-95.

| Tour | Days away from UK* | Tests | ODIs/T20 | Other matches |
|---|---|---|---|---|
| **By boat** | | | | |
| 1946-47 (A/NZ) | 221 | 6 | 0 | 23 |
| **By boat and plane** | | | | |
| 1950-51 (A/NZ) | 201 | 7 | 0 | 23 |
| 1954-55 (A/NZ) | 217 | 7 | 0 | 21 |
| 1958-59 (A/NZ) | 163 | 7 | 0 | 20 |
| 1962-63 (A/NZ) | 176 | 8 | 0 | 24 |
| **By plane** | | | | |
| 1965-66 (A/NZ) | 156 | 8 | 0 | 24 |
| 1970-71 (A/NZ) | 143 | 8 | 1 | 24 |
| 1974-75 (A/NZ) | 146 | 8 | 3 | 20 |
| 1978-79 (A) | 117 | 6 | 4 | 16 |
| 1982-83 (A/NZ) | 139 | 5 | 13 | 9 |
| 1986-87 (A) | 130 | 5 | 14 | 11 |
| 1990-91 (A) | 123 | 5 | 8 | 18 |
| 1994-95 (A) | 116 | 5 | 4 | 16 |
| 1998-99 (A) | 118 | 5 | 12 | 11 |
| 2002-03 (A) | 103 | 5 | 10 | 10 |
| 2006-07 (A) | 103 | 5 | 11 | 6 |
| 2010-11 (A) | 102 | 5 | 9 | 5 |
| 2013-14 (A) | 103 | 5 | 8 | 5 |
| 2017-18 (A/NZ) | 160 | 7 | 14 | 8 |

* From day of departure from UK to day of return; in a few cases these are approxima-
tions. Between 1946-47 and 1962-63, some players would sail while others flew, mainly
on the return journey; the days away from the UK therefore varied. The 'days away'
figure is generally calculated from the date of departure until the time by which most
if not all the party had returned. The figure for 1982-83 does not include an additional
three days in Sharjah for a benefit match en route home.

# CHAPTER 26

# English Cricket Opens Its Doors
## Tony Greig and the revolution of 1968

When Tony Greig made his debut for England against the Rest of the World at Trent Bridge in 1970 – a series of matches that at the time were viewed as holding Test status – his selection caused a stir. The son of a Scottish father posted to South Africa during the Second World War and who settled there afterwards, Greig was born and spent the first 19 years of his life in Queenstown before being offered a season's trial by Sussex. Mike Buss, his college coach, played for the county and gained him his initial introduction; Greig in his autobiography described Buss as 'the first English coach to "bring home" a South African schoolboy cricketer'. At the end of his trial season, Greig was offered a three-year deal which he repaid with 1,193 runs and 63 wickets in his first summer, but he and Buss faced resentment from the old guard in the Hove dressing-room at the threat Greig posed to their places. The hostility only motivated him further.

At the end of his third season, Greig was advised by Billy Griffith, MCC secretary, that after another 12 months he would be eligible to play for England, but thought little of it as he did not regard himself as good enough; he retained these doubts up to the point of his selection. Going into that first match in Nottingham, Greig was also troubled by another matter. 'My second worry flowed from an undercurrent of resentment which was directed at me and might have been found anywhere from the south coast to Yorkshire,' he wrote. 'Here I was, a 23-year-old upstart with a broad South African accent, taking a place in the England side which many believed I was not entitled to. It was the English authorities who had elected to give me a chance, and by doing so they earned my admiration. It would have been very easy for them to ignore me and avoid the risk of inflating the anti-South Africa balloon. But they stuck by the rules . . . knowing even as they pencilled in my name that it was a controversial selection.'

Nor would the resentment subside. 'As I improved my standing in English cricket, I received the odd nasty letter advising me in firm terms to go back where I had come from,' Greig added. 'It was something I learned to live with and ignore.' A report in *The Times* announcing the Test squad appeared under the headline 'Surprise By Selectors: Greig in England Test party', in which John Woodcock, while outlining the case for Greig's inclusion, expressed the view, 'It would be nice if he had learnt his early cricket over here.' On his first day of Test cricket, Greig took four for 59, and as Basil D'Oliveira also took four for 43, England had what Woodcock termed 'their two South African exiles' to thank for dismissing the Rest of the World for under 280. 'Here was irony indeed,' he added, in acknowledgement of the Rest of the World series having replaced a scheduled visit by the ostracised South Africa.

Greig, though he quickly became an automatic selection for England, said that he also felt that his South African background would be a powerful factor against him ever captaining the side. In fact, he was appointed to replace Mike Denness in 1975 in the midst of a crisis triggered by a heavy defeat in the first Test of a home series against Australia that followed hard on the heels of a 4-1 hammering Down Under engineered by the pace and hostility of Dennis Lillee and Jeff Thomson. 'I still believe I only got the captaincy because there was no one else in contention,' Greig later wrote. 'If there had been, the Lord's authorities would have been diplomatic and protected themselves by appointing him rather than me – and I would not have uttered a word of complaint.'

However, Alec Bedser, the chairman of selectors, viewed Greig's dynamism as a precious asset and as a consequence was prepared to forgive some of his more impulsive actions. These included his response to being denied a slip catch off Ajit Wadekar in Madras (now Chennai) during his first England tour to India and Pakistan in 1972–73, which the England captain Tony Lewis described in his diary as 'atrocious behaviour', and his run-out of Alvin Kallicharran in the West Indies the following winter, when Kallicharran failed to ground his bat as he left the crease at the close of play in Trinidad (England withdrew the appeal overnight).* Some felt Denness's diffidence in not reversing Greig's action immediately was partly to blame and that if the appeal had not been withdrawn the match would have been abandoned. Donald Carr, who managed both these tours, also stood by Greig. 'With Greig in the driving seat,' Bedser wrote, 'there was every reason for the growing feeling that England were on course as a major Test power.' But for other events, this judgement might have proved correct.

There were, though, swift and direct consequences to Greig's appointment. John Hampshire, recalled to the England side after a long absence for Greig's second Test match in charge, after the game in Leeds, 'let it be known . . . that he did not want to play for England again under the captaincy of one whom he considered to be a South African'. Nor did he.

Greig's original selection for England was different from D'Oliveira's inasmuch as he had a choice about which country he might play for, whereas D'Oliveira, as a victim of South Africa's racial segregation, did not. Greig alluded to this choice some years later when he said, 'Just say I feel I have two countries and regard myself as lucky' – a position a number of other cricketers from Britain's former colonies were to enjoy. Few if any within the English cricketing system appeared to begrudge D'Oliveira pursuing a career with England, which came through the direct encouragement of Tom Graveney, a player with whom he would eventually compete for a place in the Test XI.

While the two of them were touring Pakistan with an international

---

* Bob Willis, one of Greig's England team-mates, wrote that it would have been 'almost unthinkable' for an English-born cricketer to have run out a batsman as he left the field, 'but for all his commitment to the side, Greigy was no more English than Allan Lamb, Chris Smith or Basil D'Oliveira'.

team, Graveney urged D'Oliveira, who had been playing Lancashire league cricket since 1960, to believe he was good enough not only for county cricket but Test cricket, and subsequently persuaded him to join his own county, Worcestershire. Like Greig, D'Oliveira needed convincing of his worth in his adopted environment but, as Greig would, he scored a hundred on his championship debut and within little more than a year was playing his first Test match for England. How much at home D'Oliveira felt in the England team is a moot point though, Fletcher observing that he did not have any particular friend in the dressing-room. 'No Test player has had to overcome such tremendous disadvantages along the road to success as the Cape Coloured D'Oliveira,' stated *Wisden* in 1967.*

When it emerged, two years into Greig's captaincy of England, that he had not only signed for Kerry Packer's breakaway World Series Cricket but also recruited other England players for Packer, his perceived betrayal of English cricket was explained by some as down to him never having been English in the first place. This argument was also used against Kevin Pietersen when it emerged in 2012 that he had asked to miss some England games in order to take part in the Indian Premier League. Questions were similarly asked about the commitment to England of the Irish-born Eoin Morgan when, with the ECB's blessing, he missed England games to play in the IPL, some of them after his appointment as one-day captain, and when against ECB advice he opted out of a tour of Bangladesh on security grounds. However, such supposed acts of betrayal were not the preserve of foreign-born players: the rebel English tours of South Africa in 1982 and 1990 were organised and led by Geoff Boycott, Graham Gooch, Mike Gatting and David Graveney, a stalwart county spin bowler and nephew of Tom Graveney – all 'true blue' Englishmen.

While there were those who disliked Greig opting to play for his

---

* D'Oliveira sought to enhance his credentials in the eyes of the English cricketing authorities by knocking three years off his age when he negotiated joining Worcestershire. He was thought to be 31 on Test debut; in fact, he was 34 years old then and 40 at the time of his 44th and last Test in 1972, the year in which *Wisden* first published his correct birthdate. D'Oliveira died in 2011 but lived to see England and South Africa resume cricketing ties in 1992 and compete for the Basil D'Oliveira Trophy in Tests from 2004–05.

adopted country rather than his place of birth, administratively his credentials could not be contested. He fulfilled the four-year residential requirement and was also armed with a British passport through paternal origin. D'Oliveira's case was similarly bolstered by his having taken out British citizenship on the advice of Alf Gover, the manager of the international team he played for in Pakistan, for ease of travel. The right of access to the UK of citizens of Commonwealth or former Commonwealth countries had been a contentious political issue since a huge increase in immigration in the early 1960s. Henry Brooke, the Conservative Home Secretary, stated in 1963 that it was a basic right of British citizens to enter the country but this claim was sorely tested when thousands of Asians started being forced out of Kenya in 1967, the crisis that prompted Enoch Powell's notorious 'rivers of blood' speech. In March 1968, a controversial new act was passed: henceforth, full citizenship was available only to those seeking entry who had a parent or grandparent born, adopted or naturalised in the UK. All this equipped those foreign-born cricketers who qualified for a British passport with a powerful moral argument and the path taken by D'Oliveira and Greig was to be trodden by more.

English cricket had only a few years earlier shied away from picking a foreign-born player who had qualified for England by residence. Roy Marshall, a white Bajan, had played four Test matches for West Indies on a tour of Australia and New Zealand in 1951–52 and, after playing in the Lancashire leagues, qualified for Hampshire and married an Englishwoman. He believed his chances with West Indies had ended with his omission from a tour of New Zealand in 1956. Looking for a solution to the problem as to who should open the England innings, Gubby Allen's selection panel debated at the start of the 1959 season whether Marshall might be the answer. They decided against. 'It was unanimously agreed not to invite RE Marshall to play for England,' a minute of their selection meeting read. 'It was felt that it was undesirable to invite a cricketer to play for England who had been born abroad and had learned all his cricket in, and had played for, the country of his birth before coming to England.'

However, three years later, shortly before the start of an early-season match between MCC and Surrey at Lord's, Marshall was approached by Walter Robins, who had taken over from Allen as chairman of selectors, and asked whether he would be interested in playing for England; Robins had his eye on an experienced opener for the forthcoming tour of Australia in the winter of 1962-63. Marshall asked for time to think about it but indicated that he was keen. However, as Marshall recounted in his book *Test Outcast*, later in the day Robins returned to withdraw his offer. 'I'm sorry,' he said. 'I've made some inquiries and apparently you cannot play for England. A decision on this was made some years ago and I had forgotten about it.' Marshall had in fact twice since joining Hampshire been approached by West Indies about playing for them again but he had declined because under the rules then in place he would have made himself ineligible for county cricket; however, no such risks attached to him agreeing to play for England. As Marshall himself pointed out in his autobiography, despite England's stated reservations, under ICC rules he was qualified to play for England.

Ten years on, the climate had significantly changed, and England were actively pursuing another West Indies opening batsman at Hampshire. Gordon Greenidge spent the first 14 years of his life on Barbados before moving to Reading with his family. After some early struggles – which by his own account included some racial abuse from second XI team-mates – he developed into one of the most productive batsmen in county cricket, being the leading run-maker in the championship in 1973, and was bitterly disappointed not to have been chosen for the West Indies tour of England that year. Towards the end of the season, Charles Knott, chairman of Hampshire's cricket committee, approached him at Bournemouth on behalf of England's selectors to see if he would be interested in playing for them. 'England must have sensed that they stood a chance of persuading me,' wrote Greenidge, who had considered whether he should perhaps seek to play for England instead. 'I made it clear to him [Knott] that if I was still being ignored in a year or two, then I would be only too pleased to switch allegiance.'

In the event, Greenidge was chosen by West Indies the following year; he scored 93 and 107 in his first Test and went on to become the most prolific opening batsman they have ever had, and a particular scourge of English bowling. The TCCB, and later the ECB, did their best to ensure they did not miss out on many more like Greenidge over the years that followed.

Running parallel to these developments were a number of changes which spiced up the English game and revived public interest. One was the embrace of limited-overs cricket which added much-needed urgency to all forms of the game: in the space of nine years from 1963, three domestic one-day tournaments were created, bolstered by sponsorship and television coverage, while in 1972 England began one-day internationals against touring teams for the Prudential Trophy, which led to the introduction of the World Cup in England in 1975, also sponsored by Prudential.

The domestic competitions were hugely popular, particularly the Sunday league which was inspired by the success of the International Cavaliers 40-over matches sponsored by Rothmans. The Cavaliers matches involved England players such as Ted Dexter, Colin Cowdrey and Tom Graveney as well as overseas stars Garry Sobers and Graeme Pollock, and were the brainchild of Dexter and Bagenal Harvey, an agent and impresario, who in the late 1940s had helped Denis Compton capitalise on his fame by making him the £1,000 poster boy of Brylcreem. Rothmans also sponsored a late-season 'World Cup' at Lord's in 1966 and 1967, three 50-overs matches involving an England XI (all of them Test players), a Rest of the World XI and the touring West Indies in the first year and Pakistan in the second. The television coverage of the Cavaliers matches was more informal than Test cricket, featuring interviews with players before and after play, and this was replicated in the league. The all-star element of the Rothmans Cavaliers games also fed into another change of even greater significance in its long-term impact on the England team: a new rule allowing counties to immediately register overseas players. Things were never the same again.*

---

* Officially, the greater access to overseas players and the introduction of the Sunday league arose out of the 1967 Clark Report. The Cavaliers matches quickly died out after the start of the Sunday league, although Dexter's decision to stick by the Cavaliers initially meant he stopped playing for Sussex.

Previously it had been difficult for overseas cricketers to play in the county championship. They had to serve a two-year qualification period, itself reduced from three years only in 1962. Not until after 1962 either could a player appear in Test cricket for the country of his birth without disqualifying himself again: it was these restrictions which prevented Roy Marshall accepting invitations to play for West Indies once he had embarked on a career with Hampshire. For those fully engaged in Test cricket, the county game was effectively off limits.* However, in November 1967 the counties voted to waive the two-year requirement in the case of one overseas player per county who would be allowed to register immediately without losing his right to play Test cricket; once that player had been at the club two years, counties could sign another overseas player. Soon enough, counties had several foreigners on their staffs, though they were restricted to fielding no more than two at once. Only the behemoth Yorkshire chose not to take advantage of this liberalisation, preferring to stick with their long-standing practice of picking players born within county boundaries. They found themselves so severely handicapped that they did not win another championship until 2001, by which time they had finally scrapped their import ban.

This large-scale admittance of overseas players into county cricket proved beneficial to England's opponents, who had previously struggled to cope in English conditions. Now, their best players became accustomed to the discipline of a long English season. Their batsmen were equipped with the skills to deal with the moving ball and their bowlers developed the arts of bowling an English length, and how to seam and swing the ball in this particular environment. English pitches no longer held the terrors of old. Of the West Indies team that won the inaugural World Cup final in England in 1975, all 11 had experience of county cricket; when West Indies returned

---

* This arrangement was not simply for the benefit of English cricket; foreign boards did not want to lose significant numbers of players to the county game. By the 1960s, though, attitudes were changing and Australia admitted foreign stars to the Sheffield Shield before England did so in the county championship. Tony Lock, Colin Milburn and Tom Graveney all played Australian state cricket.

the following year for five Tests – and crushed England 3-0 – they often took the field with eight men who had played for counties.

The Pakistan side that in 1982 recorded the nation's second Test victory on English soil, and the first since 1954, contained four key players who had honed their skills in the county game, including the captain Imran Khan. Similarly, when New Zealand achieved their first Test win in England in 1983, they were led by Geoff Howarth, who had played regularly for Surrey since 1971, while John Wright and Richard Hadlee had learned much from playing in the championship, as would Martin Crowe. Here was a major contributory factor in England losing 22 Test matches at home during the 1980s, twice as many as in any previous decade.

Alec Bedser, chairman of selectors between 1969 and 1982, grappled with the consequences of this revolution. By 1976, he reported to the TCCB his concerns not only about the sheer quantity of overseas cricketers but the number being appointed to lead county sides and the harm this was doing to the training of future England captains. Three years later, he wrote: 'It is again pointed out that the dominance of overseas players occupying the principal batting and bowling positions must have its effect on the development of English cricketers. It will have been noticed that in the first 25 of the batting and bowling averages almost 50 per cent in both sections were overseas players.' In the following season of 1980 he bemoaned the dearth of English new-ball bowling. 'Last season some 15 to 17 overseas bowlers were opening the bowling in English first-class cricket. That is almost 50 per cent of the opening attacks.' Predictably enough, the 1980s was a poor period for English fast bowlers, only four of whom claimed more than 51 Test wickets: Ian Botham, Bob Willis, Graham Dilley and Neil Foster.

The argument was not straightforward though. These imported stars injected flair and imagination into an environment that had become uniform to the point of sterility. With the influence of South Africans, West Indians and Asians, county cricket became richer and ultimately better. English players were tested in new ways and challenged to expand their skills. Some of the leading England cricketers gained considerably from rubbing shoulders with the best overseas talent: Ian Botham might not have become the big-match performer that he did had he not grown up alongside Viv Richards at Somerset, while David Gower was greatly influenced at Leicestershire by Brian Davison, a tough-minded Rhodesian.

Most tellingly of all, first- and second-generation immigrants, especially from the Caribbean islands, emerged in force, taking in part direct inspiration from the kaleidoscope of stars gracing the county game, of whom many were West Indian in origin. MCC secretary Billy Griffith had anticipated this development as early as 1966–67 when, mindful of South Africa's system of apartheid and the country's unwillingness to play host to non-white cricketers, he warned the South African Cricket Association of the impending change in the racial make-up of the England team, 'in view of the number of crick-eters of West Indies descent likely to be playing in English domestic cricket in the future'. Whether or not trouble had arisen over Basil D'Oliveira, a crisis was impending.

The first black cricketer to represent England was Roland Butcher, a cousin of Basil Butcher, the West Indies batsman. Like Gordon Greenidge, he was born in Barbados and came to England in 1967. It took time for him to be recognised and, even when he was on the Lord's groundstaff, he travelled to Bristol in order to get games for Gloucestershire second XI, sometimes sleeping there overnight in the dressing-room, before Middlesex signed him in 1974. Butcher drew inspiration from the glamorous West Indies teams of the 1960s, in which Basil played, and the even stronger ones of the 1970s. 'People [from the Caribbean] that had emigrated to the UK ... really had the sport embedded in them,' he recalled. 'That period coincided with the dominance of West Indies cricket and really drove the love of the game throughout the entire community, wherever in the world they were.' A fifty in the second of two Texaco Trophy appearances at home to Australia in 1980 sealed Butcher's place on the winter tour of West Indies where he played his first Test in his native Barbados. 'Our boy, their bat,' ran a headline in the local paper. But his batting was too freewheeling for Test cricket and he was not picked by England again after that tour.

Others soon followed him into the England side. In the early

1980s, the Middlesex side also contained Norman Cowans, who came to England from Jamaica at the age of 11, and Wilf Slack and Neil Williams, both of whom were born in St Vincent. As fast bowlers Cowans and Williams benefited from playing alongside a variety of world-class overseas fast bowlers – notably Wayne Daniel from Barbados, who would have walked into the West Indies Test team were they not so strong. All three played for England, Cowans on his third appearance taking six for 77 at Melbourne in 1982 when England won by three runs. Gladstone Small, who was also born in Barbados, might have edged out Cowans as the first black fast bowler to play Tests for England; in 1982 at the age of 20 he was called up as cover against Pakistan at Edgbaston, his home ground, but in the event did not play and had to wait another four years for a debut.

Two other fast bowlers of Jamaican stock developed at their counties alongside West Indies Test bowlers from Jamaica: David Lawrence, who at Gloucestershire opened the bowling with Courtney Walsh, and Devon Malcolm, who first settled in Sheffield but was unable to play for Yorkshire because of their import-ban and eventually broke through at Derbyshire where he was mentored by Michael Holding. As Butcher had done, Small and Malcolm returned with England in 1990 to play Tests on their native islands, Malcolm taking five wickets at Kingston, Jamaica as they recorded their first Test win over West Indies for 16 years, and Small claiming eight wickets in defeat at Bridgetown.

A number of others – though born in the UK like Lawrence – were of West Indian descent and heavily influenced by the region's cricket culture. Mark Ramprakash, whose father was Indo-Caribbean, modelled his stance at the crease on his hero Viv Richards and was helped at Middlesex in the years leading up to his England selection by batting alongside Desmond Haynes, for many years Greenidge's opening partner for West Indies. Mark Butcher – the son of an English-born father Alan Butcher (who himself opened the batting for England in one Test match) and a Jamaican mother – numbered among his boyhood heroes several West Indies players including Richards, Holding and Larry Gomes, like himself a left-handed bat. Dean Headley was the grandson of the legendary West Indies batsman George Headley and son of Ron, who also played for West Indies, though having started out as a batsman Dean was picked for England primarily as a seam and swing bowler.

Alex Tudor and Michael Carberry were childhood friends who watched the great West Indies players with awe; Tudor's hero was Curtly Ambrose, and Carberry chose to bat left-handed in calculated homage to his idol Brian Lara. Although Tudor in ten Test appearances was unable to remotely match Ambrose's feats as a bowler, he was a fine athlete before injuries ruined his career. He dismissed Steve and Mark Waugh in his debut Test in Perth in 1998 and against New Zealand at Edgbaston in 1999 achieved the highest ever score by an England nightwatchman of 99 not out. Between 1981 and 2016, 19 cricketers of Afro-Caribbean origin – 11 born in the West Indies and eight in England – debuted in Tests, ODIs or Twenty20s.*

John Holder, who came over to work on London Transport and played for Hampshire from 1968, became in 1988 the first non-white English umpire to officiate in internationals in England.

This was a rich seam of talent. Seven took five-wicket hauls in winning causes for England in Tests – Malcolm, Phillip DeFreitas and Chris Lewis doing so twice, with Malcolm's figures of nine for 57 against South Africa at The Oval in 1994 being the best for England in all Tests by an out-and-out fast bowler. Ramprakash scored 2,350 runs in Tests and Mark Butcher 4,288 runs and eight centuries, among which was an unbeaten 173 to win a Test against Australia at Leeds in 2001 when Glenn McGrath and Shane Warne were in their pomp. But most of them achieved less than they might have. Ramprakash played 52 Tests, DeFreitas 44, Malcolm 40 and Lewis 32, yet they rarely held down regular places. Indeed, during a period of instability

---

* Most of these players grew up and learned their early cricket in or around London. Six of them first played for Middlesex and another six started at Surrey. In addition, Phillip DeFreitas and Chris Lewis both attended Willesden High School before moving to Leicestershire, while Mark Alleyne came through the Haringey Cricket College before playing for Gloucestershire. Monte Lynch, who like Alleyne only played for England in ODIs, appeared in three matches against West Indies in 1988 having completed a ban for joining a rebel West Indies tour of South Africa in 1983-84. Lynch acted as 12th man for England against Pakistan at Lord's in 1987 before it was realised that his ban was still in place. Tymal Mills, whose father was from St Kitts, debuted for England in Twenty20s in 2016.

for the England team in general, they were among the players most caught up in the selectors' chopping and changing.

But the frustration was mutual. Michael Atherton, Malcolm's captain in 1994, said that Malcolm's performance at The Oval came on the back of him delivering 'the mother of all bollockings' to Malcolm for his insipid efforts with the ball on the first day. At the end of his time as chairman of selectors, Ray Illingworth wrote of Malcolm, 'He will leave county cricket as the same raw fast bowler who everyone thought they could improve', and cited Lewis as the biggest disappointment among the 40 Test players chosen during his three-year reign. Some felt Lewis only ran in hard at those batsmen he thought he could get out. Ramprakash was so desperate to succeed that he put himself under enormous pressure; his frustration at his repeated failures took a heavy toll and stretched the patience of those running the side.

Meanwhile, the more relaxed rules encouraged significant numbers of South Africans to seek to play county cricket and, in some cases, qualify for England, there being no end in sight to the anti-apartheid sports boycott. In September 1980, the TCCB's registration subcommittee confirmed that Mike Procter, who had played Tests for South Africa up to 1970 when the boycott began, and Brian Davison, who had represented Rhodesia, which did not then play Test cricket, had qualified for England by completing ten consecutive years of residence without playing again for their countries of birth. Both were 33 years old and their applications were in fact devices to enable their counties to register additional foreign-born players – in itself a matter of concern for those, like Alec Bedser, who wanted a strong pool of England-qualified players to choose from.

The subcommittee also considered more authentic requests for English status from Allan Lamb of Northamptonshire and Chris Smith of Hampshire. Both had been born and grown up in South Africa to British parents. Lamb had been advised to head for England by Eddie Barlow, himself a South African and captain of Derbyshire; Lamb eventually secured a contract at Northamptonshire. Smith's original ambition was to take over as an opening batsman at Hampshire from Barry Richards, who like him hailed from Durban. In the end, it was decided that Lamb's four-year residential qualification would be complete in 1982 and Smith's the following year.*

As by then England were searching for new talent, having imposed three-year bans on a group of players who had joined a rebel tour of South Africa, both Lamb and Smith were chosen for England almost immediately. Lamb was an almost automatic selection for ten years but Smith lasted just eight Tests, though his younger brother Robin, who also went through qualification, played 62 times and, though he was a less confident character than he appeared, like Lamb established a reputation as an exceptional player of fast bowling. Between 1984 and 1995, Lamb with six centuries and Robin Smith with three scored as many hundreds between them against the mighty West Indies pace attacks as the remaining England batsmen combined. While others scratched around to little purpose, Lamb and Smith refused to let bowlers dictate terms and had clear plans about where they were going to score runs.

Even while Lamb and Chris Smith were qualifying, the TCCB, anxious at the fast-changing demographics, began to formulate more thorough qualification rules, as well as means of restricting each county to fielding no more than one overseas player rather than two. With the counties putting their own interests ahead of the country's, this process took time. The new regulations were eventually passed only in 1984. Almost immediately these faced the threat of legal challenge and had to be revised at the TCCB's winter meeting of 1987, when the residential qualification period for foreign players without a British-born parent was cut from ten years to seven (those with British parents could qualify in four years). This decision was forced by Alvin Kallicharran – who had resided in England since his last Test appearance for West Indies in 1980 and had acquired British citizenship – threatening to take his case to the High Court in an effort to play for Warwickshire as a local, but there were suspicions that the board was not unhappy to relax its stance

---

* According to *Wisden*, there were initially some doubts about the genuineness of Lamb's residence, and when the regulations were tightened in 1984 it was stated that an applicant must spend 210 nights per year in the UK during his qualification period. Lamb in fact, unlike Chris Smith, made England his permanent home, continuing to live there long after his playing days were over. 'I am an Englishman,' he told *The Cricketer* in May 2017.

in order to accommodate another batsman who was a near-certainty to play for England once the rules allowed.

Graeme Hick had the previous year, at 20, become the youngest batsman ever to score 2,000 runs in an English first-class season and, having been born in Rhodesia, he had made it plain he wished to qualify for a country that played Test cricket. Although England were his preferred choice, he was also being courted by New Zealand, whose qualification period of four years looked attractive alongside England's ten. Harry Greenway MP had lobbied for the TCCB to relax its rules on Hick's behalf and Hick himself had publicly declared: 'I don't know how long I can hang on.' By bringing forward the end of his qualifying period from 1994 to 1991, the TCCB persuaded Hick to commit to England, though in April 1989 questions were raised as to whether he had actually spent the required 210 nights a year in England since 1984; the TCCB ruled that he had.

Hick's problem was that by the time he was eligible, expectations had reached impossible heights: his career average exceeded 60 and he had 57 first-class centuries to his name. Not since WG Grace had an England batsman approached his first Test with such a body of work behind him. Like many other outsiders who joined the England ranks, the demands of his situation took their toll. Unfortunately for him, his first series was against a powerful West Indies pace attack who quickly unpicked technical flaws against short-pitched bowling. He was a shy, unassuming personality unused to not succeeding. 'I started badly and was always playing catch-up,' he reflected in retirement. 'I put myself under a lot of unnecessary pressure.'

A curious case was that of Ian Greig, Tony's younger brother by nine years, a less gifted all-rounder who trod the same path from South Africa to Sussex and played two Tests in 1982. In September 1989, and by now leading Surrey, he became a contender for the England captaincy only for the TCCB to apparently discover from ICC that Greig had forfeited his residential qualification (achieved in four years as the son of a British father) by living in Australia for 18 months in the mid-1980s. This was a nuance that affected no other player.

The first England Test team with more than half the XI born outside the country took the field in Antigua in 1990: by birth, three were

West Indians, two South Africans and one Indian.* The following year at Headingley, when Hick made his long-awaited debut, the number rose to seven: two were born in South Africa, two in the Caribbean, and one each in Rhodesia, Kenya and Wales. By the time of the 1992 World Cup, eight of the 14 members of the squad had been born abroad. When, at an eve-of-final dinner in Melbourne, the evening's entertainment included someone impersonating Her Majesty the Queen in rather poor taste, and Graham Gooch, the captain, and Ian Botham walked out in protest, the Pakistan captain Imran Khan, sitting at a nearby table, leapt on the moment with relish: 'Look, only the colonials are left!'† Keith Fletcher, who became England manager shortly after this, said Graham Gooch and Mike Gatting 'were not over-keen on picking cricketers who were from other countries'. He himself seemed to take a similar view; writing in 2005, he questioned whether the growth in foreign-born players was a good thing for the national team: 'Even if [foreign-born] players had lived in England from a young age, some did not necessarily identify with it. National identity was being watered down ... I wonder to what extent we would have been worse off without these individuals.' Fast bowler Neil Foster echoed these sentiments: 'We don't have a truly English side.'

The regulations needed to be legally sound but the TCCB reducing the number of overseas players was not necessarily the solution to England's faltering results. Bob Woolmer, who played and coached at county and international level for 40 years, cited the decision as one of several factors contributing to the further decline of English cricket in the 1990s. Others shared the view that the more top-quality players that took part in the county game the smaller the step up to Test cricket. Other factors were at play, but the removal of so many West Indians from county cricket also played its part in weakening the West Indies Test team and eroding interest among Afro-Caribbean

---

* The England team that toured the Caribbean in 1990 actually contained five players born in the West Indies: Phillip DeFreitas, Ricardo Ellcock, Chris Lewis, Devon Malcolm and Gladstone Small. Within days of arriving, Ellcock broke down with a stress fracture of the back and never actually took the field for England.

† This resulted in one of Ian Botham's wittier put-downs. Criticised by the then Australia Prime Minister Paul Keating for his walk-out, Botham responded: 'I'm very proud of my heritage. And, unlike Mr Keating, I do have one.'

communities in Britain. 'The game is dying amongst us,' Alex Tudor was quoted as saying in 2008.

The multicultural nature of the England team after 1980 was in fact admirable; no other Test team was like this and some such as Australia arguably ought to have better represented the ethnic diversity of its society. But with some individuals exploiting the system for their own ends, administrators were constantly required to refine the regulations. When Andrew Symonds, who was born in Birmingham but grew up in Australia, declared an intention to qualify for England, as he had to do in order to play for Gloucestershire as a local, only to turn down a place on an England A tour because he had decided after all to pursue a career with Australia as a 'fair dinkum Aussie', the TCCB redrafted its regulations to include a clause requiring players to state they had no 'desire or intention to play cricket for any country outside the European Community' and would not seek to do so. This was still open to abuse, however, as desires and intentions could change; Australian fast bowler Ryan Harris was, by his own admission, 'not entirely forthcoming . . . about my intentions' when he joined Sussex in 2007, and had to make an embarrassing withdrawal moments before the start of his first match when news of his plans to play state cricket broke in Australia. Harris subsequently became a scourge of England batsmen in Ashes battles.*

South African cricketers continued to come to England in large numbers because of the comparative strength of sterling over the rand and because of the positive discrimination affecting white players in post-apartheid South Africa. They were also viewed positively by English county sides because, like Australians, they tended to develop faster as youngsters. Those with British parentage could qualify for

---

* Controversy also arose over another Anglo-Australian player. Martin McCague was born in Northern Ireland but grew up in Australia and played first for Western Australia before joining Kent. Qualified by birth, he made his debut for England in 1993. Although McCague was later labelled 'the rat who joined the sinking ship' by the Australian media, the Australian board raised McCague's case at an ICC meeting in July 1993, calling for a mandatory requalification period for players spending most of their life in one country opting to play for the country or region of their birth. 'I feel English,' McCague said, to which Allan Border, the Australia captain, responded: 'To me, he's Australian.'

England relatively swiftly, and those with a European parent could through the Kolpak ruling of 2004 play for a county free of overseas status. Although this latter category did not have a direct bearing on the England team, it heightened the sense of a system struggling for control, even after the ECB incentivised counties to pick England-qualified players through special fee payments. In 2008 more than 70 county cricketers were not qualified for England; by 2017, this figure was in the low sixties, or about one in seven of the total.

When Craig Kieswetter, born in Johannesburg, was named in an England Lions squad in January 2010 shortly after England had just won a Test series (in South Africa) with the help of four players born in South Africa, the national selector Geoff Miller conceded there was an issue: 'We have got to the stage where we are very careful on that [the number of South Africans in the team], and we will be. I wouldn't say he [Kieswetter] is the last, but we will monitor it.' As it happened, within weeks Kieswetter was fast-tracked into England's squad for the World Twenty20, a tournament which they went on to win with a top three consisting of Kieswetter, Michael Lumb and Kevin Pietersen, all of whom were born in South Africa. However, before Miller's reign as national selector ended, the ECB attempted to reassert control by announcing that in future anyone over the age of 18 would require seven years to qualify for England; for those under 18, four years of residence remained sufficient. Keaton Jennings was judged to have begun his qualification a matter of days before introduction of the seven-year rule on 25 April 2012. This made him eligible by 2016 and in December that year he marked his first appearance with a century against India in Mumbai. Like Jonathan Trott and Kieswetter, Jennings represented South Africa Under-19s before relocating to England.*

Miller and his panel hardly helped themselves though when they picked with such alacrity in 2008 a cricketer such as Darren Pattinson, born in England but raised in Australia and with only six championship appearances for Nottinghamshire behind him. If Pattinson had

---

* Kieswetter was in fact sounded out about his international ambitions by South Africa coach Mickey Arthur as early as 2009, but Kieswetter told him he was set on playing for England.

genuine ambitions to represent England he kept them well hidden, and no sooner was he picked than his father came out and described him as a proud Aussie: 'He's Australian, Darren.' Two years later, England head coach Andy Flower and fast-bowling coach David Saker approached Darren's younger brother James to see whether he would be interested in playing for England, even though his claims were even more tenuous; though he too possessed a British passport through his parentage, he had been born in Melbourne. He did not take the approach seriously and subsequently played for Australia.

For those who grumbled about the England team lacking a true identity – and there were plenty – there was no realistic chance of turning back the clock to the days when the national XI routinely contained only men of English stock. This actually happened in each of the first three Tests in Australia in 2017-18, but only because the team's star all-rounder Ben Stokes, born in New Zealand, was suspended; before that the last time England fielded 11 UK-born players in a Test was in Sri Lanka in December 2003. Moreover, in late 2018, the ECB announced it was cutting its qualification period for foreign-born cricketers from seven years to three, the shortest it had been since 1909, to align it with the ICC's new minimum qualification period. The first beneficiary was expected to be Jofra Archer, born in Barbados to a British father and Bajan mother, who played for West Indies Under-19s before relocating to Sussex.

## England's Foreign-Born Players

Of England's 690 Test cricketers, 97 were born outside England. Of these, 33 were born elsewhere in Britain or Europe (including 14 in Wales, 8 in Scotland and 7 in Ireland); 19 in Asia or the Far East; 13 in Australasia; 13 in the Americas or Caribbean; and 19 in Africa. More than half of the 97 players made their debuts from 1981 onwards. In the era of amateurs and professionals before 1962, and excluding the four Australians who appeared in early matches in South Africa, 25 of the 29 players born outside England were amateurs, suggesting they were viewed differently from professionals, who were expected to meet strict qualification rules for county cricket let alone England – foreign-born amateurs were seemingly accepted as 'English' as a matter of class rather than race. Also, mobility was something more readily available to the wealthy; a number of the amateurs belonged to families serving in the colonies.

The year given is that of the player's Test debut; those who captained England in Tests, ODIs or Twenty20s are in bold. Those in italics played only in early Tests against South Africa subsequently accorded Test status.

| Rest of GB/ Europe | Asia/Far East | Australasia | Americas/WI | Africa |
|---|---|---|---|---|
| **1877-1939** | | | | |
| L Hone 1879 | Ranjitsinhji 1896 | *JJ Ferris* 1892 | **Lord Harris** 1879 | – |
| **TC O'Brien** 1884 | EG Wynyard 1896 | *WL Murdoch* 1892 | **PF Warner** 1899 | |
| *JEP McMaster* 1889 | RA Young 1907 | *SMJ Woods* 1896 | **FR Brown** 1931 | |
| G MacGregor 1890 | NC Tufnell 1910 | *AE Trott* 1899 | | |
| **FL Fane** 1906 | **DR Jardine** 1928 | **GOB Allen** 1930 | | |
| AS Kennedy 1922 | Duleepsinhji 1929 | | | |
| IAR Peebles 1927 | Nawab of Pataudi 1932 | | | |
| MJ Turnbull 1930 | ERT Holmes 1935 | | | |
| **CF Walters** 1933 | NS Mitchell-Innes 1935 | | | |
| JC Clay 1935 | | | | |
| ADG Matthews 1937 | | | | |

| Rest of GB/ Europe | Asia/Far East | Australasia | Americas/WI | Africa |
|---|---|---|---|---|
| **1946-1980** | | | | |
| AJ Watkins 1948 | GM Emmett 1948 | – | – | BL D'Oliveira 1966 |
| WGA Parkhouse 1950 | **MC Cowdrey** 1954 | | | **AW Greig** 1972 |
| **DB Carr** 1951 | JA Jameson 1971 | | | PH Edmonds 1975 |
| **ER Dexter** 1958 | RA Woolmer 1975 | | | |
| WE Russell 1961 | | | | |
| JDF Larter 1962 | | | | |
| IJ Jones 1964 | | | | |
| PI Pocock 1968 | | | | |
| **MH Denness** 1969 | | | | |
| **AR Lewis** 1972 | | | | |
| **1981-2019** | | | | |
| VP Terry 1984 | RD Jackman 1981 | AR Caddick 1993 | RO Butcher 1981 | PWG Parker 1981 |
| JG Thomas 1986 | **N Hussain** 1990 | JER Gallian 1995 | NG Cowans 1982 | **AJ Lamb** 1982 |
| SL Watkin 1991 | DA Reeve 1992 | **AJ Hollioake** 1997 | WN Slack 1986 | DR Pringle 1982 |
| H Morris 1991 | MM Patel 1996 | BC Hollioake 1997 | GC Small 1986 | IA Greig 1982 |

| Rest of GB/Europe | Asia/Far East | Australasia | Americas/WI | Africa |
|---|---|---|---|---|
| PM Such 1993 | U Afzaal 2001 | GO Jones 2004 | PAJ DeFreitas 1986 | CL Smith 1983 |
| MJ McCague 1993 | OA Shah 2006 | TR Ambrose 2008 | DE Malcolm 1989 | NV Radford 1986 |
| RDB Croft 1996 | | BA Stokes 2013 | CC Lewis 1990 | RA Smith 1988 |
| GM Hamilton 1999 | | SD Robson 2014 | NF Williams 1990 | GA Hick 1991 |
| SP Jones 2002 | | | JE Benjamin 1994 | **AJ Strauss** 2004 |
| Amjad Khan 2009 | | | CJ Jordan 2014 | **KP Pietersen** 2005 |
| **EJG Morgan** 2010 | | | | MJ Prior 2007 |
| WB Rankin 2014 | | | | IJL Trott 2009 |
| | | | | NRD Compton 2012 |
| | | | | GS Ballance 2014 |
| | | | | KK Jennings 2016 |
| | | | | TK Curran 2017 |

The following players born outside England appeared only in ODIs or Twenty20s:

| | |
|---|---|
| Rest of GB/Europe: | DR Brown 1997, EC Joyce 2006 |
| Asia/Far East: | VS Solanki 2000 |
| Americas incl WI: | MA Lynch 1988 |
| Africa: | JWM Dalrymple 2006, C Kieswetter 2010, MJ Lumb 2010, JW Dernbach 2011, SC Meaker 2011, JJ Roy 2014 |

# CHAPTER 27

# Kerry Packer and the Years of Rebellion

## Greig, Boycott and Botham test the TCCB's patience

The financial conditions under which England's players operated had long been unsatisfactory and inadequate. Although home one-day internationals were sponsored, and there had been a few ad hoc arrangements to reward team and individual performances, England's Test matches were generally viewed by the authorities as not requiring anything as vulgar as monetary stimulation.* In real terms the value of England's match fees for home Tests fell sharply in the quarter-century from 1948 to 1973, the purchasing power of the pound dropping by two-thirds while the fee rose from £75 to

---

* Horlicks in 1966 put up £500 for the team winning the series between England and West Indies and £2,000 for various individual batting and bowling performances in the five Tests, of which West Indies collected £1,700 and England £800; in 1967 the company handed out £1,350 worth of individual prizes to England and the same amount to their opponents, but no team prize. In 1970, backing from Guinness meant that each of the five England v Rest of the World matches was worth £2,000 to the winners, and the series winners took an additional £3,000; as the Rest of the World side won the series 4–1, the England players received only £2,000. In 1974, Globtik Tankers sponsored the England–India Test series, England picking up £1,800 and India £600.

£150. By the early 1960s, professional cricketers' earnings had fallen behind the average manual wage.

When Tony Lewis captained England on a four-month tour of India and Pakistan in 1972–73, he received just £1,300. He had not played Test cricket before and was grateful for the opportunity, but he noted that this amount was a lot less than he could have earned from free-lance writing and broadcasting had he stayed at home. Longer-serving England players found it easier to reject such terms: Lewis only got his chance because Ray Illingworth, England's regular captain, turned down the tour on the grounds that he was 40 years old and needed a rest (the old prejudices against Asia tours appeared to be still alive and kick-ing; he wrote in his autobiography, 'the thought of an eight-Test tour of Pakistan and India was not particularly inviting'), while MJK Smith also ruled himself out of leading the side.* Geoff Boycott declined Lewis's invitation to be his vice-captain and did not tour either.

In a similar vein, in 1969 Tom Graveney defied the instructions of chairman of selectors Alec Bedser and took himself off on the rest day of a Test in Manchester to appear in a match in Luton in aid of his own benefit. Graveney was suspended for the next three Tests, a punishment that served to bring down the curtain on an England career that spanned 18 years and 79 matches. Graveney had been paid £1,000 to play in Luton and was unrepentant. Asked what he would do if the situation arose again, he replied: 'I would do exactly the same thing. I owe it to my family.' Keith Fletcher, who played the first of 59 Tests in 1968, wrote many years later: 'It is hard to convey now the prevalent feeling in the 1960s and 1970s that cricketers should play for the love of the game ... the crowds were big enough to attract enough revenue to pay the players more than trifling sums.'

Disaffection was widespread but players struggled to express their dissatisfaction in co-ordinated fashion. At the instigation of Fred Rumsey, a left-arm fast bowler at Somerset and Worcestershire

---

* The tour had been put back by a year on government advice because of political turbulence in Pakistan and the Indian state of Bengal caused by the Bangladesh war of independence, which may have contributed to some players not putting themselves forward. The selectors initially approached 42 players about their availability to fill 16 places.

who played five Tests for England, the Cricketers' Association (the Professional Cricketers' Association from 1996) had been formed in 1967 in the face of opposition from the cricketing establishment with the aim of improving conditions for all professional cricketers, who were paid less than the national average, had no guarantee of winter employment, and did not enjoy any insurance or pension schemes.* To an extent, loyalty to the system was secured by the awarding of a benefit season to those who gave long service. The association's first notable success came in 1975 when a threat of industrial action underpinned its demands for the players to receive a share of television and radio income; the TCCB acquiesced.

The TCCB was changing, but only slowly. With the board's creation in 1968, a public-relations and promotions subcommittee was set up and chaired by Raman Subba Row, the former England batsman, who had acquired some marketing expertise in his business career since retiring as a player in 1961 and had been working in a similar role at Surrey. At The Oval, he and Bernie Coleman – who would succeed him as TCCB marketing chairman in 1974 and stay for 18 years – had developed a keen sense of the game's commercial potential through the advent of sponsorship and broader TV coverage. Within a few years, perimeter advertising had been introduced at Test matches, while in 1972 an ancient regulation that only one photographer could be permitted behind the bowler's arm at Tests was finally scrapped, greatly facilitating better newspaper coverage.

'Until that time, English Test grounds were closed shops,' wrote Patrick Eagar, who did more than any other photographer to bring an intimacy to England's cricketers. 'One photographic agency, Sport and General, had the contracts at Lord's and Headingley; another, Central Press, did the other four [Test] venues.' Sport and General paid a 'remarkably small fee' in return for which they had to cover every Lord's game, even public-schools' fixtures. Once it was discovered that Eagar had breached the citadel by photographing the Leeds Test of 1965, he and others were kept out for another seven years.

---

* Other England players who attended the first meeting of the Cricketers' Association were Arthur Milton, Alan Oakman, Eric Russell, Roger Prideaux and Ken Taylor.

Peter Lush, another with a marketing background, was recruited in 1974 as secretary of public relations and was the instigator in an overdue hike in Test-match ticket prices. 'Even an increase of £1 made a big difference,' he recalled, 'but we got a lot of opposition from MCC and Gubby Allen.' Allen, he added, 'seemed to be opposed to anything that needed modernising and changing'. Early steps would also be taken towards players being more accessible to live TV; Lush described the interviews Geoff Boycott gave on the balcony at Headingley after scoring his hundredth first-class hundred in the 1977 Test and those by Ian Botham and Bob Willis in 1981 as 'breaking new ground'.

Ahead of the 1969 season, the newfangled TCCB had taken a hard line in its negotiations with the BBC over TV coverage of the series against West Indies. According to Jack Bailey, an MCC assistant secretary and future long-serving secretary, who was also involved in the process, 'it was explained that we were trying to establish a proper base for the televising of Test matches, which the committee believed had been undersold to an extraordinary degree in the past'. The deal was concluded only three weeks before the first Test, but resulted in the board receiving twice as much for two years as it had previously received over four. In 1975, an offer of £95,000 from the BBC to televise four home Tests against Australia was rejected and ultimately led to an improved deal worth £270,000 to cover that series and the five Tests against West Indies in 1976 – hence the Cricketers' Association demanding a greater share. By way of comparison, in the three years from 1956 to 1958, which included a visit by Australia, BBC paid just £30,000. 'What we had to do was drag people into the 20th century. There were constant rows with the BBC about money,' Coleman said.

With Test-match pay as meagre as it was, the benefit season was just as important a feature in the careers of England players as it was for county stalwarts, as Tom Graveney's behaviour in 1969 demonstrated. Geoff Boycott's decision to withdraw from the England team during the 1974 season was influenced by various factors – one of them a chronic problem dealing with left-arm medium-pace bowling – but was perhaps not unconnected to it being his benefit year.

The £20,639 his benefit yielded, then a record for a Yorkshire player, helped cover the loss of England earnings during what proved to be a three-year absence.

Some prominent players were obliged to go to undignified lengths to supplement their cricketing wages. When the 1968-69 tour of South Africa was cancelled, Keith Fletcher, who had made his England debut the previous summer and was looking forward to his first Test tour, had instead to go before a tribunal to explain the seasonal nature of his work in order to claim benefits. When Middlesex won the championship in 1976, Mike Brearley's side demanded money for interviews and photographs, while the following winter Tony Greig and his England players raised eyebrows by selling pictures of themselves during a tour of India, for which the typical fee was just over £2,000. It was clear that something was profoundly wrong but, as Justice Slade noted in his High Court verdict in favour of Kerry Packer in November 1977, the cricket authorities appeared blind to the interests of the players.

The revolution, when it came, required the agency of an outside party whose interests happened to converge with those of the players. Packer, as an Australian television mogul, had his own dispute with cricket's rulers, having been rebuffed in his efforts to secure the broadcasting rights to international cricket in Australia even though he had offered more money than the Australian Broadcasting Corporation, the traditional rights-holder. He also had issues with the TCCB, having successfully bought the Australian rights to the 1977 Ashes in England for £150,000 but been denied them for the 1981 series because the TCCB concluded that the rights were the Australian board's to dispose of.* Packer's response was that if he could not screen official Test matches, he would sign up players and venues to stage his own 'Supertests' to show on his Channel Nine service – if necessary in conflict with authorised Test cricket.

The alacrity with which many of the world's best players accepted his terms showed how unhappy they were with their lot. The

---

* Under the 1977 deal, Packer made available £20,000 in prize-money. In the event, purely on match results, England's players took £9,500 and Australia £6,500.

Australian players – with Ian Chappell, the former national captain, as their abrasive spokesperson – had long been obliged to support themselves by holding down regular day jobs outside their cricketing commitments and were in a protracted battle with the Australian board.* The Pakistanis had recently threatened to strike over pay during a home series against New Zealand and the West Indies players did not think twice when offered $20,000 for three months' work. 'When I saw what Packer was offering, it was a no-brainer,' Joel Garner said. 'The difference was so vast it was unbelievable.' With his eye for a business opportunity, Packer saw what the game's administrators could not. 'Cricket,' he said, 'is short of money, and the organisation of the game is denying the best players in the world opportunities to earn what they deserve. This is not a panacea that will solve cricketers' financial problems overnight. It is, though, the biggest step taken by cricketers to try to find that solution.'

One of Packer's readiest allies was Tony Greig, who was approached shortly after leading England in the Centenary Test in Melbourne in March 1977, a highly charged and ultimately epic contest watched by a crowd that included more than 200 past participants in Ashes contests and which freakishly resulted in a win for Australia by 45 runs, thereby replicating the outcome of the first Test match 100 years earlier. That match followed a full England tour of India which had been a triumph for both Greig's inspirational leadership and the team, whose wins in Delhi, Calcutta and Madras sealed the series with two matches in hand. Greig, having noted the ability of India's batsmen to deal with spin bowling on the 1972-73 tour, boldly opted to build his attack on pace, supported by Derek Underwood's left-arm spin, and on occasions his own off-breaks, with the upshot that they captured 95 wickets between them in five matches.†

Greig's hundred in the heat of Calcutta despite battling a fierce

---

* One of the earliest to identify a looming crisis in Australian cricket was Kerry Packer's father Frank, who during England's 1965-66 tour informed the visiting captain MJK Smith that cricket was dying in Australia.
† When Keith Fletcher, a member of Greig's 1976-77 side, returned to India as captain in 1981-82 he attempted to replicate this strategy, fielding only one spinner in three of the six Tests. The tactic failed abjectly.

temperature was a remarkable exhibition of will-power and courage. Greig not only signed up with Packer but, along with Chappell, acted as his chief recruiting agent. Greig helped bring to Packer's table Alan Knott and Underwood, both of whom also represented England in the Centenary Test, and John Snow, who had played the last of his 49 Tests the previous summer. Two other England players joined at a later stage, Dennis Amiss and Bob Woolmer, both of whom also played in Melbourne.

Speaking in Hove after the broad extent of Packer's plans leaked out during the early days of Australia's tour (the probable intention was to make them public at the time of the first Test), Greig correctly anticipated that his actions would cost him the England captaincy but he was another who could not afford regrets: 'I could have said, "Okay, I'm captain of England. I'm all right." That would have been selfish,' he said. 'I have laid my captaincy on the table as a sacrifice. If it's taken away from me I will then live with my decision. The plight of the modern cricketer is certainly not the best. Many who've been playing eight years or more are living on the breadline. In the winter they go abroad coaching, leaving their families behind. Test cricketers are not paid what they are worth.' When in the winter of 1975–76 England had been without a Test tour, Greig had taken himself off to earn money playing grade cricket in Sydney, an extraordinary state of affairs for a modern England captain.*

Although there was general shock at the scale of the Packer breakaway, recent England captains expressed sympathy for the players who had signed, among them Ted Dexter, who owed his early retirement to the lack of money in the game, and Ray Illingworth, who said: 'If I had been offered a contract I would have considered it very carefully.' Mike Denness, Greig's immediate predecessor, even

---

* Greig was instrumental in the introduction of the minimum wage in county cricket in 1978, the TCCB being unwilling to discuss the matter with the players' union until Greig proposed all players take the field 30 minutes late in a round of Sunday league matches in protest. The winter of 1975–76 was the fourth in ten years (1966–67, 1969–70 and 1971–72 being the others) in which England did not undertake a Test tour, but there has been only one winter since when that has happened and that was in 1988–89 when a tour of India was cancelled. After Packer's intervention, national cricket boards were at greater pains to keep their top players employed and active.

joined Packer's ranks as manager of the Rest of the World side. The problems were more profound than simply money. The players had little respect for the game's administrators and scant faith in their judgement, and they were increasingly prepared to defy their decree.

Disillusion at the way the England team was run, and in particular the decision to make Denness captain for the West Indies tour of 1973-74 and keep him in post afterwards, was reckoned to be another factor in Boycott's self-imposed exile. Fletcher reckoned there was a general lack of support for Denness among senior members of the team, of whom he would have counted as one. Fletcher indicated that others included Knott and Underwood, who played with Denness at Kent and rated him more highly as a one-day captain. Once Denness took the drastic step of dropping himself during a heavy series defeat in Australia the following winter, Boycott and others doubtless felt vindicated. Boycott wrote in his autobiography that at the time of the first Test against India in 1974, after which Boycott withdrew from the team, 'it was glaringly obvious that Denness wanted about as much to do with me as the Black Death'.

Greig's own rationale for joining Packer included a sceptical analysis of how long he might remain England captain. Recalling his initial conversations with Packer, he summarised his attitude thus: 'I'm nearly 31 years old. I'm probably two or three Test failures from being dropped from the England team. Ian Botham is going to be a great player and there won't be room in the England Test team for both of us. England captains such as Tony Lewis, Brian Close and Colin Cowdrey, Ray Illingworth, Mike Denness and perhaps a few more, all lost the captaincy before they expected to do so. I won't be any different.'*

Another major gripe was the stricture on how long wives were permitted to join their husbands on tour, with Knott saying this had played a particular part in his decision to join Packer. Knott had kept wicket for England in all but one Test match home and away

---

* Greig's claim that he knew Botham to be a great player in the making at the time of his decision to join Packer is, however, questionable. Botham had played some ODI matches for England during the 1976 season but he had been omitted from the winter tour of India and Australia, partly on Greig's say-so.

since the winter of 1967-68, and by May 1977 had played more Tests overseas for England than anyone except Colin Cowdrey and Walter Hammond. He testified during the court case about the strain touring life had placed on his marriage and how close it came to forcing his withdrawal from the tour of India and Australia in 1976-77. Underwood felt similarly, as did Fletcher.

Underwood was a unique style of bowler, a slow left-armer who actually bowled at near to medium pace, which only made him all the harder to counter; he was phenomenally accurate and knew how to capitalise on a variety of surfaces, from dust bowls in Asia to the rain-affected pitches in England which provided him with many of his most famous triumphs in Test cricket, starting with his seven wickets for 50 against the clock in the Oval Test of 1968. Geoffrey Boycott described him as having the face of a choirboy, the demeanour of a civil servant, and the ruthlessness of a rat catcher. Underwood was as fastidious about his cricket as Knott and had himself toured regularly since 1969; only Fred Titmus had ever bowled more balls for England overseas. After some arduous tours, Fletcher had also started considering whether he wanted to tour if his family could not be with him for at least some of the time. His family had joined him in Australia in 1970-71 but it had effectively wiped out his entire tour fee.

This was a complex debate. Cricketers were themselves divided on the matter: some felt they were happier and performed better when they had their wives with them, while others took the view that families acted as a distraction and eroded esprit de corps. Historically, England captains had been permitted to bring out their wives for longer on tour, if not the whole tour, than rank-and-file members who were restricted to seeing their partners for much shorter periods: this tradition dated back to the days of WG Grace and Pelham Warner taking their brides to Australia.* The fact was that by the

---

* Inevitably, the presence of families provided ammunition for critics. Johnny Douglas in 1920-21 stood accused of spending too much time with his family when England lurched from one Test defeat to another. The presence of MJK Smith's wife and two young children in Australia in 1965-66 was described by Lyn Wellings in *Wisden* as a 'crippling additional burden' on his captaincy.

1970s society had changed and couples were much less willing to put up with long periods of enforced separation. Greig described the attitude of the English cricket authorities as 'disgraceful' and called the 21-day limit on wives staying with their husbands on tour as 'an appalling encroachment on the privileges of every married man', adding: 'My feelings were never a secret to the men in power.' Also, even if a player's family were allowed to join him, they did so purely at his cost. Henry Blofeld, in his book chronicling the first year of the Packer split, noted: 'The stark fact remained for the establishment to digest that a system which had reared players over a number of years and had turned them into international figures was unable to produce feelings of loyalty.'

Packer, by contrast, could not have been more loyal or considerate towards his recruits and, having listened to their concerns, made unconditional provision for families to join them. Knott, for instance, was provided with a flat in Sydney as a base for his family. Unlike many of Packer's innovations, though, this one was not adopted by the cricketing establishment once peace broke out. Restrictions on how much time wives and families could spend with touring players remained in place. When Peter May, as chairman of the TCCB, sat in on selection for England's next tour, to Australia in 1979-80, and learned that Knott wanted his family to be allowed to join him for several weeks during the second half of the tour, he said to the dismay of Mike Brearley, the captain: 'We can't let players dictate to us.' Knott did not tour. 'I thought it was blimpish in the extreme,' Brearley said.

Similarly, Graham Gooch turned down a tour of Australia in 1986-87 in order to spend time at home with his young family. In 1996-97, as a direct consequence of the touring party in South Africa the previous winter being joined by more than 40 wives and children over Christmas and New Year, England's captain and coach respectively Michael Atherton and David Lloyd even banned altogether wives and girlfriends joining a four-month tour of Zimbabwe and New Zealand. Lloyd admitted this was a mistake. 'Several players were openly unhappy about it from the outset,' he said. When Tim Lamb was challenged about the ban, his reply, according to an indignant Darren Gough, was: 'What would you do if you were in the army?'

During the 1990s and beyond, however, the TCCB/ECB did make more effort to ensure that when families joined the players on tour the facilities were suitable, with Medha Laud, recruited by Micky Stewart from The Oval, sent on reconnaissance visits with the express purpose of placating the players on this point.* There were still flashpoints. Alec Stewart and Darren Gough, both of whom had young families, were prevented from cherry-picking which parts of the tours of India and New Zealand they went on in 2001-02; they were told they could choose formats but not tours, with the result that Stewart did not travel at all and Gough missed all the Tests.

The following winter, the board denying the players a few days at home between an Ashes tour and the World Cup was thought to be a factor in their belligerence over not wanting to fulfil a fixture in Zimbabwe during the latter tournament. In 2006-07 Duncan Fletcher blocked the players' wishes for families to join them in the early weeks of the Ashes tour only to reach a compromise which meant families were actually with the team around the time of the first Test. Under Andy Flower and Andrew Strauss, greater efforts still were made to bring families into the fold. 'After every win, when the girls were around, we would have a family celebration together, where they could bask a little in the success of the team,' Strauss wrote. Medha Laud and the PCA were also available to help families cope with being apart for months on end. Players are now allowed to join tours late, or briefly return home, to attend the birth of children.†

The game's administrators responded to Packer's coup with moral outrage, a mood shared by the British press and public. Five days

---

* As ever, cost was a consideration. The time-honoured tradition is that host cricket boards pick up the hotel costs of 25 members of an incoming touring party; above that number, the bill is footed by the visitors. Families were therefore a financial burden on the TCCB/ECB.

† When England won the World Twenty20 in the West Indies in 2010, they only changed their XI once, when Kevin Pietersen returned home to attend the birth of his son.

after news of his plans broke in the Australian press, the Cricket Council – chaired by Freddie Brown and containing several other former amateur England captains – duly sacked Greig from his post, effectively for breach of trust although also because playing for Packer clearly threatened to cut across his England commitments. However, the Council held off until a special meeting of the ICC for a collective decision on the fate of the Packer players as a whole; with the Australian tour party mostly made up of Packer recruits it was inevitable that the Ashes series could only go ahead with the involvement of the Packer men on both sides. The ICC meeting, which concluded on the eve of the third Ashes Test, decreed that anyone signing for Packer would be banned from international cricket and urged national boards to implement similar bans at local level. Two weeks later, the TCCB duly did so. This move was formally backed towards the end of the English season by a meeting of the Cricketers' Association, although only by the narrow margin of 91-76. Some players believed that, as with the South Africa boycott, the bans amounted to a restraint on their trade, but the predominant concern was the damage a lasting split might do to the Test-match revenues on which the county game depended.

The bans were a huge mistake, especially for the TCCB – which could have waited to see how the ICC ban played out, as it was clear that Packer was intent on suing for restraint of trade – but with key posts at the ICC filled by English administrators it was natural that their attitudes were closely aligned.* Nonetheless, legally it was foolish for the TCCB to act as it did. 'To laymen it is incredible that men like Gubby Allen, for years a highly successful stockbroker, David Clark, a hard-working farmer, George Mann, a brewer of great distinction, Doug Insole, now in the building industry, Edmond King, a chartered accountant, and the other figures at Lord's who are equally well qualified in business terms should have stood so ponderously, and obviously, on their dignity,' Blofeld wrote.

Admittedly, at an early stage Raman Subba Row and Bernie

---

* The court case was officially brought on behalf of two England cricketers Tony Greig and John Snow, and the South African all-rounder Mike Procter.

Coleman, who thought an early accommodation might be the best outcome, met Packer in Brighton to see if a compromise could be reached, but they were unable to achieve one. In finding for the players in a court case spanning 32 days which saw several England cricketers testify on both sides, Justice Slade criticised the TCCB for not contracting the players all the year round, accepted that they could choose who they worked for, and said that the bans were an attempt to force them to break their contracts with Packer. With costs, the ICC and the TCCB were left sharing a bill of more than £250,000, which for the TCCB put a sizeable hole in its record profits for the 1977 season of £1.5m. Those who had little time for administrators were vindicated. Insole, the TCCB chairman, conceded, 'we've had a good stuffing.'

The TCCB's intention to serve bans, though ultimately frustrated, only heightened divisions around the counties, especially at those clubs whose players had signed for Packer. Having initially been sacked as Sussex captain, Greig was reinstated for the 1978 season, though in the end he did not appear.* Knott and Snow could not agree terms with their counties but Underwood, Woolmer and Amiss all played on. Amiss was in a particularly awkward situation at Warwickshire where committee men were also involved on committees at Lord's and took a strong line, but he nevertheless managed to top 2,000 runs in 1978. 'It was a very difficult time,' he recalled. 'People weren't talking to me [and] I found it was easier to be out in the middle than in the dressing-room ... it knocked me about but what kept me going was that I played well ... I don't know how I was able to concentrate but I did.' Though they were not formally banned from selection, predictably none was chosen for England once Packer's matches got underway.

Faced with the threat of more defections, the TCCB was compelled to find the means to pay England players better. Test fees were immediately raised to £1,000 from £210 and Cornhill Insurance

---

* The English cricketing establishment found other ways to punish Greig. The tradition was for England captains to be swiftly elected honorary members of MCC (if they were not members already) but in Greig's case they kept him waiting until 1998.

was signed as the first long-term sponsors of Test-match cricket in England: the first five-season deal starting in 1978 was worth £1.1m, rising to almost £1.9m for 1983-85. By 1991, Cornhill's support topped £1m per year.* This suggested that sponsors could be found if only the TCCB was prepared to seek them. The board argued, somewhat unconvincingly, that pay rises had been on the way in any case.†

Fees for England's first post-Packer winter tour in 1977-78 also rose to £5,000, up from £3,000 a year earlier. The enhanced sums largely had the desired effect. While the Test series with Australia in 1977 was underway, Bob Willis, Chris Old and Derek Randall (the captivating hero of the Centenary Test with a bravura innings of 174, and a brilliant fieldsman close in on either side of the wicket) all turned down approaches from Packer – Willis with the additional benefit of a renegotiated contract at Warwickshire. On the rest day of the fourth Test in Leeds Packer tried through a meeting with Mike Brearley, Greig's replacement as England captain, to recruit the entire England team but he was rejected. Packer never achieved his aim of putting together his own England team as he did Australian and West Indian XIs.‡

Another to turn down Packer was Geoff Boycott, though in convoluted circumstances. As he was not playing for England at the time, Boycott initially appeared keen to be given the captaincy of Packer's Rest of the World team, but eventually ruled himself out after it was suggested to him that Packer might stage matches during

---

* Test matches in England continued to be sponsored by Cornhill Insurance until 2000, by which point it was investing £3m per year. Cornhill were succeeded by npower (2001-2011, initially paying £3.67m a year) and Investec (2012-17, around £4.5m per year). Specsavers took over in 2018 for an unspecified sum.

† The TCCB's marketing committee had begun to bring in more business, evidenced by the additional sponsored one-day competitions, but the deals had only a modest impact on players' earnings. In 1977 it secured first-time sponsorship worth £120,000 a year from Cadbury Schweppes for the county championship, but only £27,750 of this was allocated to prize-money.

‡ Nor did Packer ever follow through on plans to stage matches in England, in large part because Justice Slade's ruling allowed Packer players, many of whom held county contracts, to continue to ply their trade in English cricket; any games Packer put on in England would have cut across that employment. Subsequently, Packer refused to engage in peace talks unless counties refrained from threats to cut off their 'rebels'.

the English season which would clash with his Yorkshire commitments.* As it transpired, Boycott at the start of the 1977 season then told the selectors he was once again available for England and two matches into the series was recalled in place of the out-of-form Amiss. By scoring 107 and 80 not out at Trent Bridge, followed by 191 at Headingley (his hundredth first-class century), Boycott proceeded to play a central role in England overwhelmingly regaining the Ashes against an Australia team theoretically at full strength but actually riven by Packer.

His rehabilitation did not stop there: the following winter, following a freak injury to Brearley who broke his arm batting in Pakistan, Boycott found himself standing in for four Tests as captain. However, as widely anticipated, he proved temperamentally unsuited to the role and ended up presiding over England's first Test defeat to New Zealand during a three-match series in which he spent almost 14 hours scoring 166 runs.† 'Tactically he was good, but he was too wound up in his own game to be a great captain,' John Lever said.

In terms of defections to Packer, England were not as badly affected as Australia or West Indies but nevertheless lost the equivalent of half a team's worth of good players. Fortunately, Boycott's return compensated for Amiss's absence while Ian Botham, Bob Taylor and Phil Edmonds proved high-quality replacements for Greig, Knott and Underwood. Taylor was not as good a batsman as Knott but he too was a superb keeper who deserved a lengthy run in the Test team; having won one cap in New Zealand in 1970-71 through the kindness of Ray Illingworth, who rested Knott to allow him to play,

---

* Jim Laker, the former England player-turned-BBC commentator, also turned down a five-figure offer from Packer when he was asked to join his broadcasting team, though he too said he did not blame the players for taking the money. Dickie Bird, the English umpire, rejected an approach in July 1977.

† Boycott's instinctive caution caused ructions during the Christchurch Test when it came to the timing of a second-innings declaration and led to claims that Ian Botham deliberately ran out Boycott on the fourth evening because Boycott's pedestrian batting was hindering the search for quick runs. Over the years the veracity of this claim has been questioned by several involved in the game including Bob Willis, Clive Radley, John Lever and Boycott himself, as well as Ewen Chatfield of New Zealand, but the popularity of the story reflects the frustration Boycott's blinkered approach created.

Taylor added 56 more caps between 1977 and 1984.* Clive Radley briefly matched Woolmer's talent for painstaking scoring.

Greig had been a leader of rare ability, but as it turned out Brearley – seasoned by seven years as Middlesex captain – proved even better: as a tactician and manager of men he was as good as England had ever had. He was a tough and uncompromising opponent but within his own dressing-room had a refreshingly consensual style. He was happy to follow good suggestions if presented with them: when England were struggling in the pivotal fourth Test in Sydney in 1978-79, he took up Mike Hendrick's suggestion that the team discuss the match situation at every session; the game was turned round and won by 93 runs.

Where Brearley was not so strong was as a player and, despite the success of the team, his place in the side was a recurring topic of debate. He conceded this threatened his ability to lead. 'Batting at Test level was a struggle for me,' he said. 'Sometimes you didn't feel like showing yourself on the field. I didn't. By Melbourne in 1978-79 [the Test before Sydney] I'd scored 65 runs in six first-class innings and then made 1 and 0. I didn't feel like motivating people. If you're captain, you'll probably survive a bit longer if the team are doing all right.'

Fortunately for Brearley, England did do all right, in part because they were fortunate in the way their fixtures fell: during the two years of the Packer split, they met a very weak Australia home and away and won 3-0 and 5-1, and also played home and away series against moderate sides from Pakistan and New Zealand. Overall, England went unbeaten in six series, winning 14 and losing only two of their 23 matches.

Their most fraught period came when they toured Pakistan with feelings at their most raw. The court judgment had just been made

---

* Taylor also kept wicket for England as a substitute during a Test at Lord's in 1986, aged 45 and two years after he had retired from first-class cricket. Bruce French, the appointed keeper, was incapacitated by a blow to the head while batting and Taylor was summoned from a sponsor's tent on the ground. Using borrowed kit except for his own gloves which were in his car, Taylor kept for 74 overs until a current county keeper could be found in Bobby Parks of Hampshire; this was as close as Parks, whose grandfather and father both played for England, got to playing Test cricket.

against the cricket authorities and Packer's World Series Cricket was underway in Australia. Pakistan had seen four senior players signed up by Packer and with the decisive third and final Test against England looming in Karachi their selectors, possibly acting with the encouragement of General Zia, announced three days before the game that they were considering fielding three Packer men, Mushtaq Mohammad, Imran Khan and Zaheer Abbas. In the event, it was decided that these players could only play if they apologised and agreed to put Pakistan first, which they did not do, but before that point was reached the prospect of them playing sent shockwaves through the England camp.

Those England players who had turned down Packer or voted in favour of banning Packer men in the Cricketers' Association meeting were particularly vocal. Others, though they had not been in favour of bans, objected to the idea of Packer men cherry-picking their fixtures. Once they had held an emergency meeting, Brearley read out a statement saying that the touring team was unanimously opposed to Packer players being considered for official Tests. Brearley was personally against the England players refusing to play the match in Karachi if Pakistan went ahead and chose their Packer men, but as he was by that point incapacitated by a broken arm and about to head home, this was something over which he had little influence. Doug Insole, the chairman of the TCCB, pleaded by phone with Boycott, the acting captain, to go ahead with the game, but Boycott made it clear to both Insole and Pakistan officials that the team was opposed to playing against players he publicly branded as 'disloyal traitors'.

The tension was hardly eased by England having to train alongside the Pakistan squad with the Packer players among them. Only at 10.15pm on the eve of the Test did the Pakistan board pull back, otherwise England might have refused to fulfil a Test for the first time since Lord Harris's side scratched the second match of their series following a riot in Sydney a hundred years earlier. The Karachi Test went ahead and ended in the dullest of draws, none of the five-and-a-half-hour days producing more than 176 runs.

That Pakistan pulled back from fielding Mushtaq, Imran and Zaheer was a big blow to the Packer camp which felt that creating divisions within the establishment fold was the best way to win the war. Amid suspicions that England had brought pressure to bear on Pakistan, Tony Greig criticised Boycott in a Sydney newspaper column, saying that 'Boycott has the uncanny knack of being where fast bowlers aren't', a reference to Boycott having missed series when England were up against Dennis Lillee and Jeff Thomson for Australia and the West Indies pair of Michael Holding and Andy Roberts, though this was hardly a fair description of Boycott's Test career as a whole.* Greig's remarks led to Sussex sacking him as captain for a second time and the TCCB fining and suspending him for the first two months of the 1978 season; less than four weeks after his return, Greig withdrew from English cricket altogether.

Unsurprisingly, when peace came it was as a result of talks between the previously implacable foes of the Australian board and the Packer camp. The Australian board had been particularly hurt by a second season of Packer matches which stole much of the attention away from an Ashes series in which an unrecognisable Australia Test team was beaten 5-1 and attendances tailed off alarmingly as the public tired of seeing their side beaten (the six Tests drew a total gate of only 370,000); even the most die-hard of loyalists would have struggled to deny that the standard of play in the Packer matches was higher. However, the deal was made without reference to officials at the TCCB and the ICC who had been striving for a solution, or those opponents Australia intended to play under the arrangement it came to with Packer's Channel Nine which committed touring teams to a hectic schedule of Tests and day–night one-dayers. The Australian board not only awarded Packer broadcast rights to Australia's home matches for the next three years (a deal he subsequently extended several times), but granted PBL Sports Pty Ltd, another Packer organisation, exclusive rights to promote the game for the next ten years. The Australian board unilaterally heralded the deal as 'in the

---

* Subsequent to Greig's charge, Boycott faced a strong Australia pace attack in 1979-80 and scored 176 runs in three Tests, second only to Ian Botham, and 663 runs in nine Tests against the all-powerful West Indians in 1980 and 1980-81, second only to his opening partner Graham Gooch. He also only began wearing a helmet in 1979, later than many of his England colleagues.

best interests of Australian and international cricket' but not everyone shared its enthusiasm. 'It was hard to avoid the sense of being hijacked twice in a couple of years: first by Packer and now by the Australian Cricket Board,' wrote Jack Bailey, secretary of MCC and the ICC.

Top cricketers who had responded well to life under Packer – when they were expected to perform like full-time professional sportsmen while being paid accordingly – discovered they were to be worked even harder on returning to official cricket. The next Australian season saw both England and West Indies tour for series of three Tests each running in parallel, interspersed with ODI matches (including in Sydney the first official day–night internationals) that formed part of a protracted triangular tournament. The players from all three sides voiced their dissatisfaction with the scheduling. Mike Brearley, the England captain, found himself having to defend the TCCB's rejection of certain playing conditions that had applied in World Series Cricket when this was properly a job for tour manager Alec Bedser; as a consequence, Brearley was portrayed as a 'whingeing Pom' and subjected to unedifying abuse from drunken spectators who became a tawdry feature of the early day–night games.*

Brearley wrote later that he might have softened some of the hostility had he engaged with spectators rather than ignored them, but concluded, 'crowds have become more unkind, opinionated and noisy'. Brearley had already made himself unpopular with Australians during the 1978-79 tour for reneging on an agreement to spare designated tail-end batsmen – two per side – short-pitched bowling. During the second Test in Perth, Brearley's bowlers abandoned the policy after Geoff Dymock, Australia's No.10, held out in a lengthy partnership with Peter Toohey. 'I was disappointed that

---

* Among the features to which the TCCB and Brearley objected were coloured clothing, white balls and fielding restrictions. However, by posting ten men on the boundary, including the wicketkeeper, in a successful bid to deny West Indies victory in England's first-ever floodlit ODI in Sydney, Mike Brearley expedited the universal application of restrictions on field-placings. Brearley said he was following a tactic he had seen used in a county match in 1972 by MJK Smith; Ted Dexter had also adopted the move in early Gillette Cup matches. English domestic cricket introduced the 30-yard fielding 'circle' in 1981.

this gentlemen's agreement was broken,' wrote Graham Yallop, the Australia captain.*

The TCCB had further indicated its displeasure by refusing to play for the Ashes in the three Tests in 1979–80 (all of which were lost). Although the idea of concurrent Test series was scrapped, other elements of the Packer vision would dominate international cricket in the 1980s, among them short-pitched bowling, sledging, the pressuring of umpires, and a win-at-all-costs mentality. One-day internationals, previously an unobtrusive part of the calendar, became a constant feature: before World Series Cricket, England had only ever played 23 ODIs; by 1983, they were almost playing that many in one year, although they did not play day–night games outside Australia until 1993.

More constructively, Packer's television coverage dramatically enhanced the experience for viewers. He employed around a dozen cameras, when in the mid-1970s the norm for the BBC covering Tests in England was only four, and he also introduced the practice of deploying cameras from behind the bowler's arm at both ends of the ground. With close-up shots of combatants, and microphones situated next to the stumps, he brought the star players more to life. Packer's greatest shove to the game was stardom, uneasy territory for Englishmen, but some such as Botham and Randall responded by celebrating wickets and catches theatrically, as Greig already did.

The TCCB did not learn the lessons of Packer well enough. The board discussed in 1978 introducing winter contracts for the leading England players, as Justice Slade had indicated it should, and

---

* Such agreements arose out of playing regulations agreed for the first World Cup in 1975 which stipulated that short-pitched balls passing over the heads of batsmen would be called wides and non-recognised batsmen would be spared bouncers. Brearley had already abandoned the agreement during a home series against Pakistan in 1978 when Iqbal Qasim, a nightwatchman, was targeted on the fourth morning by bouncers from Bob Willis and struck in the mouth. 'I'm sorry he was hit in the face but he had batted for 40 minutes,' Brearley said. The 'gentlemen's agreement' was replaced by Law 42:8 of the 1980 code of the Laws of Cricket which contained a clause relating to the bowling of fast short-pitched balls constituting an attempt to intimidate the striker: 'The relative skill of the striker shall also be taken into consideration.' How rigorously umpires have applied the clause has been a matter of debate.

'option contracts' were taken up by 12 players that year, but this proved to be mere window-dressing. Four years later nothing was in place to legally prevent some of those players joining a rebel tour of South Africa between the end of a winter tour and the start of the 1982 season.

This was a ground-breaking venture, the first of several tours of its kind, but it cannot have taken the board by surprise. South African cricket representatives would come to London around the time of ICC annual meetings and tell the world's media of the steps they had taken or were taking to meet the demands they were told were necessary if South Africa were to rejoin the ICC, and their efforts had gone unrewarded. Moreover, by the summer of 1981 Doug Insole had told the South Africans bluntly that the TCCB thought they were wasting their time. 'Until apartheid goes, you can forget about getting back into world cricket,' he said. 'England cannot support you. If we did, it would be the end of English cricket. The black nations would not play against us.'

The hostility of the India–Pakistan–West Indies bloc was stronger than ever, bolstered by the Gleneagles Agreement of 1977 precluding sporting contact with South Africa. This had been reinforced by the cancellation of England's Test in Guyana in March 1981 when the government there objected to the presence in the touring team of Robin Jackman, who had spent several winters playing and coaching in South Africa. There would be another flashpoint a few months later when India's prime minister Mrs Gandhi raised objections on similar grounds to two members of England's squad, Geoff Boycott and Geoff Cook, entering the country, even though the ICC deemed it acceptable to visit South Africa in a personal capacity. Mrs Gandhi's comments led to frantic diplomatic efforts to avoid a cancellation of the tour amid fears that it would herald a black/white split in the international game. Only 11th-hour statements from Boycott and Cook expressing their abhorrence of apartheid saved the day.

South Africa's cricketing isolation was now so extensive and firm that many within the game were aware that a sanctions-busting tour was a real option; the TCCB even wrote to England players warning of the consequences of joining such an enterprise. In fact, work had begun on assembling a touring English XI as early as the previous winter when Peter Cooke, a Lancashire-born league cricketer who had settled in South Africa, tapped up players during England's tour of West Indies in early 1981. Cooke then renewed contact during the tour of India, where some players became so disenchanted by the tedium of the cricket and what they saw as home-town umpiring in front of enormous crowds that they willingly listened to Cooke's overtures.*

After losing the first Test in Bombay (now Mumbai) in the only match of the series to produce a positive outcome, England took the rare step of lodging an official protest at the umpiring of KB Ramaswamy, who did not stand again in the Tests. In the next Test in Bangalore, the captain Keith Fletcher was so incensed at being given out caught behind attempting a sweep that he flicked off the bails with his bat as he departed (an act for which he subsequently apologised to the Indian board). Fletcher later wrote that he was out authentically just once in seven dismissals in six weeks. Graham Gooch fared little better and was so disenchanted that he was all for abandoning the tour and heading home, but was eventually persuaded to stay and even scored a hundred in the fifth of the six Tests. Even so, the fact that South Africa managed to recruit five members of that tour party plus another six players who had appeared in Tests or ODIs for England the previous summer, showed how poor relations remained between the players and the board, even after the Packer-induced pay rises. News of the rebel tour broke shortly after England's Test tour of India and Sri Lanka ended.

Some players such as Boycott – who, having emerged from the Packer affair with his reputation enhanced, was now ironically the chief recruiter – and four who had previously signed for Packer in Amiss, Knott, Underwood and Woolmer, were coming to the end of their international careers and were unconcerned about possible punishments. In fact, sanctions were by no means guaranteed given

---

* It was estimated that the Test in Calcutta was watched by a crowd of 394,000, surpassing the highest officially audited figure of 350,532 recorded for the Australia v England Test in Melbourne in 1936-37.

the failure of the authorities to impose legally enforceable bans on those who joined World Series Cricket. For those who had played for England only fleetingly, the tour was a chance to earn good money – anything from £10,000 to £40,000 depending on seniority – for a few weeks' work.

Boycott's conduct was particularly contentious. Not only was he opting to go and play in South Africa so soon after speaking out against apartheid in order to placate Mrs Gandhi, he had severely tested the patience of the England management during the India tour by declaring himself unwell and therefore unable to field during the fourth Test in Calcutta (now Kolkata), only to be spotted on a local golf course. Fletcher and Raman Subba Row, the tour manager, demanded an apology, only for Boycott to reply that he thought he ought to resign and go home. 'For a player to do this was quite extraordinary but we agreed, providing Boycott apologised to his colleagues, which he did by spearing a note with a fruit knife into a beautiful piece of Indian furniture,' Fletcher wrote. 'It was quite obvious that he did not want to be in India and neither I nor the team wanted him there.' In the previous Test in Delhi, Boycott had achieved a long-standing ambition by becoming the leading run-scorer in Test cricket, but few have left an England tour in such ignominious fashion.*

A few England players turned down the South Africa tour, including Ian Botham and David Gower, although anecdotal evidence suggests their thinking was at least in part influenced by their agents convincing them of the likely negative commercial impact on their young careers. Strikingly, Fletcher turned down £45,000 to join the tour but his failure to inform the TCCB of what was afoot – although he only learned of the plans at a late stage – was unjustly held against him. When the incoming chairman of selectors Peter May began work a few weeks later, he chose to make his mark by replacing Fletcher as captain with Bob Willis and dropping him from the side altogether in favour of younger men. Fletcher was devastated

---

* The officially stated reason given at the time of Boycott's departure, ten weeks into a 16-week tour, was 'physical and mental tiredness'.

and said that if the South Africans came back with another offer he would go. (They didn't.)

Nor were relations between board and players improved by the TCCB – under pressure from the anti-apartheid bloc – imposing three-year bans on the rebels in order 'to preserve international multi-racial cricket'. India and Pakistan had threatened not to tour England that summer if they were going to be made to play against the rebels, West Indies were vocal in their support, and a World Cup on English soil loomed the followed year. The bans went directly against a recent ICC agreement that on no account should one country be allowed to influence the team selection of another. As a result, England were deprived of the services of some significant players, most vitally Graham Gooch but also others such as John Emburey and John Lever. Unsurprisingly, they relinquished the Ashes in Australia the following winter, and were hammered 5–0 at home to West Indies in 1984.

During this period of suspensions, those left playing for England, having been threatened with a midnight curfew in Australia in 1982–83 on pain of £1,000 fines, made an ill-disciplined tour of New Zealand in 1984 which led to newspaper allegations of, among other things, recreational drug-taking. A TCCB investigation concluded that the allegations were unsubstantiated but Botham, who was the chief target for the tabloids, two years later admitted to the central claim of a *Mail on Sunday* report that he had smoked dope. By then he had already been convicted during the winter of 1984–85, when he took a winter off from touring, of possessing cannabis.* As a result of Botham's admission that he had at various times in his early 20s casually smoked pot, in part 'to get off the sometimes fearful treadmill of being an international celebrity', the TCCB banned him from all cricket for two months of the 1986 season, as a consequence of which he missed four ODIs and five Tests.

No cricketer apart from Greig had a greater talent for crossing swords with the cricketing establishment than Botham, who was

---

* This incident prompted the TCCB to introduce random drug-testing in professional cricket in England.

raised and educated in Yeovil before being sent by Somerset to spend two summers on the MCC groundstaff where he bridled at being required to bowl at members in the nets. Like Greig, Botham also tested the TCCB's regulations regarding the writing of ghosted newspaper columns. These had been relaxed slightly from the days when active England players were prevented for the whole season from writing about a series in which they were involved; now they could only not put their name to articles during the period of the matches themselves. Greig had fallen foul of this in 1977 when he was critical of the Old Trafford Test pitch in an unauthorised article for the *Sun* published on the first day of the match; his club Sussex fined and reprimanded him for not acquiring clearance from the TCCB. Botham was also recruited by the *Sun* at an early stage of his England career and during the 1982–83 tour of Australia was fined for criticising the local umpires.

Shortly after this, attempts by Donald Carr, the TCCB secretary, to prevent Botham writing his column during the World Cup were successfully thwarted by the newspaper, leading the *Sun* to write in a triumphant leader, 'This is a free country. Who is he [Carr] to tell the public what they may and may not read?' This opened the door to columns by numerous England players appearing during Test matches over the years that followed. In 1984, Botham was fined £1,000 for making derogatory remarks about Pakistan on BBC radio.

## How England's Home Test Match Fees Have Risen

England's professional players were generally paid £10 per home Test match appearance up to 1896 and after that £20 until the First World War. During the 1930s and 1940s, fees varied according to the opposition and whether the match was scheduled for three, four or five days. The fee for Australia Tests was £30 in 1921, £40 in 1930, £50 in 1938 and £75 in 1948. By the 1950s, fees were standardised, although over time supplements were introduced for the captain and players who had been capped 10, 20 or 30 times, etc.

| 1957-65: | £100 |
| 1966-69: | £120 |
| 1970-73: | £150 |
| 1974: | £160 |
| 1975: | £180 |
| 1976 | £200 |
| 1977: | £210 |
| 1978: | £1,000 |
| 1979: | £1,200 |
| 1980: | £1,400 |
| 1988: | £1,600 |
| 1996: | £2,850 |
| 2004: | £5,500 |
| 2008: | £6,000 |
| 2017: | £12,500 |

## England's Left-Arm Fast/Medium Bowlers

John Lever, who took 30 wickets at 17.03 in six Tests in his debut winter of 1976-77, was one of the few left-arm fast or fast-medium bowlers to have had significant success for England at Test level. Only five of them have taken 50 wickets and none has managed 100. Of the 47 bowlers to claim 100 wickets for England, 35 are right-armers (28 fast or fast-medium bowlers, six off-spinners, one leg-break/googly bowler) and 12 left-armers (all spinners). Lever might have taken 100 wickets had he not joined a rebel tour and been banned for three years. His figures of seven for 46 in the first innings of his debut match in Delhi remain the best by an England left-arm 'quick' bowler.

Left-armers have generally had most success bowling over the wicket and swinging the ball into the right-hander or pushing it across him – a difficult art to master and one that militates against bowling at high pace. Some of the fastest left-armers have also been among the most erratic. Ryan Sidebottom's lack of pace was held against him by Duncan Fletcher, who dismissed him as 'a good honest county-standard bowler'; in fact, when he played regularly under a subsequent regime, Sidebottom gave England a control and penetration they had been lacking.

The following have played five or more Tests as specialist left-arm fast or medium bowlers since 1897.

| Bowler | Span | Tests | Wickets | Average |
|--------|------|-------|---------|---------|
| George Hirst | 1897-1909 | 24 | 59 | 30.0 |
| Frank Foster | 1911-12 | 11 | 45 | 20.6 |
| Nobby Clark | 1929-34 | 8 | 32 | 28.1 |
| Bill Voce | 1930-47 | 27 | 98 | 27.9 |
| Jeff Jones | 1964-68 | 15 | 44 | 40.2 |
| Fred Rumsey | 1964-65 | 5 | 17 | 27.1 |
| John Lever | 1976-86 | 21 | 73 | 26.7 |
| Mark Ilott | 1993-95 | 5 | 12 | 45.2 |
| Alan Mullally | 1996-2001 | 19 | 58 | 31.2 |
| Ryan Sidebottom | 2001-10 | 22 | 79 | 28.2 |
| Sam Curran | 2018-19 | 9 | 15 | 34.2 |

Since September 2001, Ryan Sidebottom and Sam Curran are the only specialist left-arm fast/fast-medium bowlers to play Tests for England but six have appeared in white-ball internationals in that period, following a general belief that right-handers struggle with the ball angled across them: Sidebottom (25 ODIs, 18 Twenty20s including all seven matches when England won the World Twenty20 in 2010), Harry Gurney (10, 2), David Willey (42, 27), Reece Topley (10, 6), Tymal Mills (0, 4), Curran (2, 0). Since May 2014, England have played at least one left-armer in 89 out of 145 white-ball matches.

*To 1 May 2019*

# CHAPTER 28

# Gooch, Botham and the Cult of Fitness

## The rise of the backroom staff

One England cricketer in particular was sensitive to another important aspect to the Packer revolution. Graham Gooch had endured a long struggle to establish himself as a Test cricketer and, having waited 22 Tests to score his first century, identified that he needed to be physically fitter if he was to survive at the top level. Indeed, he said he first realised he needed to be slimmer, stronger and more mentally alert when Essex promoted him to open the batting in 1978. He was a big man and prone to put on weight. It was in the interval between home and away series against the might of West Indies that he started to train with West Ham's footballers and to become obsessive about early-morning runs. This novel regime met with scepticism from some team-mates, including the England captain Ian Botham, who were used to being left to their own devices. 'You could've turned up for that tour [to the West Indies in 1981] without doing a stroke of work for three months and then be expected to compete with a great side in gruelling conditions,' Gooch recalled. 'A player would say he had been to the nets in his local area three times a week and nobody could disprove that.' Gooch's new approach was vindicated when he scored 460 runs in four Tests, including two hundreds, against the best attack in the world.

Gooch was convinced he was doing the right thing: he, like other England players, had witnessed at close quarters the transformation in approach of the West Indies squad when they toured England in 1980, a year after peace was struck between Packer and the cricket authorities. West Indies arrived with their own specialist fitness guru, Dennis Waight, a former rugby league trainer from Sydney who had been detailed to work with Packer's West Indian XI, and they were convinced of the beneficial effects of his tailored drills on their fitness, stamina and concentration.

Gooch lived by his new-found work ethic for the rest of his career. It was one he pursued alone but when he became England captain in the late 1980s, he worked in conjunction with Micky Stewart, the team manager, on modernising the way the England team prepared. This involved training camps at Lilleshall and players reporting to regional centres to work with coaches and former England cricketers. It was a risk, but one he felt worth taking: 'If my way didn't work, they would get someone else.' By the time the team left for their next Test assignment, to the Caribbean in 1990, Gooch 'was satisfied we would be the fittest England side to go on tour'.

Against the odds, England came within a whisker of holding West Indies to a 2-2 draw in their own back yard; only blatant time-wasting orchestrated by Desmond Haynes, the stand-in West Indies captain, denied them victory in Trinidad when on the final afternoon West Indies bowled only 17 of the 30 overs required of them. 'I know that most of the players from the other nations have watched us very closely over the years,' Viv Richards wrote in 1991. 'They have watched the way we train and our attitude towards fitness ... [they] look on in amazement at our workloads. It is good to see it rubbing off on people like Graham Gooch who, in England, seems to be changing the image of the cricketer into that of a genuinely fit sportsman.'

It was not a smooth process, though. With support from Ted Dexter as head of the England committee, Gooch and Stewart left out both Botham and David Gower – two high-profile cricketers with loyal followings – from the West Indies tour in what Gooch described as a deliberate attempt 'to get away from the champagne-set image'. Stewart's view was that Botham was simply not fit enough for a Test tour. They decided to still accommodate him as far as one-day cricket was concerned and allowed him to turn up late (because he was appearing in pantomime) for the lead-in to the World Cup in Australia and New Zealand in 1992, provided he stuck to a prescribed training programme. (He nevertheless turned up looking overweight.)

In a long tournament in which they made all the early running, England physically flagged towards the end, Wasim Akram describing them as looking 'shattered' in the field during their defeat to Pakistan in the final. Gower, meanwhile, was not so much unfit as reluctant to train. Armed with sublime gifts of instinct and timing, he had never had much time for practice but his reputation also came to depend on his 'naturalness'. 'There was a temptation to play to the image, partly because it was fun to do so and partly because it saved having to change into something that I felt, deep down, I wasn't – and never would be,' he said.

Gower was restored to the Test team for the tour of Australia in 1990-91, but there he fell foul of the management when as a prank he and a junior member of the team, John Morris, took to the skies in a Tiger Moth and buzzed the ground at Carrara, where England were playing a mid-tour warm-up match. Gower was fined £1,000 but worse still, having scored hundreds in the previous two Tests, his form collapsed. Told to go away and score runs if he wanted to stay in the side, the harder Gower tried to replicate Gooch's steeliness the more he struggled. 'I found achieving that ultra-professional approach the hardest thing in the game,' he said. Gower played only three more Tests before his career was effectively terminated by his omission from the India and Sri Lanka tour of 1992-93, a moment that for many represented an inspirational player being sacrificed on the modish altar of perspiration. Some hailed Gooch as England's most impressive captain since Mike Brearley, but Brearley himself once termed Gooch's captaincy one of 'earnest and occasionally morose style'.

'We laid the foundations for what you see in the England set-up now,' Gooch said some 20 years later. 'The fitness, the monitoring of fitness, the nutrition, it was the birth of all that on a team scale. Before then, individuals had sorted themselves out.' He added: 'It was a time of change and for some people the change was unpalatable. You still had a bit of the attitude of "I play cricket to get fit". And that's important. You do need to get the right amount of cricket. But I've never seen a cricketer become a worse player for being fitter and stronger.'

Gooch also took the radical step of overhauling his batting method at the age of 36. Troubled by Terry Alderman's swing bowling in 1989, he withdrew from the England side during the Ashes series of that year. He subsequently stood taller, and moved less, about the crease, with dramatic consequences. He averaged 51.6 in Test cricket from this point, having previously averaged 36.9.

The quality and quantity of fast bowling on offer made the 1980s a tough decade for Test batsmen, and the necessity of wearing helmets – essential for safety in such an era – only added to the challenge. Only two batsmen made scores of more than 240 during this decade, Javed Miandad of Pakistan and Graham Yallop of Australia, and Gooch's own mighty 333 against India at Lord's in 1990 was easily England's biggest individual effort since 1974. At Headingley in 1991, Gooch played arguably the greatest innings by an England batsman of modern times when on a pitch offering an attack of Malcolm Marshall, Curtly Ambrose, Courtney Walsh and Patrick Patterson assistance, and with wickets falling at the other end, he held firm for seven and a half hours; his unbeaten 154, in a team total of 252, was the decisive factor in England's first home win over West Indies since 1969.*

Gooch credited his personal fitness regime with extending his own Test career: he was still playing for England at the age of 40 and actually scored a Test double-hundred at that age, the only batsman

---

* Although like most batsmen Gooch wore a helmet as standard, he only once attached a visor, when faced by a rampant West Indies attack on a corrugated surface at Kingston, Jamaica in 1986. Patsy Hendren in the 1930s wore a bespoke item of protective headgear against West Indies, and Mike Brearley in 1977 was the first England batsman of the modern era to follow suit in a Test match, using a moulded skullcap that he wore beneath a conventional cap. By 1978 fibre-glass helmets were commonly available but take-up among international players was only gradual. Bob Willis damaged his neck while batting with a heavy helmet at Edgbaston in 1982 and missed the following Test. Batting helmets became compulsory for all England players in April 2016.

from any country to do this since 1951. He later applied his devotion to training as a batting coach with Essex and England, by which time the younger generations were becoming far more receptive to such ideas. Gooch played an important role in mentoring Alastair Cook, the fittest and most prolific England batsman of the modern era. Cook broke many of the England batting records Gooch set.

Another contemporary of Gooch's had already improved himself by working independently on his physical and mental conditioning. Bob Willis, by his own admission largely uncoached in the mechanics of bowling fast, returned home early from the tour of Australia in 1974-75 with knee trouble and also broke down the following summer in England. Although he returned to the England side and had a successful tour of India in 1976-77, Greig criticised Willis's lack of stamina after the Centenary Test, telling him he should be able to bowl like Dennis Lillee, 'But you're always knackered after five overs ... You should get fitter.' Willis was hurt but knew Greig was right and responded by beginning to work with a doctor of hypnotherapy based in Sydney, Arthur Jackson, who advised that he take up long-distance running and provided him with cassette tapes that enabled Willis to hypnotise himself at home. Willis used them for the rest of his career and, whereas he had played 24 Tests in the previous six years, he was to appear in 66 over the next seven and retired as the leading wicket-taker in England's history. Jackson's success with Willis led to other England players visiting him on subsequent tours of Australia, to the consternation of Brearley, the captain, and Bernard Thomas, the team physiotherapist.*

Thomas had accompanied every England Test tour since Pakistan in 1968-69 and from 1977 also attended every home Test match; as such he was the first person with a medical or fitness background to be associated with the team on a permanent basis. His first sport was gymnastics, in which he acted as a top-flight trainer and judge, and he had little understanding of cricket but, having set up a physiotherapist practice in Birmingham, he was approached by MJK Smith

---

* Possibly one symptom of Willis's untutored method was a tendency to over-step; he bowled more no-balls (939) than any other bowler in Test history.

to treat injured Warwickshire players, a role that was then extended to England. 'That was the terms of reference,' Thomas recalled. 'But I became conscious that the blokes weren't necessarily that fit. I introduced the warm-up on the field before play. The purpose was not to get them fit as such but to get them warmed up and mentally attuned to what they were going to do. You couldn't run them flat out and then hope to get a full day's cricket out of them. After 15 minutes or so, I'd hand them over to the captain, who would then delegate them their ball skills.' Thomas was not a trainer in the style of Dennis Waight, and players – though they might have disliked what Willis described as his 'square-bashing mentality' – did not fear his routines as many did those of Waight.

The independent regimes undertaken by Gooch and Willis showed that Thomas was not providing them with all that they felt they needed, but he nevertheless oversaw an improvement in the general fitness and match-readiness of England players, especially fast bowlers and wicketkeeper Alan Knott, though Brearley recalls Thomas even trying to teach him – a batsman – how to run better by running towards him, pulling on a rope. Geoff Arnold credited Thomas with keeping him fit enough to play 34 Tests, most of them in a three-year period between 1972 and 1975. Thomas also advised the selectors about whether a player could be patched up for action or ought not to be risked. 'Thomas's most significant contribution to the England team ... was in the field of prevention,' Brearley wrote. 'Bowlers who had constantly suffered from muscle injuries ... became less prone to such breakdowns.'

But a rudimentary system was far from infallible. Mike Hendrick, whose England career was hindered more than most by fitness issues, was not properly tested ahead of the 1979–80 tour of Australia and he broke down after bowling three overs.* There was doubt ahead of the Headingley Test of 1981 about Willis's fitness and when the

---

* Among Hendrick's misfortunes with injuries was an incident during a Test against Pakistan in 1974 while he was being given a massage during a rainbreak, when part of the ceiling in the Lord's pavilion collapsed, hurting both himself and Richard Nicholas, the masseur. Hendrick's wounds were only minor but they prevented him taking the field when play restarted.

selectors met and sought Thomas's opinion he could not be located; fortunately, they kept their options open and in the end Willis not only played but produced one of the most famous of all match-winning spells for England. Brearley said the episode taught the selectors to be better informed about injuries ahead of their meetings. Also, during Thomas's last series with England in 1985, he advised against Richard Ellison playing at Edgbaston because of a chest virus but Ellison shrugged it off, played and took ten wickets. Willis had a long association with Thomas through Warwickshire and England and felt he wielded too much influence for someone not versed in the game: apart from sitting in on selection, he sometimes acted as assistant manager on tour. 'By definition, this gave him a say in areas of cricket-making policy,' Willis added.*

One member of the side Thomas did not need to help much was the young Ian Botham who, for all the concern he caused the England management over his lack of fitness towards the end of his career, began as a superb athlete, equipped with great suppleness and extraordinary stamina as a bowler – he could swing the ball prodigiously – and great agility as a fielder and catcher. If Botham later gave training sessions and gym work short shrift, it was because he had not needed them when he was in his pomp; his mistake was not realising, as Gooch did, that if he wanted to prolong his career he needed to work on his fitness more, not less, as the years passed. The enormous workload he got through in his first five years of Test cricket took their toll, as did a back injury which first manifested itself in 1980.

Some of his feats of endurance bear comparison with those by any England seam bowler in any era: he carried the attack in oppressive heat in Sydney in 1979 when Willis and then Hendrick were off the field suffering from sickness and dehydration, and the following winter got through 173.1 overs in three Tests in Australia, including a staggering 80.5 in Perth, before moving on to Mumbai for the

---

* Bernard Thomas's most important and best-remembered moment was when he saved the life of the New Zealand tail-end batsman Ewen Chatfield, when the helmet-less Chatfield was struck over the temple by a short ball from Peter Lever during the Auckland Test in 1975. Thomas's swift action prevented Chatfield swallowing his tongue.

Jubilee Test against India where he took 13 wickets on a generously green-tinged pitch as well as scoring a century; in the second innings, he bowled unchanged for two sessions. Hardly less astonishing was bowling 89 overs in the Oval Test of 1981 which capped a series in which he had already pulled off a string of barely credible heroics. In all, he scored 14 hundreds and took 27 five-wicket hauls in Tests but none of these occurred after his 32nd birthday. One of the issues for Botham's captains to that point was whether he should be allowed to bowl long spells of medium-pace or kept back for bursts of livelier speed. Brearley in particular had a talent for cajoling faster spells out of him. David Gower used him as a 'shock' bowler in the 1985 Ashes to great effect.

The pity was also that, as an iconic figure to whom so many young players looked for a lead, Botham later showed a reluctance to train which may have made it all the harder for the likes of Gooch and Stewart to create a new culture of hard work.

England teams first found the need for the regular services of a masseur on tours of Australia when the long hours spent travelling across a vast country by train could be as punishing on the body as the cricket. Arthur Gilligan's side in 1924-25, for example, recruited Tom Langridge, a physical training expert from Sydney. Frederick Toone, reflecting in 1930 on his experiences of managing three England tours of Australia, wrote: 'An expert masseur always accompanies the team, and is constant in his attentions. The need of such services can be judged when it is said that, apart from the strains of continuous match play, we had on the last tour [in 1928-29] to spend between 20 and 30 nights on the train.'

Tom Langridge was still being used as masseur by Walter Hammond's team in 1946-47 and, according to Hammond's deputy Norman Yardley, did a good job, but by 1950 Yardley was arguing that it was time for a masseur to accompany every team from England, if not a physical trainer who could bring into shape cricketers who could get 'very soft and bloated' from a long outward voyage. He said that the advent of five-day Test matches meant England cricketers had to be possessed of greater physical stamina than of old and questioned whether Ranjitsinhji, though a great batsman, would be worth his place in a five-day Test against a modern Australia team, as he had been 'physically slight and was sometimes lazy in the field'. Only first-rate fielders and those able to withstand barracking should be taken on tours of Australia. In fact, it was not until Len Hutton's tour of 1954–55 that MCC finally agreed to find the money for England to take to Australia a qualified masseur in Harold Dalton of Essex.

A few county coaches appreciated the particular needs of certain players such as fast bowlers, among them Jimmy Iremonger who helped Harold Larwood and Bill Voce at Nottinghamshire. He advised them about diet as well as giving technical assistance with such things as feet placement and establishing that Larwood's run-up should consist of 14 paces over 20 yards. But with so little done to physically prepare players, it was hardly surprising that occasionally some were ruled out through lumbago, which was essentially just stiffness and might have been treated had a masseur been on hand. Maurice Leyland was judged to be suffering from lumbago and declared unfit for the Leeds Test in 1935 not much more than an hour before the start, triggering a frantic search for a suitable replacement. Eventually Yorkshire batsman Arthur Mitchell was located in his garden and rushed to the ground by car; unfazed, he scored fifties in both innings and fielded brilliantly. Leyland was well enough to play in the Gentlemen v Players fixture at Lord's the day after the Test finished. Ironically, for that series against South Africa the cost of a masseur had been added to the items that the Board of Control for Test Matches expected each ground authority to make provision for when hosting a Test, though 'not exceeding £5', but there is no evidence that a masseur was made available at Headingley.

Dalton played a crucial role in one of England's most famous Ashes-winning series in 1954–55. He had chanced to be in the Caribbean the previous winter but the Board of Control for Test Matches turned down a request from the tour management to use his services on the grounds of cost. Fortunately, this was not the case when it came to the Australia tour, where Dalton took under his wing Brian Statham and Frank Tyson, the fast bowler who (ably supported by Statham) tipped the series England's way. Dalton not only managed Tyson's calf and foot niggles but – reasoning that it was too hot to eat normal meals during matches – also put him onto a lunchtime diet of two raw eggs beaten up in milk or orange juice, sometimes spiked with a measure of sherry. 'It is not exactly appetising,' Tyson wrote, 'but it is sustaining.' Combined with a shortened run-up, this served to keep Tyson going through five Tests. 'Harold Dalton ... was set loose on him [Tyson] as though he was being tuned up for a world heavyweight title fight,' Colin Cowdrey recalled.

Dalton was probably the first to bring some rudimentary science to England players' diets and lifestyle; on earlier tours, players were largely left to their own devices and the guidance of their captain. Hydration in sport was barely acknowledged until the 1950s and from the earliest days England teams touring Australia saw champagne and beer as valuable forms of sustenance. Tom Richardson, one of England's strongest bowlers turned publican, drank more beer than any cricketer alive or dead according to Ben Travers, the playwright, in *94 Declared,* published in 1981. Tiger Smith, who kept wicket for England from 1911 to 1913, recalled that fast bowlers drank a couple of pints before play so that they sweated freely, and said that he himself regularly had a beer before the start. Arthur Carr at Nottinghamshire fed Harold Larwood beer to get an extra yard out of him. Talking of his tour of Australia in 1932-33, Larwood said: 'I used to drink a drop of beer and I think that helped me tremendous [sic].' It is now accepted that beer in the evening might make a sportsman – at the very least – stiffer the next day.

Dalton accompanied subsequent England tours to South Africa, West Indies and the subcontinent, and ahead of the West Indies tour of 1959-60 Geoff Dyson, a renowned athletics coach who worked with three British Olympic teams, was recruited to prepare the players, but the fitness of England players was not addressed in co-ordinated fashion until Thomas's time. When on the outward voyage to Australia in 1962, Gordon Pirie, a former British Olympic 5,000-metre silver-medal winner, was found to be among the passengers, and Ted Dexter asked him to organise some daily drills for the players, it met with a hostile reception, especially from Fred Trueman, who had bowled more than 1,100 overs during the English season and viewed the boat journey as an opportunity to rest. Trueman firmly rejected Pirie's suggestions regarding ways to strengthen his legs or improve his diet, and when Pirie instructed the players to run round the perimeter of the deck, Trueman and Cowdrey took to cutting through a passageway to shorten the circuit. Nor did the players take kindly to Pirie, having enjoyed the team's hospitality, criticising them after he disembarked, telling an Australian newspaper they were an 'unfit, paunchy bunch of barflies'. 'Some of our old soldiers were positively mutinous,' Dexter recalled. However, John Woodcock, recalling the England players he encountered from the mid-1950s, remembers them as very unfit by modern standards, smoking and drinking a lot. David Lloyd drank a pint of beer during the lunch break after batting through the first session of his debut Test at Lord's in 1974; he was out shortly after the re-start.

The dawn of the Graham Gooch–Micky Stewart era confronted the uncomfortable fact that England's cricketers were not fit enough for the post-Packer world of international cricket, but it was not until the mid-1990s that it was acknowledged that different players, and especially fast bowlers, needed different regimes, and that much more needed to be done if England teams were to cope with Test matches played without rest days. Ray Illingworth on his appointment as chairman of selectors in 1994 said that he thought 'too much time was spent in what I saw as the wrong sort of training'. David Lloyd, who became England coach two years later, alluded to England's 'justifiably poor reputation for injuries, especially afflicting bowlers, in the early 1990s'.

As a separate issue, Keith Fletcher as head coach regretted not firing Dave Roberts as physio after the India tour of 1992-93; Roberts went through until the Australia tour of 1994-95 after which he filed a critical report to the board stating that the pre-match preparations had not been rigorous enough, partly a response to sarcastic comments from the captain Michael Atherton, who knew Roberts from Lancashire, about them being '20 minutes of aimless exercise'. Fletcher felt Roberts's criticisms reflected badly on him.

The following winter Illingworth brought in Yorkshire physiotherapist Wayne Morton, who made his presence felt in South Africa and at the World Cup, and soon had alongside him England's first strength-and-conditioning coach in Dean Riddle who, like Morton, had a background in rugby league. At the start of their first winter together, with Lloyd now head coach, Morton and Riddle took the players to Portugal for a fitness camp and 'left them in no doubt that they were not there for a holiday'. Even so, during that winter, the failure of the bowlers to remove the New Zealand No.11 Danny Morrison in Auckland, where he held out for nearly three hours with Nathan Astle to secure a draw, was an indictment of their condition, Darren Gough confessing to Lloyd that he had simply run out of puff. 'The players, I concluded, were not physically fit enough, nor as mentally strong as other teams,' Lloyd stated.

Atherton – though he attributed the team's plethora of injuries to over-playing and advocated central contracts as a means of controlling workloads – appreciated Morton's tailored work in reducing injuries and improving fitness, as did Lloyd and Gough, the team's leading fast bowler at the turn of the century. 'Being England physio is a big job,' Gough wrote in his autobiography. 'The physio is the person who is entrusted with your worries and doubts, as well as your body and its niggles. He has to be something of a faith-healer, treating you both mentally and physically ... you must have complete faith and trust in him.' Others, though, did not care for the confrontational style of Morton and Riddle – Dominic Cork and Mark Ramprakash notably failed to do the fitness work required of them – and in 1999 Morton and Riddle were released from England duty amid reports that Morton, like Thomas before him, wielded too much power and was 'getting above himself'.

The focus on fitness only sharpened with the advent of central contracts in 2000 and a national cricket academy, which was the brainchild of Hugh Morris, the ECB's performance director and former England opening batsman, and set up with the aid of Lottery funding. After two winters renting the facilities of the Australian academy in Adelaide, the national academy took up permanent residence at Loughborough University in 2003. One of the academy's early purposes under the stern eye of its first director Rod Marsh, the former Australian wicketkeeper, was to improve the fitness levels of the best young cricketers even before they got to the England team. Only later did it morph from unforgiving training camp to a place where skills could be honed with the aid of specialist coaches and cutting-edge technology. Some among the first intake were not that keen on the regime and when Andrew Flintoff was called away to join England's Test tour of India he was looked upon enviously for his 'escape'. Steven Harmison benefited from the academy because it introduced him to bowling coach Troy Cooley but he refused to go back after Christmas that same winter.

When head coach Duncan Fletcher and physiologist Nigel Stockill teamed up with a new Test captain in Michael Vaughan in 2003 they used a low-key tour of Bangladesh to work on the fitness and physical conditioning of the squad. 'The team worked harder [in Bangladesh] than any other side with which I have been involved,' Fletcher wrote in 2007. 'This was right up Nigel Stockill's alley. In the past his job as physiologist had been made very difficult when the captain and senior players had been reluctant to train hard.' Vaughan had to battle the ECB for the team to be given its first full-time masseur/masseuse. 'When I got the captaincy in 2003 I wanted the team to be fitter and on my first tour as captain to Bangladesh that was my drive,' he said. 'I realised the standard [of fitness in international cricket] was rising and also I believed fitness drives an ethic of hard work. It drives a mentality that you can be tough and do things that you don't want to do. I wanted to make them a tougher team. I had to fight hard to get a masseuse. The ECB didn't want to pay for one and I demanded that they did. The ECB said no, so I said, "Not a problem, we'll pay for it ourselves". The ECB realised that would probably come out. All of a sudden they paid for it.'*

Getting Flintoff (who in his early years as an England cricketer sometimes weighed well over 17 stone) fit was one of the key factors behind his exceptional all-round success in 2004 and 2005, when he was a pivotal figure in England winning 16 Tests across the two years

---

\* Vaughan credits Dominic Cork with introducing the ice-bath into the England dressing-room during a Test against West Indies at Lord's in 2000. 'When he first filled the Lord's bath with ice cubes one evening we all took the piss out of him ... Within a few years everyone was jumping in and out.'

and regaining the Ashes after eight straight series losses to Australia. Similarly, the turning point in Steve Harmison's career came directly after the Bangladesh tour which he left early. While England toured Sri Lanka, Harmison got fit training with the Newcastle United players under Bobby Robson. Rejoining the team for the West Indies tour, Harmison ran amok in the first Test in Jamaica and took 67 wickets in the next 12 months. Once Flintoff and Harmison retired in 2009, it proved easier for Andrew Strauss and Andy Flower to create a new culture in which the players were expected to achieve and maintain a high level of fitness. Samit Patel was overlooked for the 2011 World Cup because he did not meet the required fitness standard. It also became common for fast bowlers, especially young ones still in their developmental stage, to be taken out of cricket to work on their strength and conditioning. Stuart Broad and Steven Finn missed Tests in 2010 for this purpose.

## Those Who Made England's Touring Cricketers Fitter

For many years, England touring teams were typically accompanied only by a manager and perhaps an assistant. After the First World War they recruited the Australian Bill Ferguson to act as baggage-man and scorer, a role he filled on six tours of Australia as well as elsewhere, and also began using local masseurs to treat players. The first English masseur to travel with the team to Australia was Harold Dalton in 1954-55. Not until Bernard Thomas toured in 1968-69 was a permanent arrangement made with a physiotherapist. Wayne Morton was the first physiotherapist to bring in a strength-and-conditioning coach.

The first doctor to travel with an England Test team was Dr Philip Bell in 1995-96; within a few years it was standard for a doctor to join major tours. At the instigation of chairman of selectors Ted Dexter, the Reverend Andrew Wingfield Digby spent three years as the team's pastor and toured in 1992-93. Dr Steve Bull began in 1997 a long association with the team as psychologist, initially to 'engender togetherness' among the players; more recently Dr Mark Bawden filled this role, usually travelling with the team during the early weeks of a tour.

Dr Peter Gregory was appointed the ECB's first full-time chief medical officer in 2002.

| Physiotherapist | Strength & conditioning (or physiologist) | Masseuse/masseur |
|---|---|---|
| Bernard Thomas 1968-69 to 1984-85 (14 winters) | Dean Riddle 1996-97 to 1998-99 (3 winters) | Vicky Byrne 2004-05 (1 winter) |
| Laurie Brown 1985-86 to 1991-92 (6 winters) | Nigel Stockill 1999-2000 to 2006-07 (8 winters) | Mark Saxby 2005-06 to 2018-19 (14 winters) |
| Dave Roberts 1992-93 to 1994-95 (3 winters) | Mark Spivey 2007-08 (1 winter) | |
| Wayne Morton 1995-96 to 1998-99 (4 winters) | Sam Bradley 2007-08 to 2008-09 (2 winters) | |
| Dean Conway 1999-2000 to 2001-02 (3 winters) | Huw Bevan 2009-10 to 2013-14 (5 winters) | |
| Kirk Russell 2002-03 to 2010-11 (9 winters) | Phil Scott 2014-15 to 2018-19 (5 winters) | |
| Ben Langley 2011-12, 2012-13 (2 winters) | | |
| Craig de Weymarn 2013-14 to 2018-19 (6 winters) | | |

# CHAPTER 29

# Television Contracts and Ground Redevelopments
## The rise and fall of Durham

The staging of international cricket in England underwent a fundamental shift in the 1970s and 1980s. Just as professionalisation made itself felt on the field, so commercialisation took hold off it, though its tentacles had a direct impact on the way the game on the pitch was experienced. Previously advertising amounted to not much more than manufacturers' logos on bats, pads and gloves, and perimeter hoardings, but Cornhill Insurance's support for home Test matches marked a sea change. For a start, Cornhill and other advertisers demanded hospitality boxes from which to view the game, which altered the demographic of the crowd. But everything, it was realised, could be put up for sale and over the coming years everything would be: space on the England players' shirts, caps and boots, space on the sightscreens, outfields and stumps. Players became brand ambassadors for luxury cars, private investment banks and water suppliers. In 1991, Tetley Bitter became the first sponsors of England tours, initially paying £3m to finance three winters and then renewing with a deal worth £9m over five years, significant sums at the time. In return, the England players wore Tetley Bitter logos on their shirts.

An enhanced spectator experience also became a priority, as in part it had to following the publication of the Taylor Report in 1990 into safety at sports stadiums. This was good news in many respects, with more comfortable seating, and more of it under cover from the elements, and a wider choice of food and drink. Crucially, too, the use of better wicket covering and the installation of better drainage facilities meant a greater likelihood of play for the crowd to watch. Warwickshire made a concerted effort to find better covering equipment, investing in research in 1963 and subsequently deploying the 'Brumbrella', which covered the entire playing area at Edgbaston, but the major development was the ECB underwriting the cost of re-laid outfields with integrated drainage systems involving layers of stone, gravel and sand. This followed MCC's successful overhaul of the playing area at Lord's in 2002; the Lord's system was reckoned to be capable of draining two inches of rain in an hour and proved itself impressively equal to a biblical deluge on the second day of the 2007 Test against India. Much less play was lost through waterlogged grounds. Electronic scoreboards and replay screens became standard features at the major venues by the late 1990s, following the lead set by the Melbourne Cricket Ground in the early 1980s.

But the experience, while in many respects better, also became more sanitised. Following a series of incidents in the 1970s which made the ground authorities more mindful of security, the playing area became sacrosanct and an invisible barrier was created between performers and public. Two London Tests in 1973 saw frequent pitch invasions by noisy though peaceable West Indian supporters. 'The players were mobbed and pitch trampled on, but fortunately with the weather dry the pitch stood up well,' *Wisden* reported of the Oval match.

However, things were more serious at Lord's, where in a separate incident on the Saturday afternoon a hoax bomb scare resulted in an 85-minute interruption and a crowd of 28,000 being ordered to leave the ground. With an IRA bombing campaign underway in London at the time, MCC had no choice but to treat the threat seriously. In fact, many spectators stayed in the ground and were moved onto the outfield while police searched the terraces (the West Indies players returned to their hotel nearby and the England team sheltered in a tent behind the pavilion).* Later, as England followed on, Geoff Boycott was, in the words of John Woodcock in *The Times*, 'jostled and harassed' by fans as he left the field after being caught hooking into the hands of long leg off the last ball of the day. He jostled them back. 'The police did all they could to protect Geoff at the end of the day, which was very difficult for them,' England selector Brian Taylor said. 'I think the behaviour of some of the crowd left much to be desired. The way they kept coming on the ground made life hazardous for the police and the stewards.' When play resumed on the Monday, the crowd were confined to the stands, although after West Indies completed a huge victory thousands of West Indians again took to the field.

Two years later England's six major venues were subjected to an unprecedented wave of multiculturalism when eight teams (three white, five non-white) took part in the inaugural World Cup, in which pitch invasions and banners featured strongly. A few weeks later there was another serious breach of security during the Headingley Test when four supporters of George Davis, a minicab driver jailed the previous year for his alleged part in a robbery in which a policeman was shot, vandalised the pitch on the fourth night of the game against Australia, digging holes near the popping crease and pouring oil around the area of a good length. It emerged that the night-guard at the ground consisted of just one policeman, who went off duty at 6.30am unaware of the damage.† The captains Tony Greig and Ian Chappell briefly discussed switching the game to an adjacent pitch but the final day's play was quickly abandoned; Australia were 220 for three, chasing 445, but in any case late-morning rain would have spoiled the chances of a positive result.

The TCCB summer meeting of 1976 spent much of its time discussing noise at that summer's West Indies Tests which was

---

* Another bomb alert led to a 14-minute delay in play on the first morning of the Headingley Test of 1974.

† The previous Test match at Lord's also witnessed, emerging from the Tavern Stand on the fourth day, the first streaker at an international cricket match in England.

considered 'sometimes intimidatory to players and umpires'; both captains appealed for relative quiet at The Oval. Patience was further tested when, during the space of a month in 1984, West Indians joyously poured onto the outfield at The Oval sporting 'blackwash' banners in celebration of Clive Lloyd's team becoming the first visiting side to beat England 5-0 on their own soil. Then, a group of demonstrators acting on behalf of Tamils in Sri Lanka invaded the field at Lord's during Sri Lanka's first Test in England, waving flags and lying down on the square. Michael Holding, who played in the 1976, 1980 and 1984 Tests at The Oval, knew it was no coincidence that West Indies' visits saw such exuberant crowds. 'The Oval being quite close to Brixton meant that the West Indians just kept turning up. They loved it here because they could really show their support for the team. They could have their musical instruments and drums – a proper carnival. Those days, we didn't have all this furore around safety and whether people would get hurt and attacked, so it was pretty much a free-for-all.'

The sense that pitch invasions were a general problem out of control was endorsed by an incident during an England Test match in Perth in 1982, when Terry Alderman, the Australia bowler, tackled one of a group of Union Jack-waving intruders and dislocated his bowling shoulder. He missed the rest of the series. Fighting then broke out among English and Australian supporters, and Greg Chappell took the Australian players off the field until order was restored.

The upshot of such incidents was that spectators were increasingly discouraged from sitting on the grass around the boundary's edge, barred from running onto the playing area during or after play, and told they could not fly flags or play musical instruments.* In fact, in a spat that revisited the battle-lines between MCC and the TCCB

---

* Flags and banners were barred partly because they might carry political statements or obstruct the view of other spectators. Ground regulations for England venues included lists of prohibited items, of which one for Lord's was typical: 'Flags and banners ... musical instruments, klaxons, rattles, fireworks, firearms, weapons ... and other articles which, in the club's reasonable opinion, may be dangerous, offensive, hazardous and/ or constitute an annoyance to spectators are ... prohibited.' Unlike other grounds, Lord's also prohibits fancy-dress costumes and oversized hats. Its ban on flags extends to dressing-room balconies, as several visiting international teams have discovered.

as to who should control international matches at Lord's, MCC secretary Jack Bailey tried to insist that spectators should continue to sit on the grass rather than allow the space to be given over to advertising hoardings, but Raman Subba Row warned him, 'Jack, Lord's will lose Test matches if you don't go along with it.' A culture of high ticket prices and credit-card bookings further narrowed the type of cricket supporter willing or able to come through the gates. Brixton's West Indians who had previously bought tickets for the whole community could no longer do so, but nor were they as keen to attend once instruments were banned. Barring a craze for fancy-dress (permitted only in designated areas and generally on specified days), there was simply less colour and diversity, especially at the two corporatised London venues. Audiences were predominantly white, middle-class and male.*

One of the earliest indications that maximising revenues might trump other considerations came when the TCCB followed the Australian pattern by expanding a home Ashes series from five matches to six in 1981, and then – on the back of that success, thanks largely to Ian Botham's heroics in that series – gave consideration to staging two matches in the 1985 series at Lord's, where receipts were routinely much greater than elsewhere. Only after debate at the board's spring meeting of 1984 was the idea shelved. 'It was felt that while an extra game at Lord's might bring in more money, provincial centres, which have spent heavily in recent years on improving their facilities, deserved every encouragement,' *Wisden* reported. Old Trafford would have been the ground to miss out and it had already experienced three Test-free summers out of the previous seven. In seasons when twin tours were staged, it was accepted practice that Lord's would host both visiting teams, leaving five other venues competing for four Tests. This problem would resurface.

Soon, the landscape was permanently changed by the entry into the television market of satellite broadcaster Sky. This sort

---

* In an effort to buck this trend and better serve families and their large Asian popula-tion, Yorkshire announced they were cutting ticket prices for adults for the 2018 Test against Pakistan to £20. Research carried out for ECB in 2018 revealed the average age of attendees to home Test matches was 47.

of intervention had been sought for some time by the marketing men Bernie Coleman and Subba Row, who by this stage had risen to chairman of the board (a telling indication of the TCCB's new priorities). Sky negotiated rights to exclusive coverage of England's tour of West Indies in 1990, the first time an England Test series overseas had been shown in its entirety, and this proved the start of a long-standing relationship: Sky has shown every Test match England have played away from home ever since except for the Ashes winter of 2017-18 when BT secured the rights on a one-off basis.*

The value of Sky's original deal was relatively modest at around £2m per year, but their involvement drove up the value of broadcasting contracts considerably over the years that followed. From 1992-94, broadcast rights brought the TCCB around £5m each year, and from 1995-98 almost £15m per annum. The second of these deals might have yielded even more but there was fierce opposition from the National Heritage Committee (among others) to the possibility of England's home Tests being lost to terrestrial television. In the event, Sky did not bid for home Tests, though it added to its portfolio exclusive rights to England's home one-day internationals. 'We had to negotiate against a backdrop of the Heritage Committee's recommendation,' Brian Downing, chairman of the board's marketing committee, said at the time. 'We think it is a restraint of trade.' BBC thus continued to show home Tests, although only until 1998 when it was outbid by Channel 4, another terrestrial service, who broadcast all home Tests with the exception of one match each season which was shown on Sky. This arrangement lasted until 2005 and was initially worth more than £25m per year.

Sky's overseas coverage played a part in encouraging travelling support to follow England around the world, a phenomenon no other international team enjoyed to the same extent. The self-termed 'Barmy Army' became a noisy and not always welcome presence, although the players said they appreciated their backing. 'Their endless mantras . . . can only detract from everyone else's enjoyment.

---

* Sky Television, which struck the deal to cover the series in the Caribbean, merged with British Satellite Broadcasting in November 1990 to form BSkyB (later Sky).

They always seem inappropriate to the moment,' wrote Matthew Engel of English support in the Caribbean in 1998.

The enhanced investment improved the financial position of English cricket, but only modestly at first. Lord MacLaurin estimated that when in 1997 he took over as chairman of the ECB, a streamlined body which took over the functions of the TCCB, Cricket Council and National Cricket Association, the board was operating on a budget of only around £28m. 'You cannot do much with that,' he said. 'We really had to think about where we could get more.' This led to protracted negotiations with the department for Culture, Media and Sport and the partial delisting of Test cricket under the 1999-2002 deal and full delisting from 2006 onwards, when Sky claimed exclusive coverage of all England Tests in a deal worth around £55m per year.

The removal of cricket from mainstream television created heated debate but ECB administrators, led by Giles Clarke, who as chair of the marketing committee was instrumental in the wholesale shift to satellite, were convinced they had no choice. 'The professional game here would have died,' Clarke said. The price was undeniably a heavy one: whereas an average 4.7 million watched the last two sessions of the classic 2005 Ashes series on Channel 4, the peak figure on Sky during the 2013 Ashes was only 1.3 million. When research revealed how unrecognisable most of the top England players were with youngsters, the ECB became determined to return live cricket in some form to terrestrial TV under the 2020-24 contract. 'We have no ambition to be the richest, most irrelevant sport in this country,' Tom Harrison, the ECB's chief executive, said. Harrison duly delivered some live cricket back to the BBC, although the only live England men's matches were two Twenty20s per summer; all other men's internationals remained with Sky in a deal worth about £220m per year.*

In truth, the end of the BBC's 60-year association with Test cricket in England was no more than it deserved. The TCCB had

---

* The BBC was also contracted to show highlights of all home Tests, one-day internationals and Twenty20s, as well as live coverage of ten of the 38 matches in a new domestic short-form tournament, plus women's internationals.

long been impatient with the BBC's poor resourcing and only with the board's prompting did the BBC start to show all balls from behind the bowler's arm in 1989 and assist third umpires in making decisions on stumpings and run-outs in 1993 (even though as long ago as 1987 it had, embarrassingly, insufficient cameras to show Ian Botham running out Imran Khan). When the incident involving Michael Atherton apparently applying dirt to the ball at Lord's in 1994 occurred, the BBC had left the cricket to show racing from Ascot and the first pictures were seen by viewers in South Africa; this footage was only shown in the UK after the game, merely helping to fuel what was by then a media frenzy.

In its last year of live coverage, the BBC was using only 13 cameras at Test matches whereas in their early years of covering Tests in England both Channel 4 and Sky used twice as many. From an early stage, Sky's cameras with 50 frames per second offered conclusive proof on line-calls, as well as being able to show how the ball rotated. 'For many years, its presentation of cricket has been ... complacent and dreary,' Matthew Engel wrote of the BBC in 1999. 'Many new techniques for broadcasting the game have been developed in the past two decades ... So far as I am aware, not a single one has emanated from the BBC.' The BBC's successors started using the revolutionary Hawk-Eye ball-tracking system in 2001.*

What these ever-more-valuable contracts did was fix the national team at the centre of English cricket. Broadcasters had no wish to put on their screens a team that could not play well, and therefore resources had to be made available to ensure England's best players did themselves justice. This was the prime reason behind the introduction of central contracts and the exponential growth in their value: everyone was incentivised to make the England team a success. The country's top cricketers had never had it so good.

What also served the broadcasters' needs was an expansion in England's fixture list and from 2000 it grew significantly. That year,

---

* BBC generally, though not always, held onto radio rights for England games. Commercial station TalkSport covered several England Test tours from 2001–05 and 2018–19. They also secured the rights for major overseas series from 2019–21.

England embarked on a home schedule that typically involved seven Tests, around ten one-day internationals and, from 2005, Twenty20s. Whereas previously the first Test of the summer had never taken place before 27 May, it was now brought forward by anything up to three weeks, with the earliest start date of 6 May set in 2009.* Floodlit matches also became a feature. England's first day–nighter on home soil took place at Old Trafford on 13 July 2000, although with Zimbabwe all out for 114 and England knocking off the runs in 20.3 overs, the match was finished by 7.30pm and the lights were barely needed. By 2009, all the major English venues were equipped with floodlights and had hosted a day–night ODI or international Twenty20; in August 2017, Edgbaston became the first England ground to stage a day–night Test match.†

The growth in international fixtures created feverish competition to host games among the established England venues as well as encouraging others with ambitions to join the big time – notably Durham, Cardiff and Southampton. In the frenzy of spending that followed, several grounds got themselves into difficulties, in Durham's case with dire consequences.

The situation led the ECB, under pressure from some of the newer clubs, to set up in 2005 a Major Match Group to determine which grounds should be allocated fixtures. Host clubs wanted the security of knowing they would be staging England matches for the foreseeable future; though some received the guarantees they were looking for, others did not. The group's methodology was opaque and in many eyes was unsatisfactory, particularly in respect of clubs being asked to make blind bids.

Only after Durham needed bailing out in 2016 did Colin Graves, the ECB chairman, indicate that the system would be scrapped. In

---

* These early-season conditions proved hugely to England's advantage against teams who were typically among the weaker in Test cricket (high summer was reserved for bigger opposition). In 21 Tests between 2000 and 2016 that started in England before 27 May, England's record was won 17, drew 4, lost 0.

† The last major grounds to stage floodlit internationals were Lord's and The Oval, both of which staged their first day–night games during the World Twenty20 in June 2009. Lord's, which faced tight restrictions from local residents on the use of floodlights, has only ever staged one England day–night ODI, against Pakistan in September 2010.

future, established venues were to be compensated £500,000 for each season in which they did not host Tests, although this became a bone of contention with some counties after it emerged Glamorgan received an advance payment of £2.5m for forgoing its place altogether on the Test roster for 2020–24. 'I want to change the process so the risk is taken away from the grounds and that risk is shared by the ECB,' Graves said. 'If you have a Test match every year guaranteed then you are in a far better shape [than those that don't]. That has to change as well so everybody is treated the same.' Instead, the ECB would take a percentage of ticket revenue, 50 per cent for Tests at Lord's, 40 per cent at The Oval and 30 per cent for games elsewhere.

## How England's Grounds Have Coped With Bad Weather

Cricket and the English weather have never had a great relationship but thanks to improved ground covering and drainage, and the advent of floodlights, less play is lost than was once the case. Since May 1993, only 16 whole days have been lost to bad weather in 173 Tests in England (including two Pakistan v Australia Tests in 2010). This compares to 55 days lost in 230 Tests between 1948, when five-day Tests were introduced, and 1992, and 26 days lost in 117 Tests between 1880 and 1947 that were mainly scheduled over three or four days (including three Australia v South Africa Tests in 1912). Seven whole days were lost during the four-match series against Pakistan in 1954 and four days during the 1926, 1938, 1958, 1964, 1980 and 1987 seasons.

A policy of refunding spectators only for whole-day washouts was expanded following protests at Edgbaston in 1992 when only two balls were bowled on the second day; spectators were merely offered free entry for the final day of a game already ruined. A Small Claims Court subsequently found against the TCCB, and 4,000 ticket-holders were refunded £62,500. Three years later, the TCCB gave full refunds for spectators who bought fourth-day tickets at the same ground after England were beaten by West Indies in seven sessions on a pitch England captain Michael Atherton termed 'diabolical'.

| Ground | Scheduled Tests | Whole days lost |
|---|---|---|
| Old Trafford | 80* | 29 |
| Lord's | 137 | 20 |
| The Oval | 101 | 15 |
| Headingley | 77 | 13† |
| Trent Bridge | 63 | 10 |
| Edgbaston | 51 | 8 |
| Chester-le-Street | 6 | 2 |
| Cardiff | 3 | 0 |
| Southampton | 3 | 0 |
| Sheffield | 1 | 0 |

Geoff Cook ranks among the most important cricketers England have produced in the modern era. Born and educated in Middlesbrough, he made only seven Test appearances as an opening batsman in the early 1980s, and six of those came when several candidates were barred for making a rebel tour of South Africa, but after a 20-year career at Northamptonshire, eight as captain, he returned to the North-East to help Durham prepare to join the county championship in 1992. After winning four Minor Counties titles between 1975 and 1984, Durham were admitted as the 18th first-class county in December 1990 in a vote in which only Sussex, who abstained, withheld support.‡ Cook, returning on the understanding that he would eventually be director of cricket, captained the club in their final season as a Minor County and then led the second XI for two seasons as they strove to bring through its best young talent.

---

* Old Trafford's 80 Test matches include a three-day Test in 1890 and four-day Test in 1938 which were totally washed out. These seven days are included in the total of whole days lost.

† Headingley's days lost does not include the final day of the 1975 Test when the pitch was sabotaged by vandals.

‡ Among those who spoke out against Durham's admission was a young England player Michael Atherton, who argued in 1991 that there were already too many counties.

For the next 20 years, Cook devoted himself off the field to nurturing cricketers not only from Durham but also Northumberland and Cumbria, areas that between them had previously produced outstanding players – among them Andrew Stoddart, Tom Graveney, Colin Milburn, Bob Willis and Peter Willey – who had been obliged to pursue first-class careers elsewhere. Northamptonshire in particular had maintained close scouting links with the region, and Milburn, Willey and Cook were among many who migrated there. Another was left-arm swing bowler Simon Brown, who returned to Durham and in 1996 became the county's second Test cricketer after Ian Botham, who in 1992 played the last three of his 102 Tests as a Durham player. Durham cricketers who subsequently won England caps were all nurtured by the club. Cook played a central role in the identification and development of Steve Harmison, Paul Collingwood, Graham Onions, Mark Wood and Ben Stokes, all of whom would contribute to Ashes-winning England sides. Harmison and Wood both played for Northumberland youth teams, and Stokes for Cumbria age-groups, before being scouted by Cook. Between 1996 and 2016, only Yorkshire, with 14, had more England Test debutants than Durham's nine, and only Surrey, Sussex and Yorkshire could match their three championship titles.

Only in respect of their ambitions for their new Riverside headquarters at Chester-le-Street, opened in 1995, did Durham overreach themselves. Among the provisos attached to their elevation to first-class status, Durham were told by the TCCB that they must build a new ground rather than continue on the club grounds they had used thus far, but their officials interpreted this as encouragement to create a Test-match venue, and when Durham got into financial difficulty in 2016 this misunderstanding became a point of contention. 'They told us to build a first-class ground and in my view a first-class ground had to be for Test-match cricket,' Bob Jackson, a club director at the time, said. 'Don Robson was chairman and he always wanted to have Test-match cricket here.' Tom Moffat, a director for 15 years and honorary treasurer, said: 'I don't think it was ever stated it had to be a Test-match ground . . . but all the time there was this dream that we were going to build a Test-match ground, one of the best grounds in the country.'*

Durham eventually staged six Tests between 2003 and 2016, all of them won by England, but the four that were staged against less glamorous opposition before mid-June averaged total gates of just 25,000. The Test against Sri Lanka in May 2016, for which Durham bid £923,000, proved the death knell. Five months later, with the club burdened by debts of more than £7m, most of which was owed to the ECB and Durham County Council, a bail-out package was arranged which involved, among sundry other penalties attached to domestic competitions, Durham forfeiting its Test-match status.

Two other new international grounds fared little better. Glamorgan, having bought Sophia Gardens in Cardiff outright in 1995, announced plans in 2006 for a new pavilion, media centre, grandstand and further covered seating in a £9.4m redevelopment backed by the Welsh Assembly with the aim of securing Test status in time for the 2009 Ashes. To general surprise, the ECB duly awarded the ground the first Test of that series, on the back of a £3.2m bid. With the game lasting a full five days – as England's last-wicket pair of James Anderson and Monty Panesar survived 69 balls to secure a draw – the attendance topped 75,000.

However, by 2014 Glamorgan had debts of £17m which the club negotiated down by 70 per cent after 12 months of discussions with the chief creditors Cardiff City Council, Allied Irish Bank and former chairman Paul Russell; by 2018, long-term debt had been reduced to £2.5m. Glamorgan hosted another Australia Test in 2015 but it had no further Tests planned and seemed happy to recast itself, like Bristol, as a venue for ODIs and international Twenty20s.

Hampshire in 1997 began building a new ground at West End outside Southampton, designed by Michael Hopkins & Partners and initially costing £24m, which – despite the help of lottery funding – pushed

---

* Some reports stated that Durham were under direct instruction to build an international ground but no documentary evidence has been found to support such claims. Tom Moffat's book *The Impossible Dream . . . Come True: The story of how Durham County Cricket Club attained First Class Status in 1992* (2009) republished the key correspondence between Durham and the TCCB, which is inconclusive.

the club into serious financial difficulties even before the venue became operational. Local businessman Rod Bransgrove stepped in with a large amount of money and the club was restructured as a public limited company. The ground staged its first Test match against Sri Lanka in 2011, but like Chester-le-Street it appeared to face insuperable logistical problems as an out-of-town venue. The ground was sold to Eastleigh Borough Council in 2012 for £6.5m and by 2017 the club's debts of £10m were considered manageable. When the venues for England's home internationals for 2020-24 were announced, no Test matches were scheduled for Cardiff or Southampton.

The clubs that ran the six established international grounds undertook some of the heftiest redevelopments, leaving most under severe financial strain. They had little choice but to diversify their businesses and turn themselves into multi-purpose venues capable of staging concerts, conferences and events. Old Trafford, like Southampton, gave over space to a Hilton hotel and – along with every other first-class county headquarters bar Lord's, Edgbaston and Trent Bridge – sold naming rights to their ground. Some of these decisions proved highly lucrative; Lancashire and Surrey both enjoyed healthy revenues from outside cricket, with Surrey becoming the richest county in the country with a turnover of almost £33m and pre-tax profits of £1.6m in 2017.

Trent Bridge in 1998 unveiled a new Radcliffe Road Stand and cricket centre costing £7.2m, paid for by a £5m grant and £2.5m loan, and in 2002 opened a new Fox Road Stand. On the back of the increased capacity, Nottinghamshire signed a deal with the TCCB that kept international cricket at the ground until at least 2011. The club proved particularly susceptible to losses in years when it did not host a Test, as happened in 2016 when it reported a loss of £741,000. Modest improvements were made in 2017-18 to the Radcliffe Road Stand, which was reputed to have had a significant impact on the swing-bowling properties of the ground. From 1998, its 18 Tests produced only three draws – one of which was played on a freakishly lifeless surface for the India match in 2014 which earned a rare 'poor' marking from the ICC match referee – and 28 five-wicket hauls for fast bowlers. Seven of these were taken by James Anderson and two by Stuart Broad, whose figures of eight for 15 in 2015, when Australia were dismissed for 60 before lunch on the first day, were the best by a fast bowler in Ashes Tests.*

The Oval secured an even lengthier staging agreement on the back of plans to develop the Vauxhall End of the ground with the huge OCS Stand. The deal was struck in 2002 and was to last 20 years and the building work began two years later at a cost of £25m. Other developments included the Bedser Stand, which housed new dressing-rooms, and the Ken Barrington Centre on one side of the pavilion, and on the other side the Laker-Lock Stand and Peter May Stand, built at a cost of £10m and unveiled in 2016. The pavilion itself, with a portico designed by Adam Architecture, was renovated in 2012-13 at a cost of £2m. In 2017, Surrey declared an aspiration to signifi-cantly expand capacity to 40,000 by 2023; this was partly a response to exploratory plans to play Twenty20 matches and World Cup games in 2019 on drop-in pitches at the nearby London Stadium (venue for the Olympic Games in 2012). In the 1980s and 1990s the pitches with their trampoline bounce had a reputation for being among the best in the country for fast bowlers, but this was subsequently lost and batting became easier at The Oval than any other regular Test ground in England.† Various developments at the Vauxhall End cut into what had been a huge playing area: in the first Test staged in England in 1880, Australia's George Bonnor, batting at the pavilion end, was caught at long-on by Fred Grace off a hit measured at 115 yards.

An arrangement that had allowed Yorkshire to host a Test every year at Headingley since 1961 – a reward for consistently good attendances – came to an end in 1989 and the club was subsequently told that if it was to enjoy another long-term staging agreement it would need to purchase the ground outright rather than continue leasing it from the Leeds Cricket, Football and Athletic Company. This it did in 2005 for £13m with the help of a £9m loan from Leeds

---

* Although Anderson did not enjoy bowling at Trent Bridge during the bore-draw in 2014, he nevertheless again stole much of the limelight by making the highest score by an England No.11 of 81 in the course of a Test-record last-wicket stand of 198 with Joe Root.
† In Tests at The Oval since 2000, batsmen have averaged 36.56, more than at any other regular venue in England, and scored five double-centuries in 19 matches; at Lord's they averaged 33.75 with seven double-centuries in 33 matches.

City Council, but by this point, though a new East Stand had been built, the ground had fallen well behind other major venues in terms of redevelopment and the club only narrowly escaped foreclosure.

A key figure in a new management team was businessman Colin Graves, who chaired the club for many years before taking over as ECB chairman in 2015, and to whose family trust Yorkshire owed about £17m by 2017. The players' dressing-rooms were moved into a modern block above the club offices in 1964 and later into the Football Stand, originally built in 1932, before a controversial new pavilion costing £21m was completed in 2010. It seemed better designed for use by Leeds Metropolitan University, which owned most of the building, than cricket. An even more ambitious redevelopment was given the go-ahead in 2017 when funding was agreed for a new Football Stand, which backed onto a ground shared by rugby union and rugby league sides and was therefore a complex scheme requiring the agreement of several parties. Yorkshire's share of the costs was expected to be £16.5m but the scheme was necessary to secure England matches at Headingley beyond 2019, when the ground's staging agreement ended. Capacity would rise from 15,500 to 18,350.

The Headingley slope which uniquely among England Test grounds runs straight down the line of the square (as opposed to across it, as at Lord's) was levelled off slightly at the top end after the building of the Carnegie Pavilion but it continued to be a challenging place to bowl fast, with rhythm often hard to find whether running down the slope or up it. Fred Trueman preferred to bowl up the hill. Bob Willis ran down it during his heroic spell to win the Test in 1981. Stuart Broad and James Anderson both struggled until they switched in 2016: with Broad coming down the hill and Anderson up it, they shared 15 wickets against Sri Lanka. Modern Headingley pitches have been stubbornly resistant to spin and, although they have tended to offer good pace and carry, the key for the quicker bowler is whether the skies are overcast or not.* A fast outfield, too, allows little margin

---

* Three of the four instances in Tests in England of captains losing after declaring in the third innings have occurred at Headingley: Norman Yardley v Australia in 1948, Adam Gilchrist v England in 2001 and Joe Root against West Indies in 2017. The other instance was David Gower v West Indies at Lord's in 1984.

for error. Along with Edgbaston, since 2000, Headingley has been the fastest-scoring of England's regular Test grounds.

Edgbaston in the late 1990s acquired, partially with the help of lottery funding, a new cricket centre and the Eric Hollies Stand at a cost of £2m, but a new pavilion complex was long overdue by the time work began on the South and West Stands at a cost of £32m, £20m of which was loaned by Birmingham City Council. Previously, the dressing-rooms were so closely housed, and their partition walls so thin, that opposing teams could hear each other's livelier conversations (such as an alleged row between Ricky Ponting and Shane Warne over Ponting's decision to bowl first in the 2005 Ashes Test). The redevelopment was completed in 2011 but that same year Warwickshire received a big blow when the Major Match Group chose not to award Edgbaston a Test against Australia in 2013 or India in 2014. Nevertheless, the ground continued to generate the most vibrant and partisan atmosphere of any England home venue and remained a firm favourite with the home players. As well as being an established venue for major one-day internationals, it also became the usual home to the county Twenty20 finals days. However, by 2017 Warwickshire had debts of £27m.

Lancashire, jolted into ground improvements by losing out to Cardiff for an Ashes Test in 2009, endured a protracted legal battle over the proposed redevelopment of Old Trafford that by 2011 pushed the club to the brink of bankruptcy. Crisis was averted and in 2017, after a process lasting nine years, the ground's transformation was complete. It included The Point conference and event facility built by Gavin Elliott of BDP, a hotel, a new players' pavilion and media centre, and a facelift for the old Victorian pavilion. It cost £60m, some of which was raised with the assistance of the local council and Greater Manchester Authority.* The club held debts of about £25m, but was already returning regular annual profits through its restructured business; its profit for 2017 was £2.35m.

---

* Old Trafford was the Test-match ground worst hit by bombing during the Second World War. A fundraising appeal raised £25,000 but this was insufficient to meet plans for a new pavilion; in the end it was simply repaired, with the enhancements including improved dressing-rooms.

One consequence of the redevelopment was that the pitch was turned 90 degrees, meaning that like most cricket pitches it pointed north–south and no longer east–west, which had led to occasional issues with the setting sun interrupting play. Pitches – which used to be quick, helped reverse swing and spun – lost some of their pace after the change. In 2017, the old pavilion end was named the James Anderson End, the first instance in England of an end at a major venue being formally named after a Test cricketer; in its earlier alignment one end had become informally known as the Statham End because the road behind was Brian Statham Way.

As hosts of a Test match to every touring team, Lord's was most keenly under pressure to justify its position, a pressure it felt all the more acutely because of the memories of the long-standing acrimony created by MCC ceding powers to the TCCB. Even in Lord MacLaurin's time as chairman there were threats of Test matches being taken away from Lord's, while Duncan Fletcher at the start of his reign as England coach was sufficiently unhappy about the poor practice facilities that he threatened to move training sessions to Finchley. Only then did MCC 'wise up their act'.

However, Lord's possessed advantages which were hard to ignore. Not only was it regarded as the home of cricket – a reputation unimpaired by the ICC's decision in 2005 to move its offices to Dubai – but Lord's Tests had a cachet all their own, and as a London venue, like The Oval, it had much less trouble selling tickets than grounds in the provinces. Tickets sales alone could generate £5m.* At MCC's annual general meeting in 2016, club president Roger Knight highlighted the ability of Lord's to sell Test matches even in the difficult early-season weeks of May and June, claiming that in the three seasons from 2013 to 2015, attendances for Lord's Tests (including members) had totalled 342,000 whereas three Tests outside London attracted fewer than 110,000 spectators.

Unsurprisingly, in modernising itself, Lord's experienced none of

---

* Although Middlesex County Cricket Club are only tenants of MCC, the terms of tenancy are generous and they are paid a guaranteed sum by MCC from each Test match played at Lord's as compensation for loss of revenue during those periods.

the financial crises endured elsewhere, although MCC sometimes worked in partnership with sponsors. The undistinguished Tavern Stand, originally put up in the 1860s, was rebuilt in 1967. The Mound Stand was rebuilt by Hopkins Architects in 1987, the newly named Compton and Edrich Stands in 1990, and the main Grand Stand in 1997. Constructors working on the Compton and Edrich Stands famously came under fire when Kapil Dev struck four successive sixes to save the follow-on for India in 1990. Problems with the sightscreens, or the lack of a proper one at the Pavilion End, which could make batting treacherous against taller fast bowlers, were finally solved. A new media centre – designed by Future Systems and its Czech architect Jan Kaplicky, and constructed in Pendennis Shipyard – cost £5m and was built in time for the 1999 World Cup. It was the first all-aluminium, semi-monocoque building in the world and was awarded the Stirling Prize. The Warner Stand, originally built in 1958, was redeveloped by Populous at a cost of £25m and opened in 2017.

However, MCC made a serious error when it allowed itself to be outbid at auction by development company Rifkind, who in 1999 bought for just £2.35m a 999-year lease on disused railway tunnels at the Nursery End of the ground (though not the land above), leading to almost 20 years of bitter wrangling, and some high-profile resignations, about how best to develop this part of the ground. Rifkind proposed a deal which would enable it to construct flats there in exchange for £150m (£15m of which was to be used as a sweetener to MCC members) which could be used by the club for further ground development. Eventually, in 2017 the committee recommended and the membership endorsed its own plan to rebuild various stands and facilities paid for out of the club's own funds. The first phase was a £50m redevelopment of the Compton and Edrich Stands planned for 2019-21 which would add 2,500 seats.

Whether or not the arrangement of new stands was a factor, Lord's became a haven for seam and swing bowling and even when the ball didn't do much there was always the slope to work with, assisting slip catches when the bowling was from the Nursery End and lbws from the Pavilion End (against right-handed batsmen). Traditionally the Pavilion End is the preferred choice for fast bowlers, with the prevailing wind offering further assistance. From 2000 onwards, England won twice as many matches at Lord's as at any other home ground (though admittedly they played more often there); ten different England fast bowlers claimed five-fors.

## Test Attendances in England

Modern concerns about the popularity of Test cricket are not reflected in attendance figures for England's home matches, which have seen a decade-on-decade rise over the last 50 years. Attendances enjoyed a boom in the immediate period after the Second World War, boosted by the peace-time enthusiasm to watch sport, demobilised soldiers on leave and the transition to five-day matches. Ground authorities also shamelessly packed in the crowds, even pushing in the boundaries to accommodate spectators on the grass verges (a practice that continued into the 1970s). Hence daily attendances sometimes topped modern capacities: 40,000 watched the fourth day at Headingley in 1948 and 34,000 the fifth day at Old Trafford in 1961. The Ashes series of 1948 and 1953 both drew more than 500,000 spectators.

Some of the weaker teams proved a harder sell, especially with TV coverage becoming more comprehensive, and even the move to split tours in 1965 failed to arrest a downturn for sides other than Australia and West Indies. The first Test against New Zealand in 1965 drew just 21,000 to Edgbaston (though inclement weather played its part; it was so cold that players were served hot drinks), and the final Test of their tour four years later was watched by only 20,000 at The Oval ('the crowds must have been the smallest ever to watch a Test match in London,' John Woodcock wrote in *The Cricketer*). India's visit to Old Trafford in 1974 drew only 19,700, which *The Cricketer* reported to be the lowest attendance for a five-day Test in England. The following month, the ground was stripped of its automatic right to stage an Ashes Test. Things were little better in Australia, where the average daily attendance for the 1970-71 series of 20,540 (or 102,700 for a match lasting five days) was the lowest for an incoming Ashes tour since 1920-21.

The advent of six-match series against the bigger sides saw total gates return above 400,000 for the first time in 1993, and then (following the move to seven Tests per summer) to regularly beyond half a million: 546,450 watched the Tests in 2001, 568,484 in 2004 and 584,586 in 2011, then 637,931 in 2013, when ironically it was commonly reported after the England team retained the Ashes that they had become disengaged from the public. The biggest factor behind these rises was ground redevelopment. The regular capacities of the six main grounds in 2018 were as follows: Lord's 29,000, The Oval 25,700, Edgbaston 24,550, Old Trafford 19,600, Trent Bridge 17,000 and Headingley 15,500.

| Ground | England Tests | Total gate | Average gate | Best gate |
|---|---|---|---|---|
| 1980s | | | | |
| Lord's | 15 | 1,053,471 | 70,231 | 93,329 v Aus 1985 |
| Old Trafford | 8 | 410,355 | 51,294 | 80,000 v Aus 1981 |
| The Oval | 10 | 502,604 | 50,260 | 63,600 v Aus 1981 |
| Headingley | 10 | 451,194 | 45,119 | 54,018 v Aus 1985 |
| Edgbaston | 7 | 330,434 | 47,205 | 55,750 v Aus 1981 |
| Trent Bridge | 7 | 264,446 | 37,778 | 50,010 v Aus 1981 |
| Total | 57 | 3,012,504 | 52,851 | – |
| 1990s | | | | |
| Lord's | 14 | 1,269,186 | 90,656 | 111,938 v WI 1995 |
| The Oval | 10 | 645,901 | 64,590 | 71,301 v WI 1995 |
| Headingley | 8 | 472,067 | 59,008 | 70,450 v Aus 1993 |
| Edgbaston | 9 | 493,232 | 54,804 | 72,693 v Aus 1997 |
| Old Trafford | 8 | 437,856 | 54,732 | 87,829 v Aus 1997 |
| Trent Bridge | 8 | 321,348 | 40,169 | 52,199 v WI 1995 |
| Total | 57 | 3,639,590 | 63,853 | – |

| Ground | England Tests | Total gate | Average gate | Best gate |
|--------|---------------|------------|--------------|-----------|
| **2000s** | | | | |
| Lord's | 20 | 1,886,408 | 94,320 | 142,945 v Aus 2009 |
| The Oval | 10 | 872,151 | 87,215 | 106,790 v Aus 2005 |
| Cardiff | 1 | 75,510 | 75,510 | 75,510 v Aus 2009 |
| Edgbaston | 9 | 610,936 | 67,882 | 101,538 v Aus 2009 |
| Old Trafford | 8 | 510,288 | 63,786 | 111,657 v Aus 2005 |
| Trent Bridge | 9 | 518,116 | 57,568 | 65,583 v Aus 2005 |
| Headingley | 9 | 480,850 | 53,428 | 71,256 v Aus 2001 |
| Chester-le-St | 4 | 125,492 | 31,373 | 54,556 v WI 2007 |
| Total | 70 | 5,079,751 | 72,568 | – |
| **2010s** | | | | |
| Lord's | 18 | 1,948,071 | 108,226 | 140,111 v Ind 2011 |
| The Oval | 9 | 823,641 | 91,516 | 113,145 v Aus 2013 |
| Edgbaston | 7 | 477,520 | 68,217 | 93,795 v Ind 2011 |
| Trent Bridge | 8 | 501,631 | 62,704 | 85,035 v Aus 2013 |
| Old Trafford | 5 | 305,216 | 61,043 | 121,137 v Aus 2013 |
| Southampton | 3 | 150,788 | 50,263 | 55,676 v Ind 2018 |
| Cardiff | 2 | 95,684 | 47,842 | 59,358 v Aus 2015 |
| Chester-le-St | 2 | 92,268 | 46,134 | 62,958 v Aus 2013 |
| Headingley | 7 | 295,220 | 42,174 | 56,005 v WI 2017 |
| Total | 61 | 4,690,039 | 76,886 | – |

(excluding Pakistan v Australia Tests at Lord's and Headingley in 2010)
*Source: ECB/Wisden*

# CHAPTER 30

# Who Runs the Team?

## Micky Stewart paves the way to England becoming the 19th county

Micky Stewart's appointment as England's first full-time manager was the start of a major overhaul of the way the national team was run. It was a process that spanned almost 15 years and was effectively complete when a group of 12 leading players were placed under contract for the 2000 season – a practice soon expanded to all year round – thereby transferring their control from county to country. From this point, the England team was a permanent entity, staffed by full-time players and a full-time head coach, holding more regular meetings and playing a much larger set of fixtures.

There would be further changes, such as the introduction in 2007 of a managing director as well as the addition of further specialist coaches, but the steps taken between 1986 and 2000 were the transformative ones. Administrators, including the chairman of selectors, were gradually removed from the day-to-day affairs of the team, which were run instead by the head coach and captain. Michael Vaughan, who made his debut in the first Test in 1999 in which Duncan Fletcher and Nasser Hussain worked together as coach and captain, and eventually succeeded Hussain as captain, recalled: 'The captain and coach provided the direction of the side and created the spirit, and a management group of senior players helped drive the ethic and culture.' It was unarguable that the team was in better shape as a result and that the captain's load, which had been overbearing at times, was eased.

The path from Micky Stewart to Duncan Fletcher was far from smooth, however. In fact, there was an extraordinary amount of turbulence as the modernisation drive took two steps forward and one, two or even three steps back. It was fundamentally a matter of establishing trust between the head coach (originally known as the cricket manager) and the captain and players, and between them and the many facets of administration above them such as selectors, board members and county executives. Such relationships had always been a potential source of tension but matters were complicated by the arrival of a cricket manager/head coach in whom so much power would eventually be invested.

Some players were sceptical that the team even needed managing. Free spirits such as David Gower, Ian Botham and Phil Edmonds felt they could look after themselves and were suspicious of the football-style regimentation of life under Stewart. Michael Atherton, among others, believed that the onus would always be on the players and there was a limit to what others could contribute. These attitudes persisted, and inevitably there were clashes between some players and coaches. The head coach's first job therefore was to win over the confidence of his charges and in particular to forge a close working relationship with the captain. Stewart teamed up well with Mike Gatting and Graham Gooch, but not Gower. There was also good chemistry between Keith Fletcher and Gooch, and David Lloyd and Atherton, in their cases through friendships developed at their counties, respectively Essex and Lancashire.

Establishing where one person's responsibilities ended and another's began was at the heart of many of the problems, with the press quick to pick up on signs of confusion or discord, or simply mixed messages – which naturally only added to the difficulties. Lord MacLaurin, who came in as chairman in the winter of 1996-97, was appalled at the lack of proper leadership. 'The English cricket establishment laid claim to everything except its own shortcomings ...

all too often it was Them (the players) rather than Us (the administrators) who were held to be at fault.'

The greatest crises of this period – such as the Mike Gatting–Shakoor Rana incident at Faisalabad in 1987 – were exacerbated by differences in opinion among the hierarchy over how best to proceed. Ray Illingworth as captain had been adroit in man-management but as chairman of selectors and manager in the mid-1990s he failed to grasp the importance of presenting a unified front. His public criticism of colleagues and players created unnecessary difficulties. Patrick Whittingdale, who headed a fund-management firm which put £3m into English cricket, withdrew their sponsorship in 1995 specifically because of the way Illingworth operated, saying 'criticism of the players through the media is bad man-management and simply does not get the best out of the players'. He made direct reference to Illingworth's handling of Atherton and Angus Fraser, a key bowler.*

In the late 1990s, David Lloyd, as England coach, felt acutely that he and the team were not receiving the support from board members at Lord's, and suggested Tim Lamb, the chief executive, 'saw his responsibility as running a smooth ship for the contentment of the county chairmen who elected him, rather than offering wholehearted support to those who were out in the field doing their best for the national team'. In his report on the Australia tour of 1998-99, Lloyd stated: 'There is a view [among the England players and coaches] that there is a lack of support from home base.'

Eventually these problems were resolved, but not before England plumbed new depths. An international summer that began with MCC members staying away from a World Cup opening ceremony that preceded England's match against Sri Lanka because they were charged for admission (which meant they missed seeing Prime Minister Tony Blair speaking in the rain into a non-functioning microphone) ended with Hussain being roundly booed when he was interviewed on the balcony at The Oval. 'I knew they were not

---

* Whittingdale first got involved with English cricket in 1989-90 when he sought to prevent future England cricketers joining rebel tours of South Africa by sponsoring them through the winter; the first recipients were Nasser Hussain and Martin Bicknell. Whittingdale also invested in enhancing the coaching of England players.

booing me; I was a symbol of what had been a terrible shemozzle of a summer ... the booing made me more determined. I knew how much people cared.'

It did not help that England were so weak. With better players, stability might have been easier to achieve. Gower, Botham and Allan Lamb were finished with international cricket by 1992, and Gooch and Gatting by 1995; Robin Smith went the following year. The bowling was chronically short of firepower, with no established match-winners. Keith Fletcher, manager/coach from 1992 until 1995, claimed 'we fielded some of the weakest teams in the history of English cricket', and Illingworth, who started work as chairman in 1994, echoed his sentiments, saying he inherited little from Ted Dexter except a new captain in Atherton. Fletcher estimated that Phillip DeFreitas and Martin McCague, who opened the attack for England against Australia at Brisbane in 1994, 'probably constituted the weakest new-ball pair in the history of matches between the two countries'.

When David Lloyd started as head coach his view was that 'the team was not very good, [and] there was no established base to work from'. A long-running search for a genuine batting and bowling all-rounder – 'the next Ian Botham' – was not resolved until Andrew Flintoff began turning in consistent performances in 2003. Out of necessity, Alec Stewart, Micky's son, helped balance the side by turning himself into a capable wicketkeeper-batsman, but to do so he sacrificed a career as a free-flowing opening batsman good enough to score twin centuries in Barbados when West Indies were still a force to be reckoned with.* Stewart was nevertheless England's leading Test run-scorer in the 1990s.

Revealingly, perhaps the most celebrated England innings of the period was one that saved a match rather than won it: Atherton's ten-hour back-to-the-wall resistance to deny South Africa in

---

* Stewart, who scored 118 and 143 at Barbados in 1994, is one of the only two visiting batsmen to score twin hundreds in a Test in West Indies, the other being Sunil Gavaskar of India in Trinidad in 1971. Stewart was the only batsman to score two centuries in the same match against West Indies anywhere between 1978 and 2004, when their pace attack was at its peak.

Johannesburg. Three years later, Atherton came out on top in a fero-cious duel with Allan Donald at Trent Bridge to set up an England win, although only after surviving a concerted appeal for a gloved catch to the keeper. That England ultimately won that series was largely due to them finally assembling a potent pace attack in the shape of Fraser, Darren Gough and Dominic Cork: it was their first series win against major opposition since the victory in Australia in 1986–87 that had kicked off Micky Stewart's reign.

There had been talk of a 'Mr Cricket' taking charge of the England team since at least the mid-1970s. As it happened, Tony Greig and Mike Brearley, who led England for most of the period between 1975 and 1981, were both strong captains less in need of assistance than most in managing players but, skilled though he was, even Brearley appreciated a good tour manager when he was given one, as when Doug Insole took charge of the 1978–79 tour of Australia. 'Doug was a terrific support,' he said. 'He was happy to talk at length to people who were having difficulties. He could be firm and supportive, and made sure people felt happy and well. He looked after the team in a way that other managers didn't do. Some thought it was a PR job where you cemented relations [with the host country]. He was subtle, sensitive and helpful.'

A no-less-significant figure was Ken Barrington, the former England batsman, who carved out a coaching role not previously seen, both during home Test matches after becoming a selector in 1976 and as tour manager in 1976–77 and 1977–78 before going to Australia in 1978–79 as Insole's assistant. By popular demand he also went as assistant manager to West Indies in 1980–81; there, tragically, and to the devastation of the players, he collapsed and died at the age of only 50 early on the second morning of the Barbados Test. The team dutifully committed to completing the match after lining up on the outfield for a minute's silence; England were beaten by 298 runs. If anyone was a precursor to the full-time cricket manager/coach it was Barrington. However, it was only after several subsequent tours under different captains and managers fared less happily that steps were taken to place someone with Insole's or Barrington's sort of qualities alongside the captain on a permanent basis.

The tipping point was a period of four winters between 1981 and 1986 which saw player rebellion and indiscipline in various guises: the hatching of a rebel tour of South Africa, allegations of drug-taking in New Zealand which ultimately resulted in Botham serving a two-month playing ban, and a tour of the Caribbean so lacking in urgency that Gower, the captain, sat out the first warm-up match and sanctioned optional nets even as his team crashed to a 5-0 defeat. A few months later, England were beaten in home series by India and New Zealand for the first time. The team became a laughing stock. 'Whenever you went to a dinner in England,' Micky Stewart recalled, 'the speaker or comedian always used to take the mickey out of the England cricket side.'

The TCCB concluded that there was a need for more organisation and firmer leadership, and that it could not expect the captain, however capable or well intentioned, to deliver improvements alone. In August 1986, following an interview with Insole, now chairman of the TCCB cricket committee, and Donald Carr, the board's chief executive, Stewart was appointed to a role later agreed as cricket manager and focused on 'organisation, preparation and discipline'. Stewart – who had played eight Tests in the early 1960s mainly as an opener and might have appeared more but for the emergence of John Edrich and Geoff Boycott – had since occupied a managerial role at Surrey and was convinced, unlike Ray Illingworth who was sounded out but wanted more authority, that he could make what he wanted of the job. Sure enough, after his first successful winter, he was offered a contract for three years and ended up staying for six, although he was plagued by administrative interference and poor playing results and came close to quitting in 1989.

Stewart had the bearing of a sergeant-major but was generally kindlier than that, certainly to the younger players. He demonstrated what a good manager or coach might contribute, especially on the tours of Australia in 1986-87 and West Indies in 1989-90 when Gatting and Gooch respectively were on their first tours as captain and several members of the squad were touring for the first time. He worked hard to develop a sense of togetherness and in Australia secured the commitment of some strong-minded senior players, including two former captains in Botham and Gower, telling them that they would need to score most of the runs and take most of the wickets if the series was to be won.* He asked Botham to take under his wing some of the younger bowlers and got him involved in training by organising a lot of football warm-ups. Botham's support was particularly important as Gatting had tended to perform better for England when Botham was not around; his breakthrough series occurred in India in 1984-85 on a tour Botham missed.

Stewart also took a close hand in developing on-field tactics, improving fielding and bringing greater discipline to the bowling unit. 'Things were planned in more detail than they had been on previous tours and that took huge pressure off the captain,' said Bill Athey, who opened the batting in 1986-87. Robin Smith and Gladstone Small, who toured in 1989-90, said Stewart helped them understand the game better. 'Micky was an anchor for England: a stable character with lots of experience, excellent ideas and good man-management,' Gooch said. 'The word "manager" would be right. He dealt with everything that's needed to run an international cricket team.' Stewart himself said his first task was to boost confidence. 'When I came in, they'd just lost three series on the trot and they'd put up with so much media criticism,' he said. 'I'd never known a group of such talented people, in sport or in business, where the level of confidence was so low.'

Stewart also had one eye on the long-term development of the England side, though some of his ideas, such as a national academy to replicate the Australian model created in 1987-88, could not be implemented until much later when money finally became available. 'Micky was a visionary and very much ahead of his time,' said Medha Laud, who has been involved in the administration of the England side for 30 years. 'What were regarded as new ideas when they were introduced later originated with him. They were claimed as novel

---

* Aware of the criticism of his laissez-faire approach as captain, Gower got a T-shirt printed with the words 'I'm in charge', which he then presented to his successor when Gatting was appointed in his place.

ideas, but in fact had been discussed years earlier. The frustration was that the finance wasn't there to put them in place. I sometimes wonder just what he would have done had he had the money that the game is awash with now.'

The biggest source of difficulty was the reluctance of administrators to allow those appointed to run the team to get on with their jobs without hindrance. For generations, men in suits sitting in MCC or TCCB committee rooms at Lord's had been used to taking the important day-to-day decisions affecting the England team, and the habit died hard. They may have agreed to a full-time team manager but they had not agreed to a corresponding diminution in their own powers. The chairman of selectors who had previously acted as something of a team manager during the home season found his sphere of influence shrinking. Where responsibility lay in the event of a major crisis was unclear. As chance would have it, a year after the Ashes were retained in Australia, circumstances arose during a tour of Pakistan that tested to the full the new chain of command. The results were chaotic and the consequences were still playing out almost ten years later.

Even before the tour, relations between England and Pakistan, barely recovered from the Packer-related tensions of the 1977-78 series, were fraught, mirroring the antithetical nature of their cricket on the field: England methodical, Pakistan mercurial. In 1982, Pakistan narrowly failed to win the deciding Test at Headingley and were convinced that a controversial umpiring decision by David Constant to give out Sikander Bakht cost them the match. Imran Khan, the captain, called it 'truly bizarre'. India, possibly in retaliation to English complaints about the umpiring in India, had successfully asked the TCCB for Constant not to stand in England in 1982 (though the TCCB paid him his fee), but Pakistan's request about Constant and Ken Palmer not officiating in their five-Test series in 1987 was rebuffed, despite the long-standing convention on this point. Haseeb Ahsan, the Pakistan manager, made sure the matter became public and labelled Constant 'a disgraceful person', while AC Smith, the TCCB's ponderous chief executive, read a statement of support in the Test-match panel from the broader community of English first-class umpires. Pakistan nevertheless achieved their first series win in England.

There had also been some acrimonious meetings between the sides in one-day cricket, including one a few weeks earlier at the World Cup, the first held in Asia, in which England and Australia made the final at the expense of hosts India and Pakistan. (England's eventual defeat in the final pivoted on Gatting's error in reverse-sweeping his first ball from Allan Border's part-time rollers.) When England then began their tour by winning the ODI series 3-0, Micky Stewart and Peter Lush, the tour manager, were confidentially advised that with elections looming General Zia had issued instructions that under no circumstances were Pakistan to lose the Test series. That message inveigled itself into the touring team's psyche. 'We were never going to win, no matter how well we played,' Bill Athey recalled, before adding none too cryptically: 'I'm not sure if it was political.'*

English fears about the local umpiring appeared to be confirmed by a string of adverse decisions during an innings defeat in the first Test in Lahore. Stewart estimated that nine of England's 20 wickets were 'umpired out'; after being given out caught behind off a delivery he was convinced he did not touch, Chris Broad had to be persuaded to leave the field by Gooch, his partner. In the second Test at Faisalabad, England totalled 292 despite suffering what Stewart calculated as four more bad decisions, and with Pakistan 106 for five late on the second day they were well on top and pushing to squeeze in as many overs as they could before stumps.

Then, in the penultimate over, when Gatting made a late adjustment to his field, having advised the batsman accordingly, umpire Shakoor Rana intervened from square leg, calling out, 'Stop, stop!' and accusing Gatting of cheating for waving his hand. Gatting explained that he had only been gesturing to David Capel that he

---

* Politics had a habit of intruding on England tours of Pakistan. Tony Lewis's 1972-73 side found that British support for India over the Indo-Pakistani war led to what Keith Fletcher described as 'open resentment towards us wherever we went'.

had come up too far from deep square leg. Shakoor appeared about to return to his position when he accused Gatting, according to various witnesses, of being 'a fucking cheat'. At that, Gatting pitched into a full-blown verbal row which saw both men gesticulating at one another.

Some sort of rapprochement was clearly needed but Stewart noted in his diary that back at the hotel that evening rumours quickly circulated that the umpires would not stand, nor the Pakistan players take the field, the next day. When a compromise was set in motion in which both men would apologise, the process swiftly broke down when (according to most accounts) Javed Miandad, the Pakistan captain, encouraged Shakoor to stand firm. Gatting and his players took the field on the third day but neither the Pakistan team nor Shakoor appeared: never before had an England Test match been brought to a halt in such fashion.

Throughout the third blank day and the rest day that followed, feverish diplomatic activity continued to try and resolve the impasse; Stewart in a letter home described the lines between Faisalabad and London as 'red-hot all night'. With no live TV coverage of the series in England, the TCCB at Lord's was not well placed to form a sound judgement; one of the few images it had to go on was a photograph taken by Graham Morris, the only English cameraman on the ground at the time, which showed Gatting and Shakoor in the midst of their set-to, which hardly painted the England captain in a favourable light. 'The reaction of the "establishment" was one of horror that the captain could be involved in such an incident but Lushy and I soon made them aware of all the facts,' Stewart wrote. 'I am sure that there are still some at Lord's who think that we should swallow our pride as Englishmen and show a stiff upper lip but in the longer term I am sure that our stand will serve the game better as far as future tours of Pakistan are concerned.'

The next day, he noted in his diary, 'Instructions received from Lord's for Gatt to apologise if no other solution can be reached.' Such a prospect was not well received by the players, Stewart adding: 'Feeling very strong about Gatt's apology ... UNANIMOUS that players won't take field if Gatt's is only apology. It looks like a

STRIKE!!' The England players were in fact in favour of abandoning the tour altogether and it was only after pleading from Stewart and Gatting, who met them individually at 7.30am on the fourth morning, that they agreed to continue. Once Gatting handed over a scruffy note of apology ('for the bad language used during the 2nd day of the Test Match at Fisalabad [sic]') the game continued.* Shorn of a day, Pakistan having refused to make up the lost time, the game petered out into the tamest of draws. Another drawn game in Karachi gave Pakistan the series.†

The TCCB strove in vain to smooth over all trace of the Faisalabad fracas. Its initial response was feeble. As it happened, a routine board meeting was scheduled for the rest day in Faisalabad but, far from devote its attentions to how the issue might be resolved, the board first worked its way through standard business, leaving only 40 minutes at the end to debate events in Pakistan. Afterwards, the chairman Raman Subba Row told the media, 'every effort must be made to restart the match tomorrow.' Subba Row in fact phoned General Safdar Butt, the Pakistan board president, and was assured the matter would be sorted, but nothing was done.

During the final Test, Subba Row and AC Smith arrived in Karachi and during their visit Subba Row informed Lush that the players would each receive a 'hardship bonus' of £1,000. It was meant as a gesture of support but the impression it created was that the players, who on the day the game resumed issued a statement of 'unanimous protest' at Gatting being forced by the TCCB into an unconditional apology, had demanded the money in return for completing the tour. Stewart called the bonus 'absolutely ridiculous' and Subba Row's unilateral action was not well received by the players or colleagues on the board. Although a letter from Shakoor Rana to Gatting was eventually forthcoming, it contained expressions

* Ted Corbett, an English journalist working for the *Daily Star*, acted as a conduit between Gatting and Shakoor to get the match restarted, the paper running the headline: 'How our man saved the Test series'.
† The Shakoor Rana–Mike Gatting spat triggered a widespread debate with Gatting being castigated by some, supported by others. Former England batsman Tom Graveney said: 'They [Pakistan] have been cheating us for 37 years and I think the tour should be called off.'

of regret but not an apology, and as a result Peter Lush, somewhat questionably, chose not to make it public.

Then, six months later, in another decision that was widely criticised, the board removed Gatting from the captaincy after he had been accused by the *Sun* newspaper of being involved in late-night frolics at the team hotel at Rothley Court on the rest day of the first Test against West Indies. It did this despite accepting Gatting's account that no sexual impropriety had occurred. The board said he had 'behaved irresponsibly' by inviting a barmaid to his room.

In fact, other considerations may well have been at play: even before Gatting was named in the revelations, he was in hot water with the board for planning to include his side of the Faisalabad episode in his forthcoming autobiography *Leading from the Front*. Had the book never appeared, Gatting might have been swiftly reinstated, but it was too late for that. His efforts to remove the contentious passages in the book – due for serialisation in the *Sunday Times* before the second Test – were unsuccessful, and placing the chapter on Pakistan under the byline of his ghostwriter Angela Padmore failed to spare him a £5,000 fine for failing to secure TCCB consent for publication. In what might be seen as another attempt to detoxify the Pakistan situation, at the end of the season David Constant, so recently supported, was dropped from England's Test panel at the age of only 46, though he continued to officiate in ODIs until 2001 and in first-class cricket until 2006. Keith Fletcher later suggested the TCCB 'had not supported [Constant] as they should have done following complaints from Pakistan'.

With the Gatting–Stewart partnership prematurely broken up, Peter May and his selection panel made frantic efforts to stabilise the team. John Emburey, Gatting's vice-captain, was appointed in his place but as a spinner he was vulnerable to being left out on tactical grounds. After two defeats, he was replaced by Chris Cowdrey, who was having a good season leading Kent but as a front-foot player was ill-suited to dealing with the West Indies pace attack. Cowdrey's credibility was further undermined by suspicions of nepotism: not only was he Colin Cowdrey's son but May's godson. He turned up at Headingley to find himself denied entry by the gatekeeper and was then kept waiting at the toss by Viv Richards; England duly sank to another heavy loss. A foot injury gave the selectors an excuse for immediately getting rid of Cowdrey and, to his chagrin, he never heard from them again. The baton then passed to Gooch for the final Test of the series, where – despite a more spirited showing – England were beaten again, completing a 4-0 loss. Extraordinarily, England had in the space of one summer employed four different Test captains.*

Stewart was happy at the prospect of working with Gooch as he believed Gooch shared his outlook on how England should prepare and play, but Gooch's original tenure proved short-lived when the India government, in anticipation of England's winter tour, raised objections to him captaining the side once it learned that he had to extricate himself from an arrangement to play domestic cricket in South Africa having previously indicated he had no intention of going back there. Within 48 hours of the England touring team being named, the tour was cancelled. This was not a surprise – England had been warned by an Indian official during a one-day tournament in Sharjah in 1987 that former South Africa rebels such as Gooch and Emburey could be a problem – but the loss of a major tour represented another big blow to the TCCB's relations with the non-white bloc.† 'It is not generally known, but we were as close as a whisker from having no one to play against,' Subba Row recalled.

In an effort to prevent further costly cancellations in future, Subba Row worked hard at the ICC in the months that followed, hammering out ground-rules on what was, and what was not, acceptable to member countries regarding playing contacts with South Africa, and bans in the case of breaches. These most hurt the many English players who coached there. 'The interests of English

---

* In addition, Derek Pringle acted as stand-in captain when Graham Gooch temporarily left the field during the Oval Test.

† Attempts to arrange a tour of New Zealand in place of the cancelled India trip were also scuppered by the South African links of some England players. An itinerary of two Tests and a triangular one-day series also involving Pakistan was scrapped after Pakistan refused to play against an England squad that contained eight players on a United Nations blacklist.

players were sacrificed to keep international cricket alive,' said Mike Procter, the former South Africa all-rounder and coach of the first post-apartheid side.

Complication piled upon complication. When Peter May resigned as chairman of selectors, the board, at Subba Row's instigation, replaced his panel with an England committee responsible for all aspects of England team affairs chaired by another famous former Test captain in Ted Dexter, although someone of lower profile operating quietly and efficiently in the background might have served better. To his credit, during his four years in office Dexter would facilitate some of the reforms necessary for manager and coach to do their jobs better, but ultimately he was forced out a year ahead of time not only by a third successive Ashes series defeat but by the concerted opposition of a group of county chairmen who felt he had been appointed without sufficient consultation and wielded too much power.

Some of the players, too, found 'Lord Ted', with his enthusiasm for motorbiking into Lord's, a little too eccentric for their taste, but he was regarded with affection by at least two of the England captains he worked with. Dexter had his reservations about Gooch – whom he unfortunately described as a 'wet fish' before knowing he would have to work closely with him – and therefore supported Stewart's wish for a return to Gatting. However, under the new structure, a power of veto was invested in the chairman of the board's cricket committee, Ossie Wheatley. At Subba Row's urging, Wheatley privately applied it in respect of Gatting because of the unforgivable sin of arguing with an umpire. This got Dexter's reign off to the worst possible start and was another heavy blow to Stewart.

Gatting quickly learned of what had happened but nobly kept the matter to himself. Without explaining that it had relevance to his own position, he publicly raised the matter of Wheatley's power of veto with AC Smith at the Cricketers' Association's annual meeting. Jack Bannister, who was at the meeting, listened to Smith 'insist that, while the veto was in existence, he was sure it would never be used', and explain that 'it was there because the counties want it', before repeating 'it would never be used'. News that the veto had indeed been applied eventually emerged through the leaking of Dexter's end-of-season report.

Disenchantment was most deep-seated among the players. David Gower, who was reappointed captain in Gatting's place for the home series against Australia, only discovered he was not first-choice captain during the course of the series and the discovery did nothing to improve his relations with Stewart, with whom he had never been ideologically in tune. With England comprehensively outplayed and again beaten 4-0, Gower was under pressure from the outset and his defensive mood was typified by his decision to walk out of a press conference on the Saturday of the Lord's Test in order to keep a West End theatre appointment rather than continue being the target of hostile questioning. Selection, which had been chaotic in May's last season, was no more stable in Dexter's first, which saw 29 players chosen in six Tests, one more than in six matches the previous summer. 'There was no stability,' Emburey said. 'The players didn't have any confidence. Every match you went into, you were looking over your shoulder. It was a dreadful feeling.' Gladstone Small said the players felt those at the TCCB wouldn't leave the cricket to the players: 'There was far too much politicking going on in the background.'*

Unsurprisingly, when the South Africa cricket board began planning another rebel tour, the idea was well received among English players even though they knew the price would be seven-year bans. Emburey was an early point of contact and the scheme was spoken about among a wide circle of players: when Angus Fraser made his debut in the third Test of the 1989 series he was aware of clandestine chats at the back of the dressing-room. Gower, as captain, was deliberately kept out of discussions but Dexter and Stewart got wind of the rumours; however, when all the names emerged they were surprised

---

* There was further embarrassment for English cricket when between the fifth and sixth Tests against Australia an England XI travelled to Amstelveen to play two one-day matches against a Netherlands XI on a matting pitch. The side was virtually an England second XI, contained eight past or future Test cricketers and was accompanied by the regular management team of Micky Stewart and Peter Lush. It lost the first match by three runs before extracting revenge in the second.

at the calibre of the recruits: nine of the 16 players confirmed hours before the Ashes were surrendered at Old Trafford had played for England that summer, including three members of the XI involved in that game.

Fraser described how one of them, Neil Foster, believing his days as an England cricketer were numbered, ran in to bowl with tears in his eyes. 'They were all fed up with the hierarchy,' Stewart said. The most striking inclusion was Gatting, who conceded disillusion- ment had got the better of him. 'I'd been cast adrift by England, I'd been lied to, I'd been dragged through the mud unnecessarily, I'd not had the support of the board when I needed it . . . I wish I hadn't had to go. I loved playing for England.' Not that Gatting was alone: two other England captains of recent vintage, Emburey and Chris Cowdrey, were also in the party.* One of the early beneficiaries of the exodus was the young Lancashire batsman Michael Atherton, brought in for a debut in the following Test in Nottingham; he had acted as 12th man at Old Trafford and, like Fraser, heard whispered talk of the South African plans.

The players were recruited to make two tours of South Africa but plans were rapidly overtaken by events. The first tour, which began in January 1990, was hampered from the outset by public demonstra- tions, which had recently been made legal in South Africa, and then a few weeks into the tour Nelson Mandela was released from prison as the apartheid system finally collapsed. South Africa returned to international cricket the following year and the bans on the rebel players were lifted: Gatting, Emburey and Foster, among others, were all to play for England again.

The counties did not simply grumble about Dexter. They felt Stewart and Gooch, reunited late in 1989, were also too powerful and so a fourth selector, Dennis Amiss, was added to the panel in 1992 to counter their duopoly. Later that year, eyebrows were further

---

* Among the original recruits were two non-white players in Phillip DeFreitas and Roland Butcher but they met with such a backlash that they extricated themselves from their contracts, though with difficulty. DeFreitas played another 31 Test matches for England. Butcher was partly dissuaded by the imprecations of his Jamaican-born Middlesex team-mate Norman Cowans.

raised at the nature of the arrangement by which Keith Fletcher succeeded Micky Stewart: even Fletcher's supporters conceded his five-year deal at £50,000 per annum was too generous. Then, when Dexter stepped down, objections were raised to the speed with which the TCCB executive committee lined up MJK Smith to take over: the counties not only forced a proper election but got the England committee scrapped altogether and its duties split among two other bodies – an old-style selection panel and a development committee (later known as the England Management Advisory Committee). The veto that Ossie Wheatley had so controversially wielded was removed from the cricket committee chairman and passed to the chairman of the board (with whom it still resides today).

However, the upshot of this revolt was merely the creation of an autocracy. Ray Illingworth, who had stayed close to the game since retiring as a player through his work with the BBC and *Daily Express*, was a ready recruit to the cause of stopping the 'old boys network', and duly beat Smith in a postal ballot of the counties in 1994 to become the oldest incoming chairman of selectors for 40 years. Illingworth sought and was granted significant powers and over the next two and a half years wielded his authority with gusto. He held a veto over the selection of every player except the captain and also saw it as his brief to keep the captain's authority in check. In a book on Illingworth's reign as chairman, written in collaboration with its subject, Jack Bannister wrote: 'The new man's first task would be to break down the top-heavy influence of the captain – even a young man like Atherton, whose stamp had been firmly put on the touring party to the West Indies.' Only five survivors of that tour played in the next Test match. Illingworth also made it a general aspiration to field five bowlers, preferably including two spinners, which was a practice he had often adopted as captain, whereas Atherton, like Gooch, was inclined to favour six batsmen.

The media made much of the differences of opinion between Illingworth and Atherton. Relations were troubled in respect of the tour of Australia in 1994-95, starting with Illingworth's refusal to bow to Atherton's wish to pick Angus Fraser from the outset. (Fraser joined later as an injury replacement and did well.) Illingworth later offered some criticisms of the team from afar before joining the tour, while Atherton seemed to suggest in an interview with the *Mail on Sunday* that he would prefer the final say in selection.

After the tour, however, they agreed to sort things out between them in private, although as far as press and public were concerned their relationship plumbed new depths when on the eve of the second Test against West Indies the following summer Illingworth dramatically reselected the team, dropping the wicketkeeper Steve Rhodes from the squad picked by the selectors (including Atherton) in order that Alec Stewart, originally chosen as a batsman, could keep wicket, thereby making room for five bowlers. Newspapers claimed he had belittled Atherton but after England's brilliant victory – expedited by Stewart's fine catch to dismiss Brian Lara – Atherton declared he had been content with the switch. Illingworth admitted it was 'certainly the most controversial decision I have ever made in cricket'.* *Wisden* described it as 'an unprecedented display of autocracy by Illingworth and the manner in which he did it outraged many'.

By then, Illingworth had no less dramatically seen off Keith Fletcher, who following the Australia tour was released by the TCCB from the last two years of his contract. He had lost five of his seven Test series as manager. In another highly questionable executive decision, Illingworth thereafter incorporated Fletcher's managerial role into his other duties. This move was driven by the evident confusion over the chain of command in Australia as well as Fletcher's waning influence over the players. 'It became clear that this team is not big enough for both of them,' Alan Lee wrote of Illingworth and Fletcher in *The Times* before Fletcher's sacking. 'He [Fletcher] has become an ever-more nondescript figure, and although he has

---

* Illingworth later explained that he was motivated to switch keepers after learning that Stewart was not, contrary to initial impressions, unwilling to keep wicket and open the batting. Stewart had kept wicket in the first Test of the series and batted No.5 but the plan was now for him to move up to open. Stewart broke his right index finger in the next Test on a controversially lively pitch at Edgbaston which saw three England players suffer fractures, but when he next played as a batsman-keeper after that, in August 1996, it marked the start of a long-term pattern as faith in Jack Russell waned: Stewart kept wicket in 66 out of 76 Test matches between then and his retirement in 2003, generally batting in the middle order.

not lost the affection of the players, he can no longer relate to the majority, nor they to him.' Illingworth's view was that if the chairman of selectors managed abroad, he would exert more authority over the players than Fletcher managed, and the board's executive committee concurred. It was nonetheless an extraordinary decision. As Jack Bannister put it, 'No one man has had so much power in English cricket at selection and managerial level.'

It quickly proved a sorry mistake. The charge levelled at Fletcher of being unable to connect to the players might equally have applied to Illingworth when the following winter England toured South Africa, losing the Test series 1-0 and the one-dayers 6-1, before moving on to the subcontinent for a World Cup campaign that was an unmitigated disaster. For the first time, England were dumped out of the tournament before the semi-final stage as Sri Lanka raced almost halfway to their 50-overs target of 236 in their first 13 overs and ultimately won with 56 balls to spare. After returning home, Illingworth quit as manager, tacitly admitting that, at 63, he was too old for the job. Atherton had already concluded that he should not continue with the two jobs. David Lloyd, who was close to Atherton and effectively took over the job vacated by Illingworth, although it was now recast as head coach, said: 'If he is honest, I think he [Illingworth] will admit that it simply had not worked when he put the tracksuit on to try and combine his roles. The game had moved on since his days, largely in methods of preparation; Raymond was reluctant to move on with it.'*

His winter was also marred by a breakdown in relations with Devon Malcolm, who took the brunt of the criticism in the deciding Test in Cape Town for his inability to separate South Africa's last-wicket pair, which arguably cost England the match. Under instruction to pepper Paul Adams, South Africa's No.11, Malcolm managed only one genuine bouncer. 'I couldn't believe what I saw,' Illingworth wrote. 'He didn't even seem to run in with any aggression ... He sank without displaying any trace of the fight and spunk we were entitled to

---

* Illingworth did not help himself by appointing as assistants in South Africa John Edrich and Peter Lever who were also perceived to be out of touch with the modern game.

expect from a strike bowler.' Malcolm resorted to giving his account of events in the *Daily Express* and when Illingworth responded in kind in his ill-timed book with Jack Bannister published in the early weeks of the 1996 season Illingworth was fined £2,000 plus £500 costs for bringing the game into disrepute and severely reprimanded for disclosing confidential views he and other selectors, including Atherton, held about other players. No English cricket administrator had published so frank a book while in office. Illingworth's fine was overturned on appeal but the affair cast a long shadow over his final summer and denied him due credit for having turned England into a harder team to beat, in Test cricket if not one-dayers.

There was little sympathy. Keith Fletcher, who believed Illingworth had engineered his removal, spikily attested that Illingworth had put back English cricket 'by a good two years through not under-standing the modern-day player'. Not that he thought Illingworth was as certain in his opinions as was generally believed: 'He liked to say things afterwards but when he was chairman he didn't make that many decisions. He could sit on the fence when he felt like it.' Nor did MJK Smith – beaten in the vote for chairman of selectors – hide his disapproval of Illingworth's methods, with Smith's county Warwickshire being instrumental in David Graveney being put forward to challenge Illingworth as head of selection in the spring of 1996. Smith was 'particularly vociferous' in canvassing for a new chairman. In the event, Graveney withdrew his candidacy over a potential conflict of interest but returned to win the election a year later, by which time Illingworth was ready to step down.

Just as administrators and coaches had to adjust to the changes in the way the team operated, so did the players. Crucially, some of those who were cutting their teeth in the early days of the Gooch–Stewart regime absorbed the lessons well and stayed around to carry England forward into the next era. Michael Atherton, against Australia at Nottingham in 1989, and Alec Stewart and Nasser Hussain, both at Kingston, Jamaica in 1990, made their Test debuts within the space of three matches and were still playing for the side into the 21st cen-tury, although Atherton's later years were hampered by chronic back trouble. Between them they captained England in 112 out of 113 Test matches between 1993 and 2003 (the exception came when Mark Butcher stood in for an injured Hussain at Old Trafford in 1999) and in differing ways were central figures in a long-awaited revival. In a difficult era, careers as long as theirs were not easily achieved. Angus Fraser – for many years the side's most dependable bowler despite losing some of his nip as a result of a serious hip injury that sidelined him for a year – debuted two games before Atherton.

Atherton and Stewart were often portrayed as different characters and rivals from opposite ends of the country, a reworking of the old North–South split. This was partly because they were both candidates to succeed Gooch as captain and the story only gained momentum from a farcical run-out in Mumbai when neither man wanted to give way. But they had more in common than separated them. Both were exceptionally tough, Stewart after spending several formative winters playing grade cricket in Perth (a path that became popular with aspiring England cricketers). Both, too, had immense powers of concentration, Atherton as a batsman and Stewart as someone who kept wicket in 82 of his 133 Tests while maintaining a high standard of run-scoring. As opening partners on 50 occasions in Tests, they worked very well together.

Stewart was briefly Gooch's vice-captain but it was to 25-year-old Atherton whom the selectors turned first, believing he had a shrewd cricket brain. They were right. 'He soon demonstrated the tactical nous that would make him as competent a captain as Nasser Hussain – perhaps a better one when it came to man-management,' Keith Fletcher wrote. 'Atherton could be hard on somebody who stepped out of line but he would not bawl that person out in front of everybody else.' David Lloyd concurred, saying Atherton 'was never shy of expressing a view to a player, telling him he'd messed up. Generally, he would do this privately rather than in earshot of the entire team, but he would do it firmly, too – and then, so far as he was concerned, the matter would be finished.' Even when by his own admission he was mentally shot and in no fit state to be captaining England, he gave a tactically accomplished performance as Australia were thwarted by 19 runs at The Oval in 1997.

Stewart, when he took over from Atherton in 1998 on a generous 14-month term through to the end of the 1999 World Cup, was more regimented in approach but similarly intolerant of anyone going off-message. Whereas his father grew impatient of maverick players, Alec appeared to simply prefer not to pick them altogether. Notably, neither Phil Tufnell nor Andrew Caddick played in any of Stewart's 11 Tests as official captain even though they were the bowlers Atherton handled so astutely that day at The Oval. Stewart admitted later that he had been wrong about Caddick, who was to develop into a more consistent and mentally tougher Test-match bowler.

Hussain – a protégé at Essex of Gooch, who spotted his fighting qualities at an early stage – was the most intriguing of the three. He spent six years waiting for a proper run in the side, during which time (when he was often on the fringe of the XI) he behaved like the angry young man he was, berating Atherton for not giving him a chance in any of the five Tests of the Caribbean tour of 1993-94. The idea that he might one day captain the side was unthinkable. Once he returned, the coach David Lloyd said it still took him 18 months to appreciate what made him tick.

'Nasser probably caused me as many anxieties as David Gower caused Micky Stewart – not because they are remotely similar but because neither fits easily into the doctrines of team togetherness,' Lloyd wrote in 2000. 'I know now that the coach needs to offer space and scope to such players but that the trick is to persuade them to observe the team ethic for just long enough to present a united front . . . There was a time when I could not envisage him captaining the side and commanding the essential respect of his peers but he has come to realise that an awareness of the needs of others is part of being a cricketer.' Hussain himself credited Duncan Fletcher, the head coach he worked with when he became captain, with changing his outlook. 'He taught me . . . that there was a way of being successful different from the one I had always aspired to: the team way, the right way. And he made me a better person.' Having been a maverick himself, Hussain was determined as captain to accommodate the best players regardless: 'My attitude was, if someone can play, let's pick them and it will be up to me to ... deal with any shortcomings they may have.' He could be a martinet though.

As the team moved towards a more professional outlook, Hussain was not the only difficult player who needed bringing into line. A cricket manager or head coach was not going to get far if he failed to impose discipline, and sponsors would be reluctant to back a team with a bad image. There were wider requirements too: in November 1991, the ICC introduced match referees equipped with powers to punish on-field misbehaviour. Before central contracts especially, some England players were less inclined than they would be later to obey management writ; they primarily saw themselves as county cricketers or as their own masters. In his report of the 1996–97 tour of Zimbabwe and New Zealand, Lloyd wrote, 'we needed to get away from players managing the managers.' He had encountered various instances of players who, in his words, 'Thought it acceptable in a team situation to say: "I don't do that". My answer, unfailingly, was: "You do now" ... Too many England players had grown up taking liberties.'

This culture dated back at least to Ian Botham's early days when a number of incidents occurred, which had not resulted in disciplinary action.\* England's on-field behaviour had been generally poor during the troubled years since the Shakoor Rana affair. A few weeks after showing himself reluctant to leave the field in Lahore, Chris Broad had smashed his bat into his stumps after playing on for 139 during the Bicentennial Test in Sydney (a match to mark 200 years since the settlement of Australia). This act of dissent earned him a fine of £500.† Soon after that, Graham Dilley was fined £250 in New Zealand for loudly swearing on the field.

Meanwhile, Botham, who had announced that the 1986–87 tour of Australia would be his last, spent the following winter playing for

---

\* One instance in which Botham was cleared of wrongdoing involved a charge of actual bodily harm arising out of an incident in Scunthorpe during a night out with some Scunthorpe FC team-mates in December 1980. Botham actually went to West Indies as captain the following month with the charge hanging over him. He was subsequently found not guilty at a hearing in September 1981.

† After retiring as a player, Chris Broad surprised a few people by becoming a long-serving ICC match referee between 2003 and 2018.

Queensland and en route from Melbourne to Perth for the Sheffield Shield final was arrested on charges of assault and offensive behaviour on the flight. He appeared in court on the eve of the final and was bailed, later being fined £350. Queensland subsequently terminated his contract and fined him £2,000 for a series of incidents which included missing training, breaking a drinks curfew and swearing at spectators. England as a result did not pick him for an ODI series against West Indies at the start of the 1988 season; an expected recall for the Tests was ruined when he broke down injured and missed the rest of the season. He also lost his newspaper column with the *Sun*.

Sometimes there was no clear-cut punishment available such as fines. England took Phil Tufnell to Australia in 1994-95 after it appeared he had put some problems with a former girlfriend behind him, but when they resurfaced during the opening warm-up in Perth he responded by trashing his hotel room. The management was minded to send him home but when Tufnell discharged himself from hospital procedurally all they could do was give him a warning. Tufnell recovered and played four of the five Tests.

One of the reasons Illingworth was keen to take over managerial duties after that tour was because he wanted to tackle misconduct: during the Adelaide Test, Chris Lewis had been fined by the match referee for pointing a batsman to the pavilion. When 18 months later Lewis turned up late for a Test match at The Oval, claiming a puncture to his Mercedes convertible but failing to phone in to explain the delay, and having been late for practice two weeks earlier, the response was draconian. He was dropped from the Texaco Trophy squad, overlooked for England's winter tours despite having had a good summer, and debarred against the wishes of Lloyd and captain Alec Stewart for the World Cup the following season. Lewis responded by dismissing Illingworth and his fellow selectors as 'full of shit'. He made only two more appearances for the national side.[*]

There were also high-level discussions about sending home Dominic Cork – who had struggled to live up to an eye-catching

---

[*] In 2009 Lewis was jailed for 13 years for smuggling liquid cocaine worth £140,000 into Britain. He was released in June 2015.

debut series against West Indies – from New Zealand in 1997 following some persistently boorish behaviour. Michael Vaughan, who played alongside Cork a few years later, said of him: 'I was never quite sure how deep his confidence actually ran. He always seemed to intimidate lesser opponents, but the bigger ones were not put off.' Lord MacLaurin, who was in the early weeks of his chairmanship of the ECB, attended the Wellington Test and told Lloyd that Cork's conduct 'did not fit [the] image of what an England cricketer should be'. Lloyd dissuaded MacLaurin from ejecting Cork from the tour on the grounds that it would overshadow the later games; instead Cork received an uncomplimentary tour report and a visit from MacLaurin at his home in Derby.*

Around the same time, Graham Thorpe, who was regarded as the stand-out England batsman of his generation but who generally struggled to conform with management demands, declined to attend a three-day pre-season bonding camp in Oxford on the grounds that, in Lloyd's words, 'Graham believed his time was his own until cricket resumed.' An early morning phone call from Tim Lamb, the ECB chief executive, instructed him to get himself to Oxford immediately and when he did so he was taken aside by MacLaurin and advised who was in charge of whom. A few weeks later Thorpe scored 138 in the first Test against Australia in a stand of 288 with Hussain, who made a double-century. However, he lapsed into his old ways two years later when he was fined for refusing to attend a World Cup function.

Ironically, the most highly publicised disciplinary incident of the period involved Atherton, after TV cameras spotted him rubbing dirt into the ball during the Saturday of the Lord's Test against South Africa in 1994. To make matters worse, it transpired he had not been fully frank in his first meeting with Peter Burge, the former Australia batsman turned match referee, failing to tell him that he used dirt in his pocket to dry his hands, which left Burge to conclude that there

---

* An upshot of an earlier visit by MacLaurin to England's winter tour – this time to Harare – was that he instructed the scrapping of the practice of players (other than captain and vice-captain) sharing hotel rooms.

was no case to answer. Chairman of selectors Illingworth felt that, unless England themselves acted, Atherton would face sanctions from the ICC; Illingworth therefore decided to punish his captain both for breaking the spirit of the game (though he did not think Atherton had done anything illegal) and for concealment.

Amid sweltering temperatures Illingworth and Atherton held a press conference in the Lord's pavilion on the Sunday evening, by which time the Test had been lost. Atherton confessed to hiding part of the truth from Burge, and Illingworth said he was fining him £1,000 on each count, the maximum sums available. Illingworth had by then spoken to Burge, who said that had he known the full facts he would have suspended Atherton for two games, but agreed in the light of Illingworth's punishments to take no further action. What helped Atherton's cause was that the umpires did not believe that the condition of the ball had been changed. Bannister estimated that Illingworth saved Atherton his job: 'It is unlikely that the board would have kept him in office after censure and punishment by a match referee.' In fact, the next day, with a public debate raging about his actions, Atherton phoned Illingworth to tell him he was thinking of resigning but, after being urged to take more time and having then consulted some trusted allies, Atherton concluded a few days later that he would continue.*

Other adjustments had to be made. Tetley, and after them Vodafone, expected more in terms of personal appearances from players than earlier sponsors had done and this required a change of mindset from England's management – men whose primary focus was on getting things right on the field – as well as the players themselves. The fact that TV was now covering every game also fuelled the demands of newspapers for their own fresh angles.

The TCCB had introduced its first media manager in the late 1980s but it was not until mid-1997 that a media officer, Brian Murgatroyd, was assigned to the team on a full-time basis. Prior to

---

* Later in the series Atherton became the first England player to be punished under the ICC's new code of conduct when Burge fined him 50 per cent of his match fee for showing dissent after being given out lbw at The Oval.

his appointment, the Press Association correspondent acted as a de facto liaison officer between the team manager and the cricket writers. He would be passed the names of the selected England XI and sometimes interview players on behalf of the press pool, although even after Murgatroyd's arrival players were not routinely put up for interview: until central contracts obliged them to do the ECB's bidding, players remained their own agents. It was more common for an England manager such as Keith Fletcher to take questions from the media with the captain speaking at the end of the game. David Lloyd also worked in this way until, to his disquiet, the ECB called on him less often in Australia in 1998-99 amid fears he might say the wrong thing after some recent foot-in-mouth episodes.* The final stand-off came in the early weeks of central contracts when the players, having won the Leeds Test in two days, agreed only after hard negotiation to give interviews to help Sky fill its schedules.

Atherton had little time for some sections of the press, Lloyd believing he deliberately cultivated a grumpy image in 'perverse reaction to what he considered the excesses of the tabloid press', and hardly helped his cause after the 'dirt in the pocket' affair by having a dig at the 'gutter press' during the next game, in which he battled heroically for 99. Alec Stewart made greater efforts to be accessible, although he rarely said much of interest, and Hussain was more media-friendly still, believing (probably correctly) that his life would be easier if he kept the press on side.

The Acfield Report of 1996 reiterated that selectors could not work in the media – something that kyboshed David Lloyd's enthusiasm for Ian Botham becoming a selector – but extraordinarily Hussain managed to maintain a national newspaper column throughout his time as England captain and used it to promote policy. Hussain admitted he caused concern to David Graveney, the chairman of selectors ('He was paranoid about me leaking anything to the paper I wrote for; but the truth was, he used to leak far more himself about selectorial

---

* Since Brian Murgatroyd (1997-99), England's principal media officers on Test tours have been Andrew Walpole (1999-2012), James Avery (2005-11), Rhian Evans (2012-16) and Danny Reuben (2016 to date).

matters'), and conceded it was a mistake when, after resigning as one-day captain in 2003, he wrote a piece outlining his remaining goals as Test captain.*

Managers and coaches had their own issues dealing with the greater media scrutiny. Micky Stewart and Lloyd both identified closely with their players and struggled to remain emotionally detached from events. When David Lawrence suffered a horrific injury in New Zealand in 1992, shattering his kneecap, Stewart shoved aside a TV crew member as he helped stretcher Lawrence from the field.

Lloyd even more spectacularly lost the plot in his first overseas Test as coach when, with the help of some bowling wide of off stump which went unchecked by the umpires, the match in Bulawayo ended with the scores level after England made a bold attempt to score 205 in 37 overs. Afterwards, Lloyd stormed into the umpires' room before being pushed out again, then visited the match referee, before accusing local official Ian Goggin of being 'an absolute disgrace'. When he was goaded by two people who turned out to be the parents of Alistair Campbell, the Zimbabwe captain, 'I reacted badly ... I stuck one finger up at them.' Tim Lamb took him severely to task, saying his remarks to Goggins tarnished the reputation of the team. Then, at The Oval in 1998, Lloyd was asked during a TV interview about the action of Muttiah Muralitharan: 'I said if it was legal, then let's all do it.' This earned him a written, and effectively final, warning. By mutual consent, following a meeting with MacLaurin ahead of the event, Lloyd stepped down after the World Cup in June 1999.

Lloyd did important work in the modernisation process. He pushed for greater use of video analysis, even though some baulked at the cost, and insisted on ending in 1996 such archaic practices as tossing a coin with the opposition on the eve of home Tests to decide

---

* When he took over from Hussain as Test captain, Michael Vaughan gave up his column with the *Daily Mail* when his contract expired nine months later. Kevin Pietersen retained a column with the *News of the World* during his brief spell as England captain, but when Andrew Strauss was appointed in 2009 the ECB contractually put an end to such practices in respect of England captains.

whether to use Dukes or Reader balls, when England's preference was for the Dukes. He also remained an insistent advocate of central contracts. Keith Fletcher had reported to the board in 1995 that county cricket was not – despite the recent transition to four-day championship matches – properly developing Test cricketers and his views were consistently echoed by Atherton.* These views were reiterated by Lloyd at the end of the 1997 Ashes series, in which England had fallen away badly after winning the first Test. 'I told the board that in order to prepare adequately for Test cricket, our players needed rest and quality practice time with the best available coaches, on the best possible surfaces ... we must have players contracted to the board, so that we could manage them on a daily basis.'

Finally, in Lord MacLaurin they found someone of the same mind and, once a new broadcast deal worth £103m over four years was signed in October 1998, the finance became available. MacLaurin had by then brought in Simon Pack, a former army officer with no background in sport, to map out a broad management structure for the England team. Pack became infamous for mistaking Duncan Fletcher for Dav Whatmore during interviews for the coaching position in 1999, but he as much as anyone was the architect of central contracts, even if their introduction was eventually formalised by a working party chaired by Don Trangmar of Sussex.†

Duncan Fletcher was not the first choice to take over as England head coach in 1999. Lord MacLaurin was keen on former England player Bob Woolmer, then working with South Africa, but Woolmer effectively ruled himself out. However, Fletcher turned out to be the ideal choice. Not only did he come in at the right time, with so many previously troublesome issues ironed out, but he was also the right type of personality to benefit from the new landscape.

---

* The county championship switched to a mix of three-day and four-day games in 1988 and then to a wholly four-day programme in 1993, both moves designed to improve standards at international level. A move to two divisions followed in 1999.
† The Trangmar Report's recommendation that England's leading players should be centrally contracted to the ECB, with the players' counties compensated for their absences, was voted through 12-7 by the First Class Forum in May 1999.

A southern African with an independent streak and a wariness of those with whom he was unfamiliar, he did not bother to cultivate close relationships with the game's administrators who in the past had intruded into the affairs of the England team and who, he quickly discovered, 'were dealing with many issues in an old-fashioned and blinkered manner'. Fletcher recalled in his autobiography how he went to see Tim Lamb about acquiring a full-time assistant and Lamb had suggested Don Bennett, who had just retired as a coach at Middlesex and was 66 years old. 'His response staggered me ... demonstrating beyond doubt to me that there were those within the ECB hierarchy who did not have their finger on the pulse of international cricket and the way it was moving forward.' Fletcher described it as a huge mission to get the ECB 'to think only of making decisions which would help England win cricket matches'. He did not find his ideal assistants until Matthew Maynard and Troy Cooley joined him in late 2004.

Fletcher preferred to spend his time ensconced in the England team 'bubble', in the dressing-room and in nets, and bothered little with county cricket. As county cricket by this point was held in low regard, this did not much matter, although the removal of England players from county cricket continued to be a bone of contention for many years and Fletcher became the focal point of the counties' grievances. 'The counties still felt a huge amount of ownership over the players, as well as an unhealthy cynicism about what happened to them while they were on England duty,' Andrew Strauss wrote in his autobiography. 'Fletcher was bloody-minded enough to lock horns with the counties and effectively bypass them when it came to picking and working with England players. His belligerent attitude to the counties made him few friends.' The absence of the leading England players was widely seen as a major factor in the effective downgrading of the county championship to a development competition.

Fletcher instinctively sought to back the players with whom he shared the 'bubble', and was careful not to undermine them in public as some others in his position had done before – for example, sticking by Hussain's controversial decision to bowl first in Brisbane in 2002 – but he expected his authority to be backed in return. Ties were further cemented by him setting up a management group, usually containing the captain and three senior players, to help with decision-making. He was even cool in his dealings with David Graveney, the chairman of selectors, and Rod Marsh, the first director of the national academy from 2001 to 2005, although they were natural sources of information about emerging players. Indeed, he was seemingly prepared to take the opposite view to Marsh as a point of principle and they clashed in particular over the choice of England wicketkeeper after Alec Stewart's retirement. In 2004, Fletcher unilaterally dropped Chris Read, whom Marsh had championed, in favour of Geraint Jones midway through a tour of West Indies in a move reminiscent of Illingworth's at Lord's in 1995.* Graveney's opinions were so little sought that by the time of what proved to be Fletcher's last tour as coach Graveney was obliged to visit Australia in a personal capacity. He was not consulted even when some tricky selection decisions presented themselves.

Fletcher's one point of contact at Lord's was David Morgan, whom he knew from his time at Glamorgan, where he coached until England came knocking. He was lucky in this respect and also in the fact that Hussain, the new England captain, was also anti-establishment by temperament. Fletcher cultivated with Hussain, and later Vaughan, a crucial feeling of togetherness. 'Team England' was born, a concept Fletcher deliberately kept mysterious to outsiders in order to make the players feel even more special. 'The media were intrigued to know what was going on behind the scenes, especially when players started talking about what a profound effect he [Fletcher] was having, but they could never put their finger on it,' wrote Strauss, who added that this approach suited Fletcher's nature: 'He was essentially a quiet, introverted leader and communication was not his strong point.' It would be a while, though, before Fletcher's weaknesses came to be seen to outweigh his strengths.

---

* Two years later, when Fletcher was without his close ally Michael Vaughan, he was outvoted on the choice of wicketkeeper, and Read briefly returned at Jones's expense.

## England's Years of Drought

England endured the two longest losing sequences in their history during the modern era: one against West Indies spanning seven series between 1976 and 1990, and another against Australia from 1989 to 2003. One of the hallmarks of these setbacks was the resignations they triggered among captains, chairmen of selectors and coaches. During the 33 Tests against West Indies, only Graham Gooch (1,717 runs at 41.9) topped 1,000 runs at an average of more than 40, and in 44 Tests against Australia only Graham Thorpe did so (1,235 runs at 45.7). England's bowlers dismissed West Indies in both innings only five times and Australia nine times.

## v West Indies

| Series | Won | Lost | Drawn |
|---|---|---|---|
| 1976 (h) | 0 | 3 | 2 |
| 1980 (h) | 0 | 1 | 4 |
| 1980-81 (a) | 0 | 2 | 2 |
| 1984 (h) | 0 | 5 | 0 |
| 1985-86 (a) | 0 | 5 | 0 |
| 1988 (h) | 0 | 4 | 1 |
| 1989-90 (a) | 1 | 2 | 1 |

## v Australia

| Series | Won | Lost | Drawn |
|---|---|---|---|
| 1989 (h) | 0 | 4 | 2 |
| 1990-91 (a) | 0 | 3 | 2 |
| 1993 (h) | 1 | 4 | 1 |
| 1994-95 (a) | 1 | 3 | 1 |

| Series | Won | Lost | Drawn |
|---|---|---|---|
| 1997 (h) | 2 | 3 | 1 |
| 1998-99 (a) | 1 | 3 | 1 |
| 2001 (h) | 1 | 4 | 0 |
| 2002-03 (a) | 1 | 4 | 0 |

## England's Captains 1975-99

England's win percentages in the 1980s and 1990s were the lowest in any complete decades of Test cricket in their history: they won 20 out of 104 matches in the 1980s (19.2 percent) and 26 out of 107 in the 1990s (24.3 per cent). They won 18.8 per cent of the 32 Tests played in the 1940s when matches resumed after the Second World War in 1946.

| Captain | Period | P | W | L | D | Win % |
|---|---|---|---|---|---|---|
| JM Brearley | 1977-81 | 31 | 18 | 4 | 9 | 58.1 |
| RGD Willis | 1982-84 | 18 | 7 | 5 | 6 | 38.9 |
| GA Gooch | 1988-93 | 34 | 10 | 12 | 12 | 29.4 |
| *AJ Stewart | 1993-2001 | 15 | 4 | 8 | 3 | 26.7 |
| *MA Atherton | 1993-2001 | 54 | 13 | 21 | 20 | 24.1 |
| AW Greig | 1975-77 | 14 | 3 | 5 | 6 | 21.4 |
| DI Gower | 1982-89 | 32 | 5 | 18 | 9 | 15.6 |
| KWR Fletcher | 1981-82 | 7 | 1 | 1 | 5 | 14.3 |
| MW Gatting | 1986-88 | 23 | 2 | 5 | 16 | 8.7 |
| IT Botham | 1980-81 | 12 | 0 | 4 | 8 | 0.0 |

*Minimum: 7 Tests**

---

\* Atherton (in 2001) and Stewart (in 2000 and 2001) both led the side in two Tests after their official terms as captain ended in 1998 and 1999 respectively.

# CHAPTER 31

# Split Squads, At Last

## Adam Hollioake, Alec Stewart and pay disputes

One of the most important reforms of the 1990s was the decision to treat the England one-day team as a separate entity from the Test XI, and one worthy of distinct selection policies and strategies. This was a long overdue change and might have been done earlier had cost allowed, though there was also an ingrained reluctance to accept that the requirements of the short game were different, even when England teams were playing away from home. At home, England's one-day side continued to be a hard team to beat but overseas the game was increasingly dominated by ultra-aggressive batting and in these conditions England were light-years off the pace. This became shockingly evident at the 1996 World Cup on the subcontinent where, in a famous phrase of Matthew Engel, the editor of *Wisden*, the England squad 'resembled a bad-tempered grandmother attending a teenage rave'. Shortly before the World Cup, England were beaten 6-1 in South Africa, and in the following winter they lost 3-0 in Zimbabwe. It was the first time they had failed to make at least the World Cup semi-finals. In the previous tournament they had actually made the early running in the group stage before losing the final in Melbourne to a rejuvenated Pakistan team.*

Embarrassed into action, all the more urgent as it was due to host the 1999 World Cup, the TCCB started to bring one-day internationals in England into line with those played elsewhere, where 50 overs per side (rather than 55) was the norm. It finally embraced a 15-over powerplay at the start of the innings, which was brought in in 1996, and white balls and coloured clothing, introduced in 1998. Day–night ODIs in England began in 2000. One of the domestic competitions, the Benson & Hedges Cup, was also played under the revised regulations to allow players to develop the necessary skills, although unhelpfully this tournament was disbanded in 2002.† Previously, England had tended to play one-day internationals as though they were short Test matches, with only the field-settings different, although even in that instance the TCCB initially resisted attempts to adopt fielding restrictions. The board further accepted that England needed to fulfil more ODI fixtures, especially in Asia.‡ Michael Atherton, who captained England at the 1996 World Cup, had never played one-day international cricket there before.

England gave ODI debuts to nine players during their six home Texaco Trophy matches in 1996 – two of whom, Alistair Brown and Nick Knight, scored hundreds – but the new approach was further enforced by events during the winter of 1997-98. Then, they sent a side to an 'off-shore' tournament in Sharjah for only the second time, and then in the West Indies deployed a drastically different squad for the ODIs than had done service in the Tests (seven Test players

* The 1992 tournament was also memorable for England's semi-final win over South Africa when a late rainbreak highlighted the flaws in the existing recalculation rules. South Africa's target of 22 off 13 balls became 21 off one ball. This led to the creation of the Duckworth/Lewis method, which was first used in an England v Zimbabwe match on 1 January 1997 and adopted by the ICC two years later. Under Duckworth/Lewis, South Africa would have needed 5 to win or 4 to tie the 1992 semi-final.

† Subsequent to 2002, county players were still exposed to 50-overs cricket through various domestic competitions but, in another instance of counties putting their interests ahead of the England team, from 2010 to 2013 all that was available was 20-overs and 40-overs matches.

‡ Between January 1971 and May 1996, England played 247 one-day internationals, or ten per year; since then they have played 450 ODIs, or 21 per year.

flew home, six one-day players were flown out). This was a seminal moment: previously, England touring teams had been chosen primarily with Test matches in mind, and those players had to adapt as best they could to the shorter format; as one-day methods evolved, this strategic fudge was exposed for what it was. Even at home, England had shown little inclination to look beyond their Test regulars when it would have been a simple thing to pick one-day 'specialists': the 1979 World Cup final, played on English soil, was probably lost because Geoff Boycott and Mike Brearley started too conventionally for too long in pursuit of West Indies' 286 off 60 overs. 'We got our tactics wrong,' Brearley admitted. England's top six in that match was the same top six chosen for the first Test against India a fortnight later.*

With Atherton injured at the time of the Sharjah event and then having resigned as Test captain at the end of the series in West Indies, on both these occasions the one-day captaincy was put in the hands of Adam Hollioake, who had been among the batch of newcomers in 1996. Hollioake, who was born in Melbourne and came to England at the age of 11, was a hard-hitting batsman and inventive medium-pace bowler, and his instinctiveness was well-suited to the one-day game. He had first been used by Surrey as a stand-in captain at the age of 23 and was running the side full-time by the time he was 25, when he led them to the Benson & Hedges Cup. The selectors had already tested his credentials by putting him in charge of England A. To general surprise, England won the four-team tournament in Sharjah, in what was still an unfamiliar format of floodlit cricket, when their decision to fill the lower middle order with all-rounders paid dividends, delivering their first tournament success for ten years, but they were beaten 4-1 in West Indies.

Adam Hollioake's younger brother Ben, a cricketer of greater natural talent, marked his own introduction to the England one-day side in May 1997 with a stroke-laden 63 off 48 balls against Australia

---

* The extent to which England's one-day selections merely replicated those of the Test team is shown by the fact that of the 134 players chosen to represent them in ODIs up to May 1996, only six never played Tests. They were: Mike Smith (1973-74), Jim Love (1981), Ian Gould (1983), Trevor Jesty (1983), Colin Wells (1985) and Monte Lynch (1988).

at Lord's, but his career was to be tragically cut short when he was killed in a car crash in Perth in 2002 at the age of 24.*

Having taken over the Test captaincy, Alec Stewart – whose place in the one-day side was more assured than Atherton's had been – also took charge of the one-day outfit later in the 1998 season when for the first time England hosted a triangular event with the summer's two touring sides, South Africa and Sri Lanka, who beat England in the final. However, the broader commitment to treating Test and ODIs separately survived. Ian Austin, a specialist death bowler at Lancashire, was introduced into the side to partner Darren Gough. Adam Hollioake continued as a regular member of the ODI team and in fact led the side in Kenya in October 1998 in the Mini-World Cup – the precursor to the Champions Trophy – when England received special dispensation from the ICC to send a second-string team because they were about to embark on an Ashes tour. When the 1999 World Cup came round, though, it transpired old habits died hard. On the eve of the tournament, the selectors lost their nerve and decided to open the batting with Nasser Hussain, an established Test player, and jettison Knight, who had played in 44 out of 46 ODI matches since his debut. Hussain had never before opened in a professional match and was not even in the original World Cup squad. Even Hussain conceded: 'They really should have gone with him [Knight].'

The campaign proved another miserable failure, although the switch of openers was not a major factor. More relevant was a pay dispute leading into the tournament that highlighted the need for proper player representation. Stewart as captain liaised with Simon Pack, the international teams director, on behalf of the players and believed he had an acceptable deal, though nothing was secured in writing. In the event, the players' hopes that they would all receive

---

* Ben Hollioake made his last international appearance for England in India in January 2002, two months before he died. News of his death reached the Test team while they were involved in a Test match in Wellington, New Zealand. He is the youngest of all England's Test cricketers to die. Nasser Hussain, the England captain, flew to Australia to represent the team at the funeral, which took place five days before the next Test in Auckland.

around £30,000 evaporated; the reality was closer to £12,000 – less than they were paid for a recent triangular series in Australia. They were incensed at their treatment but not well enough organised to make a coherent case; even in the final stages they were without proper legal advice and relied on a three-man delegation of players in Stewart, Angus Fraser and Neil Fairbrother. 'We caved in over our contracts fight with Lord's. Our tournament performance reflected that dispute,' Darren Gough wrote. Stewart said: 'The management tactics were sadly typical of those in many industrial disputes. Despite all our meetings, the ECB just ran down the clock because they knew that no player would go on strike ... The management waited for us to buckle and we did, signing the contracts in Canterbury [where England held their pre-tournament training camp].'

According to Hussain, Stewart himself may have erred in the original discussions: 'Stewie had agreed to a pay deal that would favour people like himself who were going to play in every game, but not necessarily the whole squad.' Stewart was warned by David Graveney, who was in the conflicted position of being both chairman of selectors and a leading figure with the Professional Cricketers' Association, that, 'my stance might tell against me later if things didn't go well on the field.' So it proved: Stewart was sacked as both ODI and Test captain shortly after the World Cup and replaced by Hussain. Nor did the players forget Pack's role. 'In his three-year stint in the job, the England team had three heavily publicised rows with the ECB over money and contracts,' Gough pointed out. The episode highlighted how ill-equipped the players were to secure improvements in pay and conditions, and subsequently players' representatives – notably Richard Bevan of the PCA – took on a more prominent role in negotiations through the Team England Player Partnership, established in 2001 to ensure the protection of players' rights. Hussain would praise Bevan as a man who 'brought so much professionalism to English cricket off the field'.*

---

\* Bevan remained as chief executive of the PCA – and thereby principal representative of the England players in contract and commercial negotiations with the ECB – until 2007, after which he took up a position as head of the League Managers Association while continuing to sit on the Team England Player Partnership management committee.

The expansion in England's playing schedule from 2000 was seen as a desirable development in terms of helping players gain experience, and enabled Duncan Fletcher to set a target that each member of the 2003 World Cup squad should have played 30 ODIs in the 12 months leading into the tournament, something that would have been impossible in earlier times. Ironically, this expansion made it harder for the coaches and captains running the side (in those instances where the same player led both Tests and ODI teams) to find the time and energy to give both spheres their full attention. Fletcher in his eight years failed to replicate the success the team had in Test matches in the one-day arena, something Michael Vaughan said left him deeply frustrated. In 2004, Fletcher was sufficiently concerned at how the one-day team was faring that he summoned a special meeting of the selectors at the Belfry at which he outlined his vision for the future, but he admitted that this 'Utopia' was only remotely approached in the home summer of 2005. A pattern emerged of a captain giving up the one-day captaincy immediately after a World Cup and carrying on in the post in Test matches, with his likely successor using ODI cricket to develop his leadership skills. Not until 2012 was a coach, Ashley Giles, expressly charged with running England's white-ball cricket, although this decision was taken in part to prolong Andy Flower's tenure with the Test team. The roles were subsequently reunited under Peter Moores.

England's fixture list became even more congested with the advent of a World Twenty20 tournament, first staged in South Africa in September 2007 and held around every two years since. It was Moores's first major tournament as head coach and, partly through his encouragement, the selectors leaned heavily on county players with specialist knowledge of Twenty20s; although every member of the 15-man squad had played international cricket before, four of them had not done so for anything between three and seven years, and achieved so little during the tournament itself that they were never seen in an England shirt again. All four matches against major opposition were lost and the most memorable moment was a young Stuart Broad being hit for six sixes in an over by Yuvraj Singh of India in a match in Durban, the first and only time this has happened to an England bowler.

In an attempt to ease England's fixture overload, the ECB moved to decouple an Ashes tour of Australia from the same winter as the World Cup, a situation that badly hurt England's performances at the 2003, 2007 and 2011 World Cups; unsurprisingly after several months in Australia, the players were running on empty even before the tournament began, weary in mind and body and sick of life in hotels. But bringing the Ashes forward by 12 months – so that it followed hard on the heels of a home Ashes in 2013 – only served to fatally undermine the mission, and an emotionally exhausted team was beaten 5-0 in the Tests. As it happened, the World Cup campaign in 2015, ahead of which England played no Tests for five months, showed no obvious benefit and England failed to make the semi-finals for the sixth successive time.

A major stumbling block continued to be the expectation among England Test captains that they also lead the ODI side, as though to not do so demeaned their status. Stewart, Atherton, Hussain and Vaughan scored only three hundreds between them in 200 ODI matches as captain.

England's unexpected victory in Sharjah soon had to be viewed in a fresh light when it emerged that Adam Hollioake had been phoned in his hotel room on the eve of the opening game and asked if he was willing to provide information to 'fixers', and possibly more. Hollioake rejected the approach. That there were corrupt bookmakers, mainly from the subcontinent, prepared to tap up international cricketers had been generally known since allegations involving the Pakistan team surfaced in the mid-1990s, and Hollioake's story came to light in the wake of the Australian board confirming in 1998 that it had secretly fined two of its biggest stars, Shane Warne and Mark Waugh, for passing on information. Warne admitted to taking three calls during the 1994-95 Ashes and responding in general terms about selection and pitches. Further evidence regarding the Sharjah tournament came when Justice Malik Qayyum produced a report into Pakistan match-fixing in 2000 and the team's eight-run defeat to Hollioake's England received a name-check. Hollioake admitted the triumph had been tainted.

Hollioake was not the only England player tapped up. During the home Tests against New Zealand in 1999, Chris Lewis – whose international career was effectively over after his poor timekeeping of the previous summer but who could justifiably be seen as a man with inside knowledge and contacts – was approached during a face-to-face meeting in Harlesden with two Indians posing as businessmen. He was asked if he would provide them with information and consider approaching England players about underperforming in the forthcoming Test at Old Trafford. The men also claimed that three England players had in the past taken bribes, including a batsman who 'had received a "substantial figure" to get himself out deliberately during a one-day international in Australia'.

The ECB had advised players to report approaches and Lewis, having first contacted his agent and solicitor, duly informed the board the next morning, but he was to express unhappiness that the ECB took so long to encourage him to go to the police. In the end, he went to St John's Wood police station, accompanied by Simon Pack, 11 days after the Test match was over; the police subsequently questioned all 11 England players who took part in the match. Lewis also felt that the board cast him as the accuser of the three players who had allegedly taken bribes whereas he was merely reporting the claim. Several months later the ECB announced that it had found no evidence of malpractice against any England cricketer, although it was unclear whether the three players were ever quizzed; it later said its investigation was closed. Lewis accused the board of 'leaving me to sink'.

By this point, with Hansie Cronje's confession in April 2000 that he had taken substantial amounts of money to manipulate some of South Africa's matches, match-fixing had exploded into a full-blown international crisis for the game. Cronje's confession in turn led to the exposure of several players from the subcontinent, where illegal and corrupt bookmaking thrived. Few direct links were established with England teams, perhaps in part because they had so rarely played on the subcontinent in recent years, although one corrupt bookmaker was quoted by an Indian policeman as saying of England and Australia, 'it is very difficult to get through to these teams. They still have that spirit that they are playing for the country.'

England were nonetheless drawn in. Among the many things to which Cronje admitted was that he had engineered a positive outcome to England's most recent Test match in Centurion, at the direct encouragement of a man who was involved with a betting company and who subsequently provided him with a leather jacket and the equivalent of £800. With the Test seemingly destined for a draw after three days of rain, Cronje proposed that South Africa declare their first innings, both sides forfeit an innings and England then chase an agreed target. Nasser Hussain and the rest of England's management were initially sceptical but agreed after Cronje twice revised his offer down to a generous 249 off 76 overs. England won by two wickets with five balls to spare, but there was little celebrating. In fact, it transpired that Hussain had contravened the Laws of Cricket by forfeiting England's first innings, and the ECB chief executive Tim Lamb conveyed a message that evening that England's non-existent first innings should be deemed declared at 0 for no wicket, despite it not having commenced. When the truth emerged, Hussain (like Hollioake) felt England's victory had been 'ruined'.*

Among several inquiries triggered by the Cronje case was one by India's Central Bureau of Investigation, whose star witness was a bookie from Delhi called Mukesh Gupta. Gupta claimed he had dealt with a number of international cricketers, among them one England cricketer, Alec Stewart. Gupta subsequently confirmed his allegations to the ICC's new anti-corruption unit led by Paul Condon, a former Metropolitan Police Commissioner, though crucially he declined to be cross-examined by lawyers representing the players. Stewart endured a torrid time – he was on an England tour of Pakistan when the CBI published its report containing Gupta's claims, and had to hold a press conference at the team hotel in Rawalpindi to deny Gupta's claims that he had paid him £5,000 for pitch and team

---

* Believing that the Centurion Test was effectively over as a contest, several England players indulged in a long session at the hotel bar on the fourth night. Darren Gough, who hit the winning runs, later admitted to being ashamed of the state he got into: 'I have never walked onto a cricket field in such a disgraceful, self-induced state of disrepair as I was that last morning ... I had already been throwing up in the dressing-room. I felt so bad, I wasn't sure whether I was still drunk or was just beginning to suffer from a hangover.'

information during England's 1992-93 tour – and he made little impact on the field. The allegations hung over him beyond that. In June, Lord Condon said in regard to Stewart's case, 'Gupta's evidence was not the only evidence but it was the principal evidence ... the CBI said [India player Manoj] Prabhakar and others made statements of confirmation.' Then in July, between the first and second Tests of the Ashes series, Lord MacLaurin, the ECB chairman, announced that the board had cleared Stewart: 'There exists no substantive evidence justifying proceedings against Alec.'*

In an effort to protect and police international cricket, the ICC's anti-corruption unit now demands access, if needed, to the phone records of all players. All teams, including England, must before a game hand in their mobile phones, which stay in a locked box during the hours of play.

## England's Split Captaincies

The decision to pick for the first time separate Test and ODI squads for the West Indies in 1997-98 also heralded a change in approach to the England captaincy. With Michael Atherton resigning the Test captaincy during the tour, the selectors opted to promote Adam Hollioake, originally named as Atherton's deputy, to lead the ODI side even though Atherton was a member of the squad. Hollioake led England in three ODIs at home to South Africa in May 1998 but was then replaced by Alec Stewart, who also took over the Test captaincy. Both Nasser Hussain and Michael Vaughan – who stayed on as Test captains after resigning

---

* Other England games mentioned in official inquiries into match-fixing around this time included several England–Pakistan ODI games: at Trent Bridge in 1992, Sharjah in 1998-99 and in the NatWest Series in 2001; also the England v Pakistan Test at Lord's in 1996. No England players were directly accused of any wrongdoing. Ali Bacher, head of the United Cricket Board of South Africa, testified to the King Commission inquiry that an Indian bookmaker had told him that the Pakistan umpire Javed Akhtar, who stood in the England v South Africa Test at Leeds in 1998 as the international panel umpire, 'was on the payroll' of fixers. Akhtar gave nine lbw decisions in the match, won by England by 23 runs, eight of which were against South Africa batsmen. Akhtar continued as an international umpire until the World Cup the following year, his last match being England v India at Edgbaston.

the ODI leadership following a World Cup – felt uneasy about the split roles, especially when the ODI team was doing well. When Vaughan quit as Test captain in 2008 he 'reiterated my belief that it had to be one man doing both jobs'. Andrew Strauss, whose long wait to become full-time captain was due to doubts about his white-ball credentials, disagreed and after becoming managing director of England cricket in May 2015 kept the captaincies separate.

There have been various periods since 1998 when the Test and ODI jobs have been officially allocated to different leaders:

| Period | Test captain | ODI captain |
| --- | --- | --- |
| *Unified under Alec Stewart (1998-99), then Nasser Hussain (1999 to 2002-03)* | | |
| May 2003-July 2003 | Nasser Hussain | Michael Vaughan |
| *Unified under Michael Vaughan (2003 to 2007)* | | |
| May 2007-Aug 2008 | Michael Vaughan | Paul Collingwood |
| *Unified under Kevin Pietersen (2008), then Andrew Strauss (2009-11)* | | |
| May 2011-Sept 2012 | Andrew Strauss | Alastair Cook |
| *Unified under Alastair Cook (2012-13 to 2014-15)* | | |
| Jan 2015-Jan 2017 | Alastair Cook | Eoin Morgan |
| Mar 2017 to date | Joe Root | Eoin Morgan |

England played their first Twenty20 in 2005 and the captaincy of that side officially resided with the ODI captain until Strauss took charge of the Test and one-day sides, at which point the Twenty20 team was led by Paul Collingwood (2009-11) and then Stuart Broad (2011-14). From May 2011 until September 2012, England thus had separate captains in each of the three formats: Strauss (Tests), Cook (ODIs) and Broad (Twenty20s). Eoin Morgan took over the Twenty20 leadership in March 2014, and since January 2015 he has been in charge of both white-ball teams.

# CHAPTER 32

# Learning the Art of Winning in Asia
## How Duncan Fletcher delivered the Ashes in 2005

Duncan Fletcher proved the perfect appointment as head coach in respect of one of the most important tasks facing him. England had not won a Test series in Asia since 1984–85 and spectacularly failed to make any sort of impact when the World Cup was held there in 1996. A little more than a year after he began work, Fletcher was due to take the side on the daunting assignment of twin tours of Pakistan and Sri Lanka. As it was their first Test winter on the subcontinent in eight years and only their second in 13 years, the group of players he was working with had little practical experience of what would be required. What everyone knew was that England teams had a woeful record against unorthodox spin, and Asia was a place where the ball turned more than anywhere else.

Fortunately, Fletcher had very specific and well-honed theories on how to play spin, while he was also to show himself adept at devising bowling strategies suited to Asian conditions, including the use of reverse swing – a skill which English cricketers had been slow to comprehend let alone master. These talents were going to be much needed because, whereas England had played only four Tests in Asia between 1987 and 2000, in the next 13 years they would play 36 Tests there. In fact, not only did England win both series in Pakistan and Sri Lanka but they drew 1-1 in India in 2005-06 before going on to win there, with Andy Flower as head coach, in 2012-13.

As it happened, these two adjustments – playing spin better, bowling reverse swing – fed directly into solving a second and even more vital challenge: regaining the Ashes, something which had taken on the aspect of the Holy Grail for English cricket. Only by taming Shane Warne's mesmeric leg-spin and by reverse-swinging the ball both ways to unpick a formidable Australian batting line-up were England able in 2005 to end a nightmarish sequence of eight successive Ashes series losses. The national celebrations that followed, culminating in an open-top bus ride around central London and a parade in Trafalgar Square, were suitably excessive.*

Usefully, directly ahead of Fletcher's first Asian winter, England showed significant signs of progress by ending an even lengthier barren run with the defeat of West Indies, a team they had not beaten in 13 series dating back to 1969. For the first time since the days of Statham and Trueman, they were able to pick the same pair of new-ball bowlers in all five Tests: Darren Gough claimed 25 wickets and Andrew Caddick 22, four of them in one over at Headingley.†

England and the ECB were not only seeking to improve the team's playing record in Asia but also to repair diplomatic relations with the Asian nations damaged over a long period. It was not only the Shakoor Rana affair that meant England returned with trepidation. The next Test series between the sides in England in 1992 had been highly inflammatory, with the England players and manager convinced – and seemingly English umpires also – that the Pakistan bowlers were tampering with the ball to facilitate reverse swing; certainly Wasim Akram and Waqar Younis got the ball reversing remarkably early and England suffered a striking number of batting collapses against the old, or middle-aged, ball. The mood was not helped by the confrontational approach of Javed Miandad, the

---

* The victory was also recognised in the New Year Honours, with Michael Vaughan awarded an OBE and the other players MBEs. Fletcher, chairman of selectors David Graveney, and team operations manager Phil Neale received OBEs, and Medha Laud became an MBE.

† Four other bowlers have taken four wickets in an over for England: Maurice Allom (v New Zealand, 1929-30), Ken Cranston (v South Africa, 1947), Fred Titmus (v New Zealand, 1965) and Chris Old (v Pakistan, 1978).

Pakistan captain, after umpire Roy Palmer warned Aqib Javed for intimidatory bowling during the Old Trafford Test.

Then, in the following Test at Leeds, Graham Gooch was given not out by Ken Palmer, Roy's brother, when replays showed him well out of his ground. But the biggest flashpoint came after the Test series when, during the fourth ODI at Lord's, umpires Ken Palmer and John Hampshire confiscated and replaced the ball used by Pakistan after they detected tampering. Although the reason why they acted as they did was denied by the TCCB and ICC, the truth came out during a libel action brought by Sarfraz Nawaz after Allan Lamb, one of the England batsmen, stated in an article in the *Daily Mirror* that the Pakistan bowlers had cheated and Sarfraz had shown him how to tamper with the ball during their time together at Northamptonshire in the early 1980s. (Lamb's comments breached his TCCB contract and earned him a £5,000 fine.) Four days into the trial, Sarfraz dropped his action after Don Oslear, the third umpire at Lord's, confirmed under oath that the ball had been changed under Law 42.5 which relates to 'changing the condition of the ball'.*

Just as the England dressing-room sometimes felt their masters at Lord's did not back them up as well as they might, so English umpires felt more might have been done by the TCCB to support them. According to Oslear, the board sought to dissuade several umpires from taking part in the trial, and he himself was dropped from the first-class list of umpires for 1994 even though by convention he was at 65 entitled to stand for one more year. John Hampshire also complained that he and Ken Palmer were effectively blackballed for their part in the incident; Hampshire was appointed to stand in only four international matches between 1993 and 1999, and Palmer in five.†

---

* Other England players who gave evidence during the trial included Robin Smith, who played in the 1992 matches, David Capel, Chris Cowdrey and Wayne Larkins. Ian Botham was about to give evidence when the trial stopped.

† Another English umpire, John Holder, protested that he was punished for reporting Graham Gooch, the England captain, for the state of the ball in the Oval Test in 1991, which he said had 'about a dozen gouges'. The TCCB denied receiving a report. Holder was dropped from the TCCB's panel of Test umpires in May 1992 and did not stand again in a Test until 2001.

However, partly as a result of the controversies in England–Pakistan Tests in 1987–88 and 1992, the ICC finally introduced in 1994 the practice of one 'neutral' umpire, drawn from an international panel, standing in each Test, one of the consequences of which was that it reduced the scope for umpires not on the panel such as Hampshire and Ken Palmer to stand in big matches.* In 2002, 'neutral' or independent umpires stood at both ends in all Tests, something which played an important part in reducing on-field disputes as well as providing fairer decision-making.†

Moreover, by the time of the Sarfraz–Lamb trial in November 1993, the TCCB had suffered a bruising setback when at an ICC special meeting it had been forced to withdraw its application to stage the 1996 World Cup in the face of a combined bid from India, Pakistan and Sri Lanka which lacked support from any other major member but nevertheless managed to garner sufficient backing from Zimbabwe and a range of associate members to win the day. AC Smith, the TCCB chief executive, described the meeting as 'fractious and unpleasant . . . the worst meeting I have ever attended'. Nothing spoke more eloquently of the way cricket's power base was shifting from London to Mumbai.

Further trouble had arisen out of the 1992 tour, too, when Imran Khan, the former Pakistan captain, admitted in a book that he had tampered with the ball in county cricket and then in newspaper articles suggested he had only copied the methods of English players and that Pakistan's accusers such as Lamb and Ian Botham lacked class and upbringing. This led the two England players to sue Imran for libel, a case they ultimately lost, though with delicious timing the case in the High Court coincided with the England v Pakistan Test

---

* Ironically, given English perceptions, Pakistan were one of the first countries to promote neutral officials, while England were seemingly reluctant to give up using their own umpires at home. The first neutral umpires stood in the Asia Cup one-day tournament in Sri Lanka in 1985–86.

† Michael Atherton, writing in *The Times* in June 2016, cited research published in the *Journal of the Royal Statistical Society* two years earlier which examined 1,000 Tests between 1986 and 2012. 'In matches with two home umpires, they found that visiting teams were 16 per cent more likely to be given out leg-before; with one neutral umpire the bias against away teams receded to 10 per cent, and with two neutral umpires there was no bias at all.'

at Lord's in 1996, with both the England captain Michael Atherton and coach David Lloyd required to give evidence on the eve of the match. In fact, because of the playing connections at Lancashire shared by Atherton, Lloyd and the Pakistan captain Wasim Akram, relations between the teams remained amicable and stayed that way for the next ten years.

England not only had Pakistan and India to deal with. Their more frequent visits to Asia were partly the result of Sri Lanka – who, after several applications, had been granted Test status in 1981 – finally being accommodated as regular opponents following their stunning World Cup win in 1996, while Bangladesh, more controversially, also joined the ranks of Test-playing nations in 2000. Earlier attempts had been made by the Asian bloc to get Sri Lanka (or Ceylon as it was known prior to 1972, when it became an independent republic) accorded Test status, but only after they won the inaugural ICC Trophy for associate nations and then beat India at the 1979 World Cup did the tide turn in their favour. England's relationship with Sri Lanka had been delicate ever since, fuelled by suspicions England were reluctant to give them their due, although Sri Lanka's civil war cost them at least one tour by England in the 1980s.

The sides only met in one-off Tests prior to 2000-01, even though Sri Lanka showed immense promise in some of them. They got themselves into a good position before losing their first Test against England in Colombo in 1982, and scored almost 500 in their first Test in England in 1984 when they were coached by former Sussex and England player Don Smith. Sri Lanka may have lacked the fast bowling to prosper in English conditions but they were a serious proposition at home, where heat and humidity added to the challenge for visiting sides; Nasser Hussain described it as 'easily the hottest place where I have played cricket'. England were soundly beaten in Colombo in their second Test there in 1993 when for the first time they came up against Muttiah Muralitharan. In Murali, Sri Lanka possessed a match-winning spinner and in Arjuna Ranatunga a captain who defended his champion from frequent accusations that his action was suspect.

This process came to a head shortly after Murali had taken 16 wickets on a subcontinental-style pitch at The Oval in 1998 to deliver Sri Lanka their first Test victory in England. In a one-day match against England in Adelaide, Ranatunga brought play to a halt for 15 minutes when Australian umpire Ross Emerson called Murali for throwing (something Emerson had previously done three years earlier). When play resumed there were several ugly incidents between the players, with England captain Alec Stewart caught on the stump microphone telling Ranatunga, 'your behaviour today has been appalling.' Ranatunga was charged with several breaches of the ICC code of conduct but, when he appeared before the match referee accompanied by lawyers arguing that suspension would be restraint of trade, he escaped with a suspended six-match ban and a small fine.

Bangladesh (formerly East Pakistan until independence in 1971) had every motivation to do well against England after the ECB alone declined to support their promotion to Test status (though MCC had made three early tours in the space of five years), but for many years they were simply not good enough to push England or any other leading side. In their first Test series in England in 2005 their collective batting and bowling averages were respectively 17.17 and 162.50. Their application was based on nothing more than a few ODI wins, one of which against Pakistan at Northampton during the 1999 World Cup had done more than any other match to fuel speculation about match-fixing, but gradually they acquired the disciplines to succeed in the longer forms of the game, especially in Asian conditions. In 2016 and 2017, they recorded first Test wins over England (inside three days in Dhaka), Sri Lanka and Australia.

In 2000–01, it helped that England were led by Nasser Hussain, who himself had been born in Madras (now Chennai) and spent seven years there before moving with his family to England. At the time of his international debut, this background – born in Asia, raised from a young age in Britain – was unique for an England cricketer. Hussain understandably viewed himself as '100 per cent English' but, unlike some of his predecessors as captain, he could not be dismissed by critics as a white man ignorant in the ways of the subcontinent.

Complaints were confined to the hard-nosed tactics he employed in an effort to make England hard to beat in conditions that were felt to be alien to them. When they had won series in Asia in the past, seam and swing bowling had played a part as well as spin, but memories of the wholesale failure of the bowling attack on the most recent visit in 1992-93 remained strong.

The series in Pakistan was won with a last-day heist in Karachi, Pakistan unexpectedly losing their last seven wickets for 87, which left England chasing 176 in rapidly fading light. Despite their opponents' desperate attempts at time-wasting, with which the international umpire Steve Bucknor had no truck, England got home in the nick of time. 'Another five minutes and it would have been complete darkness,' said Hussain, who ran the winning runs with Graham Thorpe. Pakistan had never previously lost at the National Stadium in Karachi, and England's last Test win in Pakistan had been 39 years earlier. Then, in Sri Lanka, England won despite losing all three tosses and being beaten by an innings in the first Test. It was a fractious series but that was mainly because both teams lost confidence in the umpiring of the local officials standing alongside the international panel umpires, as well as the match referee, Hanumant Singh of India.

Hussain was unable to conjure similar magic in India the following winter but, aware of the limitations of his side, he frustrated the Indian batsmen with 7-2 off-side fields and Ashley Giles bowling his left-arm spin over the wicket, which confounded Sachin Tendulkar in Bangalore and eventually led to him being stumped for the first time in his Test career. Hussain was widely criticised but with justification he claimed, 'This was the peak of my captaincy', while Tendulkar, the most-capped cricketer in Test history, rated him the best captain he came up against.*

---

\* The most serious spat involving an Englishman in respect of this tour involved Mike Denness, the former England captain-turned-match referee, who had incensed India by suspending Virender Sehwag during a recent tour of South Africa, among other punishments handed out to Indian players. In a convoluted saga, the Indian board threatened to pick Sehwag anyway for the first Test against England, which could have jeopardised the whole tour, but at the 11th hour they abided by the suspension.

Michael Vaughan built on the good work during his first tour as captain to Bangladesh and Sri Lanka in late 2003, when the players were drawn closer through a fitness drive and two immense rearguard actions to secure draws in Galle and Kandy. An improvement in team spirit was now manifesting itself. Morale had been low for much of the 1990s and some of the newer generation detected remnants of the old mindset among those who still survived. Shortly after he departed as coach, David Lloyd wrote that two players new to the England team, Chris Read and Aftab Habib, had been 'traumatised' by the atmosphere in the dressing-room. 'I knew how those youngsters felt as they spent time amongst senior players who had grown to regard the dressing-room as their own domain and, in some cases, the game as a job.'

Steve Harmison also found the environment unwelcoming when he joined the team in 2002, and cited Andrew Caddick as an example of someone suffering chronic insecurity. 'He was bitter at the end,' Harmison said. 'I don't believe he enjoyed other people's success. I never thought he was out there to help me.' Marcus Trescothick credited Duncan Fletcher with bringing the players together, which he described as 'not easy because there were quite a few older, experienced players, and the cricket was lingering on from years before', but Vaughan's role was probably the crucial one in putting the players at ease in the fraught environment of international sport. 'He never gave the impression that he took it too seriously, which is probably why he was so popular with the players when he followed Nasser Hussain's more combative leadership,' Strauss wrote in his autobiography. 'There was a calmness about him, an ability to take all the pressure on his shoulders and spare the rest of the team from its effects.' Vaughan's decision-making was clear, brave and inventive.

Hussain's approach of telling the team what to do became outmoded, as the players moved forward on a more consensual basis. 'I thought that my first objective [on becoming Test captain in 2003] ought to be to make sure that those playing under me were really enjoying their cricket,' Vaughan wrote in his autobiography. 'Under Nasser I had the sense that we were not expressing ourselves out in the middle as much as we should have been. Perhaps there was a bit too much fear in the air, the kind that drove him on, and it was transmitting itself to the players.'* Of the Sri Lanka tour, he added: 'It was the first building block in the campaign to beat the Australians, purely because we had been able to identify characters who could fight.'

Duncan Fletcher, the best technical coach the team have had, assisted many England players in improving their methods against spin bowling and especially in their efforts to deal with the two greatest spinners of the era in Muralitharan and Warne. In particular, he encouraged them to develop a trigger movement called the forward press that got them into the right position to play the ball at an early stage, which he argued was especially important when playing spin. He also helped them to cultivate sweeps and slog-sweeps which he saw as key against top-quality spin (though not against the skiddy Indian leg-spinner Anil Kumble) whether playing in the subcontinent or elsewhere. Above all, he gave them a coherent game plan for the first time.

Fletcher first introduced his theories in Pakistan in 2000-01. Michael Atherton, though he had already played more than 100 Tests, was a ready convert, telling Fletcher he was judging the length of the ball much better. Graham Thorpe, a naturally fine player of spin, was another who took to Fletcher's methods and brought his own ideas into the mix by suggesting the team scuff up net pitches in order to replicate the worn surfaces they might encounter in matches. For Muralitharan, the whole group would sit down together to study super slo-mo replays of his methods. Thorpe, having scored a hundred against Pakistan in Lahore, struck an aggressive 46 in England's run-chase in Kandy and followed up with one of the

---

* Vaughan detected in Hussain's behaviour back in the ranks during the Sri Lanka tour evidence of him 'suffering some sort of delayed reaction to handing over the captaincy': Hussain pulled out of the Galle Test through illness only to attempt to declare himself fit at the 11th hour after Paul Collingwood had already been told he would be playing in his place; then, in Kandy, Hussain called Muralitharan a cheat 'in pretty choice language'. Duncan Fletcher recalled that the night before the winter tour squad was named, Hussain spent the evening staring at him during a dinner. 'He barely took his eyes off me all night.'

most exceptional batting performances ever seen in an England shirt when, in crippling humidity in Colombo, he scored 113 out of a team score of 249 in the first innings and 32 as they lost six wickets chasing down 74 in the second.

Fletcher also helped Marcus Trescothick and Nasser Hussain in Sri Lanka in 2001, when both scored hundreds, then Paul Collingwood in Sri Lanka two years later, and Andrew Strauss during the Ashes series in 2005. Trescothick called on Fletcher's expertise more than most players and credited him with knowing his game better than anyone else and being able to spot flaws no one else would know were there. Strauss developed a method of padding away Warne's deliveries from round the wicket with the assistance of the Merlyn bowling machine, which England used in training that summer after Vaughan and Fletcher tested it at Loughborough and deemed it a success. Vaughan – who, like Thorpe, scored Test hundreds against Murali in Sri Lanka and Warne in Australia – wrote of Fletcher: 'He was the first batting coach I had ever listened to who spoke so well about playing spinners and he was always prepared to go against accepted theories ... He changed a lot of things in my game, and I know that other players of my era will also swear that there was a touch of coaching genius about him.'

In an appreciation of Fletcher's contribution to the England team in *Wisden*, in 2008, Strauss wrote: 'His ideas became so much of a blueprint for England cricket over the time he was in charge that I defy any recent player to stand up and say he didn't learn anything off Duncan Fletcher, whether he played one Test or a hundred ... All batsmen, without exception, were shepherded into a dark room at some stage early in their England career, to listen to Fletcher's theories on playing spin.'

One of the decisive factors in England's Ashes victory – aside from the important fact that they batted first in four of the five games – was the fearless way Kevin Pietersen dealt with Warne. Pietersen was willing to use his height (he was 6ft 4in) and long reach to get to the pitch of the ball and slog-sweep, and twice deposited Warne into the Mound Stand during his debut appearance at Lord's. During the series as a whole he hit Warne for eight sixes, sometimes fetching the ball from outside off stump to do so, and scored 153 runs off the 231 balls he faced from him, getting out only three times. Warne noted from his earliest encounters with him in county cricket that Pietersen was clear in his approach: 'He picked every delivery. He jumped onto the front foot when I bowled a flipper. He knows exactly what's going on.'

Strauss said of Pietersen: 'His play against Shane Warne in 2005 announced him as the team's most ambitious and destructive player of spin in modern times.' His ferocious assault on both Warne and Brett Lee, Australia's fastest bowler, on the final, luminous afternoon of the series at The Oval finally determined the outcome in England's favour. Pietersen was every bit as belligerent against Murali, whom he forced into packing his leg-side field, and would then reverse-sweep him through the vacant off side. Pietersen even broke new ground by switch-hitting: flipping his stance at the crease and his grip on the bat into those of a left-hander to take advantage of the relatively unprotected off side of the field. He first did this in an ODI against New Zealand at Durham in 2008 but to greatest effect during a brilliant century at Colombo in 2012.*

Another convert was Alastair Cook, who also scored hundreds against Murali and Warne on their home patches and by 2017 had made nine centuries in Asia, an England record. Cook in fact scored a hundred in his first Test match against India in Nagpur but he admitted that his method against the best spinners was flawed and Fletcher was right to help him make what he described as 'substantial but necessary' changes. He began to play more with bat than pad and to hold his hands lower on the bat. 'Duncan encouraged me to do it his way, and the method suited me down to the ground,' Cook wrote in 2008. 'The forward press method that [he] taught me has benefited me hugely.'

Bowlers of the quality of Murali and Warne were never beaten, though. After England's victory in Sri Lanka in 2001, Murali had

---

* MCC ruled the switch-hit legal provided the batsman switched after the bowler's back foot had landed in his delivery action. Pietersen was warned by the umpires in Colombo for not doing this, although whether he was actually guilty of this offence was much debated.

developed a doosra by the next time they visited two years later, and he became an altogether harder proposition, especially for left-handers.* Warne, similarly, bounced back from the loss in 2005, delaying his retirement plans to take on England again at home in 2006–07 and conjuring a remarkable last-day win from a seemingly hopeless situation in Adelaide in 2006, nine England wickets tumbling for 60 either side of lunch. That series loss was to expedite Fletcher's departure after eight years.

Ignorance about how reverse swing was achieved, as well as some fairly plain cases of illegal ball-tampering, fuelled suspicions that it could only be brought about by cheating and may have held back attempts to make the ball reverse by legitimate means. Various ploys had been adopted over the years to keep one side of the ball shiny for longer in order to generate conventional swing but these had little to do with achieving reverse. After Bob Massie took 16 England wickets at Lord's in 1972, it was suspected that lip balm had helped him and lip balm duly became fashionable among English bowlers, but England did not have anyone who could genuinely swing the ball apart from Basil D'Oliveira and no one was able to replicate Massie's hooping swing.

When England were swung out by part-timer Mudassar Nazar of Pakistan at Lord's in 1982, they suspected foul play, but three of Mudassar's six wickets were taken with the first new ball. After the game, the balls were examined by Donald Carr, TCCB secretary, and it was found that 'no unusual substance had been used'. Similarly, John Lever, a conventional swinger of the ball, was accused of using Vaseline-impregnated gauze to assist him during the tour of India in 1976–77, when he swung England to victory in the first Test in Delhi and took 26 wickets in the five Tests. In the intense heat of Madras (now Chennai), Lever and Bob Willis wanted help with

---

* Murali developed his doosra during a spell at Kent in 2003. Until this point, few Sri Lankans had been recruited to county cricket: Murali himself had played for Lancashire in 1999 and 2001, and Aravinda de Silva had a successful season with Kent in 1995, but English counties were generally slow to sign them, perhaps reflecting the cool relations at national board level. Before Sri Lanka achieved Test status, Gamini Goonesena played for Nottinghamshire, and Stanley Jayasinghe and Clive Inman for Leicestershire.

keeping sweat out of their eyes; physio Bernard Thomas provided them with the gauze but it did not stay in place and Lever threw it down behind the stumps. Bishen Bedi, the India captain, who with England 2-0 up was under pressure for his job, accused England of cheating and a stressful controversy ensued.* The English traditions of conventional swing and seam movement off grassed, gripping surfaces died hard, but the realisation eventually dawned that in an era of covered pitches (as opposed to uncovered ones, as was commonly the case in England for many years) fast bowlers needed to find new ways to manipulate the old ball.

Whatever the reason, when it came to reverse swing, England were slow to catch on. Darren Gough, the most ebullient character in the dressing-room for much of the 1990s, was the first England bowler to show real expertise. Gough was relatively short for a fast bowler and naturally bowled a lot of yorkers, which helped the process, as well as bowling at the death in one-day matches when the ball was old, but his inspiration came from watching Waqar Younis on TV during the 1992 Tests and playing against Wasim Akram when Yorkshire faced Lancashire. Gough was bowling when Michael Atherton was caught on camera putting dirt from the footholds onto the ball during the Lord's Test in 1994, Gough's first summer as an England player, and according to Atherton's account Gough was getting reverse swing at the time. 'He [Gough] tells Sals [Ian Salisbury] and me to make sure we keep our sweaty hands off the rough side of the ball ... I use the dust to keep my hands and the ball dry three or four times.'

Gough could not then manipulate the ball as Wasim and Waqar could, but he improved and reverse swing played an important role in his success overseas. He took 41 wickets in eight Tests in Australia and in the winter of 2000-01 captured ten wickets in Pakistan and 14 in Sri Lanka, where he was named man of the series, at an overall

---

* Lever's father suffered a heart attack shortly after the incident, which Lever said he felt was brought on by press intrusion. 'I found it very hard to forgive Bedi for stirring it up the way he did.' Lever, who conceded some Vaseline may have unintentionally got onto the ball, said the local Indian balls used during the series were hand-wound and easily went out of shape, helping them to swing extravagantly.

average of 22.58. 'He would have played for England in any period,' said Keith Fletcher, his first England manager. Craig White, a Yorkshire team-mate of Gough's who bowled with a side-on, slingy action and for a brief period with genuine speed, also became expert at reverse and played an important part in the wins in Pakistan and Sri Lanka.

Simon Jones, who was sent on the first national academy draft to Adelaide in 2001–02 at Fletcher's insistence, took the art to another level. He also had a skiddy action suited to reverse swing and while in Adelaide was encouraged to experiment with it at the instigation of Troy Cooley, a fast-bowling coach who was actually working with Australia at the time but was brought in by academy director Rod Marsh and would soon switch to the England camp on a full-time basis.* 'I had the natural speed to bowl it, and the right sort of action to make it work ... Troy told me to have a mess around with it, and I got it right away,' Jones recalled. He added: 'I learned how to reverse it not just into the right-handed batsman – the easiest delivery to bowl – but to move it away, too.'

Jones played his first Test, against India in 2002, alongside White and both were reckoned to have got the ball reverse-swinging during that game, but Duncan Fletcher said that Jones's ability to reverse-swing the ball both ways first manifested itself during the Test against New Zealand at Lord's two years later: '[He] opened a lot of people's eyes.' The likes of Gough and White had mainly reversed the ball in to the right-hander, not away. Vaughan even got in the habit of only calling on Jones when the ball reverse-swung, once ignoring him for two and a half sessions at Port Elizabeth in 2004, but gradually realised he was also an asset when it came to conventional swing.

Then, during the 2005 Ashes, Andrew Flintoff, who had already developed a reputation as an accurate, defensive bowler, also

---

* Troy Cooley was the first specifically designated fast-bowling coach assigned to the England team, although Bob Cottam (1998–99 to 2000–01) and Graham Dilley (2001–02 and 2002–03) had toured as assistant coaches in effectively that capacity. Cooley worked with England from 2004–06 and was followed by Kevin Shine (2006–07), Ottis Gibson (2007–10), David Saker (2010–14) and Gibson again (2015–17). England went to the Ashes in Australia in 2017–18 without a full-time bowling coach, using Shane Bond as a consultant, then appointed Chris Silverwood on a full-time basis.

acquired the ability to reverse-swing the ball both ways. Fletcher said that Flintoff had never previously shown that he could swing the ball away from the right-hander in reverse fashion before, and at Edgbaston – where England won a nail-biting game by two runs – came the first clear indication that the Australians were going to struggle with reverse swing: 'Flintoff and Simon Jones ... caused all manner of problems.' The most spectacular evidence actually came in the next Test at Old Trafford, a ground where an abrasive square made it conducive to reverse. There, Flintoff from round the wicket took the ball away from the left-handed Simon Katich before jagging one back into him as he shouldered arms, while Jones, who took six for 53 in the first innings, also bowled Michael Clarke shouldering arms on the final afternoon. 'These were not batsmen who knew which way the ball was swinging,' Fletcher noted. Flintoff and Jones devised with Fletcher's help a general tactic of going round the wicket to Australia's left-handers, which worked well during the series, particularly in the case of Flintoff bowling at the dangerous Adam Gilchrist, who had often hurt England before. Flintoff also touched new heights with the newer ball as well and bowled an over of astonishing ferocity to remove Justin Langer and Ricky Ponting at Edgbaston with a ball that was only 13 overs old.

Reverse swing was not the only weapon at the disposal of one of the best pace attacks England had ever put into the field. The opening pair of Matthew Hoggard and Steven Harmison posed serious and contrasting problems: Hoggard swung the ball conventionally, mainly away from the right-hander, though he could also get the ball to 'hold up', while Harmison generated steepling bounce from his tall frame; when he got his rhythm right, as he did for much of 2004 in particular, he was a formidable proposition, dynamically one of the best fast bowlers England have ever possessed. Harmison, Hoggard, Flintoff and Jones played 16 Tests together between March 2004 and August 2005 of which England won ten and lost two; in all but two they were supported by Ashley Giles, a utilitarian spinner who performed a vital defensive role by bowling a tight leg-stump line from over the wicket – another Fletcher plan. The first time the

'Fab Four' played together, in Jamaica, Harmison took seven for 12 as West Indies were blown away for 47; towards the end, Harmison was bowling to a possibly unprecedented field for an England fast bowler of seven slips and gullies, and a short leg.

By 2005, the England team as a whole understood how disciplined they had to be to get the ball into the right state for reverse, which meant being assiduous about keeping sweaty palms off the dry side of the ball and keeping it off the lusher, damper areas of the field. Fletcher said that during his time as Glamorgan coach in 1997, Waqar Younis, their overseas player, had advised, 'try to keep sweaty palms off the ball and pick it up with two fingers on the seam.' England appointed Marcus Trescothick as 'ball manager' and few others apart from him and the bowlers were allowed to touch it. Picking out the right ball from an assorted box of 12 before the innings was also important, with Simon Jones reckoning 'the darker the ball, the harder it is for the batsman to spot which side is which once it starts reversing'. Bowlers also learned to mask the ball with their spare hand as they ran in, denying the batsman a sight of which way they were holding the ball and therefore which way it might swing.

When England went to Australia in 2006-07 without the injured Jones, they struggled to get the ball reversing, so they worked hard on remedying that when they returned in 2010-11, becoming even more meticulous than they had been in 2005. 'The art of reverse swing was a central part of our preparation for the tour,' Andrew Strauss, the England captain, explained. 'We needed to be very clear on how we were going to get the ball reversing . . . apart from Matt Prior, the only two guys to touch the ball were Alastair Cook and Jimmy Anderson. No one else was to shine the ball or do anything other than get it back to them . . . Once all 11 of you are clued in, it's amazing how protective you become of it.'

Reverse swing played a big part in England's victory in Durban in 2009 and in two of their three victories in that Ashes series: at Melbourne, a good ground for reverse since the introduction of drop-in pitches in the late 1990s, and Sydney, when Anderson, Tim Bresnan and Chris Tremlett were all difficult to play. Ahead of that series, Anderson also added another weapon to his armoury that was to prove invaluable: a 'wobble-seam' ball. It involved holding the ball with the seam horizontal and fingers splayed: the seam wobbled in flight and depending on which part of the seam hit the ground could jag left or right, with no visible clues available to the batsmen in advance. It was to serve Anderson well. England's dominance was near-total: all three of their victories were achieved by an innings, a unique achievement in an Ashes series. Anderson's mastery of reverse swing was also a factor in the series win in India in 2012-13 even though the spinners Graeme Swann and Monty Panesar were the match-winners in Mumbai.

England's relationship with the Asian sides improved on the playing front but diplomatically the ECB went through a difficult period with its Indian counterparts as the India board established itself as the most powerful force in the game. Harmony was restored over two particular incidents. The first was the decision to complete England's tour of India after the terrorist attacks on Mumbai in November 2008, among the targets of which was the Taj Palace hotel at which the England team was due to stay for one of two scheduled Tests. The England players were in Bhubaneshwar at the time, involved in the ODI series. They initially flew home, then to Abu Dhabi to train and await security advice, before returning to India to play the Tests (at different venues from those originally planned) after a two-week hiatus.

The second incident was India's reciprocal gesture to go ahead with a Test in Birmingham in 2011 despite rioting in the city. In both cases, the teams were afforded additional protection. 'The board decision to go back to India was made after considerable consultation,' said Giles Clarke, ECB chairman from 2007-15. 'The PCA were first-class and there was great leadership from Kevin Pietersen [the England captain]. If there was one decision during my eight years that was critical for world cricket this was it ... Admiration goes to the players who had the vision and courage to do it.'

This was an important moment in the story of the England team on a broader calculus. At a delicate time, there was clear leadership from Hugh Morris, a former Glamorgan and England opening batsman who had been appointed to the new post of managing director of England cricket in 2007, and Reg Dickason, a former Queensland policeman and the ECB's chief security officer, itself a position that did not exist prior to 2006. Working closely with Sean Morris, the chief executive of the PCA, they made a thorough assessment of the risks and decided that, with the Indian government offering presidential levels of security, it was safe to return. Although some players, including Andrew Flintoff and Steve Harmison, initially had doubts about safety – and there were also concerns about whether it was appropriate to play an international cricket match in India so soon after more than 160 people had been killed, or to play such a game within a ring of military steel – in the end the entire squad agreed to go back. The matches in Chennai and Mohali passed off peacefully and, despite the disruption and lack of match practice, England gave a good account of themselves, dominating the first game in Chennai in stifling humidity until India turned the tables by chasing down 387 thanks to brilliant batting from Virender Sehwag and Sachin Tendulkar.

Rarely had a security crisis affecting the team been handled so impressively. Historically, England teams have tended to complete tours unless there was overwhelming reason not to, and when safety concerns arose decisions were usually taken by the tour manager in conjunction with Lord's and the local British embassies or consulates. In the early stages of the tour of India and Pakistan in 1972-73, the team received what the captain Tony Lewis described as a 'flood of threats' by mail from Black September, the Palestinian terrorist group which had murdered 11 Israeli athletes at the Olympic Games in Munich less than three months earlier. 'The first stated that Lewis, Knott and Amiss would be murdered,' Lewis noted in his diary, before adding: 'Donald Carr [the tour manager] and I told no one but asked that the tour should be rated Top Security and so we are to live the whole visit under heavy police and army security.'

Shortly before the team left India for the next leg of their tour, Carr received a telegram which read: 'Do not let Amiss play in Pakistan. B. S.' This led to Amiss being given his own personal bodyguard. 'I was introduced to him on our arrival in Pakistan and afterwards became accustomed to being shadowed everywhere,' Amiss stated.

'In the morning I would poke my head out of the bedroom door and he would be there, his gun at the ready. At night, in the hotel dining-room, he would sit unobtrusively at an adjacent table.' It did Amiss no harm: in Lahore, he scored his maiden Test century at the 22nd attempt and followed up with 158 in Hyderabad and 99 in Karachi.*

Perhaps the most questionable decision to continue a tour was in India in 1984–85 when inside the space of four weeks Mrs Indira Gandhi, the Indian prime minister, was assassinated and Percy Norris, the British deputy high commissioner who had hosted a party for the players only the night before, was shot dead in the street. Both incidents occurred within a few miles of where the players were staying. Apparently on the advice of the Foreign Office and having been assured of greater security, England nonetheless proceeded with the first Test match in Bombay (now Mumbai) a few days later and unsurprisingly were beaten, but remarkably they recovered to win the series, which passed off without further incident. At one of their crisis meetings, the players were confronted by the tour manager Tony Brown throwing down a pile of passports and, according to Graeme Fowler, telling the players 'we could all fuck off then'. When during the 1992–93 tour communal violence flared following the destruction of the Ayodhya temple, a more cautious approach was taken and England's ODI in Ahmedabad was cancelled.

Following the terrorist attacks of 11 September 2001, another England tour of India, due to begin two months later, came under review. Initially the ECB arranged for the players to be briefed by security experts, but after that their concerns were chiefly dealt with by officials from the PCA and the ECB whose knowledge of security issues was hardly comprehensive (according to the captain Nasser Hussain, 'the ECB kept on monitoring the situation and promised to keep us totally informed of any new developments or Foreign Office advice'). The players' trust in the board waned when Darren Gough asked Tim Lamb what contingency plans were in place to

---

* This was the start of a golden two-year run for Amiss, who in 1974 scored 1,379 Test runs, then an England record for a calendar year, including a nine-and-a-half-hour marathon of 262 not out to save a Test in Jamaica.

get the team home should an incident occur and failed to receive a satisfactory answer. The players were told they could make an individual choice over whether they joined the tour and if they decided to stay home it would not be held against them; Andrew Caddick and Robert Croft eventually chose not to go.

The absence of someone attached to the team who commanded the players' confidence and was qualified to dispense proper security advice was even more acutely felt two years later when England were due to play a World Cup match in Zimbabwe, where President Robert Mugabe's confiscation of white farms had created intense debate in Britain, as the former colonial power. England had previously toured Zimbabwe (formerly Rhodesia and a region that had provided Test cricketers to the South Africa team before independence in 1980) three times since playing their first internationals there in 1996-97, but Mugabe's programme had been accelerated and, amid growing violence, compensation to the dispossessed farmers had been scrapped.*

The prospect of an England team representing the country there at such a time met with widespread opposition and, as captain, Hussain in particular was sensitive to the moral dilemma. During a long tour of Australia that led straight into the World Cup, Hussain was kept informed of the mood at home by two injured players Andrew Flintoff and Ashley Giles. When Hussain and his squad reached South Africa, they sought advice from the ICC and the ECB, both of whom insisted that the match in Harare could only be cancelled on security grounds, not moral ones. Whether it was safe was a matter of opinion: in devoting the first 22 pages of his autobiography to the crisis, Hussain recounted how the head of ICC security thought it was safe for England to go but a director of Kroll, an American intelligence company recruited by the ICC, seemed less sure.

---

* Zimbabwe had been a constant thorn in England's side since their elevation to the ranks of the Test teams in 1992. They beat England at the 1992 World Cup and won five of the first six ODI meetings between the sides including all three games on England's 1996-97 tour when, according England head coach David Lloyd, 'There were references ... wherever we went, to the fact that our board had not supported their application for full Test status'.

The ECB started out convinced it was safe, only to change its mind at the 11th hour. England head coach Duncan Fletcher, who travelled on a Zimbabwe passport and had family living there, believed it would be safe. But the players were alarmed when Richard Bevan, their PCA representative, came forward with evidence of a letter from 'the Sons and Daughters of Zimbabwe' which threatened, 'Come to Zimbabwe and you will go back to Britain in wooden coffins!' The ECB had already discounted it and Fletcher also felt it was a hoax. But such was the confusion and mistrust that Hussain's relationship broke down altogether with Tim Lamb. Fletcher advised the players to go but left the final decision to them and they voted unanimously against going. England duly forfeited the points from the game and this ultimately cost them their place in the later stages of the tournament. 'It was without doubt the most traumatic time of my life,' Hussain wrote. Fletcher said: 'If there was one slight element of frustration in my mind it was that I doubted whether the players really knew what the situation was like in Zimbabwe.'

When England toured Zimbabwe 18 months later for a series of one-day internationals – under threat of a fine if they did not fulfil their commitments under the ICC's future tours programme – Michael Vaughan, Hussain's successor, avoided getting embroiled in the same kind of debate. 'Going to Zimbabwe was not a great thing to do in the eyes of many and ... struck a raw nerve in our country. However, you are getting into something of a moral maze when entering an issue such as this, and making complex ethical judgements is not what we [cricketers] are trained to do.'* The English cricket authorities would dearly have liked the government to instruct them not to play in Zimbabwe but the government's hand was stayed for

---

* The players were again given an individual choice about making the tour but agreed to stick together and go, though the selectors decided to rest three frontline players in Marcus Trescothick, Steve Harmison and Andrew Flintoff. When Harmison and Flintoff subsequently broke ranks by announcing that they would have refused to go had they been picked, the management was incensed. The tour briefly came into doubt when the Zimbabwe government banned a group of journalists accompanying the team from entering the country. When Vaughan's team announced that in that case they would not tour, the Zimbabwe authorities eventually reversed the decision.

fear of compensation claims. However, the ECB subsequently made it clear that they would not play Zimbabwe again in bilateral series until the regime in Zimbabwe changed. The only meeting between the sides came at the World Twenty20 in South Africa in 2007.

The ECB hired a private security firm when the team toured Pakistan in 2005 before Dickason was recruited on a full-time basis. Since then the players have generally been happy to follow his advice, which has extended to safety at the Indian Premier League and other domestic tournaments. However, against his guidance Eoin Morgan and Alex Hales declined to tour Bangladesh in 2016-17 following a recent bomb blast in a bakery in Dhaka. Those players who did go were protected by hundreds of commandos and police. But there was no repeat of the chaos that surrounded the 2003 World Cup.

## England's British Asians

Raman Subba Row was the first British-born Asian to play for England. His Indian father came to study law in Britain, where he met his future wife and chose to stay. Raman himself – like his father and the three Indian princes who played for England in earlier times – enjoyed a conventional English education, in his case attending Whitgift and Cambridge. Nasser Hussain was the first England cricketer of Asian origin who broke this privileged pattern; born in Madras (now Chennai), he moved to England with his parents as a youngster. Today, South Asians make up one-third of all recreational cricketers in England though still only 4 per cent of county professionals and 5 per cent of first-class coaching posts. In 2013, Sport England gave the ECB £20m with the aim of further harnessing the enthusiasm of the South Asian community, and in 2016 Lord Kamlesh Patel of Bradford became the first Asian to sit as an ECB director. In 2018, the ECB introduced bursaries for young Asians seen as future county and England players.

Three cricketers with Asian backgrounds (Moeen Ali, Samit Patel and Adil Rashid) were members of England's Test XI against Pakistan in Sharjah in 2015 and four (Moeen, Rashid, Haseeb Hameed and Zafar Ansari) played two Tests together in India in 2016.

## Born abroad, played university and county cricket in England

| Name | Birth | Parental origin | England career* |
| --- | --- | --- | --- |
| Ranjitsinhji | Sarodar 1872 | India | 1896-1902 |
| Duleepsinhji | Sarodar 1905 | India | 1929-31 |
| Nawab of Pataudi | Pataudi 1910 | India | 1932-34 |

## Born in England, parents having moved to Britain

| Name | Birth | Parental origin | England career* |
| --- | --- | --- | --- |
| Raman Subba Row | Streatham 1932 | Andra Pradesh/England | 1958-61 |
| Aftab Habib | Reading 1972 | India/Pakistan | 1999 |
| Kabir Ali | Birmingham 1980 | Rawalpindi | 2003-06 |
| Sajid Mahmood | Bolton 1981 | Rawalpindi | 2004-09 |
| Monty Panesar | Luton 1982 | Ludhiana | 2006-13 |
| Ravi Bopara | Newham 1985 | Punjab | 2007-15 |
| Samit Patel | Leicester 1984 | Kenyan Asian/Gujarat | 2008-15 |
| Adil Rashid | Bradford 1988 | Pakistan Kashmir | 2009-19 |
| Ajmal Shahzad | Huddersfield 1985 | Pakistan | 2010-11 |
| Moeen Ali | Birmingham 1987 | Pakistan Kashmir | 2014-19 |
| Zafar Ansari | Ascot 1991 | Lahore/England | 2015-16 |
| Haseeb Hameed | Bolton 1997 | Gujarat | 2016 |

---

* Tests, one–day internationals and Twenty20s

Born abroad, moved to England with family

| Name | Birth | Parental origin | England career* |
|------|-------|-----------------|-----------------|
| Nasser Hussain | Chennai 1968 | India/England | 1989-2004 |
| Min Patel | Mumbai 1970 | Ugandan Asian/Indian | 1996 |
| Vikram Solanki | Udaipur 1976 | India | 2000-07 |
| Usman Afzaal | Rawalpindi 1977 | Rawalpindi | 2001 |
| Owais Shah | Karachi 1978 | Pakistan | 2001-09 |
| Dmitri Mascarenhas | Perth 1977 | Sri Lanka | 2007-09 |
| Amjad Khan | Copenhagen 1980 | Pakistan | 2009 |

Every player played Tests except Solanki and Mascarenhas, who only appeared in ODIs and Twenty20s.

## England's Test Results in Asia

England have found Asia one of the toughest of all places to visit. They have never won against Pakistan at their second home of the United Arab Emirates and have won only twice in Pakistan itself. Their most productive venues are all in India: they have recorded three victories in Madras/Chennai, Bombay/Mumbai, and Delhi. They are unbeaten in seven Tests in Delhi but have not played there since 1984, partly because of concerns over air pollution. After visiting the 1992-93 tour as chairman of selectors, Ted Dexter questioned whether smog played a part in England's defeat in Kolkata and they have played only one Test there since.

---

\* Tests, one–day internationals and Twenty20s

| Region | Period | P | W | L | D |
|--------|--------|---|---|---|---|
| India | 1933-2016 | 60 | 13 | 19 | 28 |
| West Pakistan (v Pakistan) | 1961-2005 | 22 | 2 | 4 | 16 |
| *East Pakistan (v Pakistan) | 1962-69 | 2 | 0 | 0 | 2 |
| United Arab Emirates (v Pakistan) | 2012-15 | 6 | 0 | 5 | 1 |
| Sri Lanka | 1982-2018 | 16 | 7 | 5 | 4 |
| *Bangladesh | 2003-16 | 6 | 5 | 1 | 0 |
| Total | | 112 | 27 | 34 | 51 |

* England played five Tests in the city of Dacca (later Dhaka): two when it was part of East Pakistan and three after East Pakistan became Bangladesh.

# CHAPTER 33

# The Rise of Player Power
## Flintoff and Pietersen, the IPL and the Stanford fiasco

The Ashes win of 2005 had a far-reaching impact on the England team. The principal players – Kevin Pietersen and Andrew Flintoff and to a lesser extent Michael Vaughan – were turned into celebrities and commodities, capable of commanding their own weighty personal sponsorship deals rather than relying solely on team endorsements. Their earnings could be calculated in the millions. As captain, Vaughan was sensitive to the shift. 'I was worried about the effects of what we had been through,' he wrote. 'In all professional sports teams there is talk about money, but I quickly noticed more discussion than usual about the commercial deals among us . . . I suspected the team was going to be harder to manage, and one aspect of it was that individual sponsorships were now at such a level that players would focus on them rather than on what they had to do for the team's collective backers.'

Peter Moores, who took over as head coach in May 2007, was also struck by the conflict between the individual and collective: 'The Ashes had become so big. Rather than being cricketers, there was something more to players. The marketing guys wanted to get their hands on them, there was all sorts going on, and that needed to be looked at. Had we got English cricket at the top of the list or had it got lost in all these other things? As players, were we doing the things we should to be the best? Individual agendas are fine – they just can't go above the team.' Andrew Strauss reckoned the team was guilty of hubris.

Vaughan was different from Flintoff and Pietersen. He took the change of circumstances in his stride. He was also a natural leader. He was in Brearley's class as a man-manager – not least in the way he handled Flintoff and Pietersen – and a cool decision-maker under pressure. Flintoff and Pietersen wanted the England captaincy in part for the kudos it brought. Both were singularly ill-equipped to make a success of it.

As a public event, the Ashes was taken to another level, fuelled by hopes of a repeat of the drama of '05 (it never happened). What was lost by the removal of cricket from terrestrial television in the UK was made up for by the growth of 24-hour news networks and the advent of social-media platforms such as Twitter. The ECB even struck a deal with Cricket Australia in 2011 to insert an additional Ashes series into the traditional four-year, home-and-away cycle between 2013 and 2017: this served to decouple England's tour of Australia from World Cup winters, but also conveniently boosted the coffers of both boards.

All this placed the players under more pressure than ever, which inevitably took its toll. Marcus Trescothick, who had borne the brunt of Australia's new-ball attack in 2005, suffered panic attacks and depression in Pakistan and India the following winter, and when he arrived in Australia for the 2006–07 series he found sleep near-impossible. He was soon heading home. 'The pressure [of the Ashes] had certainly contributed to Marcus Trescothick having to go home, in effect ending his England career,' Strauss assessed. Something similar would happen to Jonathan Trott during the back-to-back Ashes series of 2013 and 2013–14, he too returning home in the early weeks, in his case after one Test at Brisbane, with what was termed a stress-related illness.

Trott had been struggling badly during the first series in England, both with the short-pitched ball and the strain of his role at No.3, reducing him to tears on several occasions. 'Just briefly, I considered driving my car into the Thames or into a tree,' he wrote in his autobiography. 'That way I could get out of the ordeal ... as soon as I put my tracksuit on, it was like a trigger. I was going back into that arena, that pressure cooker, that place of judgement.' Asked if the relentless schedule was the main factor, Trott replied: 'I'd say 50-50.' Pietersen echoed his sentiments: 'We were worn down [by the time of the Brisbane Test]. The schedule of the England team does that to you. It's relentless.'

During the 2006-07 series, there were various indicators that the Ashes contest was no longer an ordinary cricketing event. Steve Harmison bowled the first ball of the series straight to second slip, and after England lost the match by a huge margin they let slip a strong position in the next Test in Adelaide, where Australia were 65 for three, then 286 for five, in reply to England's 551 for six declared. On the last day, needing only to bat reasonably positively for two sessions to make the game safe, England froze so badly they added only 70 in 54 overs and suffered one of their most demoralising defeats. A team missing not only Trescothick but the injured Vaughan and Simon Jones went on to lose the series 5-0, their first whitewash by Australia in 86 years, and Flintoff, the stand-in captain, came under acute pressure.

'I was supposed to be this character who was unflappable,' Flintoff recalled. 'I was having a drink with my dad on Christmas Eve [two days before the fourth Test] and as we made our way home I started crying my eyes out. I told him I'd tried my best but that I couldn't do it any more, I couldn't keep playing. We talked and I dusted myself down and carried on. But I was never the same player again. I was captain of England and financially successful. Yet instead of walking out confidently to face Australia in one of the world's biggest sporting events, I didn't want to get out of bed, never mind face people.' When it had first become clear that Vaughan's knee injury would prevent him taking part, Flintoff had been desperate to take the job.

Such a heavy defeat, so soon after the euphoria of 2005, had complex and lasting consequences. Vaughan, having been away from the team for more than a year, returned for a triangular ODI series and, fearing coming across as schoolmasterly, he let the players enjoy themselves. 'It arguably resulted in too much partying among the team over a period of weeks,' he said. A crushing one-day defeat to Australia in Adelaide compelled Duncan Fletcher to issue an apology to fans; then Flintoff turned up to a practice session in Sydney so hungover that Fletcher had to give him a major dressing-down. Counter-intuitively, despite practising less and spending more time on the beach or in the bar, the team found themselves playing better and actually ended up winning the event.

However, this only confirmed them in their drinking culture, which carried over into the World Cup in the West Indies. After an opening defeat to New Zealand in St Lucia, the players and some backroom staff went out drinking and the *News of the World* reported that Flintoff had to be rescued from a pedalo in the early hours – something he denied, though he conceded 'water was involved'. Flintoff was dropped from the next match against Canada and stripped of the vice-captaincy. After failing to win a match against major opposition and being outplayed by South Africa in a game they had to win to stay in the tournament, the players were booed off the field in Bridgetown by their own supporters.

Almost immediately, Fletcher quit and early the next year David Graveney was replaced as chairman of selectors. The ECB commissioned a review into the Ashes defeat led by Ken Schofield, a Scotsman and former director of the PGA European tour; his panel contained six former England cricketers-turned-administrators or media pundits. Few of Schofield's 19 main recommendations were radical; most related to the management or development of current or future England captains, players and coaches. His suggestion that there should be less international cricket was ignored. The most significant upshot was the creation of a managing director of England cricket who would be accountable for the performance of the national teams and act as a bridge between the team and the board, taking the weight off the head coach in the event of disciplinary issues or diplomatic crises such as Zimbabwe which dogged Fletcher. Hugh Morris, the ECB's deputy chief executive and a member of Schofield's panel, was chosen from 50 applicants to fill a role that had a wider remit then than it would do later under Paul Downton (2013-15), Andrew Strauss (2015-18) and Ashley Giles (2019-), all of whom focused more narrowly on the affairs of the men's national teams.

The Schofield Report smacked of window-dressing. England were the No.2 ranked side in Tests and the reasons they lost the Ashes were obvious: Australia were a very strong side motivated by revenge, and England were without several of their best players. Fletcher was also exhausted after nearly eight years in charge and his relationship with the players had deteriorated. 'He got sick of defending us,' said Geraint Jones, who played all his 34 Tests as wicketkeeper under Fletcher. 'He got worn down by all the media pressure and that changed his outlook on people.' Vaughan concurred: 'By the end of Duncan's coaching reign quite a few of the players had negative things to say about some of the things he did . . . not speaking to them in the right fashion or not speaking to them at all.' He added: 'Fletch always found it difficult to relate to, and to coach, the guys he felt were never going to be a big part of his team. He tended to put all his energies into the men he thought were going to be big players for him and that was probably one of his weaknesses – communication with the lesser guys.'

Above all, Flintoff proved a poor stand-in captain. He was only chosen after much debate. With Flintoff himself handicapped by an ankle problem, Strauss had led the side at home to Pakistan but Fletcher cast the decisive vote in favour of Flintoff, who had captained well at short notice in India where England salvaged a 1-1 draw with a hard-earned victory in Mumbai. He also wanted the job and was the senior man: Strauss, after all, had broken into the Test team only two years earlier after developing slowly at Middlesex. But the Fletcher–Flintoff relationship was fragile, Strauss reckoning that by the time Flintoff was made captain they weren't speaking much. 'As the tour progressed, Fletcher and Flintoff became more and more distant from each other,' he stated.

The official tour report, quoted in Steve James's *The Plan*, highlighted the extent of Flintoff's failure. Beforehand, it had been agreed that the team must take on 'a challenging, aggressive persona rather than a non-confrontational, friendly one' of the sort which might invite sledging. 'The captain clearly did/does not believe in this approach,' it said. 'The end result appears to have been a degree of disillusion and frustration for those players who believed in and aimed to carry out the original policy.' The only players who displayed aggressive personas were Pietersen (though only at first) and Paul Collingwood. Fletcher outlined Flintoff's shortcomings, including his fondness for a drink, when he published his autobiography within months of leaving his job, sparking accusations that he – like Ray Illingworth before him – was betraying dressing-room secrets.

Morris identified Peter Moores as Fletcher's successor, a former wicketkeeper who had coached Sussex to their first championship in 2003 and run the national academy at Loughborough since 2005; he was, however, without international experience as player or coach and was appointed without the position being widely advertised. Moores felt empowered by the Schofield Report to shake things up and, as Vaughan would note, 'go in a fresh direction, with a brand new set of players'.

At the end of a winter working with Moores in Sri Lanka and New Zealand, Vaughan wrote in his diary: 'Peter has been a little bit disrespectful of the old regime ... He wants to change everything including personnel,' adding: 'Peter's constant talk about stats and averages makes me feel uncomfortable ... His style seems to be out of a book.' Under Moores, past performances were cast aside, something which Strauss, like Vaughan, admitted unnerved him; within a few months, Strauss was dropped for the Sri Lanka tour before returning to salvage his England career with a century in Napier. Some younger players flourished, though, including James Anderson and Stuart Broad, who were given their first extended runs in the Test side after being brought in at Wellington to replace Matthew Hoggard, who never played again, and Steve Harmison.

As captains, Vaughan and Collingwood had most difficulty with Moores's tireless positivity. Whereas Fletcher had seen himself as counsellor, Moores wanted authority for off-field affairs as well as a say in on-field matters, as though every captain would be as ineffectual as Flintoff. 'I get the feeling he would like a young captain that he can control and brainwash,' Vaughan noted in another diary entry. When Moores imposed a full training session on Collingwood's 50-over side after a tied match in Napier, it marked a split with many of the senior players who had been comfortable with Vaughan's relaxed and instinctive style of leadership under Fletcher. Strauss, who joined the New Zealand tour for the Tests, observed: 'What is required . . . is a coach who is able to calm players down, allowing them to play to their strengths and instilling confidence in their methods . . . energy conservation, both mental and physical, is very much the order of the day for the players not out there in the middle. Moore's philosophy . . . ran very much counter to that.'

Four months later, Vaughan privately decided, even while the series with South Africa was still alive, that he was going to quit the captaincy. When South Africa chased down 281 to win the next Test at Edgbaston, Vaughan publicly announced his resignation. By this time, Collingwood had independently concluded that he too would step down as leader of the white-ball teams.* When Moores heard of the double resignation, he described it as 'an exciting time'. Vaughan sat out the final Test but hoped to return as player; however, after failing to secure a place on the winter tour of the Caribbean or for the home series against West Indies leading into the 2009 Ashes, he retired altogether.

The famous Test team that went through 2004 unbeaten, winning 11 out of 13 games, and then reclaimed the Ashes in 2005 was a distant memory. The only regulars from that period who were left were Pietersen, Strauss and Ian Bell. Flintoff, increasingly hampered by fitness issues, missed many more games than he played and he, too, joined the exodus when he announced after the first Test against Australia that the series would be his last. With typical elan, he bowled an epic last-day spell to seal the first win over Australia

---

* There were various factors behind Collingwood's decision. He had been struggling for form and was haunted by a controversy six weeks earlier when he declined to withdraw a run-out appeal against New Zealand's Grant Elliott in an ODI at The Oval despite Elliott being knocked over in a collision with Ryan Sidebottom. Collingwood chose not to take the hint dropped by umpire Mark Benson, who asked, 'Do you want to uphold the appeal, bearing in mind the spirit of the game?' But Collingwood would return as Twenty20 captain the following year under a different regime.

at Lord's since 1934, and contributed a crucial direct-hit run-out of Ricky Ponting in the decisive victory at The Oval, where he bowed out alongside Harmison.

Pietersen's appointment as Test and ODI captain appeared a natural solution as it reunited the two roles, but in truth it represented an even bigger gamble than making Moores coach.* Putting Strauss in charge of the Test team and Pietersen at the helm of the white-ball sides would have been a sounder bet. To compound the concerns that already existed about Pietersen's priorities, a revolution in players' earning-power had been triggered by the launch of the Indian Premier League in April 2008, a franchised Twenty20 domestic tournament with almost bottomless pockets. Its ambition was to recruit the world's best players and, although it was agreed that No Objection Certificates would be needed from national boards, such were the sums on offer that any board withholding clearance risked alienating its players. Stars such as Pietersen and Flintoff were obvious targets and sure to attract huge deals; the problem was that the IPL season overlapped with the start of England's home internationals.

The ECB – reluctant in any case to accept that the cricket world should further fall into India's orbit, especially in respect of a format the ECB had created – decided to release players for only limited periods. This merely served to discourage franchises from signing England players and fuel resentment among those who might have secured lucrative deals had they been given the all-clear. No centrally contracted England players appeared in the first IPL season.

As a counter-strategy, the ECB tried to forge its own Twenty20 deals and in June 2008 announced an arrangement with Allen Stanford, a Texan businessman who had previously tried without success to persuade the Indian, Australian and South African boards,

---

* Vaughan's resignation was not best timed as far as the succession was concerned. He publicly quit on Sunday 3 August 2008 and England's next Test began four days later. Pietersen met Peter Moores that day and was appointed within 24 hours. As was the case when Moores was picked as coach, alternatives were not broadly canvassed. Subsequent changes of captain and coach have followed more diligent procedures, with the ECB having succession plans in place.

as well as the ICC, to put up national sides against his own Stanford All Stars, which was essentially a West Indies XI but carrying his name. The failure of these negotiations should have been a warning. Chief executive David Collier represented the ECB in discussions with Stanford which resulted in a five-year deal of staggering proportions: the England team would play an annual winners-take-all match against a Stanford XI worth $1m per man as well as a quadrangular Twenty20 event in England also involving West Indies, Sri Lanka and New Zealand.

The ECB hosted a launch party at Lord's which involved Stanford landing a helicopter on the Nursery ground and a Perspex crate displaying what was purported to be $20m. Ian Botham was among the 'legends' recruited to Stanford's cause. The England players were naturally excited at the prospect of earning life-changing sums but there were concerns that the IPL and Stanford might encourage them to turn their backs on Test cricket. 'Test and four-day cricket has become the least important game to the players,' Vaughan noted. At Collier's prompting, Vaughan and Collingwood, as Test and ODI captains at the time, along with the PCA, gave a cautious endorsement of the deal, although the players' lawyers Harbottle & Lewis issued a letter outlining the England team's reservations.

There were also concerns, more widely expressed, about the moral probity of the England team being put out for hire: the purpose of an international team was to represent the nation in international fixtures, not to be bought for exhibition matches. 'To call it cricket at all will be difficult,' Steve James wrote. '[It] will be the night cricket is turned into reality TV.' The ECB later conceded that the team that played the All Stars in the first (and what proved to be only) winners-take-all match in Antigua in November 2008 should have done so under another name such as a Kevin Pietersen XI. As the match approached, the England camp also faced awkward decisions about how to divide up any winnings; it was eventually agreed most of the money would go to the 11 who took the field, with a small amount shared among non-playing squad members and coaching staff. Unease about the nature of the venture duly transmitted itself to the performance: England were all out for 99 and lost by ten wickets.

The ECB had hoped the Stanford plan would satisfy the players' urge to go to the IPL, but within days of the deal being unveiled Pietersen publicly advocated them still taking advantage of the IPL, precisely why there was concern at his elevation to the England captaincy two months later. 'KP would have to convince the players that he genuinely cared for the team and his team-mates, and that he wasn't doing the job purely for his own advancement,' Strauss assessed. 'Although we had all appreciated his precocious talents and his ability to turn a match on its head, there were still question marks about his commitment to the team ... He was very much the superstar, and superstars often like to separate themselves from the mere mortals around them.' Michael Atherton, by now a journalist and commentator, predicted that Pietersen's captaincy would end in tears.

It crashed faster than anyone could have anticipated. The problem was that Pietersen, like Vaughan and Collingwood, had long had issues with the way Peter Moores operated. Even a preliminary meeting between the two men when Pietersen became captain could not improve matters. 'It was already obvious to everybody that he [Pietersen] and Peter Moores did not get on at all,' Strauss observed. 'They were barely on speaking terms ... if it was going to work out some hasty patching-up of their relationship was required.' But by the time of the Test matches in India – rearranged after the Mumbai attacks in late 2008 – things were worse than ever, Strauss noting that the issues between them had become an open topic of discussion among team and support staff. (Pietersen would describe Moores in his 2014 autobiography as someone who 'was tapping on our heads like a woodpecker all day, every day', and 'like a human triple espresso – so intense'). Before the first Test, Pietersen told Giles Clarke, the chairman of the board, that Moores had to be removed (he favoured appointing Graham Ford, a long-standing ally from South Africa, in his place). Shortly after the tour, while holidaying in South Africa over the Christmas and New Year period, Pietersen sent an email to the board to reiterate that he could not lead the team to West Indies if Moores stayed in post.

A date was set for Pietersen to meet Hugh Morris and David

Collier on his return but, before that could happen, word leaked to the media that Pietersen wanted Moores removed, making it impossible to hammer out a resolution behind closed doors.* With the rift public, the ECB could fix it by backing neither Pietersen, which would be seen as a victory for player power, nor Moores, which would be to ignore the discontent he had aroused among the wider squad. (Vaughan had already spoken to Morris at the end of the New Zealand tour about his unease over Moores.) The only practical solution was to sack both men, and this was what was agreed at an executive meeting of the board on 6 January.

Pietersen had reason to feel aggrieved. He had merely expressed views about Moores that he knew others shared. His mistake was to be so strident in his demands.

He soon had cause for further disenchantment when he was bought in the auction for the IPL's second season in a deal that would have earned him $1.55m had he been allowed to play a full season but, because of the ECB's restrictions, he was able to earn only about half that amount (though this was of course still a staggeringly lucrative arrangement considering the time involved). Flintoff was bought for the same price under the same terms. The auction took place while England were involved in the first Test of their series in West Indies, with news of the deals coming through shortly before play on the third day in Jamaica. Whether or not the outcome of the auction proved a distraction is unclear, but little more than 24 hours later England capitulated for 51, the third-lowest total in their history, to lose the match by an innings.

Ten days later, while England were on his cricketing base of Antigua, Allen Stanford was exposed as a fraud and his financial empire collapsed, seriously discrediting the ECB's Twenty20 strategy (a point highlighted by the ECB expunging all reference to him in its annual report for 2008).† Collier's future was discussed by the ECB board but he survived, as did Clarke, who had signed

---

* The source of the leak was much speculated upon, but suspicions that it came via a party with an interest in Pietersen's demands being made public were inaccurate.
† Three years later, Stanford was found guilty of multiple charges of fraud and jailed for life.

off on the deal; nonetheless, the scandal stuck to their names. In defence of the ECB's reluctance to involve itself in the IPL, both Pietersen and Flintoff developed injury problems linked to their debut seasons at the tournament. Pietersen aggravated an Achilles tendon problem and subsequently broke down two Tests into the Ashes series, while Flintoff was badly hampered by a damaged knee which necessitated surgery, ruling him out of two home Tests against West Indies and the World Twenty20 and contributing to his early retirement from Tests.

Flintoff turned down the ECB's offer of an incremental contract to cover white-ball matches, saying he wanted to go freelance, but injuries continued to get the better of him, and his plans didn't work out. He never played for England again in any format. With the England management striving to cultivate a new sense of togetherness and higher standards of fitness, his departure was not widely mourned within the group. Although Pietersen attracted greater controversy, there were those who felt Flintoff was the more difficult figure in a dressing-room environment and that the celebrity that came his way after 2005 changed him.

Pietersen played for England for another five years but his relationship with the ECB never fully recovered from the manner of his removal as captain and his performances were not as consistently good, though he played a number of breathtakingly brilliant innings.* By 2012, when he was signed by Delhi Daredevils in an IPL deal that would have been worth £1.3m if he had played the whole season, the board's continued insistence on releasing him for only three of the eight weeks of the tournament created an incendiary mood. Shortly after returning from the IPL, Pietersen told the ECB that he was retiring from ODI cricket. He had hinted at doing this two years earlier, and the previous year he had been left out of a home ODI series against India. He wanted to continue playing Twenty20s but contractually this was not permitted; the board did

---

* After the loss of the captaincy, Pietersen averaged 44.5 in Tests, whereas previously he had averaged 50.5; in ODIs, in which he appeared far less often, he averaged 30.3 rather than 48.4.

not want England players quitting 50-overs cricket to cash in on Twenty20 riches, so he was obliged to withdraw from all international white-ball cricket. Pietersen then indicated that he might be willing to rescind his decision in return for missing two home Tests against New Zealand to play more of the IPL in 2013, an idea given predictably short shrift.

Matters came to a head during a Test against South Africa at Headingley. 'On the practice days he seemed completely withdrawn, as though he was consciously distancing himself from the rest of the team, and on the first day of the game itself . . . he seemed determined to let everyone in the ground know just how unhappy he was,' Strauss wrote in his autobiography published a few months later. 'As captain, I could not let it go and I called him into a back room to make it clear that his behaviour was unacceptable. I was completely shocked by his lack of contrition and his apparent hostility . . . It was almost as if he was trying to engineer an excuse to turn his back on the team.'

Two days later, Pietersen played an innings of 149 off 214 balls that was astonishing in its brutality, but he continued to behave bizarrely and in a press conference after the game suggested that the next Test, the final one of the summer, could be his last. 'It's tough being me in this dressing-room,' he said. 'It's tough playing for England.' Perhaps sensing he was about to be dropped for his disruptive behaviour, Pietersen said he was willing to recommit to England after all, and at a meeting with Strauss finally seemed contrite about what had happened. However, media reports that Pietersen had sent text messages to South Africa players, the content of which was unclear but which were at least critical of Strauss and possibly even contained information on how to get him out – claims which Pietersen did not categorically refute or apologise for at first – led to him being dropped after all.

Pietersen was soon restored to the side but, as was the case after his removal as captain, relations with the team management and board never fully recovered. (His relationship with Andy Flower, the new head coach, had not been helped by him proposing, when he first demanded Moores's removal as coach, that Flower and the rest of the backroom staff go as well.)* He admitted to sending 'provocative' texts but denied they included details on how to get Strauss out; Strauss himself later accepted this denial. In his second Test match back, Pietersen played another astonishing innings of 186 off 233 balls on a turning pitch in Mumbai, which played a big part in England taking the series 2-1 after going one down. But after that Pietersen played only 12 more Tests and nine more ODIs during a period in which he was increasingly troubled by a chronic knee problem, scoring only one more hundred before being permanently axed across all three formats following the 5-0 defeat to Australia in 2013-14.

Paul Downton – who had spent most of his time working in the City since playing the last of his 30 Tests as a wicketkeeper in 1988, before succeeding Hugh Morris as managing director – took the decision to excommunicate Pietersen after consulting Flower and Alastair Cook, the captain, among others. 'I and other people wanted people who were just purely focused on playing cricket for England,' he said. 'The accusations made were that Kevin wasn't 100 per cent focused on playing for England.' Downton conceded that Pietersen was not alone: an ageing group of players was 'maybe a little bit distracted in terms of commercial opportunities'. Graeme Swann, too, would later echo some of Pietersen's criticisms of what he felt was Cook's clichéd dressing-room leadership. But Pietersen alone paid the price. After retiring from international cricket in 2018, Cook clarified that he personally had not advocated Pietersen's permanent removal from the England teams, but favoured dropping him only for a short period. Downton's justification had been flimsier than it sounded.

The decision to remove a leading England player from all future

---

* A contributory factor in Pietersen's rehabilitation was the sense that other players in the dressing-room had not behaved well towards him, supporting a spoof Twitter account called @KPGenius. Several senior players were warned about their conduct, and part of Pietersen's reintegration into the side involved face-to-face meetings with them. Strauss admitted that he and Flower ought to have asked the players to stop following the Twitter account, set up by a friend of some Nottinghamshire players, but they had thought it innocuous. Pietersen himself had been guilty of using Twitter in an inadvisable manner and been fined as a result: in 2010 he was critical of the decision to leave him out of two England Twenty20s in order to play a championship match, and in 2012 he criticised the TV commentary of former England batsman Nick Knight.

selection on grounds other than performance was without precedent and caused a storm of protest which destabilised both the team and Cook's captaincy. Among those who spoke out in support of Pietersen was Flintoff. They were never particularly close – two big egos sharing the same dressing-room – but they had much in common. When the England team held a clear-the-air meeting following the 51 all out in Jamaica, Flintoff spoke in defence of Pietersen when he was challenged about his own celebrity lifestyle. After Pietersen's sacking as a player, Flintoff said: 'If England win he gets applauded ... If we lose, it's as if it's his fault ... Lose 5–0 in Australia and it falls on someone to be the scapegoat. In 2006–07 it was me ... Sometimes you need help as a player, an arm around you, or someone to back you. Kevin deserved that. It wasn't just him out there.'

Flintoff and Pietersen were two of the great England players of their generation, but by turning themselves into commodities they became detached from the heart of the team. Even in retirement they seemed estranged. Though there would not be a resolution until 2015, their cases raised issues about whether the ECB could or should accommodate the wishes of its top players to take part in the big Twenty20 leagues. It seemed that central contracts did not necessarily mean the board had full control of its players.

## England's Cricket Managers and Head Coaches

England have had cricket managers and head coaches since Micky Stewart was the first appointed to such a role in 1986, with Peter Moores serving two terms. In December 2012, the head coach duties were divided between Andy Flower (Tests) and Ashley Giles (ODIs and Twenty20s). This arrangement lasted until April 2014, when they were reunified under Moores. There have been two brief periods of caretakers during home seasons: in 1999, David Graveney oversaw four Test matches and in 2015 Paul Farbrace was in charge for two Tests, five ODIs and one Twenty20. Farbrace was assistant coach both to Moores during his second term and then until March 2019 to Trevor Bayliss; he was the first to fill such a role.

| Manager/coach | Reign | Age | Test/ODI/T20 | | | Major wins/highlights* |
|---|---|---|---|---|---|---|
| Micky Stewart | 1986-92 | 54-59 | 58 | 91 | – | Ashes 1986-87<br>CWC finals 1987 1992<br>NZ 1991-92 |
| Keith Fletcher | 1992-95 | 48-50 | 26 | 23 | – | |
| Ray Illingworth | 1995-96 | 62-64 | 11 | 16 | – | |
| David Lloyd | 1996-99 | 49-52 | 34 | 54 | – | NZ 1996-97 SA 1998 |
| Duncan Fletcher | 1999-07 | 51-58 | 96 | 166 | 4 | WI 2000 2003-04 2004<br>Pak/SL 2000-01<br>CT final 2004<br>SA 2004-05 Ashes 2005<br>Pak 2006 |
| Peter Moores | 2007-08 | 44-46 | 22 | 36 | 10 | WI 2007 |
| Andy Flower | 2009-14 | 40-45 | 66 | 84 | 39 | Ashes 2009 2010-11 2013<br>WT20 winners 2010<br>Pak 2010<br>Ind 2011 2012-13 |
| Ashley Giles | 2012-14 | 39-41 | – | 29 | 19 | CT final 2013 |
| Peter Moores | 2014-15 | 51-52 | 10 | 29 | 2 | Ind 2014 |
| Trevor Bayliss | 2015-19 | 52-56 | 53 | 76 | 33 | Ashes 2015<br>SA 2015-16 2017<br>WT20 final 2016<br>Ind 2018<br>SL 2018-19 |

CWC = ICC World Cup
CT = ICC Champions Trophy
WT20 = ICC World Twenty20

*Figures correct to 1 May 2019*

---

\* Major Test series defined as ones of four or more matches at home and three matches away.

# CHAPTER 34

# The World's Best-Equipped Team

## Andy Flower, winning in Australia and 'bowling dry'

England had gone through almost three years of captains and coaches not seeing eye to eye, or worse. These difficult times played a large part in shaping the approach and ultimately the success of the partnership that followed between Andrew Strauss and Andy Flower. Both men had witnessed the turmoil at close quarters, Strauss as a member of the team and Flower as an assistant coach to Moores from the autumn of 2007. Given all that had happened, the rise of the England side from the point when this pair came together in January 2009 was astonishing. Over the next two and a half years, England won eight Test series out of nine and drew the other one. The wins included Ashes series home and away, the latter being England's only Ashes series win in Australia of the last 30 years. England also won the World Twenty20 in 2010, their first major white-ball trophy, with Flower the coach and Paul Collingwood, persuaded back into a leadership role, as captain. England rose from

No.5 to No.1 in Tests by August 2011 and from No.6 to No.1 in ODIs by August 2012.*

Flower, born in Cape Town to southern African parents, was initially appointed as caretaker for the West Indies tour because there was no time for the ECB to make a considered choice, which after the way Moores's hasty promotion turned out seemed like an all the more necessary step. But Flower quickly demonstrated he had the skills required to restore order. After the tour was over, he was among four people interviewed for the full-time job and was the stand-out candidate. Apart from a distinguished playing career for Zimbabwe, Flower could point to 20 years of coaching, including a spell at the ECB's national academy, which was where Moores got to know him. Flower's gifts were varied but his real talent was in man-management, which was what was needed after all the recent turbulence. He was willing to challenge, and occasionally drop, big-name players and strong characters. 'He is conspicuously in charge,' wrote Steve James in 2012. Unlike some of his predecessors, Flower was capable of speaking with clarity and authority to players and press.

Flower and Strauss grasped the need to create stability and harmony within the playing group, and above all a sense of responsibility. 'The main issue with the regime of Peter Moores was that the management and support staff were just too hands-on ... the players did not have enough control in the process,' Strauss wrote. 'Too often it felt like a teacher/pupil relationship ... If the players were never allowed to make decisions off the pitch, why should anyone expect them to make good decisions on the pitch?' As it happened, out of a disastrous first Test in which England were routed for 51 in Jamaica, an opportunity immediately presented itself for a frank discussion about what was going wrong. A recurring theme was players not buying into a team ethos. Reflecting on how the team managed to rise to such

---

* The ICC formally introduced Test rankings in 2003 and ODI rankings in 2002 using a system created by David Kendix, an English actuary; the ICC has also applied the system retrospectively, starting with Tests in 1952 and ODIs in 1981. England have led the Test rankings for five spells (Jun 1955-Feb 1958, Aug-Dec 1958, Jan 1970-Jan 1973, Feb 1979-Aug 1980, and Aug 2011-Aug 2012) and ODI rankings seven times for a total of 36 months before they went top again in May 2018.

great heights by 2011, Strauss added: 'The players, who could easily have found themselves being sidetracked by self-interest and personal agendas, did a tremendous job buying into the idea that the team had to come first.' Various devices were found to reinforce the message, including visits to war cemeteries in Flanders, when a stone cricket ball was laid at the grave of Colin Blythe, and a bonding trip to Germany.

In fact, the recent shared traumas brought the players closer together and made them more resilient in adversity. Facing a fight for survival at Cardiff in the Ashes opener of 2009, the lower order managed to hold out on the final afternoon despite England being five down at lunch, Paul Collingwood batting 82.5 overs for 74 and the last-wicket pair of James Anderson and Monty Panesar surviving the last 69 balls. Similarly, later in the series, the team bounced back from a heavy defeat at Leeds to come out on top in a must-win game at The Oval. England's unity trumped Australia's superior individual performances. Further Cardiff-style escapes followed in South Africa the following winter, when the tenth-wicket pair twice held on to secure draws: Collingwood and Graham Onions for 19 balls in Centurion and Graeme Swann and Onions for 17 balls in Cape Town.

The greatest escape of all during Strauss's time was England batting through all of the fourth day and most of the fifth to save a Test in Brisbane, in the process losing only one wicket, that of Strauss himself for 110. After that, the team took around with them a large, blown-up photograph of the Gabba scoreboard showing 517 for one, Cook 235 not out, Trott 135 not out, and gave it pride of place in the dressing-room. Later, after Cook became captain, another great escape followed in Auckland in 2013, when they began the last day four wickets down in the fourth innings. On that occasion, the final pair of Matt Prior, who was at the crease for 57.1 overs, and Panesar negotiated 19 balls together.

A further test of team unity came with the spot-fixing scandal involving Pakistan in England in 2010. News that Salman Butt, the captain, and two of his fast bowlers Mohammad Amir and Mohammad Asif had deliberately arranged to bowl no-balls in exchange for money broke on the third evening at Lord's. With England already close to victory, the game was quickly concluded the next morning, in front of 20,000 in a surreal atmosphere, but the teams (minus the three suspects) then played out five ODIs in a mood of tension and mistrust. Following the third game at The Oval, Ijaz Butt, the Pakistan board chairman, in an absurd attempt to deflect attention from his own crisis, suggested England's batting collapse indicated they had thrown the match. Upset that their integrity had been brought into question, the England players held a crisis meeting at their London hotel and only agreed to play the remaining fixtures in the series after concluding that a boycott would merely turn them into the news story; instead, they put out a statement expressing 'surprise, dismay and outrage' at Butt's comments. Strauss described the team sticking together at such a stressful time as 'one of the defining moments of my captaincy'.*

The new management team may have inherited a messy situation, but the raw materials at their disposal were exceptionally good. Bell, Collingwood, Cook, Pietersen and Strauss were all experienced players by 2007, and to his credit Moores had subsequently brought on not only Anderson and Broad but Prior and Swann too. All nine of these players went on the tour of West Indies in a squad picked before Strauss and Flower took over, and although Anderson and Swann did not start the series they were back in the side for good by the end. Bell was dropped after the fiasco in Jamaica but would soon return. This group would be fundamental to the success that followed: the only one of them to leave the scene before Strauss himself did so at the end of the 2012 season was Collingwood, who played his last games for England in all formats in early 2011.

The first significant addition to the Test team came when Jonathan Trott marked his debut at The Oval in 2009 with a match-shaping, Ashes-winning century, but even he had already played for England before in Twenty20s. That said, only one of these players stood in the top ten of the ICC's Test rankings at the point the regime changed; they might turn out to be champions, but worked still needed to be done to get them to that position. Pietersen's later claim that Flower never developed anyone on his watch was wide of the mark.

---

* Not that the fourth ODI at Lord's, the day after the crisis meeting, passed off without incident. Before play, Jonathan Trott was involved in an altercation with Wahab Riaz in the nets in which Trott hit Riaz with his pad, an incident for which Trott was disciplined.

The batting was to prove particularly powerful. Having been axed in the Caribbean, Bell was told to get hardier and was dispatched for gruelling training sessions with Reg Dickason, the team's security manager. 'It wasn't technically that I was struggling,' Bell recalled. 'It was about how to make myself tougher and physically better. Reg put me in a tough place.' Bell found that the fitter he became, the better he concentrated. In the two years from 2009 to 2011, Bell averaged 68.50 in Tests, more than any other England batsman during that period. Only Cook, with 12, scored more hundreds than Bell's eight. Trott was next with six. Cook for many years rarely had trouble concentrating, especially while he had Strauss for an opening partner. He was immensely fit from the time he joined the team as an emergency replacement in India in early 2006, scoring 60 and 104 not out in his first match, and had the added advantage that he did not sweat, so batting for long periods in heat and humidity was less of an inconvenience than it was for most players.

For about four years from 2009 to 2013, Trott almost matched Cook for application, and in the process solved the problematic No.3 position as the tough guy who calmly saw off the new ball, soaking up pressure for the team. Trott would score more runs there than any England batsman except Wally Hammond. The middle order was also versatile with Pietersen and Prior to counter-attack and Collingwood to provide ballast. Much of the credit for the improvement was due to Graham Gooch, who joined as batting coach for the tour of Australia in 2010-11 and stayed three years; where Duncan Fletcher had taught batting technique, Gooch taught how to construct big innings. During the run to No.1, England batsmen between them made 18 scores of 150 plus, seven of which were double-centuries, while the team amassed 14 totals of 500 or more, including an all-time high in Australia of 644 and their highest in a time-limit Test of 710 for seven declared against India.

The seam attack also touched exceptional heights. Anderson and Broad were the dominant figures but they were well supported by Tim Bresnan, Graham Onions, Steven Finn and Chris Tremlett. Anderson was first picked by England at the age of 20 and played 16 Tests under Duncan Fletcher, but more than most had lived in Flintoff's shadow and thrived as more responsibility came his way; the breakthrough moment was when he and Broad, his junior by four years and with one Test cap to his name, were jointly recalled in New Zealand in 2008. Anderson and Broad would play more than 100 Tests together and take more Test wickets as a pair than any fast-bowling combination in history.

Anderson, the shorter built of the two, could swing the ball late to devastating effect. Broad was tall and sought to exploit the bounce he generated, though at his peak he also shaped the ball away from the right-hander. Anderson was the more reliable, Broad on his day the more devastating. Broad went through occasional periods where he lost his best length but he had a knack of rediscovering form when the selectors' axe was hovering. With about one-third of all specialist batsmen in the modern game left-handers, they both had a bigger challenge than many of their predecessors in constantly adjusting their lines of attack and became expert at the novel tactic of coming round the wicket to them. Their skill with the Dukes ball was central to England maintaining an outstanding record at home, where they were beaten in only four series out of 34 between 2002 and 2018. It was harder for Anderson and Broad overseas where the Dukes ball was not used (except in West Indies) and there was usually less movement through the air and off the pitch, but with the help of fast-bowling coaches Ottis Gibson and David Saker they learned how to cope; Anderson especially turned himself into a master craftsman in all conditions. The best of the support seamers was Bresnan, another skilful operator.

The player who gave Strauss's bowling attack its crucial balance, though, was Graeme Swann, an off-spinner who had first toured at the age of 20 before he was ready, but who after several years of county cricket came back equipped with fearlessness, strategic nous and away-drift to the right-handers.* What marked him out from most modern English off-spinners was that he spun the ball sharply, would bowl an attacking line outside off stump, but could also

---

* Swann, who did not impress Duncan Fletcher on the one tour he made under him to South Africa in 1999-2000, could be categorised in his younger days as among the non-conformists of whom the England management was wary as it strove to impose discipline. Another was Samit Patel, a talented all-rounder who regularly failed to meet the basic levels of fitness asked of him; he played only six Tests.

conduct holding operations in the first innings of Tests when the pitch was less in his favour.

Swann benefited from two external factors. One was the sheer number of left-handers available to bowl at in international cricket, whose outside edges came under threat from the off-spinner. Few English off-spinners had ever enjoyed such luxury. (A rare instance arose in the Caribbean in 1973-74 when Tony Greig turned from his usual medium-pacers to genuine off-breaks after the first Test: he took 24 wickets in four Tests, including 13 in the final match in Trinidad; 11 of them were left-handers). Swann took four wickets in each innings when Australia were beaten at The Oval in 2009, and the following winter took five-wicket hauls in winning causes in Durban and Chittagong, a feat he would accomplish eight more times in his career. Swann generally preferred to operate alone and when he was paired with a second spinner it rarely bore fruit; a notable exception came at Mumbai in 2012 when he and Panesar took 19 wickets between them on a pitch that turned from the first day.

The other thing that helped Swann, and spin bowlers across the board, was the introduction by degrees from early 2009 of the Decision Review System, which drew on TV replays and technological aids to assist teams in making a set number of unsuccessful challenges to umpiring decisions. DRS began only weeks after Swann made his Test debut in Chennai, where he took the wickets of Gautam Gambhir and Rahul Dravid in his first over. The system educated umpires that, in respect of lbw appeals, more balls than had been generally supposed would have gone on to hit the stumps. This led to more lbws being given and to batsmen playing spin differently: not daring to risk their pads as a second line of defence, they thrust their bats out further, which brought edges into play. Swann took 70 wickets with lbws, only one fewer than the three most successful England off-spinners before him – Jim Laker, Fred Titmus and John Emburey – combined.*

---

* Monty Panesar, a left-arm spinner, also took a relatively high proportion of his Test wickets with lbws (42 out of 167). He played most of his 50 Tests before DRS was introduced but even during his early career TV companies were using various technological gizmos, including Hawk-Eye, that would underpin DRS; this may have persuaded umpires to give more decisions in the bowlers' favour.

Swann's ability to provide control over long periods meant Strauss's England were able to broach little-chartered territory by fielding a four-man attack, a strategy that was fundamental to their success. Historically England had rarely played only four frontline bowlers, especially in hotter climes, chiefly because it needed not only a world-class spinner but also levels of fitness among the bowling group that had rarely if ever been achieved in the past. Nor had they won a five-Test series in Australia with only four bowlers before they did so in 2010-11 (although in 1911-12 they made little use of a fifth bowler in the four matches they won).

When they were in possession of a genuine all-rounder there was no need to select only four bowlers; the problem occurred when there was not such a player available and a balance had to be struck between having enough batsmen and bowlers. There were recurring debates between captains such as Vaughan and Strauss who favoured five bowlers, and generally got their way, and coaches such as Moores and Flower who wanted only four. When Flintoff was unavailable for the Leeds Test of 2009, England went with five bowlers but this left their batting weak and they were bowled out on the first day for 102, condemning them to a heavy defeat.

Once Flintoff retired, rather than risk a repeat, England picked six batsmen and four bowlers (plus wicketkeeper) in all of their next 24 Tests except for one in Bangladesh where they wanted an additional spinner. The power vested in the four-man unit, dominated by the established trio of Anderson, Broad and Swann, appeared to breed arrogance, because it acquired a reputation as a confrontational group. 'Sometimes as a team they might have appeared fractured on the field, because they could shout and bawl at each other when mistakes were made,' Steve James wrote. 'It was by far the most unattractive aspect of the side that went to number one.' Kevin Pietersen visited this issue in his score-settling autobiography published in October 2014. Pietersen claimed that during both Strauss and Cook's captaincies the bowlers and wicketkeeper Matt Prior held undue sway in the dressing-room and fielders who made mistakes were forced to apologise in front of the team (a charge confirmed by others). 'Certainly at some stages frustrations probably boiled over, but that was only because people were desperate to succeed,' Cook conceded.

Strauss and Flower also benefited from a bigger backroom staff, something fought for by Fletcher and built on under Moores, who by 2008 had supplemented the fast-bowling coach with a batting coach and fielding coach, a post that had been advocated by the Schofield Report. By 2010-11, a spin-bowling coach was also working with the team. Fielding coach Richard Halsall, who worked with the team from 2008 to 2011, built a strong partnership with Huw Bevan, who was promoted from Loughborough in 2009 to work as England's strength-and-conditioning coach. The impact of their work could be seen in the athleticism in the field during the World Twenty20 win in 2010 and the Ashes win in Australia, and in Prior's general agility and awareness around the stumps.

Psychologists Steve Bull and Mark Bawden, who came on board in 2010, also took on more prominent roles, helping the team prepare for major events such as the Ashes, which they compared to an Olympic Games in terms of the work required ahead of the event. Bawden also worked directly with individuals such as Cook, who credited him with turning around his form in 2010, and Broad, to whom he gave mental rituals to help him stay in control during pressure-cooker moments. Eventually, the backroom staff outgrew the playing staff. By 2011, the ECB was spending £31.1m on all its England teams and development squads. In 2017 the figure was £30.4m.

The most far-reaching change was in respect of data analysis. England teams had drawn on rudimentary methods of studying technique and strategy since at least the days of Bill Ferguson and his scoring charts in the 1920s. By the 1990s, the better-resourced international teams were investing in video analysts, and David Lloyd was an enthusiastic supporter. When England toured Australia in 1998-99, the ECB's Nick Slade sat up through the night in London collating video packages which were couriered to the batting and bowling groups for study before the next Test. Later, Malcolm Ashton, originally recruited as tour scorer by Ray Illingworth, was reassigned under Duncan Fletcher to video duties which involved making 20-minute presentations to the team before play (thus ending a long tradition of scorers accompanying England on tour).

Gradually the responsibility for 'feedback analysis' passed to someone equipped with technical skills who could offer the team additional support on tour; Tim Boon and Mark Garaway, who oversaw analysis from 2004 to 2009, both had coaching credentials. Fletcher reckoned England led the field in analysis by the time of the 2005 Ashes when Boon put together footage of how players were dismissed and what happened in the lead-up to those dismissals. When Boon was seconded to the World XI in Australia a few months later, Fletcher was nervous that others might learn of England's methods. Even so, by later standards the science remained basic and both Fletcher, with a superb eye for spotting technical glitches in a player's method, and Vaughan, who as captain trusted gut instinct, remained children of the pre-data period.

Flower's appointment of Nathan Leamon in the summer of 2009 took things to another level. The analysis department at Loughborough had expanded with Moores's encouragement and Flower was in tune with such developments; at his interview for head coach, Flower had advocated more American-style statistical analysis. Technology was already playing its part in enhanced training methods through the Hawk-Eye ball-tracking system, ProBatter (a virtual-reality machine which simulated facing different bowlers), and TrackMan (which calculated the revolutions imparted on the ball by spinners). Leamon was a former Cambridge mathematician and director of coaching at Eton, and in his new role he began to challenge received wisdom on all manner of cricketing issues such as selection, the toss, the balance of the team, declarations and analysis of opposing sides. His database took in every ball bowled in Tests since the mid-2000s and drew heavily on information provided by Hawk-Eye; from these sources he wrote a computer program that enabled him to 'war game' forthcoming Test matches across a range of differing scenarios, thereby providing Flower and Strauss with an estimation of their chances of success should they pursue a particular course.

He used Hawk-Eye data to draw pitchmaps for opposing batsmen, breaking down the target area into 20 blocks of 100cm x 15cm, and telling the bowlers which were the best blocks to aim at for particular opponents. 'We feed into the simulator information about pitches and the 22 players who might play, and it plays the game a number of times and tells us likely outcomes,' he explained. 'It helps us in strategy and selection. I've back-checked the program against more than 300 actual Tests and it is accurate to within four or five per cent.' In the World Twenty20 final in 2016, the idea of opening the bowling with Joe Root's part-time off-spin against Chris Gayle originated with Leamon; Root dismissed Gayle and Johnson Charles with his first three balls. Early in his time with England, Leamon also made a presentation to the team about what they needed to do to get to No.1. Strauss credited Leamon with having a massive impact on the way the England team understood the game and stated, 'Better use of statistics helped us win a lot of games.'[*]

When Strauss took over as captain, his instinct was to be cautious – something that drew criticism when he delayed declarations in the West Indies and opted not to enforce the follow-on against Australia at Lord's – but he felt he could not decide upon a way of playing until he could identify what came most naturally. Leamon, again, was recruited to help. 'One of the issues we have always grappled with as an England team is that of identity,' he wrote. 'What was England's cricket about? To me, this was a vitally important question, because if we could answer it, we would always have something to fall back on when things were difficult and it would allow us to follow our own path ... Over time, it became apparent that the method that worked best for us was one of containment ... By concentrating on starving the opposition of runs, they [the bowling attack] would be able, as a unit, to create enough pressure to induce a batsman into making a mistake ... I was surprised that this strategy worked as well and as consistently as it did, on all sorts of different wickets ... Guys who didn't like to be

---

[*] The idea that everything was controllable may have encouraged Strauss and Flower to pursue more rigorously instructions to Test groundsmen in England to prepare surfaces favouring the home side. Certainly in 2009 directions were sent to Bill Gordon at The Oval to produce a spin-friendly pitch for a match England needed to win. 'Some might say that preparing wickets to suit your bowling attack is against the spirit of the game, but to me that is what home advantage is all about,' Strauss wrote later.

dominated tended to be the most susceptible ... We were merely sticking to what we did best. We had found what the England cricket team's unique strength was.' Such a strategy was hardly new – Greg Chappell of Australia did something similar on a slow pitch in Melbourne in 1980 when he adopted field-settings that Mike Brearley said represented 'rigorous containment' – but that was not the point. As Strauss reasoned, it suited England's game. They would term it 'bowling dry'.

This was the key to winning in Australia in 2010-11. Although the batsmen ran up big first-innings totals in Adelaide, Melbourne and Sydney, England bowled first in each of those games and also in Perth (where they lost), and dismissed Australia for 280 or fewer in every game, destroying them for 98 in Melbourne. These performances created the openings for the batsmen to exploit, which they did to such good effect that England's three victories were all by innings margins. (By close of play on Boxing Day in Melbourne, Cook and Strauss had taken England to 157 for no wicket, to complete the most one-sided first day in Test history.) Such was the emphasis on containment that Finn, the leading wicket-taker after three matches, was dropped because he was considered too expensive and Bresnan, his replacement, justified his inclusion with a miserly opening spell that helped set the tone for the rout at the MCG.

In the light of subsequent events it is important to note that England's pace bowlers not only kept things tight, and made good use of reverse swing, but they also extracted good bounce on Australia's harder surfaces: Broad, Finn and Tremlett were all tall men. England had in the past thrived in Australia when they had at their disposal some of the few bowlers of genuine pace they have produced – Larwood, Tyson, Snow – but bounce was an asset too, especially on the harder surfaces in Brisbane and at the WACA in Perth, where the heavily clay-based soil made it for many years one of the fastest pitches in the world. England's poor record in these two cities reflected both their inferior firepower with the ball relative to Australia but also the struggles their own batsmen had adjusting to the extra bounce compared with home.

England returned to Australia in 2013-14 and 2017-18 equipped with some tall fast bowlers but they lacked the discipline and skill to replicate the suffocating methods of Strauss's team. Moreover, Australia learned well the lessons of their defeat: in 2010-11 only Mike Hussey showed the necessary patience to counter the frustration tactics, but four years later they made an all-out assault on Swann, who was in any case in decline, to pile more pressure on the seamers, while in 2017-18 Steve Smith and Shaun Marsh showed immense application to outstay Joe Root's defensive tactics. Smith's Australia scored more slowly than in any home series for 20 years but nevertheless ran up in Perth and Sydney two of the three biggest totals made against England in Australia. 'It was a series of patience and perhaps our batsmen had the better patience,' Smith said. Bowling dry looked like a busted flush.

The Flower era unravelled by degrees after the Test team reached No.1. One problem was what to aim for after the summit had been scaled. There was talk of creating a legacy, of becoming the best England team of all time, but it was too abstract a concept to take hold. Also, the next assignment to play Pakistan on slow, turning pitches in the United Arab Emirates was tricky. The changes of approach wrought by the DRS that had so helped Swann got into the minds of the batsmen, who suffered such a collective loss of confidence that all three Tests were lost – the one in Abu Dhabi after England were left chasing fewer than 150 to win. Led by one of Trott's best innings in Galle, they rallied in Sri Lanka a few months later, paving the way for the win in India later in the year, but by then there were indications beyond Pietersen's rucking, and Strauss's retirement, of the group fragmenting.

During the India tour it was announced that Flower was handing responsibility for the white-ball teams to Ashley Giles, who since retiring as a player in 2007 had coached Warwickshire. The relationship was never equal, with Flower, as Test coach, having first call on senior players whose rest periods were generally allocated during one-day series.* The idea was supposedly that Flower would have

---

* Rest periods had been in vogue since 2010 when several senior players sat out Test matches against Bangladesh, including Strauss who temporarily handed over the captaincy to Cook, with a view to keeping them fresh for the Australia tour.

more time for broad planning but strategy became more, not less, confused. England chose to play their home Tests of 2013 on dryer than usual pitches in the belief that Swann gave them an advantage. Against New Zealand at Leeds, they even chose not to enforce the follow-on to give them practice at bowling last ahead of the Ashes: Swann finished with ten wickets in the game, a unique occurrence for an England spinner in a Test in England in May, but weather almost denied them the win. In the early weeks of the 2013-14 tour of Australia, it emerged that an 82-page document had been compiled outlining the team's dietary requirements. Flower's regime had started with players urged to take more responsibility; it ended with them feeling overly dependent on the head coach.

The bottom line was that most of the team had been around a long time and Flower's second tour of Australia – and almost certainly his last assignment before stepping down – was a mission too far for everyone. A group of players that had just beaten Australia well at home had little left to give; it was a tour that marked the end not only of Flower and Pietersen, but also of Swann, Prior and Bresnan, and although Trott returned for three Tests in 2015 he was effectively finished as well. 'That group of players had been together for a very long time, all of them maybe a little bit distracted in terms of commercial opportunities,' Downton told the BBC a few months later. 'We had such a settled group for so long it's very difficult not to become stale ... maybe as a collective the team got into a mindset where they felt they were better than they were ... maybe all the success they'd had built what turned out to be a false cocoon around them.'

## England Overseas 1877-2019

England have played Tests overseas on 64 grounds: 15 in India, eight in South Africa, eight in New Zealand, eight in West Indies, six in Australia, six in Pakistan, five in Sri Lanka, four in Bangladesh, three in the United Arab Emirates (for matches against Pakistan) and two in Zimbabwe; the Bangabandhu stadium in Dacca (later Dhaka) staged matches involving England as a 'home' ground to Pakistan (in 1962 and 1969) and Bangladesh (in 2003). England have played Tests on drop-in pitches in Melbourne (since 1998-99), Adelaide (since 2013-14), Auckland (since 2001-02) and at the now-defunct AMI Stadium in Christchurch (in 2001-02).

The following are the venues at which England have had their best win percentages and worst loss percentages (minimum of seven matches):

## Highest win percentage

| Ground | Period | P | W | L | D | Win % |
|---|---|---|---|---|---|---|
| Port Elizabeth | 1889-2004 | 9 | 5 | 1 | 3 | 55.6 |
| Lancaster Park, Christchurch | 1930-2002 | 15 | 8 | 1 | 6 | 53.3 |
| Cape Town | 1889-2016 | 20 | 9 | 5 | 6 | 45.0 |
| Feroz Shah Kotla, Delhi | 1951-84 | 7 | 3 | 0 | 4 | 42.9 |
| Sydney | 1882-2018 | 56 | 22 | 27 | 7 | 39.3 |
| Kingsmead, Durban | 1923-2015 | 16 | 6 | 1 | 9 | 37.5 |
| Wankhede, Mumbai | 1977-2016 | 8 | 3 | 4 | 1 | 37.5 |

England are unbeaten in six visits to Green Park, Kanpur between 1952 and 1985 (W1 D5).

## Highest loss percentage

| Ground | Period | P | W | L | D | Loss % |
|---|---|---|---|---|---|---|
| WACA, Perth | 1970-2017 | 14 | 1 | 10 | 3 | 71.4 |
| Gabba, Brisbane | 1933-2017 | 21 | 4 | 12 | 5 | 61.9 |
| Adelaide Oval | 1884-2017 | 32 | 9 | 18 | 5 | 56.3 |
| Chepauk, Chennai | 1934-2016 | 9 | 3 | 5 | 1 | 55.6 |
| *Melbourne | 1877-2017 | 56 | 20 | 28 | 8 | 50.0 |
| Wankhede, Mumbai | 1977-2016 | 8 | 3 | 4 | 1 | 50.0 |
| Sydney | 1882-2018 | 56 | 22 | 27 | 7 | 48.2 |

England never won in seven visits to the Recreation Ground, Antigua (W0 L3 D4), though they came within one wicket of doing so in 2009 in a match arranged at two days' notice after their inaugural Test at the Sir Vivian Richards Stadium was abandoned after 1.4 overs because of an unfit outfield. The Jamaica Test of 1998 was also abandoned (after 10.1 overs) owing to an unfit pitch.

## England's Captains 1999-2019

In terms of win percentage Michael Vaughan, Andrew Strauss and Joe Root rank among England's most successful captains, only eight of whom have led the side in ten or more Tests and won 48 per cent: WG Grace 61.5 per cent, Douglas Jardine 60.0, Mike Brearley 58.1, Percy Chapman 52.9, Root 51.9, Vaughan 51.0, Peter May 48.8 and Strauss 48.0.

England's overall win percentages in the 2000s and 2010s were the highest in any complete decades of Test cricket since 1900 apart

---

* Melbourne's figures do not include a scheduled Test in 1970–71 which was abandoned without a ball bowled because of rain. The only other England Test overseas completely washed out was at Guyana in 1989–90.

from the 1950s: they won 55 out of 129 matches in the 2000s (42.6 per cent) and 54 out of 117 in the 2010s (46.2 per cent). Both figures partly reflected there being fewer draws than in the past; again the only comparable decade in this respect to the 2000s (26.6 per cent draws) and 2010s (18.0 per cent draws) is the 1950s. Of the 83 Tests England played in the 1950s, they won 47.0 per cent and drew 26.5 per cent.

| Captain | Period | P | W | L | D | Win % |
| --- | --- | --- | --- | --- | --- | --- |
| JE Root | 2017-19 | 27 | 14 | 11 | 2 | 51.9 |
| MP Vaughan | 2003-08 | 51 | 26 | 11 | 14 | 51.0 |
| AJ Strauss | 2006-12 | 50 | 24 | 11 | 15 | 48.0 |
| AN Cook | 2010-16 | 59 | 24 | 22 | 13 | 40.7 |
| N Hussain | 1999-2003 | 45 | 17 | 15 | 13 | 37.8 |
| KP Pietersen | 2008 | 3 | 1 | 1 | 1 | 33.3 |
| A Flintoff | 2006-07 | 11 | 2 | 7 | 2 | 18.2 |

*Minimum: 3 Tests*

# CHAPTER 35

# Strauss's White-Ball Revolution

## How England's one-day batsmen
## found their muscle

Andrew Strauss officially returned to work with England cricket in early May 2015, two years and nine months after retiring as a player. As was the case when he took over as captain, there was a crisis to manage. The break-up of the exceptional Test team he had helped assemble, and the acrimony generated by Kevin Pietersen's sacking, had taken a heavy toll. With 15 wins and 28 losses, 2014 was England's worst calendar year of modern times: it was the only year between 2009 and 2017 in which they lost more matches than they won, and they had never lost so many matches in any year in their history.

However, despite the whitewash in Australia, the real concern was not with the condition of the Test team, which had shown signs of regeneration and beaten India 3-1 over five matches in the biggest series England had played since the Ashes. The principal issue related to England's white-ball performances.

They had just failed at a World Cup for the sixth time in a row, a record unmatched by any major side over the same period. Crushed by the eventual finalists Australia and New Zealand in their opening games, and knocked out at the group stage when they were unable to beat Bangladesh in Adelaide, they had looked an outmoded and anxiety-riddled outfit. They had also squandered a winning position in the Champions Trophy final of 2013 when in a rain-shortened game at Edgbaston, they got within 20 of their target with six wickets and 16 balls in hand. 'We just capitulated,' said Eoin Morgan, whose dismissal started the collapse.

Similarly, at the World Twenty20 in Bangladesh in March 2016 they had failed to advance beyond the first phase, their embarrassment compounded by a heavy loss to the Netherlands. Defeat to the Dutch was bad in itself but it also had profound consequences, ruining the chances of Ashley Giles stepping up from white-ball duties to succeed Andy Flower as overall head coach and encouraging Paul Downton to come to the questionable conclusion that he should reappoint Peter Moores instead. Moores had not worked in international cricket since his previous stint with England, his credentials resting on having coached Lancashire to a championship title in 2011. To compensate for his shortcomings, he was given a full-time assistant, Paul Farbrace, a former county player and coach who had acquired a good reputation working for several years with the Sri Lanka national side.

Moores's previous handling of England's one-day cricket had been conservative in the extreme. For his first match in charge, an early-season fixture against Scotland in Aberdeen, he passed up an opportunity to experiment and opened the batting with Alastair Cook and Ian Bell, neither of whom offered the explosiveness most sides sought at the top of the order (ICC changes to fielding restrictions in October 2012 meant that England needed to update the methods by which they had reached No.1 earlier that year, with greater emphasis on attacking batting). After the trauma of the Australia tour, there had been a case for removing Cook from the ODI team altogether but under Moores he soldiered on at the helm of Test and one-day sides.

When England lost a match against Sri Lanka at Leeds that they dominated in the early stages, Cook came close to stepping down from the Test job of his own accord, only his wife Alice dissuading him, and for several weeks thereafter – during which most former

England captains in the commentary boxes thought he should go – his grip on the job faltered before runs against India at Southampton marked a turnaround in fortunes. There was no respite in the ODI arena, though, where losses came thick and fast. At the end of the summer, Moores and the selectors debated Cook's future but held off making a change, only to axe him after a 5-2 series loss in Sri Lanka eight weeks out from the World Cup. That left his replacement Eoin Morgan little time to find his feet, and to make matters worse Moores rejigged his line-up for the opener against Australia at the 11th hour. As Strauss would point out, Moores's tactical knowledge and strategic shortcomings were ruthlessly exposed during the tournament.

There were other factors to consider. The ECB had a new chairman in Colin Graves as well as a new chief executive in Tom Harrison, whose background in marketing and the sales of cricket broadcasting rights had been a key factor in his appointment. Their mission was to reshape the county game to accommodate a new domestic white-ball tournament that would appeal to a broader audience: market research had revealed a disconnection between the professional game and a young population who no longer recognised the nation's top cricketers. The theory was that one-day stars were now the best if not the only means of making cricket a compelling brand with the wider public. In 2017, Graves and Harrison duly persuaded the 18 counties to support a new short-form competition and then sold the combined broadcast rights for that event and England's home internationals for 2020 to 2024 for more than £1 billion, but in early 2015 there was still a strong feeling that the England team needed to reinvent itself if this mission was to be successful. Supporters wanted to see a certain style of play from their England sides: 'Courage, bravery and commitment are words that came out of the study,' Harrison said. 'It's not uniquely about victory.' But further failure at major ODI and Twenty20 tournaments was no longer acceptable. Shortly after the World Cup ended, Harrison sacked Downton, paving the way for Strauss's return.

Strauss's first act was to sack Moores. He had every justification. A few days earlier in Barbados, England had lost a Test match in three days to a West Indies side they were widely expected to beat, but because of the defeat in Bridgetown the three-match series was drawn 1-1. Strauss in any case knew enough from his first-hand experience of Moores's first term, as well as the evidence of the World Cup, to know that Moores was not the man to lead the sort of revolution he proposed to initiate. As a player, Strauss was a Test cricketer first and a one-day player second, but since then he, like the ECB, had undergone a Damascene conversion. That Strauss was prepared to remove the head coach so close to a home Ashes series betrayed the urgency of his mission, as did the way news leaked of Moores's fate while he was in Dublin for an ODI against Ireland.[*]

It was in choosing a replacement that Strauss took his most radical step. Trevor Bayliss, like Moores, had never played international cricket; nor, as an Australian, did he have experience of playing or watching county cricket. But he had an excellent track record as a white-ball coach in Australian domestic cricket and at the IPL, as well as during four years as head coach of Sri Lanka, whom he had taken to the World Cup final in 2011. In Bayliss, Strauss saw someone who could revive England's ODI and Twenty20 cricket, and potentially take them to glory when the World Cup was staged on English soil in 2019. By appointing him, Strauss was confirming his determination to scrap the second-class status the English game had historically bestowed on limited-overs cricket. He also indicated that he expected the Test and one-day squads to become more distinct, with fewer players overlapping formats. As a consequence, in September 2016 central contracts were split between Tests and one-dayers, with ten awarded for red-ball cricket and 11 for white. Only four players were given contracts for both categories.

As captain, Strauss had devoted much thought to what style of play worked best for England as a Test team, but when it came to

---

[*] Four days later, at his unveiling as managing director at Lord's, Strauss unsurprisingly ruled out a recall for Kevin Pietersen, who had taken encouragement from Graves's talk of a clean slate and the previous day scored a triple-century for Surrey at The Oval. Trust, Strauss explained, remained an issue. 'Over the 16 months since his [Pietersen's] last appearance in an England shirt, little has happened to heal the wounds from the fallout over his omission, and the inflammatory comments in his book about current team members cannot be overlooked easily.'

limited-overs cricket there was general agreement among most sides that the top three in the batting order had to be aggressive in approach. England's problem was that in home conditions the ball tended to move around more than elsewhere, which meant top-order batsmen needed sound techniques. This requirement had led to some unnecessarily cautious selections, especially when playing overseas where the new ball was less of a problem. When England won the World Twenty20 in the West Indies in 2010, their top three of Craig Kieswetter, Michael Lumb and Pietersen were by English standards unusually belligerent and the quick runs they scored were a major factor in the final outcome, but even then lessons were not learned. At the World Cup the following year, when England were soundly beaten in the quarter-finals by Bayliss's Sri Lanka, the orthodoxy of Strauss himself, Ian Bell and Jonathan Trott at the top of the order contrasted sharply with the audacity of the Sri Lankan openers, who between them knocked off their side's target of 230 with more than ten overs to spare.

If England's batsmen were to play with the necessary freedom and fearlessness, they needed to know they had the support of the management, and the steadfast backing they received was one of the principal hallmarks of the new regime. 'It's not often you get free rein to be as adventurous as you like,' Morgan said. Strauss also accepted that the old resistance to English players taking part in the IPL and other overseas Twenty20 competitions had to be abandoned. Now he believed that the best way for players to improve their white-ball skills was to be exposed to the sort of high-pressure situations these tournaments provided on a daily basis.

Strauss rationalised that if someone could show an ability to soak up pressure in the IPL or Big Bash they would cope with the first morning of an Ashes series. There was also an element of realpolitik in his position: denying the top stars access to these tournaments was an increasingly untenable position for a national board to hold; the best players might simply walk away from England and take the T20 dollar. Morgan, Jos Buttler, Ben Stokes and Chris Woakes, among others, were subsequently given more opportunities to play in these events, with Buttler, Stokes and Woakes even given leave to miss two

ODIs against Ireland in 2017 in order that they could remain at the IPL.* Later that year, Dawid Malan provided support for the theory that an ability to cope with high-intensity situations was transferable by earning Test selection on the back of an innings of 78 off 44 balls on Twenty20 debut and soon after scoring 140 against Australia in a Test match in Perth.

The speed with which England's one-day performances improved took everyone by surprise. In June 2015, in the first ODI of the new era, they topped 400 for the first time despite losing Jason Roy to the first ball of the innings; later in the same series against New Zealand they recorded what was then their highest successful chase, reaching a target of 350 with six overs to spare. In August the following year, they smashed the world record for ODIs with a total of 444 for three against Pakistan at Trent Bridge. Alex Hales made 171 of that total – an individual best for England, surpassing Robin Smith's mark of 167 which had stood since 1993. Hales did not stay on the summit for long: in January 2018, Roy struck 180 against Australia in Melbourne. In June 2018, they improved on their own record by racking up 481 for six against Australia, also at Trent Bridge. Then, in the space of a week in the West Indies in February 2019, they recorded their highest winning total batting second of 364 in Barbados and their highest total anywhere overseas of 418 for six in Grenada.†

By March 2019, England had in the space of less than four years made a greater number of ODI totals of 325 or more than they had in the previous 44 years; there had also been 13 instances of batsmen scoring centuries in fewer than 75 balls, whereas there had been only four previously. Five of these 17 came from the bat of Buttler who,

---

* The ECB's more liberal stance had an immediate impact. In three seasons of IPL from 2016 to 2018, a total of 15 England internationals were signed by franchises, whereas only ten had taken the field in the eight previous years of the tournament. Ben Stokes attracted the biggest prices at both the 2017 and 2018 auctions, £1.7m and £1.4m.

† In July 2015, early in England's white-ball revolution and in the face of mounting scores, ICC attempted to give fielding sides help by scrapping the second batting powerplay (usually taken during overs 36-40) and allowing five fielders rather than four outside the circle in last ten overs. This reduced the run-rate in the final 15 overs but not overall scoring levels.

like Morgan, credited an array of innovative sweep and ramp shots to having played a variety of different ball sports in his youth. By the age of 27, he was arguably the most brilliant and destructive one-day batsman England had ever had. The only disappointment within the dressing-room was that England did not turn this new-found domination into major trophies. Early in 2016, they reached the World Twenty20 final in Kolkata, a game they looked set to win until the last over when Stokes, defending 19, had his first four balls thrashed for six by Carlos Brathwaite of West Indies. Strong favourites to lift the Champions Trophy on home soil in 2017, they were beaten in the semi-finals by Pakistan when they failed to adapt to a slow pitch in Cardiff that made expansive strokeplay difficult.

Morgan proved the ideal captain to embrace the new approach. Having grown up around Dublin and played for Ireland until he was 22, he came at things with a different perspective and developed an early affinity with short-form cricket. Like Buttler, he displayed a rare ability to stay calm and make the right decisions amid the cauldron of a difficult run-chase. 'He was prepared to bring new answers to old problems,' Ed Smith, a Middlesex team-mate and future national selector, said. One England colleague, Moeen Ali, said Morgan would never countenance a backward step. 'Sometimes you would play a big shot, get out, and you'd have your head down in the changing-room, embarrassed, but he'd be like, "No, no, that's the best way,"' he said. 'He'd rather we got out caught on the boundary than blocking.' Buttler called Morgan 'a cricket revolutionary'.

Occasionally, in reaching for the stars, the batting imploded. At Lord's in 2017, England squandered six wickets in the first five overs of the match against South Africa and lost decisively. In Dunedin the following winter they were beaten after losing eight in 64 balls having cruised at 267 for one. Then, in St Lucia in 2019, they were dismissed for 113 in just 28.1 overs, their shortest-ever innings batting first in a one-day international in which the allotted overs were not reduced by rain. Nonetheless, England won 12 out of 15 bilateral series between June 2016 and March 2019, their only losses being in a three-match series in India and a one-off game against Scotland in Edinburgh.

# England in ODI Cricket 1971-2019

England have generally been strong at home in one-day international cricket but only since the change of approach in 2015 have they improved their record on the road. Even the decision after the 1996 World Cup to identify one-day specialists, and select distinct Test and one-day squads on tour, failed to have an impact.

|  | P | W | L | Tie | NR |
|---|---|---|---|---|---|
| **January 1971-May 1996** | | | | | |
| Home | 89 | 56 | 31 | 1 | 1 |
| Away/Neutral | 158 | 70 | 82 | 0 | 6 |
| Total | 247 | 126 | 113 | 1 | 7 |
| **May 1996-May 2015** | | | | | |
| Home | 166 | 81 | 72 | 2 | 11 |
| Away/Neutral | 231 | 102 | 122 | 4 | 3 |
| Total | 397 | 183 | 194 | 6 | 14 |
| **May 2015-March 2019** | | | | | |
| Home | 42 | 30 | 9 | 1 | 2 |
| Away/Neutral | 40 | 23 | 14 | 0 | 3 |
| Total | 82 | 53 | 23 | 1 | 5 |

*Up to 1 May 2019*

## CHAPTER 36

# Root's Red-Ball Gamble
## Test team adopts one-day style

The freewheeling approach of the one-day side had a profound influence on England's Test match cricket. Encouraging players to be one-day specialists and allowing them more time in domestic Twenty20 leagues only reduced their scope for developing as long-form cricketers. Eoin Morgan largely gave up playing championship cricket after 2015, while Jos Buttler and Jason Roy played only a handful of four-day championship games each summer; Adil Rashid and Alex Hales withdrew from championship cricket altogether in 2018.* In the case of Buttler, this was particularly contentious as he was widely thought capable of transferring his skills to the Test arena.

These issues were not unique to England. There were fears that the Twenty20 leagues were siphoning off both players and public interest from bilateral international cricket across the world, though the point may have been exaggerated: as many international fixtures were being played in 2018 as was the case before the arrival of the IPL in 2008. But those who played Tests and ODIs for England had undergone such a radical change in one arena that it was unsurprising it

---

* Another cricketer lost to England who could have made an impact at Test level was James Taylor, who played seven Tests and 27 ODIs between 2012 and 2016 before he was forced to retire at the age of 26 with a heart condition.

contaminated the other. England's Test match batting lacked patience and results fluctuated wildly between big wins and massive losses.

The wisdom of the whole white-ball project, and Trevor Bayliss's credentials as a red-ball coach, were called into question by successive 4-0 Test series defeats in India and Australia, after which Bayliss confirmed more than once, despite several requests from the ECB to stay on longer, that he would not continue beyond the Ashes in September 2019.

When the heavy defeat in Australia was followed by a catastrophic display on the first morning of a series in New Zealand, which saw England in Auckland slump to 27 for nine and 58 all out, and ultimately to defeat by an innings and 49 runs, Joe Root, who had been captain for 13 matches but was still searching for a distinctive leadership style, decided he would henceforth take Morgan's ODI side as his blueprint. Root knew from personal experience the success the one-day team had had piling pressure onto the opposition through aggressive and fearless batting.

Replicating this approach in Test cricket was risky and Root concluded that, for the batsmen to play with the necessary freedom, his line-up would need to bat deep. This played to the team's strength in all-rounders, but made it difficult for some bowlers who offered little with the bat to hold down places. The new strategy took shape at a team meeting ahead of the Christchurch Test. '[This] was where we stripped things back,' Root explained some months later. 'We'd had a really tough time . . . and it was a chance for us to start something. It felt like a breakthrough moment. We're learning from the one-day side. Eoin says, "Go and play with freedom." The guys embraced that and we saw a big improvement very quickly. Understanding how we want to play in certain situations gives us a lot of clarity.'

Three weeks after that meeting, Ed Smith came in as the new national selector, with greater powers than his predecessor James Whitaker to devise policy, and concurred with Root's new philosophy. Among Smith's earliest acts was to recall to the Test side Buttler and Rashid, established stars of England's white-ball teams who had not played first-class cricket, let alone Test cricket, for more than nine months. At a stroke, the Test team's personnel became more closely aligned to that of the shorter format sides. After two matches, Buttler was promoted to Root's vice-captain, a position Ben Stokes forfeited following the incident outside a nightclub in Bristol in September 2017. Stokes, however, remained a key figure in the dressing-room and it was Root, Buttler and Stokes – all three born within ten months of each other and who first played together at an Under-19 World Cup in 2010 – who largely drove things forward.

It was not just a matter of how the team performed on the field. The players vouched to improve team culture in the wake of the Bristol affair and allegations of drinking among the players, minor though these were, during the Australia tour. They had also seen the Australians suffer mass sackings and resignations following a ball-tampering scandal in South Africa, which served as a reminder of how easily an apparently successful team could unravel. 'We want to leave this team in a better place than when we first came into it,' Root said. 'It's part of being an England cricketer. It covers more than just the cricket itself.' An incident in a Test match in St Lucia in February 2019 demonstrated how Root was prepared to follow through on his words when he took issue with Shannon Gabriel, the West Indies fast bowler, over comments he made when Root was batting. Gabriel had said: 'Why are you smiling at me? Do you like boys?' Root's reply, which was picked up on the stump mic, was: 'Don't use it as an insult. There's nothing wrong with being gay.' Root was widely praised for his action after his comments became public.

Root quickly made clear his new approach on the field in the summer of 2018. After England lost badly to Pakistan at Lord's, where they were dismissed twice in 140.3 overs, and the batting group then held a meeting ahead of the second game in Leeds, Alastair Cook proposed that they should look to bat time. For Cook, this was a revisiting of an argument he had had with Bayliss during a Test in Visakhapatnam in 2016, when Cook and Haseeb Hameed had batted time when Bayliss would have preferred his batsmen to look to score runs. At Leeds, Cook's view had not changed, but, as captain, Root's view prevailed.

'My reasoning was that if we batted for a period of time then the runs would come,' Cook wrote later. 'Rooty took the opposite view: we can't go into our shells, it's not how long we bat for but how many runs we can score. Two things struck me. First, this was a bold approach. Second, Joe was clearer than he had ever been about how he wanted his side to play.' England won in Leeds and went on to beat India 4-1 in a series that began with them playing, and winning in thrilling fashion by 31 runs, the 1,000th Test match in their history at Edgbaston. The policy of packing the side with batsmen paid dividends as Buttler contributed 510 runs in the seven home Tests mostly from No.7, while Sam Curran scored 292 runs never batting higher than No.8. Cook, the last of the old-school accumulators, announced his retirement from Test cricket ahead of the final match against India – and went out on a well-merited high by batting almost 11 hours and scoring 71 and 147.*

More audaciously still, Root's team won all three Tests in Sri Lanka to record England's first overseas whitewash in a series of more than two matches since New Zealand in 1962-63. The pitches on which these Tests were played heavily favoured spin bowling, but Root – acting on the guidance of Bayliss and assistant coach Paul Farbrace, who had coached in Sri Lanka in the past – encouraged his players to be positive from the outset: in the first session of the series in Galle, England scored 113 runs and, although they lost five wickets, they forced back the fields and, after regrouping in the second session, added 122 runs in the third.

Their approach in the second Test in Kandy was even more daring. There, led by Root and Buttler, they scored 636 across two innings at more than four runs an over with heavy use of the sweep and reverse sweep. Historically, English sides had been reluctant to play the sweep shot in Asia, partly because of technical shortcomings and partly because, in the era of 'home town' umpiring, they feared being given out lbw if they missed. But since the advent of the Decision Review System, the sweep and the reverse sweep, which had grown

---

* In the 2019 New Year Honours list, Cook became the eleventh England cricketer to be knighted. The others were Stanley Jackson, Pelham Warner, Charles Aubrey Smith, Jack Hobbs, Henry Leveson Gower, Len Hutton, Gubby Allen, Colin Cowdrey, Alec Bedser and Ian Botham; not all were knighted for services to cricket.

in popularity in Test cricket since 2006, no longer seemed such risky options when a batsman might well be given out lbw simply attempting a forward defensive. Root's rationale was that the more sharply the ball spun, the riskier conventional defensive play became, the more there was to gain from going on the attack. He was right: in three separate sessions in Kandy, England scored 125 runs or more, and across the course of the three Tests their run-rate was the highest it had ever been in a major series in Asia.

Root appeared to expect the same ultra-attacking method to work in the West Indies in early 2019, declaring on the eve of the series: 'You don't win games by batting long periods of time, you win games by scoring big runs.' However, on pitches with more life in them than anticipated and against a West Indian pace attack of rare quality bowling overs so slowly that their captain earned a suspension, England's batting became hopelessly disorientated in the first and second Tests. Dismissed for 77, 246, 187 and 132, they shed wickets at a rate of one every 32 balls, before showing greater application in St Lucia and recording a consolation win.

Another issue Root had to wrestle with was how to manage a bowling attack that had long been over-reliant on James Anderson and Stuart Broad, both of whom appeared to be entering the final phase of their careers. They could still be dominant when conditions were in their favour, but they were not necessarily the right men to win Tests at other times, especially outside England. In Sri Lanka, there was a compelling case for fielding three frontline spinners in each of the Tests – Moeen Ali (off-spin), Jack Leach (left-arm spin) and Rashid (leg-breaks and googlies) – but this necessitated leaving out Broad from the first and second Tests and Anderson from the third. The strategy was radical but worked brilliantly, England's spinners claiming 49 wickets in the series (compared to seven taken by their seam bowlers), the most since 1958. '[Root] said we were going to be different and that was a big, brave step,' Moeen said of the Sri Lanka tour. 'We have to do that when we go abroad. Broady and Jimmy don't have to play [every game]. It changed the mind-set of the team, in that no one is undroppable. There is a lot of pride in the fact it is not just Jimmy and Broady who can get the best players out.'

The shift in power among the bowlers in Sri Lanka may have influenced the England management's decision at the start of the West Indies series to leave out Broad while keeping faith with two of their three spinners, as well as Curran, a short-built, left-arm swing bowler who failed to make an impact with the new ball, even though, historically, Bridgetown, Barbados, was a ground on which tall, fast bowlers enjoyed success. Broad was immediately recalled but took only four wickets in the two games he played. Mark Wood, easily England's fastest bowler, was also not chosen until the third game in St Lucia, where, peaking at 94.6mph, he bowled the fastest spell of the series, and the fastest by an England bowler in at least ten years. Wood and Moeen took 13 wickets between them, which meant that, across the course of an overseas winter in which England won four Tests for the first time since 2003–04, Anderson and Broad took only 15 wickets at 35 apiece combined.

Broadly speaking, England's Test and ODI teams appeared in good shape heading into the biggest home season in their history in 2019, when they were to host a World Cup and Ashes. The only time this had happened before was in 1975 when the World Cup was being staged for the first time and was a much smaller event, and a series against Australia was arranged only as a late replacement for a cancelled South Africa tour.

Expectations were much greater than they had been then. Root's re-booted Test team had won 64 per cent of their games since their Christchurch meeting, while the ODI side had had a similar success rate during the same period, helping them to consolidate their position at the top of the rankings. Bayliss admitted to some concern as to whether the players could handle the pressure of attempting to win two such big prizes close together and said he had tried to condition them to the idea of success by regularly describing them as favourites. In February 2019, Morgan, the one-day captain, said he was comfortable with this approach. 'We've gone into every series for the last year and a half as favourites and we've grown in confidence by dealing with that. It's something we've come to terms with. We see it as a huge opportunity not only to win some silverware but inspire a new generation as well.' The World Cup was, however, set to operate to different regulations from those England preferred at home, with daytime matches (including all of England's games) due to start at 10.30am rather than 11am, the time England had moved to in 2017 with a consequent improvement in results. They had calculated that the later the start, the better the chances of their powerful batting line-up firing.

Not only the future of the national team, but also the direction of the game in England as a whole, seemed set to hang on the success or failure of this twin-pronged mission.

## England's Leading Test Groundsmen

Mick Hunt retired as head groundsman at Lord's at the end of the 2018 season, a position he had held since 1985, having previously worked on the staff in a junior capacity under his predecessor Jim Fairbrother. Hunt was in charge of preparing pitches for more England home Test matches than anyone else. Ted Leyland, who was head groundsman at Edgbaston between 1926 and 1939, prepared the pitch for a Test match in 1929 in which his son Maurice played; Leyland junior scored three.

| Groundsman | Ground | Period | Test matches |
| --- | --- | --- | --- |
| Mick Hunt | Lord's | 1984-2018 | 61 |
| Bernard Flack | Edgbaston | 1956-90 | 24* |
| Peter Marron | Old Trafford | 1983-2008 | 21 |
| Jim Fairbrother | Lord's | 1969-83 | 21 |
| Harry Brind | Oval | 1975-94 | 20 |
| Bert Lock | Oval | 1945-64 | 19 |
| Andy Fogarty | Headingley | 1996-2018 | 19 |
| Frank Dalling | Trent Bridge | 1947-75 | 19 |
| Steve Birks | Trent Bridge | 1998-2018 | 18 |

* Including one Test at Old Trafford in 1977 when he was called in as consultant.

# STATISTICAL APPENDIX

## England's Record

England in Test Matches

| Opposition | Dates | P | W | L | D | Series won/lost |
|---|---|---|---|---|---|---|
| Australia | 1877-2018 | 346 | 108 | 144 | 94 | 33/39 |
| South Africa | 1889-2017 | 149 | 61 | 33 | 55 | 21/9 |
| West Indies | 1928-2019 | 157 | 49 | 57 | 51 | 14/17 |
| New Zealand | 1930-2018 | 103 | 48 | 10 | 45 | 23/4 |
| India | 1932-2018 | 122 | 47 | 26 | 49 | 19/10 |
| Pakistan | 1954-2018 | 82 | 25 | 21 | 37 | 9/8 |
| Sri Lanka | 1982-2018 | 34 | 15 | 8 | 11 | 8/5 |
| Zimbabwe | 1996-2003 | 6 | 3 | 0 | 3 | 2/0 |
| Bangladesh | 2003-16 | 10 | 9 | 1 | 0 | 4/0 |
| TOTAL | | 1010 | 365 | 300 | 345 | |

## England in One-Day Internationals

| Opposition | Dates | P | W | L | Tie | NR | Bilateral series won/lost |
|---|---|---|---|---|---|---|---|
| Australia | 1971-2018 | 147 | 61 | 81 | 2 | 3 | 10/12 |
| New Zealand | 1973-2018 | 89 | 40 | 43 | 2 | 4 | 9/7 |
| West Indies | 1973-2019 | 101 | 51 | 44 | 0 | 6 | 9/11 |
| India | 1974-2018 | 99 | 41 | 53 | 2 | 3 | 7/9 |
| Pakistan | 1974-2017 | 82 | 49 | 31 | 0 | 2 | 12/3 |
| Sri Lanka | 1982-2018 | 74 | 36 | 35 | 1 | 2 | 5/6 |
| South Africa | 1992-2017 | 59 | 26 | 29 | 1 | 3 | 4/4 |
| Zimbabwe | 1992-2004 | 30 | 21 | 8 | 0 | 1 | 3/1 |
| Bangladesh | 2000-17 | 20 | 16 | 4 | 0 | 0 | 4/0 |
| Ireland | 2006-17 | 9 | 7 | 1 | 0 | 1 | 5/0 |
| Scotland | 2008-18 | 5 | 3 | 1 | 0 | 1 | 2/1 |
| *Others | 1975-15 | 11 | 11 | 0 | 0 | 0 | |
| TOTAL | | 726 | 362 | 330 | 8 | 26 | |

## England in International Twenty20s

2005-19: Played 108, Won 53, Lost 50, Tied 1, No result 4

---

* Afghanistan, Canada, East Africa, Kenya, Namibia, the Netherlands and United Arab Emirates

# England's Leading Test Batsmen

## Overall (5000 runs, top ten averages)

‡ denotes left–handed batsman

| Batsman | Span | Inns | Runs | HS | Average | 100 | 50 |
|---|---|---|---|---|---|---|---|
| Ken Barrington | 1955-68 | 131 | 6806 | 256 | 58.67 | 20 | 35 |
| Wally Hammond | 1927-47 | 140 | 7249 | 336* | 58.45 | 22 | 24 |
| Jack Hobbs | 1908-30 | 102 | 5410 | 211 | 56.94 | 15 | 28 |
| Len Hutton | 1937-55 | 138 | 6971 | 364 | 56.67 | 19 | 33 |
| Denis Compton | 1937-57 | 131 | 5807 | 278 | 50.06 | 17 | 28 |
| Joe Root | 2012-19 | 147 | 6685 | 254 | 49.51 | 16 | 41 |
| Geoff Boycott | 1964-82 | 193 | 8114 | 246* | 47.72 | 22 | 42 |
| Kevin Pietersen | 2005-14 | 181 | 8181 | 227 | 47.28 | 23 | 35 |
| ‡Alastair Cook | 2006-18 | 291 | 12472 | 294 | 45.35 | 33 | 57 |
| ‡Graham Thorpe | 1993-2005 | 179 | 6744 | 200* | 44.66 | 16 | 39 |

## Openers (3000 runs, top ten averages)

| Batsman | Span | Inns | Runs | HS | Average | 100 | 50 |
|---|---|---|---|---|---|---|---|
| Herbert Sutcliffe | 1924-35 | 83 | 4522 | 194 | 61.10 | 16 | 23 |
| Len Hutton | 1937-55 | 131 | 6721 | 364 | 56.47 | 19 | 31 |
| Jack Hobbs | 1908-30 | 97 | 5130 | 211 | 56.37 | 14 | 27 |
| Dennis Amiss | 1972-77 | 69 | 3276 | 262* | 53.70 | 11 | 9 |
| Geoff Boycott | 1964-82 | 191 | 8091 | 246* | 48.16 | 22 | 42 |
| Michael Vaughan | 2002-08 | 72 | 3093 | 197 | 45.48 | 10 | 9 |
| ‡Alastair Cook | 2007-18 | 278 | 11485 | 294 | 44.86 | 31 | 55 |
| Alec Stewart | 1990-99 | 77 | 3348 | 190 | 44.64 | 8 | 17 |
| ‡John Edrich | 1963-76 | 82 | 3430 | 310* | 44.54 | 8 | 14 |
| Graham Gooch | 1978-95 | 184 | 7811 | 333 | 43.88 | 18 | 41 |

## Nos 3-4 (3000 runs, top ten averages)

| Batsman | Span | Inns | Runs | HS | Average | 100 | 50 |
| --- | --- | --- | --- | --- | --- | --- | --- |
| Ken Barrington | 1960-68 | 84 | 4993 | 256 | 67.47 | 20 | 19 |
| Wally Hammond | 1927-47 | 118 | 6437 | 336* | 61.30 | 21 | 19 |
| Denis Compton | 1937-57 | 98 | 4617 | 278 | 51.30 | 13 | 24 |
| Peter May | 1951-61 | 95 | 4274 | 285* | 49.69 | 12 | 21 |
| Ted Dexter | 1959-68 | 68 | 3169 | 205 | 49.51 | 6 | 18 |
| Kevin Pietersen | 2006-14 | 141 | 6609 | 227 | 48.95 | 19 | 28 |
| Tom Graveney | 1951-69 | 72 | 3180 | 258 | 47.46 | 9 | 8 |
| Jonathan Trott | 2009-13 | 81 | 3517 | 226 | 46.89 | 8 | 17 |
| Joe Root | 2013-19 | 99 | 4272 | 254 | 45.44 | 9 | 29 |
| ‡David Gower | 1978-92 | 147 | 5842 | 215 | 42.64 | 11 | 30 |

## Nos 5-7 (2250 runs; excluding wicketkeepers)

| Batsman | Span | Inns | Runs | HS | Average | 100 | 50 |
| --- | --- | --- | --- | --- | --- | --- | --- |
| Ian Bell | 2004-15 | 105 | 4389 | 199 | 51.63 | 16 | 22 |
| ‡David Gower | 1978-92 | 54 | 2316 | 200* | 49.27 | 7 | 9 |
| ‡Graham Thorpe | 1993-2005 | 102 | 3896 | 200* | 47.51 | 11 | 21 |
| Colin Cowdrey | 1954-71 | 66 | 2796 | 154 | 46.60 | 7 | 16 |
| Basil D'Oliveira | 1966-72 | 64 | 2425 | 158 | 42.54 | 5 | 15 |
| Tony Greig | 1972-77 | 89 | 3453 | 148 | 40.62 | 8 | 19 |
| Paul Collingwood | 2003-11 | 101 | 3672 | 186 | 39.91 | 9 | 17 |
| ‡Ben Stokes | 2013-19 | 87 | 3090 | 258 | 35.93 | 6 | 17 |
| Ian Botham | 1978-92 | 148 | 4977 | 208 | 34.80 | 14 | 21 |
| Andrew Flintoff | 1998-2009 | 121 | 3631 | 167 | 32.41 | 5 | 25 |

## Wicketkeepers (1500 runs)

| Batsman | Span | Inns | Runs | HS | Average | 100 | 50 |
|---------|------|------|------|-----|---------|-----|-----|
| Les Ames | 1929-39 | 67 | 2387 | 149 | 43.40 | 8 | 7 |
| Jonny Bairstow | 2013-18 | 73 | 2814 | 167* | 40.78 | 5 | 14 |
| Matt Prior | 2007-14 | 123 | 4099 | 131* | 40.18 | 7 | 28 |
| Alec Stewart | 1991-2003 | 145 | 4540 | 173 | 34.92 | 6 | 23 |
| Alan Knott | 1967-81 | 149 | 4389 | 135 | 32.75 | 5 | 30 |
| Jim Parks | 1960-68 | 64 | 1876 | 108* | 32.34 | 2 | 9 |
| ‡Jack Russell | 1988-98 | 86 | 1897 | 128* | 27.10 | 2 | 6 |
| Godfrey Evans | 1946-59 | 133 | 2439 | 104 | 20.49 | 2 | 8 |

## Nos 8-11 (1000 runs; excluding wicketkeepers)

| Batsman | Span | Inns | Runs | HS | Average | 100 | 50 |
|---------|------|------|------|-----|---------|-----|-----|
| Graeme Swann | 2008-13 | 76 | 1370 | 85 | 22.09 | 0 | 5 |
| John Emburey | 1978-95 | 73 | 1212 | 75 | 21.26 | 0 | 8 |
| Ashley Giles | 1998-2006 | 81 | 1421 | 59 | 20.89 | 0 | 4 |
| ‡Stuart Broad | 2007-18 | 179 | 2991 | 169 | 19.17 | 1 | 12 |

# England's Leading Test Bowlers

## Overall (175 wickets, top ten averages)

| Bowler | Span | Tests | Wickets | Best | Average | 5wi | 10wm |
|---|---|---|---|---|---|---|---|
| Sydney Barnes | 1901-14 | 27 | 189 | 9-103 | 16.43 | 24 | 7 |
| Jim Laker | 1948-59 | 46 | 193 | 10-53 | 21.24 | 9 | 3 |
| Fred Trueman | 1952-65 | 67 | 307 | 8-31 | 21.57 | 17 | 3 |
| Brian Statham | 1951-65 | 70 | 252 | 7-39 | 24.84 | 9 | 1 |
| Alec Bedser | 1946-55 | 51 | 236 | 7-44 | 24.89 | 15 | 5 |
| Bob Willis | 1971-84 | 90 | 325 | 8-43 | 25.20 | 16 | 0 |
| Derek Underwood | 1966-82 | 86 | 297 | 8-51 | 25.83 | 17 | 6 |
| John Snow | 1965-76 | 49 | 202 | 7-40 | 26.66 | 8 | 1 |
| James Anderson | 2003-19 | 148 | 575 | 7-42 | 26.93 | 27 | 3 |
| Angus Fraser | 1989-98 | 46 | 177 | 8-53 | 27.32 | 13 | 2 |

## Right-arm fast or fast-medium (150 wickets)

| Bowler | Span | Tests | Wickets | Best | Average | 5wi | 10wm |
|---|---|---|---|---|---|---|---|
| Sydney Barnes | 1901-14 | 27 | 189 | 9-103 | 16.43 | 24 | 7 |
| Fred Trueman | 1952-65 | 67 | 307 | 8-31 | 21.57 | 17 | 3 |
| Brian Statham | 1951-65 | 70 | 252 | 7-39 | 24.84 | 9 | 1 |
| Alec Bedser | 1946-55 | 51 | 236 | 7-44 | 24.89 | 15 | 5 |
| Bob Willis | 1971-84 | 90 | 325 | 8-43 | 25.20 | 16 | 0 |
| Maurice Tate | 1924-35 | 39 | 155 | 6-42 | 26.16 | 7 | 1 |
| John Snow | 1965-76 | 49 | 202 | 7-40 | 26.66 | 8 | 1 |
| James Anderson | 2003-19 | 148 | 575 | 7-42 | 26.93 | 27 | 3 |
| Angus Fraser | 1989-98 | 46 | 177 | 8-53 | 27.32 | 13 | 2 |
| Darren Gough | 1994-2003 | 58 | 229 | 6-42 | 28.39 | 9 | 0 |
| Ian Botham | 1977-92 | 102 | 383 | 8-34 | 28.40 | 27 | 4 |

| Bowler | Span | Tests | Wickets | Best | Average | 5wi | 10wm |
|---|---|---|---|---|---|---|---|
| Stuart Broad | 2007-19 | 126 | 437 | 8-15 | 29.05 | 16 | 2 |
| Andrew Caddick | 1993-2003 | 62 | 234 | 7-46 | 29.91 | 13 | 1 |
| Matthew Hoggard | 2000-08 | 67 | 248 | 7-61 | 30.50 | 7 | 1 |
| Steve Harmison | 2002-09 | 62 | 222 | 7-12 | 31.94 | 8 | 1 |
| Andrew Flintoff | 1998-2009 | 78 | 219 | 5-58 | 33.34 | 3 | 0 |

## Left-arm fast or fast-medium (50 wickets, top four averages)

| Bowler | Span | Tests | Wickets | Best | Average | 5wi | 10wm |
|---|---|---|---|---|---|---|---|
| John Lever | 1976-86 | 21 | 73 | 7-46 | 26.72 | 3 | 1 |
| Bill Voce | 1930-47 | 27 | 98 | 7-70 | 27.88 | 3 | 2 |
| Ryan Sidebottom | 2001-10 | 22 | 79 | 7-47 | 28.24 | 5 | 1 |
| George Hirst | 1897-1909 | 24 | 59 | 5-48 | 30.00 | 3 | 0 |

## Right-arm orthodox spin (100 wickets, top seven averages)

| Bowler | Span | Tests | Wickets | Best | Average | 5wi | 10wm |
|---|---|---|---|---|---|---|---|
| Jim Laker | 1948-59 | 46 | 193 | 10-53 | 21.24 | 9 | 3 |
| Graeme Swann | 2008-13 | 60 | 255 | 6-65 | 29.96 | 17 | 3 |
| David Allen | 1960-66 | 39 | 122 | 5-30 | 30.97 | 4 | 0 |
| Ray Illingworth | 1958-73 | 61 | 122 | 6-29 | 31.20 | 3 | 0 |
| Fred Titmus | 1955-75 | 53 | 153 | 7-79 | 32.22 | 7 | 0 |
| Moeen Ali | 2014-19 | 58 | 177 | 6-53 | 36.37 | 5 | 1 |
| John Emburey | 1978-95 | 64 | 147 | 7-78 | 38.40 | 6 | 0 |

## Left-arm orthodox spin (100 wickets, top nine averages)

| Bowler | Span | Tests | Wickets | Best | Average | 5wi | 10wm |
|---|---|---|---|---|---|---|---|
| Bobby Peel | 1884-96 | 20 | 101 | 7-31 | 16.98 | 5 | 1 |
| *Johnny Briggs | 1884-99 | 33 | 118 | 8-11 | 17.75 | 9 | 4 |
| Colin Blythe | 1901-10 | 19 | 100 | 8-59 | 18.63 | 9 | 4 |
| Hedley Verity | 1931-39 | 40 | 144 | 8-43 | 24.37 | 5 | 2 |
| Tony Lock | 1952-68 | 49 | 174 | 7-35 | 25.58 | 9 | 3 |
| Derek Underwood | 1966-82 | 86 | 297 | 8-51 | 25.83 | 17 | 6 |
| Wilfred Rhodes | 1899-1930 | 58 | 127 | 8-68 | 26.96 | 6 | 1 |
| Phil Edmonds | 1975-87 | 51 | 125 | 7-66 | 34.18 | 2 | 0 |
| Monty Panesar | 2006-13 | 50 | 167 | 6-37 | 34.71 | 12 | 2 |

## Wrist spin (45 wickets, top six averages)

| Bowler | Span | Tests | Wickets | Best | Average | 5wi | 10wm |
|---|---|---|---|---|---|---|---|
| Tich Freeman | 1924-29 | 12 | 66 | 7-71 | 25.86 | 5 | 3 |
| Walter Robins | 1929-37 | 19 | 64 | 6-32 | 27.46 | 1 | 0 |
| Ian Peebles | 1927-31 | 13 | 45 | 6-63 | 30.91 | 3 | 0 |
| Len Braund | 1901-08 | 23 | 47 | 8-81 | 38.51 | 3 | 0 |
| Doug Wright | 1938-51 | 34 | 108 | 7-105 | 39.11 | 6 | 1 |
| Adil Rashid | 2015-19 | 19 | 60 | 5-49 | 39.83 | 2 | 0 |

All six of the above bowled right–arm wrist spin. Johnny Wardle bowled two styles of left–arm spin: broadly, wrist spin overseas (45 wickets at 20.0 in 13 Tests, which would place him third in the above table) and orthodox spin at home (where his record was 57 wickets at 20.70 in 15 Tests). Overall, he took 102 wickets at 20.39 in 28 Tests between 1948 and 1957.

---

\* Briggs's record includes 21 wickets against South Africa in two matches only subsequently regarded as of Test status.

# England's Leading Fielders

## Wicketkeepers (100 dismissals)

| Wicketkeeper | Span | Inns | Caught | Stumped | Total | Average |
| --- | --- | --- | --- | --- | --- | --- |
| Jonny Bairstow | 2013-19 | 79 | 150 | 11 | 161 | 2.04 |
| Geraint Jones | 2004-06 | 66 | 128 | 5 | 133 | 2.02 |
| Matt Prior | 2007-14 | 146 | 243 | 13 | 256 | 1.75 |
| Jack Russell | 1988-98 | 96 | 153 | 12 | 165 | 1.72 |
| Alec Stewart | 1991-2003 | 141 | 227 | 14 | 241 | 1.71 |
| Bob Taylor | 1971-84 | 106 | 167 | 7 | 174 | 1.64 |
| Alan Knott | 1967-81 | 174 | 250 | 19 | 269 | 1.55 |
| Jim Parks | 1960-68 | 80 | 101 | 11 | 112 | 1.40 |
| Godfrey Evans | 1946-59 | 175 | 173 | 46 | 219 | 1.25 |

## Fielders (80 catches, top ten averages)

| Fielder | Span | Innings | Caught | Average |
| --- | --- | --- | --- | --- |
| Tony Greig | 1972-77 | 107 | 87 | 0.81 |
| Graeme Hick | 1991-2001 | 115 | 90 | 0.78 |
| Paul Collingwood | 2003-11 | 124 | 96 | 0.77 |
| Wally Hammond | 1927-47 | 154 | 110 | 0.71 |
| Marcus Trescothick | 2000-06 | 139 | 95 | 0.68 |
| Ian Botham | 1977-92 | 179 | 120 | 0.67 |
| Andrew Strauss | 2004-12 | 189 | 121 | 0.64 |
| Joe Root | 2012-19 | 151 | 91 | 0.60 |
| Graham Thorpe | 1993-2005 | 179 | 105 | 0.59 |
| Alastair Cook | 2006-18 | 300 | 175 | 0.58 |

## Leading ODI batsmen (2,750 runs, top strike-rates)

| Batsman | Span | Inns | Runs | HS | Average | Rate | 100 |
|---|---|---|---|---|---|---|---|
| **Post-1996** | | | | | | | |
| Jos Buttler | 2012-19 | 105 | 3387 | 150 | 40.80 | 118.34 | 7 |
| ‡Eoin Morgan | 2009-19 | 180 | 6069 | 124* | 39.66 | 92.59 | 11 |
| Andrew Flintoff | 1999-2009 | 119 | 3293 | 123 | 31.97 | 89.14 | 3 |
| Kevin Pietersen | 2004-13 | 123 | 4422 | 130 | 41.32 | 86.70 | 9 |
| Joe Root | 2013-19 | 119 | 5090 | 133* | 50.90 | 86.69 | 14 |
| ‡Marcus Trescothick | 2000-06 | 122 | 4335 | 137 | 37.37 | 85.21 | 12 |
| ‡Andrew Strauss | 2003-11 | 126 | 4205 | 158 | 35.63 | 80.94 | 6 |
| **Pre-1996** | | | | | | | |
| Allan Lamb | 1982-92 | 118 | 4010 | 118 | 39.31 | 75.54 | 4 |
| ‡David Gower | 1978-91 | 111 | 3170 | 158 | 30.77 | 75.15 | 7 |
| Graham Gooch | 1976-95 | 122 | 4290 | 142 | 36.98 | 61.88 | 8 |

## Leading ODI bowlers (75 wickets, top strike-rates)

| Bowler | Span | Matches | Wkts | Best | Average | SR | Econ |
|---|---|---|---|---|---|---|---|
| **Pace bowlers** | | | | | | | |
| Liam Plunkett | 2005-19 | 78 | 116 | 5-52 | 30.66 | 31.2 | 5.88 |
| Andrew Flintoff | 1999-2009 | 138 | 168 | 5-19 | 23.61 | 32.7 | 4.33 |
| Chris Woakes | 2011-19 | 84 | 116 | 6-45 | 31.62 | 33.8 | 5.61 |
| Stuart Broad | 2006-16 | 121 | 178 | 5-23 | 30.13 | 34.3 | 5.26 |
| Steven Finn | 2011-17 | 69 | 102 | 5-33 | 29.37 | 34.8 | 5.06 |
| James Anderson | 2002-15 | 194 | 269 | 5-23 | 29.22 | 35.6 | 4.92 |
| Darren Gough | 1994-2006 | 158 | 234 | 5-44 | 26.29 | 35.9 | 4.38 |
| **Spin bowlers** | | | | | | | |
| Adil Rashid | 2009-19 | 83 | 128 | 5-27 | 29.74 | 31.9 | 5.58 |
| Graeme Swann | 2000-13 | 79 | 104 | 5-28 | 27.76 | 36.6 | 4.54 |
| John Emburey | 1980-93 | 61 | 76 | 4-37 | 30.86 | 45.0 | 4.10 |

*All figures correct up to 1 May 2019*

# SOURCES IN TEXT

For the sake of space, I have confined sources listed here to the identification of direct quotations. Where sources are identified in the text, or where quotations are drawn from match or tour reports in the relevant edition of *Wisden*, they are not listed here; other quotations that are not identified in the text or here were widely available in contemporary media sources. Where reference was made in the text to meetings of the Board of Control for Test Matches in England, which operated from 1898 to 1968, the minutes were generally to be found in the MCC library. Similarly, references to decisions taken by, or correspondence relating to, MCC committee meetings or England selection meetings in the period up to 1968, when control of the England team passed to the Test and County Cricket Board, were also usually drawn from papers available in the MCC library. One handicap was the absence of documentary material from the era of the TCCB (1968-96) while its successor body, the England and Wales Cricket Board, declined to make public its records since 1997.

### 1. Band of Brothers

'vast bank of information ...' Steve James, *The Times*, 20 February 2017
'mask of positivity' Michael Vaughan, p.7
'Far from throwing my hat in the air ...' *Harold Gimblett: Tormented Genius of Cricket*, p.93
'I believe that very few players do enjoy it ...' Doug Insole, pp.132-133
'It wasn't a collective effort ...' Keith Fletcher, interview with the author; see also *Captain's Innings: An Autobiography*, p.5
'I had been used to the buzz and banter ...' David Lloyd, p.86
'The increase in the amount of cricket ...' Vaughan, interview with the author

### 2. Gentlemen v Players

'During all the years I have edited Wisden ...' Sydney Pardon, Notes by the Editor, *Wisden* 1922
'In the event of no amateur being selected in the first six ...' MCC library archive

'The upper-middle class had hijacked cricket at the highest level,' Peter Wynne-Thomas, *The History of Cricket*, p.124

'The first Test match,' Pelham Warner, *The Cricketer*, 4 June 1921

'possibly in an attempt to give Sydney some social status ...' Alan Gibson, *The Cricket Captains of England*, p.20

'so arranged that if a Player wants to watch ...' George Lohmann, *Cricket*, 30 July 1896

'he was one of us' and 'Warner always wanted the pros to look up to him ...' Tiger Smith, p.31; CB Fry 'didn't understand our feelings' ibid., p.12

'I have heard some English captains ...' Joe Darling, *The Willow Wand*, p.98

'more democratic views on captaincy ...' Derek Birley, ibid., p.92

'In general-ship the Australians are easily first ...' Jim Phillips, *The Australian*, quoted in *Cricket*, 30 November 1899

'some of the men were drunk ...' Victor Cohen, *Poverty Bay Herald*, 4 January 1894

For details of the Read-Logan dispute see Keith Booth, *A Class Act: Walter Read, Surrey Champion*; also *Wisden* 2016, p.405

'No collection shall be allowed ...' letter from Board of Control for Test Matches, 17 February 1902, MCC library archive

'Players chosen for England should be allowed to travel ...' Sydney Pardon, Notes by the Editor, *Wisden* 1926

'avoid all-night journeys,' *Wisden* 1936, p.352

'many an "amateur", so termed ...' Albert Knight, *The Willow Wand*, p.73

'these miserable and hateful labels ...' Knight, *Jack Hobbs: England's Greatest Cricketer*, p.71

'with the weather we experienced there this was almost a necessity,' Andrew Stoddart, *The Cricket Captains of England*, p.66

'three essential players' and 'Had I been told ...' *A Flick of the Fingers: The Chequered Life and Career of Jack Crawford*, p.137 and p.133

'some saw socialist revolution on the way' Eric Midwinter, *Dimming of the Day: The Cricket Season of 1914*

### 3. 'WG' Lights the Spark

'the distinction between gentlemen and players was never a matter of money ...' Derek Birley, *The Willow Wand*, p.15

'damn bad captain,' James Southerton, *Amazing Grace: The Man who was WG*, p.106

'If he hadn't taken Grace out ...' *'Give Me Arthur': A Biography of Arthur Shrewsbury*, p.112

'Men who were noted for their coolness ...' Charles Alcock, *The Father of Modern Sport: The Life and Times of Charles W Alcock*, pp.219-220

### 4. Demon Spofforth and the Australians

'Every man was animated by one thought ...' Pelham Warner, writing in the *Westminster Gazette,* quoted in *Wisden* 1913, p.540

'The Australians have mastered the art of bowling ...' Lord Harris, quoted in James D Coldham, p.46

'colonial obeisance to English class niceties' and 'ensuing spirit of amity' Gideon Haigh, p.29

### 5. Boom Time

'many a ball which would ordinarily have been fielded for two, scored four' *Bobby Abel: Professional Batsman*, p.66

'Lord's has scarcely before been the scene ...' *The Times*, 23 June 1896

'News was telegraphed every few minutes ...' Simon Rae, *WG Grace*, p.381

'urge the means for providing as much accommodation as possible ...' MCC library archive

'I cannot see why the MCC should be so reluctant to build a proper press box ...' Sydney Pardon, Notes by the Editor, *Wisden* 1901

'the long-leg or third-man view should not have been inflicted ...' Norman Preston, Notes by the Editor, *Wisden* 1959

'To save our skins we started play at 5.20 ...' Roland Ryder, 'Trials of a County Secretary', *Wisden* 1936

'These were the cricketers who became the heroes ...' Ric Sissons, p.124

'The best places for following the game have been given ...' *The Times*, 30 March 1898

'always one of the worst in England' Hobbs, Ric Sissons, p.252

'To see play from the pros' room at Lord's ...' Alec Bedser, p.145

'but they probably think it too much trouble ...' Patsy Hendren, 'Reflections', *Wisden* 1938

'As the players went to the wicket there was an outbreak of cheering ...' Malcolm Lorimer and Don Ambrose, p.47

'Some of the hits that passed for boundaries ...' Jack Fingleton, *Next Man In*, p.101

### 6. Hawke, Warner and the Amateur Coup

'Pray God, no professional shall ever captain England' Lord Hawke, *Lord Hawke: A Cricketing Legend*, p.9

'I do not remember a single instance of a plain, unmistakable failure ...' Neville Cardus, *Manchester Guardian*, 20 August 1938

'the cleverest bowler in my time,' Archie MacLaren, quoted in Derek Hodgson, p.62

'He gave to professional cricket a status of dignity and pride ...' JM Kilburn, *Lord Hawke: A Cricketing Legend*, p.11

'The Odysseus of cricket ...' Pelham Warner, ibid., p.8

'expensive habits ... feasting and merrymaking' Alfred Shaw, *The Players: A Social History of the Professional Cricketer*, p.117

'Everyone who is at all behind the scenes in cricket ...' Sydney Pardon, Notes by the Editor, *Wisden* 1903

'If the matches in future were arranged on the principles he suggested ...' Hawke's speech at Bedale, *Cricket*, 12 May 1898

'the most abused man of the day,' Charles Alcock in *Cricket*, quoted in Plum Warner, p.34

'MacLaren was a pessimist by nature ...' Warner, *Lord's 1787-1945*, pp.119-120

'a spendthrift who got everything he could out of his tour ...' Bill Ferguson, pp.83-84

'In this hope they may have been slightly disappointed ...' Alan Gibson, *The Cricket Captains of England*, p.64

### 7. The Myth of Captaincy

'a master of field placing,' Michael Down, p.171

'vision, vitality, and intensity,' AG Moyes, p.24

'an iron and joyless captain ...' Michael Down, p.173

'any problems arose because he seldom appreciated ...' Percy Fender, *The Final Over: The Cricketers of Summer 1914*, p.13

'My god, look what they've sent me!' For the origins of this comment see Michael Down, p.88

'the greatest innings I ever saw ...' Frank Chester, 'Thirty Years an Umpire', *Wisden* 1954

'Such a proceeding would never for one moment ...' *'Give Me Arthur': A Biography of Arthur Shrewsbury*, p.126

'a man for every type of wicket ...' Pelham Warner, *How We Recovered the Ashes*, p.265

'This move, which occasioned such comment ...' *Cricket*, 25 February 1904

'The locals felt so aggrieved ...' Patrick Ferriday, p.157

'as big as a tray,' Frank Chester, 'Thirty Years an Umpire', *Wisden* 1954

'although not much more than a slow turner ...' *England v Australia: A compendium of Test Cricket between the countries 1877-1968*, p.180

'The Australians had a holy dread ...' EW Swanton, *Gubby Allen: Man of Cricket*, p.184

'The decision rested on the weather ...' Gubby Allen, ibid., p.189

'the powers-that-be in the TCCB ...' Keith Fletcher, *Captain's Innings: An Autobiography*, p.126

### 8. Lord Harris's South African Deal

'a larger return than had ever been shown ...' Martin Meredith, p.303

'Chamberlain was chilly and blunt ...' James D Coldham, p.98

'to bring the counties into closer touch with the MCC' MCC in 1904, *Wisden* 1905

'that the counties are so strongly in favour ...' MCC library archive

'the strengthening of the bonds ...' Abe Bailey, *The History of Cricket,* p.133

'The Boers did not feel either welcome or inclined ...' Richard Holt, p.227

### 9. Speed, Swing and Spin

'the best fast bowler I ever saw' Jack Hobbs in obituary of Neville Knox, *Wisden* 1936

'Tom Richardson swept down on us ...' George Giffen, *Giants of the Game*, pp.183-184

'obviously scared' *Bobby Abel: Professional Batsman*, p.65

'The idea of letting England go into the field ...' Sydney Pardon, Notes by the Editor, *Wisden* 1910

'much too observant of what he thought was public opinion,' CB Fry, *Life Worth Living*, p.234

'small jealousies and petty pique' *The Times*, 21 June 1909 'betrayed England to Australia,' *Bailey's Magazine*, quoted in *Barclays World of Cricket*, p.337

'He wanted Jayes, but Haigh was given him!' Beldam, quoted in Michael Down, p.120

'Yet [they] could make the ball swerve and seam off the pitch ...' Tiger Smith, p.109

'Sometimes when the wind was in the right direction,' George Hirst, *The Great All-Rounders,* p.19

'not notably high' JM Kilburn, p.67

'the exaggerated cult of Hirst as a bowler,' Home Gordon, *Sins of Omission: The Story of The Test Selectors 1899-1990*, p.181

'the sort of ball a man might see ...' Charles Macartney, *The Times,* 14 April 1953

'the best leg-break bowler in history,' HS Altham, *The Cricket Captains of England*, p.27

'Mr Simpson-Hayward has been a great success,' *The Times*, 28 February 1910

## 10. The Culture of the Cap

'the design being three lions ...' MCC library archive, MCC committee minutes, 2 March 1908

'a cap for all England' Philip Barker, 'The Return of the Cable Knit', *Wisden* 2017

'approved by MCC to be entitled to wear,' MCC library archive, MCC committee minutes, 28 October 1907

'The honour of wearing the England cap ...' Jack Hobbs, 'Personal Impressions', *Wisden* 1935

'owing to restrictions on the use ...' Ian Peebles, *Batter's Castle*, p.169

'I just took one that fitted me,' Nick Knight, *Tiger by the Tail: A Life in Business from Tesco to Test Cricket*, p.184 and p.188

'I wouldn't fancy a career in one of those ...' *The Cricketer*, September 2016

## 11. Hobbs and Rhodes

'I had the inferiority complex to a marked degree,' Jack Hobbs, *Jack Hobbs: England's Greatest Cricketer*, p.23

'a VIP who was in a sense a hired servant on a low wage,' Ric Sissons, p.91

'I was only half the player after the war,' Jack Hobbs, *Jack Hobbs: England's Greatest Cricketer*, p.177

## 12. The Shock of Gregory and McDonald

'Never in my life did I have bowlers like Armstrong ...' Percy Fender, *PGH Fender*, p.110

'In older days the area in and around the stumps ...' Pelham Warner, *Cricket Between the Wars*, p.105

'My whole later career was based upon what happened in France,' Lionel Tennyson, *The Final Over: The Cricketers of Summer 1914*, p.139

'so nervous that he could hardly hold his bat ...' *It's Not Cricket: A History of Skulduggery, Sharp Practice and Downright Cheating in the Noble Game*, p.149

'Johnny, the selectors are telling me to have a go ...' Doug Insole, *Barclays World of Cricket*, p.337

'radiated a debonair gaiety ...' and 'stood higher than that of any predecessor' Ian Peebles, *Barclays World of Cricket*, p.148

'Our teams suffered a good deal ...' Sydney Pardon, Notes by the Editor, *Wisden* 1922

'Both these bowlers made the ball fly high ...' Bert Oldfield, *Jack Hobbs: England's Greatest Cricketer*, p.194

'If I am beaten all ends up and get away with it ...' Herbert Sutcliffe, ibid, p.215

'leave the new ball alone,' ibid, p.229

'I knew we'd found the right opener for England,' Jack Hobbs p.229

'kept the ball popping and turning ...' Frank Chester, ibid, p.290

'his standing was such that ...' John Arlott, ibid, p.297

'Their partnership almost amounts to ...' Arthur Gilligan, ibid, p.275

'A batsman dare not "cover-up" ...' Sydney Pardon, 'Success of the LBW experiment', *Wisden* 1936

'I have perhaps succumbed to the new lbw rule ...' Herbert Sutcliffe, p.43

'Does Jack really think that an action which robs the bowler ...' Harold Larwood, *Bodyline Autopsy*, p.21

'Have no mercy ... Give 'em hell,' Bill Bowes, p.78-79

'hit a few men,' Wilfred Rhodes, *Bodyline Autopsy*, p.204

'If the Australians are to be tackled ...' Neville Cardus, ibid., p.52

### 13. West Indies, New Zealand and India Join the Club

'I have from the very outset regarded these tours ...' Frederick Toone, 'Australian Tours and their Management', *Wisden* 1930

'the sporting instinct that brought us safe through the Great War,' Sir Theodore Cook, *The Willow Wand*, p.87

'How can you play for England?' quoted in 'The Duleep Papers', *Wisden Cricket Monthly*, January 1996

'submitting in reasonable time for the approval of the Imperial Cricket Conference ...' *Wisden* 1932, pp.41–42

'as matches played between sides duly selected ...' *The Times*, 29 July 1926

'Naturally men earning their living by the game ...' Stewart Caine, Notes by the Editor, *Wisden* 1927

'satisfy the hosts and for the prestige of international cricket,' *Wisden* 1949, p.913

'that at no time was the standard of West Indies cricket underrated,' ibid., p.915

'The West Indians should flay him alive,' CLR James, *The Development of West Indies Cricket*, Volume 1 p.53

### 14. Professionals Flex Their Muscles

'Mr Warner, I love a dog-fight!' and 'And by heaven! These Yorkshiremen do ...' Herbert Sutcliffe and Pelham Warner, *Cricket Between the Wars*, p.40

'are far beyond the dreams of the average county cricketer' Fred Root, *The Players: A Social History of the Professional Cricketer*, p.209

'He was puissant in back and long in arm ...' Frank Tyson, *Cricket: Picture from the Past* 'a major step in the elevation of the professional cricketer ...' John Arlott, *The Players: A Social History of the Professional Cricketer*, p.214

'Where there is a pretty lady, you will find Herbert,' Les Ames, *Jack Hobbs: England's Greatest Cricketer*, p.214

'the greatest of modern times,' Don Bradman, *Edging Towards Darkness: The Story of the Last Timeless Test*, p.28

'The whole crusade against the so-called dividing line ...' EHD Sewell, *Jack Hobbs: England's Greatest Cricketer*, p.19

'it gave us a better chance to discuss tactics,' Jack Hobbs, ibid., pp.275-276

'All concerned seemed determined that nothing should be left to chance ...' Pelham Warner, *Cricket Between the Wars*, p.15

'once I'd sorted out with the amateurs ...' Tiger Smith, p.63

'When on tour, amateurs and professionals "mix" splendidly ...' Patsy Hendren, 'Reflections', *Wisden* 1938

'still more than we do,' Jack Hobbs, *Jack Hobbs: England's Greatest Cricketer*, p.71

'I never felt so humiliated ...' Cec Parkin, *The Players: A Social History of the Professional Cricketer*, p.229

'Pray God, no professional shall ever captain England,' and 'I love and admire them all ...' *Lord Hawke: A Cricketing Legend*, p.9

'disparaging to professionals,' Mike Marqusee, *Anyone But England*, p.102

'gratuitous insult to the main body of professional cricketers,' Percy Fender, *PGH Fender*, p.142

'for the sake of England,' *The Cricketer*, July 2017

'did what me and Jack told him,' Wilfred Rhodes, *Jack Hobbs: England's Greatest Cricketer*, p.292

'to boss their own fellows,' *Jack Hobbs: England's Greatest Cricketer*, p.276

'For the sake of the professional cricketer, he should have accepted,' Herbert Sutcliffe, *Express Deliveries*, quoted in *Jack Hobbs: England's Greatest Cricketer*, p.335

'I never counted the captain in the Yorkshire side ...' Maurice Leyland, *Summer's Crown: The Story of Cricket's County Championship*, p.133

'You couldn't captain a box of bloody lead soldiers,' Tommy Mitchell, *Cricket My World*, p.90

'It was considered that a professional of such wide experience ...' *Wisden* 1933, p.348

## 15. Jardine Creates the First System

'relentless Napoleonic attitude,' Arthur Mailey, *Bodyline Autopsy*, p.239

'He was a keen student of the game ...' Pelham Warner, *Cricket Between the Wars*, p.103

'he is very efficient,' Pelham Warner, letter home to wife, quoted in *Plum Warner*, p.128

'a stern master but every inch a man,' and 'he planned for us, he cared for us, he fought for us,' Herbert Sutcliffe, *Bodyline Autopsy*, p.72

'my friend and greatest of captains,' Bill Bowes, ibid., pp.88-89

'and put the thought into his batsman's head ...' ibid., p.288

'should certainly have reported to me that he was not fit,' Douglas Jardine, *In Quest of the Ashes*, p.168

'Well! I burst and said a good deal ...' Gubby Allen, *Bodyline Autopsy*, p.146

'definitively and absolutely,' and 'utterly loyal to their captain,' ibid., p.214

'a terrible little coward of fast bowling,' *Gubby Allen: Bad Boy of Bodyline?*, p.57

'It was won because Australia's batsmen cannot play fast bowling ...' Harold
    Larwood, *Body-Line? An Account of the Test Matches between England and Australia
    1932-33*, p.135

'Bodyline was not an incident ...' CLR James, p.188

'I've nothing to apologise for ...' *Harold Larwood: The Authorised Biography of the
    World's Fastest Bowler*, p.211

'as to their attitude ...' *Wisden* 1938, p.775

'For the first time in my cricket career ...' Percy Fender, *PGH Fender*, p.150

'I don't want to see you, Mr Warner ...' Bill Woodfull, and also for reports of events
    on the Saturday in Adelaide, *Bodyline Autopsy*, pp.185-193

'large sections of both countries are embittered,' Bill Woodfull, *Bodyline Autopsy*,
    p.220

'wish to propose a new law or rule ...' and 'we would consent with great reluctance,'
    MCC cable, *Bodyline Autopsy*, p.222

'would be hustled into cars at close of play,' Christopher Martin-Jenkins, p.11

'that when inviting anyone to play for England ...' *The Times,* 20 April 1921

'I refuse to play in any more Tests ...' *Harold Larwood: The Authorised Biography of the
    World's Fastest Bowler*, p.215

'It was then decided that as I was under contract to the *Daily Mail* ...' Bob Wyatt,
    p.154

'they will find themselves a very unpopular side ...', *Plum Warner,* p107

'double personality' and 'abhorrent to him in English county cricket ...' *Pelham
    Warner,* p.115

'profoundly unhappy,' Bob Wyatt, *Bodyline Autopsy*, p.63

'if certain critics had not made such an effeminate outcry ...' Harold Larwood, *Body-
    Line? An Account of the Test Matches between England and Australia 1932-33*, p.33

'Looking back, the Australians perhaps made too much fuss ...' Jack Fingleton, *Gubby
    Allen: Bad Boy of Bodyline?*, p.71

'departing from the agreement,' *Bodyline Autopsy*, p.402

'And what do you say as captain?' For details of the Wyatt-Bowes exchange, see
    *Express Deliveries*, p.120 (although Bowes wrongly identifies the match as MCC v
    Australians, in which he did not play)

'Australia, by practically claiming the right to make laws ...' *Barbados Advocate*, 2
    August 1933 quoted in *The Cambridge Companion to Cricket*

'cricket is doomed in Australia,' Dr Allen Robertson, *Bodyline Autopsy*, p.81

'For many years after Larwood went out of the game ...' Wally Hammond, *Cricket's
    Secret History,* quoted in *The Willow Wand*, p.215

'The effect on the counties generally ...' Findlay Commission, *Wisden* 1938, p.66 and
    p.179

'A Test match today is an imperial event ...' Pelham Warner, *Cricket Between the Wars*,
    p.35

'the ashen-faced young Yorkshireman ...' EW Swanton, *Jim: The Life of EW Swanton*,
    p.61

'were never seriously considered,' Christopher Martin-Jenkins, p.132

'one eye on the set and the other watching play . . .' Norman Yardley, p.204
Accusations of BBC 'one-sidedness', Jack Fingleton, p.240

### 16. The Welsh Connection

'It was the right thing to do . . .' Andrew Strauss, *The Times*, 20 February 2017
'We were not only playing for Glamorgan . . .' Tony Lewis, promotional boards at the
  Swalec Stadium, Cardiff
'the national team of Wales,' Robert Croft, *South Wales Evening Post*, 8 April 2016
'Nobody spoke to me . . .' Allan Watkins, *Summer's Crown: The Story of Cricket's
  County Championship*, p.170
'They might appear in Wales once in a couple of seasons . . .' Don Shepherd, *Class of
  '59 From Bailey to Wooller: The Golden Age of County Cricket*, p.76
'noting the obstinate refusal . . .' Marqusee, *Anyone But England*, p.23
'Nationality is a difficult subject for him,' Peter O'Reilly, *Sunday Times*, 7 May 2017

### 17. On the Mat

'where the climatic and other conditions permit,' *The Times*, 21 August 1929
'a good heavy pair of lawn-tennis boots . . .' William Chatterton, *A Class Act: Walter
  Read, Surrey Champion*, p.93
'a monotonous study of brick red,' and 'Players unused to these conditions . . .' Ernie
  Hayes, *Jack Hobbs: England's Greatest Cricketer*, p.100
'red gravel and looked like a huge hard tennis court,' Ian Peebles, *Batter's Castle*, p.74
'very good, all of them . . .' Johnny Douglas, *The World of Cricket*, 18 April 1914
'the ball roughs up very much more quickly . . .' Ian Peebles, *Batter's Castle*, p.74
'Schwarz, Faulkner and Vogler were suited exactly by the matting wickets . . .' Jack
  Hobbs, *Plum Warner*, p.54
'He was practically unplayable on matting . . .' Jack Hobbs, *SF Barnes: Master Bowler*,
  p.117
'for sustained interest I have never seen better . . .' Ian Peebles, *Talking of Cricket*, p.175

### 18. England's Talent for Attrition

'English batsmen seem to be infected . . .' Freddie Brown, 'Batsmen Must Be Bold',
  *Wisden* 1954
'I am strongly advocating that six days . . .' Arthur Gilligan, 'Five or Six Day Tests?',
  *The Cricketer*, 20 August 1938
'Time being of no consequence . . .' Sydney Pardon, Notes by the Editor, *Wisden* 1903
'The great crowd . . . were so stunned . . .' *The Cricketer*, 7 August 1948
'an unbroken run of draws . . .' Hubert Preston, Notes by the Editor, *Wisden* 1950
'Such tactics could in time kill first-class cricket . . .' Norman Preston, Notes by the
  Editor, *Wisden* 1960
'the severe ordeal of games played to a finish . . .' Stewart Caine, Notes by the Editor,
  *Wisden* 1927
'in a quietly determined, self-denying way . . .' EW Swanton, *Swanton in Australia with
  MCC 1946-1975*, p.53

'neglected to persevere with the attack ...' Monty Noble, p.178

'the three weaker cricketing countries,' Norman Preston, Notes by the Editor, *Wisden* 1968

'a straight knockout fight,' Iain Wilton, p.273

### 19. Hammond's Sacrifice

'It is common knowledge ...' Wilfrid Brookes, Notes by the Editor, *Wisden* 1939

'I would almost have given my ears for it,' Wally Hammond, *Cricket My Destiny,* p.136

'I suffered from hero-worship,' Walter Hammond, p.92

'sagacious and inspiring captain,' Wilfrid Brookes, Notes by the Editor, *Wisden* 1939

'ill-equipped temperamentally as a leader ...' EW Swanton, *Gubby Allen: Man of Cricket,* p.212

'Hammond showed unmistakably that he was well fitted ...' Wilfrid Brookes, Notes by the Editor, *Wisden* 1939

'He maintained rigid discipline ...' Louis Duffus, *Walter Hammond,* p.87

'a great slayer of moderate bowling ...' Bob Wyatt, p.155

'That's a bloody fine way to start,' and 'I thought it was a catch ...' Wally Hammond, *Bradman's War,* pp.40–41

'all-night binge,' Charles Williams, p.45

'enormous extraneous duties,' and 'He would be a player like the rest ...' Norman Yardley, p.215 and p.216

'He displayed tact and diplomacy ...' Clif Cary, ibid., p.121

'If he had stayed in Test cricket too long ...' Gerald Howat, ibid., p.121

'Our visit has done something to cement the relationship ...' Wally Hammond, ibid., pp.122–123

'Apparently it is only the nominal status ...' Wally Hammond, *The Willow Wand,* p.133

'honourable pay and compete on equal terms ...' *Wally Hammond: The Reasons Why,* p.237

### 20. The Politicisation of Test Cricket

'The Lord's Test was the scene ...' Hilary Beckles, Volume One, p.109

'the near-exact expression ...' *Wounded Tiger: A History of Cricket in Pakistan,* p.31

'West Indians from all walks of life ...' Brian Halford, p.40

'I sometimes wonder ...' Frank Tyson, *A Typhoon Called Tyson,* p.73

'As a sporting attraction, cricket in the 1950s ...' Malcolm Knox, p.384

'in a high state of nationalistic fervor ...' Peter May, p.152

'the second most controversial tour ...' *Fred Trueman: The Authorised Biography,* p.117

'or, as a Victorian would have put it ...' Trevor Bailey, from *Calypso Kings, Dark Destroyers: England–West Indies Test Cricket and the English Press, 1950 to 1984* by Stephen Wagg, quoted by Usha Iyer, p.129

'The MCC team of 1954 pushed British prestige ...' Frank Worrell, *It's Not Cricket,* p.32

'Some of the language directed against our players ...' Clyde Walcott, ibid., p.9

'There are few signs of willingness to help Pakistan ...' *The Times,* 2 June 1950

'We have won! We have won!' Alf Gover, *Wounded Tiger: A History of Cricket in Pakistan*, p.104

'traditionally England's oldest opponents,' ICC minutes of 1960 meeting, Usha Iyer, p.65

'They now clearly rank as one of the three Great Powers ...' Alan Ross, the *Guardian*, 29 June 1963

'The status quo was retained,' *The Times*, 19 July 1962

'might be construed as an insult to full member countries,' Murray and Merrett, p.78

'This, thought Alan, too bemused to do anything ...' Jim Laker, *Basil D'Oliveira Cricket and Conspiracy: The Untold Story*, p.15

'The situation suddenly changed ...' EM Wellings, pp.4–5

'His inclusion was a guess ...' Frank Tyson, *A Typhoon Called Tyson*, p.175

'When I read that, I went cold ...' *Tom Cartwright: The Flame Still Burns*, pp.150–152

'What is more important than votes ...' David Sheppard, 'The D'Oliveira Case', *Wisden* 1969

'the English public concluded ...' John Arlott, *Cricket on Trial: John Arlott's Cricket Journal 3*, p.252

'What about Subba Row?' *Raman Subba Row: Cricket Visionary*, p.84

'Peter was very upset with David ...' Virginia May, *Peter May: A Biography*, p.166

'I firmly believe that South African cricket ...' Peter May private letter, February 1983, MCC library archive

## 21. How Hutton and May Made England Hard to Beat

'He became one of the shrewdest observers ...' Cyril Washbrook in obituary of George Duckworth, *Wisden* 1967

'The relationship between Hutton and Compton ...' Alan Gibson, *The Cricket Captains of England*, p.182

'I have not been so deeply touched ...' Neville Cardus, quoted in *The Cricketer*, June 2017

'Ay, and what's more you're not getting paid ...' Len Hutton, *MCC The Autobiography of a Cricketer*, p.61

'He became convinced that successful cricket ...' JM Kilburn on Hutton, p.41–42

'Do you think you can learn to hate ...' David Sheppard, *Peter May: A Biography*, p.110

'We've got to do 'em ...' Godfrey Evans, *It's Not Cricket*, p.9

'straight, honest, flexible ...' Alec Bedser, p.145

'The business of waiting for what seemed like hours ...' Richie Benaud, p.18

'He was accused of keeping a brake on the game ...' Colin Cowdrey, p.67

'Black patches, not previously apparent, were visible ...' Frank Tyson, *A Typhoon Called Tyson*, p.113

'the ultra-cautious policy ...' Norman Preston, Notes by the Editor, *Wisden* 1954

'cricket in handcuffs,' Denis Compton, p.121

'Their presence at times is very embarrassing ...' Len Hutton, tour report, MCC library archive

'He played it so superbly ...' and 'His idea, I suspect ...' Colin Cowdrey, pp.57–59

'His streak of isolationism ...' ibid., p.57

'Gubby says that he also made it a condition ...' Peter May, p.83

'became fully captain of England ...' Colin Cowdrey, p.98

'There was no, "us and them" ...' Fred Trueman, *Peter May: A Biography*, p.107

'He never forgives anybody who lets him down ...' Doug Insole, p.24

'There was no doubt in my mind ...' Jim Laker, *19 for 90: Jim Laker*, p.155

'Peter, at his best, combined the drive ...' Trevor Bailey, *Peter May: A Biography*, p.106

'He was a fervent admirer of Hutton ...' Jim Laker, *19 for 90: Jim Laker*, p.163

'crammed himself into the mould of Hutton,' and, 'another couple of years ...' Alan
    Gibson, quoted in *Peter May: A Biography*, p.109

'there was little observable difference in their approaches,' Gibson, *The Cricket
    Captains of England,* p.201

'The chairman informed him of the committee's determination ...' notes of selection
    meeting, quoted in *Gubby Allen: Man of Cricket*, p.269

'with the notable exception of Mr EW Swanton ...' Peter May tour report, MCC
    library archive

'courtesy and co-operation personified ...' Doug Insole, p.61 and p.55

'Colin kicked him to death ...' *It's Not Cricket*, p.188

'English cricket had settled into a depressing groove ...' EM Wellings, p.3

'all international games in England a near farce,' Bill Bowes in *The Cricketer*, quoted
    in *It's Not Cricket*, p.217

'there was no such abundance of Test-class batsmen ...' Peter May, p.96

'there was not a fast bowler in England ...' Doug Insole, pp.10–12

'Statham obliterates opposing batting like the inexorable flood tide ...' JM Kilburn,
    p.52

'Sometimes he was like Alec Bedser ...' Johnny Wardle, and 'He had a bigger heart,'
    Ray Illingworth, in obituary of Bob Appleyard, *Wisden* 2016

'Godfrey Evans behind the stumps ...' Frank Tyson, *A Typhoon Called Tyson*, pp.78–79

'tamed the best attacking batsmen in the world ...' Doug Insole, p.25

'We certainly had the bowlers ...' Peter May, p.112

'By unshakeable tradition fast bowlers ...' Colin Cowdrey, pp.86–87

## 22. Selectors: Too Close or Not Close Enough?

'It seems rather sad that ...' John Arlott, *Test Match Diary 1953*, p.43

'It is possible Hutton might not have been ...' Jack Fingleton, p.156

'My brain seems to be muzzy ...' Brian Close correspondence to John Anderson,
    quoted in *Sunday Times*, 4 March 2018

'Surely the position is not as bad as all that,' *Peter May: A Biography*, p.119

'Selectors in the natural order of things ...' Alec Bedser, p.103

'has the last word about any doubtful name,' Wally Hammond, *Cricket My Destiny*,
    p.136

'Robins Robins Robins ...' cited in *Twin Ambitions*, p.164

'It is clearly wrong ...' Doug Insole, *Barclays World of Cricket*, p.336

'The last thing selectors want to do ...' and 'over the years I invariably found
    captains ...' Alec Bedser, p.164

'It was rare I didn't get what I wanted,' Mike Brearley, *The Art of Captaincy*, p.88

'ingrained notion of selection,' Keith Fletcher, *Captain's Innings: An Autobiography*, p.50

'the worst decision Atherton made ...' ibid., p.61

'Most of the time if not 100 per cent ...' Trevor Bayliss, press conference, London, 29 June 2017

'The chairman wants more [grass] off ...' Brian Scovell, p.26

'A team which plays regularly together ...' CB Fry, *Before the Lights Went Out: The 1912 Triangular Tournament*, p.158

'not watching much,' *Gubby Allen: Man of Cricket*, p.91

'a fatal tendency to flash at rising balls ...' Norman Yardley, p.205

'the lesson of that day remains for future selections ...' ibid., p.209

'there were certain people ...' Bob Wyatt, *Lost Voices of Cricket*, p.28

'Selectors offered no public reasons for their decisions ...' Alex Bannister, 'My Life Reporting Cricket', *Wisden* 1980

'What the selectors did not know ...' Wally Hammond, *The Willow Wand*, p.144

'It does little to improve the morale of a touring team ...' Frank Tyson, *A Typhoon Called Tyson*, pp.190–191

'This amateur–professional apartheid ...' ibid., p.193

'form of legalised deceit', and the death of 'humbug and the need for petty deception,' Charles Williams, p.169

'quite extraordinary' and 'there was an immediate impression ...' Doug Insole, p.117 and p.121

'my most prized cricketing possession,' Doug Insole, *Class of '59 From Bailey to Wooller,* p.211

'I honestly felt he could not see enough cricket ...' Ray Illingworth, *One-Man Committee: The complete story of his controversial reign*, p.27

'gin-swilling dodderers,' *Ian Botham: The Power and the Glory,* p.276

'over a nice dinner, with some bottles of decent wine' and 'I'm told it has always been this way ...' David Lloyd, p.130

'They did not as a rule give technical opinions ...' EW Swanton, *Gubby Allen: Man of Cricket*, p.290

'imperial enterprises' and 'men of good character,' Frederick Toone, 'Australian Tours and their Management', *Wisden* 1930

'in the unfortunate position of having to apologise ...' MCC library archive

'bohemian jollities,' *Edging Towards Darkness: The Story of the Last Timeless Test*, p.155

'as a pair, they had apparently behaved atrociously ...' *The Art of Captaincy*, p.90

'a dreadful selectorial blunder,' Keith Fletcher, *Ashes to Ashes: The Rise, Fall and Rise of English Cricket,* p.30

'Basil D'Oliveira is a very nice chap ...' Colin Cowdrey, MCC library archive

'If the management of that previous tour ...' Doug Insole, *Basil D'Oliveira Cricket and Conspiracy: The Untold Story*, p.201

'an absolutely genuine selection process,' *Class of '59 From Bailey to Wooller,* p.210

'were severely damaged,' *Basil D'Oliveira Cricket and Conspiracy: The Untold Story*, p.133

## 23. The Rise of the Umpire

'I thought [they] went too far in their appealing . . .' Frank Chester, *How's That!*, p.33

'the English temperament is the safest . . .' ibid., p.40

'I know South Africa to their dying day . . .' Peter May, p.94

'blazingly angry,' Wally Hammond, *It's Not Cricket*, p.26

'any umpire objected to on previous occasions . . .' MCC cable, *Before the Lights Went Out: The 1912 Triangular Tournament*, p.157

'His presence in a match between England and Australia,' WA Bettesworth, *Cricket*, 30 November 1905

'one of the outstanding Test umpires of all time,' Frank Chester, *How's That!*, p.189

'on several occasions it was simply disgraceful,' *Tom Richardson: A Bowler Pure and Simple*, p.66

'terrible,' Tiger Smith, p.35

'I expressed a very strong wish . . .' and 'at times inaccurate . . .' Gubby Allen, *Gubby Allen: Man of Cricket*, p.205

'Umpiring was not too good, on the whole,' Johnny Douglas, *The World of Cricket*, April 1914

'A small number of people attempted to rush the ground . . .' *The Times*, 29 February 1904

'Len never had a greater moment . . .' Denis Compton, *Fred Trueman: The Authorised Biography*, p.111

'appalling, though I do not for one moment . . .' Len Hutton, tour report, MCC library archive

'That's the fourth f***ing time . . .' Tom Graveney, *Fred Trueman: The Authorised Biography*, p.114

'I have never known any company of cricketers . . .' ibid., p.115

'Any instructions for tomorrow's game, Skipper?' *The Cambridge Companion to Cricket*, p.205

'they were not prepared to say,' Norman Preston, Notes by the Editor, *Wisden* 1959, p.75

'The very thing which is helping to damage cricket . . .' Leslie Smith, 'The Throwing Controversy', *Wisden* 1961

'a little bit funny,' *Gubby Allen: Man of Cricket*, p.260

'he can certainly generate a great deal of speed . . .' Frank Tyson, *A Typhoon Called Tyson*, p.166

'Umpires who had called a bowler for throwing . . .' Peter May, p.153

'I sometimes see the 1958–59 tour . . .' ibid., p.152

'diabolical,' Frank Tyson, *Class of '59 From Bailey to Wooller*, p.60

'a very strong report to Lord's,' Peter May, p.154

'I cannot remember an occasion . . .' ibid., pp.154–155

'known throughout the cricketing world . . .' Doug Insole, letter to Billy Griffith, 3 October 1966, MCC library archive

'If they will not accept decisions, there is no point carrying on,' Arthur Fagg, *It's Not Cricket*, p.190

'reprehensible,' John Woodcock, *The Times*, 13 August 1973

'Having the ball thrown at you from 18 yards . . .' Peter May, p.152

## 24. The Fight for the Soul of the Game

'never seemed able to make a decision ...' *Yorkshire and Back: The Autobiography of Ray Illingworth*, p.63

'hadn't the powers of concentration ...' ibid., p.63

'Of all the really top-class batsmen ...' Doug Insole, p.31

'As a man he could be shy at times ...' Micky Stewart, p.144

'sick of the biased attitude and incompetence ...' John Snow, p.3

'his mistakes were generally made ...' and 'for the benefit of the millions now viewing on television ...' *Gubby Allen: Man of Cricket*, pp.266-267

'ordered Brown to give Trueman a wide berth ...' *Fred Trueman: The Authorised Biography*, p.149

'Much unofficial – and some quasi-official – opposition ...' *Arlott and Trueman on Cricket*, p.101

'There were ... two senior members whose attitude ...' *Gubby Allen: Man of Cricket*, p.234

'just about the worst decision ever to come out of Lord's ...' EW Swanton, quoted in *The Cricketer*, March 2004

'extraordinary histrionics,' and 'military style discipline,' Colin Cowdrey, p.99

'public dressing down of his captain ...' ibid., p.101

'You ain't no bloody business in 'ere. Get out!' Fred Trueman, *MJK Smith: No Ordinary Man*, p.47

'Apart from a few formal greetings ...' Colin Cowdrey, p.101

'Britain's national summer game ...' Richard Holt, p.113

'As manager and selector, he became cantankerous ...' Mike Brearley, *The Art of Captaincy*, p.205

'The pity was that as he grew older ...' Peter May, p.141

'was condemned to ultimate failure as a captain ...' Ray Illingworth, quoted in 'The Inscrutable MCC' by Rob Steen, ESPNcricinfo, 1 March 2017

'Until they learn to treat cricket ...' Leslie Smith, *The Cricketer*, Spring Annual 1962

'The press came down on me like a ton of bricks ...' Colin Cowdrey, p.72

'We want a captain ...' Walter Robins, *Lord Ted: The Dexter Enigma*, p.99

'The appointment of Dexter as captain ...' EM Wellings, p.3

'influence Dexter towards the right sort of play,' ibid, p.5

'I had to do all the work ...' Alec Bedser, *Class of '59 From Bailey to Wooller*, p.232

'If your captain says to you in Melbourne ...' Fred Titmus, ibid., p.93

'Gentlemen, I wish this to be an entirely informal tour ...' Duke of Norfolk, quoted in 'What have we here? The eccentric Pom' by Ian Wooldridge, *Benson and Hedges Test Series Official Book 1986–87 The Clashes for the Ashes*

'the first really obvious and overt example ...' Doug Insole, *Class of '59 From Bailey to Wooller*, p.211

'He couldn't skipper a rowing boat,' Brian Sellers, *Twin Ambitions*, pp.142-143

'I had been everywhere ...' Ted Dexter, *Lord Ted: The Dexter Enigma*, p.147

'an outstanding reader of opposition techniques ...' Tony Lewis, p.169

'Effectively I was a professional,' MJK Smith, *Class of '59 From Bailey to Wooller*, p.136

'This must be the oddest England side ever ...' John Woodcock, *The Times*, 22 January 1964

'You're kidding, aren't you?' *Micky Stewart and the Changing Face of Cricket*, p.152

'within half an hour of playing in a Test match,' Henry Blofeld, *Over and Out: My Innings of a Lifetime with Test Match Special*, p.118

'It appeared as though all you wanted ...' Doug Insole, *Playing It Straight*, p.102

'Barrington set the cricket clock back to the Dark Ages ...' Keith Miller, ibid., p.103

'unworthy and discreditable motives,' *Wisden* 1969, p.160

'on a slow flat wicket when nothing was happening ...' Ray Illingworth, *Class of '59 From Bailey to Wooller*, p.101

'The general rumour in Trinidad ...' MCC library archive; also *Sunday Times*, 13 November 2011

'Crawford phoned me ...' Brian Close, *Class of '59 From Bailey to Wooller*, p.248

'the ability of administrators ...' Clark Report, *Wisden* 1967, p.106

'after an hour, we were no nearer a mutual understanding ...' John Snow, *Lasting the Pace*, p.33

'There were days when Cowdrey didn't even turn up ...' *Yorkshire and Back: The Autobiography of Ray Illingworth*, p.64

'was by some distance ...' Bob Willis, *Lasting the Pace*, p.34

'I was forced to tell him ...' Ray Illingworth, *One-Man Committee*, p.4

'You can't caution him,' Ray Illingworth, quoted in *Sydney Morning Herald,* 'Cricket Umpire Stood No Nonsense', 7 February 2017

'Snowy joined in ...' Ray Illingworth, quoted in obituary of David Clark, *Wisden* 2014

'more of a like mind,' *Lasting the Pace*, p.33, and 'a more enlightened method of choosing the manager ...' *One-Man Committee*, p.4

'They were strict about schoolwork ...' Joe Root, interview with the author

'I was one of three amateurs ...' Bob Barber, *MJK Smith: No Ordinary Man*, p.71

## 25. Leaving, On a Jet Plane

'I think they still had the Munich air crash in mind ...' *Tom Cartwright: The Flame Still Burns*, p.111

'as though we were just off to Agincourt ...' Colin Cowdrey, p.55

'No such lovely, leisurely, luxurious start ...' and 'Nearly a month at sea on a crowded ship ...' *Swanton in Australia with MCC 1946-1975*, p.22

'At Cairo we landed on the Nile ...' Godfrey Evans, quoted in obituary of Evans, *Wisden* 2000

a 'yellow-green' Len Hutton, *Colin Cowdrey*, p.62

'More time was spent in getting from place to place ...' *Cricket in Many Climes*, p.177

'I have had Turkish baths and massage ...' *Gubby Allen: Bad Boy of Bodyline?*, p.13

'It was a small ship ...' Godfrey Evans, *The Gloves Are Off*, p.65

'The idea that it gave you a chance ...' MJK Smith, *Raman Subba Row: Cricket Visionary*, p.69

'Twenty to thirty hours at a stretch ...' *'Give Me Arthur': A Biography of Arthur Shrewsbury*, p.99

'The whole tour means a round journey ...' Frederick Toone, 'Australian Tours and their Management', *Wisden* 1930 'sanctioned and encouraged,' Peter Oborne, *Wounded Tiger: A History of Cricket in Pakistan*, p.195

'we were no longer cricketers, it seemed . . .' Keith Fletcher, ibid., p.198

'in no uncertain terms . . .' and 'probably the most nerve-wracking in my life' John Snow, ibid., p.200

'Personally, I never felt as though I was really in danger . . .' Keith Fletcher, interview with the author

'a mob, having made its way out from the city . . .' John Woodcock, *The Times*, 10 March 1969

'It is too much to expect the same nucleus of 12 or 13 players . . .' John Woodcock, *The Times*, 21 January 1964

'I think it wrong to stage Test matches without a rest day . . .' Mike Brearley, *Phoenix from the Ashes*, p.19

'It is not a cricketing decision . . .' *Lasting the Pace*, p.172


## 26. English Cricket Opens Its Doors

'the first English coach to "bring home" a South African . . .' Tony Greig, *My Story*, p.53

'My second worry flowed from an undercurrent of resentment . . .' ibid., pp.91–92

'As I improved my standing in English cricket . . .' ibid., p.89

'It would be nice . . .' John Woodcock, *The Times*, 27 June 1970

'their two South African exiles,' and 'Here was irony indeed,' John Woodcock, *The Times*, 3 July 1970

'I still believe I only got the captaincy . . .' Tony Greig, *My Story*, p.89

'atrocious behaviour,' Tony Lewis, *The Cricketer*, December 2012

'With Greig in the driving seat . . .' Alec Bedser, p.95

'let it be known . . . that he did not want to play for England again . . .' Henry Blofeld, *The Packer Affair*, p.40

'Just say I feel I have two countries . . .' Tony Greig, *Wisden* 1975, p.87

'almost unthinkable,' and 'but for all his commitment . . .' Bob Willis, p.53

'No Test player has had to overcome such tremendous disadvantages . . .' *Wisden* 1967, pp.75–76

'It was unanimously agreed not to invite RE Marshall . . .' *Gubby Allen: Man of Cricket*, p.269

'I'm sorry,' he said. 'I've made some inquiries . . .' Roy Marshall, *Test Outcast*, p.151

'England must have sensed that they stood a chance . . .' Gordon Greenidge, *The Man in the Middle*, pp.56–57

'It is again pointed out . . .' and 'Last season some 15 to 17 overseas bowlers . . .' Alec Bedser, pp.171–172

'in view of the number of cricketers of West Indies descent . . .' *Wisden* 1969, p.75

'People [from the Caribbean] that had emigrated to the UK . . .' Roland Butcher, *Independent*, 23 February 2017

'He will leave county cricket . . .' Ray Illingworth, *One-Man Committee*, p.350

'I don't know how long I can hang on,' Graeme Hick, *The Times*, 23 October 1986

'I started badly and was always playing catch-up,' Graeme Hick, *Sunday Times*, 9 August 2015

'Look, only the colonials are left!' Derek Pringle, interview with the author, 3 May 2017

'were not over-keen on picking cricketers ...' and 'Even if players had lived in England ...' Keith Fletcher, *Captain's Innings: An Autobiography*, p.68

'We don't have a truly English side,' Neil Foster, *Anyone But England*, p.22

'The game is dying amongst us,' Alex Tudor, 'Afro-Caribbean Cricket in England: Decline of a Proud Tradition,' by Dean Wilson, *Wisden* 2009, p.61

'not entirely forthcoming ... about my intentions,' Ryan Harris, *Rhino*, p.84

'I feel English,' Martin McCague, and, 'To me, he's Australian,' *Anyone But England*, pp.22–23

'We have got to the stage where we are very careful ...' Geoff Miller, various newspaper reports, 11 January 2010

'He's Australian, Darren,' *Daily Mail*, 19 July 2008

## 27. Kerry Packer and the Years of Rebellion

'the thought of an eight-Test tour of Pakistan and India ...' Ray Illingworth, *Yorkshire and Back*, p.96

'I would do exactly the same thing ...' Tom Graveney, *The Times*, 20 June 1969

'It is hard to convey ...' Keith Fletcher, *Captain's Innings: An Autobiography*, pp.3–4

'Until that time, English Test grounds were closed shops ...' Patrick Eagar, *Wisden* 2000, p.33

'Even an increase of £1 made a big difference ...' Peter Lush, interview with the author

'it was explained that we were trying to establish a proper base ...' Jack Bailey, p.42

'What we had to do was drag people into the 20th century ...' *Raman Subba Row: Cricket Visionary*, p.122

'When I saw what Packer was offering ...' Joel Garner, *Supercat: The authorised biography of Clive Lloyd*, p.115

'Cricket is short of money ...' *The Packer Affair*, p.68

'I could have said, "Okay, I'm captain of England" ...' Tony Greig, ibid., p.43

'If I had been offered a contract ...' Ray Illingworth, ibid., p.115

'it was glaringly obvious ...' Geoff Boycott, quoted in *The Autobiography: Anything But Murder*, p.83

'I'm nearly 31 years old ...' Tony Greig, the Cowdrey Lecture, quoted on 'Kerry Packer: The Revolution That Changed Cricket', BBC Radio 5 Live, 2 May 2017

'an appalling encroachment on the privileges of every married man ...' Tony Greig, *My Story*, pp.79–80

'The stark fact remained for the Establishment ...' Henry Blofeld, *The Packer Affair*, p.58

'We can't let players dictate to us,' Peter May, and 'I thought it was blimpish in the extreme,' Mike Brearley, Brearley interview with the author

'Several players were openly unhappy ...' David Lloyd, p.170

'What would you do if you were in the army?' Tim Lamb, quoted in *Dazzler: The Autobiography*, p.181

'After every win, when the girls were around ...' Andrew Strauss, *Driving Ambition*, p.209

'To lay-men it is incredible ...' *The Packer Affair*, pp.64-65

'we've had a good stuffing,' Doug Insole, cited in obituary of Insole, *The Times*, 8 August 2017

'It was a very difficult time,' Dennis Amiss, speaking on 'Kerry Packer: The Revolution That Changed Cricket', BBC Radio 5 Live, 2 May 2017

'Tactically he was good, but he was too wound up in his own game ...' John Lever, *Boycs: The True Story*, p.168

'Batting at Test level was a struggle for me,' Mike Brearley, interview with the author

'disloyal traitors,' Geoff Boycott, *Boycs: The True Story*, p.167

'Boycott has the uncanny knack of being where fast bowlers aren't,' Tony Greig, ibid., p.167

'in the best interests of Australian and international cricket,' and 'It was hard to avoid the sense ...' *Conflicts in Cricket*, p.115

'crowds have become more unkind, opinionated and noisy,' Mike Brearley, *The Art of Captaincy*, p.227

'I was disappointed that this gentlemen's agreement was broken,' Graham Yallop, p.45

'I'm sorry he was hit in the face ...' Mike Brearley, quoted in *The Australian,* 23-24 December 2017

'Until apartheid goes ...' Rodney Hartman, p.175

'For a player to do this was quite extraordinary ...' Keith Fletcher, *Ashes to Ashes: The Rise, Fall and Rise of English Cricket*, p.135

'to get off the sometimes fearful treadmill ...' *Ian Botham: The Power and the Glory*, p.273

'This is a free country ...' the *Sun*, obituary of Donald Carr, *The Times*, 13 June 2016

## 28. Gooch, Botham and the Cult of Fitness

'You could've turned up for that tour ...' Graham Gooch, *Captaincy*, p.16

'If my way didn't work ...' ibid., p.15

'was satisfied we would be the fittest England side ...' ibid., p.16

'I know that most of the players from the other nations ...' Viv Richards, *Hitting Across the Line*, pp.145-6

'to get away from the champagne-set image,' Graham Gooch, *Ian Botham: The Power and the Glory*, p.303

'There was a temptation to play to the image ...' David Gower, *An Endangered Species: The Autobiography*, p.18

'I found achieving that ultra-professional approach ...' ibid., p.22

'earnest and occasionally morose style,' Mike Brearley, *Micky Stewart and the Changing Face of Cricket*, p.298

'We laid the foundations for what you see in the England set-up now,' Graham Gooch, ibid., p.282 and p.284

'But you're always knackered after five overs ...' Tony Greig, *Lasting the Pace*, p.73

'That was the terms of reference,' Bernard Thomas, interview with the author

'square-bashing mentality,' Bob Willis, p.77

'Thomas's most significant contribution to the England team ...' Mike Brearley, *The Art of Captaincy*, p.57

'By definition, this gave him a say ...' Bob Willis, p.77

'An expert masseur always accompanies the team . . .' Frederick Toone, 'Australian Tours and their Management', *Wisden* 1930

'very soft and bloated,' Norman Yardley, p.216

'physically slight and was sometimes lazy . . .' ibid., p.214

'It is not exactly appetising . . .' *In the Eye of the Typhoon: Recollections of the Marylebone Cricket Club tour of Australia 1954-55*, p.xiii and pp.107-108

'Harold Dalton . . . was set loose on him . . .' Colin Cowdrey, p.64

'I used to drink a drop of beer . . .' Harold Larwood, cited in 'Quiet Man Dealt in Terror at 100mph' by Graeme Wright, *Independent on Sunday*, 23 July 1995

'unfit, paunchy bunch of barflies,' Gordon Pirie, quoted in *Endurance: The Extraordinary Life and Times of Emil Zatopek* (2016), p.298

'Some of our old soldiers were positively mutinous,' Ted Dexter, p.94

'too much time was spent . . .' *One-Man Committee*, p.18

'justifiably poor reputation for injuries . . .' David Lloyd, p.270

'20 minutes of aimless exercise,' *Ashes to Ashes: The Rise, Fall and Rise of English Cricket*, p.88

'left them in no doubt . . .' David Lloyd, p.170

'The players, I concluded, were not physically fit enough . . .' ibid., p.195

'Being England physio is a big job,' Darren Gough, p.234

'getting above himself,' ibid., p.235

'The team worked harder . . .' Duncan Fletcher, *Behind the Shades: The Autobiography*, pp.225-6

'When I got the captaincy in 2003 . . .' Michael Vaughan, interview with the author

'When he first filled the Lord's bath with ice cubes . . .' Michael Vaughan, p.60

## 29. Television Contracts and Ground Redevelopments

'jostled and harassed,' and 'The police did all they could . . .' *The Times*, 27 August 1973

'sometimes intimidatory to players and umpires,' *Wisden* 1977, p.1083

'The Oval being quite close to Brixton . . .' Michael Holding, 'Our Home Away from Home', *The Nightwatchman*, Spring 2017

'Jack, Lord's will lose Test matches . . .' Raman Subba Row, *Raman Subba Row: Cricket Visionary*, p.144

'It was felt that while an extra game at Lord's . . .' *Wisden* 1985, pp.1240-1242

'We had to negotiate . . .' Brian Downing, *The Times*, 17 August 1994

'Their endless mantras . . .' Matthew Engel, *Wisden Cricket Monthly*, April 1998

'You cannot do much with that,' Lord MacLaurin, *The Times*, 3 January 2017

'The professional game here would have died,' Giles Clarke, *The Cricketer*, September 2016

'We have no ambition to be the richest, most irrelevant sport . . .' Tom Harrison, 'Cricket Seeks Bigger Crowd in T20 Shake-Up', *Financial Times*, 18 March 2017

'For many years, its presentation of cricket . . .' Matthew Engel, Notes by the Editor, *Wisden* 1999

'I want to change the process . . .' Colin Graves, 'Graves Points New Way Forward To Help Counties Survive', *Daily Telegraph*, 17 November 2016

'They told us to build a first-class ground . . .' Bob Jackson, interview with the author

'I don't think it was ever stated . . .' Tom Moffat, interview with the author

'wise up their act,' Duncan Fletcher, *Behind the Shades: The Autobiography*, p.145


## 30. Who Runs the Team?

'The captain and coach provided the direction . . .' Michael Vaughan, interview with the author

'The English cricket establishment laid claim . . .' Ian MacLaurin, p.183

'criticism of the players through the media . . .' Patrick Whittingdale, *One-Man Committee*, p.199

'saw his responsibility as running a smooth ship . . .' David Lloyd, p.184

'there is a view that there is a lack of support . . .' ibid., p.248

'I knew they were not booing me . . .' Nasser Hussain, pp.257–258

'we fielded some of the weakest teams . . .' Keith Fletcher, *Ashes to Ashes*, p.4

'probably constituted the weakest new-ball pair . . .' ibid., p.67

'the team was not very good . . .' David Lloyd, p.133

'Doug was a terrific support,' Mike Brearley, interview with the author

'Whenever you went to a dinner in England,' Micky Stewart, *Micky Stewart and the Changing Face of Cricket*, p.239

'Things were planned in more detail . . .' Bill Athey, ibid., p.237

'Micky was an anchor for England . . .' Graham Gooch, ibid., p.295

'When I came in, they'd just lost three series . . .' Micky Stewart, ibid., p.234

'Micky was a visionary and very much ahead of his time,' Medha Laud, interview with the author

'truly bizarre,' Imran Khan, p.55

'We were never going to win,' Bill Athey, *The Cricketer*, October 2017

'a fucking cheat,' Nick Cook, *Raman Subba Row: Cricket Visionary*, p.153

'red hot all night,' *Micky Stewart and the Changing Face of Cricket*, p.257

'The reaction of the "establishment" . . .' and 'Instructions received from Lord's . . .' ibid., p.258

'open resentment towards us wherever we went,' Keith Fletcher, *Captain's Innings: An Autobiography*, p.39

'for the bad language used during the 2nd day . . .' Mike Gatting, *It's Not Cricket*, p.196

'every effort must be made to restart the match . . .' Subba Row, *Raman Subba Row: Cricket Visionary*, p.155

'unanimous protest,' ibid., p.155

'absolutely ridiculous,' Micky Stewart, ibid., p.259

'How our man saved the Test series,' obituary of Ted Corbett, *The Cricketer*, October 2017

'They [Pakistan] have been cheating us for 37 years . . .' Tom Graveney, *Raman Subba Row: Cricket Visionary*, p.154

'had not supported [Constant] as they should have . . .' Keith Fletcher, *Ashes to Ashes*, p.181

'It is not generally known . . .' Raman Subba Row, *Peter May: A Biography*, p.167

'The interests of English players were sacrificed . . .' Mike Procter, *Raman Subba Row: Cricket Visionary*, p.164

'insist that, while the veto was in existence ...' *One-Man Committee*, pp.15–16

'There was no stability ...' John Emburey, *Micky Stewart and the Changing Face of Cricket*, p.266

'There was far too much politicking ...' Gladstone Small, ibid., p.266

'They were all fed up with the hierarchy,' Micky Stewart, ibid., p.272

'I'd been cast adrift by England ...' Mike Gatting, ibid., p.273

'old boys network,' *One-Man Committee*, p.106

'The new man's first task ...' ibid., p.20

'It became clear that this team ...' ibid., p.181

'No one man has had so much power ...' ibid., p.6

'If he is honest, I think he will admit ...' David Lloyd, p.130

'I couldn't believe what I saw ...' Ray Illingworth, *One-Man Committee*, pp.283–284

'by a good two years ...' Keith Fletcher, *Ashes to Ashes*, p.98

'He liked to say things afterwards ...' Fletcher, interview with the author

'particularly vociferous,' *One-Man Committee*, p.309

'He soon demonstrated the tactical nous ...' Keith Fletcher, *Ashes to Ashes*, p.75

'was never shy of expressing a view ...' David Lloyd, p.139

'Nasser probably caused me as many anxieties ...' ibid., pp.144–145

'He taught me ... that there was a way of being successful ...' Nasser Hussain, pp.440–441

'My attitude was, if someone can play, let's pick them ...' ibid., p.101

'we needed to get away ...' and 'Thought it acceptable ...' David Lloyd, pp.189–190

'full of shit,' Chris Lewis, *The Times*, 29 July 1998

'I was never quite sure ...' Michael Vaughan, p.60

'did not fit [the] image ...' and 'Graham believed his time was his own ...' David Lloyd, p.189

'It is unlikely that the board would have kept him in office ...' *One-Man Committee*, p.102

'perverse reaction to what he considered ...' David Lloyd, p.139

'gutter press,' *One-Man Committee*, pp.117–118

'He was paranoid about me leaking ...' Nasser Hussain, p.237

'an absolute disgrace,' and 'I reacted badly ...' David Lloyd, pp.183–186

'I said if it was legal ...' ibid., p.234

'I told the board that in order to prepare adequately ...' ibid., pp.199–200

'were dealing with many issues ...', 'His response staggered me ...' and 'to think only of making decisions ...' *Behind the Shades: The Autobiography*, p.138

'The counties still felt a huge amount of ownership ...' Andrew Strauss, *Driving Ambition*, p.131

'The media were intrigued to know ...' and 'He was essentially a quiet, introverted leader ...' ibid., pp.133–134

## 31. Split Squads, At Last

'resembled a bad-tempered grandmother ...' Matthew Engel, Notes by the Editor, *Wisden* 1997

'We got our tactics wrong,' *The Art of Captaincy*, p.23

'They really should have gone with him [Knight],' Nasser Hussain, p.239

'We caved in over our contracts fight ...' Darren Gough, p.210

'The management tactics were sadly typical ...' Alec Stewart, p.214

'Stewie had agreed to a pay deal ...' Nasser Hussain, p.233

'my stance might tell against me ...' Alec Stewart, p.219

'In his three-year stint in the job ...' Darren Gough, p.212

'brought so much professionalism ...' Nasser Hussain, p.4

'had received a "substantial figure" ...' Chris Lewis, 'Mr Big Told Me Three of My England Team-Mates Were on the Take', *News of the World*, 16 April 2000

'leaving me to sink,' Chris Lewis, *Caught: The full story of cricket's match-fixing scandal*, p.130

'it is very difficult to get through to these teams ...' ibid., p.195

'Gupta's evidence was not the only evidence ...' Lord Condon, ibid., p.202

'There exists no substantive evidence ...' Lord MacLaurin, ibid., p.203

'I have never walked on to a cricket field ...' Darren Gough, p.242

'reiterated my belief ...' Michael Vaughan, p.5

## 32. Learning the Art of Winning in Asia

'fractious and unpleasant ... the worst meeting I have ever attended,' AC Smith, *Wisden* 1994, p.1292

'about a dozen gouges,' John Holder, p.306

'easily the hottest place where I have played cricket,' Nasser Hussain, p.305

'your behaviour today has been appalling,' Alec Stewart, p.209

'100 per cent English,' Nasser Hussain, p.24

'Another five minutes and it would have been complete darkness,' *Wisden* 2002, p.1051

'This was the peak of my captaincy,' ibid., p.345

'I knew how those youngsters felt ...' David Lloyd, *Daily Telegraph*, 16 August 1999

'He was bitter at the end,' Steve Harmison, p.121

'not easy because there were quite a few older, experienced players ...' Marcus Trescothick, 'What Duncan Did For Us', *Wisden* 2008

'He never gave the impression ...' Andrew Strauss, *Driving Ambition*, pp.174–175

'I thought that my first objective ...' Michael Vaughan, p.127

'It was the first building block in the campaign ...' ibid., p.328

'suffering some sort of delayed reaction ...' ibid., p.166

'in pretty choice language,' ibid, p.166

'He barely took his eyes off me all night,' Duncan Fletcher, *Behind the Shades: The Autobiography*, p.226

'He was the first batting coach ...' Michael Vaughan, p.69

'His ideas became so much of a blueprint for England ...' Andrew Strauss, 'What Duncan Did For Us', *Wisden* 2008

'He picked every delivery ...' Shane Warne, *On Pietersen*, p.62

'His play against Shane Warne in 2005 ...' Andrew Strauss, ibid., p.62

'substantial but necessary,' and 'Duncan encouraged me to do it his way ...' Alastair Cook, pp.91–92 and p.214

'He tells Sals and me to make sure ...' Michael Atherton, p.107

'He would have played for England in any period,' Keith Fletcher, *Ashes to Ashes*, p.71

'I found it very hard to forgive Bedi . . .' John Lever, 'The Secrets of Ball-Tampering: Hell for Leather' by Derek Pringle, *Wisden* 2017, p.80

'I had the natural speed to bowl it . . .' and 'I learned how to reverse it . . .' Simon Jones, p.95 and p.115

'[He] opened a lot of people's eyes,' Duncan Fletcher, *Ashes Regained: The Coach's Story*, p.114

'Flintoff and Simon Jones . . . caused all manner of problems,' Fletcher, *Behind the Shades*, p.274

'These were not batsmen . . .' Fletcher, *Ashes Regained*, p.116

'try to keep sweaty palms off the ball . . .' Waqar Younis, *Behind the Shades*, p.274

'the darker the ball . . .' Simon Jones, p.115

'The art of reverse swing . . .' Andrew Strauss, *Winning the Ashes Down Under: The Captain's Story*, pp.165–167

'The board decision to go back to India . . .' Giles Clarke, *The Cricketer*, September 2016

'flood of threats,' Tony Lewis, *The Cricketer*, December 2012

'I was introduced to him on our arrival . . .' Dennis Amiss, p.25

'we could all fuck off then,' Graeme Fowler, *Flying Stumps and Metal Bats*, p.41

'the ECB kept on monitoring the situation . . .' Nasser Hussain, p.338

'There were references . . . wherever we went . . .' David Lloyd, p.176

'It was without doubt the most traumatic time of my life,' Nasser Hussain, p.1

'If there was one slight element of frustration . . .' Duncan Fletcher, *Behind the Shades*, p.213

'Going to Zimbabwe was not a great thing to do . . .' Michael Vaughan, p.190

### 33. The Rise of Player Power

'I was worried about the effects . . .' Michael Vaughan, p.266

'The Ashes had become so big . . .' Peter Moores, interview with the author, September 2010

'The pressure [of the Ashes] had certainly contributed . . .' Andrew Strauss, *Driving Ambition*, p.124

'Just briefly, I considered driving my car . . .' Jonathan Trott, *Unguarded: My Autobiography*, p.29

'I'd say 50–50,' Trott, quoted in the *Guardian*, 4 October 2016

'We were worn down . . .' Kevin Pietersen, quoted in *Unguarded: My Autobiography*, p.61

'I was supposed to be this character who was unflappable,' Andrew Flintoff, speaking on 'Hidden Side of Sport', BBC Radio, 11 January 2012

'It arguably resulted in too much partying . . .' Michael Vaughan, p.293

'water was involved,' Andrew Flintoff, interview on Sky Sports News, 19 March 2007

'He got sick of defending us,' Geraint Jones, *The Plan: How Fletcher and Flower Transformed English Cricket*, p.138

'By the end of Duncan's coaching reign . . .' and 'Fletch always found it difficult . . .' Michael Vaughan, p.334 and p.347

'As the tour progressed . . .' Andrew Strauss, *Driving Ambition*, p.123

'go in a fresh direction ...' Michael Vaughan, p.329-330

'Peter has been a little bit disrespectful ...' ibid., p.357

'I get the feeling he would like a young captain ...' ibid., p.357

'What is required ...' Andrew Strauss, *Driving Ambition*, pp.157-158

'an exciting time,' Michael Vaughan, p.6

'Test and four-day cricket ...' Michael Vaughan, p.362

'To call it cricket at all will be difficult,' Steve James, 'A Reality Show of Sickening Vulgarity', *Sunday Telegraph*, 14 September 2008

'KP would have to convince the players ...' Andrew Strauss, pp.177-178

'It was already obvious to everybody ...' ibid., p.177

'was tapping on our heads like a woodpecker ...' and 'like a human triple espresso ...' Kevin Pietersen, p.16 and p.18

'On the practice days he seemed completely withdrawn ...' Andrew Strauss, pp.312-313

'It's tough being me in this dressing-room,' Kevin Pietersen, ibid., p.314

'I and other people wanted ...' and 'maybe a little bit distracted ...' Paul Downton, interview on *Test Match Special*, BBC Radio, 22 May 2014

'If England win he gets applauded ...' Andrew Flintoff, *Daily Mail*, 7 February 2014

### 34. The World's Best-Equipped Team

'He is conspicuously in charge,' Steve James, p.321

'The main issue with the regime of Peter Moores ...' Andrew Strauss, *Driving Ambition*, pp.197-198

'The players, who could easily have found themselves ...' Strauss, ibid., p.293

'one of the defining moments of my captaincy,' Strauss, ibid., p.242

'It wasn't technically that I was struggling,' Ian Bell, *The Plan*, p.221

'Sometimes as a team they might have appeared fractured ...' Steve James, p.332

'Certainly at some stages frustrations probably boiled over ...' Alastair Cook, BBC TV interview, 12 October 2014

'We feed into the simulator ...' Nathan Leamon, 'Flower Happy to Play Numbers Game', *Sunday Times*, 21 August 2011

'Better use of statistics helped us win ...' Andrew Strauss, *Driving Ambition*, pp.204-205

'One of the issues we have always grappled with ...' Andrew Strauss, ibid., pp.287-289

'rigorous containment,' Mike Brearley, *The Art of Captaincy*, p.203

'Some might say that preparing wickets ...' Andrew Strauss, *Driving Ambition*, pp.222-223

'It was a series of patience ...' Steve Smith, press conference, Sydney Cricket Ground, 8 January 2018

'That group of players ...' Paul Downton, interview on *Test Match Special*, BBC Radio, 22 May 2014

### 35. Strauss's White–Ball Revolution

'We just capitulated,' Eoin Morgan, *Wisden Cricket Monthly*, February 2018

'Courage, bravery and commitment ...' Tom Harrison, 'There was never way back for KP', *Sunday Times*, 17 May 2015

'Over the 16 months since his last appearance ...' Andrew Strauss, *Sunday Times*, 17 May 2015

'It's not often you get free rein ...' Eoin Morgan, press conference, Melbourne, 13 January 2018

'He was prepared to bring new answers ...' Ed Smith, 'Leader In Exile' by Peter O'Reilly, *Sunday Times*, 7 May 2017

'Sometimes you would play a big shot ...' Moeen Ali, *Sunday Times*, 14 May 2017

# BIBLIOGRAPHY

Allen, David Rayvern, *Cricket on the Air* (BBC Books, 1985)

Allen, David Rayvern, *Jim: The Life of EW Swanton* (Aurum, 2004)

Altham, HS and Swanton, EW, *A History of Cricket* (George Allen & Unwin, 1938)

Amiss, Dennis, *In Search of Runs: An Autobiography* (Hutchinson, 1976)

Anderson, James, *Jimmy: My Story* (Simon & Schuster, 2012)

Arlott, John, *Test Match Diary 1953* (James Barrie, 1953)

Arlott, John, *Cricket on Trial: John Arlott's Cricket Journal 3* (Heinemann, 1960)

Arlott, John (ed), *The Great All-Rounders* (Pelham, 1969)

Arlott, John, and Fred Trueman, *Arlott and Trueman on Cricket* ed by Gilbert Phelps (BBC Books, 1977)

Arlott, John, *Basingstoke Boy* (Collins Willow, 1990)

Atherton, Michael, *Opening Up: My Autobiography* (Hodder & Stoughton, 2002)

Bailey, Jack, *Conflicts in Cricket* (Kingswood Press, 1989)

Barker, Ralph, and Irving Rosenwater, *England v Australia: A compendium of Test Cricket between the countries 1877-1968* (Batsford, 1969)

Barrington, Ken, *Playing It Straight* (Stanley Paul, 1968)

Bassano, Brian, *MCC in South Africa 1938-39* (JW McKenzie, 1997)

Bassano, Brian, *Mann's Men: The MCC team in South Africa 1922-23* (JW McKenzie, 2001)

Bateman, Anthony, and Jeffrey Hill (editors), *The Cambridge Companion to Cricket* (Cambridge University Press, 2011)

Baxter, Peter, *Test Match Special* (Queen Anne Press, 1981)

Beckles, Hilary McD, *The Development of West Indies Cricket* (Vols 1 and 2; Pluto Press, 1998)

Bedser, Alec, *Twin Ambitions* (Stanley Paul, 1986)

Benaud, Richie, *Willow Patterns* (Hodder & Stoughton, 1969)

Berry, Scyld, and Rupert Peploe, *Cricket's Burning Passion: Ivo Bligh and the Story of the Ashes* (Methuen, 2006)

Berry, Scyld, *Cricket: The Game of Life* (Hodder & Stoughton, 2015)

Birley, Derek, *The Willow Wand* (Queen Anne Press, 1979)

Birley, Derek, *A Social History of English Cricket* (Aurum, 1999)

Blofeld, Henry, *The Packer Affair* (Collins, 1979)

Blofeld, Henry, *Over and Out: My Innings of a Lifetime with Test Match Special* (Hodder & Stoughton, 2017)

Booth, Keith, *The Father of Modern Sport: The Life and Times of Charles W Alcock* (Parrs Wood Press, 2002)

Booth, Keith, *A Class Act: Walter Read, Surrey Champion, ACS Lives in Cricket* (Association of Cricket Statisticians and Historians, 2011)

Booth, Keith, *Tom Richardson: A Bowler Pure and Simple, ACS Lives in Cricket* (Association of Cricket Statisticians and Historians, 2012)

Bose, Mihir, *A History of Indian Cricket* (Andre Deutsch, 1990)

Bowes, Bill, *Express Deliveries* (Stanley Paul, 1949)

Bradman, Don, *Farewell to Cricket* (Hodder & Stoughton, 1950)

Brearley, Mike, *Phoenix from the Ashes* (Hodder & Stoughton, 1982)

Brearley, Mike, *The Art of Captaincy* (Hodder & Stoughton, 1985; 1987 edition)

Briggs, Asa, *Victorian Cities* (Odhams, 1963)

Brodribb, Gerald, *The Croucher: A Biography of Gilbert Jessop* (London Magazine Editions, 1974)

Brodribb, Gerald, *Next Man In* (Pelham, 1985)

Brooke, Robert, *FR Foster: The Fields Were Sudden Bare, ACS Lives in Cricket* (Association of Cricket Statisticians and Historians, 2011)

Burns, Michael, *A Flick of the Fingers: The Chequered Life and Career of Jack Crawford* (Pitch Publishing, 2015)

Campbell, RH, *Some Statistics Concerning Cricket Casualties* (Australian Broadcasting Commission 1933)

Cardus, Neville, *Cardus on Cricket* (Souvenir Press, 1977)

Cashman, Richard, *Australian Cricket Crowds: The Attendance Cycle. Daily Figures, 1877-1984* (Kensington, 1984)

Catton, JAH, *Wickets and Goals* (Chapman & Hall, 1926)

Chalke: Stephen, *At the heart of English cricket: The Life and Memories of Geoffrey Howard* (Fairfield Books, 2001)

Chalke, Stephen, and Derek Hodgson, *No Coward Soul: The Remarkable Story of Bob Appleyard* (Fairfield Books, 2003)

Chalke, Stephen, *Tom Cartwright: The Flame Still Burns* (Fairfield Books, 2007)

Chalke, Stephen, *Micky Stewart and the Changing Face of Cricket* (Fairfield Books, 2012)

Chalke, Stephen, *Summer's Crown: The Story of Cricket's County Championship* (Fairfield Books, 2015)

Chester, Frank, *How's That!* (Hutchinson, 1956)

Clarke, John, *With England in Australia: the MCC Tour 1965-66* (Stanley Paul, 1966)

Coldham, James D, *Lord Harris* (Allen & Unwin, 1983)

Coldham, James P, *Lord Hawke: A Cricketing Legend* (Crowood Press, 1990)

Compton, Denis, *End of an Innings* (Oldbourne Press, 1958)

Cook, Alastair, *Starting Out: My Story So Far* (Hodder & Stoughton, 2008)

Cowdrey, Colin, *MCC The Autobiography of a Cricketer* (Hodder & Stoughton, 1976)

Dellor, Ralph, and Stephen Lamb, *Lost Voices of Cricket* (Bene Factum Publishing, 2014)

Dexter, Ted, *Ted Dexter Declares: An Autobiography* (Stanley Paul, 1966)

Douglas, Christopher, *Douglas Jardine: Spartan Cricketer* (Allen & Unwin, 1984)

Down, Michael, *Archie: A Biography of AC MacLaren* (Allen & Unwin, 1981)

Duckworth, Leslie, *SF Barnes: Master Bowler* (Hutchinson, 1967)

Duckworth, Leslie, *Holmes and Sutcliffe: The Run Stealers* (Hutchinson, 1970)

Edwards, Alan, *Lionel Tennyson: Regency Buck* (Robson Books, 2001)

Evans, Godfrey, *The Gloves Are Off* (Hodder & Stoughton, 1960)

Fay, Stephen, and David Kynaston, *Arlott, Swanton and the Soul of English Cricket* (Bloomsbury, 2018)

Fender, Percy, *Defending the Ashes* (Chapman & Hall, 1921)

Ferguson, Bill, *Mr Cricket* (Nicholas Kaye, 1957)

Ferriday, Patrick, *Before the Lights Went Out: The 1912 Triangular Tournament* (Von Krumm Publishing, 2011)

Fingleton, Jack, *The Ashes Crown the Year* (Collins, 1954)

Fletcher, Duncan, *Ashes Regained: The Coach's Story* (Simon & Schuster, 2005)

Fletcher, Duncan, *Behind the Shades: The Autobiography* (Simon & Schuster, 2007)

Fletcher, Keith, *Captain's Innings: An Autobiography* (Hutchinson, 1983)

Fletcher, Keith, *Ashes to Ashes: The Rise, Fall and Rise of English Cricket* (Headline, 2005)

Foot, David, *Wally Hammond: The Reasons Why* (Robson Books, 1998)

Foot, David, *Harold Gimblett: Tormented Genius of Cricket* (Heinemann, 1982; reprinted 2003)

Frith, David, *My Dear Victorious Stod: a Biography of AE Stoddart* (Lutterworth Press, 1977)

Frith, David, *Silence of the Heart: Cricket Suicides* (Mainstream, 2000)

Frith, David, *Bodyline Autopsy* (Aurum, 2002)

Fry, CB, *Life Worth Living* (Eyre & Spottiswoode, 1939)

Gatting, Mike, *Leading from the Front* (Queen Anne Press, 1988)

Geddes, Margaret, *Remembering Bradman* (Viking, 2002)

Gibson, Alan, *Jackson's Year* (Cassell, 1965)

Gibson, Alan, *The Cricket Captains of England* (Cassell, 1977)

Gooch, Graham, with Patrick Murphy, *Captaincy* (Hutchinson, 1992)

Gough, Darren, *Dazzler: The Autobiography* (Michael Joseph, 2001)

Gower, David, *An Endangered Species: The Autobiography* (Simon & Schuster, 2013)

Greenidge, Gordon, *The Man in the Middle* (David & Charles, 1980)

Greig, Tony, *My Story* (Hutchinson, 1980)

Guha, Ramachandra, *A Corner of a Foreign Field: The Indian History of a British Sport* (Picador, 2002)

Haigh, Gideon, *Stroke of Genius, Victor Trumper and the shot that changed cricket* (Simon & Schuster, 2016)

Halford, Brian, *Edgbaston: Fifty Tests* (2017)

Hamilton, Duncan, *Harold Larwood: The Authorized Biography of the World's Fastest Bowler* (Quercus, 2009)

Hammond, Walter, *Cricket My Destiny* (Stanley Paul, 1946)

Hammond, Walter, *Cricket My World* (Stanley Paul, 1948)

Hammond, Walter, *Cricket's Secret History* (Stanley Paul, 1952)

Harmison, Steve, *Speed Demons* (Trinity Mirror Sport, 2017)

Harris, Ryan, *Rhino* (Hardie Grant, 2014)

Hartman, Rodney, *Ali: The Life of Ali Bacher* (Viking, 2004)

Hignell, Andrew, *100 Greats: Glamorgan County Cricket Club* (NPI Media, 2000)

Hignell, Andrew, *100 First-Class Umpires* (The History Press, 2003)

Hill, Alan, *Peter May: A Biography* (André Deutsch, 1996)

Hill, Alan, *Brian Close: Cricket's Lionheart* (Methuen, 2002)

Holder, John, and Andrew Murtagh, *Test of Character: The Story of John Holder, Fast Bowler and Test Match Umpire* (Pitch Publishing, 2016)

Holt, Richard, *Sport and the British: A Modern History* (Clarendon Press, 1989)

Howat, Gerald, *Walter Hammond* (HarperCollins, 1984)

Howat, Gerald, *Plum Warner* (HarperCollins, 1987)

Hussain, Nasser, *Playing with Fire: The Autobiography* (Michael Joseph, 2004)

Illingworth, Ray, *Yorkshire and Back: The Autobiography of Ray Illingworth* (Queen Anne Press, 1980)

Illingworth, Ray, with Jack Bannister, *One-Man Committee: The complete story of his controversial reign* (Headline, 1996)

Insole, Douglas, *Cricket From the Middle* (Heinemann, 1961)

James, CLR, *Beyond a Boundary* (Hutchinson, 1963)

James, Steve, *The Plan: How Fletcher and Flower Transformed English Cricket* (Transworld, 2012)

Jardine, Douglas, *In Quest of the Ashes* (Hutchinson, 1933)

Jones, Simon, *The Test: My Life, and the Inside Story of the Greatest Ashes Series* (Yellow Jersey, 2015)

Kelner, Martin, *Sit Down and Cheer: A History of Sport on TV* (John Wisden & Co, 2012)

Khan, Imran, *All Round View* (Chatto & Windus, 1988)

Kilburn, JM, *Sweet Summers: The Classic Cricket Writing of JM Kilburn* (edited by Duncan Hamilton; Great Northern Books, 2008)

Knox, Malcolm, *Bradman's War* (Robson Press, 2013)

Kynaston, David, *Bobby Abel: Professional Batsman* (Secker & Warburg, 1982)

Laker, Jim, *Over to Me* (Frederick Muller, 1960)

Larwood, Harold, *Body-Line? An Account of the Test Matches between England and Australia 1932-33* (Elkin Matthews & Marrot, 1933)

Lazenby, John, *The Strangers Who Came Home* (Wisden, 2015)

Lazenby, John, *Edging Towards Darkness: The Story of the last Timeless Test* (Wisden, 2017)

Lee, Alan, *Lord Ted: The Dexter Enigma* (Gollancz, 1995)

Lemmon, David, *Johnny Won't Hit Today: A Cricketing Biography of JWHT Douglas* (Allen & Unwin, 1983)

Lever, JK, and Pat Gibson, *JK Lever: A Cricketers' Cricketer* (Collins Willow, 1989)

Lewis, Tony, *Taking Fresh Guard: A Memoir* (Headline, 2003)

Lister, Simon, *Supercat: The authorized biography of Clive Lloyd* (Fairfield Books, 2007)

Lloyd, David, *The Autobiography: Anything But Murder* (Collins Willow, 2000)

Lock, Tony, *For Surrey and England* (Hodder & Stoughton, 1957)

Lorimer, Malcolm, and Don Ambrose, *Cricket Grounds of Lancashire* (Association of Cricket Statisticians, 1992)

Lynd, Robert, *The Sporting Life* (Grant Richards, 1922)

Lyttelton, RH (with CB Fry, George Giffen and WJ Ford) *Giants of the Game* (1899)

McGlew, Jackie, *Cricket for South Africa* (Hodder & Stoughton, 1961)

McKinstry, Leo, *Boycs: The True Story* (Partridge Press, 2000)

McKinstry, Leo, *Jack Hobbs: England's Greatest Cricketer* (Yellow Jersey, 2011)

MacLaurin, Ian, *Tiger by the Tail: A Life in Business from Tesco to Test Cricket* (Macmillan, 1999)

Marqusee, Mike, *Anyone But England: Cricket, Race and Class* (Verso Books, 1994)

Marshall, John, *Headingley* (Pelham Books, 1970)

Marshall, Roy, *Test Outcast* (Pelham Books, 1970)

Martin-Jenkins, Christopher, *Ball By Ball: The Story of Cricket Broadcasting* (Grafton, 1990)

Mason, Ronald, *Warwick Armstrong's Australians* (Epworth Press, 1971)

May, Peter, *A Game Enjoyed* (Stanley Paul, 1985)

Meredith, Martin, *Diamonds, Gold and War: The Making of South Africa* (Simon & Schuster, 2007)

Miller, Douglas, *MJK Smith: No Ordinary Man, ACS Lives in Cricket* (Association of Cricket Statisticians and Historians, 2013)

Miller, Douglas, *Raman Subba Row: Cricket Visionary* (Charlcombe Books, 2017)

Moffat, Tom, *The Impossible Dream . . . Come True: The Story of how Durham County Cricket Club attained First Class Status in 1992* (FRO Print & Design, 2009)

Moore, Andrew, *The 'Fascist' Cricket tour of 1924-25, Australian Society for Sports History Publications* (May 1991)

Moyes, AG, *A Century of Cricketers* (Harrop, 1950)

Murray, Bruce, and Christopher Merrett, *Caught Behind: Race and Politics in Springbok Cricket* (University Kwazulu Natal Press, 2004)

Noble, MA, *The Fight for the Ashes 1928-29* (Harrap, 1929)

Oborne, Peter, *Basil D'Oliveira Cricket and Conspiracy: The Untold Story* (Little, Brown, 2004)

Oborne, Peter, *Wounded Tiger: A History of Cricket in Pakistan* (Simon & Schuster, 2014)

Pakenham, Thomas, *The Boer War* (Weidenfeld & Nicolson, 1979)

Parkinson, Justin, *The Strange Death of English Leg Spin: How cricket's finest art was given away* (Pitch Publishing, 2015)

Pawle, Gerald, *RES Wyatt: Fighting Cricketer* (Allen & Unwin, 1985)

Peebles, Ian, *Talking of Cricket* (Museum Press, 1953)

Peebles, Ian, *Batter's Castle* (Souvenir Press, 1958)

Peebles, Ian, *Patsy Hendren* (Macmillan, 1969)

Peel, Mark, *Ambassadors of Goodwill: MCC Tours 1946-47–1970/71* (Pitch, 2018)

Pietersen, Kevin, *KP: The Autobiography* (Little, Brown, 2014)

Pringle, Derek, *Pushing the Boundaries: Cricket in the Eighties* (Hodder & Stoughton, 2018)

Rae, Simon, *WG Grace* (Faber & Faber, 1998)

Rae, Simon, *It's Not Cricket: A History of Skulduggery, Sharp Practice and Downright Cheating in the Noble Game* (Faber & Faber, 2001)

Ramprakash, Mark, *Strictly Me: My Life Under the Spotlight* (Mainstream, 2009)

Rendell, Brian, *Gubby Allen: Bad Boy of Bodyline?* (2004)

Rendell, Brian, *Walter Robins: Achievements, Affections and Affronts, ACS Lives in Cricket* (Association of Cricket Statisticians and Historians, 2013)

Richards, Viv, *Hitting Across the Line* (Headline, 1991)

Ryan, Christian, *Feeling is the Thing that Happens in 1000th of a Second: A Season of Cricket Photographer Patrick Eagar* (Riverrun, 2017)

Sandford, Christopher, *The Final Over: The Cricketers of Summer 1914* (History Press, 2014)

Scoble, Christopher, *Colin Blythe: Lament for a Legend* (Sportsbooks, 2005)

Scovell, Brian, *19 for 90: Jim Laker* (History Press, 2006)

Searle, Chris, *Pitch of Life: Writings on Cricket* (Parrs Wood Press, 2001)

Sewell, EHD, *A Searchlight on English Cricket* (Robert Holden, 1926)

Sissons, Ric, *The Players: A Social History of the Professional Cricketer* (Kingswood Press, 1988)

Smith, EJ, as told to Pat Murphy, *'Tiger' Smith of Warwickshire and England* (Lutterworth Press, 1981)

Snow, John, *Cricket Rebel: An Autobiography* (Hamlyn, 1976)

Sobers, Garry, *My Autobiography* (Headline, 2002)

Statham, Brian, *Cricket Merry-Go-Round* (Stanley Paul, 1956)

Stewart, Alec, *Playing for Keeps* (BBC Books, 2003)

Strauss, Andrew, *Winning the Ashes Down Under: The Captain's Story* (Hodder & Stoughton, 2011)

Strauss, Andrew, *Driving Ambition: My Autobiography* (Hodder & Stoughton, 2013)

Streeton, Richard, *PGH Fender* (Faber & Faber, 1981)

Sutcliffe, Herbert, *How to Become a First Class Batsman* (Herbert Sutcliffe, 1949)

Swanton, EW, *Swanton in Australia with MCC 1946-1975* (Collins, 1975)

Swanton, EW (general editor), *Barclays World of Cricket* (Collins, 1980)

Swanton, EW, *Gubby Allen: Man of Cricket* (Hutchinson, 1985)

Sweetman, Simon, *Dimming of the Day: The Cricket Season of 1914* (Association of Cricket Statisticians and Historians, 2015)

Synge, Allen, *Sins of Omission: The Story of The Test Selectors 1899-1990* (Michael Joseph, 1990)

Tendulkar, Sachin, *Playing It May Way: My Autobiography* (Hodder & Stoughton, 2014)

Tennant, Ivo, *Graham Gooch: The Biography* (HF & G Witherby, 1993)

Tomlinson, Richard, *Amazing Grace: The Man who was WG* (Little, Brown, 2015)

Travers, Ben, *94 Declared* (Elm Tree Books, 1981)

Trott, Jonathan, *Unguarded: My Autobiography* (Sphere, 2016)

Tyson, Frank, *A Typhoon Called Tyson* (Heinemann, 1961)

Tyson, Frank, *In the Eye of the Typhoon: Recollections of the Marylebone Cricket Club tour of Australia 1954-55* (Parrs Wood Press, 2004)

Vaughan, Michael, *Time to Declare* (Hodder & Stoughton, 2009)

Walcott, Clyde, with Brian Scovell, *Sixty Years on the Back Foot* (Weidenfeld & Nicolson, 1999)

Warner, Pelham, *Cricket in Many Climes* (Heinemann, 1900)

Warner, Pelham, *How We Recovered the Ashes: An Account of the 1903-04 MCC Tour of Australia* (1904; Methuen 2003 edition)

Warner, Pelham, *Cricket Between the Wars* (Chatto & Windus, 1942)

Warner, Pelham, *Lord's 1787-1945* (Harrap, 1946)

Warner, Pelham, *Long Innings: The Autobiography* (Harrap, 1951)

Waters, Chris, *Fred Trueman: The Authorised Biography* (Aurum, 2011)

Waters, Chris, *10 for 10: Hedley Verity and the Story of Cricket's Greatest Bowling Feat* (Wisden, 2014)

Wellings, EM, *Dexter v Benaud: MCC Tour of Australia 1962-3* (Bailey Brothers & Swinfen, 1963)

Westcott, Chris, *Class of '59 From Bailey to Wooller: The Golden Age of County Cricket* (Mainstream, 2000)

Wigmore, Tim, and Miller, Peter, *Second XI: Cricket In Its Outposts* (Pitch Publishing, 2015)

Wilde, Simon, *Caught: The full story of cricket's match-fixing scandal* (Aurum, 2001)

Wilde, Simon, *Ian Botham: The Power and the Glory* (Simon & Schuster, 2011)

Wilde, Simon, *On Pietersen* (Simon & Schuster, 2014)

Williams, Charles, *Gentlemen & Players: The death of amateurism in cricket* (Weidenfeld & Nicolson, 2012)

Williams, Jack, *Cricket and Broadcasting* (Manchester University Press, 2011)

Williams, Marcus (and others), *Test Match Grounds of the World* (Collins Willow, 1990)

Willis, Bob, *Lasting the Pace* (Collins Willow, 1985)

Wilson, Jonathan, *Inverting the Pyramid: The History of Football Tactics* (Orion, 2008)

Wilton, Iain, *CB Fry: An English Hero* (Richard Cohen Books, 1999)

Winder, Robert, *Bloody Foreigners: The Story of Immigration to Britain* (Abacus, 2013, revised edn)

Wisden Cricketer, The, *Flying Stumps and Metal Bats: Cricket's Greatest Moments – by the People Who Were There* (Aurum, 2008)

Woolmer, Bob, *Woolmer on Cricket* (Virgin Books, 2000)

Wyatt, Bob, *Three Straight Sticks* (Stanley Paul, 1951)

Wynne-Thomas, Peter, *'Give Me Arthur': A Biography of Arthur Shrewsbury* (Arthur Barker, 1985)

Wynne-Thomas, Peter, *The Complete History of Cricket Tours at Home & Abroad* (Hamlyn, 1989)

Wynne-Thomas, Peter, *The History of Cricket* (Stationery Office, 1997)

Yallop, Graham, *Lambs to the Slaughter* (New English Library, 1979)

Yapp, Nick, *Cricket: Pictures from the Past* (Collins & Brown, 1991)

Yardley, Norman, *Cricket Campaigns* (Stanley Paul, 1950)

# ACKNOWLEDGEMENTS

This was my twelfth book and the hardest undertaking. No one in modern times has attempted a comprehensive account of the England national team and I quickly discovered why, such was the breadth of the topic, spanning more than 140 years and a cast of several hundred characters. Inevitably I have drawn in part on the work of others. More than 400 players who have represented England at international level are mentioned in the text: many make only a brief appearance and even some of those who had significant careers for their country receive – of necessity – relatively short assessments. These are players who have generated some excellent biographies and autobiographies. Many tours undertaken or hosted by England have also had books written about them, in some cases more than one; I sometimes deal with them in a paragraph or two.

There has been a vast body of research done in modern times, which contributes to the need for a wholesale revision in our understanding of England team affairs. Fresh material, too, is being unearthed all the time. Of particular value is the work of the Association of Cricket Statisticians and Historians (www.acscricket. com), which produces a quarterly journal, as well as a series of booklets called *Famous Cricketers* and *Lives in Cricket* which provide studies of many prominent England players. The ACS's sister website www. cricketarchive.com is also a vital source of information. The archives, in some cases online, of specialist magazines *Cricket* (1882-1914), *The*

*Cricketer* (1921 to date) and *Wisden Cricket Monthly* (1979–2003 and 2017 to date) offer vital contemporary accounts of England matches and developments. Another wonderful resource is http://test-cricket-tours.co.uk, which gives detailed analysis of Test tours, their personnel and itineraries. The MCC library at Lord's holds minutes and accounts of many meetings, as well as correspondence, relating to England matters. An excellent study of the post-war developments of the ICC was found in *Decolonization and the Imperial Cricket Conference, 1947-65: A Study in Transnational Commonwealth History?* by Usha Iyer, a Doctorate of Philosophy thesis at the University of Central Lancashire.

As cricket correspondent of the *Sunday Times*, I have interviewed dozens of past and present England cricketers and administrators over the past 20 years, in addition to which I spoke to many more in the course of writing this book. I have reported more than 250 England Test matches for *The Times* and *Sunday Times* since 1995, and to an extent writing a history of the England team feels like an extension of a curiously itinerant day job which I share with colleagues on other national newspapers and websites, some of whom have seen England play even more than I have. Scyld Berry has attended 450 England Tests, more than the incomparable John Woodcock once did for *The Times*. Michael Atherton has played in, commentated and reported on more than 300, as has Vic Marks of the *Observer* and *Guardian*, and Derek Pringle, formerly of the *Independent* and *Daily Telegraph*. John Etheridge of the *Sun* has probably attended more England internationals of all descriptions than anyone else.

There is no shortage, therefore, of people better qualified for this task, but at least I was able to pick their brains and seek their advice, as I did with many others. They include: Geoff Arnold, Mark Arthur, Malcolm Ashton, Peter Baxter, Tim Boon, Geoff Boycott, Mike Brearley, Derek Brewer, Giles Clarke, Matthew Engel, Keith Fletcher, David Frith, CS Gamage, David Gower, David Graveney, Gideon Haigh, Steve Harmison, Richard Heller, Bob Jackson, Medha Laud, David Lloyd, Peter Lush, Colin Maynard, Tom Moffat, Graham Morris, Brian Murgatroyd, JT Murray, Min Patel, Neil Robinson (MCC librarian), Joe Root, Andrew Sansom, Mike

Selvey, MJK Smith, Andrew Strauss, Peter Such, Graeme Swann, Bob Taylor, Ivo Tennant, the late Bernard Thomas, Huw Turbervill, Michael Vaughan, James Whitaker and Peter Wynne-Thomas; also Tom Harrison, Jenny Smith and Andrew Walpole at the ECB. My particular thanks to Ian Marshall of Simon & Schuster and my indefatigable copy editor Charlotte Atyeo, to David Luxton, my agent, for keeping the faith even when I didn't, to Alex Butler and Nick Greenslade at the *Sunday Times* and to Gayle, Freddie, Lily and Eve for their love, fortitude and forgiveness.

# INDEX